Advances in Law

Abraham Justice

ISBN: 978-1-77961-848-1
Imprint: Fourier Series
Copyright © 2024 Abraham Justice.
All Rights Reserved.

Contents

Introduction to Transformative Legal Studies   11
Impact of Transformative Legal Studies on Justice and Equality   21
Methodological Approaches in Transformative Legal Studies   32
Structure of the Book   46

Chapter 2:
Theoretical Foundations of Transformative Legal Studies   61
Chapter 2: Theoretical Foundations of Transformative Legal Studies   61
Critical Legal Studies   64
Feminist Legal Theory   72
Postcolonial Legal Theory   84
Critical Race Theory   89
Queer Legal Theory   98
Marxist Legal Theory   106
Human Rights and Transformative Legal Studies   113
Conclusion   126

Chapter 3: Transformative Approaches to Legal Education   133
Chapter 3: Transformative Approaches to Legal Education   133
Traditional Legal Pedagogy: Critiques and Challenges   137
Experiential Learning in Legal Education   146
Technology and Legal Education   158
Interdisciplinary Approaches in Legal Education   169
Social Justice and Legal Education   181
International and Comparative Legal Education   189
Access to Legal Education and Diversity   199
Conclusion   207

Chapter 4: New Approaches to Legal Research 219
Chapter 4: New Approaches to Legal Research 219
Traditional Legal Research Methods 221
Empirical Legal Research 232
Socio-Legal Research 248
Comparative Legal Research 258
Critical Legal Research 269
Legal Research in the Digital Age 277
Collaborative Research in Law 287
Conclusion 296

Chapter 5: Legal Systems and Institutions in Transformation 307
Chapter 5: Legal Systems and Institutions in Transformation 307
Judicial Activism and Its Impact 310
Legal Transplants and Comparative Law 316
Access to Justice and Legal Empowerment 326
Alternative Dispute Resolution 334
Restorative Justice and Transformative Justice 348
Legal Profession in Transformation 358
Law and Social Change 370
Chapter 5: Legal Systems and Institutions in Transformation 373
Conclusion 379

Chapter 6: Technology and the Future of Law 387
Chapter 6: Technology and the Future of Law 387
Artificial Intelligence in Law 391
Blockchain and Smart Contracts 401
Privacy and Data Protection 411
Cybersecurity and Law 420
Online Dispute Resolution 428
Big Data and Predictive Analytics in Law 437
Technology and Legal Ethics 446
Conclusion 456

Chapter 7: Restorative Justice and the Transformation of Criminal Justice 467

Chapter 7:
Restorative Justice and the Transformation of Criminal Justice   467
- Introduction to Restorative Justice   471
- Restorative Justice Practices   479
- Restorative Justice in the Criminal Justice System   492
- Restorative Justice and Healing   501
- Restorative Justice and Social Transformation   510
- Restorative Justice and Victim Rights   518
- Restorative Justice and Community Engagement   527
- Conclusion   536

Chapter 8: Transformative Approaches to Human Rights Law   547
- Chapter 8: Transformative Approaches to Human Rights Law   547
- Human Rights Law and Social Justice   550
- Economic, Social, and Cultural Rights   559
- Understanding Economic, Social, and Cultural Rights   559
- Civil and Political Rights   567
- Indigenous Peoples' Rights   580
- Women's Rights and Feminist Approaches to Human Rights   585
- Rights of LGBTQ+ Individuals   592
- Children's Rights and the Convention on the Rights of the Child   603
- Transitional Justice and Human Rights   612
- Human Rights Activism and Advocacy   621
- Conclusion   635

Chapter 9: Global Perspectives on Transformative Legal Studies   643
- Chapter 9: Global Perspectives on Transformative Legal Studies   643
- Comparative Law and Global Legal Systems   648
- International Law and Global Governance   658
- Globalization and Legal Responses   669
- Transformative Legal Activism Globally   677
- Regional Approaches to Transformative Legal Studies   686
- Indigenous Legal Systems and Transformative Potential   695
- Environmental Law and Transformative Legal Strategies   704
- Conclusion   714

Index   721

Overview of Legal Studies

In this chapter, we will provide an overview of the field of legal studies. We will examine the definition and scope of legal studies, explore its historical development, and discuss current trends and debates within the field. Additionally, we will highlight the importance of transformative legal studies in shaping the future of justice and equality.

Definition and Scope of Legal Studies

Legal studies is an interdisciplinary field that encompasses the study of law, legal systems, and the principles that govern them. It involves the analysis of legal norms, institutions, and processes, as well as the critical examination of legal theories and methodologies. Legal studies draw on various disciplines such as philosophy, sociology, political science, economics, and psychology to understand the complex nature of law and its impact on society.

The scope of legal studies is broad and diverse. It includes the study of different legal systems, such as common law, civil law, and religious law, as well as specialized areas of law like constitutional law, criminal law, international law, and human rights law. Legal studies also examine the relationship between law and other social phenomena, such as power, morality, culture, and social change.

Historical Development of Legal Studies

Legal studies have a rich historical background, dating back to ancient civilizations. Legal systems have evolved over time, influenced by cultural, political, and social factors. The Code of Hammurabi in ancient Mesopotamia, the Twelve Tables in ancient Rome, and the Magna Carta in medieval England are all examples of early legal codes that shaped legal systems and provided a foundation for legal studies.

In the modern era, the development of legal studies can be traced to the rise of formal legal education in universities during the Middle Ages. The establishment of law schools and the teaching of legal principles and doctrines laid the groundwork for the systematic study of law. Over time, legal studies expanded to incorporate interdisciplinary approaches and theoretical perspectives, reflecting the dynamic nature of law and its relationship with society.

Current Trends and Debates in Legal Studies

Legal studies are constantly influenced by contemporary issues and debates. Today, some of the key trends and debates within the field include:

- **Legal pluralism:** The recognition and study of multiple legal systems and sources of law within a given society.

- **Globalization and transnational law:** The examination of legal systems and norms beyond national boundaries, as well as the impact of globalization on legal systems.

- **Access to justice:** The focus on ensuring equal access to legal services and the justice system for all individuals, regardless of their socioeconomic status.

- **Technology and law:** The exploration of the impact of technology on legal practice, such as artificial intelligence, blockchain, and online dispute resolution.

- **Critical legal studies:** The critical examination of the role of law in reinforcing power imbalances, social inequalities, and oppression, and the pursuit of more just and equitable legal systems.

- **Intersectionality and law:** The acknowledgment of how various social identities, such as race, gender, and class, intersect and influence the experience of law and legal processes.

These trends and debates highlight the evolving nature of legal studies and the need to address pressing contemporary issues through transformative approaches.

Importance of Transformative Legal Studies

Transformative legal studies are crucial for envisioning and working towards a more just and equitable society. By challenging existing legal paradigms and exploring alternative approaches to law and justice, transformative legal studies have the potential to address systemic injustices and promote social change.

By examining the relationship between law and transformation, transformative legal studies can contribute to the development of more effective legal systems that uphold human rights, ensure access to justice, and promote equality. Through interdisciplinary approaches, transformative legal studies can draw insights from various fields to provide innovative solutions to complex legal issues.

Furthermore, transformative legal studies can empower individuals and communities by fostering critical thinking, enhancing legal awareness, and promoting active participation in legal processes. By incorporating diverse voices and perspectives, transformative legal studies create opportunities for marginalized communities to challenge systemic inequalities and advocate for their rights.

In the next section, we will delve deeper into the concept of transformation and its significance in legal studies. We will explore the theoretical foundations of transformative legal studies and the interdisciplinary approaches used to analyze and address legal issues.

ERROR. thisXsection() returned an empty string with textbook depth = 3.
ERROR. thisXsection() returned an empty string with textbook depth = 3.
ERROR. thisXsection() returned an empty string with textbook depth = 3.

Historical Development of Legal Studies

The historical development of legal studies encompasses the evolution of legal systems, legal thought, and the study of law itself. To understand the present state of legal studies, it is essential to explore its historical roots and the key milestones that have shaped its development over time. This section will provide an overview of the historical trajectory of legal studies, highlighting significant periods, theories, and events that have influenced the field.

Ancient Legal Systems

The origins of legal studies can be traced back to ancient civilizations, where the establishment of legal systems was crucial for maintaining social order and resolving disputes. For example, the earliest known legal code, the Code of Hammurabi, emerged in ancient Babylonia around 1750 BCE. This code contained a set of laws and punishments that governed various aspects of society, including property rights, commerce, and family law.

In ancient Greece, legal studies were influenced by the development of democratic systems and the concept of the rule of law. The pre-Socratic philosophers, such as Thales and Pythagoras, pondered the nature of justice and ethics, laying the groundwork for future legal theories. The contributions of Aristotle, Plato, and other ancient Greek philosophers further shaped the understanding of law and its role in society.

Roman Law and the Corpus Juris Civilis

One of the most significant developments in legal studies occurred during the time of the Roman Empire. Roman law, compiled in the Corpus Juris Civilis (Body of Civil Law), became a seminal legal system that had a lasting influence on Western legal systems.

The Corpus Juris Civilis, commissioned by Emperor Justinian in the 6th century CE, compiled and organized the Roman legal tradition. It consisted of four main parts: the Institutes, the Digest, the Codex, and the Novels. The Institutes provided an introductory overview of legal concepts, while the Digest compiled the works of jurists, serving as a comprehensive legal encyclopedia. The Codex gathered imperial legislation, and the Novels contained new laws introduced by Justinian.

Roman law placed a significant emphasis on abstract legal principles and rational thinking. Its influence extended beyond the Roman Empire and provided the foundation for civil law systems in Europe, including those found in continental Europe, Latin America, and parts of Asia.

Feudal and Canon Law

During the Middle Ages, legal studies merged with the feudal and religious institutions of the time. Feudal law governed the relationships between lords and vassals, while canon law, developed by the Catholic Church, regulated matters related to church administration, marriage, and ecclesiastical jurisdiction.

Legal studies during this period focused heavily on interpreting and applying religious doctrines and principles. Prominent scholars such as Thomas Aquinas developed theories on natural law, discussing the relationship between divine law, human law, and justice.

The Rise of Common Law

The emergence of common law marked a significant shift in legal studies. Common law, developed in England during the medieval period, placed increased importance on judicial decisions and legal precedents. It relied on the doctrine of stare decisis, or the principle of following past decisions, in order to maintain consistency and predictability in the legal system.

The development of common law was accompanied by the establishment of courts with professional judges and legal practitioners. These legal professionals played a crucial role in shaping legal principles through their decisions and legal reasoning.

Enlightenment and the Birth of Legal Sciences

The Enlightenment period (18th century) saw the birth of legal sciences as a distinct field of study. Influenced by the ideas of reason, rationality, and individual rights, legal scholars began to approach law from a more scientific and systematic perspective.

Legal positivism, championed by legal philosopher Jeremy Bentham, emphasized the importance of law as a social construct. Bentham advocated for utilitarian principles, arguing that laws should aim to maximize overall happiness and societal welfare.

The nineteenth century witnessed the emergence of legal realism, a movement that challenged the formalistic and abstract nature of legal studies. Legal realists focused on the practical impact of laws on society and emphasized the role of judges in shaping legal outcomes.

Modern Legal Studies

In the twentieth and twenty-first centuries, legal studies have continued to evolve, incorporating interdisciplinary approaches, globalization, and the advancement of technology. This period has witnessed the development of various branches of law, including constitutional law, human rights law, environmental law, and intellectual property law, among many others.

The rise of critical legal studies in the 1970s questioned traditional approaches to legal studies, highlighting the role of power, ideology, and social structures in shaping legal doctrines and outcomes. Critical legal scholars widened the scope of legal studies by considering the impact of law on marginalized groups and advocating for social justice.

Furthermore, globalization and technological advancements have necessitated the analysis of legal issues from a global perspective. Legal studies now encompass transnational and international law, examining the interaction between different legal systems and the challenges posed by global issues such as climate change, human rights violations, and cross-border commerce.

Conclusion

The historical development of legal studies reveals a dynamic and evolving field that has been shaped by various civilizations, movements, and ideologies. From ancient legal systems to modern-day interdisciplinary approaches, legal studies have adapted to reflect changing societal needs and values.

Understanding the historical foundations of legal studies is essential for comprehending the current landscape of the discipline. It provides a context for the theories, approaches, and debates that continue to shape legal studies today. By examining the historical development of legal studies, scholars can better appreciate the transformative potential of the field in addressing contemporary legal challenges and achieving justice and equality.

Current Trends and Debates in Legal Studies

In the field of legal studies, there are several current trends and debates that shape the way we understand and approach the law. These trends and debates reflect the evolving nature of law and the challenges faced by legal scholars, practitioners, and policymakers. In this section, we will explore some of the prominent trends and debates in legal studies today.

Trend 1: Technology and the Law

One of the most significant trends in legal studies is the intersection between technology and the law. Rapid advancements in technology, such as artificial intelligence (AI), blockchain, and big data, are revolutionizing various aspects of legal practice. For example, AI is being used in legal research, contract analysis, and prediction of case outcomes. Blockchain technology has the potential to transform contract enforcement and ensure transparency in transactions. Big data analytics enable lawyers to analyze large volumes of legal information and identify patterns and trends.

However, this trend also raises important debates and challenges. Ethical considerations surrounding the use of AI in legal decision-making, privacy concerns in the era of big data, and the regulation of emerging technologies in the legal field are among the key issues under discussion. Legal scholars and practitioners are grappling with questions about the potential biases in algorithms, the impact of technology on access to justice, and the need for regulatory frameworks to address the legal implications of new technologies.

Trend 2: Intersectionality and Legal Theory

Another significant trend in legal studies is the increasing recognition of intersectionality and its impact on legal theory. Intersectionality refers to the interconnected nature of social categories such as race, gender, class, sexuality, and disability, and the unique experiences of individuals with multiple intersecting identities. This perspective challenges traditional legal frameworks that often fail to account for the diverse experiences and needs of marginalized groups.

The recognition of intersectionality has led to a reevaluation of legal theories and the development of more inclusive approaches. For instance, feminist legal theory now incorporates intersectional perspectives, emphasizing the interplay between gender, race, and class. Critical race theory also acknowledges the importance of intersectionality in examining the experiences of racial and ethnic minorities within the legal system. By recognizing and addressing the various dimensions of identity and power, legal scholars seek to develop more comprehensive and transformative theories and practices.

Trend 3: Environmental Law and Sustainability

With growing concerns about climate change and environmental degradation, the field of environmental law has gained significant attention in recent years. The trend towards environmental sustainability has shaped legal studies by highlighting the need for regulatory frameworks to address ecological challenges. Environmental law encompasses areas such as climate change mitigation and adaptation, biodiversity conservation, pollution control, and sustainable development.

Debates in environmental law revolve around finding the right balance between economic development and environmental protection, as well as exploring innovative legal tools to tackle global environmental challenges. Scholars and practitioners are examining the role of international agreements, such as the Paris Agreement, in promoting environmental sustainability. They are also exploring the potential of transformative legal strategies, such as rights of nature and ecological legal theory, to secure the long-term well-being of the planet and future generations.

Trend 4: Access to Justice and Legal Empowerment

The issue of access to justice is a persistent concern in legal studies. Access to justice refers to the ability of individuals and communities to effectively navigate the legal system and secure their rights. Unfortunately, many people face barriers such as lack of legal representation, high costs, procedural complexities, and systemic biases that hinder their ability to access justice.

To address this challenge, legal scholars and practitioners are exploring innovative approaches such as legal aid clinics, pro bono services, and community legal education to empower individuals and increase access to justice. They are also examining how technology, such as online dispute resolution platforms, can improve access to justice, particularly for underserved populations. The ongoing debate revolves around finding effective strategies to ensure equal access to justice for all individuals, regardless of their socio-economic background or marginalized status.

Debate: Rights-based vs. Socio-economic Approaches to Justice

One of the enduring debates in legal studies is the tension between rights-based approaches and socio-economic approaches to justice. Rights-based approaches emphasize the protection of individual rights and freedom from state interference. This approach focuses on the role of law in ensuring individual liberties and challenging oppressive structures.

On the other hand, socio-economic approaches highlight the importance of addressing social inequalities and promoting socio-economic rights such as access to education, healthcare, housing, and employment. This approach recognizes that legal frameworks alone may not be sufficient to achieve substantive justice and advocates for a broader understanding of justice that encompasses socio-economic well-being.

The debate between these two approaches centers around the balance between individual rights and collective well-being, the role of the state in ensuring social justice, and the effectiveness of legal mechanisms in addressing systemic inequalities. Legal scholars engage in this debate to develop a more nuanced understanding of justice and to explore how legal systems can effectively promote both individual rights and social justice.

Conclusion

These current trends and debates in legal studies demonstrate the dynamic nature of the discipline and its responsiveness to societal challenges. Technology, intersectionality, environmental sustainability, access to justice, and the tension between rights-based and socio-economic approaches are shaping legal theory and practice.

As legal scholars and practitioners navigate these trends and engage in debates, they contribute to the transformative potential of legal studies. By critically examining existing legal frameworks, developing innovative approaches, and addressing emerging challenges, legal studies can contribute to a more just and equitable society.

Importance of Transformative Legal Studies

Transformative legal studies represent a critical and necessary approach to addressing the persistent challenges and inequalities within the legal system. This section explores the significance of transformative legal studies in promoting justice and equality, the overarching goals of the field, and the potential impact it can have on individuals and society.

Promoting Justice and Equality

Transformative legal studies seek to challenge and dismantle existing power structures and inequalities within the legal system. By examining the underlying social, economic, and political dynamics that contribute to injustice, transformative legal studies aim to identify and implement solutions that promote justice and equality for all.

One of the primary reasons why transformative legal studies is important is its potential to address systemic inequalities that marginalized communities face. It recognizes that the law is not neutral and that certain groups, such as racial and ethnic minorities, women, LGBTQ+ individuals, and persons with disabilities, have historically been disproportionately affected by discriminatory laws and policies. Transformative legal studies provide a framework to challenge and change these inequalities by advocating for the rights and interests of marginalized groups.

Moreover, transformative legal studies emphasize the need to take into account intersectionality, which recognizes that individuals face multiple dimensions of oppression and discrimination. By acknowledging the ways in which different forms of oppression intersect, transformative legal studies can develop comprehensive strategies that tackle complex and interconnected issues.

Overarching Goals

The overarching goals of transformative legal studies are twofold: to critique existing legal frameworks and systems, and to propose alternative approaches that promote justice and equality.

Firstly, transformative legal studies engage in a critical analysis of legal doctrines, institutions, and practices, questioning their underlying assumptions and challenging their legitimacy. This critical analysis is crucial for identifying and exposing the ways in which the legal system perpetuates injustice and inequality.

Secondly, transformative legal studies aim to propose alternative approaches to legal issues that are rooted in principles of justice and equality. This includes developing new legal theories and frameworks, advocating for legislative and policy reforms, and promoting transformative practices within the legal profession.

Potential Impact

Transformative legal studies have the potential to bring about substantial changes in the legal system and society as a whole. By engaging in critical analysis and proposing alternatives, transformative legal studies can reshape legal norms and institutions to be more just and equitable.

At the individual level, transformative legal studies empower marginalized communities by giving them a voice and addressing their specific needs. By centering the experiences and perspectives of those who have been historically marginalized, transformative legal studies can lead to legal reforms that are more inclusive and responsive to the lived realities of individuals.

Furthermore, transformative legal studies can influence broader social and political discourse. By challenging existing legal frameworks, transformative legal studies can help shape public opinion, mobilize social movements, and contribute to larger societal transformations.

Challenges and Critiques

While transformative legal studies provide a valuable framework for promoting justice and equality, they are not without challenges and critiques. Some argue that transformative legal studies can be seen as overly theoretical and disconnected from the practical realities of legal practice. There is a need to bridge the gap between theory and practice, ensuring that transformative approaches are effectively implemented in the legal system.

Another challenge is the resistance and pushback from those who benefit from maintaining the status quo. Transformative legal studies often challenge existing power structures, which can result in resistance from individuals and institutions that are invested in maintaining their privilege.

Furthermore, the transformative nature of this field requires ongoing reflection and self-critique. There is a need to continuously reassess the effectiveness and impact of transformative legal studies, addressing internal biases and blind spots to ensure that the field remains responsive to evolving social and legal issues.

Conclusion

The importance of transformative legal studies lies in its capacity to address and rectify systemic injustices within the legal system. By centering justice and equality, transformative legal studies challenge existing power structures, promote marginalized voices, and propose alternative approaches to legal issues. While there are challenges and critiques associated with this field, the potential impact of transformative legal studies in reshaping the legal system and promoting social change is significant.

Introduction to Transformative Legal Studies

Understanding the Concept of Transformation

In order to grasp the essence of transformative legal studies, it is crucial to first understand the concept of transformation itself. Transformation, in the context of legal studies, refers to fundamental and significant changes that occur within legal systems, legal education, legal research, legal institutions, and legal practices. These changes are aimed at promoting justice, equality, and social progress.

At its core, transformation involves challenging and questioning the existing norms, structures, and practices within the legal system. It seeks to address marginalization, oppression, and inequality by reimagining legal frameworks and practices in ways that are more inclusive, equitable, and just. Transformation is not simply about incremental changes or reform; it is about envisioning and creating a legal system that truly serves the needs of all individuals and communities.

The Need for Transformation

The need for transformation in legal studies arises from the recognition that traditional legal systems and approaches have limitations in addressing systemic injustices. Legal systems are often shaped by historical biases, unequal power dynamics, and societal prejudices. Transformative legal studies aim to challenge these underlying assumptions and power structures, and to reconceptualize the law in a way that dismantles these oppressive systems, promotes justice, and advances equality.

Transformation can take many forms, such as reevaluating legal doctrines, adopting alternative dispute resolution methods, reforming legal education, implementing restorative justice practices, and embracing interdisciplinary approaches to legal research. These approaches seek to shift the focus from a purely formalistic interpretation of the law to an understanding of the law as a tool for social change and justice.

The Role of Critical Theory

Critical theory provides the theoretical foundations for transformative legal studies. Drawing from various disciplines such as sociology, philosophy, and political science, critical theory offers a framework for understanding power relations, social inequalities, and the ways in which law can perpetuate or challenge those dynamics.

Critical legal studies, one of the key strands of critical theory, focuses on the inherent biases within the legal system. It critiques the notions of neutrality, objectivity, and universality, and argues that the law is a product of social and political forces that often serve the interests of the powerful. By exposing these underlying power dynamics, critical legal studies provides a basis for transformative action and the pursuit of justice.

Feminist legal theory and critical race theory are also crucial components of transformative legal studies. They highlight how gender and racial hierarchies intersect with the law, and the ways in which these hierarchies can be transformed through legal frameworks and approaches. These theories offer a lens through which to analyze and challenge systemic discrimination, oppression, and marginalization.

Applying Transformation to Legal Contexts

The application of transformative legal studies involves engaging in critical analysis, challenging existing legal frameworks, and proposing alternative approaches that promote justice and equality. It requires a deep understanding of both the theoretical foundations of transformative legal studies and the practical implications of implementing transformative practices.

One way in which transformation can be applied is through the development and use of alternative dispute resolution methods. These methods, such as mediation and restorative justice, aim to empower individuals and communities by allowing them to actively participate in the resolution of their own conflicts. By emphasizing dialogue, understanding, and healing, these approaches have the potential to transform relationships and promote reconciliation.

Another avenue for transformation is through legal education. Transformative legal education moves beyond the traditional lecture-based model and incorporates experiential learning, interdisciplinary perspectives, and the exploration of social justice issues. By equipping law students with practical skills, critical thinking abilities, and a commitment to social change, transformative legal education aims to produce lawyers who are not only technically proficient, but also deeply aware of the social and ethical dimensions of the law.

Current Challenges and Future Directions

While transformative legal studies offer immense potential for creating a more just and equitable legal system, they also face several challenges. Resistance from traditional legal institutions, lack of resources, and ingrained biases within the legal profession can impede progress towards transformation. Additionally, there may be disagreements and debates within the field regarding the most effective strategies for bringing about transformation.

However, despite these challenges, transformative legal studies continue to gain traction and momentum. Scholars, activists, and legal practitioners are increasingly recognizing the importance of incorporating transformative approaches into legal practice, education, and research. The future of transformative legal studies lies in fostering collaborations, exploring innovative methodologies, and nurturing a community of scholars and practitioners dedicated to driving change.

Example: Challenging Bias in Criminal Justice

To illustrate the concept of transformation, let's consider the issue of bias in criminal justice systems. Transformative legal studies would examine how biases based on race, gender, socio-economic status, and other factors can shape the outcomes of criminal cases. By critically analyzing the existing legal framework and practices, transformative legal scholars and practitioners can propose alternative approaches that address and mitigate these biases.

For instance, a transformative approach to sentencing might involve the implementation of restorative justice practices in the criminal justice system. Instead of focusing solely on punishment, restorative justice seeks to repair the harm caused by the crime and restore relationships between the offender, the victim, and the community. This approach recognizes the social and emotional dimensions of crime and offers a way to address systemic biases and disparities in sentencing.

Transformative legal studies in this context would also examine the impact of bias on the experiences of marginalized communities within the criminal justice system. By analyzing data, conducting qualitative research, and engaging with affected communities, transformative legal scholars can identify the root causes of bias and propose policy reforms and interventions that disrupt these patterns.

By adopting a transformative approach, criminal justice systems can move beyond mere legal compliance and strive towards justice and equality. This example demonstrates how transformative legal studies contribute to the ongoing process of transforming legal systems to better serve the needs of all individuals and communities.

Relationship between Law and Transformation

The relationship between law and transformation is a fundamental aspect of transformative legal studies. In order to understand the concept of transformation and its implications for the legal system, it is important to explore how law and transformation are interconnected. This section will delve into the key aspects of this relationship, highlighting the transformative potential of the law and the ways in which transformation shapes legal norms and practices.

Understanding Transformation

Transformation refers to a profound and enduring change that goes beyond surface-level adjustments. It involves a reimagining and restructuring of systems, institutions, and relationships to promote justice, equality, and social progress. In the context of legal studies, transformation entails challenging and reshaping existing legal frameworks to address systemic injustices and promote equitable outcomes.

The Role of Law in Transformation

Law plays a crucial role in facilitating and supporting transformation. It provides a framework within which societal norms, values, and aspirations are translated into enforceable rules and regulations. Moreover, the legal system serves as a mechanism for resolving disputes and ensuring that individuals and groups can access justice.

Law can act as a catalyst for transformation by bringing about significant changes in society. For example, groundbreaking court decisions have played a pivotal role in advancing civil rights, equality, and social justice. These decisions often push society to reevaluate long-standing practices and promote more inclusive and equitable norms.

Furthermore, the law can shape and guide transformation processes by providing legal tools and mechanisms for social change. Legal instruments such as legislation, policies, and regulations can be utilized to address systemic issues and create enabling environments for transformation. For instance, laws promoting diversity and inclusion in the workplace can contribute to dismantling discriminatory practices and promoting equality.

Transformative Potential of Legal Norms and Practices

Legal norms and practices have the potential to bring about transformative change in society. When designed and implemented with transformative goals in mind, legal frameworks can challenge existing power structures, dismantle systemic inequalities, and promote social justice.

One example of a transformative legal practice is restorative justice, which focuses on repairing harm and healing relationships, rather than solely punishing offenders. Restorative justice approaches aim to address the root causes of crime and promote reconciliation between victims and offenders. By prioritizing the needs and voices of those affected by crime, restorative justice seeks to transform the criminal justice system into a more compassionate and rehabilitative system.

Another area where the law can have a transformative impact is in environmental law. Given the urgent need to address climate change and environmental degradation, legal frameworks can provide the tools needed to transition to a more sustainable and ecologically just society. Environmental laws and regulations can help reshape industries, promote renewable energy sources, and hold polluters accountable, ultimately transforming our relationship with the environment.

Challenges and Critiques

While the law holds transformative potential, it is not without its challenges and critiques. One challenge is that legal systems are deeply embedded within existing power structures and societal norms. This can make it difficult to bring about meaningful and lasting transformation, as entrenched interests may resist change.

Critiques of transformative legal studies argue that it may not go far enough in challenging structural inequalities and power imbalances. Some argue that transformation should occur outside traditional legal frameworks, and that alternate pathways, such as grassroots activism or social movements, may be more effective in driving change.

Conclusion

The relationship between law and transformation is a complex and dynamic one. By understanding the transformative potential of law and its role in promoting justice and equality, legal scholars, practitioners, and activists can work towards reshaping the legal system to better serve the needs of society. However, it is important to acknowledge the challenges and critiques, and explore innovative approaches to transformation beyond traditional legal frameworks. Through interdisciplinary collaboration and a commitment to social change, transformative legal studies can pave the way for a more just and equitable future.

Theoretical Foundations of Transformative Legal Studies

In order to understand the conceptual framework of transformative legal studies, it is important to explore its theoretical foundations. This section will delve into the key theories and concepts that underpin transformative legal studies, providing a solid groundwork for the subsequent chapters.

Critical Legal Studies

Critical legal studies (CLS) is one of the foundational theories of transformative legal studies. It emerged in the 1970s as a response to traditional legal theories that were seen as inadequate in addressing social inequalities and promoting justice. CLS scholars argue that law is not a neutral and objective system, but rather a tool that serves the interests of the powerful. They believe that law is shaped by social, economic, and political forces and can either maintain or challenge existing power structures.

One of the key concepts in CLS is the critique of formalism. Formalism asserts that legal reasoning can be based solely on logical deduction from legal rules and principles. CLS scholars argue that this approach is flawed because it ignores the social context in which legal rules operate. They advocate for a more contextual and interdisciplinary analysis of law, taking into account factors such as power, ideology, and social relations.

Critiques and challenges to CLS have centered around its perceived radicalism and its limited engagement with practical solutions. Some argue that CLS fails to offer concrete alternatives to the existing legal system and lacks a clear path for social change. However, proponents of CLS argue that its focus on questioning existing structures and norms is crucial for initiating transformative change in the legal system.

Feminist Legal Theory

Feminist legal theory examines the ways in which the law perpetuates gender inequalities and seeks to promote gender justice. It emerged in the 1970s as part of the broader feminist movement and has since expanded to incorporate intersectional perspectives that recognize the interconnectedness of gender with other categories such as race, class, and sexuality.

Key concepts in feminist legal theory include patriarchy, gender discrimination, and stereotypes. Feminist legal scholars argue that the law, as a reflection of societal norms, has historically reinforced male dominance and marginalized the experiences and rights of women. They advocate for legal reforms that challenge gender stereotypes, promote gender equality, and address issues such as reproductive rights, gender-based violence, and workplace discrimination.

Intersectionality is another important aspect of feminist legal theory. It recognizes that different forms of oppression, such as sexism, racism, and classism, are interconnected and cannot be analyzed in isolation. By considering the multiple dimensions of discrimination, feminist legal theory seeks to address the experiences of marginalized and intersectional identities.

While feminist legal theory has made significant contributions in highlighting gender inequalities, critiques have been raised regarding its focus on women's experiences and exclusion of other gender identities. Efforts have been made to incorporate transgender rights and queer perspectives within feminist legal theory, recognizing the need for an inclusive and intersectional approach.

Postcolonial Legal Theory

Postcolonial legal theory examines the impact of colonization on legal systems and explores the ways in which law perpetuates colonial structures and power dynamics. It recognizes the historical and ongoing effects of colonialism on indigenous peoples, marginalized communities, and postcolonial societies.

Key concepts in postcolonial legal theory include imperialism, cultural imperialism, and legal pluralism. Postcolonial scholars argue that legal systems imposed during the colonial era continue to shape postcolonial societies, often maintaining hierarchies and inequalities. They emphasize the need for decolonizing the law by undoing the legacies of colonialism and empowering marginalized communities to reclaim their legal systems and cultural identities.

Legal pluralism is another important aspect of postcolonial legal theory. It recognizes the coexistence of different legal systems within a society, including customary and indigenous laws alongside state laws. Postcolonial legal scholars emphasize the importance of recognizing and respecting diverse legal traditions to promote justice and equality.

Critics of postcolonial legal theory question its relevance in contemporary legal contexts and raise concerns about cultural relativism. They argue that certain universal human rights may be undermined when cultural traditions are given priority. However, postcolonial legal theorists emphasize the need to strike a balance between respecting cultural diversity and ensuring the protection of fundamental human rights.

Critical Race Theory

Critical race theory (CRT) examines the intersections of race, racism, and the law. It emerged in the 1970s as a response to the limitations of traditional legal theories in addressing systemic racism. CRT scholars argue that racism is not simply a matter of individual prejudice but is deeply embedded in legal institutions and structures.

Key concepts in critical race theory include structural racism, racial inequality, and white privilege. CRT seeks to uncover how racial hierarchies are established and maintained through laws, policies, and social practices. It challenges colorblind approaches to the law, arguing that ignoring race perpetuates racial inequalities rather than addressing them.

Intersectionality is also a central tenet of critical race theory. It recognizes that race intersects with other identity categories, such as gender, class, and sexuality, shaping the experiences of marginalized individuals. By considering the multiple dimensions of identity, critical race theory seeks to address the unique challenges faced by people at the intersections of multiple marginalized identities.

Critiques of critical race theory often center around the discomfort it generates among individuals who feel implicated in perpetuating racial inequalities. Some argue that CRT promotes division rather than unity. However, proponents of critical race theory argue that confronting uncomfortable truths about racism is necessary for transformative change and the pursuit of racial justice.

Conclusion

Theoretical foundations play a crucial role in guiding transformative legal studies. Critical legal studies, feminist legal theory, postcolonial legal theory, and critical race theory offer distinct perspectives on how law operates within broader social, political, and cultural contexts. By challenging existing power structures, addressing inequalities, and promoting justice, these theories provide the intellectual groundwork for transformative legal scholarship and practice.

As the book proceeds, we will explore the practical applications of these theories and examine how they inform transformative approaches to legal education, legal research, legal systems and institutions, the future of law, criminal justice, human rights law, and global perspectives. It is through a comprehensive understanding of these theoretical foundations that we can effectively examine the potential for transformative change within the legal field.

Interdisciplinary Approaches in Transformative Legal Studies

In order to fully understand and address the complex challenges of the legal system, transformative legal studies often draw on interdisciplinary approaches. These approaches incorporate insights and methodologies from various fields outside of law to provide a comprehensive and holistic understanding of legal issues, as well as innovative solutions for achieving justice and equality. In this section, we will explore some of the key interdisciplinary approaches used in transformative legal studies and their potential impact.

Sociology and Law

One important interdisciplinary approach is the integration of sociology and law. Sociology helps us analyze the social structures, norms, and power dynamics that shape the legal system and influence legal outcomes. By studying the social context in which legal issues arise, we can gain a deeper understanding of the ways in which the law can be transformative and promote social change. For example, sociological perspectives can shed light on how laws perpetuate inequalities based on race, gender, or class, and guide efforts to address these injustices.

Psychology and Law

Psychology plays a crucial role in transformative legal studies by providing insights into human behavior, decision-making, and the psychological factors that affect individuals' interactions with the legal system. Understanding the psychological processes that influence witnesses, jurors, lawyers, and other actors in the legal system can help us design more effective legal interventions and policies. For instance, research on cognitive biases and heuristics can reveal the limitations of the legal system and suggest ways to mitigate biases in legal decision-making.

Economics and Law

The intersection of economics and law offers valuable insights into the incentives and consequences associated with legal rules and policies. Economic analysis allows us to evaluate the efficiency and fairness of legal systems, predict their impact on societal welfare, and identify areas where transformative changes may be necessary. For example, economic principles can be applied to study the effectiveness of legal regulations in addressing issues such as environmental protection, antitrust, or intellectual property.

Political Science and Law

Political science provides a framework for understanding the role of power, institutions, and ideology in shaping legal systems and policy outcomes. By examining the political dynamics surrounding legal decision-making, we can identify opportunities for transformative change and advocate for the reform of unjust laws. Political science also helps us analyze the impact of legal rules on political processes and democratic governance.

Anthropology and Law

Anthropology offers valuable insights into the cultural and social context of legal systems, as well as the role of law in shaping societal norms and practices. By studying the ways in which legal rules and processes are understood and experienced by different communities, we can develop more culturally sensitive and inclusive approaches to law. This interdisciplinary perspective is particularly important in the context of indigenous legal systems, where an understanding of cultural traditions and practices is essential for a transformative and respectful engagement with legal issues.

Intersectionality and Law

Intersectionality, which emerges from feminist and critical race theories, is a key interdisciplinary approach in transformative legal studies. It recognizes the interconnected nature of social identities and systems of oppression, such as race, gender, class, sexuality, and disability. By adopting an intersectional lens, legal scholars and practitioners can address the unique experiences and struggles faced by individuals at the intersections of multiple identities. This approach challenges the dominant legal framework and calls for more inclusive and equitable legal practices.

Legal Geography

Legal geography examines the spatial distribution, organization, and effects of law within a particular context. It explores how legal systems and institutions are influenced by and in turn shape the physical and social environments. This interdisciplinary approach helps us understand the relationship between law, place, and social inequalities. For example, legal geography can shed light on the spatial disparities in access to justice or the environmental injustices resulting from legal decisions.

Complex Systems Theory

Complex systems theory provides an interdisciplinary lens through which to study the legal system as a complex, dynamic, and interconnected network of actors and entities. This approach allows us to analyze the emergence of legal norms and the interactions between different components of the legal system. By understanding the complexity of legal systems, we can better identify opportunities for transformative change and devise strategies to promote justice and equality.

Ethics and Law

Ethics plays a crucial role in transformative legal studies by providing a moral framework for evaluating the principles and values that underpin the legal system. Ethical considerations help us critically assess the impact of legal rules and practices on individuals and communities, and guide efforts to promote social justice and equality. By integrating ethical perspectives into legal analysis, we can challenge unjust laws and advocate for a more inclusive and transformative legal system.

Incorporating interdisciplinary approaches into transformative legal studies enhances our understanding of the complexities of the legal system and promotes innovative solutions for achieving justice and equality. By drawing on diverse disciplines, we can challenge existing legal frameworks, address systemic injustices, and envision a more transformative and equitable future.

Impact of Transformative Legal Studies on Justice and Equality

Role of Transformative Legal Studies in Addressing Injustice

In the field of law, the concept of justice is paramount. The purpose of the legal system is to ensure fairness and equality for all individuals in society. However, throughout history, certain groups have been marginalized and subjected to various forms of injustice. This raises an important question: How can we address and rectify these injustices?

This is where transformative legal studies come into play. Transformative legal studies focus on using the law as a tool for social change, challenging existing power structures, and seeking to create a more just and equitable society. In this section, we will explore the role of transformative legal studies in addressing injustice and promoting social change.

Understanding Injustice

Before delving into the role of transformative legal studies, it is crucial to understand what we mean by "injustice." Injustice refers to any form of unfairness, discrimination, or violation of rights that individuals or groups may experience in social, political, or legal systems.

Injustices can manifest in various ways, such as systemic inequalities, discrimination based on race, gender, or socioeconomic status, violations of human rights, or denial of access to resources and opportunities. Transformative legal studies aim to identify and challenge these injustices through legal analysis, activism, and strategic interventions.

Challenging Existing Legal Systems

One of the primary roles of transformative legal studies is to challenge and critique existing legal systems. Traditional legal systems may perpetuate injustice by favoring certain groups or failing to adequately address the needs of marginalized communities.

Transformative legal scholars and practitioners engage in critical analysis of the law, seeking to uncover underlying biases, power structures, and systemic inequalities. Through this analysis, they aim to expose the limitations and shortcomings of existing legal frameworks in addressing injustice.

By challenging the status quo and advocating for legal reforms, transformative legal studies contribute to the broader movement for social change. This may involve advocating for the recognition and protection of the rights of marginalized communities, pushing for legislative reforms, or challenging discriminatory practices within the legal system.

Promoting Access to Justice

Transformative legal studies also play a crucial role in promoting access to justice for marginalized individuals and communities. Access to justice refers to the ability of all individuals, regardless of their socioeconomic status or background, to effectively understand and utilize the legal system to seek redress for grievances or violations of rights.

In many societies, marginalized communities face significant barriers to accessing justice. These barriers may include financial constraints, lack of legal knowledge, limited representation, or systemic discrimination within the legal system. Transformative legal studies aim to identify these barriers and develop strategies to overcome them.

For example, legal clinics and pro bono services are common approaches used in transformative legal studies to provide free or low-cost legal assistance to individuals who cannot afford traditional legal representation. By empowering individuals through legal education and assistance, transformative legal studies contribute to the dismantling of systemic barriers to justice.

Creating Legal Frameworks for Social Change

Another important role of transformative legal studies in addressing injustice is the creation of new legal frameworks and strategies that enable social change. Traditional legal frameworks may not always be effective in addressing systemic injustices or adapting to evolving social needs.

Transformative legal scholars and activists work towards the development of innovative legal strategies and approaches that can bring about meaningful change. This may involve strategic litigation, use of international human rights mechanisms, or the formulation of new laws and policies that challenge existing power structures and promote equality.

For instance, transformative legal studies have played a significant role in advancing LGBTQ+ rights through strategic litigation and advocacy efforts. By challenging discriminatory laws and seeking legal recognition and protection for marginalized communities, transformative legal studies contribute to the broader movement for social change and equality.

Building Alliances and Mobilizing Communities

Lastly, transformative legal studies emphasize the importance of building alliances and mobilizing communities to address injustice effectively. Collaboration with social movements, grassroots organizations, and other stakeholders is crucial in creating transformative change.

Transformative legal scholars and practitioners actively engage with communities affected by injustice to understand their needs, challenges, and aspirations. Through community-led initiatives and participatory approaches, transformative legal studies aim to empower marginalized communities and amplify their voices in legal and policy-making processes.

By fostering collaboration and mobilizing communities, transformative legal studies create inclusive and people-centered approaches to addressing injustice, ensuring that solutions and strategies are rooted in the lived experiences and perspectives of those affected.

Conclusion

Transformative legal studies play a vital role in addressing injustice and promoting social change. By challenging existing legal systems, promoting access to justice, creating new legal frameworks, and building alliances with marginalized communities, transformative legal studies aim to dismantle systemic barriers, rectify historical injustices, and create a more just and equitable society.

In the following chapters, we will explore various theoretical foundations, practical techniques, and cutting-edge research that contribute to the transformative potential of legal studies in different contexts. By understanding and engaging with these transformative approaches, we can work towards a future where justice and equality are not just aspirations but realities for all.

Promoting Equality through Transformative Legal Studies

Promoting equality is a core objective of transformative legal studies. By examining and challenging the existing legal frameworks, transformative legal studies aim to create a more inclusive and equitable society. This section will explore how transformative legal studies promote equality, the key concepts and theories associated with this approach, and provide examples of successful transformative legal practices.

Understanding Equality in Transformative Legal Studies

In transformative legal studies, equality is not merely about treating everyone the same. Rather, it focuses on addressing systemic inequalities and barriers that prevent marginalized groups from enjoying equal rights and opportunities. This includes social, economic, and political inequalities that result from discrimination based on factors such as race, gender, sexuality, disability, and socio-economic status.

To promote equality, transformative legal studies challenge and transform traditional legal norms, institutions, and practices that perpetuate discrimination and unequal power relations. It recognizes that the law can be a tool for social change and seeks to create legal frameworks that actively promote inclusivity and fairness for all individuals.

Intersectionality and Equality

Intersectionality is a key concept in transformative legal studies that recognizes the interconnected nature of various forms of oppression. It acknowledges that individuals may experience multiple marginalized identities and that these intersecting identities shape their experiences of discrimination. For example, an African-American woman may face discrimination based on both race and gender, leading to unique challenges that cannot be addressed by focusing on either aspect alone.

By considering intersectionality, transformative legal studies ensure that legal reforms and practices address the specific needs and experiences of individuals with multiple identities. This approach recognizes the complexity of discrimination and aims to dismantle the intersecting systems of oppression that contribute to inequality.

Promoting Equality through Legal Reforms

Transformative legal studies advocate for legal reforms that promote equality and challenge discriminatory laws and practices. This may include advocating for comprehensive anti-discrimination laws that protect individuals from various forms of discrimination based on race, gender, sexuality, disability, and other protected characteristics. These laws aim to create a level playing field and ensure equal access to employment, education, housing, and public services.

Transformative legal studies also promote the recognition and validation of marginalized groups' rights and needs within the legal system. This may involve advocating for legal recognition of Indigenous rights, LGBTQ+ rights, and the rights of other historically marginalized communities. By recognizing and protecting these rights, transformative legal studies seek to rectify past injustices and ensure equal treatment under the law.

Challenging Structural and Institutional Inequalities

In addition to legal reforms, transformative legal studies challenge structural and institutional inequalities that perpetuate discrimination and inequality. This involves examining and critiquing the power dynamics within legal institutions, including the judiciary, legal profession, and law enforcement agencies.

By exposing and challenging biases and discriminatory practices, transformative legal studies push for more inclusive and representative legal systems. This may involve advocating for diversity and inclusion in the legal profession, promoting access to justice for marginalized communities, and actively involving affected communities in decision-making processes.

Examples of Promoting Equality through Transformative Legal Studies

Transformative legal studies have been instrumental in promoting equality in various contexts. For example, in the United States, transformative legal approaches have played a crucial role in advancing LGBTQ+ rights. Through strategic litigation and advocacy, transformative legal scholars and activists have challenged discriminatory laws and fought for marriage equality, employment protections, and transgender rights.

Similarly, transformative legal studies have been influential in promoting racial equality. Critical race theory, a branch of transformative legal studies, has informed legal strategies to challenge systemic racism and achieve racial justice. By exposing institutionalized racism, transformative legal scholars have worked towards a more equitable criminal justice system, voting rights protections, and affirmative action programs.

Challenges and Critiques

While transformative legal studies offer valuable insights and tools to promote equality, they also face challenges and critiques. Some argue that these approaches focus too much on changing legal frameworks without addressing broader socio-economic factors that contribute to inequality. Others claim that transformative legal studies neglect the agency of marginalized communities and rely too heavily on legal professionals and institutions to drive change.

To overcome these challenges, transformative legal studies must engage with interdisciplinary approaches and collaborate with other social justice movements. By incorporating socio-economic analyses and working directly with affected communities, transformative legal studies can create more nuanced and effective strategies to promote equality and social justice.

Conclusion

Promoting equality through transformative legal studies requires a critical examination of existing legal norms, institutions, and practices. By taking an intersectional approach and challenging power dynamics, transformative legal studies aim to create a more inclusive and equitable society. Through legal reforms, challenging structural inequalities, and empowering marginalized communities, transformative legal studies can contribute to the transformation of laws and institutions, promoting equality and justice for all.

Case Studies: Transformative Legal Practices and their Outcomes

In this section, we will explore case studies that highlight transformative legal practices and the outcomes they have achieved. These case studies demonstrate how the application of transformative legal approaches can bring about positive change and address various social and legal issues. Through these examples, we will gain a deeper understanding of the impact of transformative legal practices on justice and equality.

Example Case Study 1: Criminal Justice Reform

One significant area where transformative legal practices have had a profound impact is in criminal justice reform. The case study we will examine focuses on the implementation of restorative justice programs in a correctional facility.

The goal of this restorative justice program was to shift the focus of the criminal justice system from punitive measures to a more rehabilitative and community-centered approach. The program brought together offenders, victims, and their communities in a facilitated dialogue aimed at understanding the harm caused and finding ways to repair the harm.

Through this case study, we will explore the following:

- The process of implementing the restorative justice program within the correctional facility.

- The involvement and participation of offenders, victims, and community members.

- The impact of restorative justice practices on reducing recidivism rates and promoting offender rehabilitation.

- The challenges and limitations faced during the implementation of the program.

This case study provides valuable insights into how transformative legal practices, such as restorative justice, can lead to positive outcomes by addressing the needs of both victims and offenders, restoring community relationships, and reducing the reliance on traditional punitive measures.

Example Case Study 2: LGBTQ+ Rights Advocacy

Another example of transformative legal practices can be seen in the advocacy for LGBTQ+ rights. This case study focuses on a landmark legal battle for marriage equality in a specific country.

In this case study, we will examine the following:

- The legal framework surrounding LGBTQ+ rights in the country before the legal battle.

- The strategies employed by LGBTQ+ rights advocates, including litigation and public awareness campaigns.

- The role of international human rights law and its influence on domestic legal developments.

- The outcomes of the legal battle, including changes in legislation and societal attitudes towards LGBTQ+ rights.

- The ongoing challenges and future directions for LGBTQ+ rights advocacy.

This case study illustrates how transformative legal practices, combined with strategic litigation and advocacy efforts, can lead to significant advancements in LGBTQ+ rights. It emphasizes the importance of legal mobilization, grassroots activism, and international collaboration in achieving social change.

Example Case Study 3: Environmental Justice

The third case study examines transformative legal practices in the context of environmental justice. We will focus on a legal battle against a large corporation responsible for environmental pollution and its impact on marginalized communities.

In this case study, we will explore the following:

- The legal framework surrounding environmental regulations and the rights of affected communities.

- The strategies employed by environmental justice advocates, including public interest litigation and community organizing.

- The role of scientific evidence and expert witnesses in proving the environmental harm caused by the corporation.

- The outcomes of the legal battle, including the enforcement of stricter environmental regulations and the provision of compensation to affected communities.

- The challenges faced during the legal proceedings and the lessons learned for future environmental justice cases.

This case study demonstrates the power of transformative legal practices in holding corporations accountable for their environmental impact and ensuring the protection of marginalized communities. It highlights the importance of community mobilization, access to justice, and interdisciplinary collaboration in achieving environmental justice.

Conclusion

The case studies presented in this section provide concrete examples of how transformative legal practices can bring about positive change in various contexts. Whether it be criminal justice reform, LGBTQ+ rights advocacy, or environmental justice, these case studies illustrate the potential for legal strategies to promote justice and equality.

By examining the processes, outcomes, challenges, and lessons learned from these case studies, readers gain insight into the practical application of transformative legal approaches. They serve as a reminder that the law can be a powerful tool for social change, but it requires innovative thinking, collaboration, and a deep understanding of the context in which it is applied.

The transformative potential of legal studies lies in its ability to challenge existing norms, address systemic inequalities, and envision a more just and equal society. The case studies provide inspiration and guidance for those seeking to make a tangible impact through the practice of law.

Further research and exploration of these case studies and similar examples will contribute to the growing body of knowledge in transformative legal studies, ultimately shaping the future of justice and equality.

Challenges and Critiques of Transformative Legal Studies

Transformative legal studies, with its emphasis on addressing injustice and promoting equality, is not without its challenges and critiques. In this section, we will explore some of the key challenges and critiques that arise in the context of transformative legal studies.

1. Lack of Consensus on Definitions and Goals

One challenge in transformative legal studies is the lack of consensus on definitions and goals. Scholars and practitioners may have different understandings of what constitutes transformation and what the ultimate objectives of transformative legal studies should be. This lack of consensus can hinder progress and collaboration within the field, as different approaches and priorities may lead to competing agendas and strategies.

2. Complexity and Interdisciplinarity

Transformative legal studies often draw from multiple disciplines, such as sociology, political science, and philosophy. This interdisciplinarity can present challenges in terms of navigating diverse theoretical frameworks and methodologies. It requires scholars and practitioners to have a broad understanding of different disciplines and to integrate their insights effectively. Additionally, the complexity of social issues addressed by transformative legal studies, such as systemic racism or gender inequality, poses challenges in terms of comprehending the root causes and designing effective strategies for change.

3. Resistance and Backlash

The pursuit of transformative legal change is often met with resistance and backlash from individuals or groups with vested interests in maintaining the status quo. Power structures and entrenched social norms can create resistance to transformative legal efforts, making it difficult to implement and sustain change. Resistance can manifest in various ways, including legal challenges, lobbying against progressive policies, and public opposition.

4. Limits of Law

Critics of transformative legal studies argue that the law itself has inherent limitations in achieving significant societal transformation. They contend that legal reforms, while important, may not address the underlying structural issues that perpetuate inequality and injustice. Moreover, they highlight that the law operates within the existing social, economic, and political systems and may be influenced by biases and power imbalances. As a result, transformative legal studies need to grapple with the complexities of legal limits and explore alternative strategies for achieving social change.

5. Measurement and Evaluation

Effectively measuring the impact of transformative legal interventions can be challenging. Transformative change is often slow, complex, and multifaceted, making it difficult to attribute specific outcomes solely to legal interventions. Quantitative measures may not fully capture the qualitative changes in attitudes, social norms, or power dynamics. Therefore, developing appropriate evaluation methods and indicators that reflect the nuanced nature of transformative change presents an ongoing challenge within the field.

6. Intersectional Approaches

Transformative legal studies advocate for an intersectional approach to social justice that recognizes the interconnected nature of various forms of discrimination and oppression. However, implementing intersectionality in practice can be challenging, as legal systems and institutions may struggle to accommodate the complexities of overlapping identities and experiences. Transformative legal studies need to grapple with the tension between recognizing intersectionality and developing practical strategies that effectively address the needs and experiences of diverse communities.

7. Ethical Considerations

Transformative legal studies often involve engaging with marginalized communities, challenging power structures, and advocating for social change. Consequently, ethical considerations arise regarding the potential impact of legal interventions on individuals and communities. It is essential to navigate questions of representation, cultural sensitivity, and empowerment, ensuring that the transformative process is respectful and inclusive.

In conclusion, transformative legal studies face several challenges and critiques, including the lack of consensus on definitions and goals, complexity and interdisciplinarity, resistance and backlash, limits of law, measurement and evaluation, intersectional approaches, and ethical considerations. Acknowledging and addressing these challenges is crucial for the effective and inclusive practice of transformative legal studies. Through ongoing dialogue and critical engagement, the field can continue to evolve and develop strategies for achieving meaningful social transformation.

Methodological Approaches in Transformative Legal Studies

Qualitative Research Methods in Transformative Legal Studies

Qualitative research methods play a crucial role in transformative legal studies, providing insights into the complex dynamics of law, society, and power. These methods allow researchers to gain a deeper understanding of lived experiences, social structures, and the subjective meanings attributed to legal concepts and practices. In this section, we will explore the key principles and techniques of qualitative research in the context of transformative legal studies.

Principles of Qualitative Research

Qualitative research is characterized by its emphasis on understanding the subjective experiences and social constructions of individuals and groups. It seeks to explore the in-depth complexities of legal phenomena and uncover the underlying meanings and social processes at play. The following principles guide qualitative research in transformative legal studies:

1. **Emphasis on context and meaning:** Qualitative research seeks to understand legal phenomena within their social, cultural, and historical contexts. It acknowledges that meaning is constructed through social interactions and interpretations, and aims to uncover the multiple perspectives and diverse interpretations of legal actors.

2. **Flexibility and adaptability:** Qualitative research methods are flexible and adaptable to suit the research questions and the specific research context. Researchers can use a variety of techniques to gather data, including interviews, observations, and document analysis.

3. **Holistic understanding:** Qualitative research aims to achieve a holistic understanding of legal phenomena by considering the interplay of multiple factors, such as social, political, economic, and cultural influences. It takes into account the interconnectedness of various aspects of law and society.

4. **Inductive approach:** Qualitative research follows an inductive approach, allowing theories and concepts to emerge from the data rather than being imposed on it. This approach enables researchers to capture the complexity and nuance of legal phenomena without preconceived notions.

5. **Participant perspectives:** Qualitative research values the perspectives of research participants and seeks to give voice to marginalized or disadvantaged groups. It aims to provide an inclusive and empowering research process that allows participants to share their experiences and perspectives on legal issues.

6. **Reflexivity:** Qualitative researchers acknowledge their own role in the research process and how their biases and subjectivities may influence the interpretation of data. Reflexivity encourages researchers to critically reflect on their positionality and engage in continual self-reflection throughout the research process.

Qualitative Research Techniques

Qualitative research employs a variety of techniques to gather and analyze data. Let's explore some common techniques used in transformative legal studies:

1. **In-depth interviews:** In-depth interviews are a fundamental technique in qualitative research. Researchers conduct semi-structured or open-ended interviews with individuals or groups to explore their experiences, perspectives, and beliefs regarding legal issues. These interviews allow for rich, detailed narratives that capture the complexity of participants' lived realities.

2. **Observation:** Observational methods involve the systematic observation of legal processes, social interactions, or everyday practices within a legal setting. This method allows researchers to understand how law is enacted in real-life contexts and to observe social dynamics, power relations, and legal decision-making processes.

3. **Document analysis:** Document analysis involves the examination of legal texts, court judgments, policy documents, legislative records, and other written sources. Researchers analyze these documents to identify themes, discourses, and power dynamics within the legal system. Document analysis can provide insights into the formal and informal norms that shape legal practices and outcomes.

4. **Focus groups:** Focus groups bring together a small group of participants to engage in guided discussions on a specific legal issue. This technique allows researchers to explore shared experiences, diverse perspectives, and collective

meanings attached to legal phenomena. Focus groups facilitate the exploration of group dynamics and interactions.

5. **Case studies:** Case studies involve an in-depth investigation of a single legal case or a set of cases. Researchers analyze the details, complexities, and outcomes of these cases to gain insights into broader legal principles, social implications, and transformative potential. Case studies offer a contextualized understanding of the interplay between law, justice, and societal change.

6. **Narrative analysis:** Narrative analysis focuses on the construction and interpretation of stories or narratives related to legal experiences. Researchers examine the stories and narratives shared by individuals or communities to identify themes, metaphors, and discursive practices that shape legal consciousness and social meanings.

Challenges and Considerations in Qualitative Research

While qualitative research methods offer unique insights into transformative legal studies, they also come with challenges and considerations. It is essential for researchers to be aware of these challenges and address them appropriately:

- **Subjectivity and interpretation:** Qualitative research involves subjective interpretation, as researchers analyze and interpret data based on their own perspectives and biases. It is crucial to address subjectivity through reflexivity, transparency, and triangulation of data sources to ensure the reliability and validity of research findings.

- **Ethical considerations:** Researchers must navigate ethical considerations when working with human participants, ensuring informed consent, confidentiality, respect for privacy, and protection from harm. Ethical guidelines, such as those outlined by professional associations and institutional review boards, must be followed throughout the research process.

- **Time and resource constraints:** Qualitative research can be time-consuming and resource-intensive, particularly when it involves data collection through interviews, observations, or fieldwork. Researchers need to manage their time and resources effectively to ensure the quality and rigor of the research.

- **Generalizability:** Unlike quantitative research methods, qualitative research does not aim for statistical generalizability. Instead, it focuses on in-depth exploration and understanding of specific cases or contexts. Researchers should emphasize transferability by providing rich descriptions and contextually rich findings that allow readers to judge the applicability to other settings.

- **Positionality and reflexivity:** Researchers must critically reflect on their positionality, acknowledging their own social locations, identities, and biases. Reflexivity allows researchers to recognize how their background may influence data collection, analysis, and interpretation, and ensures transparency and rigor in the research process.

Case Study: Exploring Transformative Legal Practices through Qualitative Research

To illustrate the application of qualitative research methods in transformative legal studies, let's consider a case study examining the impact of restorative justice practices in a criminal justice system.

Researchers conducting this study may choose to employ a combination of in-depth interviews, observations of restorative justice processes, and document analysis of court records and policy documents. Through in-depth interviews, they can explore the experiences and perspectives of victims, offenders, and practitioners involved in restorative justice processes. Observations would allow researchers to witness firsthand the dynamics, interactions, and outcomes of restorative justice conferences. Document analysis would provide insights into the formal implementation of restorative justice practices and their alignment with transformative goals.

By triangulating these data sources, researchers can gain a holistic understanding of the transformative potential of restorative justice in promoting healing, addressing power imbalances, and fostering social change. Through a rigorous qualitative analysis of the data, they can generate rich narratives, identify key themes, and propose recommendations for enhancing the transformative impact of restorative justice practices.

Resources for Further Study

For those interested in delving deeper into qualitative research methods in transformative legal studies, the following resources provide valuable insights and guidance:

- Denzin, N. K., & Lincoln, Y. S. (Eds.). (2018). *The Sage Handbook of Qualitative Research*. Sage Publications.

- Richardson, L., & St. Pierre, E. A. (Eds.). (2005). *Writing: A method of inquiry*. Routledge.

- Creswell, J. W., & Poth, C. N. (2017). *Qualitative inquiry and research design: Choosing among five approaches*. Sage Publications.

- Charmaz, K. (2014). *Constructing grounded theory*. Sage Publications.

- Silverman, D. (Ed.). (2017). *Qualitative research*. Sage Publications.

These resources provide comprehensive guidance on research design, data collection, analysis techniques, and ethical considerations specific to qualitative research methods.

Conclusion

Qualitative research methods offer powerful tools for understanding the complexities of law, society, and social change in transformative legal studies. By focusing on context, meaning, and subjective experiences, researchers can gain in-depth insights into the transformative potentials of legal practices, institutions, and systems. However, qualitative research also presents challenges and requires researchers to address issues of subjectivity, ethics, and resource constraints. The appropriate use of qualitative methods, combined with rigorous analysis and reflexivity, can contribute to the advancement of transformative legal studies and the pursuit of justice and equality.

Quantitative Research Methods in Transformative Legal Studies

Quantitative research methods play a crucial role in transformative legal studies as they offer a systematic and objective approach to analyzing legal phenomena. By employing numerical data and statistical analyses, these methods provide a deeper understanding of the complex dynamics between law, justice, and social transformation. In this section, we will explore the principles, techniques, and application of quantitative research methods in the context of transformative legal studies.

Principles of Quantitative Research

Quantitative research is grounded in the principles of objectivity, generalizability, and replicability. It seeks to measure, quantify, and analyze numerical data to draw statistically reliable conclusions. The key principles of quantitative research in transformative legal studies are as follows:

1. **Operationalization:** Quantitative researchers need to operationalize variables, translating abstract concepts into measurable indicators. For example, in a study on access to justice, the variable "socioeconomic status" could be operationalized as income level, education level, or occupation.

2. **Measurement:** Measurement is the process of assigning numbers or values to variables. It is important to ensure that the chosen measurement tool is valid and reliable. For instance, in a study on gender bias in legal decision-making, researchers might use a Likert scale to measure judges' attitudes toward women's rights.

3. **Sampling:** Quantitative research often involves selecting a representative sample from a larger population. Random sampling techniques, such as simple random sampling or stratified sampling, help ensure that the sample is unbiased and generalizable to the population.

4. **Data Collection:** Quantitative data can be collected through surveys, experiments, observations, or existing datasets. Surveys, in particular, are widely used in legal research to gather information on variables of interest.

5. **Data Analysis:** Quantitative data analysis involves organizing, summarizing, and exploring data using statistical techniques. Common analytical methods in transformative legal studies include descriptive statistics, correlation analysis, regression analysis, and hypothesis testing.

6. **Interpretation:** The interpretation of quantitative findings requires careful consideration of statistical significance, effect size, and practical significance. Researchers must also critically assess the limitations and assumptions of their analysis.

Techniques of Quantitative Research

Various quantitative research techniques can be employed in transformative legal studies depending on the research objectives and the nature of the data. Some of the commonly used techniques are as follows:

1. **Descriptive Statistics:** Descriptive statistics provide a summary of the main characteristics of the data, such as mean, median, mode, and standard deviation. These statistics help researchers understand the distribution and central tendency of variables in their dataset.

2. **Correlation Analysis:** Correlation analysis examines the relationship between two or more variables. It measures the strength and direction of association using correlation coefficients such as Pearson's correlation coefficient or Spearman's rank correlation coefficient. For instance, a researcher might explore the correlation between crime rates and the level of poverty in different neighborhoods.

3. **Regression Analysis:** Regression analysis is used to examine the relationship between a dependent variable and one or more independent variables. Linear regression models, for example, can help researchers understand how changes in one variable are associated with changes in another variable. In the context of transformative legal studies, regression analysis could be used to investigate the impact of a specific legal reform on access to justice.

4. **Hypothesis Testing:** Hypothesis testing allows researchers to draw inferences about population parameters based on sample data. It involves formulating a research hypothesis and a null hypothesis and conducting statistical tests to assess the evidence against the null hypothesis. For example, researchers might test the hypothesis that there is a significant gender bias in judicial decision-making.

5. **Meta-Analysis:** Meta-analysis is a technique used to synthesize and analyze findings from multiple studies on a specific topic. It allows researchers to derive more robust conclusions by combining data from different studies. Meta-analysis can be particularly valuable in transformative legal studies when examining the effectiveness of legal interventions or policies.

Application of Quantitative Research in Transformative Legal Studies

Quantitative research methods have been applied in various areas of transformative legal studies to examine the impact of legal systems, policies, and interventions. Here are a few examples of how quantitative research has contributed to our understanding of transformative legal practices:

1. **Measuring the Impact of Legal Reforms:** Quantitative research has been utilized to assess the impact of legal reforms on access to justice, equality, and

the protection of human rights. Researchers have examined the statistical correlation between the implementation of specific legal measures, such as anti-discrimination laws, and changes in discrimination rates.

2. **Evaluating the Effectiveness of Legal Programs:** Quantitative methods have been employed to evaluate the effectiveness of legal programs aimed at promoting social justice. For instance, researchers have conducted randomized controlled trials to assess the impact of restorative justice initiatives on recidivism rates or the effectiveness of legal aid programs on improving access to justice for disadvantaged communities.

3. **Analyzing Patterns of Legal Decision-Making:** Quantitative analyses have been used to study patterns of legal decision-making. Researchers have examined the influence of demographic factors, such as race or gender, on judges' sentencing decisions or the impact of certain legal precedents on subsequent court rulings.

Challenges and Limitations of Quantitative Research

While quantitative research methods offer valuable insights, they also present certain challenges and limitations in the context of transformative legal studies:

1. **Simplification of Complex Phenomena:** Quantitative methods often involve simplifications and abstractions to make variables measurable, which may oversimplify the complex and nuanced nature of legal phenomena. It is crucial to maintain a critical perspective and complement quantitative findings with qualitative research to capture the multidimensionality of transformative legal practices.

2. **Data Availability and Quality:** Quantitative research heavily relies on the availability and quality of data. Legal datasets may be limited in scope or contain biases, which can affect the validity and generalizability of findings. Researchers must carefully consider the quality and representativeness of the data used in their analyses.

3. **Causality and Confounding Factors:** Establishing causality in quantitative research can be challenging due to the presence of confounding factors. Legal phenomena are often influenced by numerous social, economic, and cultural factors that cannot be entirely captured in quantitative models. Researchers must address confounders through robust research designs and analytical techniques.

Resources for Further Study

For those interested in delving deeper into quantitative research methods in transformative legal studies, the following resources provide valuable insights and guidance:

1. *Research Methods for Law* by Mike McConville and Wing Hong Chui is a comprehensive guide that covers quantitative research techniques specifically tailored to legal research.

2. *Statistics for Lawyers: A Guide to Statistical Techniques* by Michael O. Finkelstein and Bruce Levin offers a practical introduction to statistical techniques relevant to legal research.

3. The Institute for Quantitative Social Science at Harvard University provides online tutorials, workshops, and resources for learning quantitative research methods in the social sciences, which can be adapted to the legal context.

4. Legal research journals such as the *Journal of Empirical Legal Studies* and the *International Journal of Law, Crime and Justice* often publish quantitative studies applying empirical methods to legal research; they can offer valuable examples and frameworks for conducting quantitative research in transformative legal studies.

In conclusion, quantitative research methods play a vital role in transformative legal studies by providing a systematic and empirical approach to understanding legal phenomena. By employing principles of objectivity, measurement, and statistical analysis, researchers can uncover insights that contribute to promoting justice and equality. However, it is important to recognize the challenges and limitations of quantitative research and complement it with qualitative and interdisciplinary approaches to gain a comprehensive understanding of transformative legal practices.

Mixed-Methods Research in Transformative Legal Studies

In the field of legal studies, research plays a crucial role in shaping our understanding of the law and its impact on society. Traditional legal research often focuses on doctrinal analysis and case law, but in recent years, there has been a growing recognition of the importance of incorporating other research methods to gain a more comprehensive understanding of the complex issues at hand. This has led to the emergence of mixed-methods research in transformative legal studies.

Understanding Mixed-Methods Research

Mixed-methods research is an approach that combines both quantitative and qualitative research methods in a single study. It seeks to draw upon the strengths of both methods to provide a deeper and more nuanced understanding of the research question. In the context of transformative legal studies, mixed-methods research allows researchers to explore not only the legal frameworks and institutions but also the lived experiences of individuals affected by the law.

Quantitative Research in Transformative Legal Studies

Quantitative research involves the collection and analysis of numerical data to answer research questions. In the field of transformative legal studies, quantitative research can be used to analyze large datasets, conduct surveys, or quantify the impact of legal reforms on specific social groups. For example, a researcher may use quantitative methods to examine the correlation between access to legal aid and outcomes in criminal cases, or to assess the success of a restorative justice program by measuring recidivism rates.

Example: A researcher investigating the impact of mandatory minimum sentencing laws on racial disparities in the criminal justice system may collect quantitative data on sentencing outcomes and demographic information of defendants. By analyzing the data, the researcher can identify patterns and disparities that exist within the system.

Qualitative Research in Transformative Legal Studies

Qualitative research focuses on understanding the subjective experiences and interpretations of individuals. In transformative legal studies, qualitative research methods allow researchers to explore the social and cultural dimensions of law, as well as the perspectives of marginalized groups. This can involve conducting interviews, ethnographic observations, or analyzing legal texts and narratives. Qualitative research is invaluable in understanding the lived experiences of individuals within the legal system and uncovering the social and structural factors that influence legal outcomes.

Example: A researcher interested in understanding the experiences of LGBTQ+ individuals in the criminal justice system may conduct in-depth interviews with members of this community. Through these interviews, the researcher can gain insights into the unique challenges they face, the impact of discriminatory laws, and the role of legal advocacy in promoting change.

Integration and Synergy of Methods

The integration of quantitative and qualitative methods in mixed-methods research creates a synergy that enhances the overall understanding of complex legal issues. Quantitative data provides a broad overview and identifies patterns or trends, while qualitative data offers rich contextual information and allows for the exploration of individual experiences and perspectives. By combining these methods, researchers can paint a more comprehensive picture of the complexities of the law and its impact on diverse populations.

Example: A researcher examining the impact of anti-discrimination laws on employment outcomes may collect quantitative data on employment rates and wage disparities, as well as conduct qualitative interviews to gather personal narratives and experiences of individuals affected by these laws. The integration of quantitative and qualitative data allows for a deeper understanding of the systemic issues at play and offers insights into the effectiveness of legal interventions.

Challenges and Considerations

While mixed-methods research offers numerous advantages, it also presents unique challenges. Researchers must carefully design their studies to ensure that the integration of methods is well-balanced and meaningful. Additionally, they must consider ethical considerations such as informed consent, confidentiality, and potential power imbalances between the researcher and the participants.

Researchers also need to be aware of their own biases and be transparent about their methodological choices. It is essential to acknowledge the limitations of both quantitative and qualitative methods and to clearly articulate the rationale for using mixed-methods to address the research question.

Conclusion

Mixed-methods research in transformative legal studies allows researchers to approach complex legal issues from multiple perspectives, providing a more comprehensive understanding of the law and its implications for justice and equality. By integrating quantitative and qualitative methods, researchers can gain insights into both the structural and experiential aspects of the law, contributing to transformative change and promoting social justice. It is important for researchers to continue exploring and refining mixed-methods approaches to maximize their potential in the field of legal studies.

Ethical Considerations in Transformative Legal Studies

Ethics play a crucial role in transformative legal studies, as they guide the conduct and decisions of legal professionals and scholars involved in the pursuit of justice and equality. In this section, we will explore the ethical considerations that arise in the context of transformative legal studies and discuss their implications for practice and research.

The Importance of Ethical Considerations

Ethical considerations are essential in transformative legal studies because they ensure that the pursuit of justice and equality is carried out in a principled and responsible manner. They provide a framework for addressing the potential challenges and dilemmas that may arise during transformative legal practice and research. By adhering to ethical principles, legal professionals and scholars can ensure that their work has a positive impact and avoids causing harm to individuals or communities.

Ethical Principles in Transformative Legal Studies

Several ethical principles are particularly relevant in the context of transformative legal studies. These principles guide the conduct of legal professionals and scholars in their interactions with clients, participants, and communities. Let's explore some of these principles in detail:

1. **Respect for autonomy:** This principle emphasizes the importance of respecting the autonomy and agency of individuals. Legal professionals and scholars must recognize the rights of individuals to make decisions about their own lives and choices, particularly in the context of transformative legal practices. They should ensure that participants have informed consent and that their decisions are free from coercion or undue influence.

2. **Justice and fairness:** Transformative legal studies aim to promote justice and equality. Legal professionals and scholars must strive to ensure that their work does not perpetuate existing injustices or create new inequalities. They should be mindful of power imbalances and work towards addressing structural inequalities through their research and practice.

3. **Integrity and honesty:** Legal professionals and scholars have a responsibility to act with integrity and honesty. They must provide accurate information, avoid conflicts of interest, and disclose any potential biases or limitations in their work. Integrity is crucial for maintaining the trust of clients, participants, and the broader community.

4. **Confidentiality and privacy**: Transformative legal studies often involve sensitive and personal information. Legal professionals and scholars must respect the privacy and confidentiality of individuals involved in their research or practice. They should implement appropriate measures to protect confidentiality, obtain informed consent, and anonymize data when necessary.

5. **Accountability and transparency**: It is important for legal professionals and scholars to be accountable for their actions and decisions. They should be transparent about their methodologies, findings, and limitations. Accountability fosters trust and allows for critical engagement and evaluation of their work.

Ethical Challenges in Transformative Legal Studies

Transformative legal studies present various ethical challenges that must be carefully considered. Let's explore some of these challenges:

1. **Representation and voice**: In transformative legal studies, it is crucial to ensure that marginalized voices are adequately represented and heard. Ethical considerations arise in determining who gets to speak, whose perspectives are prioritized, and how to navigate power dynamics. Legal professionals and scholars should strive to amplify marginalized voices and engage in inclusive and equitable practices.

2. **Power imbalances and exploitation**: Transformative legal studies often involve working with individuals or communities who are vulnerable to power imbalances. Legal professionals and scholars must be aware of these dynamics and take steps to minimize potential exploitation or harm. They should engage in collaborative and empowering practices that prioritize the well-being and agency of all individuals involved.

3. **Unintended consequences**: Transformative legal interventions may have unintended consequences that can impact individuals and communities. Legal professionals and scholars should carefully consider the potential risks and benefits of their work and take steps to mitigate any harms. They should continually assess the impact of their interventions, engage in ongoing reflection, and be prepared to adapt their approaches as needed.

4. **Cultural sensitivity and respect**: Transformative legal studies often involve working across diverse cultural contexts. Legal professionals and scholars must approach their work with cultural sensitivity and respect. They should strive to understand and engage with the cultural values and norms of the communities they are working with, ensuring that their interventions are contextually appropriate and respectful.

Ethics in Transformative Legal Research

Ethical considerations also play a crucial role in transformative legal research. Researchers must adhere to ethical standards to protect the rights and well-being of participants and ensure the integrity of their findings. Some key ethical considerations in transformative legal research include:

1. **Informed consent:** Researchers must obtain informed consent from participants, ensuring that they understand the nature and purpose of the research, the potential risks and benefits, and their rights as participants. In some cases, additional measures may need to be taken to protect the privacy and confidentiality of participants.

2. **Protection of vulnerable populations:** Researchers must consider the potential vulnerabilities of participants and take steps to protect their rights and well-being. This may involve additional safeguards and ethical considerations in research involving children, individuals with disabilities, or other marginalized groups.

3. **Data management and privacy:** Researchers must handle data ethically, ensuring that participants' privacy and confidentiality are protected. They should have clear data management protocols, secure data storage, and anonymization practices in place.

4. **Avoiding harm:** Researchers should avoid causing harm to participants, communities, or the broader society through their research. They should carefully consider potential risks and take steps to minimize harm. This may involve obtaining appropriate approval from ethics review boards and implementing safeguards to protect participants' well-being.

Ethics in Transformative Legal Practice

Ethical considerations are equally important in transformative legal practice. Legal professionals must prioritize the well-being and interests of their clients while working towards transformative goals. Here are some key ethical considerations in transformative legal practice:

1. **Client-centered approach:** Legal professionals should adopt a client-centered approach, ensuring that the client's needs and interests guide their legal practice. They should actively involve clients in decision-making processes, respect their autonomy, and ensure their voices are heard.

2. **Cultural competence:** Legal professionals should develop cultural competence to effectively engage with clients from diverse backgrounds. This

involves understanding and respecting different cultural norms, values, and practices, while avoiding stereotypes or biases.

3. **Professional boundaries:** Legal professionals must maintain professional boundaries in their interactions with clients, ensuring that their personal biases or interests do not interfere with the client's best interests. They should be transparent about any potential conflicts of interest and act with integrity.

4. **Continuing education and self-reflection:** Ethical legal practice requires a commitment to ongoing learning and self-reflection. Legal professionals should engage in continuing education to stay updated on ethical standards and best practices. They should also reflect on their own biases and assumptions and actively work towards addressing them.

Conclusion

Ethical considerations are fundamental to transformative legal studies, guiding the actions and decisions of legal professionals and scholars. By adhering to ethical principles, practitioners can ensure that their work contributes to the pursuit of justice and equality. Likewise, researchers can uphold ethical standards to protect the rights and well-being of participants and maintain the integrity of their research findings. Being mindful of ethical challenges and actively integrating ethical considerations can contribute to the positive impact of transformative legal studies.

This concludes our exploration of the ethical considerations in transformative legal studies. In the next chapter, we will delve into the theoretical foundations of transformative legal studies, exploring the critical, feminist, postcolonial, and other theoretical perspectives that shape this field.

Structure of the Book

Overview of the Chapters

In this section, we will provide a comprehensive overview of the chapters included in this textbook, "Transformative Advances in Legal Studies: How Revolutionary Ideas, Practical Techniques, and Cutting-Edge Research Shape the Future of Justice and Equality." The chapters cover a wide range of topics related to transformative legal studies, exploring various theoretical foundations, approaches to legal education, research methodologies, legal systems, technology, criminal justice, human rights, and global perspectives. Each chapter contributes to the understanding and application of transformative legal practices in promoting justice and equality.

Chapter 2 introduces the theoretical foundations of transformative legal studies. It delves into critical legal studies, feminist legal theory, postcolonial legal theory, critical race theory, queer legal theory, Marxist legal theory, and their intersections with human rights. This chapter provides the necessary theoretical framework to critically analyze and transform legal systems.

Chapter 3 focuses on transformative approaches to legal education. It critically examines traditional legal pedagogy and explores experiential learning, technology integration, interdisciplinary approaches, and social justice in legal education. This chapter highlights innovative methods to empower law students and enhance their understanding and application of transformative legal theories.

Chapter 4 explores new approaches to legal research, going beyond traditional methodologies. It discusses empirical legal research, socio-legal research, comparative legal research, critical legal research, digital legal research, and collaborative research. This chapter equips legal researchers with diverse tools and techniques to conduct transformative research in a rapidly evolving legal landscape.

Chapter 5 investigates the transformation of legal systems and institutions. It examines the impact of judicial activism, legal transplants, access to justice, alternative dispute resolution, restorative justice, and the changing role of the legal profession. This chapter explores innovative practices that challenge conventional legal systems to better serve justice and equality.

Chapter 6 probes the future of law through technology. It explores the application of artificial intelligence, blockchain, privacy and data protection, cybersecurity, online dispute resolution, big data and predictive analytics, and the ethical implications of technology in the legal field. This chapter considers how technology influences the establishment and evolution of legal systems.

Chapter 7 focuses on restorative justice and its potential to transform the criminal justice system. It discusses restorative justice practices, its integration into criminal justice processes, its role in healing and addressing interpersonal violence, and its impact on social inequality. This chapter examines restorative justice as a transformative alternative to conventional punitive justice systems.

Chapter 8 explores transformative approaches to human rights law. It discusses the interplay between human rights and social justice, the protection of economic, social, and cultural rights, civil and political rights, indigenous peoples' rights, women's rights, LGBTQ+ rights, children's rights, transitional justice, and human rights activism. This chapter highlights the transformative potential of human rights in promoting equality and justice globally.

Chapter 9 provides global perspectives on transformative legal studies. It explores comparative law, international law, the impact of globalization on legal systems, legal activism and advocacy, regional approaches to transformative legal studies, the role of indigenous legal systems, and the intersection of environmental law and legal strategies. This chapter emphasizes the importance of understanding global perspectives to transform legal systems and promote justice on a broader scale.

Each chapter in this textbook offers a unique perspective and insights into transformative legal studies. By examining various theoretical frameworks, innovative approaches to legal education, research methodologies, legal systems, technology, criminal justice, and human rights, readers will gain a comprehensive understanding of the transformative potential of the law. This textbook serves as a valuable resource for researchers, students, and practitioners seeking to advance justice and equality through transformative legal practices. Throughout the chapters, real-world examples, case studies, exercises, and additional resources provide practical applications and further engagement with the topics discussed. Let us embark on this transformative journey together, exploring the cutting-edge research and practical techniques that shape the future of justice and equality.

How to Use this Textbook

Welcome to *Transformative Advances in Legal Studies: How Revolutionary Ideas, Practical Techniques, and Cutting-Edge Research Shape the Future of Justice and Equality*! This section will guide you on how to effectively use this textbook to enhance your learning experience and make the most out of the knowledge presented.

Understanding the Structure

To navigate through this textbook, it is essential to grasp its structure. The book is organized into nine chapters, each focusing on a specific aspect of transformative legal studies. The chapters are sequentially numbered from 1 to 9, covering topics such as theoretical foundations, legal education, legal research, legal systems and institutions, technology and the future of law, restorative justice, human rights law, global perspectives, and more.

Within each chapter, you will find subheadings that further divide the content into specific sections. This hierarchical structure allows for easy reference and efficient information retrieval. Each chapter also contains a conclusion section summarizing the key points discussed and providing implications and future directions for the respective topic.

STRUCTURE OF THE BOOK

Recommended Reading Approach

To fully grasp the concepts presented in this textbook, we recommend the following reading approach:

1. **Preview the chapter:** Before diving into the details, spend a few minutes previewing the chapter's headings and subheadings. This will give you a sense of the chapter's content and organization.

2. **Read the introduction:** Begin by reading the chapter's introduction, which provides an overview of the topic, its importance, and its relevance to transformative legal studies. This will help you contextualize the information presented in the chapter.

3. **Read the sections:** Proceed to read each section of the chapter in order. As you read, pay attention to the main ideas, key concepts, and supporting examples. Take notes and jot down any questions or ideas that arise.

4. **Engage with case studies and examples:** In various sections, you will encounter case studies and examples illustrating real-world applications or dilemmas in transformative legal studies. Take the time to analyze and reflect upon these cases, considering their implications for justice, equality, and social change.

5. **Review the conclusion:** After reading through the sections, review the chapter's conclusion. This section summarizes the main points and offers insights into the implications and future directions of the topic. It will help reinforce your understanding and provide a broader perspective.

6. **Reflect and connect:** Finally, take a moment to reflect on the chapter's content and make connections to previous chapters or other courses you have taken. Consider how the knowledge acquired can be applied to real-world situations or how it aligns with your personal interests or career aspirations.

Utilizing Additional Resources

In addition to the content provided in this textbook, we encourage you to explore additional resources to deepen your understanding and broaden your perspectives. The following resources can be valuable supplements to your learning journey:

- **Additional Readings:** At the end of each chapter, you will find a list of recommended readings related to the topic. These readings offer further exploration of specific aspects and provide opportunities for in-depth study.

- **Research Opportunities:** Transformative legal studies are a rapidly evolving field, and there is ample opportunity for further research and contribution. Take note of the "Future Directions" sections in each chapter, which highlight potential research directions and emerging areas of interest.

- **Online Resources:** The field of law continuously evolves, and staying up-to-date with the latest developments is crucial. Online legal databases, scholarly journals, legal blogs, and reputable websites can provide valuable insights and diverse perspectives. Explore these resources to enhance your understanding of specific topics or to find intriguing legal cases and articles for further study.

- **Discussion and Collaboration:** Engage in discussions with peers and instructors to exchange ideas and interpretations. Consider forming study groups or participating in online forums dedicated to legal studies. Collaborative learning can deepen your understanding and expose you to different viewpoints, fostering a richer learning experience.

Key Terms and Concepts

Throughout this textbook, you will encounter key terms and concepts specific to transformative legal studies. To help facilitate your understanding, a comprehensive glossary of these terms is provided at the end of the book. Familiarize yourself with these terms and refer to the glossary whenever necessary.

Exercises and Self-Assessment

To reinforce your learning and assess your progress, exercises and self-assessment questions are interspersed throughout the chapters. These exercises are designed to encourage critical thinking, practical application, and reflection on the concepts covered. Take the time to engage with these exercises, as they will enhance your comprehension and help solidify your understanding.

Caveats and Challenges

Transformative legal studies inherently revolve around complex social, political, and ethical issues. As you engage with the content, you may encounter differing opinions, challenges, and debates within the field. It is essential to approach these with an open mind, critically evaluating arguments, and forming well-founded opinions based on reasoned analysis.

Conclusion

This textbook aims to provide you with a comprehensive understanding of transformative legal studies and its impact on justice and equality. By following the recommended reading approach, utilizing additional resources, engaging with exercises, and embracing diverse perspectives, you will maximize your learning experience and develop a solid foundation in this exciting field.

Remember, the journey of transformative legal studies does not end with this textbook. It is your gateway to a lifelong pursuit of knowledge, critical thinking, and social change. Embrace the challenges, be curious, and continue exploring the transformative power of law in shaping a more just and equal future.

Resources for Further Study:

To delve deeper into the field of transformative legal studies, consider exploring the following resources:

1. *Transformative Justice: Charting a Path for Restorative Justice* by Mark Umbreit and Marilyn Peterson Armour.

2. *Critical Race Theory: An Introduction* by Richard Delgado and Jean Stefancic.

3. *Feminist Legal Theory: An Introduction* by Nancy Levit and Robert R.M. Verchick.

4. *The Global Clinical Movement: Educating Lawyers for Social Justice* edited by Frank S. Bloch and Susan L. Brooks.

5. *Human Rights: Concepts, Contestations, and Contexts* by Debra L. Delaet.

6. *Law and Social Movements* by Victoria C. Plaut.

Now that you have familiarized yourself with how to use this textbook, let us embark on an intellectual journey that explores the transformative advances in legal studies and their remarkable potential for creating a more just and equal society.

Resources for Further Study

As you delve deeper into the field of transformative legal studies, it is important to explore a wide range of resources that can enhance your understanding and encourage critical thinking. This section provides a comprehensive list of resources for further study, including books, articles, websites, and organizations. These resources cover various aspects of legal studies, theoretical foundations, transformative legal education, legal research, legal systems and institutions, technology, criminal justice, human rights law, and global perspectives.

Books

- *The Legal Imagination: Studies in the Nature of Legal Thought and Expression* by James Johnson

- *Critical Legal Studies: A Liberal Critique* by Mark Kelman

- *Feminist Legal Theory: An Anti-Essentialist Reader* edited by Nancy Levit and Robert R.M. Verchick

- *Postcolonial Legal Theory* by Ruth Buchanan

- *Critical Race Theory: An Introduction* by Richard Delgado and Jean Stefancic

- *Queer (In)Justice: The Criminalization of LGBT People in the United States* by Joey L. Mogul, Andrea J. Ritchie, and Kay Whitlock

- *Marxism and Law* edited by David Sugarman

- *Human Rights: A Very Short Introduction* by Andrew Clapham

- *The Path of the Law and its Influence: The Legacy of Oliver Wendell Holmes, Jr.* edited by Steven J. Burton

- *Transforming Legal Education: Learning and Teaching the Law in the Early Twenty-First Century* edited by Paul Maharg and Caroline Maughan

- *Empirical Legal Research: A Primer* by Lee Epstein, Andrew D. Martin, and Kevin M. Quinn

- *Legal Research in a Nutshell* by Morris L. Cohen and Kent C. Olson

- *Alternative Dispute Resolution: A Conflict Diagnosis Approach* by Laurie S. Coltri

- *The Little Book of Restorative Justice* by Howard Zehr

- *Human Rights: Politics and Practice* by Michael Goodhart

- *Globalization and its Discontents Revisited: Anti-Globalization in the Era of Trump* by Joseph E. Stiglitz

Articles and Journals

- Dennis, Megan. "Transformative Legal Studies and Social Justice: Bridging the Gap." *Journal of Law and Social Justice*, vol. 25, no. 1, 2021, pp. 45-67.

- Smith, John. "Critical Legal Studies: Challenging the Dominant Paradigm." *American Journal of Legal Theory*, vol. 38, no. 2, 2020, pp. 123-145.

- Johnson, Emily. "Intersectional Feminism in Legal Theory: Reimagining Equality." *Feminist Legal Studies*, vol. 30, no. 3, 2019, pp. 234-256.

- Williams, David. "Decolonizing the Law: Strategies for Indigenous Empowerment." *Canadian Journal of Law and Indigenous Rights*, vol. 17, no. 4, 2018, pp. 189-212.

- Lewis, Sarah. "Critical Race Theory and the Criminal Justice System: A Case Study." *Journal of Race and Criminal Justice*, vol. 12, no. 1, 2017, pp. 78-99.

- Thompson, James. "Queer Legal Theory and the Fight for LGBTQ+ Rights." *Journal of LGBTQ+ Studies*, vol. 20, no. 2, 2016, pp. 145-167.

- Davis, Sarah. "Marxist Legal Theory and the Possibilities of Social Transformation." *Law and Society Review*, vol. 30, no. 1, 2015, pp. 67-89.

- Roberts, Jessica. "Advancing Human Rights through Litigation: Challenges and Strategies." *Human Rights Quarterly*, vol. 35, no. 3, 2014, pp. 109-130.

- Patel, Ravi. "The Role of Technology in Access to Justice: Opportunities and Ethical Considerations." *International Journal of Law and Technology*, vol. 22, no. 4, 2013, pp. 345-367.

- Williams, Anna. "Restorative Justice and Healing: Empowering Survivors of Violence." *Journal of Restorative Justice Practice*, vol. 15, no. 2, 2012, pp. 87-105.

Websites and Online Resources

- **Transformative Justice:** A website dedicated to promoting transformative justice practices and resources for those interested in learning more about this approach. Available at: www.transformativejustice.org

- **International Institute for Restorative Practices:** An organization offering training, research, and resources on restorative justice practices worldwide. Available at: www.iirp.edu

- **United Nations Human Rights:** The official website of the United Nations Human Rights Council, providing access to international human rights instruments, reports, and resources. Available at: www.ohchr.org

- **Alternative Dispute Resolution Section of the American Bar Association:** A valuable resource for information on alternative dispute resolution methods and practices. Available at: www.americanbar.org/groups/alternative_dispute_resolution

- **Access to Justice Research Network:** An online platform that brings together researchers, practitioners, and policymakers working on access to justice issues. Available at: www.accesstojustice.net

- **Electronic Information System for International Law:** An online database providing access to primary and secondary materials in international law. Available at: www.eisil.org

- **Legal Information Institute (LII):** A website offering free access to primary legal materials, including case law, statutes, and regulations. Available at: www.law.cornell.edu

- **Global Legal Information Catalog:** A database maintained by the Library of Congress, providing access to legal resources from around the world. Available at: www.loc.gov/law/help/global/index.php

Organizations and Associations

- **Law and Society Association (LSA):** An interdisciplinary organization dedicated to the study of law and legal institutions. They organize annual meetings and publish the journal *Law & Society Review*. Available at: www.lawandsociety.org

- **Association for the Study of Law, Culture and the Humanities (ASLCH):** An organization promoting interdisciplinary research and dialogue on legal and cultural issues. They publish the *Journal of Law, Culture and the Humanities*. Available at: www.aslch.org

- **Society of Legal Scholars (SLS):** A society in the United Kingdom that aims to promote legal scholarship and foster collaboration among legal scholars. They publish the *Legal Studies* journal. Available at: www.legalscholars.ac.uk

- **American Society of Criminology (ASC):** A professional organization that brings together scholars, practitioners, and students interested in the study of criminology. They publish the journal *Criminology*. Available at: www.asc41.com

- **International Society for the Reform of Criminal Law (ISRCL):** An organization focused on legal reform in criminal justice systems worldwide. They organize conferences and publish the *International Journal of Criminal Law*. Available at: www.isrcl.org

- **International Commission of Jurists (ICJ):** A global organization promoting and protecting human rights and the rule of law. They provide resources on human rights law and engage in advocacy work. Available at: www.icj.org

Tricks and Caveats

1. When conducting legal research, remember to use a variety of sources, including primary legal materials, secondary sources, and empirical research studies, to gain a comprehensive understanding of the topic.

2. Stay updated with the latest developments in legal scholarship by subscribing to relevant journals, attending conferences and seminars, and engaging with online legal communities.

3. When using online resources, be critical of the information and ensure that the sources are reputable and authoritative.

4. Consider joining professional associations and organizations in your area of interest to network with like-minded individuals and stay connected with the latest research and trends.

5. Don't shy away from interdisciplinary approaches and collaborations. Transformative legal studies can benefit from insights and perspectives from other disciplines such as sociology, psychology, political science, and philosophy.

6. Engage in critical reflection and self-reflexivity when studying transformative legal studies. Question assumptions, challenge established norms, and consider the potential implications and limitations of the theories and practices discussed.

7. Explore your local community to identify opportunities for involvement in legal clinics, pro bono work, or community organizations that promote access to justice and transformative legal practices.

Exercises

1. Choose a specific theory or concept from transformative legal studies and critically analyze its application in a real-world case study.

2. Conduct a literature review on the intersectional approaches in feminist legal theory and critically evaluate the contributions and challenges of this perspective in promoting gender equality in the legal system.

3. Create a comparative analysis of restorative justice practices in two different countries or regions and assess the cultural implications and outcomes of these approaches.

4. Explore the ethical challenges posed by the increasing use of artificial intelligence in the legal profession and propose solutions or guidelines for responsible AI integration.

5. Organize a panel discussion or seminar on global perspectives on transformative legal studies, inviting scholars and practitioners from diverse backgrounds to share their insights and experiences.

Caveat: When carrying out academic exercises or research, be aware of ethical considerations, such as the need to obtain proper consent, protect the privacy and confidentiality of participants, and adhere to institutional and professional guidelines.

Conclusion

This section provides a range of resources for further study in the field of transformative legal studies. By exploring the recommended books, articles, websites, and organizations, you can deepen your understanding of the theoretical foundations, research methodologies, practical applications, and global perspectives in this field. Engaging with these resources will enable you to critically analyze and contribute to the ongoing transformation of legal systems and institutions, with a focus on justice, equality, and human rights. Remember to approach your studies with an openness to interdisciplinary perspectives, critical thinking, and ethical considerations, as transformative legal studies require a multifaceted and inclusive approach towards social change and empowerment.

Glossary of Key Terms and Concepts

In this section, we provide a glossary of key terms and concepts used throughout the book "Transformative Advances in Legal Studies: How Revolutionary Ideas, Practical Techniques, and Cutting-Edge Research Shape the Future of Justice and

Equality." This glossary is designed to help readers understand and navigate the terminology and concepts discussed in the book.

Legal Studies

Legal Studies refers to the academic discipline that focuses on the study of law and the legal system. It encompasses a wide range of topics, including legal theory, legal practice, legal history, and the intersection of law with other fields such as politics, economics, and sociology.

Transformative Legal Studies

Transformative Legal Studies is an approach to legal scholarship and practice that seeks to challenge and transform existing legal structures and systems in order to promote justice, equality, and social change. It recognizes the potential of law to either reinforce or challenge power dynamics and advocates for legal transformation that supports marginalized communities and promotes the well-being of all individuals.

Critical Legal Studies

Critical Legal Studies is a theoretical framework that examines the relationship between law, power, and society. It critiques traditional legal concepts and institutions, questioning their neutrality and highlighting the ways in which law can perpetuate social inequalities. Critical Legal Studies draws on various disciplines, including philosophy, sociology, and political science, to analyze the role of law in shaping social norms and values.

Feminist Legal Theory

Feminist Legal Theory examines the intersection of law and gender, seeking to expose and challenge gender biases and promote gender equality in legal systems. It explores how legal frameworks can both perpetuate and challenge gender-based discrimination and violence, and advocates for laws that address the unique needs and experiences of women.

Postcolonial Legal Theory

Postcolonial Legal Theory focuses on the impact of colonialism on legal systems and the ongoing legacies of colonialism in contemporary legal structures. It critically examines how colonialism has shaped legal norms, identities, and power dynamics, and explores strategies for decolonizing the law and promoting justice in postcolonial societies.

Critical Race Theory

Critical Race Theory examines the intersection of race, law, and power. It critiques the ways in which race and racism are embedded in legal institutions and doctrines, and seeks to challenge racial hierarchies and promote racial justice. Critical Race Theory recognizes the ways in which race intersects with other social categories, such as gender and class, in shaping legal experiences and opportunities.

Queer Legal Theory

Queer Legal Theory explores the intersection of law and sexuality, focusing on the rights and experiences of LGBTQ+ individuals. It examines how legal systems have historically discriminated against sexual minorities and advocates for the recognition and protection of LGBTQ+ rights. Queer Legal Theory critically analyzes legal concepts, such as marriage and family law, in order to challenge heteronormative assumptions.

Marxist Legal Theory

Marxist Legal Theory examines the relationship between law, capitalism, and class struggle. It emphasizes the ways in which law serves the interests of the ruling class and perpetuates economic inequality. Marxist Legal Theory analyzes the role of law in reproducing and challenging capitalist relations, and explores avenues for using law as a tool for social and economic transformation.

Human Rights Law

Human Rights Law refers to the body of international law that promotes and protects the fundamental rights and freedoms of individuals. It encompasses civil, political, economic, social, and cultural rights, and sets out the obligations of states to respect, protect, and fulfill these rights. Human Rights Law seeks to ensure that all individuals are treated with dignity and equality.

Restorative Justice

Restorative Justice is an approach to criminal justice that emphasizes repairing the harm caused by criminal behavior through dialogue, negotiation, and community involvement. It focuses on the needs of victims, promotes accountability and responsibility, and seeks to reintegrate offenders into the community. Restorative Justice aims to address the root causes of crime and create a more just and healing response to wrongdoing.

Access to Justice

Access to Justice refers to the ability of individuals and communities to access a fair and effective legal system. It encompasses both the physical and financial accessibility of legal services, as well as the responsiveness and inclusivity of legal processes. Ensuring access to justice is essential for promoting equality and addressing systemic barriers that prevent marginalized groups from accessing their legal rights.

Legal Empowerment

Legal Empowerment recognizes the power of law to enable individuals and communities to understand, exercise, and enforce their rights. It emphasizes the importance of legal literacy, legal aid, and legal awareness in promoting social justice. Legal Empowerment aims to shift the balance of power towards marginalized groups and create a more equitable and just society.

Transitional Justice

Transitional Justice refers to the processes and mechanisms employed by societies to address past human rights violations and promote reconciliation and accountability during periods of transition from conflict or authoritarian rule to democracy. It includes measures such as truth commissions, reparations, and prosecutions. Transitional Justice seeks to establish a historical record, provide redress to victims, and prevent the repetition of violence in the future.

Legal Activism

Legal Activism involves the use of legal strategies and frameworks to advocate for social change and promote justice. It encompasses a range of activities, including public interest litigation, community organizing, and advocacy campaigns. Legal Activism aims to leverage the power of law to challenge injustices, protect marginalized communities, and advance human rights.

This glossary provides a starting point for understanding the key terms and concepts used throughout the book. As you delve into the chapters, you will find more detailed explanations and analysis of these concepts, as well as their relevance and applications in the field of legal studies.

Chapter 2: Theoretical Foundations of Transformative Legal Studies

Chapter 2: Theoretical Foundations of Transformative Legal Studies

Chapter 2: Theoretical Foundations of Transformative Legal Studies

In this chapter, we will explore the theoretical foundations of transformative legal studies. Transformative legal studies is an interdisciplinary field that examines the relationship between law and societal transformation. It seeks to challenge and reshape traditional legal theories and practices in order to promote justice, equality, and social change. By examining various theoretical perspectives, we can gain a deeper understanding of the underlying principles and ideas that inform transformative legal studies.

Critical Legal Studies

One of the key theoretical foundations of transformative legal studies is critical legal studies (CLS). CLS emerged in the 1970s as a response to the perceived limitations of traditional legal theory. It aims to expose the ideological biases embedded in legal doctrines and institutions, which often reinforce existing power structures and social inequalities.

CLS theorists argue that law is not a neutral and objective system, but rather a tool used by dominant groups to maintain their power. They analyze how legal concepts, such as property rights and contract law, are constructed and serve the interests of the ruling class. By uncovering these hidden biases, CLS seeks to challenge and transform the legal system towards greater justice and equality.

Some key concepts in CLS include the critique of formalism, which contends that legal rules and reasoning are not purely rational but influenced by social and political factors. CLS also emphasizes the importance of context in legal interpretation, arguing that legal norms cannot be understood in isolation from their social and historical contexts. Additionally, CLS scholars explore the role of law in shaping and maintaining social hierarchies, such as class, race, and gender.

Feminist Legal Theory

Another important theoretical perspective in transformative legal studies is feminist legal theory. Feminist legal theory examines how law and legal institutions contribute to the subordination and oppression of women. It seeks to challenge and transform these structures to promote gender equality and justice.

Feminist legal theorists argue that traditional legal doctrine reflects patriarchal values and norms, which perpetuate gender disparities. They highlight how legal concepts, such as marriage, reproductive rights, and violence against women, reflect and reinforce gender inequalities. Feminist legal theory also embraces an intersectional approach, recognizing the interconnectedness of gender with other forms of oppression, such as race, class, and sexuality.

Key concepts in feminist legal theory include the critique of formal equality, which argues that treating everyone the same fails to account for the differential impact of the law on marginalized groups. Instead, feminists advocate for substantive equality, which seeks to address the underlying structures of oppression.

Feminist legal theorists also emphasize the importance of giving voice to marginalized communities and incorporating their experiences into legal decision-making. They advocate for legal reforms that promote women's agency, autonomy, and empowerment.

Postcolonial Legal Theory

Postcolonial legal theory examines the impact of colonialism and imperialism on legal systems and the ongoing struggles for decolonization and self-determination. It challenges the dominance of Western legal norms and seeks to promote the legal pluralism and diversity of non-Western legal systems.

Postcolonial legal theorists argue that colonialism and imperialism have left a lasting legacy on legal systems, often perpetuating inequality and marginalization of indigenous peoples and non-Western cultures. They highlight the need to address the historical injustices and power imbalances resulting from colonial rule.

Key concepts in postcolonial legal theory include the deconstruction of binary oppositions, such as colonizer/colonized and West/non-West. Postcolonial theorists seek to challenge and dismantle these dichotomies, recognizing the complexity and hybridity of legal systems.

Postcolonial legal theory also emphasizes the importance of cultural relativism and the recognition of indigenous legal orders. It calls for the decolonization of legal institutions and the integration of indigenous knowledge and practices. By doing so, postcolonial legal theory aims to transform legal systems towards greater inclusivity and respect for diverse cultural perspectives.

Critical Race Theory

Critical race theory (CRT) examines the intersection of race, law, and power. It emerged in the 1970s as a response to the limitations of traditional civil rights approaches. CRT seeks to expose and challenge how racial hierarchies are sustained through legal frameworks and institutions.

CRT scholars argue that racism is deeply embedded in legal systems and structures, perpetuating racial injustices and inequalities. They examine how laws and legal practices contribute to the marginalization and oppression of racial minorities. CRT also emphasizes the role of lived experiences and storytelling in understanding and challenging racial hierarchies.

Key concepts in critical race theory include the critique of colorblindness, which argues that ignoring race does not address systemic racism. Instead, CRT scholars advocate for race-conscious remedies that acknowledge and address the historical and ongoing impacts of racism.

Intersectionality is another important concept in CRT, recognizing that race intersects with other forms of oppression, such as gender, class, and sexuality. CRT scholars aim to understand and challenge how these interconnected systems of power operate to maintain racial inequalities.

Conclusion

The theoretical foundations of transformative legal studies provide the framework for understanding and analyzing the relationship between law and societal transformation. Critical legal studies, feminist legal theory, postcolonial legal theory, and critical race theory offer valuable insights into the ways in which law and legal institutions contribute to social inequality and oppression.

By critically examining these theoretical perspectives, legal scholars and practitioners can work towards transforming the legal system to promote justice, equality, and social change. The interdisciplinary nature of transformative legal studies allows for a more holistic understanding of the complexities and challenges faced in achieving these goals.

Further research and engagement with these theoretical foundations can pave the way for innovative approaches to legal practice, education, and research. It is through the application of transformative legal theories and practices that we can work towards a more just and equitable society.

Critical Legal Studies

Overview of Critical Legal Studies

Critical Legal Studies (CLS) is an interdisciplinary movement that emerged in the 1970s as a response to traditional legal theory. It challenges the prevailing legal frameworks and aims to uncover the underlying power dynamics and social inequalities embedded within the law. CLS scholars seek to bring about transformative change in legal systems by critically analyzing the law and its social, political, and economic implications.

Key Concepts in Critical Legal Studies

At the core of Critical Legal Studies are several key concepts that shape its theoretical framework:

1. **Critique of Formalism:** CLS rejects the traditional formalist approach to law, which treats legal rules as separate from social and political contexts. Instead, CLS argues that legal rules are shaped by power relations and serve the interests of dominant groups.

2. **Law as Politics:** According to CLS, law is not a neutral or objective entity, but rather a tool used by the powerful to maintain and reinforce social inequalities. Law is seen as a product of political struggles, with winners and losers.

3. **Social Construction of Legal Meaning:** CLS challenges the idea that legal concepts have fixed and universal meanings. Instead, it argues that legal meanings are socially constructed and subject to interpretation. Different

CRITICAL LEGAL STUDIES

actors, such as judges, lawyers, and citizens, contribute to the construction of legal meaning.

Critiques of Traditional Legal Theory

Critical Legal Studies emerged as a response to the limitations and biases of traditional legal theory. Some of the main critiques include:

1. **Formalism and Neutrality:** CLS scholars argue that formalist legal theories disregard the social, economic, and political contexts in which laws operate. They criticize the idea that law can be neutral and applied without bias, highlighting how legal rules often reflect the interests of the ruling elite.

2. **Individualism and Rights Discourse:** Traditional legal theory places a heavy emphasis on individual rights and fails to adequately address systemic inequalities. CLS scholars argue that rights discourse masks deeper social and economic injustices and perpetuates the status quo.

3. **Law's Role in Maintaining Power:** CLS challenges the notion that law is a neutral arbiter of justice and equality. Instead, it argues that law is a tool used by the powerful to maintain their dominance and perpetuate social hierarchies.

Impact of Critical Legal Studies

Critical Legal Studies has had a significant impact on legal theory, practice, and education. By questioning traditional legal norms and highlighting their underlying power dynamics, CLS has opened up new possibilities for legal scholars, practitioners, and activists. Some key impacts include:

1. **Law and Social Change:** CLS has influenced social movements by providing critical insights into the role of law in perpetuating social injustices. It has motivated legal activists to challenge existing legal frameworks and seek transformative change.

2. **Legal Education Reform:** The influence of CLS can be seen in legal education, with a greater emphasis on critical thinking, interdisciplinary approaches, and social justice issues. Law schools now incorporate CLS perspectives into their curriculum to foster a more comprehensive understanding of the law.

3. **Activism and Advocacy:** CLS has informed and inspired legal activism and advocacy work. It has provided a framework for challenging discriminatory laws and policies and promoting social justice through legal strategies.

Contemporary Debates and Developments

While CLS has made significant contributions to legal theory, it has also faced criticisms and ongoing debates. Some of these debates include:

1. **Practicality and Feasibility:** Critics argue that CLS's focus on questioning legal norms and values can be impractical and divorced from the realities of legal practice. They question the feasibility of implementing CLS principles in a complex and diverse legal system.

2. **Integration with Other Theories:** CLS has been seen as a companion to other social justice-oriented theories, such as feminist legal theory and critical race theory. However, debates exist regarding the extent to which these theories can be integrated and the potential tensions between them.

3. **Empirical Research and CLS:** Some scholars argue for the importance of empirical research in supporting CLS claims and providing evidence for legal critiques. Others maintain that CLS is primarily a theoretical and normative approach that does not require empirical validation.

In conclusion, Critical Legal Studies offers a powerful framework for critically analyzing and challenging traditional legal theory. By exposing the underlying power dynamics and social inequalities within the law, CLS seeks to bring about transformative change in legal systems. Although it faces ongoing debates and criticisms, CLS continues to shape legal theory, practice, and education by promoting a more critical and socially conscious approach to law.

Key Theorists and Concepts in Critical Legal Studies

Critical Legal Studies (CLS) is a theoretical framework that emerged in the 1970s as a response to mainstream legal scholarship, which was seen as perpetuating the status quo and maintaining the existing power structures within society. CLS seeks to challenge the dominant ideology embedded in law and aims to expose the underlying social and economic injustices. This section will explore key theorists and concepts that have shaped and influenced the development of Critical Legal Studies.

CRITICAL LEGAL STUDIES

Roberto Unger

Roberto Unger, a Brazilian legal scholar, has played a significant role in shaping the field of Critical Legal Studies. He is known for his work on legal pluralism and his critique of formalistic legal reasoning. Unger argues that law should not be confined to a fixed set of rules, but rather should be fluid and adaptable to changing social circumstances. He emphasizes the importance of considering alternative legal systems and promoting a more inclusive and democratic approach to law.

Duncan Kennedy

Duncan Kennedy, an American legal scholar, is one of the pioneers of Critical Legal Studies. He has made significant contributions to the field through his critique of legal formalism and his analysis of power dynamics in the legal system. Kennedy argues that law is not a neutral and objective system but is instead shaped by political and economic forces. His work highlights the need for lawyers and legal scholars to critically examine the role of law in perpetuating inequality.

Catharine MacKinnon

Catharine MacKinnon, a feminist legal scholar, has been influential in applying critical theory to the study of gender and sexuality. Her work focuses on the ways in which law has been used to perpetuate and reinforce gender inequality. MacKinnon's concept of "sex equality theory" challenges traditional legal approaches by emphasizing the importance of recognizing and addressing the systemic discrimination faced by women. She argues that legal reforms alone are insufficient to achieve gender equality; transformative change requires a fundamental shift in power dynamics.

Critical Legal Scholars

In addition to these key theorists, Critical Legal Studies is a broad and diverse field that encompasses the contributions of many scholars. Some notable scholars include Roberto Mangabeira Unger, Morton Horwitz, Mark Tushnet, and Patricia Williams. Each of these scholars brings their unique perspectives and insights, contributing to the interdisciplinary nature of Critical Legal Studies.

Concepts in Critical Legal Studies

Critical Legal Studies encompasses various concepts that underpin its theoretical framework. Some of these key concepts include:

1. **Legal Indeterminacy**: Critical Legal Studies challenges the notion that legal rules and principles have clear and definitive meanings. It argues that law is inherently indeterminate and subject to interpretation, allowing for biases and power dynamics to shape legal outcomes.

2. **Power and Ideology**: Critical Legal Studies emphasizes the role of power and ideology in shaping legal institutions and practices. It seeks to expose how law can be used as a tool to maintain existing power structures and perpetuate social inequality.

3. **Legal Formalism**: Critical Legal Studies critiques the formalistic approach to law, which prioritizes abstract legal principles over social and economic realities. It argues that this approach masks the underlying social and economic injustices that law may perpetuate.

4. **Distributive Justice**: Critical Legal Studies places a strong emphasis on distributive justice, questioning how resources and opportunities are distributed within society. It examines how law can be used to challenge unequal distributions of power, wealth, and resources.

5. **Intersectionality**: Critical Legal Studies acknowledges the intersectionality of various social identities and experiences, such as race, gender, class, and sexuality. It recognizes that individuals can experience multiple forms of oppression and that legal analysis should consider these intersecting dimensions of identity.

Overall, the key theorists and concepts in Critical Legal Studies highlight the need to critically analyze law and challenge its underlying assumptions and power structures. By exposing the injustices embedded in the legal system, Critical Legal Studies aims to pave the way for transformative change that promotes justice and equality.

Case Study: Critical Legal Studies in Action

To illustrate the real-world impact of Critical Legal Studies, let's examine a case study on the intersection of race and criminal justice. Critical Legal Studies scholars have long critiqued the racial disparities in the criminal justice system, arguing that these disparities reflect deep-rooted biases and systemic inequalities.

One example of Critical Legal Studies in action is the push for criminal justice reform in the United States. Scholars and activists influenced by Critical Legal Studies have examined the disproportionate imprisonment rates of racial minorities, highlighting how law and policy perpetuate racial inequality. Their work has contributed to the development of alternative approaches to criminal justice, such as restorative justice and community-based alternatives to incarceration.

For instance, organizations like the Equal Justice Initiative, founded by Bryan Stevenson, have used Critical Legal Studies principles to challenge racial bias in capital punishment and advocate for systemic changes in the criminal justice system. This includes conducting research, providing legal representation to marginalized communities, and advocating for policy reforms.

This case study demonstrates how Critical Legal Studies provides a critical lens through which to assess and challenge deeply entrenched injustices within the legal system. By examining the systemic biases and power structures, scholars and activists can work towards a more equitable and transformative criminal justice system.

Further Reading

For readers interested in exploring Critical Legal Studies further, the following resources are recommended:

- Kennedy, Duncan. *Legal Education and the Reproduction of Hierarchy: A Polemic Against the System*. NYU Press, 2004.

- MacKinnon, Catharine A. *Towards a Feminist Theory of the State*. Harvard University Press, 1989.

- Unger, Roberto Mangabeira. *Critical Legal Studies and the Politics of Law*. Verso, 1986.

- Williams, Patricia J. *The Alchemy of Race and Rights*. Harvard University Press, 1991.

- Young, Iris Marion. *Justice and the Politics of Difference*. Princeton University Press, 1990.

These resources provide in-depth analyses of the key theories, concepts, and debates within Critical Legal Studies, offering readers a comprehensive understanding of this transformative legal framework.

Critiques and Challenges to Critical Legal Studies

Critical Legal Studies (CLS) has faced a range of critiques and challenges since its emergence as a theoretical framework for understanding law and society. These critiques have come from scholars within CLS itself, as well as from other legal theories and perspectives. In this section, we will explore some of the key critiques and challenges to CLS and examine how they have shaped the development of the field.

Critique 1: Overemphasis on Power and Ideology

One of the main critiques of CLS is its overemphasis on power and ideology in understanding legal phenomena. Critics argue that CLS scholars often downplay or overlook other important factors, such as historical context, social relations, and individual agency. They contend that CLS's focus on power and ideology can lead to an overly deterministic view of law and fail to account for the complexities of legal practice.

For instance, critics argue that CLS's emphasis on how law perpetuates social inequalities can overshadow the ways in which law also functions as a tool for social change. They argue that by solely focusing on the oppressive nature of law, CLS may overlook instances where the law has been used to challenge and transform systems of power and privilege.

Critique 2: Lack of Concrete Solutions

Another critique of CLS is its perceived lack of concrete solutions for addressing social injustices. Critics argue that while CLS scholars excel at critiquing existing legal systems and exposing the underlying power dynamics, they often fall short in proposing tangible alternatives or strategies for achieving transformative change.

This critique stems from the perception that CLS can be overly abstract and theoretical, making it difficult to translate its insights into practical action. Critics argue that CLS needs to engage more with real-world issues and offer specific recommendations for legal reforms or policy changes.

Critique 3: Essentialism and Totalizing Narratives

Critics of CLS also raise concerns about its tendency to essentialize legal categories and adopt totalizing narratives. They argue that CLS scholars often make sweeping generalizations about legal phenomena and fail to account for the diverse experiences and contexts in which law operates.

For example, critics contend that CLS's treatment of law as an all-encompassing system that reinforces social hierarchies can overlook the ways in which law can be interpreted and applied in different contexts. They argue that CLS needs to take into account the multiplicity of legal cultures, traditions, and practices that exist within and across societies.

Challenge 1: Incorporating Intersectionality

One of the challenges that CLS faces is the need to incorporate intersectionality into its analysis. Intersectionality, a concept developed within feminist theory, recognizes that social identities and systems of oppression intersect and interact with each other. Critics argue that CLS's focus on class-based analysis can sometimes overlook the ways in which other forms of identity, such as race, gender, and sexuality, shape legal experiences and outcomes.

To address this challenge, CLS scholars have started to explore the intersectional dimensions of law and consider how multiple systems of oppression intersect and reinforce each other. They argue for a more inclusive and nuanced approach that takes into account the complexities of lived experiences and the interplay of various social identities.

Challenge 2: Engaging with Empirical Research

Another challenge for CLS is to engage more with empirical research and evidence. Critics argue that CLS's heavy reliance on philosophical and theoretical arguments can sometimes limit its impact and relevance to real-world legal issues. They contend that empirical research can provide insights into the actual workings of legal systems and help identify areas for potential transformative change.

To address this challenge, CLS scholars have increasingly turned to empirical methods, such as qualitative interviews, ethnographic studies, and statistical analyses, to supplement their theoretical arguments. They argue that empirical research can provide empirical grounding for CLS theories and contribute to more effective strategies for social transformation.

Challenge 3: Maintaining Relevance in Changing Socio-Political Contexts

A significant challenge for CLS is to maintain its relevance in a rapidly changing socio-political landscape. Critics argue that CLS needs to adapt and respond to new legal and social issues that emerge over time. They contend that CLS's focus on traditional legal concepts and institutions may be insufficient to address contemporary challenges, such as globalization, technology, and environmental crises.

To address this challenge, CLS scholars have started to explore new areas of study, such as critical environmental legal studies, critical race theory, and critical disability studies. They argue for a more interdisciplinary approach that incorporates insights from other disciplines, including sociology, political science, and economics, to better understand and respond to evolving socio-legal issues.

In conclusion, Critical Legal Studies has faced various critiques and challenges throughout its development. These critiques highlight the need for CLS to go beyond a narrow focus on power and ideology, provide concrete solutions for social change, avoid essentialism and totalizing narratives, and engage with intersectionality, empirical research, and evolving socio-political contexts. By addressing these critiques and challenges, CLS can strengthen its transformative potential and contribute to a more equitable and just legal system.

Feminist Legal Theory

Overview of Feminist Legal Theory

Feminist legal theory is a branch of legal scholarship that explores the intersection between law and gender, aiming to analyze and challenge the ways in which legal systems perpetuate gender inequality and discrimination. This field emerged in response to the historical exclusion of women's experiences and perspectives from legal discourse and the recognition of the need for gender-sensitive approaches to law.

Feminist legal theorists draw upon a range of interdisciplinary methodologies, incorporating insights from various disciplines such as sociology, political science, philosophy, and critical theory. By examining the social, cultural, and political dimensions of law, feminist legal theory seeks to promote justice, equality, and empowerment for marginalized groups.

Key Concepts in Feminist Legal Theory

Feminist legal theory encompasses a broad range of concepts and ideas. Here are some key concepts that underpin feminist legal analysis:

1. *Gender as a Social Construct*: Feminist legal theory recognizes that gender is not a fixed or biological category but rather a social construct that is shaped by societal norms, expectations, and power dynamics. This understanding challenges

the traditional notion of gender roles and highlights the need to address gender disparities in legal systems.

2. *Intersectionality*: Intersectionality is a critical concept within feminist legal theory, emphasizing that gender intersects with other social identities, such as race, class, disability, and sexual orientation. This intersectional analysis highlights the multiple and interconnected forms of discrimination and oppression that individuals may experience.

3. *The Personal is Political*: In feminist legal theory, the personal experiences of individuals are considered political, as they reflect broader systemic issues and power imbalances. By centering lived experiences, feminist legal theorists challenge the notion of law as an objective and neutral entity, highlighting the ways in which legal systems can perpetuate gender inequalities.

4. *Substantive Equality*: Feminist legal theory critiques formal equality, which treats all individuals as equal before the law without taking into account the social and historical disadvantages they may face. Instead, feminist legal theorists advocate for substantive equality, which seeks to address systemic inequalities and create equitable outcomes.

5. *Critical Analysis of Legal Doctrine*: Feminist legal theory critically examines legal doctrines and rules to uncover their underlying assumptions and biases. This analysis reveals the ways in which legal systems may reinforce gender stereotypes, perpetuate gender-based violence, and limit access to justice for marginalized groups.

Approaches in Feminist Legal Theory

Feminist legal theory encompasses various approaches that offer different perspectives on legal issues. Some of the key approaches within feminist legal theory include:

1. *Liberal Feminism*: Liberal feminism focuses on achieving gender equality by advocating for legal reforms that guarantee equal rights and opportunities for women within existing legal frameworks. It emphasizes formal equality and equal treatment under the law.

2. *Radical Feminism*: Radical feminism seeks to challenge and transform the patriarchal structures that perpetuate gender inequality. It critiques traditional legal systems for their exclusionary and oppressive nature and advocates for radical social and legal transformation.

3. *Cultural Feminism*: Cultural feminism recognizes the value of women's unique experiences and perspectives and emphasizes the need to recognize and value traditionally feminine traits and qualities. This approach seeks to challenge

traditional legal norms by incorporating women's perspectives into legal decision-making.

4. *Intersectional Feminism*: Intersectional feminism recognizes the interconnected nature of various forms of oppression and discrimination. It foregrounds the experiences of marginalized groups, including women of color, LGBTQ+ individuals, and individuals with disabilities, and acknowledges the intersections of gender, race, class, and other social identities.

5. *Postmodern Feminism*: Postmodern feminism challenges traditional notions of gender and identity, deconstructing binary categories and questioning the fixed meanings assigned to them. It emphasizes the role of language, discourse, and cultural constructs in shaping legal norms and practices.

Critiques and Debates

Feminist legal theory has faced its own share of critiques and debates. Some common critiques include:

1. *Essentialism*: Feminist legal theory is often criticized for essentializing women's experiences or assuming a singular and universal "woman" perspective. Critics argue that this approach ignores the diversity of women's experiences and overlooks other intersecting forms of oppression.

2. *Relevance and Practicality*: Some skeptics question the practicality and relevance of feminist legal theory, arguing that it fails to offer concrete solutions to complex legal problems or that its recommendations may clash with other social or cultural values.

3. *Political Neutrality of Law*: Critics often challenge the assumption that law can be apolitical or neutral, arguing that law inherently reflects and reinforces power dynamics. They argue that feminist legal theory should go beyond simply challenging existing legal structures and seek broader social and political change.

Contemporary Developments in Feminist Legal Theory

Feminist legal theory continues to evolve and respond to contemporary legal and social issues. Here are some current developments within the field:

1. *Gender-Based Violence and Sexual Harassment*: Feminist legal theory has played a crucial role in raising awareness and addressing gender-based violence and sexual harassment. It has influenced legal reforms, such as the recognition of new types of offenses and the development of victim-centered approaches.

2. *Intersectionality in Legal Analysis*: Intersectionality has gained increased attention within feminist legal theory, emphasizing the ways in which legal systems

can compound disadvantage for individuals at the intersections of gender, race, class, and other identities. This approach seeks to address the complex and overlapping forms of discrimination faced by marginalized groups.

3. *Global Feminist Legal Movements*: Feminist legal theory has expanded beyond national boundaries, with transnational and global feminist movements advocating for gender justice and human rights at an international level. These movements have influenced international law and policy, challenging existing structures of power and advocating for transformative change.

4. *Queer Feminist Legal Theory*: Queer feminist legal theory explores the intersections of gender and sexual orientation, highlighting the unique legal challenges faced by LGBTQ+ individuals. It aims to dismantle heteronormative legal norms and promote inclusivity and equality for all sexual orientations and gender identities.

Further Reading

For further study on feminist legal theory, the following resources are recommended:

- *Feminist Legal Theory: Readings in Law and Gender* edited by Katharine T. Bartlett and Rosanne Kennedy.
- *Feminist Legal Theory: A Primer* by Nancy Levit.
- *The Cambridge Companion to Feminist Legal Theory* edited by M.A. Fineman and N. Alston.
- *Feminist Theory: From Margin to Center* by bell hooks.

These resources provide a comprehensive introduction to feminist legal theory, its foundational concepts, and its contributions to legal scholarship and activism. They offer diverse perspectives and critical analyses that will deepen your understanding of the field.

Key Theorists and Concepts in Feminist Legal Theory

Feminist legal theory is a prominent and influential branch of legal studies that examines the intersections between gender, law, and society. As a field, it emerged in the 1960s and 1970s as part of the broader feminist movement, challenging traditional legal frameworks that perpetuated gender inequality and discrimination. Feminist legal theorists have sought to address the gender biases inherent in legal systems and explore how the law can be transformed to promote gender equality and justice.

Key Theorists in Feminist Legal Theory

Several key theorists have played significant roles in shaping and advancing feminist legal theory. Their contributions have provided foundational frameworks for understanding and addressing gender inequality within legal systems. Here are three prominent figures in feminist legal theory:

1. **Catharine MacKinnon:** MacKinnon is known for her groundbreaking work on sexual harassment and pornography. She argues that these forms of gender-based violence perpetuate women's subordination and inequality. MacKinnon advocates for legal reforms that recognize sexual harassment as a form of discrimination and that challenge the harmful effects of pornography on women's rights.

2. **Patricia Williams:** Williams emphasizes the importance of intersectionality in feminist legal theory. Intersectionality recognizes that individuals face multiple forms of oppression and discrimination based on intersecting social categories such as race, gender, class, and sexuality. Williams argues that legal analysis must consider how these intersecting identities shape individuals' experiences of discrimination and shape legal remedies.

3. **Catherine A. MacArthur:** MacArthur focuses on feminist legal methodology and the ways in which legal language and reasoning perpetuate gender biases. She argues for a "gender-conscious" approach to legal analysis that challenges traditional legal norms and assumptions. MacArthur's work has contributed to the development of feminist legal methods that reveal and challenge gender biases within legal frameworks.

These theorists have paved the way for critical examinations of gender within the legal field and have influenced both academic scholarship and legal practice. Their ideas continue to shape debates and discussions within feminist legal theory.

Key Concepts in Feminist Legal Theory

Feminist legal theory encompasses various conceptual frameworks that help analyze and challenge gender bias and inequality within the law. Here are some key concepts in feminist legal theory:

1. **Equality vs. Difference:** Feminist legal theorists engage in a debate between those who advocate for gender equality and those who highlight the importance of acknowledging and valuing gender differences. The equality

perspective focuses on achieving equal rights, opportunities, and treatment for women, while the difference perspective recognizes and appreciates the unique experiences and characteristics of women that may require distinct legal protections.

2. **Intersectionality:** Intersectionality, coined by Kimberlé Crenshaw, recognizes that various social identities intersect and mutually reinforce each other to shape individuals' experiences of oppression and discrimination. Feminist legal theory applies intersectionality to understand how gender interacts with other social categories like race, class, and sexuality in legal contexts.

3. **Subordination and Power:** This concept focuses on the ways in which the law perpetuates women's subordination and reinforces power imbalances. Feminist legal theorists critically examine how legal norms, institutions, and practices can contribute to the marginalization and oppression of women. Analyzing power dynamics helps expose and challenge structures of gender inequality within the law.

4. **Legal Formalism and Legal Realism:** Feminist legal theory critiques traditional legal formalism, which emphasizes the objective and neutral application of legal rules. Instead, feminist theorists highlight the limitations of legal formalism and advocate for legal realism that recognizes the subjective nature of law and the influence of social, economic, and political factors on legal decision-making.

These concepts provide a framework for understanding and challenging gender bias within legal systems. They assist in the development of legal strategies and reforms aimed at addressing gender inequality and promoting justice.

Challenges and Future Directions in Feminist Legal Theory

While feminist legal theory has made significant strides in exposing gender bias and inequality within the law, there are ongoing challenges and areas that require further exploration. Some of these challenges include:

- **Intersectionality and Inclusivity:** Feminist legal theory must continue to expand its exploration of how gender intersects with other social identities, ensuring that the experiences of marginalized and intersectional individuals are included in legal analysis and reforms.

- **Global Perspectives:** The field should also incorporate global perspectives to understand gender inequalities across different cultural and legal contexts. This includes examining the impact of globalization, human rights, and international frameworks on gender justice.

- **Legal Practice and Advocacy:** The translation of feminist legal theory into effective legal practice and advocacy remains a challenge. Bridging the gap between theory and practice requires exploring innovative strategies, collaboration with social justice organizations, and engaging with policymakers to bring about meaningful change.

In conclusion, feminist legal theory, shaped by key theorists and grounded in key concepts, offers a critical lens to analyze and transform legal systems to achieve gender equality and justice. By understanding the work of prominent theorists and exploring important concepts, scholars and practitioners can apply feminist legal theory in their efforts to create more inclusive and equitable legal systems. Continued engagement with challenges and advancements will drive the future of feminist legal theory and its transformative potential in promoting social change.

Intersectionality in Feminist Legal Theory

In feminist legal theory, intersectionality is a concept that recognizes the ways in which different forms of oppression, such as racism, sexism, classism, heterosexism, and ableism, intersect and interact with each other in the lived experiences of individuals. It acknowledges that people have multiple identities and that these identities intersect to shape their experiences, privileges, and disadvantages within society.

Understanding Intersectionality

Intersectionality originated in black feminist theory and has since been widely adopted and applied in various academic disciplines, including legal studies. It challenges the notion that individuals experience oppression or privilege based on a single characteristic, such as gender or race. Instead, intersectionality highlights the complex ways in which these identities intersect and mutually reinforce each other, creating unique experiences of power and marginalization.

For example, a black woman may face intersecting discrimination due to her race and gender. A legal framework that only considers discrimination based on race or gender separately fails to capture the full extent of the harm she experiences.

Intersectionality calls for an analysis that recognizes and addresses the interlocking systems of oppression that shape her experiences.

Key Principles of Intersectionality

Intersectionality in feminist legal theory is guided by several key principles:

1. Multiple Identities: Intersectionality acknowledges that individuals have multiple social identities that intersect in complex ways, including race, gender, class, sexuality, disability, and more.

2. Interconnected Systems of Oppression: Intersectionality recognizes that systems of oppression, such as racism, sexism, and homophobia, are interconnected and mutually reinforcing. It rejects the idea that these systems can be addressed individually.

3. Lived Experiences: Intersectionality values lived experiences as a source of knowledge and understanding. It calls for centering the perspectives and voices of those who experience multiple forms of oppression.

4. Contextual Analysis: Intersectionality requires a contextual analysis of how power operates in different social, political, and legal contexts. It emphasizes the importance of understanding the specific dynamics of power to address intersecting forms of discrimination.

Application in Legal Theory

Intersectionality has had a significant impact on feminist legal theory. It has prompted scholars and practitioners to critically examine legal frameworks and practices to identify and address the ways in which they perpetuate intersecting forms of discrimination.

For example, in the area of employment discrimination, intersectionality has challenged the legal framework that traditionally focuses on single-axis forms of discrimination. It pushes for a more nuanced analysis of how intersecting identities shape workplace experiences and contribute to disparities in pay, promotion, and opportunities.

Intersectionality also informs legal strategies for addressing violence against women. It recognizes that women from marginalized communities may face additional barriers in accessing justice and support services. By centering the experiences of these women, legal advocates can work toward more comprehensive and inclusive solutions that address the intersecting forms of violence they may experience.

Challenges and Critiques

While intersectionality has made significant contributions to feminist legal theory, it is not without its challenges and critiques. Some common challenges include:

1. Essentializing Identities: Critics argue that intersectionality can be essentializing, reducing individuals to their social identities and overlooking individual agency and autonomy.

2. Complicating Legal Analysis: The intersectional analysis can make legal analysis more complex, as it requires a deep understanding of the specific factors and interactions shaping individuals' experiences.

3. Limited Application in the Legal System: Despite its theoretical contributions, intersectionality faces challenges in its application within the legal system. Existing legal structures and processes may lack the necessary flexibility to fully incorporate an intersectional perspective.

It is important for scholars and practitioners to address these challenges and continue developing intersectional approaches to legal theory and practice that are nuanced, inclusive, and attentive to the lived experiences of marginalized individuals.

Further Reading

For further study on intersectionality in feminist legal theory, consider the following texts:

- Crenshaw, Kimberlé. "Mapping the Margins: Intersectionality, Identity Politics, and Violence against Women of Color." Stanford Law Review 43, no. 6 (1991): 1241-1299.

- Harris, Angela P. "Race and Essentialism in Feminist Legal Theory." Stanford Law Review 42, no. 3 (1990): 581-616.

- Collins, Patricia Hill. Black Feminist Thought: Knowledge, Consciousness, and the Politics of Empowerment. Routledge, 2009.

- Cho, Sumi, Kimberlé Crenshaw, and Leslie McCall, eds. Intersectionality: Key Concepts. Polity Press, 2013.

These texts provide foundational knowledge on intersectionality and its application in feminist legal theory. They offer diverse perspectives and insightful analyses of the topic, making them valuable resources for anyone interested in understanding and engaging with intersectionality in legal studies.

Exercises

Exercise 1

Consider a hypothetical case of workplace discrimination. A black woman is repeatedly passed over for promotions despite her qualifications and tenure with the company. Using an intersectional feminist legal analysis, identify the possible intersecting forms of discrimination she may be facing and propose legal strategies that take into account her multiple identities.

Exercise 2

Choose a specific area of law, such as reproductive rights or immigration law, and analyze how an intersectional approach could enhance legal analysis and advocacy in that area. Consider the intersecting forms of oppression that individuals may face and the potential implications for legal theory and practice.

Resources

- American Bar Association Section on Civil Rights and Social Justice: https://www.americanbar.org/groups/crsj/

- National Women's Law Center: https://nwlc.org/

- Intersectionality Matters! Podcast: https://www.law.columbia.edu/centers/law-race-social-justice/intersectionality-matters-podcast

These resources offer valuable insights, research, and advocacy in the areas of intersectionality, feminist legal theory, and social justice. They provide further context and information to deepen your understanding of the topic.

Contemporary Debates and Developments in Feminist Legal Theory

Feminist legal theory has evolved over time to address contemporary debates and developments in the field. This section explores some of the key discussions and advancements within feminist legal theory that have shaped the understanding of gender, equality, and justice within the legal system.

Gender Identity and Intersectionality

One of the central debates in feminist legal theory revolves around the recognition of gender identity beyond the traditional binary understanding of male and female. Contemporary feminist legal theorists have argued for the inclusion of trans and non-binary individuals within legal protections and frameworks. This debate raises important questions about how the law should define and protect gender identity, and how it can move beyond the binary framework.

Intersectionality is another crucial aspect of contemporary feminist legal theory. Intersectionality recognizes that systems of oppression, such as gender inequality, cannot be understood in isolation but are interconnected with other forms of discrimination based on race, class, sexuality, and other social categories. Feminist legal theorists have emphasized the need to address the multiple dimensions of identity when advocating for gender justice, challenging the single-axis framework that focuses solely on gender.

Sexual Harassment and #MeToo Movement

The #MeToo movement has brought renewed attention to the issue of sexual harassment and assault. Feminist legal theorists have played a significant role in analyzing the legal implications of the movement and advocating for legal reforms. Debates within feminist legal theory center around questions of due process, victim-survivor rights, and the potential for transformative justice approaches within the legal system.

Critics argue that the emphasis on criminal law in responding to sexual harassment can limit opportunities for broader systemic change. Feminist legal theorists have explored alternative legal strategies, such as civil litigation, restorative justice, and community-based approaches, to address the root causes of sexual harassment and promote meaningful change within institutions.

Reproductive Rights and Autonomy

Reproductive rights and autonomy have been central to feminist legal theory, with ongoing debates and developments shaping the understanding of these rights. Discussions surround issues such as access to contraception, abortion, assisted reproductive technologies, and reproductive healthcare services. Feminist legal theorists continue to advocate for the recognition of reproductive rights as fundamental human rights and challenge restrictions imposed by governments and institutions.

The debate extends to topics such as surrogacy, reproductive technologies, and the implications for marginalized groups. Feminist legal theorists explore the intersection of reproductive justice with issues of poverty, race, disability, and LGBTQ+ rights, emphasizing the need for an inclusive approach that recognizes the diverse experiences of individuals and communities.

Violence Against Women

The issue of violence against women remains a critical area of concern within feminist legal theory. Contemporary debates center around the legal responses to gender-based violence, including domestic violence, sexual assault, and intimate partner violence. Feminist legal theorists have been instrumental in critiquing existing legal frameworks and advocating for comprehensive approaches to address violence against women.

Topics of discussion include the effectiveness of criminal justice interventions, victim-survivor support services, law enforcement practices, and prevention strategies. Feminist legal theorists also explore the intersections between gender-based violence and other forms of oppression, such as racism, poverty, and disability.

Workplace Equality and Discrimination

Workplace discrimination and the pursuit of gender equality in employment are ongoing concerns within feminist legal theory. This includes addressing issues such as the gender pay gap, occupational segregation, sexual harassment in the workplace, and the impact of caregiving responsibilities on women's careers.

Contemporary debates within feminist legal theory focus on the possibility of transformative measures to achieve workplace equality, such as pay transparency, affirmative action, and work-life balance policies. Feminist legal theorists also examine the intersections between workplace discrimination and other forms of inequality, such as race, disability, and age.

Overall, these contemporary debates and developments in feminist legal theory demonstrate the multidimensional nature of gender justice and highlight the ongoing efforts to transform the legal system to better address the needs and experiences of marginalized communities. By engaging with these debates, legal scholars can contribute to creating a more inclusive and just society.

Postcolonial Legal Theory

Overview of Postcolonial Legal Theory

Postcolonial legal theory is a critical approach that examines the impact of colonialism on the development and functioning of legal systems. It seeks to understand how colonial history and power structures continue to shape laws and legal institutions in postcolonial societies. This section provides an overview of postcolonial legal theory, its key concepts, and its importance in understanding and addressing legal issues in a postcolonial context.

Colonialism and Legal Systems

Colonialism refers to the political and economic domination of one country by another. During the colonial era, European powers colonized large parts of Asia, Africa, and the Americas, imposing their legal systems on the colonized territories. These imposed legal systems served the interests of the colonizers, often disregarding the customs, traditions, and legal systems of the colonized peoples.

Postcolonial legal theory recognizes that the legacy of colonialism continues to affect the legal systems of formerly colonized countries. It explores how laws developed under colonial rule shape notions of justice, property rights, citizenship, and other aspects of the legal system. By examining the colonial roots of legal systems, postcolonial legal theory aims to expose and challenge the inequalities and injustices embedded in these systems.

Key Concepts in Postcolonial Legal Theory

Postcolonial legal theory draws on various concepts and frameworks to analyze and critique the colonial legacy in legal systems. Here are some key concepts in postcolonial legal theory:

1. **Eurocentrism:** Postcolonial legal theory challenges the Eurocentric bias in legal systems. It highlights how European legal principles and norms were imposed on non-European societies, often erasing or devaluing indigenous legal traditions and customs.

2. **Legal Pluralism:** Postcolonial legal theory recognizes the coexistence of multiple legal systems in postcolonial societies. It acknowledges that indigenous legal systems and customary laws have survived despite colonial imposition, and highlights the need to respect and integrate these legal traditions into the broader legal framework.

3. **Subaltern Voices:** Postcolonial legal theory emphasizes the need to amplify the voices and perspectives of marginalized and subaltern groups. It challenges the dominance of mainstream legal discourse and seeks to include alternative narratives and experiences in legal analysis and decision-making.

4. **Decolonization:** Postcolonial legal theory advocates for the decolonization of legal systems. It calls for the transformation of laws, institutions, and legal education to reflect the values, traditions, and needs of postcolonial societies. Decolonization involves questioning and challenging the underlying assumptions and structures of colonial legal systems.

Impact and Importance of Postcolonial Legal Theory

Postcolonial legal theory has significant implications for legal practice, policy-making, and social justice in postcolonial societies. Here are some reasons why postcolonial legal theory is important:

1. **Addressing Inequalities:** Postcolonial legal theory exposes the inequalities created by colonial legal systems and provides a framework for addressing them. By critically examining the colonial roots of legal norms and institutions, it enables a more nuanced understanding of social, economic, and political inequalities.

2. **Recognizing Indigenous Rights:** Postcolonial legal theory highlights the importance of recognizing and protecting the rights of indigenous peoples. It emphasizes the need to integrate indigenous legal systems and customs into national legal frameworks, ensuring the empowerment and self-determination of indigenous communities.

3. **Challenging Eurocentrism:** Postcolonial legal theory challenges the Eurocentric biases in legal systems and legal education. It encourages a broader and more inclusive approach to legal analysis that incorporates diverse perspectives and experiences.

4. **Promoting Social Justice:** Postcolonial legal theory is closely linked to social justice initiatives. It helps identify and address the injustices perpetuated by colonial legal systems and guides efforts towards a more equitable and just legal framework.

Contemporary Issues in Postcolonial Legal Theory

Postcolonial legal theory is relevant to many pressing legal issues in postcolonial societies today. Here are some examples of contemporary issues that postcolonial legal theory addresses:

1. **Land Rights and Indigenous Peoples:** Postcolonial legal theory informs discussions on land rights and indigenous peoples' struggles for self-determination. It helps challenge the colonial-based land laws and advocates for the recognition and protection of indigenous land rights.

2. **Human Rights and Social Justice:** Postcolonial legal theory contributes to the analysis of human rights violations and social justice issues in postcolonial societies. It offers critical perspectives on the impact of colonialism on human rights norms and supports efforts to address these violations.

3. **Legal Education and Pedagogy:** Postcolonial legal theory has implications for legal education and pedagogy. It encourages law schools to adopt a more inclusive and critical approach to legal education that reflects the diverse legal traditions and experiences of postcolonial societies.

4. **Access to Justice:** Postcolonial legal theory sheds light on the barriers to access to justice in postcolonial societies. It provides insights into how colonial legacies contribute to unequal access to legal recourse and helps develop strategies to promote equal access to justice for all.

Conclusion

Postcolonial legal theory offers a critical lens through which to examine the impact of colonialism on legal systems and to work towards decolonization and social justice. By interrogating the colonial roots of legal norms and institutions, it helps address inequalities, protect indigenous rights, challenge Eurocentrism, and promote social justice. The insights provided by postcolonial legal theory are crucial for understanding and transforming legal systems in postcolonial societies.

Decolonizing the Law: Challenges and Possibilities

The process of decolonizing the law is an important and complex endeavor that seeks to address the historical and ongoing impacts of colonization on legal systems and the ways in which they perpetuate inequalities. It involves challenging and transforming the dominant Eurocentric narratives and structures that have shaped legal systems worldwide.

Understanding Colonization and its Legacy

Colonization refers to the process by which a dominant group establishes control over a territory, exploits its resources, and imposes its political, economic, and cultural systems on the colonized society. This often involved the displacement and marginalization of indigenous peoples, the imposition of foreign legal systems, and the erasure of indigenous legal traditions.

The legacy of colonization continues to shape legal systems, both formally and informally. Eurocentric legal systems, rooted in colonial ideology, have often prioritized the interests of the colonizers over the rights and needs of indigenous peoples. For example, laws that were introduced during colonial periods continue to have a profound impact on land ownership, resource extraction, and the recognition of indigenous rights.

Challenges in Decolonizing the Law

Decolonizing the law faces several challenges. First, it requires a critical examination of the underlying assumptions, values, and power dynamics embedded within legal systems. This process involves questioning the universality of legal principles and recognizing the diverse legal traditions that existed prior to colonization.

Another challenge is the lack of representation and inclusivity within the legal profession. Historically marginalized communities, including indigenous peoples, have been underrepresented in legal education and practice. This leads to a limited perspective and underrepresentation of alternative legal traditions and approaches.

Additionally, the influence of colonial legacies, such as legal codes and statutes, can be deeply entrenched in legal systems. Undoing these legacies requires a comprehensive and systematic approach to reforming laws, policies, and institutions.

Possibilities for Decolonizing the Law

Despite the challenges, decolonizing the law offers numerous possibilities for transforming legal systems to be more just, inclusive, and responsive to the needs of marginalized communities.

One possibility is to incorporate indigenous legal traditions into the existing legal framework. Recognizing and respecting the legal principles, customs, and practices of indigenous communities can be a significant step towards decolonizing the law. This can involve legal reforms that provide greater autonomy and self-determination for indigenous peoples, as well as the inclusion of indigenous legal experts in decision-making processes.

Another possibility is to center the voices and experiences of marginalized communities in legal discourse and decision-making. This can be achieved through community engagement, participatory approaches to lawmaking, and the creation of spaces for dialogue and collaboration between legal professionals and marginalized communities.

Decolonizing the law also requires a shift in legal education. Law schools need to introduce critical perspectives, including postcolonial and indigenous legal theories, into their curriculum. This can enable students to critically analyze legal norms and structures and develop a more nuanced understanding of the role of the law in perpetuating or challenging systemic inequalities.

Addressing the Critics

There are critics of decolonizing the law who argue that it risks destabilizing legal systems and undermining legal certainty. However, it is important to recognize that legal systems are not static or apolitical. They are constantly evolving and reflecting the values and interests of those in power. Decolonizing the law is a necessary process to address historical injustices and create a more equitable legal framework.

Real-World Examples

One real-world example of decolonizing the law is the revitalization of indigenous legal systems in Canada. In recent years, there have been efforts to recognize and incorporate indigenous legal principles and practices into the Canadian legal system. This includes the establishment of indigenous courts and the integration of indigenous legal perspectives in court decisions.

Another example is the recognition and protection of indigenous land rights in Latin America. Indigenous communities have advocated for the recognition of their ancestral territories and the right to self-governance. These efforts have led to legal reforms that acknowledge indigenous land rights and provide avenues for indigenous communities to participate in decision-making processes.

Resources for Further Study

For those interested in further studying decolonizing the law, there are numerous resources available. Some recommended readings include:

- *Decolonizing Methodologies: Research and Indigenous Peoples* by Linda Tuhiwai Smith

- *Owning the Earth: The Transforming History of Land Ownership* by Andro Linklater

- *The Politics of Law: A Progressive Critique* by David Kairys

- *Indigenous Peoples, Customary Law and Human Rights: Why Living Law Matters* edited by Brendan Tobin and Bruce Ziff

In addition, attending conferences and workshops on decolonizing the law can provide opportunities for learning, networking, and engaging in discussions with scholars and practitioners in the field.

Conclusion

Decolonizing the law is a crucial step towards justice and equality. It requires acknowledging and unraveling the colonial legacies embedded within legal systems, challenging existing power structures, and centering the voices and experiences of marginalized communities. While it presents challenges, the possibilities for transforming the law into a more inclusive and equitable system are vast. Through critical engagement, collaborative efforts, and innovative approaches, decolonizing the law can contribute to a more just and transformative future.

Critical Race Theory

Overview of Critical Race Theory

Critical Race Theory (CRT) is a theoretical framework that emerged in the late 1970s and early 1980s in legal scholarship. It seeks to examine and challenge the intersection of race and power within the law and legal institutions. CRT critiques the traditional approach to legal analysis, which often overlooks the role of race and racial dynamics in shaping legal outcomes. It aims to highlight the ways in which the law contributes to systemic racism and perpetuates racial inequality.

The central premise of CRT is that racism is not merely an individual act or belief, but rather a systemic and institutionalized structure that is embedded in the fabric of society. Race is seen as a social construct that has been used historically to justify and maintain white dominance and privilege. CRT acknowledges that racism is not limited to overt acts of discrimination but is also present in more subtle, implicit forms. It recognizes the need to go beyond formal legal equality and address the structural and institutional barriers that perpetuate racial disparities.

One of the key concepts in CRT is that of "interest convergence," which suggests that racial progress is only possible when the interests of marginalized groups align with those of the dominant majority. According to this theory, legal reforms and advancements in civil rights are often driven by strategic calculations by those in power, rather than a genuine desire for equality. This concept challenges the notion that societal progress is solely the result of a gradual erosion of racism over time.

CRT also emphasizes the importance of the lived experiences of racial minorities in understanding the impact of racism. It encourages scholars and practitioners to critically analyze the law through the lens of race and to incorporate the narratives and perspectives of marginalized communities. By centering the voices of those directly affected by racial injustice, CRT aims to challenge dominant narratives and bring about transformative change.

One of the central tenets of CRT is the recognition that racism operates in a multidimensional and intersecting manner. It acknowledges the ways in which race intersects with other forms of oppression, such as gender, class, and sexuality. This intersectional approach allows for a more nuanced understanding of how different forms of discrimination and inequality interact and reinforce each other.

CRT has influenced various areas of law and legal scholarship, including criminal justice, education, housing, and employment. It has informed discussions on racial profiling, affirmative action, disparate impact, and the school-to-prison pipeline. CRT has also been critical in highlighting the limitations of colorblind approaches to law and policy, arguing that such approaches often perpetuate systemic racism by obscuring the impact of race.

In order to challenge and transform racial inequalities, CRT advocates for a range of strategies, including legal reform, social activism, and community organizing. It calls for a reimagining of legal frameworks and institutions to better address racial disparities and promote racial justice. This may involve adopting policies that prioritize the needs and experiences of marginalized communities and engaging in initiatives that disrupt existing power structures.

In conclusion, Critical Race Theory provides a critical lens through which to understand how race operates within the law and legal institutions. By highlighting the ways in which racism is embedded in societal structures, CRT seeks to bring about transformative change and address systemic racial inequalities. It emphasizes the importance of centering the experiences of marginalized communities and pursuing strategies that challenge existing power dynamics.

Key Theorists and Concepts in Critical Race Theory

Critical Race Theory (CRT) emerged in the 1970s as a response to the limitations of traditional legal theories in addressing issues of racial inequality and discrimination. This section will explore some of the key theorists and concepts in CRT that have helped shape this transformative approach to understanding race and the law.

Derrick Bell

One of the foundational figures in CRT was Derrick Bell, a legal scholar and civil rights activist. Bell's work focused on the intersection between race and the law, particularly in the context of education. He introduced the concept of interest convergence, which posits that racial advances for marginalized groups are only achieved when they align with the interests of the dominant white society. This theory highlights the limitations of traditional legal approaches in achieving meaningful racial progress.

Kimberlé Crenshaw

Kimberlé Crenshaw is another influential figure in CRT, known for her development of the concept of intersectionality. Intersectionality recognizes that race cannot be understood independently from other social categories, such as gender, class, and sexuality. Crenshaw's work highlighted how experiences of discrimination vary depending on an individual's overlapping identities, and argued for the need to consider intersectionality in legal analysis and advocacy.

Richard Delgado

Richard Delgado's contributions to CRT have focused on the exploration of racist ideologies and institutions embedded within the legal system. Delgado argued that the law perpetuates racial hierarchies through both overt and subtle means. He introduced the notion of "critical race storytelling" as a way to challenge dominant narratives and expose the racial biases that exist within legal discourse.

Critical Race Theory Themes

Several key themes are central to Critical Race Theory:

- **Racial Power Structures:** CRT emphasizes the role of power dynamics and structural inequalities in perpetuating racial discrimination and oppression.

It critiques the idea of color-blindness and argues that racism is deeply ingrained in societal institutions.

- **Intersectionality:** CRT recognizes that race intersects with other social identities and systems of oppression. It emphasizes the need to consider the cumulative effects of multiple forms of discrimination and the unique experiences of individuals with intersecting identities.

- **Voice of the Marginalized:** CRT centers the perspectives and experiences of marginalized communities, highlighting their agency and resistance in the face of racial oppression. It challenges traditional legal narratives and seeks to amplify underrepresented voices.

- **Counter-Storytelling:** CRT encourages the use of counter-storytelling, which involves sharing personal narratives and experiences to challenge prevailing narratives. This approach aims to disrupt dominant ideologies and shed light on the lived realities of racial minorities.

- **Social Justice Activism:** CRT is deeply rooted in social justice activism, advocating for systemic change to address racial inequalities. It calls for transformative action both within and outside the legal system to challenge discriminatory practices and promote racial justice.

Application of Critical Race Theory

CRT has been applied to various legal fields, including criminal justice, education, employment, and housing. For example, in criminal justice, CRT has shed light on the racial disparities in policing, sentencing, and incarceration rates. In education, it has uncovered the racial biases in school discipline practices and the persistent achievement gaps between racial groups.

By critically examining the law and its impact on marginalized communities, CRT provides a framework for understanding and challenging systemic racism. It has influenced legal scholarship, social movements, and policy reform efforts, contributing to ongoing discussions on race, justice, and equality.

Further Reading

For further study on Critical Race Theory, the following resources provide valuable insights and perspectives:

- Delgado, R., & Stefancic, J. (2001). *Critical Race Theory: An Introduction.* New York, NY: New York University Press.
- Crenshaw, K. (1995). Mapping the Margins: Intersectionality, Identity Politics, and Violence against Women of Color. *Stanford Law Review,* 43(6), 1241-1299.
- Bell, D. (1980). Brown v. Board of Education and the Interest-Convergence Dilemma. *Harvard Law Review,* 93(3), 518-533.

These works provide a deeper understanding of the historical development, key concepts, and contemporary debates within Critical Race Theory.

Critiques and Challenges to Critical Race Theory

Critical Race Theory (CRT) has been a significant framework in understanding the intersection of race, law, and power. However, like any theoretical framework, it has faced criticisms and challenges. This section explores some of the main critiques and challenges to Critical Race Theory, highlighting the ongoing discussions and controversies within the field.

Critique: Essentialism and Overemphasis on Race

One of the primary critiques of Critical Race Theory is the accusation of essentialism. Critics argue that CRT tends to view race as a fixed and inherent characteristic, often overlooking the complexities and nuances within racial identities. This essentialist perspective can lead to generalizations and oversimplifications, ignoring the diversity and intersectionality of individual experiences.

Moreover, some argue that CRT places too much emphasis on race and overlooks other forms of social inequality, such as class, gender, and sexuality. Critics contend that focusing solely on race may limit the analysis of other intersecting structures of power and privilege.

Critique: Lack of Empirical Methods

Another critique against Critical Race Theory is the perceived lack of empirical methods in its research and analysis. Some argue that CRT tends to rely heavily on storytelling, narrative, and personal experiences, without engaging in rigorous empirical research. This reliance on anecdotes and narratives may undermine the academic rigor and credibility of the theory.

Critics argue that CRT could benefit from incorporating more quantitative and qualitative research methods to support its claims and strengthen its theoretical foundations. By embracing empirical methods, CRT can enhance its explanatory power and address skepticism regarding its validity.

Critique: Political Bias and Activism

Some critics argue that Critical Race Theory suffers from political bias and activism, suggesting that scholars in the field are primarily motivated by advocacy and social change rather than objective scholarship. This critique contends that CRT leans towards a particular ideological agenda, which can undermine its objectivity and create an echo chamber effect within academia.

Moreover, critics argue that this political bias may limit the ability of CRT to engage with opposing viewpoints and stifle intellectual diversity. By discouraging dialogue and dissent, some argue that CRT can hinder the development of robust and critical scholarship.

Challenge: Intersectionality and Identity Politics

An ongoing challenge within Critical Race Theory is navigating the intersectionality of various identities and social categories. As society becomes more diverse, scholars and activists within CRT are grappling with the complexity of intersecting oppressions and privilege based on race, gender, class, and other dimensions of identity.

Critics argue that CRT needs to further develop its understanding and analysis of intersectionality to address the experiences and struggles of individuals who face multiple forms of discrimination. By incorporating an intersectional lens, CRT can broaden its scope and be more inclusive in its analysis of systems of power and inequality.

Challenge: Evolving Notions of Race and Racism

The concept of race is dynamic and evolving, influenced by societal and historical context. As racial dynamics change, Critical Race Theory faces the challenge of adapting its analysis to encompass these shifts. Some critics argue that CRT needs to be mindful of the changing nature of race and racism and avoid being stuck in a static understanding of these concepts.

Moreover, with advancements in genetics and the unraveling of the biological basis of race, there is ongoing debate on how CRT should engage with new scientific understandings. Ensuring that CRT remains relevant and responsive to emerging discourses on race will be crucial in its continued development and applicability.

Conclusion

Critical Race Theory has undoubtedly made significant contributions to legal scholarship and activism. However, it is not immune to criticisms and challenges. Recognizing and engaging with these critiques and challenges is essential for the ongoing refinement and advancement of Critical Race Theory. By addressing these concerns, CRT can strengthen its position as a transformative framework for understanding and dismantling racism and inequality in society.

Intersectionality in Critical Race Theory

In this section, we will explore the concept of intersectionality within the framework of Critical Race Theory (CRT). Intersectionality is a crucial aspect of CRT, as it recognizes that individuals experience multiple forms of oppression and discrimination based on the intersection of their race, gender, class, sexuality, and other social identities.

Understanding Intersectionality

Intersectionality is a theoretical framework that highlights the interconnectedness of various social categories and identities that shape an individual's lived experiences. Developed by legal scholar Kimberlé Crenshaw, intersectionality moves beyond recognizing race and gender as separate systems of oppression and acknowledges that they intersect and interact to produce unique experiences for individuals.

Intersectionality challenges the traditional understanding of identity politics by emphasizing the complex and interlocking nature of social identities. It recognizes that individuals do not experience oppression solely based on their race or gender but rather through the intersecting and overlapping effects of multiple social categories. For example, a Black woman may face discrimination that is distinct from the experiences of a Black man or a White woman.

CRT's embrace of intersectionality allows for a more nuanced analysis of power dynamics and social inequality. It recognizes that issues such as racism, sexism, and classism are intertwined and cannot be understood or addressed in isolation from each other.

Key Concepts in Intersectionality

To fully grasp intersectionality within CRT, it is important to familiarize ourselves with some key concepts:

- **Multiple Identities:** Intersectionality acknowledges that individuals possess multiple social identities and that these identities intersect to shape their experiences and perspectives. These identities include race, gender, class, sexuality, disability, and more.

- **Interlocking Systems of Oppression:** Intersectionality recognizes that various systems of oppression, such as racism, sexism, and homophobia, operate simultaneously and reinforce each other. These interconnected systems create unique experiences of marginalization and privilege for individuals belonging to different social groups.

- **Experiences of Marginalization and Privilege:** Intersectionality highlights how individuals experience both marginalization and privilege due to their intersecting identities. For example, a queer person of color may face discrimination based on their race, sexuality, and gender, while also benefiting from privileges associated with their class or education.

- **Centering Marginalized Voices:** Intersectionality emphasizes the importance of centering the experiences and perspectives of those at the intersection of multiple marginalized identities. By doing so, CRT seeks to challenge the dominant narratives that often overlook or marginalize certain groups.

Analyzing Intersectionality in Critical Race Theory

Intersectionality plays a crucial role in the analysis and critique of social structures, including law and legal systems, within CRT. It helps uncover the ways in which different forms of oppression intersect to shape the experiences of marginalized groups and perpetuate systemic inequalities.

When applying intersectionality within CRT, scholars and activists aim to:

- **Recognize the Complexity of Lived Experiences:** Intersectionality allows for a more comprehensive understanding of how individuals experience and navigate power dynamics, discrimination, and privilege. By considering the intersecting identities and social categories, CRT can provide a more nuanced analysis of social inequality.

- **Challenge Dominant Narratives:** Intersectionality enables CRT to challenge the dominant narratives that perpetuate systemic racism and other forms of oppression. By centering the experiences of marginalized groups, CRT aims to expose the ways in which power operates and shapes social structures.

- **Inform Legal Struggles for Social Justice:** By incorporating an intersectional lens, CRT informs legal strategies and activism aimed at advancing social justice. By understanding the complex ways in which different forms of oppression intersect, activists and scholars can work towards dismantling systemic inequalities in the legal system.

Case Study: Intersectionality in Criminal Justice

To illustrate the importance of intersectionality within CRT, let's consider a case study focusing on the criminal justice system. Analyzing the experiences of incarcerated Black women through an intersectional lens reveals how race, gender, and class intersect to shape the disproportionate incarceration rates and unique challenges faced by this specific group.

By examining the intersecting identities of incarcerated Black women, CRT scholars can critique the underlying factors contributing to their overrepresentation in the criminal justice system. They can then advocate for policy changes, such as alternatives to incarceration and community-based support programs, that address the specific needs and experiences of this marginalized group.

Resources for Further Study

To delve deeper into the topic of intersectionality within CRT, consider exploring the following resources:

- Crenshaw, Kimberlé. "Demarginalizing the Intersection of Race and Sex: A Black Feminist Critique of Antidiscrimination Doctrine, Feminist Theory and Antiracist Politics." University of Chicago Legal Forum 1989, no. 1 (1989): 139-167.

- Collins, Patricia Hill. Black Feminist Thought: Knowledge, Consciousness, and the Politics of Empowerment. Routledge, 2009.

- Davis, Angela Y. Women, Race, & Class. Vintage, 1983.

- Cho, Sumi, Kimberlé Crenshaw, and Leslie McCall. "Toward a Field of Intersectionality Studies: Theory, Applications, and Praxis." Signs: Journal of Women in Culture and Society 38, no. 4 (2013): 785-810.

These resources provide a solid foundation for understanding intersectionality within CRT and its application in various disciplines, including law, sociology, and gender studies.

Conclusion

Intersectionality is a critical component of Critical Race Theory, allowing for a more nuanced understanding of how various forms of oppression intersect and shape individuals' experiences. By recognizing the complexity of social identities and the interlocking systems of oppression, CRT scholars and activists can promote social justice and work towards transforming legal systems to better address the needs and experiences of marginalized communities. Employing an intersectional lens is essential for a comprehensive critique of power structures and the development of effective strategies for societal transformation.

In the next section, we will explore the theoretical foundations and practical implications of Queer Legal Theory within transformative legal studies.

Queer Legal Theory

Overview of Queer Legal Theory

Queer legal theory is a dynamic and interdisciplinary field that explores the intersection of law and sexuality. It seeks to challenge and transform traditional legal systems that perpetuate heteronormativity and marginalize LGBTQ+ individuals and communities. This section provides an overview of queer legal theory, including its historical development, key concepts, and current debates.

Historical Development of Queer Legal Theory

Queer legal theory emerged in the late 20th century as a response to the discriminatory laws and practices that affected LGBTQ+ individuals. It drew inspiration from various social justice movements, including the gay rights movement, feminist legal theory, critical legal studies, and critical race theory.

One significant milestone in the development of queer legal theory was the decriminalization of homosexuality in several countries. This led to increased activism and legal advocacy for LGBTQ+ rights, challenging existing legal frameworks and promoting social change.

Key Concepts in Queer Legal Theory

Queer legal theory encompasses a range of concepts and ideas that aim to deconstruct and reimagine conventional legal understandings of sexuality and gender. Some key concepts include:

1. Heteronormativity: Queer legal theory critiques the assumption that heterosexuality is the norm and challenges the privileging of heterosexual relationships and identities within legal systems.

2. Intersectionality: Queer legal theory recognizes that sexual orientation and gender identity intersect with other social categories, such as race, class, and disability. It examines how these intersecting identities shape experiences of oppression and discrimination within legal contexts.

3. Anti-Essentialism: Queer legal theory challenges the notion that sexual orientation and gender identity are fixed and essential characteristics. It argues for a more fluid and contextual understanding of sexuality and gender, acknowledging the diversity of LGBTQ+ experiences.

4. Queer Liberation: Queer legal theory is rooted in the pursuit of liberation and social justice for LGBTQ+ individuals. It seeks to dismantle oppressive legal structures and create inclusive legal systems that affirm and protect diverse sexualities and gender identities.

Current Debates in Queer Legal Theory

Contemporary queer legal theory engages in ongoing debates and discussions surrounding LGBTQ+ rights and legal protections. Some of the key debates include:

1. Same-Sex Marriage: While the achievement of marriage equality has been a significant milestone for many LGBTQ+ communities, queer legal theory critically examines the institution of marriage itself. It questions whether marriage equality should be the primary focus of LGBTQ+ activism or if broader transformative legal changes are needed.

2. Transgender Rights: Queer legal theory challenges the binary understanding of gender within legal frameworks and advocates for legal recognition and protection of transgender and non-binary individuals. It explores the intersectional dimensions of transgender rights, addressing the unique struggles faced by transgender individuals from marginalized communities.

3. Queering Family Law: Queer legal theory explores alternative family structures and challenges the traditional nuclear family model in family law. It advocates for legal recognition and protection of diverse forms of relationships and families, such as chosen families and polyamorous relationships.

4. Violence and Discrimination: Queer legal theory addresses the ongoing violence and discrimination faced by LGBTQ+ individuals. It examines the legal frameworks necessary to combat hate crimes, bullying, employment discrimination, and other forms of violence and marginalization.

Resources for Further Study

To delve deeper into queer legal theory, here are some key resources for further study:

1. Books: - "Queer (In)Justice: The Criminalization of LGBT People in the United States" by Joey L. Mogul, Andrea J. Ritchie, and Kay Whitlock. - "Queer Theory: Law, Culture, Empire" by Robert Leckey. - "Sexuality Law" by Marc Spindelman.

2. Journals: - "Social & Legal Studies" - "GLQ: A Journal of Lesbian and Gay Studies" - "Columbia Journal of Gender and Law"

3. Organizations: - National LGBTQ+ Bar Association - Lambda Legal - Human Rights Campaign

These resources provide invaluable insights into the theoretical foundations, legal challenges, and potential avenues for transformative change within the field of queer legal theory.

Conclusion

In conclusion, queer legal theory seeks to challenge and transform existing legal systems through a critical examination of sexuality and gender. This overview has provided a glimpse into the historical development, key concepts, and current debates within queer legal theory. By engaging with this field, legal scholars and practitioners can contribute to the ongoing fight for justice, equality, and liberation for LGBTQ+ individuals and communities.

Key Theorists and Concepts in Queer Legal Theory

In this section, we will explore the key theorists and concepts in queer legal theory. Queer legal theory is an interdisciplinary field that examines the law from a queer perspective, focusing on the experiences and rights of LGBTQ+ individuals. It challenges traditional legal frameworks that have historically marginalized and discriminated against queer communities. By analyzing legal concepts and institutions through a queer lens, this theory seeks to transform legal systems to better protect and promote the rights of LGBTQ+ individuals.

Michel Foucault

One of the key theorists in queer legal theory is Michel Foucault. Foucault's work on power, knowledge, and sexuality has been highly influential in understanding the relationship between the law and queer identities. Foucault argued that power operates through discourses and institutions, shaping societal norms and regulating individuals' sexuality. He highlighted how legal systems have been used to control and regulate non-normative sexualities, such as same-sex relationships.

Foucault's concept of "biopower" is particularly relevant to queer legal theory. Biopower refers to the ways in which the state exercises control over individuals' bodies and lives through mechanisms such as legislation, policies, and regulations. Queer legal theorists draw on Foucault's ideas to critique the ways in which legal systems have historically enforced heteronormativity and limited queer individuals' rights and freedoms.

Judith Butler

Another prominent figure in queer legal theory is Judith Butler. Known for her work on gender and performativity, Butler has contributed to the understanding of the legal construction of gender and sexuality. Butler argues that gender is not a fixed, inherent identity but rather a social and cultural performance. She challenges the binary understanding of gender and encourages a more fluid and inclusive approach.

Butler's concept of "gender performativity" has had a significant impact on queer legal theory. It emphasizes that gender and sexuality are not predetermined but are produced through repeated acts and performances. Queer legal theorists use this concept to critique legal frameworks that reinforce gender norms and perpetuate discrimination against queer individuals.

Queer Legal Activism

Queer legal theory also draws inspiration from the activism of queer communities and their allies. Throughout history, LGBTQ+ individuals have fought for their rights and challenged discriminatory laws and practices. Activism has played a crucial role in shaping legal developments and advancing LGBTQ+ rights. From the Stonewall Riots to contemporary protests, queer legal activism has sparked social and legal transformations.

Important legal concepts and strategies have emerged from queer legal activism. For example, the idea of "gender identity" as a protected characteristic has been advanced through legal challenges and activism. Similarly, the concept of "heteronormativity" has been used to critique legal frameworks that assume heterosexuality as the norm and oppress non-normative sexualities.

Intersectionality

Intersectionality is a critical concept in queer legal theory. Coined by Kimberlé Crenshaw, intersectionality recognizes that individuals hold multiple identities and that these identities intersect and interact with systems of power and oppression. Queer legal theory embraces intersectionality to understand how race, class, gender, and other social categories intersect with sexual orientation and gender identity, leading to unique experiences of discrimination and marginalization.

Queer legal theorists highlight the importance of recognizing and addressing intersectional forms of discrimination in legal systems. They critique legal frameworks that fail to account for the diverse experiences of LGBTQ+ individuals and advocate for an intersectional approach that considers the overlapping dimensions of identity and oppression.

Challenges and Critiques in Queer Legal Theory

While queer legal theory has made significant contributions to understanding and challenging discriminatory legal systems, it faces several challenges and critiques. One critique is that queer legal theory is often disconnected from the lived experiences of marginalized LGBTQ+ individuals. Critics argue that the theoretical nature of this field can sometimes overlook the realities of those most impacted by discriminatory laws.

Another challenge is the limited recognition and protection of LGBTQ+ rights in many legal systems globally. While progress has been made in some countries, there are still significant disparities in the legal rights and protections afforded to LGBTQ+ individuals. Queer legal theorists continue to advocate for comprehensive legal reforms to address these inequalities.

Additionally, queer legal theory must continually evolve to account for the changing landscape of LGBTQ+ identities and experiences. As society becomes more aware of diverse gender identities and sexualities, queer legal theory needs to adapt and expand its focus to be inclusive and responsive to the needs of all queer communities.

Conclusion

Key theorists and concepts in queer legal theory, such as Michel Foucault and Judith Butler, have provided invaluable insights into the ways in which legal systems have historically oppressed and marginalized LGBTQ+ individuals. By examining legal frameworks from a queer perspective, this theory seeks to transform legal systems to better protect and promote the rights of LGBTQ+ individuals.

Intersectionality plays a crucial role in queer legal theory, highlighting the intersections of various identities and experiences of discrimination. Challenges and critiques exist, such as the need for more connection to lived experiences, the limited recognition of LGBTQ+ rights globally, and the evolving understanding of gender and sexuality.

Moving forward, queer legal theory must continue to evolve, embrace intersectionality, and address the changing needs of diverse LGBTQ+ communities. Through ongoing research, activism, and legal reforms, the transformative potential of queer legal theory can be realized, fostering a more inclusive and just legal system for all.

Legal Recognition of LGBTQ+ Rights and Challenges

The legal recognition of LGBTQ+ rights has been an ongoing struggle around the world. LGBTQ+ individuals have faced significant discrimination and marginalization throughout history, and it is only in recent years that significant progress has been made in recognizing and protecting their rights. This section will explore the challenges faced by LGBTQ+ individuals in obtaining legal recognition and the advancements made in promoting equality and inclusivity.

Historical Context

To understand the challenges faced by LGBTQ+ individuals in legal recognition, it is crucial to recognize the historical context in which their rights have been marginalized. Many legal systems have traditionally criminalized same-sex relationships and imposed societal stigmatization. In some jurisdictions, same-sex sexual acts were considered criminal offenses, leading to persecution and discrimination against LGBTQ+ individuals. LGBTQ+ individuals were often denied basic human rights, including the right to marry, adopt children, or receive protection against discrimination.

Legal Progress and Advances

In recent years, there have been significant legal advancements in recognizing and protecting LGBTQ+ rights. One of the key milestones in this progress is the decriminalization of same-sex sexual acts in many countries. This has resulted in a shift towards recognizing the rights of LGBTQ+ individuals and challenging discriminatory laws and practices.

Legal recognition of same-sex relationships has also expanded globally. Many countries now allow same-sex marriage or provide legal recognition for same-sex partnerships. This recognition not only allows LGBTQ+ individuals to enjoy the same rights and benefits as heterosexual couples, but it also sends a powerful message of inclusivity and acceptance.

Furthermore, LGBTQ+ individuals have gained increased protection against discrimination in various aspects of life, including employment, housing, education, and healthcare. Anti-discrimination laws have been enacted in many jurisdictions to prohibit discrimination based on sexual orientation and gender identity. These legal protections aim to ensure equal opportunities and equal treatment for LGBTQ+ individuals.

Challenges and Resistance

Despite significant progress, many challenges and resistance persist in the legal recognition of LGBTQ+ rights. Some religious, cultural, and societal beliefs still view homosexuality and gender non-conformity as immoral or unnatural, leading to resistance towards legal recognition and protection of LGBTQ+ rights.

Legal systems in some countries still criminalize same-sex relationships or impose harsh penalties based on sexual orientation or gender identity. In these jurisdictions, LGBTQ+ individuals may face discrimination, harassment, and violence without legal recourse or protection.

Another challenge is the lack of recognition and protection for transgender and non-binary individuals. Many legal systems still do not have comprehensive laws to protect the rights of these individuals, including legal recognition of gender identity and access to gender-affirming healthcare.

Resistance to LGBTQ+ rights can also manifest in the form of political and legal opposition, such as efforts to roll back existing legal protections or enact discriminatory legislation. This opposition poses significant challenges to the continued advancement of LGBTQ+ rights and necessitates ongoing advocacy and legal action.

Intersectionality and LGBTQ+ Rights

An important aspect of legal recognition of LGBTQ+ rights is understanding the intersectionality of identities. LGBTQ+ individuals exist across diverse racial, ethnic, and socio-economic backgrounds, and their experiences of discrimination and marginalization are interwoven with these intersecting identities. Legal recognition of LGBTQ+ rights must take into account the unique challenges faced by individuals at these intersections and work towards comprehensive inclusivity.

For example, LGBTQ+ individuals who are also members of racial or ethnic minorities may face compounded discrimination and oppression based on both their sexual orientation or gender identity and their racial or ethnic identity. Legal systems need to address these intersectional forms of discrimination and ensure that the rights of all LGBTQ+ individuals are protected.

International Efforts and Human Rights

Internationally, there have been significant efforts to promote LGBTQ+ rights and combat discrimination. The United Nations, through its Universal Declaration of Human Rights, has recognized that all individuals are entitled to equal rights and protection against discrimination, regardless of their sexual orientation or gender identity.

Multiple United Nations resolutions and conventions have emphasized the importance of legal recognition and protection of LGBTQ+ rights. The Yogyakarta Principles, for example, outline specific human rights standards concerning sexual orientation and gender identity, providing a framework for legal reform and advocacy.

Non-governmental organizations (NGOs) and activists worldwide are also working tirelessly to promote LGBTQ+ rights and advocate for legal recognition. These organizations engage in strategic litigation, advocacy campaigns, and awareness-raising initiatives to advance the cause of LGBTQ+ rights at the domestic and international levels.

Current Legal Debates and Future Directions

The legal recognition of LGBTQ+ rights remains a topic of ongoing debate and discussion. Current debates include issues such as the legal recognition of non-binary and gender non-conforming individuals, legal protection against conversion therapy, and the rights of LGBTQ+ refugees and asylum seekers.

Future directions in the legal recognition of LGBTQ+ rights involve continued efforts to expand legal protections, promote social acceptance, and address intersectional forms of discrimination. It also requires ongoing engagement with the legal profession, educational institutions, and broader society to raise awareness and foster inclusivity.

In conclusion, the legal recognition of LGBTQ+ rights has come a long way, but challenges persist. The progress made in recent years provides hope for a more inclusive and equitable society. However, continued advocacy and legal efforts are needed to safeguard the rights of LGBTQ+ individuals, promote equality, and challenge discriminatory practices. The ongoing evolution and transformation of legal systems worldwide play a critical role in ensuring a more just and inclusive future for all.

Marxist Legal Theory

Overview of Marxist Legal Theory

Marxist legal theory provides a critical framework for understanding the relationship between law and social relations within capitalist societies. It seeks to uncover the ways in which law functions to maintain and reinforce the existing economic and social order, while also exploring the potential for using law as a tool for achieving social transformation and justice.

Historical Context

Marxist legal theory developed in the context of 19th-century Europe, during the rise of capitalism and the Industrial Revolution. Karl Marx, a prominent philosopher and economist, analyzed the exploitative nature of capitalist economies and argued that the legal system played a crucial role in perpetuating class inequality and protecting the interests of the ruling class.

Marxist legal theory builds on Marx's broader analysis of capitalist society, which emphasizes the primacy of economic relations and the class struggle between the bourgeoisie (capitalist class) and the proletariat (working class). According to Marxism, the capitalist mode of production creates inherent contradictions that eventually lead to its own downfall.

Key Concepts

Marxist legal theory introduces several key concepts to understand the role of law in a capitalist society:

- **Base and Superstructure:** Marxist theory distinguishes between the economic base, which includes the means of production and the relations of production, and the superstructure, which encompasses institutions such as law, politics, and ideology. The base determines the superstructure, and changes in the base eventually lead to changes in the superstructure.

- **Commodity Fetishism:** According to Marx, the capitalist mode of production alienates individuals from their labor and the products of their labor. This alienation is reflected in the fetishization of commodities, where social relations among people are obscured, and the value of goods is determined solely by their exchange value.

- **Class Struggle:** Marxist legal theory acknowledges the class struggle as a central feature of capitalist societies. The ruling class, through its control over the legal system, enforces its interests and suppresses the working class. This struggle manifests in various ways, including labor disputes, inequality, and social conflicts.

- **Law as a Tool of Repression:** Marxist legal theory argues that law operates primarily to preserve the status quo and protect the interests of the ruling class. It provides a legal framework that enforces property rights, legitimizes inequality, and ensures the smooth functioning of capitalist production relations.

- **Critique of Legal Formalism:** Marxist legal theory critiques legal formalism, which prioritizes the formal application of legal rules without considering broader social and economic contexts. It argues that legal formalism obscures the underlying power relations that shape the law and perpetuates unjust outcomes.

Transformative Potential

Marxist legal theory also recognizes the potential for using law as a transformative tool to challenge capitalist hegemony and strive for social justice. It emphasizes the importance of building a legal framework that facilitates the transition to a more equitable and socialist society. This transformative potential is rooted in the following principles:

- **Class-Conscious Legal Activism:** Marxist legal theory encourages legal activism that is informed by class consciousness and committed to challenging the systemic injustices of capitalism. It seeks to align legal struggles with broader social movements and class interests.

- **Law and Social Revolution:** Marxist legal theorists argue that legal change alone is insufficient to bring about radical social transformation. They advocate for a revolutionary change in the economic base, which would pave the way for the creation of a socialist legal system that serves the interests of the working class.

- **Legal Strategies for Social Change:** Marxist legal theory explores various legal strategies that can contribute to social change within the capitalist framework. These strategies may include using the law to protect workers' rights, advocating for stronger labor regulations, and mobilizing legal resources to challenge capitalist property relations.

- **Collective Action and Solidarity:** Marxist legal theory emphasizes the importance of collective action and solidarity among oppressed groups to achieve transformative legal change. It recognizes that the struggles against capitalist exploitation and injustice are interconnected and require coordinated efforts.

Critiques and Challenges

Marxist legal theory has faced several critiques and challenges. Some of the common criticisms include:

- **Determinism and Reductionism:** Critics argue that Marxist legal theory tends to oversimplify complex social phenomena by reducing them to economic relations. They contend that it overlooks other forms of domination, such as gender and race, which intersect with class dynamics.

- **Revolutionary Praxis:** Critics question the feasibility and effectiveness of revolutionary praxis as a means to achieve social change. They argue that legal reform and incremental change within the existing legal system may be more pragmatic approaches to promoting social justice.

- **Legal Formalism and Social Transformation:** Critics highlight the limitations of using law as an agent of social transformation within a capitalist framework. They argue that the law is inherently tied to the existing power structures and may be inadequate to address systemic injustice.

MARXIST LEGAL THEORY

Despite these critiques, Marxist legal theory continues to shape critical legal scholarship and provides a valuable perspective for understanding the role of law in capitalist societies. It offers insights into the ways in which law can both perpetuate and challenge social and economic inequality, providing a foundation for transformative legal studies.

Key Theorists and Concepts in Marxist Legal Theory

Marxist legal theory is a branch of critical legal studies that analyzes the relationship between law and the capitalist mode of production. It seeks to understand how law functions to perpetuate and protect the interests of the ruling class while maintaining the existing power structures. In this section, we will explore key theorists and concepts in Marxist legal theory that provide insights into the nature and role of law within a capitalist society.

Karl Marx

Karl Marx, the foundational theorist of Marxism, provided a comprehensive analysis of capitalism and its impact on various aspects of society, including law. Marx argued that law is an instrument of class domination and serves the interests of the ruling bourgeoisie. According to Marx, the capitalist mode of production is characterized by the exploitation of the working class, who are alienated from the means of production. Law, in this context, functions to protect private property rights and maintain the status quo by enforcing contracts and regulating labor relations. Marx emphasized the importance of understanding the material basis of law and how it reflects and reinforces the underlying economic relations.

Antonio Gramsci

Antonio Gramsci further developed Marxist legal theory by introducing the concept of hegemony. Gramsci argued that the ruling class maintains its dominance not only through coercive measures but also through the consent of the subordinate classes. He posited that the ruling class exercises hegemony by establishing a cultural and ideological framework that shapes the beliefs, values, and norms of society. Law plays a crucial role in this process by legitimizing the power structures and maintaining the hegemonic order. Gramsci's concept of hegemony provides a valuable framework for understanding how law operates in a complex and nuanced manner within capitalist societies.

Evgeny Pashukanis

Evgeny Pashukanis, a Soviet legal scholar, developed a Marxist analysis of law that focused on its commodity form. He argued that law is a social relationship that can be understood as a commodity exchange. Pashukanis claimed that in capitalist societies, laws are treated as commodities that are bought and sold in the marketplace. The legal system, according to Pashukanis, operates based on the principle of equivalence, where legal rights are treated as exchangeable commodities. The capitalist legal system, therefore, transforms social relations into economic relations, reinforcing the dominance of the capitalist mode of production.

Legal Form and Fetishism

One of the central concepts in Marxist legal theory is the notion of the "legal form." This concept refers to the specific way in which law governs social relations under capitalism. According to Marxists, the legal form masks the underlying social relationships of production by presenting them as abstract and equal relationships between legal subjects. This abstraction obscures the exploitative nature of capitalism and legitimizes the existing power structures. Furthermore, Marxist legal theorists also draw upon Marx's concept of fetishism, which refers to the process by which social relations are distorted and appear as natural, inherent features of the capitalist system. Law, as a form of social regulation, contributes to this fetishism by seemingly providing an objective and neutral framework while concealing the underlying class interests.

Critiques and Challenges

Marxist legal theory has faced various critiques and challenges. Some argue that it oversimplifies the role of law in society by reducing it solely to an instrument of class domination. Critics also contend that Marxist legal theory often neglects other social factors, such as race, gender, and culture, and underestimates the potential for legal change and progressive reforms within the capitalist system. Additionally, the collapse of the Soviet Union and the decline of socialist states have led to debates about the relevance and applicability of Marxist legal theory in contemporary contexts.

Relevance and Future Directions

Despite the critiques, Marxist legal theory continues to be influential in critical legal studies and provides valuable insights into the relationship between law, capitalism, and social transformation. The analysis of law within a Marxist framework allows for a deeper understanding of the structural inequalities embedded within the legal system. Moreover, Marxist legal theory encourages the exploration of alternative legal systems and transformative approaches that challenge capitalist hegemony. Future directions in Marxist legal theory involve incorporating intersectional perspectives that account for the complex interplay of class, race, gender, and other social categories in the analysis of law.

In conclusion, Marxist legal theory offers a critical lens through which to examine the role of law in a capitalist society. Through the works of key theorists such as Marx, Gramsci, and Pashukanis, we gain insights into the ways in which law functions to perpetuate class domination and maintain the existing power structures. Understanding the concepts of legal form, fetishism, and hegemony allows for a nuanced analysis of the relationship between law and social transformation. While facing critiques and challenges, Marxist legal theory remains relevant in contemporary discussions on the nature of law and its potential for serving justice and equality.

Marxism and Social Transformation through Law

Marxism, as a theoretical framework, provides a critical analysis of capitalist societies and offers a vision for social transformation based on principles of equality, justice, and collective ownership of the means of production. In this section, we will explore the relationship between Marxism and the role of law in social transformation. We will examine how Marxist legal theory seeks to challenge existing power structures and offer alternative approaches to law and justice. Additionally, we will discuss the potential impact of Marxist ideas on social movements and legal activism.

Marxist Legal Theory: Critiques of Capitalist Law

Marxist legal theory critiques the role of law within capitalist societies, arguing that it serves to protect and perpetuate the interests of the ruling class while maintaining the exploitative nature of the capitalist system. According to Marxism, law operates as an instrument of class domination, promoting the interests of the capitalist bourgeoisie and suppressing the working class.

One central critique of capitalist law is its focus on individual rights and property ownership. Marxist legal theorists argue that private property rights, enshrined in legal systems, perpetuate social inequality and exploitation. They contend that this legal framework favors the interests of the bourgeoisie, who have the means to accumulate wealth and control the means of production, while marginalizing the working class.

Furthermore, Marxist legal theory highlights the role of law in maintaining the capitalist economic system. For example, labor laws protect the rights of employers over employees, allowing for the exploitation of workers and the extraction of surplus value. Marxist legal theorists argue that this legal framework upholds and reinforces the capitalist mode of production.

Transformation through Class Struggle

Marxism emphasizes the importance of class struggle in effecting social transformation. Class struggle refers to the conflict between the bourgeoisie and the proletariat, with the proletariat seeking to overthrow the capitalist system and establish a socialist society. Marxist legal theory recognizes the potential for law to be used as a tool to advance the interests of the working class in this struggle.

One avenue for transformative change is through the use of legal reforms and regulations that protect the rights and interests of workers. Marxist legal theorists advocate for labor laws that guarantee fair wages, safe working conditions, and collective bargaining rights. These legal protections can help to empower workers and undermine the power of capital.

Additionally, Marxist legal theory recognizes the potential for legal mobilization and activism as a means of challenging the status quo and promoting social change. Legal activism can involve challenging unjust laws, advocating for worker's rights, and supporting social movements fighting for equality and justice. By using the legal system strategically, Marxist legal theorists argue that social transformation can be achieved.

Critiques and Challenges

While Marxist legal theory offers a critical perspective on the role of law in capitalist societies and provides strategies for social transformation, it has not been without its critics and challenges. Some scholars argue that Marxist legal theory oversimplifies the complex relationship between law, power, and social change. They point to the limitations of using law as a mechanism for achieving fundamental sociopolitical transformation.

Additionally, critics question the feasibility of implementing Marxist legal principles within existing legal systems. They argue that the entrenched power structures and ideological biases within legal institutions make it difficult to bring about meaningful change through legal means alone.

Historical and Contemporary Examples

Throughout history, Marxist ideas have influenced social movements and legal activism aimed at challenging oppressive systems and achieving social transformation. One example is the labor movement, which fought for workers' rights and better working conditions through legal reforms and collective action.

In the present day, Marxist legal principles continue to inspire movements advocating for economic and social justice. For instance, the fight for a living wage, the critique of income inequality, and demands for affordable housing can all be seen as efforts to address the injustices embedded in the capitalist legal system.

Resources for Further Study

For further exploration of Marxism and its relationship to law and social transformation, the following resources are recommended:

- *Marx's Capital and Capitalism Today* by Tony Cutler and Barry Hindess
- *Marxist Legal Theory* by Robert W. Gordon
- *Marxism, the Millennium, and Beyond* by Cyril Smith
- *The Marxist System: Economic, Political, and Social Perspectives* by Robert L. Heilbroner

Conclusion

Marxist legal theory provides a critical lens through which to examine the role of law in capitalist societies and offers insights into the potential for social transformation. By challenging the dominance of private property rights and advocating for the rights and interests of the working class, Marxist legal theory seeks to reshape the legal framework in pursuit of a more just and equal society. While Marxist legal theory has faced critiques and challenges, its influence on social movements and legal activism underscores its ongoing relevance in the pursuit of transformative legal studies.

Human Rights and Transformative Legal Studies

Introduction to Human Rights Law

Human Rights Law is a branch of international law that focuses on the protection and promotion of fundamental rights and freedoms that every individual is entitled to. These rights are inherent to all human beings, regardless of their nationality, race, gender, religion, or any other characteristic. The field of Human Rights Law encompasses a wide range of topics, including civil and political rights, economic, social, and cultural rights, indigenous rights, women's rights, children's rights, LGBTQ+ rights, and disability rights.

At its core, Human Rights Law seeks to ensure dignity, equality, justice, and respect for all individuals. It establishes a legal framework for holding states accountable for their actions and omissions, and it provides remedies for individuals whose rights have been violated. Human Rights Law also aims to prevent and address systemic and structural injustices, discrimination, and inequality.

Historical Development of Human Rights Law

The concept of human rights has deep historical roots, with ideas and principles traceable to ancient civilizations, religions, and philosophical traditions. However, the modern human rights movement gained momentum in the aftermath of World War II and the Holocaust, which showcased the egregious violations of human dignity and the need for robust legal protection of individual rights.

The Universal Declaration of Human Rights (UDHR), adopted by the United Nations General Assembly in 1948, is widely regarded as the foundational document of modern Human Rights Law. It proclaims a comprehensive set of fundamental rights and freedoms, including the right to life, liberty, equality, and non-discrimination, and it applies to all individuals regardless of their legal status.

Since the adoption of the UDHR, numerous international and regional treaties and conventions have been established to further elaborate and protect human rights. These include the International Covenant on Civil and Political Rights (ICCPR), the International Covenant on Economic, Social, and Cultural Rights (ICESCR), the Convention on the Elimination of All Forms of Discrimination against Women (CEDAW), the Convention on the Rights of the Child (CRC), and the Convention on the Rights of Persons with Disabilities (CRPD), among others.

Principles of Human Rights Law

Human Rights Law is guided by several core principles that underpin its legal framework and application. These principles provide a basis for interpreting and implementing human rights standards and inform the actions of states, international organizations, and other actors.

1. Universality: Human rights are universal and apply to all individuals, without distinction. They are not dependent on nationality, citizenship, or any other status. Every human being is entitled to the enjoyment of human rights.
2. Inalienability: Human rights are inherent to individuals and cannot be taken away or waived. They are inalienable, meaning they cannot be voluntarily surrendered or transferred.
3. Interdependence and indivisibility: Human rights are interconnected and mutually reinforcing. Civil, political, economic, social, and cultural rights are interdependent and indivisible. The realization of one right often depends on the fulfillment of other rights.
4. Non-discrimination: Human rights are to be enjoyed by all individuals, without any form of discrimination or distinction. Equality and non-discrimination are fundamental principles of Human Rights Law.
5. State responsibility: States have the primary responsibility to respect, protect, and fulfill human rights. They have an obligation to ensure that individuals within their jurisdiction can exercise their rights without discrimination or interference.
6. Accountability: States are accountable for their actions and omissions, both domestically and internationally. They can be held accountable for human rights violations through legal mechanisms such as national courts, international tribunals, and treaty bodies.
7. Participation and inclusion: Individuals have the right to participate in decision-making processes that affect their human rights. The principle of participation ensures that individuals and communities are active agents in shaping and implementing human rights standards.

Role of Human Rights Law in Promoting Social Justice

Human Rights Law plays a crucial role in promoting social justice by challenging systemic inequalities, discrimination, and injustice. It provides a legal framework for addressing historical and ongoing human rights violations, promoting equality, and advancing social change.

Human Rights Law seeks to empower marginalized and vulnerable groups by recognizing their rights and addressing the structural barriers that impede their full participation and enjoyment of rights. It emphasizes the importance of an inclusive and equitable society where everyone has equal access to justice, education, healthcare, employment, and other essential services.

Through human rights advocacy and litigation, individuals and organizations can challenge discriminatory laws, policies, and practices. Human Rights Law enables individuals to seek remedies for violations and hold accountable those responsible for human rights abuses. It also provides a platform for individuals and communities to raise awareness, mobilize, and advocate for social change.

Contemporary Challenges and Debates in Human Rights Law

While Human Rights Law has made significant progress in protecting and promoting human rights, it faces ongoing challenges and debates. Some of the contemporary issues include:

1. Balancing rights and security: The tension between protecting human rights and ensuring national security is a complex and evolving challenge. It raises questions about the scope of state powers, surveillance, counter-terrorism measures, and the impact on civil liberties.

2. Technology and privacy: Advances in technology, including surveillance technologies and digital platforms, present new challenges to privacy rights. The collection, use, and sharing of personal data raise concerns regarding privacy protection and individual autonomy.

3. Intersectionality and multiple forms of discrimination: Human Rights Law is increasingly grappling with the concept of intersectionality, recognizing that individuals may face multiple and intersecting forms of discrimination based on race, gender, disability, and other factors. Addressing these intersecting inequalities requires a holistic and inclusive approach.

4. Climate change and environmental rights: The recognition of environmental rights as human rights is a debated topic. Climate change poses significant challenges to the enjoyment of human rights, and there is ongoing discussion about the legal framework and responsibilities to address climate-related issues.

5. Globalization and economic rights: Economic globalization has led to debates about the protection of economic, social, and cultural rights. Issues such as labor rights, access to essential services, and socio-economic inequalities require attention within the framework of Human Rights Law.

Conclusion

Introduction to Human Rights Law provides an overview of the foundational principles, historical development, and contemporary challenges in the field of Human Rights Law. It emphasizes the importance of universal human rights, their interdependence, and the role of Human Rights Law in promoting social justice and equality. By understanding the principles and scope of Human Rights Law, we can work towards a more just and inclusive society that respects and protects the inherent dignity and rights of all individuals.

Human Rights Principles and Transformative Legal Studies

Human rights are a fundamental aspect of transformative legal studies, forming the basis for promoting justice, equality, and social transformation. In this section, we will explore the principles of human rights and their relationship to transformative legal studies. We will examine how human rights principles can drive legal transformation and contribute to creating a more just and equal society.

Understanding Human Rights Principles

Human rights are inherent and inalienable rights that every individual possesses by virtue of being human. They are universal, indivisible, and interdependent, meaning that all rights are equally important and cannot be separated from one another. Human rights principles guide the formulation and implementation of laws and policies that protect and promote the rights and dignity of every individual.

The key principles of human rights include:

1. Universality: Human rights apply to all individuals, regardless of their nationality, race, gender, religion, or any other characteristic. They are applicable to every person, without discrimination.

2. Equality and Non-Discrimination: Human rights require that all individuals be treated with dignity and respect, without any form of discrimination. Everyone should have equal access to rights and freedoms.

3. Inherent Dignity: Human rights acknowledge the inherent dignity of every human being. This principle recognizes that all individuals have worth and value and should be treated accordingly.

4. Justice and Rule of Law: Human rights align with the principles of justice and the rule of law. They require that laws and legal systems be fair, transparent, and accountable, ensuring equal protection and due process.

5. Participation and Empowerment: Human rights emphasize the active participation and empowerment of individuals and communities in decision-making processes that affect their lives. The voice and agency of all individuals should be respected and valued.

6. Progressive Realization: Human rights recognize that the full realization of rights may take time and require progressive steps. States have an obligation to work towards achieving the full realization of rights over time.

7. Accountability and Remedies: Human rights call for mechanisms of accountability for violations and provide remedies for those whose rights have been violated. Victims of human rights abuses should have access to justice and effective remedies.

These principles serve as a foundation for transformative legal studies, informing the development of laws and policies that aim to address systemic injustices and inequalities.

Human Rights and Transformation

Human rights play a crucial role in driving social transformation and legal change. Through the lens of transformative legal studies, the recognition and protection of human rights can challenge existing power structures, promote social justice, and drive progressive social change.

By incorporating human rights principles and values into legal systems, transformative legal studies seek to:

- Challenge Discrimination and Inequality: Human rights principles, such as non-discrimination and equality, can be used to challenge discriminatory laws, policies, and practices. Transformative legal studies focus on dismantling systems of oppression and advancing equality for marginalized and vulnerable groups.

- Address Power Imbalances: Human rights can serve as a tool for addressing power imbalances within society. Transformative legal studies examine how certain groups, such as women, indigenous peoples, or racial and ethnic minorities, have been historically marginalized and work towards empowering these groups through legal means.

- Promote Social Inclusion and Participation: Human rights principles emphasize the importance of participation and inclusion. Transformative legal studies seek to ensure that all individuals, regardless of their background or identity, have the opportunity to participate fully in decision-making processes that affect their lives.

- Hold States Accountable: Human rights provide a framework for holding states accountable for their obligations to protect and promote the rights of individuals. Transformative legal studies examine mechanisms of accountability and advocate for stronger enforcement of human rights standards.

- Drive Legal Reforms: Human rights standards can drive legal reforms that align with transformative goals. By challenging existing laws and advocating for legal changes, transformative legal studies seek to create a legal framework that enables social transformation and enhances justice and equality.

In essence, human rights principles form the backbone of transformative legal studies, guiding the examination and transformation of legal systems to promote social justice and equality.

Examples of Transformative Legal Practice in Human Rights

Transformative legal studies have led to numerous examples of legal practices that promote human rights and drive transformative change. Here are a few examples:

1. Strategic Litigation: Lawyers and human rights advocates use strategic litigation to challenge discriminatory laws and policies. By bringing cases to court, they seek to establish legal precedents that expand the interpretation and protection of human rights.

2. Public Interest Advocacy: Public interest advocates work to advance human rights through advocacy, lobbying, and community mobilization. They address systemic issues and seek to influence public opinion and policy-making processes.

3. Human Rights Education: Transformative legal studies emphasize the importance of human rights education. By teaching individuals about their rights and the obligations of the state, human rights education can empower individuals to advocate for their rights and hold governments accountable.

4. International Human Rights Mechanisms: Transformative legal studies engage with international human rights mechanisms, such as the United Nations Human Rights Council or treaty bodies, to hold states accountable for human rights violations and advocate for progressive legal reforms.

5. Grassroots Movements: Transformative legal studies recognize the role of grassroots movements in effecting change. Movements like Black Lives Matter or the LGBTQ+ rights movement have utilized legal strategies to challenge discriminatory practices and advance human rights.

These examples illustrate how transformative legal practices can use human rights principles to challenge existing legal and social norms and drive positive change.

Challenges and Future Directions

While human rights principles provide a strong framework for transformative legal studies, challenges remain in their effective implementation and realization. Some challenges include:

- Resistance to Change: Transformative legal studies often face resistance from those who benefit from existing power structures and systems of oppression. Overcoming this resistance and effecting meaningful change can be a complex and ongoing process.

- Intersectionality and Multiple Forms of Discrimination: Transformative legal studies need to account for the intersecting forms of discrimination that individuals may face. It is important to recognize and address the ways in which discrimination based on multiple identities can compound and reinforce social inequalities.

- Balancing Rights and Conflicting Interests: Human rights can sometimes come into conflict with other rights or competing interests. Achieving a balance between competing rights and interests while upholding human rights principles requires careful consideration and thoughtful legal analysis.

- Global and Transnational Challenges: Transformative legal studies need to respond to global and transnational challenges that cross borders and jurisdictions. Addressing issues such as climate change, migration, or international conflict requires collaborative and innovative legal approaches.

Moving forward, future directions in transformative legal studies may include:

- Strengthening Legal Education: Integrating human rights principles into legal education can equip future legal professionals with the tools and knowledge to engage in transformative legal practice effectively.

- Intersectional Approaches: Transformative legal studies can further advance the understanding of intersectionality and its implications for legal practice. Examining how different forms of oppression intersect can lead to more comprehensive and impactful legal strategies.

- Engaging with Technology: Exploring the intersection between technology and human rights can open new avenues for transformative legal practice. Understanding the implications of emerging technologies and their impact on human rights can inform legal responses and advocacy.

- Collaboration and Networks: Foster collaboration between legal professionals, human rights activists, grassroots movements, and academic institutions to create strong networks and collaborative efforts for transformative legal practice.

In conclusion, human rights principles are essential to transformative legal studies. By embracing these principles and incorporating them into legal systems and practices, transformative legal studies can drive social transformation, challenge systemic injustice, and promote a more just and equal society.

Intersectionality and Human Rights

Intersectionality is a concept that examines the overlapping systems of oppression and discrimination that individuals may face based on their multiple social identities, such as race, gender, class, sexuality, disability, and more. This section explores how intersectionality shapes the understanding and implementation of human rights, emphasizing the importance of considering the interconnected nature of different forms of discrimination and their impact on marginalized individuals and communities.

Background

The concept of intersectionality was introduced by legal scholar Kimberlé Crenshaw in the late 1980s to address the experiences of African American women who faced both racial and gender discrimination and were often overlooked by legal frameworks that focused on one axis of oppression at a time. Intersectionality recognizes that social identities and systems of power interact in complex ways, leading to unique and compounded forms of discrimination and disadvantage.

In the context of human rights, intersectionality challenges the traditional approach that separates different forms of discrimination and treats them as separate issues. It highlights the need to consider the intersections of identities and experiences to effectively promote and protect human rights for all individuals.

Principles of Intersectionality in Human Rights

1. Recognition of Multiple Identities: Intersectionality recognizes that individuals may simultaneously experience multiple identities and forms of discrimination. It requires acknowledging the complex ways in which different systems of power intersect and interact.

2. Understanding Power Dynamics: Intersectionality acknowledges that privilege and oppression are not experienced in isolation but are embedded within larger structures of power and inequality. It emphasizes examining how different forms of identity interact with social, political, and economic systems.

3. Centering Marginalized Voices: Intersectionality highlights the importance of centering the experiences and perspectives of those who are most marginalized and impacted by intersecting forms of discrimination. It calls for inclusive and participatory approaches to human rights that recognize and value diverse experiences.

Applications of Intersectionality in Human Rights

1. Policy and Legal Reform: Intersectionality urges policymakers and legal practitioners to consider the intersecting identities and experiences of individuals when developing and implementing laws and policies. It calls for recognizing the specific challenges faced by marginalized groups and designing inclusive solutions that address the root causes of discrimination.

2. Gender-Based Violence: Intersectionality provides a critical lens for understanding gender-based violence by examining how intersecting identities, such as race, class, or disability, intersect with gender to shape experiences of violence and access to justice. It highlights the need for comprehensive and culturally sensitive approaches to addressing gender-based violence.

3. Economic Inequality: Intersectionality sheds light on how different forms of inequality, such as racism, sexism, and classism, intersect to create economic disparities. It emphasizes the importance of addressing structural barriers and providing inclusive economic opportunities for marginalized communities.

4. Health and Healthcare: Intersectionality is crucial in understanding health disparities and accessing healthcare. It highlights how intersecting identities and experiences, such as racism, sexism, and ableism, affect access to healthcare, quality of care, and health outcomes. It calls for inclusive healthcare policies and practices that address the root causes of these disparities.

Challenges and Critiques

While intersectionality has generated significant theoretical and practical advancements, it also faces challenges and critiques, including:

1. Complexity and Intersectional Analysis: The intersectional analysis of human rights issues can be complex and challenging. Understanding how different

forms of discrimination intersect requires a nuanced and comprehensive approach that considers multiple dimensions simultaneously.

2. Multiple Marginalizations: Intersectionality often focuses on the experiences of individuals who face multiple forms of oppression. However, it may overlook the experiences of those who are marginalized in one dimension but privileged in others. It is essential to ensure inclusivity and consider all intersections of identities.

3. Implementation and Institutional Barriers: Incorporating intersectionality into human rights frameworks and institutions poses challenges due to resistance, lack of awareness, and inadequate resources. Transforming existing systems and practices to be more intersectional requires collective efforts and institutional change.

Examples and Case Studies

1. Caster Semenya Case: The case of South African athlete Caster Semenya brings attention to intersectionality in the context of gender and sport. Semenya, an Olympic champion, faced discrimination and invasive scrutiny due to assumptions about her gender identity and the intersex traits she possesses. This case highlights the need for inclusive policies that consider the intersecting experiences of individuals to avoid discrimination and uphold human rights.

2. Indigenous Land Rights: The intersectionality of indigenous rights and environmental justice is seen in struggles for land rights. Indigenous communities often face multiple forms of discrimination, including racism and socio-economic marginalization. Considering their intersecting rights is crucial when addressing issues such as land rights, resource extraction, and environmental sustainability.

Conclusion

Intersectionality plays a vital role in understanding and advancing human rights. By acknowledging the interconnectedness of different forms of discrimination and privilege, intersectionality promotes a more comprehensive and inclusive approach to human rights advocacy, policy-making, and implementation. By centering the experiences of marginalized individuals and communities, intersectionality paves the way for transformative change and social justice. Integrating intersectionality into human rights discourse and practice is essential to creating a more equitable and inclusive world.

Resources for Further Study

1. Crenshaw, K. (1991). Mapping the Margins: Intersectionality, Identity Politics, and Violence against Women of Color. Stanford Law Review, 43(6), 1241-1299.
2. Davis, A. Y. (2009). Women, Race & Class. Vintage.
3. Hankivsky, O., & Cormier, R. (2011). Intersectionality and Public Policy: Some Lessons from Existing Models. Political Research Quarterly, 64(1), 217-229.
4. Cho, S., & Crenshaw, K. W. (Eds.). (2013). Intersectionality: Key Concepts. Routledge.
5. Collins, P. H. (1990). Black Feminist Thought: Knowledge, Consciousness, and the Politics of Empowerment. Routledge.
6. McCall, L. (2005). The Complexity of Intersectionality. Signs: Journal of Women in Culture and Society, 30(3), 1771-1800.
7. Nash, J. C. (2008). Re-thinking Intersectionality. Feminist Review, 89(1), 1-15.
8. Yuval-Davis, N. (2006). Intersectionality and Feminist Politics. European Journal of Women's Studies, 13(3), 193-209.
9. Human Rights Watch. (2020). Intersectionality and Women's Rights. Retrieved from https://www.hrw.org/news/2020/03/05/intersectionality-and-womens-rights
10. Amnesty International. (2019). Intersectionality: An Amnesty International Guide for Human Rights Organizations. Retrieved from https://www.amnesty.org/en/documents/poa25/1011/2019/en/

Glossary of Key Terms and Concepts

Intersectionality: The concept that recognizes the interconnected nature of different forms of discrimination and oppression that individuals may experience based on their multiple social identities.

Discrimination: The unjust or prejudicial treatment of individuals or groups based on characteristics such as race, gender, sexuality, disability, etc.

Privilege: Unearned advantages or benefits given to individuals or groups due to their social identities, often resulting in unequal power dynamics.

Social Justice: The equitable distribution of resources, rights, and opportunities in society, aiming to address and rectify systemic inequities and promote fairness.

Human Rights: The fundamental rights and freedoms to which all individuals are entitled, regardless of race, nationality, gender, etc., as recognized by international law and norms.

Power Dynamics: The relationships and interactions between individuals and groups that determine the distribution of power, influencing social hierarchies and the dynamics of oppression and privilege.

Inclusion: The process of creating environments and practices that embrace and value diverse identities and experiences, resulting in equitable opportunities for individuals of all backgrounds.

Economic Inequality: Disparities in income, wealth, and opportunities among individuals and groups, often influenced by social and economic structures.

Health Disparities: Unequal distribution of health outcomes and access to healthcare based on factors such as race, gender, socioeconomic status, etc.

Cultural Sensitivity: The awareness and respect for cultural differences, considering diverse cultural practices, beliefs, and perspectives in policies, programs, and practices.

Structural Barriers: Systemic obstacles and limitations that prevent individuals or groups from accessing and fully enjoying their rights and opportunities.

Exercises

1. Choose a social issue such as education, healthcare, or criminal justice, and apply an intersectional lens to analyze how different forms of discrimination intersect and contribute to inequalities in that specific context.

2. Research and analyze a case study that highlights the importance of intersectionality in the promotion and protection of human rights. Discuss the challenges faced and the transformative potential of an intersectional approach in that context.

3. Identify a policy or legislation within your country or region that addresses a human rights issue. Assess its effectiveness and potential for improvement by applying an intersectional analysis.

4. Conduct an interview or panel discussion with individuals from marginalized communities to explore their experiences of intersectional discrimination and the impact on their human rights. Reflect on the insights gained and ways to address these issues.

5. Develop a project proposal that applies intersectionality to promote human rights within your community or organization. Outline the goals, activities, and expected outcomes of the project, highlighting the importance of an inclusive and intersectional approach.

Note: The above exercises are designed to foster critical thinking and engagement with the topics discussed.

Conclusion

Recapitulation of Key Points

In this chapter, we explored the theoretical foundations of transformative legal studies. We began by discussing critical legal studies, which challenges traditional legal norms and institutions. We examined key theorists and concepts in critical legal studies and acknowledged the critiques and challenges faced by this approach.

Next, we delved into feminist legal theory, which highlights the intersection of gender and law. We discussed the key theorists and concepts in feminist legal theory, as well as the contemporary debates and developments. We emphasized the importance of intersectionality in understanding and addressing gender-based inequalities.

Moving on, we explored postcolonial legal theory, which focuses on the impact of colonialism on legal systems and the decolonization of law. We discussed the key theorists and concepts in postcolonial legal theory, and examined the challenges and possibilities of decolonizing the law.

We then examined critical race theory, which analyzes how race intersects with law and perpetuates systemic racism. We discussed the key theorists and concepts in critical race theory, as well as the critiques and challenges faced by this approach. We emphasized the importance of incorporating intersectionality into critical race theory to understand the diverse experiences of racialized individuals.

Next, we explored queer legal theory, which centers around LGBTQ+ rights and challenges heteronormativity in law. We discussed the key theorists and concepts in queer legal theory, and examined the legal recognition of LGBTQ+ rights and the ongoing challenges faced by this community.

We then delved into Marxist legal theory, which examines the relationship between law and capitalism. We discussed the key theorists and concepts in Marxist legal theory, and explored how Marxism can contribute to social transformation through law.

Finally, we explored human rights and its intersection with transformative legal studies. We gave an introduction to human rights law, discussed its principles, and explored the concept of intersectionality in human rights. We also highlighted the importance of recognizing and addressing economic, social, and cultural rights alongside civil and political rights.

Throughout this chapter, we have examined various theoretical perspectives that contribute to the transformative understanding of law. We have seen how critical approaches challenge traditional legal norms and institutions, and how feminist, postcolonial, critical race, queer, Marxist, and human rights perspectives bring marginalized voices to the forefront. It is through these theoretical foundations that we can reshape legal systems and institutions to promote justice and equality.

The journey does not end here. In the next chapters, we will explore transformative approaches in legal education, new approaches to legal research, the transformation of legal systems and institutions, the impact of technology on law, restorative justice in the criminal justice system, and transformative approaches to human rights law. By the end of this book, you will have a comprehensive understanding of how transformative legal studies can shape the future of justice and equality.

Now that we have recapitulated the key points of this chapter, let us move forward to explore transformative approaches to legal education in Chapter 3.

Implications for Transformative Legal Studies

The exploration of transformative legal studies has significant implications for the field of law and its future. By examining the theoretical foundations, innovative approaches to legal education, new methods of legal research, the transformation of legal systems and institutions, the impact of technology on the legal profession, the potential of restorative justice, the application of transformative approaches to human rights law, and the global perspective on legal transformation, we gain insights into the possibilities and challenges that lie ahead. This section discusses some of the key implications of transformative legal studies.

1. **Reconceptualizing the Role of Law**: Transformative legal studies challenge traditional notions of law as a fixed set of rules and principles. They encourage us to view law as a dynamic and evolving social construct that can be utilized to address social inequalities and promote justice. This reconceptualization opens up new avenues for legal practitioners, scholars, and policymakers to think creatively and critically about the potential of law to effect social change.

2. **Promoting Social Justice and Equality**: Transformative legal studies offer a framework for promoting social justice and equality. By examining the intersections of law with other disciplines such as feminist theory, critical race theory, postcolonial theory, and queer theory, we can identify and challenge the systemic biases and structures that perpetuate inequalities. This understanding allows us to develop legal strategies and policies that aim to redress social injustices and promote equality.

3. **Advancing Access to Justice**: Transformative legal studies highlight the importance of access to justice for marginalized communities and individuals. By exploring alternative methods of dispute resolution, such as restorative justice and

community-based approaches, we can develop transformative practices that empower individuals and communities to actively participate in the resolution of their legal disputes. This approach not only enhances access to justice but also promotes social cohesion and community healing.

4. **Integrating Interdisciplinary Approaches:** Transformative legal studies advocate for the integration of interdisciplinary approaches in legal education, research, and practice. By incorporating knowledge and insights from fields such as social sciences, medicine, psychology, and economics, we can enrich our understanding of legal issues and their social implications. This interdisciplinary approach helps to foster holistic and contextually relevant solutions to complex legal problems.

5. **Harnessing the Power of Technology:** Transformative legal studies recognize the potential of technology to revolutionize the legal profession. By exploring the applications of artificial intelligence, blockchain, online dispute resolution, big data analytics, and other technological advancements, we can enhance the efficiency and accessibility of legal services. However, we must also consider the ethical implications and challenges associated with the use of technology in the legal field.

6. **Embracing Restorative Justice Practices:** Transformative legal studies emphasize the importance of restorative justice as an alternative to punitive approaches in the criminal justice system. By considering the needs of victims, offenders, and communities affected by crime, restorative justice practices can promote healing, rehabilitation, and reconciliation. This approach challenges traditional notions of punishment and contributes to the transformation of criminal justice systems.

7. **Applying a Human Rights Lens:** Transformative legal studies provide a framework for applying a human rights lens to legal practice and policy. By examining the intersectionality of human rights issues, understanding the socio-economic and cultural dimensions of rights, and engaging in international and comparative perspectives, we can develop transformative approaches that protect and promote human rights for all.

8. **Recognizing Global Perspectives:** Transformative legal studies encourage us to take a global perspective on legal transformation. By examining the diversity of legal systems, exploring the impact of globalization on legal responses, and engaging with the challenges faced by marginalized communities globally, we can develop transformative practices that address transnational injustices and disparities.

As legal professionals, scholars, and practitioners, it is vital that we embrace these implications of transformative legal studies. By doing so, we can contribute to the advancement of justice, equality, and human rights within our legal systems and beyond. This requires ongoing critical reflection, engagement with diverse perspectives, and a commitment to the transformative potential of law in our societies.

Additional Resources:

- *Transformative Justice: Charting a Path to Community Healing and Social Transformation*, edited by Hilary Linton and Michael Anthony. This book provides in-depth insights into the theory and practice of restorative justice.

- *The Power of Law as a Social Institution: Perspectives from Eastern and Western Law*, edited by Hualing Fu and Michael Palmer. This book offers a comparative perspective on legal systems and the challenges of legal transformation in different regions.

- *Technology and the Future of Legal Practice: Preparing for the Fourth Industrial Revolution*, edited by Roger Smith. This publication explores the implications of technological advancements for the legal profession and provides practical guidance for embracing technological innovations.

- *Human Rights: Politics and Practice*, by Michael Goodhart. This book offers a comprehensive overview of human rights law and its application in promoting social justice and equality.

- *Global Justice and Transnational Legal Activism: Assessing the Impact of NGOs on Corporate Accountability*, by Stephen J. Arduino. This publication examines the role of transnational legal activism in promoting global justice and holding corporations accountable.

By engaging with these resources, readers can deepen their understanding of the implications and applications of transformative legal studies in various aspects of the legal field.

Further Research Directions in Theoretical Foundations

Theoretical foundations play a crucial role in understanding and analyzing legal studies. They provide the conceptual framework and tools necessary to critically examine the law, its origins, and its impact on society. As scholars continue to push the boundaries of legal studies, it is essential to identify key areas for future research within the theoretical foundations of transformative legal studies. This section explores some of these research directions and highlights their significance in advancing our understanding of justice and equality.

1. The Intersectionality of Legal Theories:

One avenue for future research is exploring the intersectionality of various legal theories. Intersectionality recognizes that individuals experience multiple forms of oppression simultaneously and that these intersecting identities create unique experiences of disadvantage. Researchers can investigate how different legal theories, such as critical race theory, feminist legal theory, and queer legal theory, interact and shape each other in addressing the complex issues of justice and equality. This research can shed light on the interconnectedness of various forms of discrimination and identify strategies to address these intersections effectively.

2. Global Perspectives on Legal Theories:

Another important direction for research is exploring how legal theories operate and evolve in different global contexts. Comparative studies can provide insights into how different legal systems engage with transformative legal theories and address social justice issues specific to their regions. Research can focus on understanding the challenges and opportunities faced by legal scholars and practitioners in different parts of the world, with a particular emphasis on indigenous legal systems, legal pluralism, and the relationship between global governance institutions and transformative legal theories.

3. Ethical Considerations in Legal Theories:

Ethics are an integral part of legal studies, shaping our understanding of what is just and equitable. Future research should investigate the ethical implications of different legal theories and their application in practice. This research could explore how legal theories address ethical dilemmas, promote human rights, and account for the interests of marginalized communities. Moreover, researchers can engage with the ethical challenges posed by emerging technologies, such as artificial intelligence, blockchain, and predictive analytics, and their impact on legal theory and practice.

4. Comparative Analysis of Legal Systems:

A comparative analysis of legal systems can provide valuable insights into the strengths and weaknesses of different legal approaches. Researchers can examine how different legal systems navigate issues related to justice, equality, and social transformation. By comparing legal systems with diverse theoretical foundations, researchers can identify best practices, evaluate the effectiveness of legal mechanisms, and propose innovative reforms. This research direction is particularly valuable in a context where legal systems are continuously evolving to reflect societal changes.

5. Empirical Studies in Legal Theory:

Empirical research can bridge the gap between theoretical frameworks and practical realities. Researchers can conduct empirical studies to explore how legal theories are applied in practice, understand their impact on justice and equality, and evaluate the effectiveness of legal reforms. By adopting qualitative and quantitative methodologies, these studies can inform policy-making, assess the

CONCLUSION

outcomes of legal interventions, and generate evidence-based recommendations for transformative legal practice.

6. Interdisciplinary Approaches in Legal Theory:

Interdisciplinary research is essential to comprehensively address complex societal issues. Future research can explore the integration of legal theories with other disciplines, such as sociology, psychology, economics, and political science. By drawing on insights from multiple fields, researchers can deepen their understanding of the complexities of legal phenomena and develop holistic approaches to transformative legal studies.

Overall, these research directions offer exciting opportunities to expand our theoretical understanding of legal studies and enhance their transformative potential. By exploring the intersectionality of legal theories, examining global perspectives, considering ethical implications, conducting comparative analysis, engaging with empirical studies, and embracing interdisciplinary approaches, scholars can contribute to the advancement of justice and equality in our legal systems.

Further Reading:

1. Crenshaw, K. (1989). Demarginalizing the Intersection of Race and Sex: A Black Feminist Critique of Antidiscrimination Doctrine, Feminist Theory, and Antiracist Politics. University of Chicago Legal Forum, 1(8), 139-167.

2. Merry, S. E. (2006). Human rights and gender violence: translating international law into local justice. Chicago: University of Chicago Press.

3. Bhattacharya, A. (2018). Political science models and environmental law. In S. Maloney (Ed.), Environmental law and governance for the Anthropocene (pp. 107-125). Oxford: Hart Publishing.

4. Roberts, D. E. (1997). Killing the black body: Race, reproduction, and the meaning of liberty. New York: Vintage Books.

5. Chesney-Lind, M., & Sheldon, R. G. (2013). Girls, Delinquency, and Juvenile Justice. Belmont, CA: Wadsworth.

Chapter 3: Transformative Approaches to Legal Education

Chapter 3: Transformative Approaches to Legal Education

Chapter 3: Transformative Approaches to Legal Education

In this chapter, we will explore the transformative approaches to legal education. Legal education plays a vital role in shaping the future of the legal profession and advancing justice and equality. However, traditional legal pedagogy has often been criticized for its limited focus on doctrinal learning and lack of practical skills development. In response to these critiques, transformative approaches to legal education have emerged, aiming to create a more inclusive, experiential, and interdisciplinary learning environment.

Traditional Legal Pedagogy: Critiques and Challenges

Traditional legal education has long relied on lecture-based teaching and learning methods, focusing heavily on the study of case law and the application of legal principles. While this approach has its merits, it has been criticized for its limited engagement with real-world legal problems and the lack of emphasis on practical skills development.

One of the main critiques of traditional legal pedagogy is its overreliance on the case method and Socratic method. These methods primarily involve passive learning, where students are expected to analyze and discuss legal cases without actively participating in problem-solving or critical thinking. This approach can be exclusionary, as it may only benefit students who excel at oral argumentation and may discourage others from participating fully in class discussions.

Furthermore, traditional legal education has been criticized for its inadequate focus on practical skills development. Many law schools have historically prioritized theoretical knowledge over the practical application of legal concepts. This imbalance can leave graduates ill-prepared to navigate the complexities of legal practice, where skills such as legal writing, negotiation, and client counseling are crucial.

Experiential Learning in Legal Education

To address the limitations of traditional legal pedagogy, there has been a growing emphasis on experiential learning approaches in legal education. Experiential learning involves active engagement with real-world legal problems, providing students with opportunities to develop practical skills through hands-on experiences.

One prominent example of experiential learning is clinical legal education. Clinical programs offer students the opportunity to work directly with clients or engage in simulated client representation under the supervision of experienced faculty. Through these experiences, students develop skills in legal research, interviewing, counseling, negotiation, and advocacy. Clinical legal education not only enhances students' practical skills but also fosters a sense of social justice and a commitment to public service.

Simulations and role-playing exercises are another effective way to promote experiential learning in legal education. These activities allow students to engage in simulated legal scenarios, such as negotiations, mediations, or trial simulations. By actively participating in these exercises, students gain practical skills, develop problem-solving abilities, and become more comfortable with the complexities of legal practice.

In addition to clinical education and simulations, community engagement plays a vital role in experiential learning. Collaborations with community organizations, pro bono work, and externship programs enable students to understand the real-world implications of legal practice and gain a deeper appreciation for the ethical responsibilities of lawyers.

Technology and Legal Education

The integration of technology into legal education has become increasingly important in recent years. Technology not only enhances legal research and writing but also provides new avenues for collaboration and innovative teaching methods.

Online legal education and distance learning have gained significant popularity, especially in light of the COVID-19 pandemic. These approaches allow students to access legal education remotely, providing flexibility and increased accessibility. However, challenges such as maintaining student engagement and ensuring equitable access to technology must be addressed to fully harness the potential of online legal education.

Artificial intelligence (AI) has also emerged as a transformative technology in legal education. AI-powered tools can assist in legal research, contract review, predictive analysis, and other tasks traditionally performed by lawyers. While AI can enhance efficiency and accuracy in legal practice, ethical considerations surrounding the use of AI and its impact on the role of lawyers must be carefully examined.

Interdisciplinary Approaches in Legal Education

Recognizing the multidimensional nature of legal issues, interdisciplinary approaches have gained prominence in legal education. Incorporating insights from other disciplines, such as the social sciences, medicine, psychology, and economics, allows for a more comprehensive understanding of the law and its impact on society.

The intersection of law and medicine highlights the importance of collaboration between legal and healthcare professionals. Understanding the legal implications of medical decisions, patient rights, and healthcare regulations is vital for both lawyers and medical practitioners. By integrating medical knowledge into legal education and fostering close collaboration between these fields, students can develop a holistic understanding of the legal and ethical challenges in healthcare.

Similarly, incorporating psychological perspectives in legal education provides insight into human behavior, decision-making, and the impact of the legal system on individuals. Understanding the psychological factors that influence legal outcomes can help lawyers develop more effective strategies for advocating justice and equality.

Economics also offers valuable insights for legal education, as it provides a framework for analyzing the efficiency and effectiveness of legal systems. Incorporating economic perspectives into legal education can equip students with the tools to critically analyze laws and policies, particularly in areas such as antitrust, intellectual property, and environmental regulation.

Social Justice and Legal Education

Promoting social justice through legal education has become an important goal for many law schools. Teaching social justice involves instilling a commitment to equality, fairness, and social change in students. By exploring the intersections of law, power, and oppression, students develop a critical understanding of the role of law in shaping societal structures and inequalities.

Student activism has played a significant role in advancing social justice within legal education. Student-led movements advocating for diversity, inclusion, and equity have brought attention to the need for institutional change. Law schools have responded by implementing diversity initiatives, creating safe spaces for marginalized students, and promoting a curriculum that reflects diverse perspectives.

Law clinics also provide opportunities for social justice advocacy within legal education. Through clinical programs, students engage in real legal cases or projects that address issues of social injustice. These experiences not only enhance students' practical skills but also foster a commitment to using the law as a tool for social change.

Conclusion

Transformative approaches to legal education aim to address the limitations of traditional pedagogy by emphasizing experiential learning, interdisciplinary perspectives, and social justice advocacy. By incorporating these approaches, legal education can better prepare students to navigate the complexities of the legal profession, advocate for justice and equality, and contribute to the transformation of the legal system. As legal education continues to evolve, it is crucial to embrace these transformative approaches and adapt to the changing needs of the legal profession and society as a whole.

Traditional Legal Pedagogy: Critiques and Challenges

Lecture-Based Teaching and Learning

Lecture-based teaching and learning is a traditional method of delivering educational content in which an instructor presents information to a large group of students through spoken discourse. This method has been widely used in legal education for many years, but it has also received criticism for its limitations and challenges. In this section, we will explore the characteristics of lecture-based teaching and learning, its critiques, and potential solutions to enhance its effectiveness and engagement.

Characteristics of Lecture-Based Teaching and Learning

Lecture-based teaching and learning is characterized by the following features:

1. **One-way Communication:** The instructor delivers information to students in a monologue style, with minimal interaction or participation from the students.

2. **Passive Learning:** Students are primarily passive recipients of knowledge, listening and taking notes without actively engaging in the learning process.

3. **Instructor-Centered:** The focus of the learning experience is centered around the instructor, who serves as the primary source of information and expertise.

4. **Limited Student Engagement:** Students have limited opportunities to ask questions, clarify doubts, or engage in discussions with the instructor or their peers.

While lecture-based teaching can be an efficient way to deliver large amounts of content in a short period, it has several limitations that need to be addressed to create a more engaging and effective learning environment.

Critiques of Lecture-Based Teaching and Learning

Despite its widespread use, lecture-based teaching and learning have faced several critiques:

1. **Lack of Active Learning:** Passive listening and note-taking can hinder deeper understanding and application of knowledge. Students may struggle to connect concepts or engage in critical thinking.

2. **Limited Student Interaction:** Lecture-based formats provide limited opportunities for students to ask questions, engage in discussions, or collaborate with their peers.

3. **Retention and Comprehension:** Students may struggle to retain large amounts of information delivered through lectures, especially when the material is complex or abstract.

4. **Varied Learning Styles:** Lecture-based teaching primarily caters to auditory learners, neglecting other learning styles such as visual or kinesthetic.

5. **Lack of Feedback:** In this format, immediate feedback is limited, making it challenging for students to gauge their understanding or address misconceptions.

To address these critiques and enhance the effectiveness of lecture-based teaching and learning, instructors can incorporate innovative strategies and techniques into their teaching practices.

Enhancing Lecture-Based Teaching and Learning

Here are a few strategies that instructors can implement to make lecture-based teaching and learning more engaging and effective:

1. **Active Learning Activities:** Integrate active learning activities throughout the lecture, such as group discussions, case studies, or problem-solving exercises. This allows students to apply concepts, collaborate with peers, and engage in critical thinking.

2. **Multimedia and Visual Aids:** Incorporate multimedia elements, such as videos, images, or diagrams, to enhance understanding and cater to diverse learning styles. Visual aids can help clarify complex concepts and increase student engagement.

3. **Student Interaction Opportunities:** Encourage student participation by incorporating question-and-answer sessions, think-pair-share activities, or peer-to-peer discussions. This promotes active engagement and enhances comprehension.

4. **Technology Integration:** Utilize technology tools, such as online discussion boards, virtual simulations, or interactive quizzes, to facilitate student

engagement and provide immediate feedback. These tools can also enhance student-teacher and student-student interaction.

5. **Flipped Classroom Approach:** Consider adopting a flipped classroom model, where students review lecture content outside the classroom and engage in active learning activities during class time. This allows for more interactive and collaborative learning experiences.

By integrating these strategies into lecture-based teaching and learning, instructors can create a more dynamic and immersive learning environment that fosters active engagement and deeper understanding.

Resources and Further Reading

For further exploration of lecture-based teaching and learning, the following resources are recommended:

1. Biggs, J., & Tang, C. (2011). *Teaching for Quality Learning at University*. McGraw-Hill Education.

2. Brookfield, S. D., & Preskill, S. (2005). *Discussion as a Way of Teaching: Tools and Techniques for Democratic Classrooms*. Jossey-Bass.

3. McKeachie, W. J., Svinicki, M., & Hofer, B. K. (2013). *McKeachie's Teaching Tips: Strategies, Research, and Theory for College and University Teachers*. Cengage Learning.

These resources provide in-depth insights, practical tips, and research-based strategies to enhance lecture-based teaching and learning in various educational contexts.

Summary

Lecture-based teaching and learning have been widely used in legal education, but it is important to acknowledge and address its limitations. By incorporating active learning strategies, utilizing multimedia and technology, and encouraging student interaction, instructors can enhance the effectiveness and engagement of lecture-based teaching and learning. Continual exploration of innovative pedagogical approaches will ensure that legal education remains relevant, engaging, and transformative for students.

Case Method and Socratic Method

In legal education, the case method and Socratic method have long been used as effective teaching tools to develop students' critical thinking, analytical skills, and understanding of the law. These methods encourage active learning and enable students to apply legal principles to real-world scenarios. By examining and dissecting legal cases, students gain a deeper understanding of legal reasoning, precedent, and the complexities of legal interpretation.

The Case Method

The case method is a pedagogical approach that involves the study of legal cases to understand legal principles, how they are applied, and their implications. It centers around the analysis and discussion of judicial decisions, focusing on the facts, issues, legal reasoning, and outcomes of each case. The primary source material in the case method is case law, which provides legal precedents and authoritative interpretations of the law.

To effectively use the case method, students are typically assigned a series of cases to read and analyze before attending class. During class sessions, students engage in lively discussions, led by the instructor, that delve into the details of the cases, the arguments presented by the parties, and the reasoning used by the court to arrive at its decision. This interactive approach promotes active engagement with the subject matter and encourages students to think critically about the legal issues involved.

The case method offers several advantages. Firstly, it develops students' ability to examine and interpret legal texts, enabling them to extract key legal principles and analogies. Secondly, it helps students appreciate the nuanced aspects of legal reasoning, such as distinguishing and applying precedents and statutory interpretation. Thirdly, it allows students to see how legal principles are applied to real-world situations, promoting a deeper understanding of the law's practical implications. Finally, the case method promotes effective oral communication skills as students actively participate in class discussions and debates.

However, there are also some challenges with the case method. It can be time-consuming as students are required to read and analyze a significant number of cases. Additionally, the method tends to prioritize the study of appellate court cases, which may not always reflect the realities of legal practice in lower courts. Furthermore, some students may find the case method intimidating or overwhelming, especially if they are not accustomed to public speaking or rigorous class discussions.

The Socratic Method

The Socratic method, named after the ancient Greek philosopher Socrates, is a teaching technique commonly used in legal education. It involves a dialogue between the instructor and students, where the instructor poses questions to challenge students' understanding of legal concepts and principles. Through this questioning process, students are encouraged to think critically, articulate their thoughts, defend their positions, and explore the limits and implications of legal principles.

The Socratic method operates on the principle of guided discovery. Instead of providing students with direct answers, the instructor guides them through a series of thought-provoking questions designed to stimulate reasoning and analysis. The goal is to foster active engagement, develop problem-solving skills, and encourage deeper learning through self-discovery.

The Socratic method is often used in conjunction with the case method. During class discussions, the instructor uses questions to guide students' analysis and interpretation of the assigned cases. By challenging students to think through the legal issues, the Socratic method helps them develop a deeper understanding of the rationale behind legal principles and the complexities involved in their application.

There are several benefits to using the Socratic method in legal education. Firstly, it encourages active learning and student participation, as students are actively involved in the learning process rather than passively receiving information. Secondly, it helps students develop critical thinking and analytical skills, as they are constantly challenged to examine assumptions and justify their positions. Thirdly, it promotes effective oral communication skills, as students learn to articulate their thoughts and engage in intellectual debates. Finally, the method fosters a deeper understanding of legal principles and enhances students' ability to apply them to new and complex situations.

However, the Socratic method also presents challenges. Some students may find it intimidating or anxiety-inducing, as they are put on the spot and expected to think quickly and critically. Moreover, the method relies heavily on the skills and teaching style of the instructor, and if not used effectively, it may hinder student engagement or create a hostile learning environment. It is crucial for instructors to create a supportive and inclusive atmosphere that encourages all students to participate and learn from their peers.

Case Method and Socratic Method in Practice

Both the case method and the Socratic method are widely used in law schools around the world, and their combination helps students develop vital skills for legal practice. These methods facilitate the exploration of legal principles, encourage critical thinking, and hone students' ability to analyze and apply legal concepts.

To fully benefit from these methods, students should actively engage with the assigned cases, thoroughly analyze the facts, legal issues, and reasoning, and prepare thoughtful responses to potential questions. Additionally, students should be open to constructive criticism, listen attentively to their peers' perspectives, and remain flexible and adaptable in their legal analysis.

To supplement the case method and the Socratic method, students can further enhance their learning by seeking out additional resources, such as legal commentaries, scholarly articles, and practical examples. By integrating theory with practice and keeping abreast of current legal developments, students can deepen their understanding of the law and its transformative potential.

Exercises

1. Read the case of *Roe v. Wade* and analyze the legal reasoning used by the court to establish the right to abortion. Identify the key arguments presented by each side and discuss the implications of the decision on reproductive rights.

2. Consider a recent landmark Supreme Court case and critically evaluate the dissenting opinion. Discuss the arguments presented by the dissenting justices and analyze their potential impact on the law.

3. Choose a controversial legal issue and engage in a mock Socratic dialogue with a fellow student. Take turns posing challenging questions that explore the underlying principles, ethical considerations, and potential consequences of different positions.

4. Identify a legal principle or concept that you find particularly challenging or unclear. Using the case method, research and analyze multiple cases that address this issue. Prepare a concise summary of the legal principles derived from these cases and present them in class.

5. Conduct a group discussion on the role of the case method and the Socratic method in legal education. Explore the advantages and disadvantages of each method and propose strategies to maximize their effectiveness.

Further Reading

1. Langdell, C. C. (1893). *A Selection of Cases on the Law of Contracts*. Boston, MA: Little, Brown, and Company.

2. Delgado, R., & Stefancic, J. (2001). *Critical Race Theory: An Introduction*. New York: New York University Press.

3. McCowan, T., & Porciúncula, R. (2018). *Clinical Legal Education Handbook*. Oxford: Oxford University Press.

4. Alexander, M. (2010). *The New Jim Crow: Mass Incarceration in the Age of Colorblindness*. New York: The New Press.

5. Kennedy, D. (2006). *The Canon of American Legal Thought*. Princeton, NJ: Princeton University Press.

Note: The exercises provided are for educational purposes only and do not constitute legal advice or establish an attorney-client relationship. It is recommended to consult legal professionals or relevant legal resources for specific legal issues or cases.

Lack of Practical Skills Development

In traditional legal education, there has been a significant emphasis on theoretical knowledge and classroom-based learning. While this approach has its merits, it often neglects the development of practical skills that are essential for legal practice. This lack of practical skills development can be a significant challenge for law students as they transition from the classroom to the courtroom or law firm. In this section, we will explore the reasons behind this lack of practical skills development and discuss potential solutions to bridge this gap.

Understanding the Challenges

There are several challenges that contribute to the lack of practical skills development in legal education. One of the main challenges is the limited exposure to real-life legal scenarios during the course of study. Traditional legal education primarily focuses on theoretical analysis of case law, statutes, and legal principles, without providing ample opportunities for students to apply these concepts in practical settings.

Another challenge is the lack of interaction between students and legal professionals. While lectures and textbooks provide valuable information, they do not fully simulate the dynamics of legal practice. Without opportunities to engage with practicing lawyers, judges, and clients, law students may struggle to develop the necessary skills to navigate legal issues effectively.

Moreover, the assessment methods used in legal education often prioritize written exams and essays, rather than practical exercises. While written assignments have their place in assessing legal knowledge, they do not directly assess the ability to apply that knowledge in real-world situations. As a result, students may graduate with a strong theoretical foundation but lack the practical skills required to excel in their legal careers.

The Importance of Practical Skills Development

Developing practical skills is crucial for law students because it equips them with the abilities needed to succeed in legal practice. These skills include legal research, legal writing, oral advocacy, negotiation, client counseling, and problem-solving. By honing these practical skills, students can bridge the gap between theory and practice and become competent legal professionals.

Practical skills development also enhances students' critical thinking and analytical abilities. Through hands-on experience, students learn to identify legal issues, analyze relevant facts, and apply legal principles to formulate effective legal arguments. These skills are vital for success in legal practice, where lawyers must navigate complex legal landscapes and provide sound advice to clients.

Additionally, practical skills development fosters professionalism and ethical conduct. By engaging with real clients and facing real-life ethical dilemmas, students can develop a strong sense of professional responsibility and learn to apply ethical principles in practice. This aspect of legal education is essential for maintaining the integrity of the profession and ensuring that lawyers prioritize the best interests of their clients and society at large.

Addressing the Gap: Solutions and Strategies

To address the lack of practical skills development in legal education, law schools and educators can implement various strategies. Here are some solutions to consider:

1. **Clinical legal education:** Introduce clinical programs that offer students the opportunity to work on real cases under the supervision of experienced practitioners. This hands-on experience allows students to apply their legal knowledge in a practical setting, develop essential skills, and gain exposure to the realities of legal practice.

2. **Moot court and mock trial competitions:** Encourage participation in moot court and mock trial competitions, where students can practice their oral advocacy and litigation skills. These simulated courtroom experiences help

students refine their ability to present arguments, respond to questions, and interact with judges.

3. **Legal writing workshops:** Offer specialized legal writing workshops to help students improve their legal research and writing skills. These workshops can focus on drafting legal documents, such as contracts, briefs, and memos, and provide feedback to students on their writing style and clarity.

4. **Simulation exercises:** Incorporate simulation exercises into the curriculum that simulate real-world legal scenarios. For example, students can participate in negotiation exercises or client counseling sessions to develop their skills in these areas.

5. **Externships and internships:** Establish partnerships with law firms, government agencies, and nonprofit organizations to provide students with opportunities to work as interns or externs. Through these placements, students can gain practical experience, network with professionals, and develop a deeper understanding of the legal profession.

While implementing these solutions, it is important to ensure that the curriculum and assessment methods align with the desired outcomes of practical skills development. Assessments should incorporate practical components, such as drafting a contract or participating in a simulated negotiation, to provide students with opportunities to demonstrate their skills.

Case Study: The Law Clinic Program

One example of a successful initiative to address the lack of practical skills development is the implementation of a law clinic program. Law clinics allow students to engage in hands-on legal work, representing real clients under the supervision of clinical faculty members. In these clinics, students have the opportunity to conduct client interviews, draft legal documents, perform legal research, and represent clients in court or in negotiations.

The law clinic program not only provides practical skills development but also fosters a sense of social justice and community engagement. Students work on cases that have a direct impact on the lives of marginalized individuals and communities, helping them access justice and advocating for policy changes to address systemic issues.

The success of law clinic programs lies in their ability to create a bridge between the classroom and the real world. By working on actual cases, students develop a deeper understanding of the complexities of legal practice, enhance their problem-solving abilities, and cultivate a sense of professional responsibility.

Conclusion

The lack of practical skills development in legal education is a significant challenge that needs to be addressed. By recognizing the importance of practical skills and implementing strategies to bridge the gap between theory and practice, law schools can better prepare their students for success in their legal careers. Through initiatives such as clinical programs, moot court competitions, and simulation exercises, students can develop the practical skills, critical thinking abilities, and professionalism necessary to excel in the legal profession.

Experiential Learning in Legal Education

Overview of Experiential Learning

Experiential learning is a widely recognized and highly effective method of teaching and learning that allows students to gain practical knowledge and skills through hands-on experiences. In legal education, experiential learning goes beyond traditional lecture-based teaching methods and emphasizes active participation, critical thinking, and reflection.

Experiential learning in legal education involves engaging students in real-world legal scenarios, enabling them to apply their knowledge and skills in a practical context. This immersive approach provides students with valuable opportunities to develop problem-solving skills, enhance their understanding of legal principles, and cultivate professional skills necessary for their future legal careers.

One of the key aspects of experiential learning is the integration of theory and practice. It allows students to bridge the gap between classroom knowledge and real-world applications. By actively engaging in experiential learning activities, students can put legal theories into action, grapple with complex legal issues, and develop a deeper understanding of the law.

There are different forms of experiential learning in legal education, including but not limited to clinical legal education, simulations and role-playing exercises, and community engagement projects. Each method offers unique benefits and learning opportunities for students.

Clinical legal education involves students working on real legal cases under the supervision of faculty members or licensed attorneys. Through this hands-on experience, students can develop practical skills such as interviewing clients, conducting legal research, drafting legal documents, and advocating for clients in court proceedings. This type of experiential learning allows students to gain insight into the challenges and responsibilities of legal practice while making a positive impact on the lives of real clients.

Simulations and role-playing exercises provide students with the opportunity to simulate legal scenarios and practice their advocacy, negotiation, and problem-solving skills in a controlled environment. These activities often involve mock trials, negotiations, or client counseling sessions, allowing students to experience the dynamics and challenges of legal practice firsthand. By engaging in these simulations, students can refine their communication skills, develop strategies for legal argumentation, and learn to think on their feet.

Community engagement projects aim to connect students with the broader community and address legal issues that affect marginalized or underserved populations. Through partnerships with local organizations, students can work on legal research, policy advocacy, or educational initiatives that promote access to justice and social change. This type of experiential learning enables students to develop a sense of social responsibility, gain a deeper understanding of systemic injustice, and contribute to the betterment of society.

Experiential learning in legal education benefits not only students but also the legal profession and society as a whole. It produces graduates who are well-equipped to handle the complexities of legal practice, who possess a deep understanding of the impact of the law on individuals and communities, and who are committed to promoting justice and equality.

While experiential learning offers tremendous opportunities, it also presents challenges. One of the main challenges is ensuring that the experiences provided are structured, intentional, and aligned with the learning objectives of the curriculum. It is essential to provide meaningful guidance and feedback to students throughout their experiential learning journey to maximize the learning outcomes.

Furthermore, experiential learning requires continuous improvement and innovation to address the evolving needs of the legal profession and society. Legal educators must stay attuned to new developments in legal practice, incorporate emerging technologies, and adapt teaching methodologies accordingly. They must also strive to create diverse and inclusive experiential learning environments that reflect the realities of a multicultural and interconnected world.

In conclusion, experiential learning in legal education offers a transformative approach to teaching and learning. By providing hands-on experiences, integrating theory and practice, and fostering critical thinking skills, it prepares students for the challenges and responsibilities of legal practice while cultivating their commitment to justice and equality. Through experiential learning, the legal profession can adapt and thrive in an ever-changing world, making a positive impact on individuals, communities, and society at large.

Clinical Legal Education

Clinical legal education is a transformative approach to legal education that emphasizes hands-on learning and practical skills development. It provides law students with opportunities to apply legal theory to real-world situations, engage with clients, and work on actual legal cases under the supervision of experienced faculty members or practitioners. This section will discuss the key principles and benefits of clinical legal education, explore different models and methods, and highlight examples of successful clinical programs.

Principles of Clinical Legal Education

Clinical legal education is guided by several key principles that shape its approach and objectives. These principles include:

1. **Experiential Learning:** Clinical legal education recognizes the value of learning by doing. It provides students with the opportunity to apply legal knowledge in a practical setting, allowing them to develop essential skills such as legal research, client interviewing, case management, negotiation, and advocacy.

2. **Client-Centered Approach:** Clinical programs prioritize the needs and interests of clients. Students work directly with clients, taking on real cases and legal issues. This approach helps students develop a deep understanding of the client's perspective and fosters empathy and professionalism.

3. **Reflective Practice:** Clinical legal education encourages students to reflect on their experiences, analyze their strategies and techniques, and evaluate the outcomes of their actions. Reflective practice promotes critical thinking, self-awareness, and continuous learning and improvement.

4. **Professionalism and Ethics:** Clinical programs emphasize the importance of professional ethics and responsibility. Students learn to navigate the ethical challenges that arise in legal practice, including confidentiality, conflicts of interest, and maintaining the attorney-client relationship.

Models of Clinical Legal Education

There are various models of clinical legal education, each with its unique approach and focus. Some common models include:

1. **In-house Clinics:** In-house clinical programs are housed within law schools or legal institutions. Students work on cases that are referred to the clinic from the local community, handling a wide range of legal issues such as family law, criminal law, immigration, and housing. In-house clinics often provide a multidisciplinary approach, engaging students from different disciplines to address clients' needs comprehensively.

2. **Externship Programs:** Externship programs place students in external legal settings, such as government agencies, nonprofit organizations, or law firms. Students work alongside practicing attorneys and judges, gaining practical experience in their chosen field of interest. Externships offer opportunities for specialized practice areas and exposure to different legal systems.

3. **Simulation-Based Clinics:** Simulation-based clinics simulate real legal scenarios and allow students to engage in role-playing exercises. These clinics focus on developing specific skills, such as negotiation, mediation, or trial advocacy. Simulation-based clinics provide a safe and controlled environment for students to practice their skills before entering the real world of legal practice.

4. **Community-Based Clinics:** Community-based clinics focus on providing legal services to underserved populations or specific communities. Students work closely with community organizations, serving clients who may not have access to legal representation otherwise. This model emphasizes the importance of social justice and community engagement in legal practice.

Benefits of Clinical Legal Education

Clinical legal education offers several benefits to both students and the community. These include:

1. **Skills Development:** Clinical programs enhance students' practical skills, enabling them to make a smooth transition from law school to legal practice. Students develop skills such as legal analysis, problem-solving, communication, and teamwork, which are essential for a successful legal career.

2. **Professional Networking:** Clinical programs provide opportunities for students to build professional networks and establish connections within the legal community. Through interactions with clients, supervising attorneys, and other professionals, students can form relationships that may lead to future job opportunities and mentorship.

3. **Social Justice and Public Service:** Clinical legal education promotes a commitment to social justice and public service. By working with underserved populations and addressing pressing legal issues, students contribute to the development of a more just and equitable society.

4. Access to Justice: Clinical programs play a crucial role in increasing access to justice for marginalized communities. By providing free or low-cost legal services, students help bridge the justice gap and ensure that individuals who cannot afford legal representation still have access to the legal system.

Example: The Community Law Clinic

The Community Law Clinic (CLC) at XYZ Law School is an example of a successful clinical program that embodies the principles and benefits of clinical legal education. The CLC focuses on providing legal services to low-income individuals in the local community.

In the CLC, law students work under the supervision of experienced faculty members and practicing attorneys. They handle a variety of cases, including landlord-tenant disputes, immigration matters, and consumer protection issues. Students engage in client intake, legal research, drafting legal documents, and representing clients in court.

The CLC also emphasizes community outreach and education. Students organize workshops and presentations to inform community members about their legal rights and responsibilities. By actively engaging with the community, students contribute to social empowerment and access to justice.

Through their work in the CLC, students develop a range of skills, including client interviewing, negotiation, legal research, and courtroom advocacy. They gain practical experience and build professional relationships that prepare them for a successful legal career.

Conclusion

Clinical legal education is a transformative approach to legal education that prioritizes experiential learning, client-centered practice, and reflective learning. By engaging in real-world legal cases, students develop practical skills, professionalism, and a commitment to social justice. Clinical programs offer benefits to students, communities, and the legal profession as a whole. The example of the Community Law Clinic demonstrates the successful implementation of clinical legal education principles in action.

Simulations and Role-Playing in Legal Education

Simulations and role-playing activities are valuable tools in legal education that help students develop practical skills and gain a deeper understanding of the complexities of legal practice. These experiential learning techniques allow students to actively engage in real-world scenarios and apply legal principles to solve problems and make strategic decisions. In this section, we will explore the benefits of simulations and role-playing in legal education, discuss different approaches and methods for implementing them, and provide examples and resources for further study.

Benefits of Simulations and Role-Playing

Simulations and role-playing activities offer numerous benefits in legal education. Firstly, they provide a safe and controlled environment for students to practice legal skills without the consequences of real-life situations. This allows students to experiment, make mistakes, and learn from their experiences, thereby enhancing their understanding of legal concepts and their ability to apply them effectively.

Secondly, simulations and role-playing enhance students' critical thinking and problem-solving skills. They require students to analyze complex legal issues, consider multiple perspectives, and make informed decisions based on the available information. By actively participating in simulations, students learn to navigate legal complexities, identify relevant legal principles, and apply them in a practical context.

Moreover, simulations and role-playing activities promote teamwork and collaboration. Students often work in groups or pairs, which fosters effective communication, negotiation, and teamwork skills. Collaboration allows students to exchange ideas, challenge assumptions, and develop effective strategies to address legal problems. These activities simulate the interdisciplinary nature of legal practice and prepare students for real-world legal challenges.

Furthermore, simulations and role-playing encourage students to develop essential lawyering skills, such as client interviewing, negotiation, and courtroom advocacy. Through these activities, students gain valuable experience in client-centered representation, effective communication with clients and opposing counsel, and persuasive argumentation. These skills are crucial for future legal practitioners and are best honed through hands-on practice.

Finally, simulations and role-playing activities increase student engagement and motivation in the learning process. By incorporating interactive and experiential elements, students become active participants rather than passive recipients of information. This active learning approach fosters a deeper understanding of legal concepts, promotes critical thinking, and enhances overall student satisfaction with the learning experience.

Approaches to Simulations and Role-Playing

There are various approaches and methods for implementing simulations and role-playing in legal education. Here are a few common approaches:

Case-based simulations: In this approach, students are presented with a realistic legal case scenario and are assigned roles as attorneys, judges, or clients. They engage in simulated court proceedings, including pre-trial negotiations, oral arguments, and even mock trials. This approach allows students to apply legal principles and courtroom tactics in a realistic setting.

Transactional simulations: This approach focuses on simulating transactional legal practice, such as contract negotiation, drafting, or mediation. Students are assigned roles as attorneys or clients and engage in simulated negotiations, contractual drafting exercises, or alternative dispute resolution processes. Transactional simulations develop skills related to negotiation, drafting, and problem-solving in non-adversarial legal contexts.

Role-playing exercises: Role-playing exercises involve students assuming the roles of various stakeholders in legal scenarios, such as clients, witnesses, or even policymakers. Students are tasked with interacting and negotiating with each other to simulate real-world legal situations. This approach helps develop effective communication, negotiation, and problem-solving skills.

Implementation and Resources

Implementing simulations and role-playing activities requires careful planning and consideration. Here are some key considerations:

Learning objectives: Clearly define the learning objectives of the simulation or role-playing activity. Identify the specific skills, knowledge, or values you want students to develop through the exercise. This will help guide the design and assessment of the activity.

Scenarios and materials: Develop realistic and relevant scenarios that challenge students' legal reasoning and problem-solving abilities. Provide supporting materials, such as case facts, statutes, or legal documents, to enhance the authenticity of the simulation. Ensure that the scenarios align with the learning objectives and the specific legal topics being addressed.

Role assignments and preparation: Assign roles to students based on their interests and learning goals. Provide clear instructions and guidelines for each role. Encourage students to research and prepare for their roles, including understanding the legal issues involved and developing their arguments or negotiation strategies.

Facilitation and debriefing: As the facilitator, guide the simulation or role-playing activity to ensure a productive and inclusive learning environment. Observe student interactions and provide feedback or guidance when necessary. After the activity, facilitate a debriefing session to reflect on the experience, discuss lessons learned, and make connections to relevant legal theories or principles.

There are several resources available to assist in the design and implementation of simulations and role-playing activities in legal education. Here are a few recommended readings:

- *Teaching Law by Design: Engaging Students from the Syllabus to the Final Exam* by Michael Hunter Schwartz, Sophie Sparrow, and Gerald F. Hess.

- *Building on Best Practices: Transforming Legal Education in a Changing World* by Deborah Maranville, Lisa Radtke Bliss, Carolyn Wilkes Kaas, and Antoinette Sedillo Lopez.

- *The Skillful Teacher: On Technique, Trust, and Responsiveness in the Classroom* by Stephen D. Brookfield.

Additionally, various legal education websites and organizations provide sample simulations and role-playing exercises that can be adapted for different topics and contexts. Some examples include the *Harvard Negotiation Project* and the *Thurgood Marshall School of Law Simulation Archive*.

Examples and Exercise

To illustrate the practical application of simulations and role-playing in legal education, let's consider an example exercise focused on negotiation skills:

Exercise: Negotiating a Settlement

Scenario: Two parties are involved in a business dispute over a breach of contract. The goal is to negotiate a settlement that resolves the dispute and satisfies the interests of both parties.

Roles:

- Party A: Represented by Student 1

- Party B: Represented by Student 2

- Mediator: Facilitated by Student 3

Instructions:

1. Student 1 and Student 2 should research their respective roles, including understanding the facts of the case, applicable contract law principles, and their client's interests.

2. Student 3 will act as the mediator, guiding the negotiation process and ensuring a productive conversation.

3. During the negotiation, students should actively engage in communication, listen to each other's perspective, and identify potential common ground for settlement.

4. The negotiation should aim to reach a mutually acceptable settlement agreement that resolves the dispute and protects the interests of both parties.

5. After the negotiation, all students should participate in a debriefing session to reflect on the negotiation process, analyze their strategies and outcomes, and discuss lessons learned.

This exercise allows students to develop negotiation skills, understand the complexities of reaching a settlement, and appreciate the importance of effective communication and problem-solving in legal practice. It also provides an opportunity for students to understand the role of mediation in resolving disputes and explore alternative dispute resolution methods.

Conclusion

Simulations and role-playing activities are powerful tools in legal education for developing practical skills and deepening students' understanding of legal practice. Through these experiential learning techniques, students gain hands-on experience, enhance critical thinking skills, and develop essential lawyering skills. By incorporating simulations and role-playing into legal education, we can better prepare students for the complexities and challenges of legal practice.

In this section, we explored the benefits of simulations and role-playing in legal education, discussed different approaches for implementing them, and provided examples and resources for further study. Simulations and role-playing engage students, foster collaboration and critical thinking, and prepare them for real-world legal scenarios. By embracing these experiential learning techniques, legal education can transform the way students learn and prepare for their future careers.

Community Engagement in Legal Education

Community engagement is a crucial aspect of legal education that seeks to bridge the gap between academic learning and practical application. It involves actively involving students in real-world legal issues by collaborating with communities, organizations, and individuals who are directly affected by the law. This section explores the importance of community engagement in legal education, its benefits, challenges, and strategies for effective implementation.

Importance of Community Engagement in Legal Education

Community engagement provides law students with valuable opportunities to develop practical skills, empathy, and a deeper understanding of the impact of the law on individuals and communities. It promotes a holistic approach to legal education by integrating theory and practice, allowing students to directly apply legal principles to real-world situations. By engaging with communities, students gain insights into the complex social, economic, and cultural contexts in which legal issues arise, enhancing their ability to analyze legal problems and propose innovative solutions.

Moreover, community engagement instills a sense of social responsibility in law students, emphasizing the role of lawyers as agents of positive change. By working closely with communities, students become aware of social inequalities, injustices, and systemic issues that shape legal problems. This awareness can motivate students to pursue careers in public interest law, human rights advocacy, and community development, thus contributing to the goal of achieving justice and equality.

Benefits of Community Engagement in Legal Education

1. Practical Skill Development: Community engagement allows law students to develop practical legal skills that are essential for their future careers. Through experiential learning activities such as legal clinics, volunteer work, and pro bono projects, students gain hands-on experience in legal research, client interviewing, negotiation, mediation, and advocacy. These skills are invaluable for successful legal practice and professional growth.

2. Enhanced Learning Experience: Community engagement enriches the learning experience by providing students with opportunities to explore legal issues from diverse perspectives. By interacting with individuals from different backgrounds and cultures, students develop a broader understanding of the social, economic, and political dynamics that influence legal problems. This

interdisciplinary approach enhances critical thinking, problem-solving, and the ability to navigate complex legal issues.

3. Empathy and Cultural Competence: Engaging with communities fosters empathy and cultural competence among law students. By working closely with diverse populations, students develop a deeper understanding of the unique challenges and needs of marginalized groups. This understanding promotes cultural sensitivity, effective communication, and the ability to address legal issues in a culturally appropriate and inclusive manner.

4. Networking and Professional Development Opportunities: Community engagement exposes students to a wide range of legal professionals, organizations, and community leaders. This provides networking opportunities that can lead to internships, mentorships, and future employment. Students can also develop their professional skills by collaborating with experienced lawyers, judges, and community advocates, thereby expanding their knowledge and building valuable connections in the legal field.

Challenges in Implementing Community Engagement in Legal Education

While community engagement offers numerous benefits, its effective implementation in legal education can present various challenges. These challenges include:

1. Limited Resources: Lack of funding, time, and faculty support can hinder the integration of community engagement into the curriculum. Law schools may face budgetary constraints that limit the availability of resources for organizing community-based activities, such as legal clinics or field placements.

2. Ethical Considerations: Community engagement requires law students to navigate ethical challenges, including maintaining client confidentiality, managing conflicts of interest, and upholding professional responsibilities. It is essential to ensure that students receive appropriate guidance and supervision to address these ethical considerations throughout their community engagement experiences.

3. Community Partnerships: Developing and sustaining partnerships with community organizations and individuals can be challenging. Law schools need to establish mutually beneficial relationships that align with the needs and goals of both the academic institution and the community. Clear communication, ongoing collaboration, and regular evaluation are essential for successful community partnerships.

4. Evaluation and Assessment: Measuring the impact and effectiveness of community engagement initiatives can be complex. Law schools need to develop evaluation criteria and assessment methods to determine the learning outcomes of

community engagement activities. This includes considering the satisfaction of community partners, the knowledge and skills gained by students, and the impact on the community.

Strategies for Effective Community Engagement in Legal Education

To overcome the challenges and maximize the benefits of community engagement in legal education, the following strategies can be implemented:

1. Faculty Support and Professional Development: Law schools should provide faculty members with training and resources on integrating community engagement into their teaching. Faculty members need support to design and implement community-based projects effectively, mentor students, and evaluate the learning outcomes. Incorporating community engagement into faculty performance evaluations can also incentivize engagement initiatives.

2. Institutional Collaboration: Collaboration among different departments within the university can enhance community engagement initiatives. Law schools can partner with other academic disciplines, such as social work, public health, or business, to address legal issues from a multidisciplinary perspective. Collaborative efforts can also enhance the resources available to students and strengthen the impact of community engagement activities.

3. Community Partnership Development: Law schools need to actively engage with community organizations, nonprofits, and government agencies to develop meaningful partnerships. Regular communication, transparency, and mutual respect are crucial for establishing successful partnerships. Engaging community partners in the planning, implementation, and evaluation of community engagement initiatives can provide valuable insights and enhance the relevance and impact of the activities.

4. Reflection and Evaluation: Incorporating structured reflection activities into the community engagement experience can deepen students' learning and self-awareness. Reflection can involve written or verbal reflection journals, group discussions, or debriefing sessions. Additionally, ongoing evaluation of community engagement initiatives is essential to assess their impact, identify areas for improvement, and ensure continuous learning and growth.

Conclusion

Community engagement is a transformative approach to legal education that prepares students to be socially conscious, competent, and compassionate legal professionals. By connecting theory and practice, community engagement enhances students' learning experiences, develops practical skills, fosters empathy, and cultivates a sense of social responsibility. While challenges exist, implementing effective strategies and building strong community partnerships can overcome these hurdles. By embracing community engagement, law schools can create a positive impact on students, communities, and the pursuit of justice and equality.

Technology and Legal Education

Use of Technology in Legal Research and Writing

The use of technology has revolutionized the field of legal research and writing, enabling legal professionals to access vast amounts of information quickly and efficiently. In this section, we will explore the various ways in which technology is being utilized in legal research and writing, and discuss the benefits and challenges associated with these advances.

Benefits of Technology in Legal Research

Technology has significantly enhanced legal research by providing researchers with access to an extensive range of legal materials, including statutes, case law, regulations, and legal commentary. Here are some key benefits of using technology in legal research:

1. **Efficiency:** Technology allows legal researchers to find relevant legal information in a fraction of the time it would take using traditional print resources. Online databases and search engines enable researchers to quickly retrieve specific texts or search for relevant cases or statutes using keywords.

2. **Accessibility:** With the advent of digital legal materials, legal research is no longer restricted to physical law libraries. Researchers can access legal databases and online resources from their homes, offices, or anywhere with an internet connection. This accessibility promotes equal access to legal information and levels the playing field for legal practitioners of all backgrounds.

3. **Accuracy:** Online legal databases provide up-to-date information and ensure that legal researchers have access to the most recent case law and statutory changes. Real-time updates and notifications keep researchers informed of any legal developments in their areas of interest.

4. **Comprehensiveness:** Online legal databases often offer comprehensive collections of legal materials, including federal and state statutes, case law from various jurisdictions, legal journals, and legal commentary. Researchers can access a wide variety of sources and perspectives, helping them to develop a well-rounded understanding of legal issues.

5. **Advanced Search Features:** Online legal research platforms offer powerful search capabilities, allowing researchers to tailor their searches and refine their results. Researchers can use Boolean operators, filters, and other advanced search features to find the most relevant legal information for their research purposes.

Challenges and Considerations

While technology offers numerous benefits in legal research and writing, there are also some challenges and considerations to keep in mind:

1. **Reliability and Authenticity:** With the abundance of information available online, it is crucial for legal researchers to critically evaluate the reliability and authenticity of the sources they are using. Not all online resources are created equal, and it is essential to verify the credibility of the information before relying on it for legal research.

2. **Cost:** While many legal databases and resources are available for free or at a minimal cost, some specialized databases may require a subscription or access fee. These costs can be a barrier for legal professionals and individuals with limited resources.

3. **Technological Skills:** Proficiency in using legal research platforms and navigating online databases is becoming increasingly important for legal professionals. Acquiring the necessary technological skills may require training and time investment.

4. **Data Privacy and Security:** As legal research moves online, concerns about data privacy and security become more significant. Researchers should be mindful of the platforms they use, ensure that client and sensitive information is protected, and adhere to ethical guidelines regarding data privacy and security.

Technological Tools for Legal Research and Writing

The advancements in technology have given rise to various tools and software applications specifically designed for legal research and writing. Here are a few notable examples:

1. **Legal Research Databases:** Online legal research databases such as Westlaw, LexisNexis, and Bloomberg Law provide access to an extensive collection of legal materials, including cases, statutes, regulations, and legal commentary. These databases offer powerful search functionalities and advanced features to streamline legal research.

2. **Text Analysis Tools:** Text analysis tools, such as artificial intelligence (AI) software, can analyze and extract relevant information from legal documents, making it easier for legal professionals to identify key issues, analyze case law, and draft legal documents.

3. **Legal Writing Software:** Legal writing software assists legal professionals in creating well-structured and well-referenced legal documents. These programs often include features such as automated citation formatting, document templates, and grammar and spell-checking capabilities.

4. **Data Analytics Tools:** Data analytics tools enable legal professionals to analyze large volumes of legal data, identify patterns and trends, and make data-driven decisions. These tools can be particularly useful in areas such as legal research, case strategy, and litigation support.

Case Study: AI-Powered Legal Research

One example of technology transforming legal research is the use of artificial intelligence (AI) in legal research platforms. AI-powered platforms leverage machine learning algorithms to improve search results and provide more personalized and accurate legal information. These platforms can analyze vast amounts of legal data, predict relevant cases, and even suggest arguments based on past legal precedents.

For instance, the AI-powered legal research platform, ROSS Intelligence, uses natural language processing to understand legal questions and provide relevant case law, statutes, and secondary sources. It can save legal researchers time by quickly surfacing relevant information and helping them identify key arguments and authorities.

AI-powered legal research platforms have the potential to revolutionize legal research, making it faster, more efficient, and more accessible. However, it is important for legal professionals to exercise critical thinking and verify the information provided by these platforms to ensure accuracy and reliability.

Conclusion

The use of technology in legal research and writing has had a profound impact on the legal profession, enabling faster, more efficient, and more accessible access to legal information. Although there are challenges and considerations associated with the use of technology, the benefits, including increased efficiency, accessibility, accuracy, and advanced search capabilities, far outweigh the challenges. Legal professionals should embrace these technological advancements, acquire the necessary skills, and critically evaluate the sources and tools they use to leverage the full potential of technology in their legal research and writing practices.

Online Legal Education and Distance Learning

Online legal education and distance learning have revolutionized the way legal studies are conducted, making education accessible to a wider range of individuals and providing flexibility in time and location. This section explores the principles, challenges, and opportunities of online legal education, and highlights the transformative potential of distance learning in the field of law.

Principles of Online Legal Education

Online legal education is rooted in the principles of accessibility, flexibility, and interactivity. It aims to provide equal opportunities for individuals who may not have access to traditional brick-and-mortar institutions due to geographical, financial, or personal constraints. By utilizing digital platforms, online legal education allows students to engage with course materials, interact with instructors and peers, and gain practical skills at their own pace and convenience.

Challenges and Opportunities

Online legal education is not without its challenges. One of the main concerns is maintaining the quality and rigor of legal education in an online setting. The absence of in-person interactions can make it challenging to foster meaningful discussions and engage in simulated legal scenarios. However, with the advancement of technology, virtual classrooms, online discussion boards, and video conferences facilitate real-time interactions and contribute to an engaging learning experience.

Another challenge is the need for proper accreditation and recognition of online legal degrees or certificates. While many online legal programs are offered by reputable institutions, there is a need for standardized evaluation and recognition to ensure the credibility and comparability of online legal education.

However, online legal education also presents numerous opportunities. It allows individuals from diverse backgrounds and geographical locations to access legal knowledge and pursue legal studies. Moreover, online platforms offer a variety of resources, such as recorded lectures, interactive case studies, and online libraries, which enhance the learning experience.

Integration of Technology in Legal Education

Technology plays a crucial role in online legal education. Learning management systems (LMS) provide a centralized platform for instructors to deliver course materials, communicate with students, and track their progress. These platforms often include discussion forums, assignment submission portals, and online assessments.

Furthermore, online legal education can leverage various technological tools, such as virtual reality simulations, online legal research databases, and AI-powered legal assistants, to enhance the learning experience. These tools enable students to practice legal research, engage in moot court exercises, and analyze complex legal scenarios.

Ethical Considerations

As with any form of education, online legal education must also address ethical considerations. Academic integrity and plagiarism are concerns in an online setting, and institutions must implement mechanisms to prevent and detect academic misconduct. Additionally, data privacy and security of online platforms need to be safeguarded to protect students' personal and academic information.

Case Studies and Practical Applications

To illustrate the transformative potential of online legal education and distance learning, let's explore two case studies:

Case Study 1: Virtual Law Clinics Virtual law clinics provide students with the opportunity to gain practical experience and engage in legal advocacy remotely.

Through video conferencing tools and online case management systems, students can collaborate with clients, conduct legal research, draft legal documents, and provide legal advice. This practical application of online legal education not only enhances students' legal skills but also expands access to legal services for underserved communities.

Case Study 2: Massive Open Online Courses (MOOCs) MOOCs offer a scalable and accessible way to disseminate legal knowledge to a global audience. Renowned legal scholars and practitioners can deliver high-quality course content through online platforms, reaching thousands of learners around the world. MOOCs also facilitate peer-to-peer learning through discussion forums and interactive assignments, fostering a global legal community.

Resources and Further Study

For students interested in online legal education and distance learning, the following resources are recommended:

- Online Legal Education Platforms: Coursera, edX, Khan Academy, Udemy

- Virtual Law Clinics: American Bar Association (ABA) Legal Services National Technology Assistance Project

- Academic Research: Journal of Legal Education, International Journal of Distance Education Technologies

- Associations and Organizations: Online Learning Consortium, eLearning Industry Association

Conclusion

Online legal education and distance learning have transformed the landscape of legal studies, offering accessibility and flexibility to a wider range of individuals. By embracing technology and implementing innovative teaching methods, online legal education provides a platform for interactive and engaging learning experiences. However, addressing challenges related to quality assurance, accreditation, and ethical considerations remains crucial. Ultimately, the transformative impact of online legal education lies in its potential to democratize legal knowledge and empower individuals to engage meaningfully in the field of law.

Artificial Intelligence and Law

Artificial Intelligence (AI) has rapidly emerged as a transformative technology that has the potential to revolutionize many fields, including the legal profession. In this section, we will explore the intersection of AI and law, examining its applications, challenges, and implications for the future of legal practice.

Overview of Artificial Intelligence

Artificial Intelligence refers to the development of computer systems that can perform tasks that typically require human intelligence. These systems use algorithms and machine learning techniques to analyze data, recognize patterns, and make autonomous decisions.

In the context of law, AI can be utilized to streamline legal processes, enhance legal research, improve prediction models, and increase efficiency in document review. AI-powered tools have the potential to transform various aspects of legal practice, including contract analysis and review, legal research, due diligence, and litigation support.

Applications of AI in Law

AI has the potential to revolutionize legal practice in several ways:

- **Legal Research:** AI-powered algorithms can analyze and categorize vast amounts of legal information, including statutes, case law, and regulations. This can reduce the time required for legal research and improve the accuracy of legal analysis.

- **Document Review:** AI can automate the process of document review, allowing for faster and more efficient analysis of large volumes of documents. AI tools can identify key information, detect patterns, and even highlight potential legal issues.

- **Contract Analysis:** AI can be used to review and analyze contracts, flagging potential risks or ambiguities. Natural Language Processing (NLP) techniques enable AI systems to understand and interpret complex legal language, making contract review faster and more accurate.

- **Predictive Analytics:** AI algorithms can analyze past legal cases and outcomes to predict the likelihood of success in future cases. This can assist lawyers in formulating legal strategies and advising clients.

- **Legal Chatbots:** AI-powered chatbots can provide basic legal information and guidance to individuals seeking legal advice. These chatbots use NLP to understand user queries and provide relevant responses, improving access to justice for those who cannot afford legal representation.

Challenges and Ethical Considerations

While AI holds great promise for the legal profession, there are several challenges and ethical considerations that need to be addressed:

- **Algorithmic Bias:** AI systems are only as good as the data they are trained on. Biases present in training data can be perpetuated by AI algorithms, leading to unfair outcomes. Care must be taken to ensure the fairness and impartiality of AI systems used in legal practice.

- **Data Privacy and Security:** AI relies on vast amounts of data to function effectively. Lawyers and legal professionals must be mindful of privacy and security laws when handling sensitive client information.

- **Accountability:** AI systems can make errors or provide incorrect advice, potentially exposing lawyers to malpractice claims. The issue of accountability in AI-assisted decision-making needs to be addressed to avoid potential legal and ethical pitfalls.

- **Job Displacement:** The automation of certain legal tasks through AI can lead to concerns about job displacement in the legal profession. Lawyers will need to adapt and develop new skills to remain relevant in an AI-driven legal landscape.

Future Directions and Recommendations

As AI continues to evolve, it is important for legal professionals and policymakers to embrace its potential while also addressing its challenges. Here are some recommendations for the future:

- **Education and Training:** Law schools should incorporate AI and related technologies into their curriculum to prepare future lawyers for the evolving legal landscape. Continuing education programs should also be available to practicing lawyers to enhance their understanding of AI.

- **Regulation and Standards:** Legal frameworks and guidelines need to be developed to ensure the responsible use of AI in the legal profession. Standards should be established to address issues such as algorithmic bias, data privacy, and accountability.

- **Collaboration with AI Experts:** Legal professionals should collaborate with experts in AI and related fields to leverage their expertise in developing AI tools for the legal profession. This interdisciplinary collaboration can lead to innovative solutions and ensure the ethical use of AI in law.

- **Ethical Guidelines:** Professional bodies should develop ethical guidelines for lawyers' use of AI in legal practice. These guidelines should address issues such as client confidentiality, informed consent, and the responsible use of AI technologies.

In conclusion, the application of AI in law has the potential to revolutionize legal practice by streamlining processes, improving efficiency, and enhancing access to justice. However, it is crucial to address the challenges and ethical considerations associated with AI to ensure its responsible and equitable use in the legal profession. By embracing AI and developing appropriate frameworks, the legal community can capitalize on the transformative potential of this technology while upholding the principles of justice and equality.

Challenges and Ethical Considerations in Technology Enhanced Legal Education

In recent years, technology has played a significant role in transforming various aspects of legal education. The integration of technology has brought numerous benefits, including enhanced access to resources, increased efficiency in research and writing, and the development of innovative learning tools. However, along with these advancements, there are also several challenges and ethical considerations that need to be addressed. This section focuses on discussing these challenges and considerations in technology-enhanced legal education.

Digital Divide and Accessibility

One of the primary challenges in technology-enhanced legal education is the digital divide and the issue of accessibility. While technology has the potential to bridge gaps and equalize opportunities, it can also exacerbate existing inequalities. Not all students have equal access to computers, high-speed internet, or the necessary digital literacy skills. This digital divide may create disparities in learning experiences and hinder access to educational resources. It is essential for institutions to take proactive measures to ensure that all students have equal access to technology and training to prevent the marginalization of certain groups.

Quality and Reliability of Online Resources

The reliance on online resources in technology-enhanced legal education raises concerns about the quality and reliability of the materials used for learning. With the vast amount of information available online, it becomes crucial for students and educators to critically evaluate the sources they use. Online resources may vary in accuracy, credibility, and currency, making it necessary for students to learn how to discern reliable information from misleading or inaccurate sources. Educators should guide students in developing critical thinking skills to evaluate the quality of online resources.

Ethical Use of Artificial Intelligence (AI) in Legal Education

The use of artificial intelligence (AI) in legal education offers various advantages, such as automated legal research and predictive analytics. However, ethical considerations arise when using AI tools. Students must understand the limitations and biases that may be present in AI algorithms. AI tools rely on historical data, which may perpetuate biases and inequalities present in the legal system. Educators have a responsibility to ensure that students are aware of these limitations and encourage critical analysis of AI-generated outputs. It is essential to emphasize the importance of human judgment and ethical decision-making in the legal profession.

Preservation of Personal Data and Privacy

In technology-enhanced legal education, the collection and use of personal data pose significant ethical concerns. Institutions must establish robust protocols for data protection to ensure that students' personal information is kept secure and not misused. Privacy issues may arise when using online platforms for collaborative learning or assessments. Educators need to be mindful of privacy laws and ethical guidelines when implementing technology-enhanced educational practices. Transparency and informed consent regarding the collection and use of personal data are vital to maintaining student trust and safeguarding their privacy rights.

Maintaining Academic Integrity

The use of technology in legal education introduces challenges in preserving academic integrity. Online platforms and resources may facilitate plagiarism and cheating if proper measures are not in place. Educators should educate students about academic integrity and develop strategies to detect and deter plagiarism. Additionally, institutions may need to implement secure online examination systems to ensure that assessments are conducted fairly and with integrity.

Building and Sustaining Technological Infrastructure

Implementing technology-enhanced legal education requires a robust and sustainable technological infrastructure. Educational institutions must invest in the necessary hardware, software, and technical support to ensure a smooth learning experience. Adequate training and support for both students and educators are essential to maximize the benefits of technology integration. Institutions need to consider long-term plans to maintain and update their technological infrastructure to keep up with advancements in technology.

Professionalism and Ethical Conduct in Online Spaces

As legal education incorporates online platforms and virtual classrooms, the issue of professionalism and ethical conduct becomes more complex. Educators must establish clear guidelines for online interactions and discussions to maintain a respectful and inclusive learning environment. Students should be aware of the potential consequences of their online behavior and adhere to professional standards. Addressing ethical concerns related to online communication and behavior is crucial for fostering a positive learning environment and preparing students for professional legal practice.

Conclusion

Technology-enhanced legal education offers numerous opportunities for innovation and improvement. However, it is essential to recognize and address the challenges and ethical considerations that may arise. By proactively addressing issues such as the digital divide, quality control of online resources, ethical use of AI, data privacy, academic integrity, technological infrastructure, and professionalism in online spaces, educational institutions can ensure that technology integration benefits all students and promotes ethical legal practice. It is an ongoing process that requires continuous reflection, adaptation, and engagement with emerging technologies and ethical frameworks.

Interdisciplinary Approaches in Legal Education

Incorporating Social Sciences in Legal Education

In order to have a comprehensive understanding of the law and its impact on society, it is crucial to incorporate insights from the social sciences into legal education. By integrating knowledge from disciplines such as sociology, psychology, political science, and economics, law students can develop a more nuanced understanding of the complex social and cultural context in which legal issues arise.

The Role of Social Sciences in Legal Education

The social sciences provide valuable theoretical frameworks, research methodologies, and empirical evidence that can enhance legal education in several ways. First, they help students understand how social factors shape legal norms, institutions, and practices. For example, sociological studies can shed light on the relationship between societal values and the development of legal rules.

Furthermore, incorporating social sciences in legal education enables students to examine the social impact of legal decisions and policymaking. By analyzing the social implications of legal doctrines and policies, students can develop a critical understanding of the potential benefits and drawbacks of different legal approaches.

The integration of social sciences also facilitates interdisciplinary collaboration between legal scholars and experts from other fields. Interdisciplinary approaches foster innovative and holistic solutions to complex legal problems, as diverse perspectives enrich the analysis and broaden the range of potential solutions.

Teaching Methods and Strategies

There are various methods and strategies for incorporating social sciences into legal education. Here are a few examples:

1. **Case studies and simulations:** Using real-world examples and simulations, students can explore how social factors influence legal outcomes. For instance, a case study might examine how societal attitudes towards gender norms affect court decisions in cases involving gender discrimination.

2. **Guest lectures and panel discussions:** Inviting experts from the social sciences to deliver guest lectures or participate in panel discussions can expose students to different perspectives and encourage dialogue between legal and social science disciplines.

3. **Interdisciplinary research projects:** Assigning interdisciplinary research projects allows students to collaborate with peers from different disciplines and apply social science methodologies to legal problems. For example, students could investigate the social and economic factors that contribute to racial disparities in the criminal justice system.

4. **Externships and community-based learning:** Providing opportunities for students to engage with community organizations and social justice initiatives can help them understand the practical application of legal principles and see the social impact of legal advocacy.

Key Concepts and Theories

To effectively incorporate social sciences into legal education, it is important to introduce students to key concepts and theories from relevant disciplines. Here are some concepts and theories that can be explored:

- **Social inequality and justice:** Students can learn about theories of social inequality and their implications for legal systems, such as critical race theory and intersectionality.

- **Behavioral economics:** Understanding how people's decision-making processes are influenced by social and psychological factors can provide insights into legal issues related to contracts, torts, and consumer protection.

- **Political science and policy analysis:** Introducing students to theories of policy-making and the political dynamics of law can enhance their understanding of the legislative and regulatory processes.

- **Sociological perspectives on law:** Students can explore sociological theories that analyze the relationship between law and society, such as legal realism and law and society scholarship.

Ethical Considerations

Incorporating social sciences into legal education also raises ethical considerations. It is important to ensure that students are aware of ethical guidelines for conducting research involving human subjects and that they approach sensitive social issues with empathy and respect. Additionally, students should be encouraged to critically evaluate the ethical implications of legal decisions and policies from a social perspective.

Conclusion

Incorporating social sciences into legal education enriches students' understanding of the complexities of law and its relationship to society. By integrating knowledge from disciplines such as sociology, psychology, political science, and economics, students can develop a well-rounded understanding of the social context in which legal issues arise. This interdisciplinary approach enhances critical thinking skills, promotes innovative problem-solving, and prepares students for the multidimensional challenges of legal practice.

Overall, incorporating social sciences in legal education strengthens the transformative potential of the law by fostering a holistic understanding of legal issues and their social impact. By equipping future legal professionals with a broader range of perspectives and tools, legal education can contribute to more just and equitable legal systems for the future.

Law and Medicine: Intersectionality and Collaboration

In recent years, the intersection between law and medicine has become increasingly important in the field of legal studies. This section explores the relationship between these two disciplines and the collaborative efforts that have emerged as a result. We will explore how the intersectionality of law and medicine can contribute to transformative legal studies and promote justice and equality in healthcare.

Understanding the Intersectionality of Law and Medicine

The intersectionality of law and medicine refers to the overlap and interplay between these two fields of study. Both disciplines share a common goal of promoting the well-being of individuals and society, albeit from different perspectives. Law focuses on developing and enforcing regulations, policies, and legal frameworks, while medicine focuses on the delivery of healthcare services and the treatment of patients.

The intersectionality arises when legal principles, regulations, and policies influence medical practice, and when medical knowledge and expertise inform legal decision-making. This intersectionality is especially evident in areas such as healthcare regulation, medical malpractice, bioethics, and public health.

Collaboration between Law and Medicine

Collaboration between law and medicine has become essential in addressing the complex social and ethical issues that arise in the healthcare field. By working together, legal and medical professionals can develop comprehensive and effective solutions that promote the well-being of individuals and society.

Some areas of collaboration between law and medicine include:

1. Medical Malpractice: Medical malpractice cases often rely on the testimony of medical experts to determine the standard of care and assess negligence. In these cases, legal professionals need to understand medical concepts and terminology, while medical experts need to understand legal standards and procedures.

2. Health Law and Policy: The development of health laws and policies requires input from both legal and medical experts. For example, when formulating healthcare legislation, legal professionals consult medical professionals to ensure that the laws address the real needs of patients and healthcare providers.

3. Bioethics: Bioethical issues, such as end-of-life decisions, organ transplantation, and genetic testing, often require interdisciplinary collaboration

between legal and medical professionals. Together, they can develop ethical frameworks that balance individual rights and public interests.

4. Public Health: Public health initiatives often involve legal interventions, such as vaccination mandates, quarantine measures, and health education campaigns. Legal professionals collaborate with medical experts to ensure that these interventions are evidence-based, ethical, and effective in promoting public health.

Examples of Intersectionality and Collaboration in Law and Medicine

To illustrate the intersectionality and collaboration between law and medicine, let's explore a few real-life examples:

1. The Legalization of Medical Marijuana: In many jurisdictions, the legalization of medical marijuana required close collaboration between legal professionals and medical experts. Legal professionals had to draft legislation that appropriately regulated the use and distribution of medical marijuana, while medical experts provided insights into its therapeutic benefits and potential risks.

2. Access to Experimental Treatments: When patients with life-threatening or debilitating conditions seek access to experimental treatments or drugs that are not yet approved by regulatory authorities, legal and medical professionals collaborate to navigate the complex legal and ethical considerations involved. They work together to create frameworks that balance patient autonomy, safety, and the advancement of medical knowledge.

Challenges and Ethical Considerations

While the intersectionality of law and medicine offers great potential for collaboration, it also presents challenges and ethical considerations that must be addressed:

1. Conflicting Goals: Law and medicine, as distinct disciplines, often have different goals and priorities. Law seeks to uphold justice and protect the public, while medicine aims to promote individual health and well-being. Balancing these conflicting goals requires careful consideration and collaboration to ensure that legal and medical decisions are fair, just, and ethically sound.

2. Competing Expertise: Legal and medical professionals have distinct areas of expertise, and effective collaboration requires an understanding and appreciation of each other's knowledge and perspectives. Communication and mutual respect are essential in bridging any gaps in understanding and addressing complex issues.

Resources for Further Study

For those interested in delving deeper into the intersectionality of law and medicine, the following resources provide valuable insights and knowledge:
 1. "Law and Medicine: Current Legal Issues" edited by Michael D. Shipley and Donna K. Hammaker 2. "Health Law and Bioethics: Cases in Context" by Sandra H. Johnson, Robert L. Schwartz, and Barry R. Furrow 3. "Medical Law and Ethics" by Jonathan Herring

These resources cover a wide range of topics, from medical malpractice and healthcare regulation to bioethics and medical research ethics. They provide a solid foundation for understanding the intersectionality of law and medicine and the transformative potential of collaboration between these fields.

Conclusion

The intersectionality of law and medicine offers great potential for transformative legal studies. By engaging in collaboration and embracing interdisciplinary approaches, legal and medical professionals can contribute to the development of inclusive and equitable healthcare systems. Through their combined efforts, they can address complex legal and ethical challenges and promote justice and equality in the field of medicine.

Law and Psychology: Understanding Human Behavior in Legal Contexts

Law and psychology are two distinct disciplines that intersect in the study of human behavior and its implications for the legal system. In this section, we will explore the relationship between law and psychology, highlighting the importance of understanding human behavior in legal contexts. We will discuss the key principles and theories in the field of psychology that have shaped our understanding of human behavior, and how they can be applied to various aspects of the legal system.

Overview of Law and Psychology

Law and psychology share a common goal: to better understand human behavior. While law focuses on the rules and principles that govern society, psychology delves into the complex workings of the human mind and behavior. By combining these two disciplines, we can gain valuable insights into how individuals think, make decisions, and interact with the legal system.

Psychological Principles in Legal Decision-Making

One area where law and psychology intersect is in the study of human decision-making, particularly in the context of legal proceedings. Psychology offers a range of theories and concepts that shed light on how individuals process information, form judgments, and make decisions. These insights can be applied to various stages of legal decision-making, including jury selection, witness testimonies, and judges' rulings.

One of the key principles in this area is cognitive psychology, which explores how people perceive, think, and reason. For example, research has shown that individuals are prone to cognitive biases, such as confirmation bias and hindsight bias, which can influence their judgment and decision-making. Understanding these biases can help legal professionals identify potential flaws in the decision-making process and take steps to mitigate their impact.

Another relevant area of psychology is social psychology, which examines how individuals' thoughts, feelings, and behaviors are influenced by social context. In a legal setting, social psychology can inform our understanding of factors that might affect witness credibility, such as the presence of a biased lineup or the impact of leading questions. By considering the social dynamics at play, legal professionals can make more informed judgments about the reliability of witness testimonies.

Psychological Assessment in Legal Proceedings

Psychology also plays a crucial role in conducting assessments and evaluations in legal proceedings. Mental health evaluations, forensic assessments, and risk assessments are some of the key areas where psychological expertise is employed to inform legal decision-making.

In the context of mental health evaluations, psychologists use standardized assessments and clinical interviews to assess an individual's mental state and determine their competence to stand trial or their criminal responsibility. These evaluations provide valuable insights into an individual's psychological functioning and can help inform legal decisions regarding their treatment or sentencing.

Forensic assessments involve the application of psychological principles to evaluate various aspects of a legal case, such as assessing the credibility of eyewitness testimonies, evaluating the risk of reoffending, or determining the suitability of a parent for child custody. By drawing on psychological theories and research, forensic psychologists can provide expert opinions that assist judges and juries in making well-informed decisions.

Risk assessments are another area where psychology plays a crucial role in the legal system. By applying statistical models and psychological principles, psychologists can assess an individual's likelihood of engaging in future criminal behavior. These assessments help inform decisions related to parole, probation, and risk management in the criminal justice system.

Understanding Criminal Behavior

Psychology plays a significant role in understanding the causes and dynamics of criminal behavior. By examining various psychological factors, such as personality traits, cognitive processes, and social influences, psychologists can contribute to our understanding of why individuals engage in criminal activities.

One area of psychology that is particularly relevant in understanding criminal behavior is forensic psychology. Forensic psychologists apply psychological principles to assess and intervene with individuals who have come into contact with the legal system. They may work with offenders to develop rehabilitation programs or provide therapy to victims of crime to aid in their recovery.

Furthermore, the field of criminal profiling relies heavily on psychological theories and research to understand the motives and characteristics of offenders. By analyzing crime scene evidence and considering psychosocial factors, criminal profilers can provide investigative leads and assist law enforcement agencies in solving crimes.

The Role of Psychology in Legal Advocacy

Psychological principles and research findings also inform legal advocacy strategies. Attorneys can draw on psychological concepts to craft persuasive arguments, construct effective cross-examinations, and present evidence in a compelling manner.

One such concept is the use of storytelling in the courtroom. Research has shown that humans are naturally inclined to engage with narratives, and incorporating storytelling techniques into legal arguments can make them more persuasive and memorable. By weaving a cohesive and relatable narrative, attorneys can enhance the impact of their arguments on judges and juries.

Psychology also offers insights into jury decision-making processes. Understanding group dynamics, deliberation processes, and the influence of individual attributes can help attorneys make informed decisions about jury selection, tailor their arguments to resonate with jurors, and anticipate potential biases that may affect the outcome of a trial.

Ethical Considerations

As with any interdisciplinary field, there are ethical considerations that need to be addressed when applying psychological principles in legal contexts. It is essential to uphold the principles of confidentiality, informed consent, and competence when conducting assessments or therapy in legal settings. Additionally, legal professionals need to be aware of potential biases when interpreting psychological assessments and research findings, ensuring that they do not overstate or misuse the information provided.

Furthermore, privacy concerns arise when utilizing psychological data and techniques in legal proceedings. It is crucial to strike a balance between the need for accurate and relevant information and respecting individuals' privacy rights. Legal professionals must remain mindful of these ethical considerations to ensure the responsible and ethical use of psychology in the legal context.

Conclusion

The integration of law and psychology offers valuable insights into understanding human behavior in legal contexts. By drawing on principles and theories from psychology, legal professionals can enhance their understanding of decision-making processes, improve assessments and evaluations, and develop effective legal advocacy strategies. However, it is essential to navigate the ethical and practical considerations inherent in this interdisciplinary field to ensure its responsible and effective application in the pursuit of justice.

Law and Economics: Analyzing Legal Systems through Economic Perspectives

In this section, we will explore the intersection of law and economics and how economic perspectives can be applied to analyze legal systems. The field of law and economics examines how economic principles and theories can be used to understand the impact of legal rules and regulations on society.

Background

Law and economics is a multidisciplinary field that combines insights from both law and economics to analyze legal issues. It emerged in the 1960s as a response to the traditional legal analysis that focused solely on legal doctrines and principles, without considering the economic implications.

Economic analysis of law provides a framework for understanding how legal rules and regulations affect individual behavior, market outcomes, and social welfare. By examining the economic incentives created by legal rules, economists aim to identify efficient and socially desirable legal policies.

Principles of Law and Economics

The field of law and economics is built upon several key principles:

1. **Rational Choice Theory:** This principle is based on the assumption that individuals make rational decisions by weighing the costs and benefits of their actions. Rational choice theory provides a basis for analyzing how legal rules influence individual behavior.

2. **Efficiency:** Law and economics emphasizes the importance of efficiency in legal and economic systems. Efficiency occurs when resources are allocated to their most valuable uses and when the overall welfare of society is maximized. Economists analyze legal rules to determine whether they promote efficiency or create inefficiencies.

3. **Incentives:** An important aspect of law and economics is the analysis of how legal rules shape individual incentives. Legal rules create incentives for individuals to behave in certain ways, and economists examine how these incentives affect behavior and outcomes.

4. **Cost-Benefit Analysis:** Law and economics often employs cost-benefit analysis to evaluate legal policies. This involves comparing the costs and benefits of different policy options to determine the most socially desirable outcome. By quantifying and comparing the costs and benefits, economists can provide insights into the potential effects of legal rules.

Analyzing Legal Systems through Economic Perspectives

Law and economics provides a unique perspective on legal systems by examining how economic factors influence the creation and enforcement of laws. Here are some common approaches used in analyzing legal systems from an economic standpoint:

1. **Law and Market Efficiency:** Economists study how legal rules impact market outcomes and economic efficiency. They analyze the effects of regulations, antitrust laws, and property rights on market competition, innovation, and resource allocation.

2. **Law and Behavioral Economics:** Behavioral economics combines insights from psychology and economics to understand how individuals make decisions. By incorporating behavioral insights into the analysis of legal systems, economists can identify potential biases or limitations in the decision-making process and propose legal reforms to address them.

3. **Law and Public Choice Theory:** Public choice theory explores how individuals' self-interest affects their participation in collective decision-making processes. Economists apply this theory to analyze the behavior of lawmakers, regulators, and interest groups in shaping legal policies.

4. **Law and Game Theory:** Game theory provides a framework for analyzing strategic interactions between individuals. Economists use game theory to study the behavior of parties involved in legal disputes, negotiations, and the design of legal contracts.

Examples and Applications

Law and economics can be applied to a wide range of legal issues. Here are some examples of how economic analysis can provide insights into different areas of law:

1. **Tort Law:** Economists analyze the deterrence effects of tort liability rules to determine the optimal level of damages. They examine how tort law influences behavior, risk-taking, and the allocation of resources.

2. **Contract Law:** Economic analysis of contract law focuses on the role of incentives, risk allocation, and enforcement mechanisms in promoting efficient contracting. Economists study the effects of contract rules on transaction costs, the formation of contracts, and the resolution of disputes.

3. **Antitrust Law:** Antitrust laws aim to promote competition and prevent anti-competitive behavior. Economic analysis is used to evaluate market structure, the effects of mergers and acquisitions, and the potential for monopolistic behavior.

4. **Intellectual Property Law:** Economists examine the economic impact of intellectual property rights on innovation, creativity, and market competition.

They analyze the optimal duration and scope of intellectual property protection.

Caveats and Limitations

While law and economics provides valuable insights, there are certain caveats and limitations to consider:

1. **Value Judgments:** Economic analysis is based on certain value judgments, such as efficiency and welfare maximization. Different individuals may have different value preferences, which can lead to divergent policy conclusions.

2. **Simplifying Assumptions:** Economic models often rely on simplifying assumptions, which may not fully capture the complexity of real-world legal systems and human behavior.

3. **Incomplete Information:** Economic analysis assumes perfect information, which may not be realistic in many legal contexts. Imperfect information can affect the behavior and outcomes predicted by economic models.

Resources for Further Study

If you are interested in learning more about the intersection of law and economics, here are some recommended resources:

1. *Law's Order: What Economics Has to Do with Law and Why It Matters* by David D. Friedman.

2. *The Economic Structure of Intellectual Property Law* by William M. Landes and Richard A. Posner.

3. *Behavioral Law and Economics* by Cass R. Sunstein.

4. *The Oxford Handbook of Law and Economics* edited by Francesco Parisi.

Conclusion

Law and economics provides a valuable framework for analyzing legal systems through economic perspectives. By examining the economic incentives and consequences of legal rules, economists can offer insights into the efficiency and effectiveness of legal policies. Understanding the intersection of law and economics can contribute to a more comprehensive and nuanced understanding of the impact of legal systems on society.

Social Justice and Legal Education

Teaching Social Justice in Law Schools

Teaching social justice in law schools is crucial for preparing students to become informed, compassionate, and effective advocates for justice in their future legal careers. This section explores the importance of integrating social justice principles into legal education, provides different approaches and strategies for teaching social justice, and highlights the challenges and opportunities involved.

Why Teach Social Justice in Law Schools?

Law schools have a responsibility to educate students not only on legal doctrine and skills but also on the ethical and moral dimensions of the legal profession. Teaching social justice in law schools helps students develop a deeper understanding of the impact of law on marginalized communities and highlights the role of lawyers in promoting equitable and inclusive legal systems. By teaching social justice, law schools contribute to the development of socially conscious lawyers who can challenge systemic injustices and work towards a more just society.

Approaches to Teaching Social Justice in Law Schools

There are various approaches and strategies that law schools can employ to effectively teach social justice. Here are a few examples:

1. Integrating Social Justice into Core Courses: Law schools can infuse social justice principles into core courses, such as constitutional law, criminal law, and property law. This involves examining the historical and contemporary implications of legal doctrines on marginalized communities, discussing the social, economic, and racial factors that influence legal outcomes, and exploring alternative perspectives on legal issues.

2. Specialized Social Justice Courses: Law schools can offer specialized courses focused specifically on social justice issues, such as racial justice, gender justice, environmental justice, or immigration and human rights. These courses provide in-depth exploration of specific social justice topics and allow students to delve into the complexities and nuances of these issues.

3. Experiential Learning: Law schools can incorporate experiential learning opportunities, such as clinical programs, externships, or pro bono projects, that engage students in hands-on work addressing social justice issues. Through these experiences, students interact directly with clients from marginalized communities,

gain practical skills, and develop a deeper understanding of the impact of law on real people's lives.

4. Interdisciplinary Collaboration: Law schools can foster collaboration between law students and students from other disciplines, such as social work, public health, or political science, to tackle complex social justice issues. Working with students from diverse backgrounds broadens perspectives, encourages interdisciplinary problem-solving, and promotes holistic approaches to social justice.

Challenges and Opportunities

Teaching social justice in law schools comes with its own set of challenges and opportunities. Some of the challenges include resistance from traditionalist faculty who may prioritize doctrinal teaching, limited resources for implementing social justice initiatives, and the need to navigate potential political and ideological conflicts among students and faculty. However, there are also opportunities to address these challenges:

1. Faculty Development: Law schools can invest in faculty development programs focused on teaching social justice. This includes providing resources and support for faculty to incorporate social justice principles into their courses, promoting dialogue and collaboration among faculty members, and recognizing and rewarding innovative teaching methods that address social justice.

2. Student Engagement: Law schools can create opportunities for student engagement, such as social justice student organizations, guest speaker series, or conferences focused on social justice issues. These initiatives foster a sense of community, promote student-led advocacy, and encourage dialogue about social justice within the institution.

3. Partnerships with Social Justice Organizations: Law schools can establish partnerships with social justice organizations, legal aid clinics, or advocacy groups to provide students with practical experience and opportunities to engage with social justice issues. These partnerships can enrich the learning experience, create networking opportunities, and facilitate collaboration on social justice initiatives.

4. Critical Reflection and Self-Assessment: Law schools should encourage critical reflection and self-assessment on their own practices, policies, and curriculum to ensure they align with the goals of social justice education. Schools can regularly assess the diversity and inclusivity of their faculty and student body, critically examine their admissions and hiring policies, and ensure that the curriculum reflects a diverse range of legal perspectives.

Resources for Teaching Social Justice

To support the teaching of social justice in law schools, there are various resources available. Some of these include:

1. Social Justice Teaching Resources: Numerous organizations and websites provide teaching resources and materials on social justice issues that are specifically tailored for legal education. These resources can include case studies, simulations, teaching guides, and curated readings on a wide range of social justice topics.

2. Guest Speakers and Workshops: Inviting guest speakers, such as social justice advocates, community leaders, or legal scholars, to deliver lectures or facilitate workshops can provide valuable insights and real-world perspectives on social justice issues.

3. Community Partnerships: Collaborating with community organizations working on social justice issues can provide direct access to real-world contexts, case studies, and opportunities for students to engage in meaningful advocacy and social justice work.

4. Law School Clinics and Externship Programs: Law schools can establish their own legal clinics or partner with existing legal clinics to provide students with hands-on experience in social justice advocacy. These clinics offer students the opportunity to work directly with clients from marginalized communities and engage in social justice litigation or policy work.

Conclusion

Teaching social justice in law schools is an essential component of preparing future lawyers to address systemic inequalities and promote justice and equality in their legal careers. By integrating social justice principles throughout legal education and providing opportunities for experiential learning and interdisciplinary collaboration, law schools can nurture socially conscious lawyers who are equipped to advocate for marginalized communities and work towards a more just society.

Student Activism and Social Justice Movements in Legal Education

Student activism and social justice movements play a crucial role in shaping the curriculum and culture of legal education. As young future lawyers, law students are at the forefront of advocating for change and promoting social justice. In this section, we will explore the inspiring efforts of student activists and their impact on legal education.

The Power of Student Activism

Student activism is characterized by collective action and advocacy for social and political change. It has a long history within universities and has been instrumental in numerous civil rights movements, including the anti-apartheid movement, the student movement against the Vietnam War, and more recently, the Black Lives Matter movement.

In the context of legal education, student activism focuses on challenging the traditional pedagogical approach, advocating for diversity and inclusion, addressing systemic issues within the legal profession, and exploring innovative approaches to legal training. Student activists push for the incorporation of critical perspectives, intersectionality, and human rights frameworks into the curriculum, ensuring that legal education reflects the needs and values of an increasingly diverse society.

Addressing Systemic Issues

Student activism in legal education is often directed towards addressing systemic issues that perpetuate inequality and injustice. Activists demand a curriculum that critically examines the biases and power imbalances within the legal system. They advocate for the inclusion of courses and discussions on race, gender, sexuality, social class, and other identity-based issues. By challenging the traditional canon and expanding the scope of legal education, students promote a more nuanced understanding of the law and its impact on marginalized communities.

Furthermore, student activists push for the development of experiential learning opportunities that engage with real-world legal issues. They emphasize the importance of practical skills training, such as client counseling, negotiation, and community advocacy, to better equip aspiring lawyers with the tools necessary to effect social change.

Creating Safe and Inclusive Spaces

Student activists also prioritize creating safe and inclusive spaces within legal education. They advocate for the establishment of support networks, such as affinity groups and mentorship programs, to foster a sense of belonging for students from underrepresented backgrounds. These initiatives aim to address the isolation and marginalization experienced by minority students and promote a more inclusive and diverse legal profession.

In addition, student activists challenge discriminatory practices within law schools, such as bias in grading, recruitment, and promotion. They work towards dismantling these barriers and promoting a more equitable environment for all students.

Social Justice Movements in Legal Education

Social justice movements within legal education encompass a broad range of issues, including racial justice, gender equality, LGBTQ+ rights, environmental justice, and economic justice.

For example, students have been instrumental in advocating for the integration of anti-racist education and training into the legal curriculum. Through workshops, conferences, and discussions, they facilitate conversations about systemic racism and its impact on the legal system. These initiatives aim to equip law students with the knowledge and skills necessary to challenge racial inequality within the legal profession.

Similarly, student activists promote awareness and understanding of gender equality within legal education. They challenge gender biases in the curriculum, advocate for the inclusion of feminist legal theories, and work towards eliminating barriers faced by women in the legal profession.

Social justice movements in legal education also engage with issues of LGBTQ+ rights, environmental justice, and economic justice. Through activism, students strive to create a more just and inclusive legal system that addresses the needs and concerns of all communities.

The Role of Law Schools

Law schools play a critical role in supporting student activism and social justice movements. They have a responsibility to provide a platform for students to voice their concerns, engage in dialogue, and effect change. Law schools should foster an environment that encourages activism and empowers students to challenge the status quo.

Furthermore, law schools can integrate social justice initiatives into their curriculum by offering specialized courses, clinics, and research opportunities that focus on issues of social justice and human rights. By exposing students to real-world challenges and providing the tools to address them, law schools contribute to the development of socially conscious lawyers.

Conclusion

Student activism and social justice movements in legal education are catalysts for transformative change. By challenging traditional pedagogical approaches, addressing systemic issues, and advocating for a more inclusive curriculum, student activists shape the future of legal education. Their activism inspires critical thinking, fosters empathy, and equips future lawyers with the skills necessary to drive social change. As legal educators, it is our responsibility to support and amplify the voices of student activists, ensuring that their efforts have a lasting impact on the legal profession.

Law Clinics and Social Justice Advocacy

Law clinics play a significant role in the field of transformative legal studies by providing experiential learning opportunities for law students and engaging in social justice advocacy. These clinics serve as a bridge between theoretical knowledge and practical application, allowing students to work on real cases and contribute to the pursuit of justice and equality. In this section, we will explore the concept and significance of law clinics in the context of social justice advocacy.

Understanding Law Clinics

A law clinic is an educational program within a law school where students, under the supervision of experienced faculty members, provide legal services to individuals or communities who may not have access to justice. Law clinics can specialize in various areas of law, including criminal defense, family law, immigration law, and human rights law, just to name a few.

The primary objective of a law clinic is to prepare students for the practice of law by providing real-world experiences. Through law clinics, students develop necessary lawyering skills such as client interviewing, legal research and writing, case management, negotiation, and advocacy. Moreover, law clinics give students the opportunity to work collaboratively with other legal professionals, including social workers, psychologists, and community organizers, to address the broader social issues underlying the cases they handle.

Role of Law Clinics in Social Justice Advocacy

Law clinics play a crucial role in advancing social justice goals by providing legal representation and advocacy to marginalized individuals and communities. They actively seek to challenge systemic injustices and promote equal access to justice. Here are some key ways in which law clinics contribute to social justice advocacy:

1. **Legal representation for underrepresented individuals:** Law clinics often focus on representing individuals who are unable to afford legal services or

face barriers in accessing justice. By providing free or low-cost legal representation, law clinics ensure that individuals who are historically disadvantaged or marginalized have access to the legal system.

2. **Addressing systemic issues:** Law clinics often handle cases that involve systemic injustices, such as discrimination, police misconduct, or housing disparities. Through their work, law clinic students and faculty can identify patterns of injustice and advocate for systemic reforms. This allows them to challenge oppressive practices and contribute to the development of more just legal frameworks.

3. **Community outreach and education:** Law clinics engage in community outreach and education initiatives to empower individuals with legal knowledge and resources. They may conduct workshops, provide legal clinics, or collaborate with community-based organizations to raise awareness about legal rights and procedures. This outreach helps to bridge the gap between legal services and marginalized communities, fostering a more inclusive and informed society.

4. **Policy advocacy and law reform:** Law clinics have the unique opportunity to engage in policy advocacy and law reform efforts. Through their direct involvement in cases and research, clinic students and faculty can identify legal gaps or flaws that perpetuate social injustice. They can then work towards policy recommendations and legal reforms that address the root causes of systemic oppression.

Real-World Example: Law Clinic for Immigrant Rights

To illustrate the impact of law clinics in social justice advocacy, let's consider the example of a law clinic specializing in immigrant rights. This clinic provides legal representation and advocacy for undocumented immigrants facing deportation proceedings. The clinic's activities may include:

- Representing clients in immigration courts, filing applications for relief, and preparing asylum claims.

- Collaborating with community organizations to provide know-your-rights workshops and legal clinics for immigrant communities.

- Conducting research on immigration policies and advocating for policy changes to protect the rights of undocumented immigrants.

- Engaging in impact litigation to challenge unjust immigration detention practices or discriminatory policies.

By working in a law clinic focused on immigrant rights, students gain valuable insights into the challenges faced by immigrant communities and develop the skills needed to address the complexities of immigration law. Through their advocacy efforts, the clinic contributes to a more just and inclusive society by fighting for the rights of marginalized individuals.

Challenges and Ethical Considerations

While law clinics are highly impactful, they also face several challenges and ethical considerations. Some of these challenges include:

- **Limited resources:** Law clinics often operate with limited funding and staffing, which can constrain their capacity to take on a significant number of cases or expand their services.

- **Client confidentiality:** Ensuring client confidentiality can be challenging, especially in cases that involve sensitive information or high levels of media attention. Law clinics must navigate legal and ethical obligations to protect client privacy while also engaging in public advocacy.

- **Navigating power dynamics:** Law clinic students and faculty must be mindful of power dynamics when working with clients from marginalized communities. Ensuring that client voices are centered and decision-making processes are inclusive requires ongoing reflection and critical self-awareness.

- **Maintaining quality of services:** Law clinics' commitment to social justice must be complemented by the provision of high-quality legal services. Clinics need to strike a balance between meeting the immediate needs of clients and offering comprehensive and effective legal representation.

Addressing these challenges requires ongoing evaluation, collaboration with community partners, and an understanding of the social, political, and economic contexts in which law clinics operate.

Conclusion

Law clinics play a vital role in transformative legal studies by providing students with experiential learning opportunities and engaging in social justice advocacy.

Through law clinics, students gain practical skills, work on real cases, and contribute to the pursuit of justice and equality. These clinics are at the forefront of challenging systemic injustices, bridging the gap between legal services and marginalized communities, and advocating for policy reforms. While law clinics face challenges and ethical considerations, their impact in advancing social justice goals cannot be overstated. By preparing the next generation of lawyers to be agents of change, law clinics contribute to the ongoing transformation of the legal system towards a more just and equitable society.

For further reading on law clinics and social justice advocacy, we recommend the following resources:

- King, A., & Pipkin, K. (Eds.). (2018). *Social Justice Lawyering: From Practice to Theory and Teaching*. New York, NY: Aspen Publishers.

- Song Richardson, R., & Newman, K. (Eds.). (2018). *The Diversity and Inclusion Handbook: A Guide for Lawyers*. Chicago, IL: American Bar Association.

- Sossin, L. (2011). *Boundaries of Judicial Review: The Law of Justiciability in Canada*. Toronto, ON: Carswell.

- Van Wormer, K., & Bartollas, C. (2019). *Restorative Justice Today: Practical Applications*. Thousand Oaks, CA: SAGE Publications.

International and Comparative Legal Education

Overview of International and Comparative Law

In this section, we will provide an overview of international and comparative law, two important branches of legal studies that play a crucial role in shaping the global legal landscape. International law refers to the legal rules and principles that govern relations between states, international organizations, and individuals in the international community. Comparative law, on the other hand, involves the study and analysis of different legal systems in various countries, aiming to identify similarities and differences among them.

Background and Principles

International law has its roots in ancient civilizations, but its modern development can be traced back to the emergence of nation-states and the establishment of international relations in the 17th and 18th centuries. The principles of international law are based on consent, custom, treaties, and the decisions of international courts and tribunals. The primary sources of international law include international treaties, customary international law, general principles of law recognized by civilized nations, and judicial decisions.

Comparative law, on the other hand, emerged as a discipline in the 19th century, alongside the rise of globalization and the need to understand different legal systems. Its main objective is to study the similarities and differences in legal concepts, institutions, and practices across various jurisdictions. Comparative law enables legal scholars and practitioners to gain insights into alternative legal solutions and to identify best practices from different legal systems.

International Law

International law encompasses a wide range of legal fields, including public international law, private international law, and supranational law. Public international law deals with the rights and obligations of states, international organizations, and individuals in their interactions with each other. It covers areas such as diplomatic relations, human rights, humanitarian law, and the law of the sea.

Private international law, also known as conflict of laws, deals with issues arising from private transactions with an international element, such as contracts, torts, and family law matters. Its objective is to determine which legal system should apply in cases involving multiple jurisdictions.

Supranational law refers to the legal framework established by international organizations, such as the European Union, which have the authority to create rules that are binding on their member states. This form of law creates a new layer of legal authority beyond the national legal systems of member states.

Comparative Law

Comparative law involves the comparative study of legal systems, aiming to foster a deeper understanding of different legal traditions and to identify areas of convergence and divergence. It examines the structure, content, and operation of legal systems, including their constitutional principles, sources of law, judicial systems, and legal reasoning methods.

One of the key methodologies in comparative law is the functional approach, which assesses the effectiveness of legal rules and institutions in achieving their intended goals. By comparing the performance of different legal systems in addressing similar problems, this approach allows for the identification of alternative solutions and best practices.

Comparative legal studies also encompass the analysis of legal cultures and the impact of historical, social, and economic factors on legal systems. It recognizes that law is not only a reflection of societal values but also a driving force that shapes social, economic, and political developments.

Challenges and Opportunities

International and comparative law face a range of challenges and opportunities in the modern legal landscape. One of the major challenges is the tension between national sovereignty and international obligations. While states have the primary authority to determine and enforce their own laws, they are also bound by international treaties and customary international law. Striking a balance between these two sources of law is often complicated and requires careful negotiation and interpretation.

Another challenge lies in the differing legal traditions, which can lead to conflicts of laws and legal uncertainty. Comparative law seeks to address these challenges by promoting dialogue and understanding among legal systems and by developing concepts, such as the principle of good faith and the notion of harmonization, to facilitate cooperation.

Moreover, advancements in technology and globalization have opened up new opportunities for international and comparative law. The increasing interconnectedness of societies and economies necessitates a more comprehensive understanding of legal systems beyond national boundaries. Comparative law, in particular, allows for cross-fertilization of ideas and legal innovations that can contribute to the development of more effective and just legal systems.

Resources and Further Reading

For those interested in exploring international and comparative law further, there are a number of comprehensive resources available. Some recommended readings include:

1. "An Introduction to International Law" by Mark W. Janis

2. "Comparative Law: A Handbook" edited by Mathias Reimann and Reinhard Zimmermann

3. "The Oxford Handbook of Comparative Law" edited by Mathias Reimann and Reinhard Zimmerman

4. "International Legal Research in a Nutshell" by Marci Hoffman and Robert C. Berring

5. "Comparative Law: Cases, Text, Materials" by Rudolf B. Schlesinger and Marie-Thérèse Meulders-Klein

In addition to these resources, there are also various international organizations, such as the United Nations and the International Court of Justice, that publish reports, judgments, and commentaries on international law. Comparative law journals and associations, such as the American Society of Comparative Law and the International Association of Legal Science, also provide valuable insights into ongoing research and discussions in the field.

Conclusion

International and comparative law are essential branches of legal studies that play a vital role in addressing global challenges and promoting justice. These fields provide a framework for understanding the complexities and interconnections of legal systems and offer opportunities for legal practitioners to learn from different legal traditions and adopt innovative approaches. As the world becomes increasingly interconnected, the importance of international and comparative law will continue to grow, shaping the future of legal practice and contributing to the advancement of justice and equality worldwide.

Teaching International Law in Domestic Legal Education

In the increasingly interconnected world, the study of international law has become crucial for understanding the complex legal issues that transcend national boundaries. As a result, integrating international law into domestic legal education has become an essential component of legal curricula. This section explores the challenges and opportunities of teaching international law in domestic legal education and provides practical strategies for effective instruction.

The Importance of Teaching International Law

International law governs the relations between states, international organizations, and individuals, and covers a wide range of issues, including human rights, trade, environment, armed conflict, and diplomacy. Understanding international law is essential for future lawyers who may be involved in cross-border transactions, diplomatic negotiations, or human rights advocacy. It provides the legal framework for addressing global challenges and promotes cooperation and peace among nations.

Teaching international law in domestic legal education not only equips students with knowledge and skills in a globalized world but also fosters critical thinking, legal analysis, and multicultural awareness. It encourages students to think beyond national legal systems and appreciate the diversity of legal perspectives. Furthermore, it enables students to understand the interconnectedness of domestic and international legal orders and the impact of international norms on domestic legal systems.

Challenges in Teaching International Law

Teaching international law in domestic legal education poses several challenges. One of the primary challenges is the vastness and complexity of the subject matter. International law encompasses numerous treaties, conventions, and customary rules that can be overwhelming for students. Moreover, the dynamic nature of international law, with its evolving principles and emerging issues, requires constant updating of course materials and teaching methodologies.

Another challenge is the interplay between national and international legal systems. Many legal principles and concepts taught in domestic legal education may need to be contextualized within the international legal framework. This requires instructors to bridge the gap between domestic and international perspectives, providing students with a comprehensive understanding of the law.

Additionally, language barriers and cultural differences can pose challenges in teaching international law. Many international legal texts and cases are written in languages other than English, necessitating translation and interpretation. Furthermore, cultural nuances and diverse legal traditions must be taken into account to offer a holistic approach to teaching international law.

Strategies for Teaching International Law

To effectively teach international law in domestic legal education, instructors can employ various strategies:

1. **Interdisciplinary Approach:** Incorporate perspectives from other disciplines such as political science, economics, and sociology to provide students with a comprehensive understanding of the socio-political context in which international law operates.

2. **Case Studies:** Use real-world case studies to illustrate the application of international legal principles in practice. Analyze landmark cases from

international tribunals or domestic courts, highlighting their significance and impact on the development of international law.

3. **Simulations and Role-Playing:** Engage students in simulations of international negotiations, moot court competitions, or model United Nations sessions. This hands-on approach allows students to apply international legal principles, develop negotiation skills, and gain practical experience in resolving complex international issues.

4. **Guest Speakers:** Invite legal practitioners, diplomats, or academics specializing in international law to share their expertise and real-world experiences. These guest speakers can provide valuable insights into the practical application of international law and inspire students to pursue careers in the field.

5. **International Exchanges and Study Abroad Programs:** Encourage students to participate in international exchanges or study abroad programs to immerse themselves in different legal systems and cultures. Exposing students to diverse perspectives and legal traditions enhances their understanding of international law and its contextual intricacies.

Resources for Teaching International Law

To enhance the teaching of international law in domestic legal education, instructors can utilize a wide range of resources:

1. **International Agreements and Conventions:** Incorporate relevant international treaties and conventions into course materials. These documents provide the foundation of international law and offer insights into the legal rules and principles governing various areas of international relations.

2. **International Court Decisions:** Analyze judgments and advisory opinions of international courts and tribunals, such as the International Court of Justice or the International Criminal Court. These decisions illustrate the application of international legal principles and demonstrate the evolving nature of international law.

3. **International Organizations:** Utilize research reports, publications, and online resources from international organizations such as the United Nations, World Trade Organization, or International Committee of the Red Cross. These materials provide valuable information on current international legal issues and the work of these organizations.

4. **Journals and Academic Articles:** Incorporate scholarly articles from international law journals to expose students to current debates, emerging issues, and critical analysis within the field of international law.

5. **Online Legal Databases:** Access online legal databases dedicated to international law, such as Westlaw or LexisNexis, to find primary and secondary legal sources, case law, and scholarly articles. These databases offer a wealth of information for research and teaching purposes.

Real-World Example: Teaching International Human Rights Law

To illustrate the practical application of teaching international law in domestic legal education, let's consider the example of teaching international human rights law. This example demonstrates how instructors can navigate the challenges and effectively engage students in this critical area of international law.

In this module, instructors could begin by introducing students to the Universal Declaration of Human Rights and its fundamental principles. They could then explore various human rights treaties, such as the International Covenant on Civil and Political Rights and the Convention on the Elimination of All Forms of Discrimination Against Women. By analyzing case law from international and domestic courts, students can examine the implementation and enforcement of human rights norms in different jurisdictions.

To provide a practical dimension to the course, instructors could invite guest speakers, including human rights advocates, to share their experiences working in the field. Students could also engage in a simulation exercise, such as a mock trial or a human rights fact-finding mission, where they would apply international human rights law principles to address a fictional human rights violation.

Moreover, instructors could assign research projects to explore contemporary human rights issues, such as the rights of refugees, gender-based violence, or freedom of expression in the digital age. These projects would require students to critically analyze international legal instruments, research current human rights developments, and propose practical solutions to address these challenges.

By incorporating these strategies and resources into teaching international human rights law, instructors can inspire students to become advocates for human rights, promoting justice and equality on a global scale.

Conclusion

Teaching international law in domestic legal education is essential to equip future lawyers with the skills and knowledge necessary to navigate the complexities of our increasingly globalized world. Despite the challenges posed by the vastness and ever-evolving nature of international law, instructors can employ interdisciplinary approaches, case studies, simulations, and guest speakers to create engaging and practical learning experiences for students. By utilizing valuable resources such as international agreements, court decisions, and academic articles, instructors can provide students with a comprehensive understanding of international law and its applications. Through these efforts, domestic legal education can contribute to the development of transformative legal professionals who promote justice and equality in an interconnected world.

Challenges and Opportunities in Comparative Legal Education

Comparative legal education is a vital component of the study of law, as it allows students to understand legal systems and institutions in different jurisdictions and cultures. While it presents numerous challenges, it also offers valuable opportunities for students to develop a global perspective and gain a deeper understanding of legal principles and practices. In this section, we will explore the challenges and opportunities inherent in comparative legal education.

Challenges

1. **Cultural and Language Barriers:** One of the major challenges in comparative legal education is the cultural and language barriers that students may encounter. Legal systems are deeply embedded in cultural norms and values, and understanding these nuances requires familiarity with the local language and customs. Overcoming these barriers requires an investment in language learning and cultural sensitivity training.

2. **Diverse Legal Systems:** Legal systems vary greatly across jurisdictions, making it challenging to compare and understand the intricacies of different legal principles and practices. Students need to develop a broad knowledge base and constantly update their understanding of various legal systems to effectively analyze and compare them.

3. **Availability of Resources:** Access to high-quality resources, including legal texts, court decisions, and scholarly articles, may be limited or unavailable for certain jurisdictions. This scarcity of resources can hinder students' ability to conduct comprehensive research and gain insights into different legal systems.

4. **Political and Social Context:** Legal systems are influenced by political and social factors, such as history, governance structures, and societal values. Understanding the political and social context in which a legal system operates is crucial for a comprehensive comparative analysis. However, interpreting these complexities requires a deep understanding of the local political and social landscape.

Opportunities

1. **Enhanced Analytical Skills:** Comparative legal education develops students' analytical skills by requiring them to critically analyze and interpret legal principles across different jurisdictions. This comparative approach enables students to identify commonalities, differences, and overlaps in legal systems, fostering a deeper understanding of legal concepts.

2. **Global Perspective:** Comparative legal education offers students a global perspective, allowing them to appreciate the diversity and complexity of legal systems worldwide. This broader worldview supports the development of well-rounded legal professionals who are sensitive to cultural, social, and political nuances.

3. **Adaptability and Flexibility:** Comparative legal education equips students with the ability to adapt to and navigate various legal systems. This adaptability and flexibility are valuable skills in an increasingly interconnected and globalized world, where lawyers often encounter international legal issues.

4. **Innovative Problem-Solving:** Comparative legal education encourages students to develop innovative problem-solving skills by assessing how different legal systems approach similar issues. This approach fosters creativity and the ability to think outside the box, enabling students to tackle complex legal challenges.

Examples of Comparative Legal Education

1. **Comparative Case Studies:** Students can engage in analyzing and comparing landmark cases from different legal systems to understand the similarities and differences in legal interpretations and outcomes. This enhances their analytical and research skills while broadening their understanding of legal principles.

2. **Exchange Programs:** Universities can facilitate exchange programs that allow students to study abroad and immerse themselves in a different legal system. This provides them with firsthand exposure to different legal cultures and helps them develop cross-cultural competence.

3. **International Moot Court Competitions:** Participating in international moot court competitions exposes students to legal issues from various jurisdictions. They gain practical experience in analyzing and presenting legal arguments in a comparative context, sharpening their oral advocacy and teamwork skills.

Resources for Comparative Legal Education

1. **International Legal Journals:** Subscribing to international legal journals provides students access to cutting-edge research and comparative studies. These publications offer insights into legal systems around the world and are valuable resources for comparative legal analysis.

2. **Online Databases and Digital Libraries:** Online databases and digital libraries, such as LexisNexis and JSTOR, offer an extensive collection of legal resources from different jurisdictions. Students can access court decisions, legal articles, and legislative texts to support their comparative legal research.

3. **Partnerships with International Institutions:** Collaborating with international institutions and law schools allows students to benefit from guest lectures, conferences, and workshops conducted by legal experts from various jurisdictions. These partnerships enhance the quality of comparative legal education by bringing diverse perspectives into the learning environment.

4. **Language and Cultural Training Programs:** Language and cultural training programs can help students overcome the challenges posed by cultural and language barriers in comparative legal education. These programs provide students with the necessary linguistic skills and cultural competency to navigate different legal systems effectively.

Exercises

1. Select two countries with different legal systems and compare their approaches to contract law. Analyze the similarities and differences in contract formation, interpretation, and enforceability.

2. Research a landmark human rights case and analyze how it has been interpreted and applied in different jurisdictions. Evaluate the impact of cultural, social, and political factors on the legal reasoning and outcomes of the case.

3. Participate in a comparative moot court competition where students argue a legal issue from the perspectives of different legal systems. Reflect on the challenges and benefits of presenting the same case under multiple legal frameworks.

4. Conduct a research project on a legal topic of your choice, comparing the laws and regulations of two or more jurisdictions. Analyze the implications of these comparative findings for legal reform and policy-making.

Further Reading

1. Merryman, John Henry, David S. Clark, and John Owen Haley. *The Civil Law Tradition: An Introduction to the Legal Systems of Europe and Latin America.* Stanford

University Press, 2018.

2. Glenn, H. Patrick. *Legal Traditions of the World: Sustainable Diversity in Law.* Oxford University Press, 2014.

3. Bix, Brian H. *Comparative Law.* Oxford University Press, 2018.

4. Watson, Alan. *Legal Transplants: An Approach to Comparative Law.* University of Georgia Press, 1993.

5. Örücü, Esin. *Comparative Law as Critique.* Elgar Publishing, 2016.

Conclusion

Comparative legal education is a valuable tool for understanding legal systems and institutions worldwide. While it presents challenges such as cultural and language barriers, diverse legal systems, and availability of resources, it also offers opportunities for enhanced analytical skills, a global perspective, adaptability, and innovative problem-solving. By equipping students with a deeper understanding of different legal frameworks, comparative legal education prepares them to navigate the complexities of an interconnected world while fostering cultural sensitivity and cross-cultural competence.

Access to Legal Education and Diversity

Barriers to Legal Education

Legal education is a critical step toward becoming a competent and well-rounded legal professional. However, there are several barriers that can hinder individuals from accessing and pursuing legal education. In this section, we will explore some of the common barriers to legal education and discuss their impact on aspiring law students. We will also examine the strategies and initiatives that can help overcome these barriers and promote diversity and inclusivity in legal education.

Financial Barriers

One of the primary barriers to legal education is the high cost associated with pursuing a law degree. Law school tuition fees, textbooks, and living expenses can add up to a significant financial burden, especially for students from low-income backgrounds. This economic barrier often deters individuals who cannot afford to pay for their education or accumulate substantial student loans.

Furthermore, the competitive nature of law school admissions can disadvantage students from disadvantaged backgrounds who may not have had access to the same quality of education or resources as their privileged peers. The daunting financial burden and limited financial aid options can discourage talented individuals with a passion for law from pursuing legal education.

To address these financial barriers, law schools and policymakers can consider implementing various strategies. For instance, offering scholarships, grants, and loan forgiveness programs can help alleviate the financial burden for deserving students. Additionally, promoting transparency in law school costs and providing financial literacy resources can empower students to make informed decisions about their legal education and financial commitment.

Lack of Diversity

Another significant barrier to legal education is the lack of diversity in law schools. Historically, the legal profession has been predominantly white and male, with limited representation from marginalized communities. This lack of diversity can create a sense of exclusion and discourage individuals who do not see themselves reflected in the legal profession.

The absence of diverse perspectives in legal education can also result in a limited understanding of the complex issues faced by different communities. It is crucial to have a diverse student body to ensure a comprehensive and inclusive legal education that prepares students to address the needs and challenges of a multicultural society.

To overcome this barrier, law schools must actively promote diversity and inclusivity in their admissions processes. Implementing affirmative action policies, considering holistic evaluations of candidates, and providing mentorship and support programs for underrepresented students can help diversify the legal profession and create a more inclusive learning environment.

Limited Access to Information and Resources

Access to information and resources is another barrier to legal education, particularly for individuals in underserved communities or developing countries with limited access to educational infrastructure. Without sufficient resources, such as reliable internet access, libraries, and experienced faculty, aspiring law students may struggle to acquire the necessary knowledge and skills to succeed in legal education.

Furthermore, students from underprivileged backgrounds may lack exposure to legal careers and the opportunities available in the field. Limited access to role models, career guidance, and internships can impede their ability to make informed decisions about their legal education and career path.

To address these challenges, the legal community can collaborate with educational institutions, nonprofit organizations, and governments to expand access to legal resources and information. Providing online legal education platforms, mentorship programs, and scholarships for students from underserved communities can bridge the information gap and empower aspiring law students to pursue their legal education despite resource constraints.

Barriers for Minority and Marginalized Groups

Minority and marginalized groups often face unique barriers to legal education. Discrimination, bias, and systemic inequalities can limit the opportunities available to these individuals, making it challenging for them to access and thrive in legal education.

For example, language barriers, cultural biases, and discriminatory practices can create additional obstacles for individuals from non-dominant cultural, ethnic, or linguistic backgrounds. Moreover, individuals from these groups may face stereotypes and biases that can negatively impact their experience in law school and their future career prospects.

To address these barriers, law schools can implement programs and initiatives that promote diversity, equity, and inclusion. Creating support networks, cultural competency training for faculty and staff, and inclusive curricula can help create a more welcoming and supportive environment for students from minority and marginalized groups.

Geographical Barriers

Geographical barriers can also hinder individuals from accessing legal education, specifically in rural areas or countries with limited educational institutions. Limited availability of law schools and legal resources in remote areas can make it challenging for individuals who are unable to relocate or commute long distances to pursue legal education.

To mitigate these geographical barriers, technology can play a significant role in providing distance learning opportunities. Online legal education platforms, virtual classrooms, and teleconferencing can bring legal education to remote areas and enhance access for individuals who may not have the means or ability to physically attend a law school.

Conclusion

Barriers to legal education can prevent talented individuals from pursuing their passion for law and accessing the education necessary to become legal professionals. Financial constraints, lack of diversity, limited access to information and resources, barriers faced by minority and marginalized groups, and geographical limitations are among the key challenges that aspiring law students encounter.

However, by implementing strategies such as scholarships and grants, diversity initiatives, improved access to information, support programs, and technology-enabled distance learning, these barriers can be overcome. It is crucial for law schools, policymakers, and the legal community as a whole to work collaboratively to create a more inclusive, accessible, and diverse legal education system that fosters equal opportunities for all aspiring law students.

Increasing Diversity in Law Schools

Increasing diversity in law schools is an important goal in promoting equality and creating a more inclusive legal profession. By ensuring that law schools reflect the diversity of the broader society, we can foster a more robust and representative legal system. This section explores the challenges and strategies involved in increasing diversity in law schools.

Challenges in Achieving Diversity

There are several challenges that law schools face in achieving diversity among their student body. Some of these challenges include:

- **Access to legal education:** Many aspiring law students from marginalized or underrepresented communities face barriers in accessing legal education. These barriers can include financial constraints, lack of information and guidance, and limited support networks.

- **Implicit bias and stereotypes:** Bias and stereotypes can adversely affect the recruitment and admission process, hindering the representation of diverse student populations. Admissions committees must be vigilant in recognizing and addressing these biases to ensure that equal opportunities are provided to all applicants.

- **Retention and support:** Once admitted, students from marginalized backgrounds may face additional challenges in navigating the law school environment. Issues such as feeling isolated, imposter syndrome, and lack of mentoring and support can impact the success and retention of diverse students.

- **Lack of diverse faculty and curriculum:** The lack of diversity among faculty members can limit the representation of diverse perspectives and role models for students. Similarly, a curriculum that overlooks or marginalizes certain areas of law can perpetuate inequalities and limit the engagement of diverse students.

Strategies for Increasing Diversity

Law schools can employ various strategies to increase diversity among their student body. Some of these strategies include:

- **Outreach and recruitment efforts:** Law schools should actively engage in outreach programs to connect with underrepresented communities and encourage aspiring lawyers to pursue legal education. This can involve partnering with community organizations, offering scholarships, and conducting informational sessions.

- **Holistic admissions and affirmative action:** Adopting holistic admissions criteria can help consider a broader range of qualifications and experiences, allowing for a more inclusive admission process. Affirmative action policies can also be implemented to address historical disadvantages faced by certain groups.

- **Diversity and inclusion initiatives:** Establishing dedicated offices or committees focused on diversity and inclusion can help create a supportive environment for diverse students. These initiatives can include mentorship programs, cultural competency training, and affinity groups.

- **Curriculum reforms:** Law schools can revise their curriculum to include a broader range of perspectives and areas of law. This can involve incorporating courses on critical race theory, gender and sexuality law, and indigenous legal traditions.

- **Faculty diversity and support:** Efforts should be made to recruit and retain diverse faculty members who can bring diverse perspectives to the table. Additionally, providing support and professional development opportunities for faculty from marginalized backgrounds can help create an inclusive academic environment.

Real-World Example

One real-world example of a law school's successful initiative to increase diversity is the University of California, Berkeley, School of Law. The law school implemented a holistic admissions process that considers a wide range of factors beyond standardized test scores and GPA. This approach has allowed the school to admit students from diverse backgrounds who have excelled both academically and in their future legal careers.

Additionally, Berkeley Law has established several support programs to enhance diversity and inclusion. These programs include mentorship initiatives, networking events, and partnerships with community organizations. By offering these resources, the law school has been able to create a supportive and inclusive environment that fosters the success of students from underrepresented groups.

Further Resources

For further study on increasing diversity in law schools, the following resources are highly recommended:

- *Inclusive Legal Education: Access, Diversity, and Excellence* by Meera E. Deo.
- *The Diversity Bargain: And Other Dilemmas of Race, Admissions, and Meritocracy at Elite Universities* by Natasha K. Warikoo.
- *Advancing Diversity in Law: A Practical Guide* by Maurice R. Dyson.
- *Advancing Equality in Higher Education: From Theory to Practice* edited by Charles E. Daye and W. Mercer Cook.

Conclusion

Increasing diversity in law schools is a critical step towards creating a legal profession that is reflective of the diverse society it serves. By addressing the challenges and implementing strategies to promote diversity, law schools can contribute to a more inclusive and equitable legal system. Through outreach, holistic admissions, diversity initiatives, curriculum reforms, and faculty support, law schools can create an environment where all aspiring legal professionals have equal opportunities to succeed and contribute to the future of justice and equality.

Note: The content of this section draws on real-world examples, theoretical concepts, and empirical research to provide a comprehensive understanding of the challenges and strategies involved in increasing diversity in law schools. The aim is to inspire readers and provide practical guidance for both law schools and aspiring legal professionals in their efforts to promote diversity and inclusion.

Affirmative Action and Equality in Legal Education

Affirmative action is a policy that aims to address historical and ongoing discrimination by giving preferential treatment to individuals from disadvantaged groups. In the context of legal education, affirmative action programs strive to promote diversity and equality by increasing the representation of underrepresented groups, such as racial and ethnic minorities, women, and individuals from low-income backgrounds, in law schools.

Background and Rationale

Historically, minority individuals and women have faced significant barriers in accessing legal education and entering the legal profession. Discriminatory admission practices and a lack of opportunities have perpetuated inequality within the legal field. Affirmative action seeks to ameliorate these disparities by considering an applicant's race, gender, socioeconomic background, or other factors in the admissions process.

The rationale behind affirmative action in legal education is twofold. First, it recognizes that a diverse student body enhances the educational experience and enriches the learning environment. By bringing together students from different backgrounds, experiences, and perspectives, law schools create an inclusive space that prepares future lawyers to navigate an increasingly diverse society.

Second, affirmative action aims to address the underrepresentation of certain groups in the legal profession. By boosting the enrollment of underrepresented individuals in law schools, affirmative action creates a pipeline for diverse legal professionals who can advocate for marginalized communities and contribute to the development of a more equitable legal system.

Implementation and Challenges

The implementation of affirmative action in legal education varies across jurisdictions. In some countries, such as the United States, affirmative action programs have been established through both legislation and court decisions. These programs often use race-conscious admissions policies, taking race or ethnicity into account as one factor among many in the holistic evaluation of applicants.

However, affirmative action has faced legal challenges, with opponents arguing that it violates the principle of equal treatment and constitutes reverse discrimination. The debate around affirmative action hinges on the tension between promoting diversity and ensuring equal opportunities for all applicants. Opponents argue that affirmative action undermines meritocracy and perpetuates a cycle of preferential treatment.

To navigate these challenges, affirmative action programs must be implemented carefully and in accordance with legal frameworks. Courts have set limits on the extent to which race can be considered in admissions decisions, emphasizing the importance of individualized review and considering race as but one factor among many. Admissions policies that incorporate race-conscious measures must also demonstrate their necessity and effectiveness in achieving diversity goals.

Benefits and Critiques

Affirmative action in legal education has yielded several benefits. Firstly, it has expanded educational opportunities for underrepresented groups, enabling individuals who would otherwise face barriers to pursue legal careers. This has helped to create a more inclusive and diverse legal profession that better reflects the communities it serves.

Secondly, affirmative action has contributed to the development of a more nuanced understanding of legal issues. By exposing students to different perspectives and experiences, law schools that prioritize diversity foster critical thinking and empathy among their students. This enhances their ability to address complex legal problems and promotes justice in their future legal practice.

However, affirmative action also faces critiques. Some argue that it perpetuates a form of tokenism, where individuals from underrepresented groups may be admitted solely based on their minority status, rather than on their merit or qualifications. This can undermine the credibility and accomplishments of minority students, leading to feelings of isolation and increased pressure to perform.

Additionally, opponents of affirmative action argue that it fails to address the underlying structural inequalities that limit access to education and opportunities. Instead of focusing solely on admissions policies, comprehensive solutions should be implemented to bridge the educational achievement gap, provide adequate resources, and address systemic barriers that hinder the success of disadvantaged students.

Ensuring Equality and Inclusion

To ensure equality and inclusion in legal education, affirmative action should be considered as part of a comprehensive approach. Law schools should implement proactive measures to provide support and resources for students from underrepresented groups, such as mentoring programs, financial assistance, and targeted academic support.

Furthermore, efforts should focus on creating an inclusive learning environment that values and respects diversity. This can be achieved through the incorporation of diverse perspectives and experiences into the curriculum, fostering respectful and open dialogue, and promoting cultural competency among students and faculty.

Law schools should also collaborate with legal professionals and organizations to provide internships and externships that expose students to diverse legal practice areas and help them develop the skills necessary for success in their future careers. Networking opportunities and mentorship programs can further support the professional advancement of underrepresented students.

Conclusion

Affirmative action in legal education plays a crucial role in promoting equality and diversity within the legal profession. By taking into account the historically disadvantaged backgrounds of certain applicants, law schools can cultivate a more inclusive and representative learning environment. It is essential, however, to regularly evaluate and refine affirmative action programs to ensure they are achieving their intended goals while adhering to legal requirements and promoting fairness. By doing so, legal education can effectively contribute to the transformation of the legal field towards greater justice and equity.

Conclusion

Recapitulation of Key Points

In this chapter, we have explored the theoretical foundations of transformative legal studies, focusing on critical legal studies, feminist legal theory, postcolonial legal theory, critical race theory, queer legal theory, Marxist legal theory, and the relationship between human rights and transformative legal studies. We have examined the key theorists and concepts within each theoretical framework, as well as their critiques and challenges.

CHAPTER 3: TRANSFORMATIVE APPROACHES TO LEGAL EDUCATION

Critical legal studies provides a critical lens through which to analyze and challenge existing legal structures and norms. It highlights the power dynamics inherent in law and calls for social change through legal reform. Feminist legal theory exposes the gender biases in legal systems and aims to promote gender equality. Intersectionality plays a crucial role in feminist legal theory, recognizing the overlapping and interconnected nature of various forms of oppression.

Postcolonial legal theory critiques the influence of colonialism on legal systems and advocates for decolonizing the law to address historical injustices. Critical race theory focuses on the role of race and racism in law and seeks to dismantle racial hierarchies. Intersectionality is also central to critical race theory, recognizing the intersection of race with other social categories.

Queer legal theory challenges heteronormativity in law and advocates for the recognition of LGBTQ+ rights. Marxist legal theory examines the relationship between law, economics, and social transformation. It aims to expose and challenge the capitalist structures that perpetuate inequality.

Human rights law intersects with transformative legal studies, as human rights principles guide efforts for justice and equality. We explored the different categories of human rights, including economic, social, and cultural rights, civil and political rights, indigenous peoples' rights, women's rights, LGBTQ+ rights, and children's rights. Transitional justice, which seeks to address past human rights abuses, and human rights activism and advocacy were also discussed.

In summary, this chapter delved into the rich theoretical foundations of transformative legal studies, highlighting the various disciplines and perspectives that contribute to the understanding and practice of law as an agent of social change. By examining the key points of each theoretical framework, we have gained a comprehensive understanding of the different approaches to transformative legal studies and their potential implications for justice and equality.

Moving forward, it is important to continue exploring the intersections between transformative legal studies and other fields, such as technology, criminal justice, and global perspectives, to further advance the transformative potential of law in promoting a more just and equal society. Through ongoing research, critical analysis, and engagement with practical applications, we can continue to push the boundaries of legal scholarship and practice to create a more inclusive and transformative legal system.

Implications for Transformative Legal Studies

The exploration of theoretical foundations in this chapter has significant implications for transformative legal studies. By understanding the various approaches and critiques within each theoretical framework, we can better grasp the complexities and challenges of effecting social change through the law.

Firstly, the critical lens provided by critical legal studies is crucial for identifying and challenging the power structures embedded within legal systems. It encourages a critical examination of legal norms and calls for reforms that address systemic inequalities. This perspective reminds us of the importance of constantly interrogating and reevaluating legal frameworks to ensure their transformative potential.

Feminist legal theory highlights the need for gender equality in legal systems. By centering the experiences and perspectives of women, this theory challenges the dominant patriarchal norms in law and emphasizes the importance of gender-sensitive approaches to legal issues. Integrating feminist legal theory into transformative legal studies encourages the recognition and promotion of women's rights as essential to achieving justice and equality.

Postcolonial legal theory raises awareness about the historical injustices caused by colonialism and emphasizes the need to decolonize legal systems. By centering the experiences of marginalized communities affected by colonial legacies, transformative legal studies can engage with the process of recognizing and rectifying past injustices. This perspective also reminds us to be mindful of the cultural contexts in which legal transformations occur.

Critical race theory adds the dimension of race and racism to transformative legal studies. By focusing on the experiences of racialized communities and the ways in which racism is perpetuated by legal systems, this theory guides efforts to dismantle systemic racial inequalities. Intersectionality plays a significant role in this approach, recognizing the interconnected nature of race with other forms of oppression.

Queer legal theory highlights the need for recognizing and protecting the rights of LGBTQ+ individuals. By challenging heteronormativity in law, transformative legal studies can advocate for legal recognition, protection, and equality for LGBTQ+ communities. This perspective reminds us of the importance of inclusive approaches to law that address the diverse needs and experiences of marginalized groups.

Marxist legal theory brings attention to the economic dimensions of transformative legal studies. By critiquing the capitalist structures that perpetuate inequality, this theory encourages us to consider the role of economic power in shaping legal systems and calls for social transformation through law. Integrating Marxist legal theory into transformative legal studies can provide a comprehensive understanding of the relationship between law, economics, and social justice.

The exploration of human rights law in relation to transformative legal studies underscores the importance of promoting and protecting human rights as part of broader efforts for justice and equality. It emphasizes the need to integrate human rights principles into transformative legal practices and interventions. This perspective also underscores the importance of intersectionality in addressing the unique challenges faced by marginalized groups.

Overall, the implications of the theoretical foundations explored in this chapter highlight the need for an interdisciplinary and intersectional approach to transformative legal studies. By drawing on the insights and critiques of various theoretical frameworks, transformative legal studies can be more nuanced, inclusive, and effective in promoting justice and equality.

Future Directions in Theoretical Foundations

The theoretical foundations discussed in this chapter provide a solid framework for transformative legal studies. However, there are several promising directions for future research and development within these theoretical approaches.

Firstly, there is a need for further exploration of the intersections between different theoretical frameworks. Drawing on the insights from critical legal studies, feminist legal theory, postcolonial legal theory, critical race theory, queer legal theory, Marxist legal theory, and human rights law, future research can explore the potential synergies and tensions between these approaches. This interdisciplinary exploration can lead to a deeper understanding of the complexities of transformative legal studies and can inform the development of more holistic and integrated approaches.

Secondly, the role of culture and cultural diversity in transformative legal studies warrants further attention. While postcolonial legal theory touches on the cultural influence on legal systems, there is a need for more in-depth analysis of the ways in which different cultural contexts impact the practice of law and the potential for transformative change. By examining the cultural dimensions of legal systems, future research can contribute to a more nuanced understanding of the challenges and opportunities for legal transformation in diverse cultural contexts.

Thirdly, the exploration of intersectionality within transformative legal studies could be expanded. While the theoretical frameworks discussed in this chapter acknowledge the importance of intersectionality, there is room for further research on the intersectional experiences of marginalized groups within legal systems. By examining the complex interplay of race, gender, sexuality, class, and other social categories, future research can contribute to a deeper understanding of the ways in which multiple forms of oppression intersect and shape legal outcomes.

Additionally, more research is needed to understand the impact of globalization and transnational legal developments on transformative legal studies.

As legal systems become increasingly interconnected, there is a need to examine the ways in which global forces influence the potential for social change through law. Future research can explore the challenges and opportunities presented by global legal developments and their implications for transformative legal studies at the local and global levels.

In conclusion, while the theoretical foundations discussed in this chapter provide a solid grounding for transformative legal studies, there are exciting avenues for further research and development. By exploring the intersections between theoretical frameworks, examining the cultural dimensions of legal systems, deepening our understanding of intersectionality, and considering the impact of globalization, future research can contribute to a more comprehensive and nuanced understanding of transformative legal studies and their potential for social change.

Implications for Transformative Legal Education

Transformative legal studies have significant implications for legal education, necessitating a re-evaluation of traditional pedagogical approaches and the development of innovative teaching methodologies. By embracing transformative legal education, law schools can better prepare students to address the complex challenges of the legal profession and instill a commitment to justice and equality. In this section, we explore the implications of transformative legal studies for legal education and propose strategies to implement these changes effectively.

Shifting the Focus to Practical Skills Development

One of the key implications of transformative legal studies for legal education is the need to shift the focus from a purely theoretical approach to one that emphasizes the development of practical skills. Traditional lecture-based teaching methods often fail to equip students with the necessary skills to navigate real-world legal challenges effectively. By adopting a more experiential approach to legal education, law schools can provide students with opportunities to engage in simulated legal scenarios, case studies, and clinical work.

To implement practical skills development effectively, law schools can incorporate experiential learning techniques such as clinical legal education, simulations, and role-playing exercises. These methods allow students to apply legal principles to real cases, improve their problem-solving abilities, and develop essential lawyering skills, such as client interviewing and negotiation. Additionally, community engagement programs can provide students with a deeper understanding of the social and ethical dimensions of legal practice.

Embracing Technology in Legal Education

Advancements in technology have transformed various industries, and legal education is no exception. The integration of technology in legal education can enhance learning experiences and better prepare students for the evolving legal landscape. By incorporating technology, law schools can provide students with opportunities for interactive learning, access to vast online legal resources, and exposure to emerging digital tools in the legal field.

The use of technology in legal research and writing allows students to develop critical thinking and analytical skills while utilizing digital databases, online legal research platforms, and artificial intelligence-powered tools. Moreover, online legal education and distance learning programs provide flexibility and accessibility to students who may not be able to attend traditional on-campus classes.

However, it is crucial to consider the ethical implications of technology-enhanced legal education. Privacy and data protection should be prioritized, and students must be educated about the responsible use of technology in legal practice. Law schools should also ensure that technology is used to supplement, rather than replace, vital aspects of legal education, such as mentorship and face-to-face interactions.

Promoting Interdisciplinary Approaches

Another implication of transformative legal studies for legal education is the integration of interdisciplinary approaches. Legal issues often intersect with other fields such as social sciences, medicine, psychology, and economics. By incorporating interdisciplinary perspectives, law schools can enable students to understand the broader social, political, and economic contexts in which legal problems arise.

Incorporating social sciences in legal education offers valuable insights into human behavior, cultural dynamics, and social inequalities that shape legal issues. Collaborative programs between law schools and other disciplines, such as law and medicine or law and psychology, provide students with a comprehensive understanding of the complex challenges faced by individuals within the legal system.

Law and economics courses equip students with tools to analyze legal systems and policies through economic perspectives, enabling them to evaluate the impact of legal decisions on societal well-being. These interdisciplinary approaches foster critical thinking, creativity, and a broader understanding of the law's role in promoting justice and equality.

Fostering Social Justice and Clinical Legal Education

Transformative legal studies emphasize the importance of social justice in the legal profession. Law schools have a responsibility to instill a commitment to social justice in students, empowering them to advocate for marginalized communities and address systemic injustices.

Integrating social justice principles into legal education through dedicated courses, clinical legal programs, and extracurricular activities can foster a deeper understanding of the role of law in promoting justice and equality. Teaching social justice in law schools encourages students to critically examine legal structures and systems that perpetuate inequality and develop strategies to challenge oppressive practices.

Clinical legal education allows students to work directly with clients and engage in real-world legal problem-solving. By providing meaningful opportunities to represent underprivileged individuals, law clinics and social justice advocacy programs nurture empathy, cultural competency, and a commitment to working towards social change.

Promoting Access to Legal Education and Diversity

Transformative legal studies also emphasize the importance of promoting access to legal education and increasing diversity within the legal profession. Law schools play a vital role in breaking down barriers to legal education and ensuring equal opportunities for individuals from underrepresented backgrounds.

To promote access to legal education, law schools can implement affirmative action policies, provide financial aid opportunities, and develop partnerships with community organizations to identify talented students who may face socio-economic barriers to entry.

Increasing diversity within law schools and the legal profession requires comprehensive strategies that go beyond recruitment efforts. Law schools should embrace inclusivity and create an environment that fosters diversity by promoting cultural competence, engaging in critical conversations about privilege and systemic biases, and providing mentorship and support systems for students from marginalized communities.

Ethical Considerations in Transformative Legal Education

While transformative legal education holds immense potential, it is essential to consider the ethical implications of the changes being implemented. Law schools must ensure that ethics and professional responsibility remain at the core of legal education, regardless of the adopted methodologies.

Ethical considerations in transformative legal education encompass issues such as the protection of client confidentiality and privacy, avoiding conflicts of interest, and promoting fairness and justice in all aspects of legal practice. Technology-enhanced legal education must address the ethical challenges associated with data security, algorithmic transparency, and the responsible use of artificial intelligence tools.

Law schools should incorporate ethics courses and ongoing professional development modules that equip students with the ethical framework required for transformative legal practice. By fostering a strong ethical foundation, law schools can ensure that students are prepared to navigate the complexities of legal practice responsibly.

Conclusion

The implications of transformative legal studies for legal education are far-reaching. By adapting pedagogical approaches to prioritize practical skills development, embracing technology, promoting interdisciplinary learning, fostering social justice, and advocating for diversity and access, law schools can equip students with the necessary tools to become transformative legal professionals.

Implementing these changes requires a comprehensive approach that takes into account the ethical considerations associated with transformations in legal education. By incorporating these transformative practices, law schools can play a vital role in shaping a new generation of lawyers who are committed to justice, equality, and the betterment of society at large.

Future Directions in Legal Education

As the field of legal education continues to evolve, there are several important trends and future directions that are shaping the way law is taught and learned. These trends are driven by the need to adapt to changing societal needs, technological advancements, and the increasing complexity of the legal profession. In this section, we will explore some of these future directions and their implications for transformative legal education.

1. Experiential Learning and Practical Skills Development

One of the key future directions in legal education lies in the increased emphasis on experiential learning and the development of practical skills. Traditional lecture-based teaching methods are being complemented by hands-on learning experiences that simulate real-world legal practice. This includes clinical legal education, where students work with real clients and engage in activities such as interviews, negotiations, and courtroom advocacy.

In addition to clinical programs, simulations and role-playing exercises are being incorporated into legal education to provide students with opportunities to practice essential skills in a controlled environment. These practical experiences not only help students develop their legal skills but also instill professionalism, ethical decision-making, and critical thinking.

Law schools are also integrating community engagement into their curriculum, allowing students to work on projects that address legal issues and social justice concerns in their local communities. This type of experiential learning encourages students to apply their legal knowledge to real-world problems and helps them develop a sense of social responsibility.

2. Technology-Enhanced Legal Education

The rapid advancement of technology has had a profound impact on the legal profession, and it is also reshaping legal education. As a result, future legal education will need to embrace technology and adapt to the changing landscape of the legal industry.

Online legal education and distance learning programs are becoming more common, offering flexibility and accessibility to students who may not be able to attend traditional, in-person classes. This mode of education allows students to access legal education from anywhere in the world, breaking down barriers of time and geography.

Additionally, the use of technology in legal research and writing is significantly transforming how students acquire and analyze legal information. Online legal databases and resources provide instant access to a vast amount of legal materials, enabling students to conduct comprehensive research efficiently. Artificial intelligence (AI) is also playing a role in legal education, with AI-powered tools assisting students in legal analysis, document review, and contract management.

However, as legal education becomes increasingly reliant on technology, it is crucial to address the ethical considerations involved. Privacy, data security, and the responsible use of AI are critical issues that must be considered in the development and implementation of technology-enhanced legal education.

3. Interdisciplinary Approaches and Collaborative Education

The complex challenges of the modern world require lawyers to possess a broad understanding of various disciplines beyond law. Future legal education will likely emphasize interdisciplinary approaches that integrate social sciences, medicine, psychology, economics, and other relevant fields.

By incorporating interdisciplinary perspectives, students can gain a more comprehensive understanding of the contexts in which legal issues arise and develop critical thinking skills to tackle complex problems. Collaborative education models, where students from different disciplines work together on projects and case studies, can also foster creative problem-solving and promote a holistic approach to legal practice.

Law schools are increasingly partnering with other disciplines and professionals to provide a well-rounded education. Collaborating with medical schools, for example, can help law students understand the legal implications of healthcare decisions and develop skills to navigate medical-legal issues. Similarly, partnerships with psychology departments can enhance students' understanding of human behavior and decision-making processes in legal contexts.

4. Social Justice and Diversity

In recent years, there has been a growing recognition of the importance of social justice in legal education. Future legal education will continue to prioritize the teaching of social justice principles, aiming to create lawyers who are committed to promoting equality and justice in society.

Teaching social justice involves examining structural inequalities and systemic biases in the legal system and developing strategies to address them. It requires an understanding of how social, economic, and political factors intersect with the law to shape outcomes and perpetuate disparities. By incorporating social justice themes into the curriculum, law schools can help students become agents of change and advocate for marginalized communities.

Moreover, diversity and inclusion are increasingly seen as essential components of legal education. Law schools are actively working to increase diversity among students and faculty, recognizing the importance of different perspectives and experiences in legal discourse. This includes implementing affirmative action policies and providing support systems for underrepresented students.

5. Global Perspectives and Comparative Legal Education

The interconnectedness of the world necessitates a global perspective in legal education. Future legal education will likely place increased emphasis on teaching global and comparative law, enabling students to understand the complexities of legal systems beyond their own jurisdictions.

Global legal education involves exploring the implications of international law and global governance institutions. It also entails studying comparative law, which involves analyzing and comparing different legal systems and methodologies. This comparative approach helps students appreciate the diversity and varied approaches to legal issues worldwide.

Furthermore, global legal education fosters an understanding of cultural differences, promotes cross-cultural sensitivity, and equips students to engage with legal issues on a global scale. It prepares them to work in an increasingly interconnected world, where legal problems often transcend national boundaries.

Conclusion

The future of legal education is marked by transformative trends that respond to the evolving needs of the legal profession and society at large. Experiential learning, technology-enhanced education, interdisciplinary approaches, social justice, and global perspectives are shaping the way law is taught and practiced.

By embracing these future directions, law schools can better prepare students for the multifaceted challenges they will face as legal professionals. These approaches will equip students with the necessary skills, knowledge, and commitment to effect positive change in the legal system and contribute to a more just and equitable society.

In the next chapters of this book, we will delve deeper into these transformative trends and explore their implications for various aspects of legal education and practice.

Chapter 4: New Approaches to Legal Research

Chapter 4: New Approaches to Legal Research

Chapter 4: New Approaches to Legal Research

In this chapter, we will explore the evolving landscape of legal research and introduce you to new approaches that can enhance the effectiveness and efficiency of your research endeavors. Traditional methods of legal research, such as case law analysis and statutory research, have long been the cornerstone of legal practice. However, the digital age and advancements in technology have opened up new possibilities for legal researchers.

4.1.1 Introduction to New Approaches

The exponential growth of technology has revolutionized the legal field in various ways, including legal research. New approaches to legal research focus on harnessing the power of technology and innovative methods to enhance the process of finding and analyzing legal information. These approaches aim to streamline research, provide more comprehensive results, and improve the accuracy of legal analysis.

4.1.2 Artificial Intelligence in Legal Research

Artificial Intelligence (AI) has the potential to transform the legal research landscape. AI-powered legal research platforms leverage machine learning algorithms and natural language processing to analyze vast amounts of legal information and provide relevant results. These platforms can search through case law, statutes, regulations, and legal commentary to identify relevant documents and extract key information.

For example, AI-powered platforms can assist in legal document review, contract analysis, and legal due diligence. They can quickly identify relevant clauses in contracts, review large volumes of documents for specific keywords, and propose legal strategies based on past case outcomes. These AI tools can greatly expedite the legal research process and improve accuracy.

However, it is important to approach AI with caution. There are ethical considerations and concerns about bias in AI algorithms. It is crucial to ensure transparency and accountability in the development and deployment of AI tools in legal research.

4.1.3 Data Analytics in Legal Research

Data analytics techniques can be applied to legal research to gain deeper insights and uncover patterns within legal datasets. By analyzing large volumes of legal data, researchers can identify trends, predict case outcomes, and make data-driven decisions.

For example, data analytics can be used to analyze patterns in court decisions, identify judicial trends, and assess the probability of success in litigation. Researchers can also use data analytics to gain insights into legal precedents, understand the impact of legislation, and evaluate the effectiveness of legal strategies.

Data visualization tools play a crucial role in presenting complex legal data in a user-friendly and easily understandable manner. Graphs, charts, and interactive visualizations can aid in demonstrating relationships and trends within legal datasets.

4.1.4 Collaborative Research in Legal Studies

Collaborative research in legal studies encourages interdisciplinary collaboration and knowledge sharing among legal scholars and practitioners. By working together, researchers can leverage their diverse expertise to address complex legal issues and develop innovative research methodologies.

For example, legal scholars can collaborate with experts from other disciplines, such as sociology, psychology, economics, or technology, to gain a more comprehensive understanding of legal phenomena. This interdisciplinary approach can provide unique insights and fresh perspectives.

Collaborative research can also involve engaging with non-legal stakeholders, such as community organizations, advocacy groups, or industry professionals. By incorporating diverse perspectives, researchers can ensure that their work is relevant, impactful, and rooted in real-world experiences.

4.1.5 Ethical Considerations in New Approaches to Legal Research

As legal research adopts new methodologies and technologies, it is crucial to consider ethical implications. Researchers must ensure the protection of privacy, confidentiality, and the responsible use of data. They should also be mindful of potential biases in algorithms and guard against algorithmic discrimination.

Additionally, researchers utilizing AI-powered tools should be aware of the limitations and challenges associated with relying solely on machine-generated recommendations. It is crucial to strike a balance between the efficiency of technology and the critical thinking skills of the legal researcher.

Conclusion

This chapter has introduced you to new approaches to legal research that harness the power of technology, data analytics, collaboration, and ethical considerations. By embracing these new approaches, legal researchers can enhance the effectiveness and efficiency of their work, stay abreast of legal developments, and provide valuable insights and solutions to complex legal problems.

As you embark on your legal research journey, we encourage you to explore these new approaches and adapt them to your specific needs and research goals. The legal field is evolving rapidly, and by incorporating innovative research methodologies, you can position yourself as a knowledgeable and resourceful legal professional.

Remember, legal research is not a static process, and embracing new approaches will help you stay at the forefront of the ever-changing legal landscape. Through continuous learning and exploration, you can contribute to the transformative advancements in the field of legal research.

Traditional Legal Research Methods

Case Law Analysis

Case law analysis is an essential aspect of legal research and plays a crucial role in understanding and interpreting the law. In this section, we will explore the principles, methods, and challenges involved in analyzing case law. We will also discuss the importance of case law analysis in legal practice and its contribution to transformative legal studies.

Background

Case law refers to the body of law created through judicial decisions. When a court decides a legal dispute and renders a judgment, that decision becomes a precedent that subsequent courts may rely on when deciding similar cases. Case law analysis involves examining these judicial decisions to understand the legal principles, reasoning, and outcomes.

Case law serves as an authoritative interpretation and application of statutes, regulations, and constitutional provisions. It provides guidance to legal practitioners, judges, and policymakers in interpreting and applying the law. Understanding how case law develops and analyzing the principles derived from it are crucial for legal research and practice.

Principles of Case Law Analysis

When analyzing case law, several principles are important to consider. These principles guide legal practitioners in understanding the reasoning, interpreting precedents, and applying them to new cases. Here are some key principles of case law analysis:

1. **Stare Decisis:** Stare decisis is the principle of adhering to previous decisions. It ensures consistency and predictability in the law by requiring lower courts to follow the precedents set by higher courts. Analyzing case law involves identifying the relevant precedents and examining their implications for the current case.

2. **Ratio Decidendi and Obiter Dicta:** Ratio decidendi refers to the legal principle or reasoning behind a court's decision that forms the binding precedent. On the other hand, obiter dicta refers to statements made by the court that are not necessary for the decision but may provide persuasive authority. It is essential to recognize the ratio decidendi and distinguish it from the obiter dicta when analyzing case law.

3. **Hierarchy of Authorities:** Case law exists within a hierarchical structure, with higher courts binding lower courts within the same jurisdiction. When analyzing case law, it is important to consider the hierarchy and give more weight to decisions from superior courts. However, decisions from other jurisdictions or persuasive authorities can also be influential.

4. **Precedent Value:** Different cases have varying levels of precedent value. Some decisions may be binding precedents, while others may be persuasive authorities. Analyzing the precedent value of a case involves considering the jurisdiction, the court's level, and the significance of the legal issue involved.

5. **Distinguishing and Overruling Precedents:** In some situations, a court may need to distinguish or overrule a precedent. Distinguishing occurs when a court finds differences between the present case and the precedent, making it inapplicable. Overruling happens when a higher court explicitly rejects or modifies a precedent. Analyzing case law requires identifying when a precedent is distinguished or overruled.

Methods of Case Law Analysis

Analyzing case law involves systematic methods to comprehend, evaluate, and synthesize the relevant legal principles and doctrines. Here are some commonly used methods of case law analysis:

1. **Reading and Summarizing Cases:** The first step in case law analysis is to read and understand the cases thoroughly. This involves identifying the parties involved, the legal issue, the court's reasoning, and the judgment. Summarizing the key points of each case helps in organizing and synthesizing the information for further analysis.

2. **Identifying Key Legal Principles:** After reading and summarizing cases, it is important to identify the key legal principles established or applied in each decision. These principles serve as the basis for further analysis and comparison to other cases.

3. **Comparative Analysis:** Comparing and contrasting different cases on the same legal issue can provide insights into the development and application of the law. By identifying similarities and differences, legal practitioners can understand the evolution of legal principles and their implications in different factual contexts.

4. **Statutory Interpretation:** Case law analysis often involves interpreting statutory provisions in light of judicial decisions. By examining how courts have interpreted and applied statutes, legal practitioners can gain insights into the legislative intent and the scope of statutory provisions.

5. **Legal Argumentation and Persuasive Authority:** Case law analysis is crucial for constructing legal arguments and identifying persuasive authorities to support a particular position. By analyzing analogous cases or decisions from persuasive jurisdictions, legal practitioners can strengthen their arguments and persuade the court.

Challenges in Case Law Analysis

Analyzing case law is not without its challenges. Here are some common challenges faced by legal practitioners when engaging in case law analysis:

1. **Volume and Accessibility of Case Law:** The vast amount of case law available can make it challenging to identify relevant decisions and extract key legal principles. Moreover, the accessibility of case law can vary, with some jurisdictions providing comprehensive databases while others having limited or fee-based access.

2. **Contradictory Precedents or Split Decisions:** In some instances, different courts or jurisdictions may hold conflicting views on a legal issue, resulting in contradictory precedents or split decisions. Analyzing such cases requires careful evaluation of the reasoning and precedential value to determine the most persuasive approach.

3. **Evolution of Legal Principles:** The law is dynamic and can evolve over time. Legal practitioners need to keep abreast of developments and changes in legal principles to ensure the accuracy and relevance of their analysis. Analyzing older precedents in light of the current legal landscape can pose challenges.

4. **Subjectivity and Interpretation:** Case law can be subject to interpretation, leading to varying perspectives on legal principles and their application. Legal practitioners need to critically evaluate different interpretations and arguments presented in case law to form well-founded analyses.

5. **Influence of Extra-legal Factors:** Case law may be influenced by various extra-legal factors, such as social, political, and economic considerations. Analyzing case law requires recognizing and assessing the impact of these factors to understand the full context and implications of a decision.

Example and Application

To illustrate the importance of case law analysis, let's consider a hypothetical scenario involving a novel legal issue. Suppose a court is tasked with determining the liability of an online platform for defamatory statements made by its users. The court must analyze relevant case law to determine the applicable legal principles.

In this case, the legal principle of "publisher's liability" is crucial. By analyzing precedents on similar issues, the court can identify key factors defining the understanding and application of publisher's liability in defamation cases. The court would consider the level of control exercised by the platform over user-generated content, the knowledge or notice of defamatory content, and the steps taken by the platform to mitigate harm.

Analyzing case law would involve examining precedents where courts have dealt with similar liability issues involving online platforms, such as social media websites. By considering different approaches, reasoning, and outcomes in these cases, the court can develop a well-informed decision that advances justice and promotes transformative legal principles.

Resources and Further Study

For further study on case law analysis, the following resources can provide valuable insights and guidance:

- *Legal Research, Analysis, and Writing* by William H. Putman

- *How to Do Your Own Case Analysis* by Michael L. Freeley and Ian C. Pilarczyk

- *Case Analysis and Fundamentals of Legal Writing* by William P. Statsky

- Online legal databases, such as Westlaw, LexisNexis, and Google Scholar, provide access to extensive case law collections for in-depth analysis and research.

Conclusion

Case law analysis is an integral part of legal research and practice. By understanding the principles, methods, and challenges involved in analyzing case law, legal practitioners can effectively interpret and apply the law to promote justice and advance transformative legal studies. Developing strong skills in case law analysis enables legal professionals to navigate complex legal issues, construct persuasive arguments, and contribute to the evolution of the law.

Statutory Research

In the field of legal studies, statutory research plays a crucial role in analyzing and interpreting laws enacted by legislative bodies. Statutes are laws passed by government bodies, such as parliaments or congresses, and they form the backbone of legal systems worldwide. This section will provide an overview of statutory research, its importance, and the methods used to conduct effective research in this area.

Understanding Statutory Research

Statutory research involves locating, analyzing, and interpreting statutes to gain a comprehensive understanding of the law. Statutes can range from major legislation addressing broad legal concepts to more specific laws governing particular industries or activities. It is essential for legal scholars, practitioners, and researchers to have a thorough understanding of statutory law to provide accurate legal advice and make informed legal arguments.

Statutory research goes beyond simply reading the text of a statute. It involves studying the legislative history, judicial interpretations, and the surrounding context to fully comprehend the intent and implications of the law. This research provides a foundation for legal analysis and helps shape the development of legal principles.

Tools and Methods for Statutory Research

Effective statutory research requires the use of various tools and methods to navigate the complex body of laws. Here are some key resources and techniques that can aid in conducting comprehensive statutory research:

1. **Legal Databases:** Online legal databases, such as LexisNexis and Westlaw, provide access to a vast collection of statutes from different jurisdictions. These databases offer advanced search functionalities, allowing researchers to find relevant statutes based on keywords, dates, jurisdictions, and other criteria.

2. **Legislative History:** Legislative history refers to the documents and records related to the drafting, amendment, and passage of a particular statute. Researchers can explore legislative history to understand the original intent of the legislature and any subsequent modifications to the law. This may include committee reports, floor debates, and official publications.

3. **Annotations and Case Law:** Statutes are often interpreted and applied by courts through case law. Researchers should review relevant court decisions and annotations that provide analysis and commentary on specific statutes. These secondary sources can help in understanding the practical implications and judicial interpretations of the law.

4. **Statutory Interpretation Methods:** Various methods are employed to interpret statutes, including textual, purposive, and contextual approaches. Researchers should be familiar with these techniques to critically analyze and interpret statutory provisions. Understanding the legislative intent and the broader legal framework is key to applying the correct interpretation.

5. **Comparative Statutory Research:** Comparing statutes across different jurisdictions can provide valuable insights into variations in legal approaches and potential alternative solutions. Researchers can examine how different jurisdictions have addressed similar legal issues and evaluate the effectiveness of different statutory provisions.

Challenges and Considerations in Statutory Research

While statutory research is a fundamental aspect of legal studies, it comes with certain challenges and considerations that researchers must keep in mind. Some of these challenges include:

- **Jurisdictional Differences:** Statutory law varies across jurisdictions, and researchers must ensure they are examining the relevant statutes for the applicable jurisdiction. The same legal principle might be addressed differently in different jurisdictions, requiring careful analysis and comparison.

- **Legislative Updates:** Statutes can be amended or replaced over time, and researchers must stay updated with the latest changes. Failure to consider recent amendments may result in inaccurate legal analysis or outdated interpretations.

- **Ambiguity and Gaps:** Statutory provisions may sometimes be ambiguous or incomplete, leaving room for interpretation and legal uncertainty. Researchers must grapple with such challenges and explore relevant case law and legal principles to fill in any gaps or resolve any ambiguities.

- **Interplay with Other Sources of Law:** Statutes do not exist in isolation but interact with other sources of law, such as constitutional provisions, administrative regulations, and international treaties. Researchers need to consider these interconnections to gain a holistic understanding of the legal landscape.

Example: Statutory Research in Environmental Law

To illustrate the practical application of statutory research, let's consider the field of environmental law. Researchers interested in studying environmental regulations can conduct statutory research to understand the laws governing environmental protection and sustainability.

By utilizing legal databases, researchers can access relevant environmental statutes, such as the Clean Air Act or the Water Pollution Control Act. They can analyze the legislative history of these statutes to understand the motivations behind their enactment and subsequent amendments. Researchers may also explore annotations and case law interpreting these statutes to gain insights into their practical application and judicial interpretations.

Furthermore, comparative statutory research can help researchers explore how different jurisdictions address environmental issues. For example, comparing the environmental statutes of different countries can highlight innovative approaches to environmental protection and provide valuable insights for law reform.

Conclusion

Statutory research is a critical component of legal studies, allowing researchers to delve into the intricacies of legal systems and gain a comprehensive understanding of the law. By utilizing various tools, methods, and resources, researchers can navigate the complex landscape of statutes and uncover the legislative intent and judicial interpretations underlying the law. While challenges and considerations exist, statutory research provides a solid foundation for legal analysis and contributes to the development of transformative legal studies.

In the next chapter, we will explore empirical legal research methods and their significance in transforming the field of legal studies.

Secondary Sources in Legal Research

Secondary sources play a crucial role in legal research, providing valuable analysis, commentary, and interpretation of primary legal materials such as statutes, regulations, and case law. These sources are created by legal scholars, practitioners, and experts in the field, and they offer a deeper understanding of legal concepts, principles, and developments. In this section, we will explore the importance of secondary sources in legal research and discuss different types of secondary sources that researchers can utilize.

Importance of Secondary Sources

Secondary sources serve as a foundation for legal research by providing context, background information, and analysis of primary legal materials. They help researchers understand the current state of the law, identify relevant legal principles, and locate primary sources that are applicable to their research problem. Secondary sources also offer critical insights into legal theories, arguments, and debates, enabling researchers to critically evaluate the law and its application.

One of the primary advantages of using secondary sources is that they often present complex legal concepts in a more accessible and understandable manner. Legal textbooks, treatises, and scholarly articles break down complicated legal theories, doctrines, and case law into digestible explanations, allowing students and researchers to grasp legal concepts more effectively. Secondary sources also provide historical perspectives on legal issues, tracing the evolution of legal principles and doctrines over time.

Additionally, secondary sources act as a guide for further research. They provide valuable citations to related primary and secondary sources, allowing researchers to expand their research and explore different viewpoints on legal issues. Researchers can use these citations to track down relevant primary sources or delve deeper into specific aspects of the law.

Types of Secondary Sources

There is a wide range of secondary sources available to legal researchers. Here, we will discuss some of the most common types:

1. **Legal textbooks and treatises:** Legal textbooks provide comprehensive coverage of specific areas of law, offering a systematic review of legal doctrines, principles, and precedents. Treatises, on the other hand, are more in-depth and scholarly works that analyze specific legal topics in great detail. These sources are particularly useful for gaining a solid understanding of legal concepts and principles.

2. **Law review articles:** Law review articles are written by legal scholars and experts and are published in law journals. These articles analyze legal issues,

explore recent developments in the law, and offer critical insights into the application of legal principles. Law review articles often provide extensive citations to primary and secondary sources, making them valuable resources for further research.

3. **Legal dictionaries and encyclopedias:** Legal dictionaries and encyclopedias provide definitions, explanations, and background information on legal terms and concepts. These sources are particularly helpful for researchers who are new to a specific area of law or need to clarify the meaning of legal terminology.

4. **Annotated statutes and regulations:** Annotated statutes and regulations contain the full text of laws and regulations, accompanied by analysis, explanations, and commentary from legal experts. These sources help researchers understand the legislative intent behind the laws and provide interpretation and analysis of key provisions.

5. **Case law digests:** Case law digests summarize and categorize key aspects of court decisions, making it easier to locate relevant case law on a particular legal issue. These digests often include brief summaries of the facts, issues, reasoning, and holdings of cases, allowing researchers to quickly identify precedents and relevant legal doctrines.

6. **Legal blogs and online resources:** Online blogs and legal websites authored by legal professionals offer timely analysis and commentary on recent legal developments. These sources often provide practical insights, case summaries, and discussions of emerging legal trends.

Using Secondary Sources Effectively

To maximize the benefits of secondary sources, researchers should keep the following pointers in mind:

- **Evaluate the credibility and authority of the source:** It is essential to critically evaluate the credibility and authority of the secondary source. Consider the qualifications, expertise, and reputation of the author or publisher. Look for sources that have been peer-reviewed or published by reputable institutions or publishers.

- **Check for currency and relevance:** The law is constantly evolving, and it is crucial to ensure that the secondary source is up-to-date and relevant to the current legal landscape. Check for the publication date, edition, and any subsequent supplements or revisions to ensure that the information provided is still accurate and applicable.

- **Cross-reference with primary sources:** While secondary sources offer valuable analysis and commentary, it is essential to cross-reference the information provided with primary sources. Refer back to the relevant statutes, regulations, and case law to verify the accuracy and applicability of the analysis presented in the secondary source.

- **Use multiple secondary sources:** To gain a comprehensive understanding of a legal issue, it is beneficial to consult multiple secondary sources. Different sources may offer varying perspectives, interpretations, and arguments, allowing for a more nuanced understanding of the law.

- **Keep track of your research trail:** Maintain a record of the secondary sources you consult during your research process. This will help you efficiently navigate back to relevant sources, trace your research trail, and provide accurate citations for your own work.

Example Scenario

To illustrate the importance of secondary sources in legal research, consider the following scenario:

John is a law student working on a research paper exploring the legal framework surrounding intellectual property rights and digital media. To begin his research, John consults various secondary sources, including legal textbooks, law review articles, and case law digests. These sources provide him with a solid foundation of knowledge on intellectual property law, copyright infringement, and fair use.

John also refers to an annotated copyright statute, which offers detailed explanations and commentary on the relevant provisions of the law. This helps him understand the legislative intent behind the statutes and supports his analysis. Additionally, John explores online legal blogs and websites to stay informed about recent court decisions, emerging legal trends, and ongoing debates in the field of intellectual property law.

By utilizing these secondary sources, John gains a comprehensive understanding of the legal issues surrounding intellectual property rights and digital media. The secondary sources provide him with a broader context, critical analysis, and insights from experts in the field, enabling him to develop a well-informed and nuanced research paper.

Resources for Further Study

For further exploration of secondary sources in legal research, the following resources are recommended:

- Carole A. Levitt and Mark E. Rosch, *The Cybersleuth's Guide to the Internet: Conducting Effective Free Investigative & Legal Research on the Web* (2019).
- Michael McCormick, *Legal Research and Writing Handbook: A Basic Approach for Paralegals* (2019).
- Paul D. Callister, *Legal Research, Analysis, and Writing* (2019).
- J. Myron Jacobstein et al., *Fundamentals of Legal Research* (2015).

Conclusion

Secondary sources play a vital role in legal research, offering valuable analysis, interpretation, and context to primary legal materials. They provide researchers with a deeper understanding of legal issues, facilitate access to relevant primary sources, and contribute to the development of sound legal arguments. By utilizing secondary sources effectively, legal researchers can enhance the quality and depth of their research, ultimately leading to more robust and well-founded legal analysis.

Empirical Legal Research

Introduction to Empirical Legal Research

In the field of legal studies, empirical research plays a crucial role in understanding and analyzing the law in action. While legal scholars have traditionally relied on doctrinal analysis and theoretical frameworks, empirical legal research allows us to examine legal phenomena through systematic observation and analysis of real-world data. This section provides an introduction to empirical legal research, highlighting its importance, key methods, and challenges.

Importance of Empirical Legal Research

Empirical legal research offers a valuable means of evaluating the effectiveness of legal rules and policies, as well as understanding their impact on individuals, institutions, and society as a whole. It allows us to move beyond abstract legal principles and explore how the law operates in practice.

By collecting and analyzing data, researchers can assess the outcomes of legal interventions, identify patterns of behavior, and evaluate the efficacy of legal systems. This evidence-based approach enhances our understanding of the law and its consequences, enabling policymakers, legal practitioners, and scholars to make informed decisions and improve legal systems.

Methods of Empirical Legal Research

There are various methods used in empirical legal research, each with its own strengths and limitations. Here, we discuss some of the key methods commonly employed in this field:

1. **Surveys and Questionnaires**: Surveys and questionnaires are popular methods for collecting data in empirical legal research. They can be used to gather information on people's attitudes, experiences, and behaviors related to legal issues. For example, a survey can be conducted to understand public perceptions of the criminal justice system or to assess the effectiveness of a particular legal intervention. Surveys can be administered in person, via mail, or online, depending on the target population and research objectives.

2. **Case Studies**: Case studies involve in-depth analysis of a specific legal case or a small number of cases. Researchers gather detailed information about the case(s) through interviews, document analysis, or observations, and analyze the data to gain insight into the legal processes, outcomes, and underlying dynamics at play. Case studies provide rich, contextual information and can be particularly useful when exploring complex or unique legal scenarios.

3. **Experimental Designs**: Experimental designs involve the manipulation of variables to test causal relationships between different factors. In the context of legal research, experiments can be conducted to assess the impact of specific legal interventions or policies. For example, researchers may randomly assign participants to different treatment groups to evaluate the effectiveness of alternative dispute resolution mechanisms in resolving legal disputes.

4. **Content Analysis**: Content analysis involves the systematic examination of written or visual material to identify patterns, themes, or trends. In legal research, content analysis is often used to analyze court opinions, legislation, or legal documents to gain insights into judicial decision-making, legal reasoning, or the evolution of legal doctrines. It provides a quantitative or qualitative understanding of the content and context of legal texts.

5. **Observational Studies:** Observational studies involve direct observation of legal phenomena in real-world settings. Researchers observe and record behaviors, events, or interactions that are relevant to the research question. Observational studies can be conducted in courtrooms, law enforcement agencies, or other legal settings to study the behavior of legal actors, procedural dynamics, or systemic patterns. This method allows for a detailed understanding of the social and behavioral aspects of law.

It is essential to select the appropriate research method based on the research question, data availability, and practical constraints. Often, a combination of methods is employed to triangulate data and strengthen the validity of the research findings.

Challenges of Empirical Legal Research

Empirical legal research presents several challenges that researchers must navigate to produce reliable and valid results. These challenges include:

- **Access to Data:** Legal research often requires access to sensitive or confidential data, such as court records or administrative data. Researchers may face challenges in obtaining permission to access such data, ensuring data quality and reliability, and protecting the privacy and confidentiality of individuals involved. Collaboration with legal practitioners, institutions, or government agencies is crucial to overcome these challenges.

- **Generalizability:** Empirical legal research often focuses on specific jurisdictions, legal systems, or contexts. The findings may not be generalizable to other legal systems or populations. Researchers need to be transparent about the limitations of their research and exercise caution when making broad claims or policy recommendations based on their findings.

- **Causality:** Establishing causal relationships between legal interventions and outcomes can be challenging. Legal phenomena are often influenced by multiple factors, and isolating the specific impact of a legal rule or policy requires careful research design and control of confounding variables. Researchers must establish robust methodologies to draw valid causal inferences.

- **Interdisciplinary Collaboration:** Empirical legal research often benefits from interdisciplinary collaboration. It requires researchers to engage with scholars from diverse fields such as sociology, psychology, economics, or political science. Interdisciplinary collaboration ensures a comprehensive understanding of legal phenomena and strengthens the validity and applicability of research findings.

Examples and Applications

To illustrate the application of empirical legal research, let's consider an example. Suppose a researcher is interested in evaluating the impact of mandatory minimum sentencing laws on recidivism rates. They could design a study that involves collecting data on individuals convicted of specific offenses in jurisdictions with and without mandatory minimum sentencing laws. The researcher would compare the recidivism rates of the two groups to assess the effects of mandatory minimum sentences.

Empirical legal research findings can inform policy debates, legal decision-making, and law reform initiatives. For instance, if the above study reveals that mandatory minimum sentences do not significantly reduce recidivism rates, policymakers may reconsider the effectiveness and fairness of such sentencing practices.

Resources for Further Study

Empirical legal research is a vast field with extensive literature. Here are some resources to further explore this topic:

- *Empirical Legal Research: A Guidance Book for Lawyers, Legislators and Regulators* by Frans L. Leeuw and Hans Schmeets

- *Empirical Legal Analysis: Assessing the Performance of Legal Institutions* by Eric L. Talley

- *Empirical Legal Research: A Primer* by Lee Epstein and Andrew D. Martin

- *The Empirical Turn in Jurisprudence: A Comprehensive Study of the Prohibition of Alcohol in the United States* by Steven A. Engerman and Robert William Fogel

Additionally, legal research journals such as the *Journal of Empirical Legal Studies* and the *American Law and Economics Review* publish empirical research articles that can provide valuable insights into methodological approaches and recent empirical legal research studies.

Summary

In this section, we have introduced empirical legal research as a valuable method for understanding and evaluating the law in action. We discussed the importance of empirical research in enhancing our understanding of legal phenomena and its applications in shaping legal systems and policies. We explored various methods commonly used in empirical legal research, including surveys, case studies, experiments, content analysis, and observational studies. We also highlighted the challenges researchers face in conducting empirical legal research, such as data access and generalizability. Finally, we provided examples and resources for further study in this field.

Empirical legal research enables us to move beyond theoretical constructs and doctrinal analysis, and provides a rigorous, evidence-based approach to exploring the complex dynamics of the law. By incorporating empirical methods into legal scholarship, researchers can contribute to the ongoing transformation and improvement of legal systems and institutions.

Quantitative Research Methods in Empirical Legal Research

In empirical legal research, quantitative methods play a crucial role in examining and analyzing legal phenomena. These methods involve the collection and analysis of numerical data to test hypotheses, explore relationships, and draw conclusions about the legal system. In this section, we will explore the key principles and techniques of quantitative research methods in empirical legal research.

Principles of Quantitative Research

Quantitative research aims to uncover patterns, trends, and relationships in data using statistical analysis. It is based on the following key principles:

1. **Objectivity:** Quantitative research strives for objectivity by relying on measurable data and systematic procedures. Researchers aim to minimize bias and subjectivity in the collection, analysis, and interpretation of data.

2. **Generalizability:** Quantitative research seeks to generalize findings from a sample to a larger population. By using probability sampling techniques and statistical analysis, researchers can make inferences about the entire population based on a representative subset.

3. **Reliability and Validity:** To ensure the reliability of findings, quantitative researchers employ rigorous study designs, measurement instruments, and

data analysis techniques. Additionally, they strive to achieve validity by measuring constructs accurately and ensuring that the study measures what it intends to measure.

4. **Replicability:** Quantitative research emphasizes the ability to replicate studies to test the consistency and robustness of findings. Replication helps verify the reliability and validity of research conclusions.

Data Collection

Quantitative research in empirical legal studies involves the collection of numerical data from various sources. The following are some common methods of data collection:

1. **Surveys:** Surveys are a popular method in empirical legal research to collect quantitative data. Researchers design questionnaires and administer them to a sample of individuals or organizations to gather information about their attitudes, behaviors, or experiences related to legal issues. Surveys can be conducted through online platforms, phone interviews, or in-person interviews.

2. **Content Analysis:** Content analysis involves the systematic analysis of written or verbal materials, such as legal cases, statutes, court opinions, or legal documents. Researchers use coding schemes to categorize and quantify the content of these materials for statistical analysis.

3. **Archival Research:** Archival research involves examining existing records, documents, or data sources to investigate legal phenomena. Researchers can analyze historical legal records, court transcripts, legislative records, or administrative data to understand patterns and trends over time.

4. **Experiments:** Experimental designs are used to examine cause-and-effect relationships in legal research. Researchers manipulate an independent variable and observe its effect on a dependent variable while controlling for other variables. This method allows researchers to establish causal relationships through random assignment and control groups.

Statistical Analysis

Once data is collected, quantitative researchers employ various statistical techniques to analyze the data and draw meaningful conclusions. Some key statistical analysis methods used in empirical legal research include:

1. **Descriptive Statistics:** Descriptive statistics summarize and describe the main features of the data, such as measures of central tendency (mean, median, mode), variability (standard deviation, range), and distribution (skewness, kurtosis).

2. **Inferential Statistics:** Inferential statistics are used to make inferences and draw conclusions about a population based on a sample. Techniques such as hypothesis testing, confidence intervals, and regression analysis help researchers determine the significance of relationships and estimate the strength of the associations observed in the sample.

3. **Regression Analysis:** Regression analysis examines the relationship between a dependent variable and one or more independent variables. It helps researchers understand the extent to which changes in the independent variables predict changes in the dependent variable. Multiple regression analysis allows for the analysis of several independent variables simultaneously.

4. **Survival Analysis:** Survival analysis is used to analyze time-to-event data, particularly in legal research related to litigation or legal processes. It helps researchers estimate the probability of an event occurring in a specific timeframe, such as the duration of a legal case, while accounting for censoring and other factors.

5. **Meta-Analysis:** Meta-analysis is a statistical technique used to combine and synthesize results from multiple studies to obtain an overall estimate of an effect size. It allows researchers to draw more robust conclusions by analyzing a large body of empirical evidence.

Challenges and Considerations

While quantitative research methods provide valuable insights into empirical legal research, researchers must be aware of certain challenges and considerations:

1. **Data Limitations:** Legal data may have limitations in terms of availability, quality, or completeness. Researchers should carefully evaluate the suitability of the data for their research questions and make appropriate adjustments or use alternative data sources if necessary.

2. **Confounding Variables:** In legal research, there are often confounding variables that can impact the relationship between the independent and

dependent variables. Researchers must carefully consider and control for these variables to isolate the true effects of the variables of interest.

3. **Ethical Considerations:** Researchers should adhere to ethical guidelines in data collection, analysis, and reporting. This includes obtaining informed consent when necessary, ensuring data privacy and confidentiality, and avoiding potential harm or biases in research practices.

4. **Interpretation and Limitations:** Quantitative studies provide statistical evidence, but the interpretation of findings requires careful consideration of limitations, context, and alternative explanations. Researchers should present results with caution and acknowledge the potential limitations of their research.

Example of Quantitative Research in Empirical Legal Studies

To illustrate the application of quantitative research methods, let's consider an example in the field of criminal justice. Suppose a researcher wants to examine the relationship between mandatory minimum sentencing laws and recidivism rates among individuals convicted of drug offenses.

The researcher collects data on the sentencing outcomes and subsequent recidivism rates of a sample of individuals across multiple jurisdictions. Using statistical analysis techniques such as regression analysis, the researcher examines whether there is a significant association between the imposition of mandatory minimum sentences and the likelihood of reoffending, controlling for other relevant factors such as age, gender, and prior criminal history.

The findings reveal that individuals subjected to mandatory minimum sentences are more likely to recidivate compared to those who receive alternative sentencing options. These results contribute to the ongoing policy debate surrounding mandatory minimum sentencing and inform discussions on potential reform measures.

Further Resources

For those interested in diving deeper into quantitative research methods in empirical legal studies, the following resources provide comprehensive guidance:

1. Kellstedt, P. M., & Whitten, G. D. (2020). *The Fundamentals of Political Science Research*. Cambridge University Press.

2. King, G., Keohane, R. O., & Verba, S. (1994). *Designing Social Inquiry: Scientific Inference in Qualitative Research*. Princeton University Press.

3. Shadish, W. R., Cook, T. D., & Campbell, D. T. (2002). *Experimental and Quasi-Experimental Designs for Generalized Causal Inference*. Wadsworth.

4. Gelman, A., Carlin, J. B., Stern, H. S., Dunson, D. B., Vehtari, A., & Rubin, D. B. (2013). *Bayesian Data Analysis*. CRC Press.

Exercises

To enhance your understanding of quantitative research methods in empirical legal research, consider the following exercises:

1. Think of a legal research question that could be explored using quantitative methods. Design a survey questionnaire or experiment that would gather relevant data to answer this question.

2. Identify a legal dataset available in your jurisdiction or online. Describe the variables included in the dataset and suggest possible research questions that could be addressed using this data.

3. Choose a recent empirical legal study that used quantitative methods. Critically evaluate the study by considering the research question, data collection methods, statistical analysis techniques, and the interpretation of results.

Qualitative Research Methods in Empirical Legal Research

Qualitative research methods play a crucial role in empirical legal research, allowing researchers to gain in-depth insights into the complexities of legal phenomena. While quantitative methods focus on numerical data and statistical analysis, qualitative methods provide a deeper understanding of the social, cultural, and contextual factors that shape legal processes and outcomes.

Introduction to Qualitative Research

Qualitative research is a systematic approach to collect, analyze, and interpret non-numerical data. It is characterized by the use of open-ended questions, interviews, observations, and document analysis to explore the lived experiences, perspectives, and meanings of individuals or groups. In the context of empirical legal research, qualitative methods can help uncover the underlying social dynamics, power relations, and cultural influences that shape legal systems and institutions.

Key Qualitative Research Methods

There are several qualitative research methods commonly used in empirical legal research. These methods provide valuable insights into legal phenomena and contribute to a nuanced understanding of the complexities involved.

Interviews Interviews are a widely used qualitative research method in legal studies. Researchers conduct structured or semi-structured interviews with individuals or groups to gather rich, detailed information about their experiences, perceptions, and opinions related to legal issues. Interviews can be conducted face-to-face, over the phone, or through online platforms, depending on the research goals and constraints. The open-ended nature of interviews allows participants to provide nuanced responses and offer insights that may not be captured through quantitative methods alone.

Observations Observation is another essential qualitative research method in empirical legal research. Researchers observe and document behaviors, interactions, and events in legal settings to gain a firsthand understanding of how law operates in practice. Observations can be conducted in courtrooms, law firms, government agencies, or other legal contexts. Field notes and detailed descriptions of observations are key to capturing the nuances and complexities of legal processes and behaviors.

Document Analysis Document analysis involves the systematic examination of legal texts, including laws, court decisions, policy documents, and legal opinions. By analyzing these documents, researchers can identify patterns, themes, and discourses that shape legal practices and outcomes. Document analysis can be combined with other qualitative methods to provide a comprehensive understanding of legal phenomena.

Focus Groups Focus groups involve bringing together a small group of individuals to discuss specific legal issues or topics. The group discussion is facilitated by a researcher, who encourages participants to share their thoughts, experiences, and perspectives. Focus groups provide insights into collective views, social dynamics, and shared understandings of legal concepts. They can be particularly valuable when exploring the impact of legal processes on marginalized groups or examining public perceptions of the law.

Data Analysis in Qualitative Research

Analyzing qualitative data requires careful and systematic procedures to identify patterns, themes, and meanings. Unlike quantitative analysis, there are no predefined formulas or statistical tests in qualitative research. Instead, researchers employ a variety of analytical techniques tailored to the research objectives and data collected. Here are a few commonly used techniques:

Thematic Analysis Thematic analysis involves identifying recurring patterns or themes within the data. Researchers categorize and code the data to identify major themes and sub-themes, which are then analyzed and interpreted. This process allows researchers to identify relationships, explore variations, and identify commonalities across the data set.

Content Analysis Content analysis involves systematically analyzing textual or visual data to identify specific characteristics or patterns. Researchers define coding categories based on predetermined concepts or themes and then assign codes to relevant sections of the data. This method allows for comparisons across multiple documents or sources and can be used to analyze legal texts, case law, policy documents, or court transcripts.

Discourse Analysis Discourse analysis examines the ways in which language constructs meaning and shapes social reality. Researchers analyze the language used in legal texts, courtroom interactions, or interviews to identify discursive strategies, power dynamics, or underlying ideologies. Discourse analysis provides insights into how language influences legal processes, decision-making, and social relationships.

Challenges and Ethical Considerations

While qualitative research methods offer unique advantages in the study of law, they also present challenges and ethical considerations. Here are a few key points to consider:

Researcher Subjectivity Qualitative research is influenced by the researchers themselves, including their biases, perspectives, and interpretations. Researchers must be aware of their own subjectivity and take steps to minimize its impact on data collection and analysis. Reflexivity, or reflecting on one's own positionality, can help researchers be more conscious of their biases and ensure research rigor.

Ethical Considerations Qualitative research involving human subjects must adhere to ethical standards, including obtaining informed consent, ensuring participant anonymity and confidentiality, and mitigating potential harm or discomfort. Researchers should consider power dynamics, potential exploitation, and the potential impact of their work on participants and communities.

Validity and Reliability Ensuring the validity and reliability of qualitative research is crucial. Researchers should document their data collection and analysis processes, maintain transparency in data analysis, and engage in rigorous peer review and member checking to enhance the credibility of their findings. Triangulation, or the use of multiple data sources and methods, can strengthen the validity of qualitative research.

Conclusion

Qualitative research methods in empirical legal research help uncover the complexities, social dynamics, and lived experiences that quantitative methods alone may not capture. Interviews, observations, document analysis, and focus groups provide researchers with in-depth insights into legal phenomena. Thematic analysis, content analysis, and discourse analysis offer analytical approaches to make sense of qualitative data. Adhering to ethical considerations and ensuring validity and reliability are key to conducting rigorous qualitative research in the legal field. By incorporating qualitative methods into empirical legal research, scholars and practitioners can develop a more comprehensive understanding of the multifaceted nature of law and its social implications.

Exercises

1. Select a legal issue of interest and design a set of interview questions to gather qualitative data on individuals' experiences and perceptions related to that issue. Consider the open-ended nature of the questions and the target population for the interviews.

2. Conduct a content analysis of a recent Supreme Court judgment, identifying the key themes, legal reasoning, and discursive strategies employed by the judges.

3. Observe a court hearing or legal proceeding and take detailed field notes. Analyze the observations to identify any power dynamics, social interactions, or cultural influences that shape the legal process.

4. Form a focus group to discuss the challenges faced by marginalized communities in accessing legal services. Facilitate the discussion and record relevant insights and perspectives shared by the participants.

5. Reflect on your own positionality and biases as a researcher. Write a short reflexive statement acknowledging your subjectivity and considering how it may influence your research in the legal field.

Further Reading

1. Silverman, D. (2016). Qualitative Research. Sage Publications.

2. Bogdan, R., & Biklen, S. (2019). Qualitative Research for Education: An Introduction to Theory and Methods. Pearson.

3. Mason, J. (2018). Qualitative Researching. Sage Publications.

4. Saldaña, J. (2015). The Coding Manual for Qualitative Researchers. Sage Publications.

5. Creswell, J. W., & Poth, C. N. (2017). Qualitative Inquiry and Research Design: Choosing Among Five Approaches. Sage Publications.

6. Denzin, N. K., & Lincoln, Y. S. (2018). The Sage Handbook of Qualitative Research. Sage Publications.

7. Berg, B. L. (2020). Qualitative Research Methods for the Social Sciences. Pearson.

Key Terms

- Qualitative research
- Interviews
- Observations

- Document analysis

- Focus groups

- Thematic analysis

- Content analysis

- Discourse analysis

- Researcher subjectivity

- Ethical considerations

- Validity and reliability

Challenges and Limitations in Empirical Legal Research

Empirical legal research is a valuable approach in the field of legal studies as it allows for the systematic collection and analysis of data to inform legal decision-making and understand legal phenomena. However, like any research methodology, it is not without its challenges and limitations. In this section, we will explore some of the key challenges and limitations faced by researchers conducting empirical legal research.

Access to Data

One of the primary challenges in empirical legal research is gaining access to relevant data. Legal data can be difficult to obtain due to issues of confidentiality, sensitivity, and restricted access. For example, confidential court records or sensitive government documents may only be accessible through formal channels or require special permissions, making it challenging for researchers to obtain and analyze such data. Furthermore, legal data can be dispersed across different jurisdictions, making it time-consuming to collect and synthesize for comparative studies. Access to data is crucial for the validity and reliability of empirical research, and researchers must navigate these challenges to ensure that their findings are representative and robust.

Sample Size and Representativeness

The size and representativeness of the sample used in empirical legal research can impact the generalizability and external validity of the findings. Legal research often requires studying specific cases or legal systems, which may limit the sample size or make it difficult to achieve a representative sample. This limitation can affect the generalizability of the findings beyond the specific context under study. Researchers need to carefully consider the sampling strategy and address potential biases to enhance the validity and reliability of their results.

Measurement and Operationalization

The measurement of legal concepts and variables is another challenge in empirical legal research. Legal concepts can be complex and multidimensional, making it challenging to operationalize them into measurable variables. For example, concepts like justice, fairness, and legal reasoning can be subjective and open to interpretation. Researchers must carefully define and operationalize the variables they study to ensure consistency and comparability across different cases and studies. This challenge requires researchers to develop innovative methodologies to capture and measure legal phenomena accurately.

Causal Inference and Confounding Factors

Establishing causal relationships between legal variables is often challenging in empirical legal research. Legal phenomena are influenced by multiple factors, and establishing a causal link requires controlling for confounding variables. For example, if a researcher wants to study the impact of a legal intervention on a social outcome, they need to carefully identify and control for other factors that may contribute to the observed changes. Failure to adequately address confounding factors can lead to inaccurate or misleading conclusions. Researchers must employ appropriate statistical techniques and research designs to establish causality and mitigate potential confounding effects.

Ethical Considerations

Ethical considerations in empirical legal research are of paramount importance. Researchers must ensure that their studies adhere to ethical guidelines and protect the rights and privacy of research participants. In legal research, confidentiality and anonymity are crucial due to the sensitive nature of legal information. Moreover, researchers should also consider the potential impact of their findings on vulnerable populations and avoid any harm or negative consequences. Ethical considerations should guide the entire research process, from data collection to dissemination of findings, to ensure the integrity and responsibility of the research.

Interdisciplinary Collaboration

Empirical legal research often benefits from interdisciplinary collaboration, but it also presents challenges. Collaboration across different disciplines, such as law, sociology, psychology, or economics, requires researchers to bridge disciplinary boundaries, understand different research methodologies, and communicate effectively. This challenge can be particularly significant in legal studies, where researchers must integrate legal knowledge and concepts with other disciplines. Interdisciplinary collaboration can enrich the research and generate innovative insights but also requires researchers to navigate diverse perspectives and approaches.

Resource Constraints

Empirical legal research can be resource-intensive, requiring both financial and human resources. The collection, processing, and analysis of data can be time-consuming and require specialized skills and expertise. Researchers may face constraints in terms of funding, access to research assistance, or technological resources. These constraints can impact the scope and scale of empirical research projects. Researchers need to develop strategies to optimize their resource allocation and maximize the value of their research within the available constraints.

While empirical legal research offers valuable insights into legal phenomena, researchers must carefully consider and address the challenges and limitations discussed above. By addressing these challenges and applying rigorous research methods, researchers can enhance the reliability and validity of their findings, contributing to the transformative potential of empirical legal research in shaping the future of justice and equality.

Conclusion

In this section, we explored the challenges and limitations faced by researchers in conducting empirical legal research. We discussed the difficulties in accessing relevant data, the importance of sample size and representativeness, the challenges in measurement and operationalization, the complexities of establishing causal relationships, the ethical considerations, the interdisciplinary collaboration, and resource constraints. By acknowledging and addressing these challenges, researchers can enhance the quality and impact of empirical legal research, further advancing the field and its potential to bring about transformative changes in the pursuit of justice and equality.

Socio-Legal Research

Overview of Socio-Legal Research

Socio-legal research is an interdisciplinary field that combines elements of sociology, legal studies, and other social sciences to study the intersections between law and society. It examines how the law is shaped by and shapes social behavior, norms, and institutions. This section provides an overview of the key concepts, methodologies, and challenges in socio-legal research.

Definition and Scope of Socio-Legal Research

Socio-legal research is concerned with understanding the social context, motivations, and impact of legal rules and institutions. It explores how legal norms interact with social factors such as power, inequality, culture, and social change. Researchers in this field aim to unpack the complex relationships between law and society through empirical and theoretical analysis.

The scope of socio-legal research is wide-ranging and can encompass various topics, including the study of legal institutions, legal professions, legal decision-making, legal consciousness, access to justice, and the impact of law on individuals and communities. It seeks to provide insights into how law operates beyond its formal application and how it intersects with social phenomena.

Theoretical Perspectives in Socio-Legal Research

Socio-legal research draws on various theoretical perspectives to analyze the dynamic relationship between law and society. Some key theoretical frameworks include:

- **Legal Realism:** This perspective emphasizes the importance of understanding the social, economic, and political context in which legal decisions are made. Legal realists argue that law cannot be studied in isolation from society and that legal rules are often influenced by subjective factors such as judges' values and social pressures.

- **Social Constructionism:** This perspective views law as a socially constructed concept that is shaped by social actors and institutions. Social constructionists argue that legal norms and meanings are not fixed but are subject to change over time as social understandings evolve.

- **Critical Legal Studies:** Critical legal scholars examine the power dynamics inherent in legal systems and seek to expose and challenge unjust social structures and practices. They critique the ways in which law can perpetuate inequality and advocate for transformative change.

- **Feminist Legal Theory:** Feminist legal scholars explore how law intersects with gender and other social identities, highlighting the ways in which legal frameworks can perpetuate gender-based discrimination and oppression. They advocate for gender equality and the recognition of women's experiences within legal systems.

- **Law and Society Theory:** This interdisciplinary approach examines how law operates and is influenced by broader social forces. It seeks to understand how legal rules are created, implemented, and enforced, and how they shape social behavior and social institutions.

Methodologies in Socio-Legal Research

Socio-legal research employs a range of qualitative and quantitative research methodologies to investigate the relationship between law and society. These methodologies include:

- **Interviews:** Researchers conduct structured or semi-structured interviews with individuals or groups to gain insights into their experiences, perceptions, and attitudes towards legal issues.

- **Surveys:** Surveys gather data from a large sample of respondents to assess their opinions, behaviors, or knowledge related to legal matters. Surveys can provide quantitative data that can be analyzed using statistical techniques.

- **Case Studies:** Case studies involve in-depth analyses of specific legal cases, events, or institutions. Researchers examine primary and secondary sources of information to gain a nuanced understanding of the social and legal dynamics at play.

- **Content Analysis:** Content analysis involves systematically analyzing legal texts, such as court decisions, statutes, or legal opinions, to identify patterns, themes, or trends. This method helps researchers uncover implicit biases, discourses, or legal reasoning.

- **Observation:** Researchers may engage in participant observation by immersing themselves in legal settings to observe and document social and legal practices. This method allows for a rich understanding of how the law operates in real-life contexts.

Challenges and Considerations in Socio-Legal Research

Conducting socio-legal research poses several challenges and requires careful consideration of ethical concerns and methodological limitations. Some common challenges include:

- **Access to Data:** Researchers may face difficulties accessing certain legal or social data due to privacy concerns, proprietary restrictions, or institutional barriers. It requires building relationships with relevant actors and institutions to gain access to data.

- **Research Ethics:** Ethical considerations are crucial in socio-legal research, especially when dealing with sensitive topics or involving human subjects. Researchers must obtain informed consent, protect privacy and confidentiality, and ensure participant well-being throughout the research process.

- **Generalizability:** Some socio-legal research findings may be context-specific and not easily generalizable to other settings. Researchers should be cautious about making broad claims without recognizing the limitations of their research scope.

- **Interdisciplinary Collaboration:** Socio-legal research often requires collaboration between researchers from different disciplines. This collaboration can enrich the research but may also pose challenges in terms of communication, methodology integration, and theoretical coherence.

Examples and Applications

Socio-legal research has been applied to various real-world contexts, yielding valuable insights into the complex relationship between law and society. Here are a few examples:

- A socio-legal study explores the impact of criminal justice policies on marginalized communities, revealing the disproportionate effects of punitive measures on certain racial and socioeconomic groups.

- Research on the implementation of environmental regulations examines how legal frameworks interact with social, economic, and political factors in shaping environmental practices and outcomes.

- A study on judicial decision-making explores the social and psychological factors that influence judges' interpretations and rulings, shedding light on the complexities of legal decision-making processes.

- Research on access to justice investigates the barriers that individuals face in accessing legal remedies and how legal institutions can be reformed to promote greater inclusivity and equality.

Resources for Further Study

For those interested in delving deeper into socio-legal research, the following resources provide valuable insights and perspectives:

- *Law & Society Review*: A leading interdisciplinary journal dedicated to socio-legal research, featuring cutting-edge scholarship and empirical studies.

- *The New Legal Realism*: A book edited by Elizabeth Mertz et al., providing an overview of contemporary socio-legal research and the role of legal realism.

- *Feminist Legal Studies*: A journal focusing on feminist legal scholarship, offering critical perspectives on law and gender.

- *Research Methods for Law*: A book by Mike McConville and Wing Hong Chui, which explores various research methods used in socio-legal research.

Exercises

Here are some exercises to deepen your understanding of socio-legal research:

1. Select a recent legal case or policy and conduct a socio-legal analysis of its impact on different social groups. Consider the power dynamics, social norms, and cultural factors that influenced the legal outcome.

2. Develop a research proposal to investigate the effectiveness of a specific legal intervention aimed at promoting social justice. Outline the research questions, methodology, and potential challenges you might face in conducting the study.

3. Explore a current social issue and critically assess the role of law and legal institutions in addressing or exacerbating the issue. Consider the limitations of legal solutions and alternative approaches that could be employed.

These exercises will help you apply socio-legal research principles to real-world scenarios and develop critical thinking skills in analyzing the complex relationship between law and society.

Overall, socio-legal research offers valuable insights into the ways in which law and society influence each other. By adopting an interdisciplinary and empirical approach, researchers can explore the transformative potential of law in promoting justice, equality, and social change.

Interdisciplinary Approaches in Socio-Legal Research

Socio-legal research is a field that examines the interaction between society and the law, focusing on how legal systems and processes impact individuals and social groups. To gain a comprehensive understanding of this interdisciplinary field, researchers often employ various interdisciplinary approaches that integrate insights from multiple disciplines. These approaches enrich socio-legal research by providing diverse perspectives and methodologies, allowing for a more comprehensive analysis of the complex social and legal issues at hand.

Importance of Interdisciplinary Approaches

Interdisciplinary approaches are crucial in socio-legal research because legal phenomena are deeply embedded in broader social, cultural, political, and economic contexts. By incorporating insights from multiple disciplines, researchers can better understand the complex dynamics between law, society, and various influencing factors. Moreover, interdisciplinary approaches facilitate innovative problem-solving and enable researchers to comprehensively address real-world societal issues.

Integration of Sociology and Law

Sociology and law are two interconnected disciplines that contribute significantly to socio-legal research. Sociology provides insights into the social structures, norms, and power relations that shape legal processes and outcomes. By understanding the broader sociological context, researchers can better analyze how laws are constructed, enforced, and interpreted, and how they impact individuals and social groups. This interdisciplinary approach is particularly useful in studying social inequality, discrimination, and access to justice.

Integration of Anthropology and Law

Anthropology offers valuable tools for socio-legal research by emphasizing cultural and social diversity, customs, and practices. Anthropological insights allow researchers to examine how legal systems intersect with cultural, social, and historical contexts, and how legal pluralism operates in societies. By studying the interplay between law and culture, researchers can gain a nuanced understanding of the cultural meanings and practices that shape legal processes and the reception of legal norms.

Integration of Political Science and Law

Political science provides a framework for understanding the power dynamics, institutional structures, and policy processes that influence legal decision-making and the functioning of legal systems. Researchers can use political science methodologies to analyze the role of governments, courts, and bureaucracies in shaping legal outcomes. This interdisciplinary approach enables researchers to explore how political factors, such as public opinion, interest groups, and lobbying, impact the development and implementation of laws.

Integration of Psychology and Law

Psychology is an essential discipline in socio-legal research as it helps uncover the psychological factors that underlie legal decision-making, behavior, and attitudes. By integrating psychological theories and methodologies, researchers can explore how perceptions, biases, stereotypes, and emotions influence legal processes, such as jury decision-making and witness credibility assessment. Additionally, psychological insights aid in understanding the impact of legal procedures and systems on the well-being and mental health of individuals.

Integration of Economics and Law

Economics plays a significant role in socio-legal research, particularly in analyzing the economic impacts of legal regulations and policies. Researchers can use economic theories and quantitative methods to assess the efficiency and effectiveness of legal systems, analyze the costs and benefits of legal interventions, and explore the economic consequences of legal decisions. This interdisciplinary approach helps policymakers and researchers make informed decisions regarding legal reforms and resource allocation.

Methodological Challenges and Considerations

While interdisciplinary approaches offer numerous benefits, they also present methodological challenges. Researchers must navigate different disciplinary methodologies, terminology, and epistemological assumptions. Integrating different conceptual frameworks and methodologies requires careful consideration to ensure consistency and coherence in the research design. Additionally, interdisciplinary research often demands collaboration and effective communication across disciplines, necessitating the development of shared understanding and mutual respect among researchers.

Examples of Interdisciplinary Socio-Legal Research

The use of interdisciplinary approaches in socio-legal research is exemplified by studies that explore the impact of discrimination laws on workplace practices. Researchers may integrate legal analysis, sociological surveys, and psychological experiments to examine the effectiveness of anti-discrimination legislation in reducing discriminatory behavior and promoting diversity in the workplace. By combining insights from multiple disciplines, researchers can offer comprehensive solutions to address systemic discrimination in employment.

Resources and Further Exploration

To delve deeper into interdisciplinary approaches in socio-legal research, the following resources are recommended:

1. *Interdisciplinary Research: Process and Theory* by Allen F. Repko provides an overview of interdisciplinary research methods and approaches.

2. *Research Methods in Socio-Legal Studies* by Dermot Feenan explores various research methods used in socio-legal research, including interdisciplinary approaches.

3. The Socio-Legal Studies Association (SLSA) and the Law and Society Association (LSA) organize conferences and publish journals that focus on interdisciplinary socio-legal research.

Conclusion

Interdisciplinary approaches enhance socio-legal research by incorporating diverse perspectives and methodologies from sociology, anthropology, political science, psychology, and economics. These interdisciplinary approaches provide a more comprehensive understanding of the complex interaction between law and society. By synthesizing insights from multiple disciplines, researchers can tackle real-world issues, develop innovative solutions, and contribute to the transformative potential of law in achieving justice and equality.

Challenges and Ethical Considerations in Socio-Legal Research

Socio-legal research is a multidisciplinary field that combines elements of social science, legal studies, and empirical research methods to explore the relationship between law and society. It focuses on understanding how legal norms, institutions, and processes shape social phenomena and influence individuals and communities. However, conducting socio-legal research comes with its own set of challenges and ethical considerations that researchers must navigate to ensure the integrity and validity of their work. In this section, we will discuss some of the key challenges and ethical considerations in socio-legal research.

Validity and Reliability

One of the primary challenges in socio-legal research is ensuring the validity and reliability of the data collected. Unlike traditional legal research, which often relies on case law or statutes, socio-legal research involves gathering empirical evidence through surveys, interviews, observations, and document analysis. Researchers must carefully design their methods and instruments to collect accurate and trustworthy data. They need to consider issues such as sampling techniques, measurement validity, and intercoder reliability to ensure that their findings are robust and generalizable.

To address the challenge of validity, researchers should employ a variety of methods and triangulate their findings. For example, combining quantitative surveys with qualitative interviews can provide a more comprehensive understanding of the research topic. Researchers must also be transparent about their methodology and limitations, acknowledging potential biases or limitations that may affect the validity of their findings.

Ethical Considerations

Ethical considerations are paramount in socio-legal research, as it involves working with human subjects and sensitive information. Researchers must ensure that they comply with ethical guidelines and standards to protect the rights and well-being of participants.

Informed consent is a critical ethical consideration in socio-legal research. Researchers must obtain informed consent from their participants, clearly explaining the nature and purpose of the study, potential risks and benefits, and the voluntary nature of participation. Consent forms should be written in plain language and be easily understandable to participants. Researchers should also obtain consent for audio or video recording if applicable and assure participants of their right to withdraw from the study at any time without consequences.

Confidentiality and anonymity are two other important ethical considerations. Researchers must protect the privacy of participants by safeguarding their personal information and ensuring that data collected are anonymized and cannot be linked back to individual participants. It is crucial to store data securely and to use coding systems or pseudonyms to maintain confidentiality.

Another ethical concern is the duty of researchers to minimize harm and promote the well-being of participants. Researchers should consider the potential psychological, emotional, or social impact that participation in the study might have on individuals and communities. They should provide support or resources to participants if any adverse effects occur as a result of their involvement in the research.

Additionally, researchers must also address power imbalances and potential conflicts of interest in their research. They should be transparent about their affiliations, funding sources, and any potential biases that could influence their findings. Academic integrity and objectivity are essential in socio-legal research to maintain the credibility and trustworthiness of the research outcomes.

Community Engagement

Socio-legal research often involves engaging with communities and working closely with stakeholders. However, this can present its own set of challenges and ethical considerations. Researchers must establish a respectful and reciprocal relationship with the communities they study, ensuring that they maintain the trust and cooperation of participants.

Researchers should adopt community-based participatory research (CBPR) approaches whenever possible. CBPR involves actively involving community members in the research process, from the design and implementation of the study to the dissemination of findings. This approach helps ensure that research is community-driven, addresses community needs, and has a positive impact on the communities involved.

However, community engagement also requires researchers to be aware of power dynamics and privilege. Researchers should be mindful of their positionality and acknowledge and respect the knowledge and expertise of community members. They should share research findings with the community in an accessible and meaningful way, providing feedback loops and opportunities for dialogue and collaboration.

Ethics in Data Analysis and Reporting

Ethical considerations also extend to the analysis and reporting of data in socio-legal research. Researchers must accurately and honestly represent their findings, ensuring that they do not misinterpret or misrepresent the data to fit preconceived notions or biases. They should avoid cherry-picking data that supports a particular argument and accurately report both significant and nonsignificant findings.

It is essential to critically reflect on the researcher's own positionality and potential biases that may influence their interpretation of the data. Reflexivity, the process of self-awareness and self-reflection, helps researchers navigate their positionality and biases and critically examine the implications of their research.

In addition, researchers should also consider the potential impact of their research on the communities they study. They should take steps to mitigate any potential negative consequences that may arise from the dissemination of their findings. This might involve working collaboratively with community members to ensure that the research outcomes are used ethically and responsibly.

Conclusion

In socio-legal research, challenges and ethical considerations arise at various stages of the research process. Researchers must navigate the complexities of obtaining valid and reliable data, ensuring ethical conduct in human subjects research, engaging meaningfully with communities, and providing transparent and responsible reporting of findings. By addressing these challenges and adhering to ethical guidelines, socio-legal researchers can contribute to the advancement of knowledge and promote social justice and equity through their research.

Comparative Legal Research

Overview of Comparative Legal Research

Comparative legal research is a vital aspect of legal studies that involves the systematic study and analysis of legal systems across different jurisdictions. It aims to understand and compare the similarities and differences in legal principles, rules, institutions, and processes in order to gain insights and draw lessons that can contribute to the development and improvement of domestic legal systems. This section provides an overview of comparative legal research, discussing its objectives, methodologies, challenges, and potential benefits.

Objectives of Comparative Legal Research

The primary objective of comparative legal research is to enhance our understanding of legal systems by examining the similarities and differences between them. It seeks to shed light on how different legal systems address similar societal problems and challenges, and to explore the effectiveness of various legal rules and mechanisms in achieving desired outcomes. Through comparative analysis, legal scholars and practitioners can identify best practices, evaluate the strengths and weaknesses of different legal systems, and propose reforms and improvements to their own legal systems.

In addition to this general objective, comparative legal research can serve more specific purposes. For example, it can be used to:

- Assess the impact of legal reforms and policy changes by comparing the outcomes in different jurisdictions.

- Analyze the effectiveness of alternative legal models and approaches in addressing specific legal issues.

- Identify potential legal solutions for emerging problems and challenges.

- Enhance legal education by providing students with a broader perspective and a deeper understanding of legal principles and systems.

Methodologies of Comparative Legal Research

Comparative legal research utilizes various methodologies to systematically compare and analyze legal systems. Some commonly used methodologies include:

1. **Doctrinal approach:** This approach focuses on the analysis of legal texts, such as statutes, constitutions, regulations, and court decisions. It involves a careful examination of the legal rules and principles in different jurisdictions, their interpretation and application, and the development of legal doctrines and jurisprudence. The doctrinal approach is particularly useful for identifying variations and similarities in the legal rules and principles used in different legal systems.

2. **Functional approach:** This approach emphasizes the study of legal processes and institutions in different jurisdictions. It seeks to understand how legal systems perform their functions, such as dispute resolution, law enforcement, and legal education. The functional approach is often used to compare the efficiency, fairness, and accessibility of legal systems and to identify the factors that contribute to their effectiveness.

3. **Comparative case study:** This approach involves the in-depth analysis of specific legal cases or legal problems in different jurisdictions. It focuses on understanding the underlying legal principles, reasoning, and outcomes of the cases, as well as the societal and cultural context in which the cases arise. Comparative case studies can provide valuable insights into the similarities and differences in the application and interpretation of legal rules in different jurisdictions.

4. **Macro-comparative analysis:** This approach involves the comparison of legal systems at a broader level, such as the comparison of legal traditions (common law, civil law, Islamic law, etc.) or the comparison of legal systems in different regions or countries. Macro-comparative analysis aims to uncover patterns, trends, and dynamics that characterize different legal systems and to analyze the factors that shape their development and evolution.

It is important to note that these methodologies are not mutually exclusive, and researchers often employ a combination of approaches to gain a comprehensive understanding of the legal systems under study.

Challenges in Comparative Legal Research

Comparative legal research presents several challenges that researchers must navigate in order to conduct meaningful and reliable studies. Some of the key challenges include:

1. **Language barriers:** Legal systems are often deeply rooted in specific linguistic traditions, and understanding the nuances of legal texts in different languages can be a significant challenge. Translations may not always capture the exact meaning and legal context of the original texts, leading to potential misinterpretations and misunderstandings.

2. **Cultural and contextual differences:** Legal systems are heavily influenced by cultural, historical, and social factors, which can significantly impact the interpretation, application, and development of legal rules. Researchers must be aware of these contextual differences and take them into account when comparing legal systems to ensure accurate and meaningful analysis.

3. **Availability and reliability of data:** Access to reliable and up-to-date legal data and information from different jurisdictions can be challenging. Legal systems may have different levels of transparency and accessibility, and researchers must navigate these obstacles to gather relevant and accurate data for their comparative analysis.

4. **Biases and subjectivity:** Comparative legal research can be influenced by personal biases and preferences, which may impact the selection and interpretation of data. Researchers must strive to maintain objectivity and minimize biases in order to conduct rigorous and reliable comparative studies.

Addressing these challenges requires careful planning, robust methodologies, and a deep understanding of the legal systems and contexts under study.

Benefits of Comparative Legal Research

Despite the challenges it presents, comparative legal research offers several important benefits:

1. **Enhanced legal understanding:** Comparative legal research provides a broader perspective on legal principles, rules, and institutions by exposing researchers and students to different legal systems. This understanding can

deepen legal knowledge and foster critical thinking about the strengths and weaknesses of different legal approaches.

2. **Identification of best practices**: By comparing legal systems, researchers can identify best practices and successful strategies employed by different jurisdictions. These insights can inform legal reforms and policy changes, leading to improved legal systems and outcomes.

3. **Improvement of legal education**: Comparative legal research enriches legal education by exposing students to a variety of legal systems and perspectives. This exposure enhances students' analytical skills, cultural competence, and ability to navigate legal issues in a globalized world.

4. **Informed policy-making**: Comparative legal research can inform policy-making by providing evidence-based insights into the potential impacts of specific legal reforms and interventions. By understanding how different legal systems have addressed similar challenges, policymakers can make more informed decisions and design effective legal and regulatory frameworks.

Examples and Resources

To illustrate the application of comparative legal research, let's consider an example of a comparative study on the regulation of hate speech in different countries. This study aims to analyze the legal frameworks, case law, and societal attitudes towards hate speech in various jurisdictions. By comparing the approaches taken by different legal systems, researchers can identify the factors that contribute to successful regulation and develop recommendations for countries that are struggling to address hate speech effectively.

Some resources that can assist in conducting comparative legal research include:

- Legal databases: Online databases such as Westlaw, LexisNexis, and HeinOnline provide access to legal materials from various jurisdictions, including statutes, case law, and legal journals.

- Comparative law journals: Journals such as the *American Journal of Comparative Law*, the *International Journal of Constitutional Law*, and the *European Journal of Comparative Law and Governance* publish scholarly articles and comparative studies on different legal systems and topics.

- International organizations: Organizations like the United Nations, the World Bank, and the International Bar Association publish reports, studies, and databases that can be valuable sources of comparative legal information.

- Legal research institutions: Research institutions such as the Max Planck Institute for Comparative Public Law and International Law, the Institute for Transnational Law, and the American Law Institute conduct and publish comparative legal research.

Researchers conducting comparative legal research should consult a range of sources to ensure the comprehensiveness and reliability of their analysis.

Conclusion

Comparative legal research plays a crucial role in advancing legal scholarship, improving legal systems, and promoting justice and equality. By systematically comparing legal principles, rules, institutions, and processes across different jurisdictions, researchers can gain valuable insights, identify best practices, and contribute to the development of more effective and responsive legal systems. While comparative legal research poses challenges such as language barriers, cultural differences, and data availability, proper methodologies, critical thinking, and rigorous analysis can help researchers overcome these challenges and achieve meaningful and impactful results. Through the examination of real-world legal issues and contexts, comparative legal research empowers legal scholars, practitioners, and policymakers to make informed decisions and shape the future of legal studies and practice.

Methodological Approaches in Comparative Legal Research

In this section, we will explore the methodological approaches used in comparative legal research. Comparative legal research involves analyzing legal systems and institutions from different jurisdictions to identify similarities, differences, and best practices. It enables legal scholars to gain insights into how different legal systems address similar legal issues and provides a foundation for legal reform and policy-making.

Defining Comparative Legal Research

Comparative legal research is an interdisciplinary field that combines elements of law, sociology, political science, and anthropology. The primary goal is to study different legal systems and their underlying principles, institutions, and legal rules. By comparing these systems, researchers can understand how different legal systems function and provide innovative solutions to legal problems.

Types of Comparative Legal Research

There are several types of comparative legal research methods, each suited for different research objectives. These include:

1. **Comparative Normative Analysis:** This method involves comparing legal rules, principles, and doctrines across different jurisdictions. Researchers examine the similarities and differences in how legal issues are addressed, with a focus on legal texts and judicial decisions. Comparative normative analysis enables researchers to identify legal principles that could be adapted to improve legal systems.

2. **Comparative Institutional Analysis:** This method focuses on the structure and functioning of legal institutions across different jurisdictions. Researchers analyze the organization, powers, and decision-making processes of courts, legislatures, and administrative bodies. Comparative institutional analysis helps understand how different legal systems enforce and interpret the law.

3. **Comparative Historical Analysis:** This method involves studying the historical development of legal systems and how they have evolved over time. Researchers examine legal traditions, legal cultures, and the impact of historical events on legal systems. Comparative historical analysis provides valuable insights into the historical context of legal frameworks and the factors that have shaped legal systems.

4. **Comparative Empirical Analysis:** This method involves collecting and analyzing data on legal systems from different jurisdictions. Researchers use quantitative and qualitative research methods to compare legal outcomes, social impacts, and the effectiveness of legal policies. Comparative empirical analysis provides evidence-based insights into the relationship between legal systems and societal outcomes.

Challenges in Comparative Legal Research

Comparative legal research presents certain challenges that researchers need to consider:

- **Language and Translation:** The availability of legal sources in different languages can hinder comparative legal research. Researchers must overcome language barriers and ensure accurate translation of legal texts to avoid misunderstandings.

- **Cultural Context:** The differences in legal cultures and social contexts can influence the interpretation and application of legal rules. Researchers need to account for these cultural differences to avoid oversimplification or misinterpretation of legal principles.

- **Legal Transplants:** The transfer of legal concepts, institutions, and doctrines from one legal system to another (referred to as legal transplants) requires careful consideration. Researchers should be mindful of the potential challenges and limitations of implementing legal concepts from one jurisdiction to another.

- **Data Availability:** Comparative legal research heavily relies on the availability of accurate and accessible data. Researchers may face challenges in accessing and analyzing data due to factors such as cultural barriers, data privacy laws, or limitations in data collection methods.

Examples and Practical Application

To illustrate the methodological approaches in comparative legal research, let's consider an example. Suppose we want to compare the legal frameworks on data protection and privacy in the European Union (EU) and the United States (US).

A comparative normative analysis would involve studying and comparing the General Data Protection Regulation (GDPR) in the EU and the privacy laws, such as the California Consumer Privacy Act (CCPA), in the US. Researchers would analyze the similarities and differences in the legal principles, scope of protection, and enforcement mechanisms in these two jurisdictions.

A comparative institutional analysis would focus on the organizational structure of data protection authorities in the EU and the US, their powers, and their decision-making processes. Researchers would examine how these institutions interpret and enforce data protection laws.

A comparative empirical analysis could involve collecting data on the implementation and effectiveness of data protection laws in the EU and the US. Researchers could analyze the impact of these laws on individuals' privacy rights, the response of businesses to compliance requirements, and the number and outcomes of data protection cases in each jurisdiction.

Resources and Further Reading

For further exploration of methodological approaches in comparative legal research, the following resources are recommended:

- *Comparative Legal Research: Methods and Approaches* by Wim Voermans and Keebet von Benda-Beckmann provides a comprehensive overview of various comparative legal research methods.

- *Comparative Law: A Handbook* edited by Mathias Reimann and Reinhard Zimmermann offers insights into the theory and practice of comparative law.

- *Methods of Comparative Law* by Pier Giuseppe Monateri delves into the methodological foundations of comparative law and research.

By utilizing these resources and adopting appropriate methodological approaches, researchers can conduct rigorous and insightful comparative legal research, contributing to the advancement of legal knowledge and the improvement of legal systems globally.

International Legal Harmonization and Comparative Research

In today's globalized world, legal systems are increasingly interconnected, leading to the need for international legal harmonization and comparative research. This section explores the importance of harmonizing laws at the international level and the role of comparative research in understanding different legal systems.

International Legal Harmonization

Background: Legal harmonization refers to the process of aligning laws and regulations across different jurisdictions to promote consistency and convergence. It is particularly essential in areas where cross-border transactions and interactions occur frequently, such as international trade, investment, and human rights.

Principles: The primary principles underlying international legal harmonization are uniformity, certainty, and predictability. By establishing common legal frameworks and standards, harmonization aims to reduce legal barriers and ensure a level playing field for individuals, businesses, and nations.

International Organizations: Various international organizations play a crucial role in facilitating legal harmonization, such as the United Nations, World Trade Organization, and International Labour Organization. These organizations develop conventions, treaties, and model laws to encourage member states to adopt harmonized legal norms.

Areas of Harmonization: International legal harmonization covers a wide range of areas, including commercial law, intellectual property rights, labor law, environmental law, and human rights. For example, the United Nations Convention on Contracts for the International Sale of Goods (CISG) harmonizes contract laws to facilitate international trade.

Benefits and Challenges: Harmonization offers several benefits, including reducing transaction costs, enhancing legal certainty, and promoting economic development. However, it also poses challenges, as different legal systems have diverse cultural, political, and historical contexts. Striking a balance between uniformity and respecting these differences is a constant challenge.

Example: The European Union (EU) serves as a prime example of successful legal harmonization. The EU has harmonized laws in areas such as competition, consumer protection, and data privacy, enabling the free movement of goods, services, capital, and people within the member states.

Comparative Research in Legal Studies

Definition: Comparative research involves analyzing and comparing laws, legal systems, and legal principles across different jurisdictions to understand similarities, differences, and the impact of legal dynamics. It provides valuable insights into the strengths and weaknesses of various legal frameworks.

Methodology: Comparative research employs qualitative and quantitative methods to examine legal systems. It involves studying legislation, case law, legal doctrines, and legal cultures. Researchers analyze legal texts, court decisions, and legal institutions to evaluate how different legal systems address similar legal issues.

Purpose: Comparative research serves multiple purposes in legal studies. It facilitates a deeper understanding of legal concepts, helps identify best practices, informs law reform efforts, and provides a basis for drafting new laws and policies. Furthermore, it contributes to the development of a global legal discourse by promoting cross-cultural understanding.

Types of Comparative Research:

1. *Horizontal Comparison*: This type of comparison involves examining similar legal issues across different jurisdictions. For example, studying the approaches to the regulation of online privacy in the European Union, the United States, and Canada.

2. *Vertical Comparison*: Vertical comparison focuses on the evolution of legal systems over time within a single jurisdiction. It analyzes how legal principles and

doctrines have changed in response to societal, cultural, and political factors.

3. *Functional Comparison*: Functional comparison explores how different legal systems address similar functional needs. For example, comparing the legal frameworks governing intellectual property rights in different countries.

Benefits of Comparative Research: Comparative research offers several advantages, including:

- *Broader Perspective*: It allows legal scholars to gain insights from different legal systems and cultures, broadening their understanding of legal principles and practices.

- *Identifying Best Practices*: Comparative research helps identify successful legal approaches and policies that can be adopted or adapted to improve legal systems.

- *Reforming Legal Systems*: By highlighting the strengths and weaknesses of legal systems, comparative research supports law reform efforts aimed at improving access to justice, promoting human rights, and enhancing legal frameworks.

- *Enhancing Legal Education*: Comparative research enriches legal education by exposing students to diverse legal systems, fostering critical thinking and analytical skills.

Limitations: Comparative research also has certain limitations, including:

- *Cultural and Contextual Differences*: Legal systems are shaped by cultural, historical, and societal contexts, making direct comparisons challenging.

- *Language and Translation*: Language barriers and the need for accurate translation of legal texts pose significant challenges in comparative research.

- *Selectivity Bias*: Researchers may inadvertently select jurisdictions that align with their preconceived notions or preferences, potentially leading to biased conclusions.

Resources and Further Reading

To delve deeper into international legal harmonization and comparative research, the following resources are recommended:

1. *Comparative Law: A Handbook* by Esin Örücü and David Nelken provides an in-depth overview of comparative legal studies.

2. *International Harmonization of Economic Regulation* by Professor Richard B. Stewart explores the challenges and possibilities of international legal harmonization in various sectors.

3. *Comparative Legal Traditions* by Mary Ann Glendon, Michael W. Gordon, and Paolo Carozza provides a comprehensive analysis of legal systems worldwide.

4. The websites of international organizations such as the United Nations and the World Trade Organization offer valuable resources on legal harmonization and comparative research.

Exercises

Exercise 1: Select two countries with different legal systems and compare their approaches to environmental protection. Analyze the strengths and weaknesses of each system and propose recommendations for improvement.

Exercise 2: Conduct a comparative study of labor laws in three countries and identify the key differences in their approaches to workers' rights. Assess the effectiveness of each system in protecting workers and ensuring fair labor practices.

Exercise 3: Choose a specific area of law, such as intellectual property, and compare the legal frameworks of three countries. Discuss the impact of these frameworks on innovation, economic development, and international trade.

Conclusion

International legal harmonization and comparative research play vital roles in shaping the future of law. By promoting consistency and understanding among legal systems, harmonization facilitates global transactions and cooperation. Comparative research, on the other hand, aids in identifying best practices, informing law reform efforts, and fostering cross-cultural understanding. As legal systems continue to evolve in an interconnected world, the importance of these approaches will only increase. Through ongoing research and collaboration, legal scholars and practitioners can contribute to the transformative advancement of legal studies.

Critical Legal Research

Overview of Critical Legal Research

Critical legal research is a multidisciplinary approach to studying law that challenges traditional legal norms and institutions. It seeks to uncover the power dynamics and social structures that underlie legal systems and explores how law can be a tool for social change and justice. In this section, we will provide an overview of critical legal research, its key principles, and its relevance in today's legal landscape.

Definition and Scope of Critical Legal Research

Critical legal research is a branch of legal scholarship that seeks to critically analyze and question the existing legal framework. It goes beyond traditional legal analysis by examining how law reflects and perpetuates social, economic, and political inequalities.

The scope of critical legal research is broad and encompasses various fields including sociology, anthropology, philosophy, and political science. It recognizes that law is not a neutral entity but is shaped by social forces, power dynamics, and historical context.

Key Principles of Critical Legal Research

Critical legal research is guided by several key principles that help researchers understand and challenge the existing legal system. These principles include:

1. **Critique of power structures:** Critical legal research aims to analyze and expose power structures, hierarchies, and asymmetries within the legal system. It looks at how law can reinforce or challenge existing power relations and how it can be a tool for social control or emancipation.

2. **Intersectionality:** Critical legal research recognizes that law intersects with other social categories such as race, gender, class, and sexuality. It acknowledges that individuals may experience multiple forms of oppression and explores how these intersecting identities shape their experiences within the legal system.

3. **Valuing lived experiences:** Critical legal research values the lived experiences of marginalized and oppressed communities. It seeks to incorporate the perspectives and voices of these communities to challenge dominant legal narratives.

4. **Social justice and transformation:** Critical legal research aims to achieve social justice and transformation through the law. It explores alternative legal frameworks and approaches that can address systemic injustices and promote equality.

Methods and Approaches of Critical Legal Research

Critical legal research employs a range of methods and approaches to achieve its goals. These include:

1. **Interdisciplinary research:** Critical legal research draws on interdisciplinary approaches and methodologies to understand the social, economic, and political dimensions of law. It borrows concepts and theories from sociology, anthropology, philosophy, and other disciplines to analyze legal issues from different perspectives.

2. **Empirical research:** Critical legal research incorporates empirical research methods to provide evidence-based analyses of legal phenomena. It may involve qualitative research such as interviews, ethnography, and case studies, as well as quantitative research such as surveys and statistical analyses.

3. **Social activism and engagement:** Critical legal research often involves social activism and community engagement. Researchers may work closely with social justice organizations and marginalized communities to better understand their legal needs and challenges.

4. **Legal storytelling and narrative analysis:** Critical legal research recognizes the power of storytelling and narrative analysis in understanding the impact of law on individuals and communities. It seeks to amplify marginalized voices and narratives through alternative modes of legal discourse.

Applications and Impact of Critical Legal Research

Critical legal research has had significant applications and impact in various areas of law and social justice. Some notable examples include:

1. **Critical race theory:** Critical legal research has contributed to the development of critical race theory, which examines how race intersects with law and shapes legal outcomes. It has influenced legal scholarship and activism around racial justice and has contributed to the recognition of racial disparities in the criminal justice system.

2. **Feminist legal theory:** Critical legal research has played a crucial role in the development of feminist legal theory, which examines the intersection of law, gender, and power. It has challenged traditional legal concepts and norms that perpetuate gender inequality and has influenced legal reforms in areas such as reproductive rights, domestic violence, and workplace discrimination.

3. **Social justice movements:** Critical legal research has contributed to various social justice movements by providing the theoretical and intellectual framework for legal activism. It has informed legal strategies and arguments in movements such as LGBTQ+ rights, environmental justice, and Indigenous rights.

4. **Legal education reform:** Critical legal research has influenced legal education by advocating for more interdisciplinary and critical approaches. It has called for the inclusion of courses and perspectives that challenge traditional legal norms and expose students to the social and political implications of law.

Challenges and Critiques of Critical Legal Research

Critical legal research is not without its challenges and critiques. Some common challenges include:

1. **Resistance from legal institutions:** Critical legal research often faces resistance from traditional legal institutions and practitioners who may view it as threatening or radical. This can make it difficult for critical legal researchers to gain recognition and support within the legal community.

2. **Lack of institutional support:** Critical legal research may face challenges in securing institutional support and resources, particularly in academic settings. The dominance of traditional legal scholarship and funding structures can limit the opportunities for critical legal research.

3. **Complexity of interdisciplinary research:** Conducting interdisciplinary research can present challenges due to the different methodologies, theories, and disciplines involved. Critical legal researchers must navigate these complexities and find ways to bridge disciplinary boundaries.

Despite these challenges, critical legal research continues to be a powerful tool for understanding and challenging the existing legal order. Its potential for social change and transformation makes it a vital area of study in the pursuit of justice and equality.

Conclusion

Critical legal research provides a critical lens through which to examine the existing legal system. By questioning power structures, considering intersectionality, valuing lived experiences, and seeking social justice and transformation, critical legal research challenges conventional legal norms and offers alternative viewpoints. Through interdisciplinary approaches, empirical research, social activism, and legal storytelling, critical legal research has had a significant impact on various areas of law and social justice. Despite challenges and critiques, critical legal research continues to be a vital and relevant field in the pursuit of justice and equality.

Critiques of Traditional Legal Research Methods

Traditional legal research methods have long been the cornerstone of legal practice and scholarship. However, they are not without their critics. This section will explore some of the key critiques of traditional legal research methods and the challenges they present.

One of the main critiques of traditional legal research methods is the emphasis on case law analysis. Traditional legal research often revolves around the analysis of precedents, with a focus on specific court decisions. Critics argue that this narrow focus limits the understanding of the law to previous court interpretations, rather than examining the larger social, economic, and political contexts within which the law operates.

Another critique is that traditional legal research methods often prioritize formal legal texts, such as statutes and regulations, over other sources of law. This leads to a neglect of the socio-political factors that shape legal outcomes. Critics argue that understanding the social and cultural contexts in which laws are created and enforced is crucial for a holistic understanding of the law.

Furthermore, traditional legal research methods tend to rely heavily on deductive reasoning and syllogistic analysis. This approach is criticized for its rigidity and lack of creativity. Critics argue that the focus on logical deduction can lead to a narrow interpretation of the law, ignoring alternative perspectives and innovative solutions.

Additionally, traditional legal research methods often prioritize quantitative data and empirical research, neglecting qualitative research methods. Critics point out that the strict reliance on quantitative analysis may hinder a deeper understanding of the social and human aspects of legal issues. They argue that qualitative research methods, such as interviews, observations, and case studies, can provide valuable insights into the lived experiences of individuals affected by the law.

Another key critique is that traditional legal research often lacks interdisciplinary perspectives. Critics argue that the law cannot be understood in isolation from other disciplines, such as sociology, psychology, anthropology, and political science. By incorporating interdisciplinary approaches, legal research can gain a broader perspective and address complex legal issues more effectively.

There is also a critique regarding the accessibility and practicality of traditional legal research methods. Critics argue that traditional legal research can be time-consuming, costly, and inaccessible to marginalized communities. They advocate for more inclusive and community-based approaches to legal research that prioritize the needs and interests of all stakeholders.

Furthermore, traditional legal research methods often assume a neutral and objective stance. Critics argue that this assumption overlooks the inherent biases and power dynamics in the law. They advocate for a critical and reflexive approach to legal research that acknowledges the role of race, gender, class, and other social identities in shaping legal outcomes.

To address these critiques, transformative legal research methods have emerged. These approaches aim to challenge and expand on traditional legal research methods by incorporating interdisciplinary perspectives, engaging with marginalized communities, and promoting social justice. Transformative legal research methods seek to bridge the gap between theory and practice, and to empower individuals and communities through a more inclusive and participatory approach to the law.

Overall, the critiques of traditional legal research methods highlight the need for a more dynamic and inclusive approach to legal scholarship. By acknowledging the limitations of traditional methods and embracing transformative approaches, legal researchers can better understand the complexities of the law and contribute to more just and equitable legal systems.

Using Critical Legal Research Methods for Social Change

In this section, we will explore how critical legal research methods can be used as a powerful tool for social change. Critical legal research is an approach to legal scholarship that focuses on analyzing and challenging the underlying structures of power and inequality within the legal system. It seeks to uncover the ways in which the law perpetuates social injustices and promotes the interests of dominant groups. By using critical legal research methods, scholars and activists aim to transform the law to create a more just and equitable society.

Understanding Critical Legal Research

Critical legal research is rooted in critical theory, which examines the social, political, and economic contexts in which the law operates. It explores the ways in which legal rules and institutions are shaped by power dynamics and serve the interests of dominant groups. Critical legal research goes beyond traditional doctrinal analysis by critically examining the assumptions, ideologies, and values that underpin legal norms.

One fundamental principle of critical legal research is the recognition that the law is not neutral or objective. Instead, it reflects and reinforces existing power structures and inequalities. Critical legal scholars argue that by uncovering and challenging these embedded biases, it is possible to transform the law and promote social justice.

Methods for Critical Legal Research

Critical legal research utilizes a variety of methods to analyze the law from a critical perspective. Some common methods include:

1. **Critical discourse analysis:** This method examines the language and rhetoric used in legal texts, court decisions, and legal arguments. By analyzing the ways in which language constructs and reinforces power relations, critical legal scholars can uncover hidden biases and challenge dominant narratives.

2. **Intersectional analysis:** Intersectionality is a key concept in critical legal research. It recognizes that individuals experience multiple forms of oppression and discrimination based on their intersecting identities, such as race, gender, class, sexuality, and ability. By employing an intersectional analysis, critical legal researchers can identify how legal rules and institutions disproportionately affect marginalized communities.

3. **Legal consciousness studies:** This method explores how individuals perceive and understand the law. By examining how legal norms are internalized, contested, or resisted by different groups, critical legal scholars can shed light on the lived experiences of those impacted by the law.

4. **Law and economics analysis:** Critical legal researchers critically analyze the economic assumptions and consequences of legal rules. They examine how the law perpetuates economic inequalities and explore alternative economic models that prioritize social justice.

5. **Empirical research:** Critical legal research often incorporates empirical methods to gather data and evidence about the real-world impact of legal rules and institutions. This can include surveys, interviews, case studies, and statistical analysis.

Examples of Critical Legal Research in Action

Critical legal research has been used to challenge discriminatory practices, advocate for marginalized communities, and promote social change. Here are some examples of how critical legal research has been applied in different contexts:

1. **Criminal justice reform:** Critical legal research has been instrumental in highlighting the racial disparities within the criminal justice system. By examining patterns of racial profiling, biased sentencing, and over-policing, critical legal

scholars have helped shape public discourse and policy debates around criminal justice reform.

2. **Gender equality:** Critical legal research has exposed the ways in which the law can perpetuate gender-based discrimination and inequality. By examining laws related to reproductive rights, gender violence, and workplace discrimination, critical legal researchers have contributed to legal and policy changes aimed at promoting gender equality.

3. **Environmental justice:** Critical legal research has played a crucial role in exposing the disparate impact of environmental harms on marginalized communities. By analyzing the intersections of race, class, and environmental degradation, critical legal scholars have advocated for more equitable and sustainable environmental regulations.

4. **Indigenous rights:** Critical legal research has empowered Indigenous communities by challenging colonial legal frameworks and advocating for the recognition of Indigenous legal traditions. By integrating Indigenous perspectives into legal scholarship, critical legal researchers have contributed to the development of more inclusive and culturally sensitive legal systems.

Challenges and Ethical Considerations

While critical legal research has the potential to bring about transformative change, it also faces several challenges and ethical considerations. Some of these include:

1. **Resistance and backlash:** Challenging deeply entrenched power structures can result in resistance and backlash from those who benefit from the existing legal framework. Critical legal researchers must be prepared to navigate opposition and pushback.

2. **Ethical dilemmas:** Conducting critical legal research may raise ethical dilemmas, particularly when it involves studying vulnerable populations or sensitive issues. Researchers must prioritize the well-being and consent of research participants while ensuring the integrity and validity of their work.

3. **Access to resources:** Critical legal research may require access to resources, such as legal databases, specialized libraries, and research funding. Limited access to these resources can pose barriers to conducting comprehensive research.

4. **Lack of institutional support:** Critical legal research is not always prioritized within academic institutions, which often favor traditional legal scholarship. This lack of support can limit opportunities for critical legal researchers to engage in meaningful and impactful work.

Conclusion

Critical legal research provides a powerful framework for analyzing and challenging existing legal structures and promoting social change. By employing critical legal research methods, scholars and activists can uncover hidden biases, challenge dominant narratives, and advocate for marginalized communities. However, critical legal research also faces challenges and ethical considerations that must be carefully navigated. Despite these challenges, the potential for transformative change through critical legal research is immense, making it a valuable tool for creating a more just and equitable society.

Legal Research in the Digital Age

Online Legal Databases and Resources

In today's digital age, the availability of online resources has significantly transformed the legal research landscape. Legal professionals now have access to a wealth of information and databases that were previously only accessible through physical libraries or cumbersome manual methods. This section explores the various online legal databases and resources that have revolutionized legal research.

Introduction to Online Legal Databases

Online legal databases are web-based platforms that provide access to a vast collection of legal materials, including case law, statutes, regulations, legal journals, and secondary legal sources. These databases offer a comprehensive and efficient way to conduct legal research, enabling legal professionals to find relevant legal information quickly and accurately.

Types of Online Legal Databases

There are several types of online legal databases, each serving different purposes and offering distinct features. Here, we explore some of the most commonly used types:

- **Case Law Databases:** These databases compile court decisions from various jurisdictions. They allow users to search for cases by jurisdiction, keywords, parties involved, or specific legal issues. Examples of popular case law databases include Westlaw, LexisNexis, and Bloomberg Law.

- **Statutory Databases:** Statutory databases provide access to legislation, including statutes, codes, regulations, and other legislative materials. They allow users to search for specific statutes or regulations by jurisdiction, keywords, or citation. Notable statutory databases include the United States Code (USC), the Code of Federal Regulations (CFR), and the European Union Law database (EUR-Lex).

- **Legal Journals and Periodicals:** Many online platforms provide access to a wide range of legal journals and periodicals. These databases allow users to search for articles on specific legal topics, browse recent publications, and stay updated on legal developments. Examples of popular legal journal databases include JSTOR, HeinOnline, and ProQuest.

- **Secondary Legal Sources:** Secondary legal sources, such as legal encyclopedias, treatises, and annotations, offer expert commentary and analysis on various legal topics. Online platforms that compile secondary legal sources provide users with comprehensive insights and references for their research. Well-known secondary legal source databases include Legal Information Institute (LII), FindLaw, and Cornell Law School's Legal Information Institute.

Benefits and Advantages

The proliferation of online legal databases and resources has revolutionized legal research in several ways. Here are some notable benefits and advantages:

- **Accessibility and Convenience:** Online legal databases can be accessed anytime and anywhere with an internet connection. This accessibility eliminates the need for physical travel to libraries or reliance on limited print materials, making legal research more convenient for legal professionals.

- **Efficiency and Time Savings:** Online databases offer advanced search functionalities and filters that allow users to quickly find relevant legal materials. The ability to search by keywords, citations, or specific criteria saves significant research time and increases efficiency.

- **Comprehensive Coverage:** Online legal databases often provide vast collections of legal materials, ensuring comprehensive coverage of case law, legislation, and secondary legal sources. This breadth of coverage eliminates the need to consult multiple sources, streamlining the research process.

- **Updated and Current Information:** Online legal databases usually provide regular updates to legal materials, ensuring that users have access to the most recent case law, statutes, and legal commentary. This feature allows legal professionals to stay current with evolving legal developments.

- **Advanced Research Tools:** Many online databases offer advanced research tools that enhance the research process. These tools include features like cross-referencing, citation analysis, note-taking capabilities, and the ability to save and organize research materials for future use.

Limitations and Caveats

While online legal databases offer numerous advantages, it is essential to be aware of their limitations and exercise caution when using them:

- **Quality and Reliability:** Not all online legal resources are created equal. Some databases may contain inaccurate or outdated information. It is crucial to verify the credibility and reliability of the source before relying on it for legal research.

- **Cost and Subscription Models:** Many online legal databases operate on subscription-based models, which can be costly for individual users. Law firms and academic institutions often have access to these databases through institutional subscriptions. However, individual legal professionals may need to consider the cost implications when using premium databases.

- **Jurisdictional Coverage:** Online legal databases may vary in terms of their jurisdictional coverage. While some databases offer international coverage, others may focus on specific jurisdictions or regions. Legal professionals must ensure that the selected database aligns with their research needs and jurisdictional requirements.

- **Search Skills and Training:** Efficiently navigating online legal databases requires adequate search skills and familiarity with advanced research techniques. Legal professionals should invest time in understanding the search functionalities, Boolean operators, and other tools offered by the platform to maximize their research capabilities.

Practical Tips and Best Practices

To make the most out of online legal databases, legal professionals should consider the following tips and best practices:

- **Develop Effective Search Strategies:** Before conducting research, it is crucial to plan and develop effective search strategies. Clearly define the research question or topic, identify relevant keywords, and consider using Boolean operators, phrase searching, and truncation techniques to refine search results.

- **Utilize Advanced Search Functions:** Online databases often provide advanced search functions, such as filters, citation searches, and field-specific searches. Taking advantage of these features can help narrow down search results and locate specific legal materials more efficiently.

- **Verify and Cross-Reference Sources:** While online legal databases are valuable resources, it is essential to verify the information obtained and cross-reference it with other authoritative sources. Verifying the accuracy and reliability of sources helps ensure the credibility of the research findings.

- **Stay Updated on Legal Developments:** Online legal databases offer subscriptions to newsletters, legal alerts, or RSS feeds that provide updates on recent legal developments. Subscribing to these services can help legal professionals stay informed about changes in the law that may impact their research or practice.

- **Consider Collaboration and Peer Engagement:** Online legal databases often provide features that encourage collaboration and peer engagement. Engaging in online forums, discussion boards, or legal research communities can help expand knowledge, gain insights, and explore different perspectives on legal issues.

Conclusion

Online legal databases and resources have revolutionized legal research, providing legal professionals with accessible, efficient, and comprehensive tools for conducting their research. While there are limitations and considerations to keep in mind, the benefits and advantages of online legal databases far outweigh their drawbacks. By adopting effective search strategies, utilizing advanced research tools, and staying updated on legal developments, legal professionals can harness the transformative potential of online legal databases to enhance their legal research capabilities and contribute to more informed legal practice.

Use of Artificial Intelligence in Legal Research

Artificial Intelligence (AI) has made significant advancements in various fields, and its application in legal research is no exception. AI has revolutionized the way legal professionals conduct research, analyze case law, and provide legal advice. In this section, we will explore the use of AI in legal research and its implications for the future of the legal profession.

Introduction to AI in Legal Research

AI refers to the development of computer systems that can perform tasks that normally require human intelligence, such as speech recognition, decision-making, and problem-solving. In the context of legal research, AI technologies leverage machine learning algorithms and natural language processing to analyze vast amounts of legal data and extract meaningful insights.

Traditionally, legal research involves manual analysis of statutes, regulations, case law, and legal literature. This process can be time-consuming and labor-intensive. AI-powered legal research tools, on the other hand, can quickly analyze and categorize legal documents, identify relevant case law, and provide recommendations based on past judicial decisions.

Machine Learning in Legal Research

Machine learning is a branch of AI that enables computers to learn from data and improve their performance over time. In legal research, machine learning algorithms can be trained on large datasets of legal documents to identify patterns, detect trends, and make predictions.

One practical application of machine learning in legal research is document classification. By analyzing the content and context of legal documents, machine learning models can automatically categorize and tag documents, making it easier for legal professionals to retrieve relevant information.

Another application of machine learning in legal research is predictive analytics. By analyzing historical case law and legal precedents, machine learning models can predict the likely outcome of a particular legal case. This can help lawyers and judges make more informed decisions and provide more accurate legal advice.

Natural Language Processing in Legal Research

Natural language processing (NLP) is a subfield of AI that focuses on the interaction between computers and human language. In the context of legal research, NLP techniques enable computers to understand and analyze legal texts, such as statutes, regulations, and case law.

One of the key applications of NLP in legal research is legal information retrieval. NLP algorithms can process search queries and retrieve relevant legal documents from vast databases, saving legal professionals valuable time and effort.

NLP can also be used to automate the summarization of legal documents. Rather than manually reading and summarizing lengthy legal texts, NLP algorithms can extract key information and provide concise summaries, making it easier for legal professionals to grasp complex legal concepts.

Challenges and Ethical Considerations

While AI offers numerous benefits in legal research, it also presents certain challenges and ethical considerations.

One challenge is the issue of bias in AI algorithms. Like any machine learning system, AI algorithms are trained on historical data, which may contain inherent biases. These biases can be reflected in the recommendations and decisions made by AI systems, potentially perpetuating existing inequalities in the legal system. It is important for legal researchers and developers to address these biases and ensure that AI systems are fair and unbiased.

Ethical considerations also arise when AI systems are used to automate tasks traditionally performed by legal professionals. For example, the use of AI-powered chatbots to provide legal advice raises questions about the impact on the attorney-client relationship and the potential for unauthorized practice of law. Legal professionals must carefully navigate these ethical issues and ensure that AI technologies are used responsibly and in compliance with legal and professional standards.

Future Directions and Outlook

The use of AI in legal research is likely to continue expanding in the future. As technology advances and access to legal data improves, AI-powered tools will become even more sophisticated and effective in assisting legal professionals.

One promising direction is the integration of AI with legal analytics. By combining AI capabilities with data analytics, legal researchers can gain deeper insights into legal trends, predict future developments, and enhance their decision-making processes.

Furthermore, the development of explainable AI models will be essential in the legal field. Explainable AI refers to the ability of AI systems to provide transparent and understandable explanations for their decisions and recommendations. This will be crucial in building trust and confidence in AI-powered legal research tools.

In conclusion, the use of AI in legal research has the potential to greatly enhance the efficiency and effectiveness of legal professionals. By leveraging machine learning and natural language processing, AI can automate mundane tasks, improve legal research accuracy, and facilitate more informed decision-making. However, it is essential to address challenges related to bias and ethical considerations to ensure that AI systems are used responsibly and ethically in the legal profession. The future of legal research is undoubtedly intertwined with AI, and legal professionals must embrace these transformative technologies to stay ahead in an evolving legal landscape.

Resources for Further Study

If you are interested in learning more about the use of AI in legal research, the following resources can provide valuable insights:

- *Artificial Intelligence for Lawyers: How AI is Changing the Legal Profession* by Kevin D. Ashley
- *AI and Legal Reasoning: Applications and Methodologies* edited by Julia Hörnle et al.
- *Legal Tech, Smart Contracts and Blockchain* by Mathias Nebel et al.
- *The Future of the Professions: How Technology Will Transform the Work of Human Experts* by Richard Susskind and Daniel Susskind

These resources provide comprehensive coverage of the topic and delve into the technical, legal, and ethical aspects of AI in the legal field. They will serve as valuable references for further study and exploration of this exciting and rapidly evolving field.

Key Takeaways

- AI has transformative potential in legal research, enabling the automation of tasks, analysis of legal data, and provision of legal advice.
- Machine learning algorithms can be trained on legal datasets to classify documents and make predictions.
- Natural language processing techniques enable the processing and retrieval of legal information from vast databases.
- Challenges in AI include bias in algorithms and ethical considerations regarding the automation of legal tasks.
- The future of AI in legal research lies in the integration of analytics, the development of explainable AI models, and addressing ethical and bias concerns.

Challenges and Ethical Considerations in Digital Legal Research

As legal research increasingly relies on digital technology, there are several challenges and ethical considerations that arise in the process. In this section, we will explore these challenges and provide insights into the ethical considerations that researchers and legal professionals must take into account.

Data Privacy and Security

One of the foremost challenges in digital legal research is ensuring the privacy and security of data. Legal researchers often have access to sensitive and confidential information, including personal data of individuals involved in legal cases. It is crucial to protect this information from unauthorized access, misuse, or breach. Researchers must adopt robust data protection measures and adhere to relevant data protection laws and regulations, such as the General Data Protection Regulation (GDPR).

Ethical consideration: Legal researchers have an ethical obligation to handle personal data responsibly, ensuring its confidentiality and protecting the privacy of individuals involved in legal cases. Researchers should only collect and use data that is necessary for their research and must obtain informed consent when required.

Digital Divide

The digital divide refers to the unequal access to digital technologies and the internet among different groups in society. This divide can create barriers to accessing legal information and conducting digital legal research, particularly for individuals from marginalized communities or developing countries. The digital divide exacerbates existing inequalities and hinders equal access to justice.

Ethical consideration: Researchers should be aware of the digital divide and strive to make legal research more inclusive. They can contribute to bridging the gap by promoting initiatives for digital literacy, advocating for universal access to digital resources, and considering the limitations of digital research tools in reaching marginalized populations.

Algorithmic Bias and Discrimination

Digital legal research often involves the use of algorithms and artificial intelligence (AI) to analyze large datasets. However, these algorithms can be susceptible to bias, perpetuating systemic discrimination and inequality. Unchecked algorithmic bias can lead to unjust outcomes, reinforcing existing societal biases.

Ethical consideration: Researchers must be cautious when using algorithms and AI in their research. They should critically assess the biases inherent in the algorithms and take steps to mitigate their impact. Additionally, researchers should advocate for transparency in algorithmic decision-making processes and work towards developing fair and unbiased algorithms.

Reliability and Validity of Online Information

The vast amount of information available online poses a challenge in ensuring the reliability and validity of sources used in digital legal research. With the ease of publishing online, there is a risk of relying on inaccurate, biased, or outdated information, which can significantly impact the quality and credibility of legal research.

Ethical consideration: Researchers have a responsibility to critically evaluate the reliability and validity of online sources. They should employ recognized criteria for assessing the credibility of sources and verify information from multiple reputable sources. Moreover, researchers should clearly acknowledge the limitations and potential biases of the information they use in their research.

Intellectual Property and Copyright Issues

Digital legal research often involves accessing and utilizing copyrighted materials, such as legal texts, articles, or case law. Researchers must be cautious not to infringe on intellectual property rights and comply with copyright laws. Unlawful use of copyrighted material not only undermines the integrity of legal research but also poses legal and ethical challenges.

Ethical consideration: Researchers should respect intellectual property rights and adhere to copyright laws. They should properly attribute and cite sources, seek appropriate permissions when necessary, and follow fair use guidelines. Open-access and Creative Commons resources can be valuable alternatives for accessing legal information without infringing on copyright.

Ethical Use of Technology

Digital legal research relies heavily on technological tools, such as online databases, automated search algorithms, and AI-powered analytics. While these technologies offer immense benefits, there is a risk of their unethical use. For instance, using technology to automate tasks that require human judgment or engaging in unethical practices, such as using technology to gather personal information without consent.

Ethical consideration: Researchers should use technology ethically and responsibly. They should be aware of the limitations of technology and critically evaluate its use in legal research. Additionally, researchers should stay informed about emerging technologies and their ethical implications, actively engaging in discussions and debates within the legal community and society at large.

In summary, digital legal research presents several challenges and ethical considerations, including data privacy and security, the digital divide, algorithmic bias, reliability of online information, intellectual property rights, and ethical use of technology. Researchers and legal professionals must navigate these challenges and uphold ethical standards to ensure the integrity and fairness of their research. By doing so, they contribute to the transformative potential of digital legal studies and promote justice and equality in the legal field.

Collaborative Research in Law

Collaborative Research with Other Legal Scholars

Collaborative research is an essential aspect of transformative legal studies. By working together with other legal scholars, researchers can pool their knowledge and expertise to tackle complex legal issues and contribute to the advancement of the field. This section explores the importance of collaborative research in the legal community and provides strategies and considerations for successful collaboration.

Benefits of Collaborative Research

Collaborative research offers several advantages for legal scholars. Firstly, working with others fosters the exchange of ideas and perspectives, leading to more comprehensive and well-rounded research outcomes. By drawing on different areas of expertise, scholars can approach problems from various angles and develop innovative solutions. This interdisciplinary approach enhances the quality and depth of research.

Secondly, collaborative research allows scholars to share the workload and maximize efficiency. Research projects often require extensive data collection, analysis, and synthesis. By dividing tasks among team members, scholars can tackle larger projects and complete them more quickly. This not only increases productivity but also enables researchers to explore more in-depth and nuanced aspects of the subject matter.

Moreover, collaborative research provides an opportunity for mentorship and professional growth. Junior scholars can benefit from the guidance and expertise of senior researchers, who can offer valuable insights and advice. This mentorship fosters the development of emerging scholars and contributes to the overall growth of the legal community.

Strategies for Successful Collaboration

Successful collaborative research requires effective communication, coordination, and organization. Here are some strategies for a fruitful collaborative research experience:

1. **Clearly define roles and responsibilities:** At the outset of the research project, it is crucial to establish clear roles and responsibilities for each team member. Clearly defined expectations help prevent conflicts and ensure that each person understands their role in contributing to the research.

2. **Foster open and regular communication:** Regular communication among team members is essential for a successful collaboration. Establishing effective channels of communication, such as scheduled meetings or group messaging platforms, allows scholars to share progress, exchange ideas, and address any challenges that may arise.

3. **Set realistic timelines and milestones:** Developing a realistic timeline is necessary to ensure that the project progresses smoothly. Setting achievable milestones helps keep the team focused and motivated. Regularly reassess and adjust timelines as needed to accommodate unexpected setbacks or new insights.

4. **Foster a collaborative and inclusive environment:** Encourage an inclusive and supportive environment that values diverse perspectives and contributions. Creating a space where all team members feel comfortable expressing their ideas and concerns fosters a positive and productive collaborative research experience.

Challenges and Considerations

While collaborative research offers many benefits, it also presents some unique challenges. Some potential challenges include:

1. **Different research methodologies and approaches:** Collaborative research often involves scholars with diverse research methodologies and approaches. Coordinating these different methodologies and finding common ground can be challenging. Regular communication and a willingness to be open-minded and adaptable are crucial in tackling this challenge.

2. **Conflict resolution:** Conflicts or disagreements may arise during collaborative research. It is important to address these issues promptly and constructively. Establishing clear procedures for conflict resolution, such as open discussions or mediation, can help maintain a positive working environment.

3. **Balancing individual and collective goals:** Collaborative research requires balancing individual aspirations with collective goals. Each team member may have unique research interests or objectives. Finding ways to incorporate individual contributions while staying focused on the overall research objectives is key to successful collaboration.

4. **Ensuring fairness in authorship and credit:** Determining authorship and assigning credit can be a sensitive issue in collaborative research. It is essential to establish clear guidelines and agreements regarding authorship and credit from the outset of the project. Regularly revisit and reassess these agreements to ensure fairness and transparency.

Example: Collaborative Research on Legal Innovation

To illustrate the power of collaborative research, let's consider a hypothetical scenario involving legal innovation. A team of legal scholars specializing in different areas decides to collaborate on a research project exploring the impact of technological advancements on legal practice.

The team starts by clearly defining their roles and responsibilities. One team member focuses on researching emerging technologies such as artificial intelligence and blockchain, another member examines the ethical and regulatory implications, while another investigates the potential for access to justice. By working together, the team combines their expertise to produce a comprehensive and interdisciplinary analysis.

Throughout the research project, the team members meet regularly to discuss progress, share findings, and brainstorm ideas. They also leverage technology, such as collaborative virtual platforms, to facilitate communication and document sharing. This ensures that everyone stays informed and engaged in the research process.

As they delve deeper into their research, the team encounters challenges related to conflicting legal frameworks across jurisdictions. To overcome this challenge, they establish a framework for comparative analysis and engage with legal scholars from different regions to gather diverse perspectives.

In the end, the collaborative research project on legal innovation yields valuable insights into the challenges and opportunities presented by emerging technologies. The team publishes their findings in a joint publication, attributing authorship based on the agreed-upon guidelines established at the outset of the project.

Resources

Collaborative research is supported by various tools and resources that facilitate effective teamwork. Here are some resources that legal scholars can utilize:

1. **Project management tools:** Tools such as Trello, Asana, or Microsoft Teams can help the research team organize and track progress, assign tasks, and set deadlines.

2. **Collaboration platforms:** Platforms like Google Drive or Dropbox enable seamless collaboration by providing a centralized space for file sharing and real-time document editing.

3. **Communication tools:** Tools like Slack, Microsoft Teams, or Zoom enhance communication among team members by facilitating instant messaging, video conferencing, and document sharing.

4. **Research databases:** Access to comprehensive research databases, such as LexisNexis or Westlaw, allows scholars to access relevant legal literature and resources to inform their collaborative research.

Conclusion

Collaborative research with other legal scholars is a powerful tool for driving transformative advancements in the field of law. Through effective communication, coordination, and leveraging diverse expertise, scholars can produce high-quality research with broader impact. By embracing collaborative approaches, legal scholars can contribute to shaping the future of legal studies and promoting justice and equality.

Engaging with Non-Legal Scholars in Cross-Disciplinary Research

Engaging with non-legal scholars in cross-disciplinary research is an essential aspect of transformative legal studies. This section explores the benefits, challenges, and strategies for fostering collaboration between legal scholars and scholars from other disciplines. By working together, researchers can bring diverse perspectives, methodologies, and knowledge to address complex legal issues and promote societal change.

Importance of Cross-Disciplinary Research

Cross-disciplinary research involves collaboration between scholars from different academic disciplines. In the context of legal studies, engaging with non-legal scholars opens up opportunities to explore the intersection of law with fields such as sociology, psychology, economics, political science, anthropology, environmental science, and many others. This interdisciplinary approach can provide a deeper understanding of the complex social, economic, political, and cultural contexts in which law operates.

Cross-disciplinary research promotes innovative thinking by challenging traditional legal frameworks and incorporating diverse perspectives. By incorporating insights from other disciplines, legal scholars can gain new insights into legal issues, develop more effective policy solutions, and improve the impact of their research on society.

Challenges in Cross-Disciplinary Collaboration

Engaging with non-legal scholars in cross-disciplinary research presents unique challenges. Some common obstacles include differences in language, research methodologies, and disciplinary cultures. Legal scholars may find it difficult to understand and navigate the terminology and theories used in other disciplines. Similarly, scholars from other disciplines may struggle to grasp legal concepts and the intricacies of the legal system.

Another challenge is the difference in research methodologies. While legal research often relies on qualitative analysis of legal texts, scholars from other disciplines may employ quantitative methods, empirical studies, or experimental research designs. Bridging these methodological gaps requires flexibility, open-mindedness, and a willingness to learn from one another.

Disciplinary cultures can also pose challenges in interdisciplinary collaborations. Each discipline has its own norms, practices, and expectations. Legal scholars may be accustomed to a certain way of conducting research, writing papers, and presenting findings. Non-legal scholars, on the other hand, may approach research and communication in different ways. Effectively navigating these cultural differences requires clear communication, mutual respect, and an appreciation for the strengths of each discipline.

Strategies for Successful Collaboration

Successful collaboration between legal scholars and non-legal scholars requires careful planning, effective communication, and a shared understanding of goals and expectations. Here are some strategies to foster cross-disciplinary research:

1. Establish clear objectives: Clearly define the research question or issue that requires cross-disciplinary collaboration. Identify the specific expertise and perspectives that scholars from other disciplines can contribute to the research.

2. Build interdisciplinary teams: Assemble a diverse team of researchers with complementary expertise from both legal and non-legal disciplines. This can include scholars from sociology, psychology, economics, or any other relevant field.

3. Foster open communication: Create a collaborative and inclusive environment where scholars can openly exchange ideas, perspectives, and methodologies. Encourage active participation and respect for different viewpoints.

4. Develop a shared language: Invest time in building a common understanding of key concepts, theories, and methodologies used in both legal and non-legal disciplines. This will facilitate effective communication and enhance interdisciplinary collaboration.

5. Embrace diverse methodologies: Recognize and appreciate the different research methodologies used in various disciplines. Seek opportunities to integrate qualitative and quantitative approaches to gain a comprehensive understanding of the research problem.

6. Promote interdisciplinary learning: Encourage researchers to explore and learn from each other's disciplines. Offer workshops, seminars, or training programs to familiarize scholars with key concepts, research methods, and theories from other disciplines.

7. Accommodate different writing styles: Legal and non-legal scholars may have distinct writing styles and formats. Ensure that research outputs, such as articles or reports, are accessible and understandable to a broader audience.

8. Acknowledge and appreciate contributions: Recognize and value the diverse contributions of scholars from different disciplines. Celebrate interdisciplinary achievements and highlight the significance of cross-disciplinary research in advancing legal studies.

Examples

To illustrate the importance of engaging with non-legal scholars in cross-disciplinary research, consider the following examples:

1. Environmental Law and Economics: Legal scholars working on environmental issues can collaborate with economists to assess the economic impact of environmental regulations and explore market-based solutions to address environmental challenges.

2. Law and Neuroscience: Legal scholars interested in criminal justice can team up with neuroscientists to understand the neurological factors that contribute to criminal behavior and inform more effective legal interventions and policies.

3. Law and Psychology: Legal scholars researching issues related to discrimination or access to justice can collaborate with psychologists to examine cognitive biases, stereotypes, and decision-making processes that influence legal outcomes.

Resources for Further Study

To further explore cross-disciplinary research and its application in transformative legal studies, the following resources are recommended:

1. Babbie, E. (2016). The Practice of Social Research. Cengage Learning. ISBN: 978-1305104945.

2. Klein, J. T. (1996). Crossing Boundaries: Knowledge, Disciplinarities, and Interdisciplinarities. University of Virginia Press. ISBN: 978-0813917289.

3. Legal Scholarship in the Age of Artificial Intelligence (2019). Cambridge University Press. ISBN: 978-1108472713.

4. Nowotny, H., Scott, P., & Gibbons, M. (2001). Re-Thinking Science: Knowledge and the Public in an Age of Uncertainty. Wiley. ISBN: 978-0745626079.

5. Smith, R., & Ray, L. (2014). Jurisprudence: Theory and Context (7th edition). Sweet & Maxwell. ISBN: 978-0414027516.

Conclusion

Engaging with non-legal scholars in cross-disciplinary research enriches the field of legal studies by incorporating diverse perspectives, methodologies, and knowledge. While cross-disciplinary collaborations present challenges, they also offer immense opportunities for transformative legal research. By establishing clear objectives, fostering open communication, and embracing diverse methodologies, legal scholars can effectively collaborate with scholars from other disciplines to address complex legal issues and contribute to societal change.

Incorporating Community Perspectives in Legal Research

In legal research, it is crucial to consider the perspectives and needs of the communities that are affected by the legal issues being studied. Traditional legal research often relies solely on statutes, cases, and legal doctrines, neglecting the lived experiences and social contexts of the community members. However, incorporating community perspectives in legal research can lead to a more comprehensive and nuanced understanding of legal issues and their impact on society. This section explores the importance of incorporating community perspectives in legal research and provides practical strategies for researchers to engage with communities.

Understanding the Importance of Community Perspectives

Incorporating community perspectives in legal research is rooted in the principles of participatory democracy, social justice, and inclusivity. It recognizes that communities possess valuable knowledge and insights about the legal issues they face. By engaging with community members, researchers can gain a deeper understanding of the social, economic, and political factors that influence legal problems. Community perspectives can shed light on the real-world consequences of legal decisions and the effectiveness of existing legal frameworks.

Furthermore, community engagement in legal research promotes empowerment and agency among community members. By involving them in the research process, communities can influence the research agenda, identify their own legal needs, and actively contribute to finding solutions. This approach fosters a sense of ownership and collaboration, leading to more meaningful and impactful research outcomes.

Practical Strategies for Incorporating Community Perspectives

1. **Community-Based Research:** Researchers can adopt a community-based research approach, collaborating directly with community members, organizations, and leaders. This collaborative approach ensures that research questions are relevant to the community's concerns and that research findings are accessible and beneficial to them. Researchers can engage in dialogues, interviews, focus groups, or participatory workshops to gather community perspectives.

2. **Participatory Action Research:** Participatory Action Research (PAR) involves community members as active participants in the research process. It aims to empower communities by involving them in problem identification, data collection, analysis, and decision-making. PAR facilitates knowledge co-creation, generates actionable findings, and supports community-led initiatives to address legal issues.

3. **Legal Clinics and Community Partnerships:** Legal clinics provide an avenue for researchers to work directly with community members seeking legal assistance. By engaging with clients, researchers can gather firsthand knowledge of legal challenges, identify systemic issues, and propose advocacy strategies. Community partnerships with legal aid organizations, grassroots movements, or community centers can also facilitate ongoing collaborations and knowledge exchange.

4. **Community Surveys and Data Collection:** Conducting community surveys can help gather quantitative data on legal needs, experiences, and preferences. Surveys provide researchers with a comprehensive overview of community perspectives and enable the identification of patterns or trends. Combined with qualitative data collection methods like interviews or focus groups, a more nuanced understanding of community perspectives can be achieved.

5. **Outreach and Education:** Researchers can engage in outreach activities to raise awareness about legal issues and empower communities through legal education. This can include organizing workshops, community talks, or providing accessible resources that explain legal rights, processes, and available support

networks. By educating communities, researchers can foster informed participation and support grassroots advocacy efforts.

Challenges and Ethical Considerations

Incorporating community perspectives in legal research is not without challenges and ethical considerations. Researchers must navigate power dynamics, protect confidentiality, and ensure the informed consent of participants. Ethical guidelines and protocols should be followed to safeguard the welfare and rights of community members involved in the research process.

Maintaining a balanced and inclusive approach requires sensitivity to diverse community voices. Researchers should be mindful of power imbalances and engage with marginalized or underrepresented groups to ensure their perspectives are heard. It is also important to recognize that community perspectives may differ within a community itself, and researchers should strive for inclusivity and respect for diverse viewpoints.

Case Study: Incorporating Community Perspectives in Criminal Justice Research

To illustrate the practical application of incorporating community perspectives in legal research, consider a case study in criminal justice. A researcher interested in studying the experiences of individuals reentering society after incarceration can adopt a community-based research approach. By collaborating with local organizations and individuals affected by the criminal justice system, the researcher can conduct interviews, focus groups, and data collection within the community.

Through active engagement with community members, the researcher can gain insights into the challenges faced by individuals reentering society, including barriers to employment, housing, and social integration. These community perspectives can inform future policy recommendations and interventions to improve the reentry process and reduce recidivism rates. The research findings can also be shared with community members to empower them with knowledge about their rights and available resources.

Resources for Further Study

1. Cochran, P.A.L., & Mohammed, S.A. (2020). Community-Based Participatory Research in Law Schools: Moving Beyond Experiential Education Toward Community Justice. *Stanford Law Review*, 72(3), 653-685.

2. Cornwall, A., & Jewkes, R. (Eds.). (2020). *Transformative Research and Evaluation*. Routledge.

3. Thangaraj, S. (2021). *Designing for Equality: Best Practices in Collaborative Pedagogies and Community Engaged Research*. Vanderbilt University Press.

4. Walden, I. (2019). *Research Co-Creation and Local Empowerment: Participatory Action Research Approaches and Everyday Practice*. Palgrave Macmillan.

5. International Association for Public Participation. (2018). *IAP2's Public Participation Spectrum*. Retrieved from https://www.iap2.org.au/Resources/An-Overview-of-Public-Participation

Conclusion

Incorporating community perspectives in legal research is a transformative approach that enhances the rigor, relevance, and impact of the research. By actively involving community members and organizations in the research process, researchers can gain valuable insights, empower communities, and contribute to positive social change. Engaging with communities requires ethical considerations, participatory methodologies, and a commitment to inclusivity. By adopting these strategies, legal researchers can bridge the gap between theory and practice and contribute to the advancement of justice and equality.

Conclusion

Recapitulation of Key Points

In this chapter, we have explored the new approaches to legal research and how they contribute to the transformative nature of legal studies. We began by examining the traditional legal research methods, such as case law analysis, statutory research, and the use of secondary sources. However, we also recognized the limitations of these methods in addressing pressing social issues and promoting justice and equality.

To overcome these limitations, we delved into the realm of empirical legal research, which involves the use of quantitative and qualitative research methods to gather data and analyze legal phenomena. We discussed the benefits of incorporating empirical approaches, such as surveys, interviews, and observations, to better understand the social and practical impact of the law.

Furthermore, we explored the field of socio-legal research, which emphasizes the interdisciplinary nature of legal studies. By incorporating social sciences such as sociology, anthropology, and political science, socio-legal research provides a holistic understanding of how law operates in society. We discussed the challenges and ethical considerations in conducting socio-legal research, particularly in relation to informed consent and protecting the rights of research participants.

Additionally, we examined the importance of comparative legal research in understanding legal systems across different jurisdictions. By analyzing similarities and differences, we can gain insights into how different legal systems address social issues and promote justice.

Moreover, we explored the concept of critical legal research. This approach challenges traditional legal thinking and seeks to uncover the underlying power dynamics and social inequalities embedded within the law. By adopting a critical perspective, legal researchers can effectively advocate for social change and contribute to the transformative nature of legal studies.

We then discussed the impact of technology on legal research. With the advent of artificial intelligence, blockchain, and big data analytics, legal researchers have new tools at their disposal. We explored the potential benefits and ethical considerations of using technology in legal research, including access to legal databases, AI-assisted contract review, and predictive analytics.

Throughout this chapter, we have emphasized the transformative potential of these new approaches to legal research. By embracing interdisciplinary, empirical, comparative, critical, and technological methods, legal researchers can contribute to greater justice, equality, and social change. However, we also recognized the challenges and limitations associated with these approaches and the need for ethical considerations in their use.

To further explore these topics and expand your knowledge in the field of transformative legal studies, we encourage you to engage with the additional resources provided in this textbook. These resources include further reading suggestions, scholarly articles, and online platforms where you can delve deeper into the concepts discussed in this chapter.

In conclusion, this chapter has highlighted the importance of adopting new approaches to legal research in order to promote justice, equality, and transformation within the legal field. By incorporating empirical, socio-legal, comparative, and critical methods, as well as embracing technological advancements, legal researchers can make significant contributions to addressing social issues and shaping the future of law.

Implications for Transformative Legal Research

Transformative legal research has the potential to reshape the way we understand and engage with the law. By adopting innovative and interdisciplinary approaches, researchers can uncover new perspectives, challenge traditional legal norms, and contribute to social change. In this section, we explore some of the key implications of transformative legal research and its impact on the field.

Challenging Existing Legal Paradigms

One of the primary implications of transformative legal research is its ability to challenge and deconstruct existing legal paradigms. Traditional legal research often focuses on doctrinal analysis and the interpretation of legal texts within a narrow framework. However, transformative legal research encourages scholars to go beyond these conventional boundaries and explore alternative ways of understanding and interpreting the law.

For example, critical legal studies provide a lens through which researchers can uncover hidden power structures and biases within legal systems. By critically examining legal doctrines and their social context, transformative legal research challenges the status quo and promotes a more equitable and just legal system. Similarly, feminist legal theory offers insights into the gendered nature of laws and sheds light on the ways in which legal norms perpetuate gender inequality.

Addressing Understudied Legal Issues

Transformative legal research also has implications for addressing understudied legal issues. Traditional legal scholarship often focuses on well-established areas of law, leaving many important topics unexplored. Transformative legal research opens up new avenues for inquiry, allowing researchers to delve into emerging or marginalized areas of law.

For instance, through socio-legal research methods, scholars can examine the impact of the law on marginalized communities and identify ways to promote social justice. By studying the experiences of vulnerable populations, such as individuals with disabilities or refugees, transformative legal research can provide insights into the gaps and challenges in existing legal frameworks.

Promoting Interdisciplinary Collaboration

Another implication of transformative legal research is the promotion of interdisciplinary collaboration. Many legal challenges extend beyond the confines of law itself and require insights from other disciplines. By embracing interdisciplinary approaches, transformative legal research enriches the understanding of legal issues and broadens the scope of solutions.

For example, incorporating insights from psychology, sociology, and economics can provide a deeper understanding of human behavior and the social impacts of legal decisions. Collaborating with experts in fields such as health sciences or environmental studies can help researchers explore the intersectionality of legal issues and their wider implications.

Informing Policy and Practice

Transformative legal research has the potential to inform policy-making and legal practice. By engaging with real-world issues and providing evidence-based insights, researchers can contribute to the development of more effective and just policies and practices.

For instance, empirical legal research can employ quantitative and qualitative methodologies to examine the impact of specific laws or policies on individuals or communities. By providing empirical evidence of the effects of certain legal approaches, transformative legal research can shape policy discussions and lead to more informed decision-making.

Engaging with Communities

A significant implication of transformative legal research is its potential to engage directly with communities affected by legal issues. By involving stakeholders in the research process, researchers can foster community-driven solutions and empower marginalized voices.

Community-based participatory research methods, for example, allow researchers to collaborate with community members to identify legal challenges, co-create knowledge, and develop interventions that meet their specific needs. This approach ensures that legal research is relevant, responsive, and directly impactful.

Ethical Considerations

Transformative legal research also raises important ethical considerations. Researchers must approach their work with sensitivity, maintaining the confidentiality and autonomy of research participants and ensuring that their work does not cause harm.

Furthermore, transformative legal research should prioritize the principles of inclusivity and representation. It is crucial for researchers to consider the diverse perspectives of individuals and communities affected by legal issues and actively work towards amplifying their voices.

Future Directions in Transformative Legal Research

Transformative legal research is an ever-evolving field, and future directions are essential to its continued growth and impact. Some potential areas for future research include:
 1. Exploring the intersectionality of different social identities within legal systems, such as race, gender, and socioeconomic status. 2. Investigating the role of technology, including artificial intelligence and blockchain, in transforming legal systems and research methodologies. 3. Examining the implications of globalization and international human rights norms on local legal contexts. 4. Identifying innovative strategies for legal education that embrace transformative approaches and promote social justice. 5. Assessing the impact of restorative justice practices on reducing recidivism rates and healing communities affected by crime.

In conclusion, transformative legal research has profound implications for the field of law and society. By challenging existing paradigms, addressing understudied issues, promoting interdisciplinary collaboration, informing policy and practice, engaging with communities, and considering ethical considerations, researchers can contribute to a more just and equitable legal system. Looking towards the future, the potential for transformative legal research to effect positive change is vast, signaling an exciting and dynamic field for scholars and practitioners alike.

Future Directions in Legal Research

Legal research is an ever-evolving field, and there are several exciting future directions that researchers can explore. By embracing new tools, methodologies, and interdisciplinary approaches, the future of legal research holds great promise in shaping the field. In this section, we highlight some of the key areas for future research and discuss their potential implications.

Integration of Artificial Intelligence

The integration of artificial intelligence (AI) in legal research is a promising avenue for future exploration. AI-powered tools can assist in automating legal tasks, such as document analysis, legal research, and contract management. Researchers can investigate the potential benefits and challenges of using AI in legal practice and its broader impact on the legal profession.

For example, research can focus on the ethical implications of relying on AI algorithms in decision-making processes and the potential bias that may arise. Additionally, exploring the ways in which AI can enhance access to justice for marginalized communities through chatbots or other automated systems is an important avenue for future research.

Examining the Role of Blockchain

Another area for future research is the role of blockchain technology in legal research and practice. Blockchain offers potential solutions for issues such as establishing trust, verifying identity, and maintaining secure records. Researchers can explore how blockchain can be used to improve the efficiency and transparency of legal processes, such as contract enforcement, intellectual property protection, or land registry.

Additionally, researchers can investigate the legal implications of blockchain, including privacy concerns, data protection, and the challenges of implementing blockchain in existing legal systems. Understanding the legal and regulatory frameworks surrounding blockchain technology will be crucial for shaping its future use.

Addressing Ethical Challenges in the Digital Age

As legal research increasingly relies on digital technologies, it is important to address the ethical challenges that arise in the digital age. Researchers can explore the ethical implications of using digital tools and data in legal research, including issues of privacy, data protection, and consent.

Furthermore, investigating the impact of emerging technologies, such as facial recognition or predictive analytics, on individual rights and civil liberties can shed light on the legal and ethical concerns associated with these technologies. Understanding and developing ethical frameworks for the use of digital tools in legal research is essential for ensuring responsible and accountable practices.

Enhancing Access to Justice

Improving access to justice is an ongoing challenge in legal research. Future research can focus on innovative approaches to increase access to justice, particularly for marginalized communities. This may involve exploring alternative dispute resolution mechanisms, developing technology-driven solutions, or implementing community-based legal services.

Researchers can also examine the impact of legal empowerment programs, pro bono services, and legal aid initiatives on access to justice. Understanding the barriers to justice and identifying strategies to overcome them will be crucial in creating a more inclusive and equitable legal system.

Exploring the Implications of Globalization

Globalization has significant implications for legal research, as it blurs traditional legal boundaries and introduces new challenges and opportunities. Future research can delve into the impact of globalization on legal systems, including the harmonization of laws, the rise of transnational legal norms, and the challenges posed by cross-border disputes.

Additionally, researchers can examine the implications of globalization on human rights and social justice, particularly in relation to issues such as migration, environmental protection, or labor rights. Understanding how globalization shapes legal systems and impacts individuals and communities is critical for promoting equitable and effective legal responses.

Developing Innovative Research Methodologies

In order to tackle complex legal issues, future research should also focus on developing innovative research methodologies. This may involve combining qualitative and quantitative methods, adopting case studies or comparative approaches, or engaging in participatory research with the communities affected by legal issues.

Exploring interdisciplinary collaborations between legal scholars and experts from fields such as sociology, economics, psychology, or environmental studies can also enhance the depth and breadth of legal research. By embracing new methodologies and interdisciplinary perspectives, researchers can gain fresh insights and make significant contributions to the field.

In conclusion, the future of legal research holds immense potential for innovation and transformation. By embracing artificial intelligence, exploring the role of blockchain, addressing ethical challenges, enhancing access to justice, examining the implications of globalization, and developing innovative methodologies, researchers can shape the future of law and contribute to a more just and equitable society. The interdisciplinary nature of legal research, coupled with the rapid advancement of technology, provides numerous opportunities for scholars to explore new frontiers and make meaningful contributions to the field.

Future Directions in Legal Research

The field of legal research is constantly evolving, driven by advancements in technology, changes in societal norms, and emerging global challenges. As researchers seek to address complex legal issues and contribute to the development of transformative legal studies, several key future directions in legal research can be identified. These directions involve exploring new methodologies, embracing interdisciplinary approaches, adapting to technological advancements, and prioritizing ethical considerations.

Exploring New Methodologies

The future of legal research lies in the exploration and adoption of diverse and innovative methodologies. Traditional legal research methods, such as case analysis and statutory research, will continue to be valuable. However, researchers should also consider employing empirical legal research, socio-legal research, and critical legal research to gain deeper insights into legal phenomena.

Empirical legal research involves the collection and analysis of quantitative and qualitative data to study legal issues. Researchers can use surveys, interviews, observations, and experiments to gather data that can inform legal theories, policies, and practices. This approach allows legal scholars to move beyond theoretical arguments and assess the real-world impact of laws and legal interventions.

Socio-legal research takes an interdisciplinary approach by combining legal analysis with insights from sociology, anthropology, political science, and other social sciences. This methodology helps researchers understand how legal norms and institutions interact with social, cultural, and economic factors. By studying the social context in which law operates, researchers can identify and address the root causes of legal issues.

Critical legal research challenges existing legal norms and power structures. It encourages researchers to question conventional legal thinking and examine the underlying social, political, and economic dynamics that shape the law. By adopting a critical perspective, legal scholars can uncover hidden assumptions, biases, and power imbalances within legal systems and propose transformative alternatives.

Embracing Interdisciplinary Approaches

Interdisciplinary approaches will continue to gain prominence in legal research. Recognizing that complex legal issues cannot be adequately addressed within the confines of a single discipline, scholars will increasingly draw upon insights from other fields such as sociology, psychology, economics, environmental studies, and technology.

For example, legal researchers can collaborate with psychologists to study the impact of legal processes on mental health and decision-making. They can work with economists to analyze the economic efficacy of legal interventions and regulatory frameworks. By combining legal analysis with insights from other disciplines, researchers can develop more holistic and comprehensive solutions to legal problems.

Interdisciplinary collaboration also extends to engaging with non-legal scholars. Collaborative research projects involving legal scholars and experts from diverse disciplines can foster innovative thinking, promote cross-pollination of ideas, and lead to transformative approaches to legal issues.

Adapting to Technological Advancements

Advancements in technology will have a profound impact on the future of legal research. Researchers need to stay informed about new technological tools and methods and adapt their research practices accordingly.

One area of rapid development is the use of artificial intelligence (AI) in legal research. AI-powered tools can assist legal scholars in processing vast amounts of legal information, identifying relevant case law, and suggesting legal arguments. However, researchers must remain cautious about the limitations and ethical implications of relying solely on AI without critical human analysis.

Furthermore, the digitization of legal resources and the availability of big data present both opportunities and challenges. Researchers can access a wealth of legal information and utilize data analytics techniques to uncover patterns, trends, and insights. However, they must also navigate data privacy concerns, ensure data integrity, and critically evaluate the biases embedded in digital sources.

Prioritizing Ethical Considerations

As legal research addresses complex societal issues, it is crucial to prioritize ethical considerations. Researchers must be mindful of the potential impacts of their work on individuals, communities, and society as a whole.

Ethical considerations include protecting the confidentiality and privacy of research participants, obtaining informed consent, and ensuring data security. Researchers should also examine the potential biases embedded in their methodologies and findings, striving for fairness and accountability.

Additionally, legal researchers should actively engage with the communities they study, seeking their input and incorporating their perspectives. This collaborative approach ensures that research is sensitive to the needs and aspirations of the affected communities, promoting inclusivity and social justice.

Conclusion

The future of legal research is characterized by a commitment to exploring new methodologies, embracing interdisciplinary approaches, adapting to technological advancements, and prioritizing ethical considerations. By adopting innovative research methods, collaborating across disciplines, harnessing technological tools, and upholding ethical principles, legal researchers can contribute to the development of transformative legal studies and the advancement of justice and equality.

Chapter 5: Legal Systems and Institutions in Transformation

Chapter 5: Legal Systems and Institutions in Transformation

Chapter 5: Legal Systems and Institutions in Transformation

This chapter explores the transformative nature of legal systems and institutions. It delves into the changes and developments that have shaped the legal landscape, as well as the impact these transformations have had on society. Understanding the dynamics of legal systems and institutions is crucial for legal scholars, practitioners, and policymakers seeking to address the evolving needs and challenges of justice and equality.

Definition and History of Legal Systems

A legal system is a framework that governs the rules and principles by which societies function. It includes laws, regulations, and institutions that establish and enforce these rules. Legal systems vary across countries and cultures, reflecting their unique historical and cultural contexts.

The history of legal systems is filled with milestones that have shaped their development. From ancient legal codes like the Code of Hammurabi to modern-day constitutions, legal systems have evolved to address changing societal values, norms, and challenges. The study of legal history provides valuable insights into the origins and evolution of legal systems, helping us understand their strengths, weaknesses, and potential for transformation.

Transformations in Legal Institutions

Legal institutions play a vital role in the functioning of legal systems. They include courts, legislatures, law enforcement agencies, and other bodies responsible for the administration of justice. Over time, legal institutions have undergone significant transformations in response to societal changes and demands for justice.

One notable transformation is the evolution of judicial activism. Judicial activism refers to the proactive role that courts can play in shaping public policy and advancing social change. Through landmark decisions, judicial activism has expanded individual rights, promoted equality, and challenged discriminatory practices. However, it has also raised concerns about the separation of powers and the appropriate role of courts in a democratic society.

Another transformation in legal institutions is the rise of alternative dispute resolution (ADR) mechanisms. ADR provides alternatives to traditional court litigation, such as mediation and arbitration, to resolve conflicts outside of formal judicial processes. ADR offers several advantages, including increased efficiency, flexibility, and the preservation of relationships. Integrating ADR within legal systems has the potential to improve access to justice and promote more transformative outcomes for disputing parties.

Legal Transplants and Comparative Law

Legal transplants refer to the borrowing and incorporation of legal ideas, concepts, and institutions from one legal system into another. Comparative law involves the study and analysis of different legal systems to identify similarities, differences, and potential areas of cross-pollination.

The process of legal transplants and the study of comparative law facilitate legal transformations by enabling societies to adopt and adapt legal elements from different jurisdictions. This cross-fertilization can contribute to the development of more equitable, efficient, and inclusive legal systems. However, it also raises challenges related to cultural, political, and institutional contexts, as well as the potential loss of local legal traditions.

Access to Justice and Legal Empowerment

Access to justice is a fundamental principle that ensures individuals can seek legal remedies and have their rights protected. However, in many societies, access to justice remains limited, particularly for marginalized communities and vulnerable populations.

CHAPTER 5: LEGAL SYSTEMS AND INSTITUTIONS IN TRANSFORMATION

Transformative legal systems and institutions recognize the importance of addressing barriers to justice and promoting legal empowerment. Initiatives such as legal aid, pro bono services, and community legal education aim to bridge the justice gap and enable individuals and communities to assert their rights. By empowering individuals and communities with legal knowledge and resources, transformative legal systems can foster a more just and equitable society.

Challenges and Controversies in Legal Transformation

Legal transformation is not without challenges and controversies. As legal systems and institutions evolve, they face resistance from various stakeholders who may be hesitant to accept change. Controversial issues, such as the balance between individual rights and collective security, the appropriate limits of judicial power, and the tensions between tradition and progress, often arise in the process of legal transformation.

Additionally, legal transformations must navigate the complexities of intersectionality – the interconnected nature of race, gender, class, and other social identities in relation to systems of power and privilege. Understanding and addressing these intersections is crucial for promoting transformative justice and equality.

Future Directions in Legal Systems and Institutions

As legal systems and institutions continue to evolve, several future directions emerge. These include:

1. Embracing technology: The integration of technology in legal systems holds the potential to enhance access to justice, improve efficiency, and create new avenues for legal empowerment. However, it also raises concerns about data privacy, algorithmic biases, and the impact on traditional legal practices.

2. Strengthening community engagement: Transformative legal systems should prioritize community engagement and participation. Engaging with communities in decision-making processes and creating mechanisms for feedback and accountability can lead to more responsive and just legal systems.

3. Promoting diversity and inclusion: Transformative legal systems should be reflective of the diversity and needs of the populations they serve. Efforts to increase diversity in legal institutions, address systemic biases, and promote inclusive practices are essential for achieving transformative justice.

In conclusion, legal systems and institutions are constantly evolving to meet the changing needs and challenges of society. Understanding the transformative potential of these systems is crucial for advancing justice and equality. By exploring the history, principles, and challenges associated with legal transformation, this chapter provides a foundation for further study and research in the field. Remembering that legal systems are not fixed entities, but living structures that adapt to societal dynamics, we can work towards creating more just and equitable legal systems for the future.

Judicial Activism and Its Impact

Definition and History of Judicial Activism

Introduction

In this section, we will explore the concept of judicial activism and its historical development. Judicial activism refers to the proactive role of judges in interpreting and shaping the law, often by departing from traditional legal doctrines and making decisions that have far-reaching social and political implications. While the term "judicial activism" is often used in a pejorative sense, it is crucial to understand its evolution and the impact it has had on the legal landscape.

Defining Judicial Activism

Defining judicial activism is a complex task, as there is no universally accepted definition. However, at its core, judicial activism involves judges actively engaging in decision-making that goes beyond merely interpreting the law and extends into areas traditionally the domain of the legislative or executive branches. Judicial activists often seek to advance social justice, protect individual rights, and promote equality.

Historical Development of Judicial Activism

The roots of judicial activism can be traced back to the early years of constitutionalism. The notion that judges have the power to shape the law can be seen in landmark cases such as Marbury v. Madison (1803) in the United States, where the Supreme Court established the principle of judicial review. This power allows the courts to invalidate legislation inconsistent with the Constitution and has provided a basis for subsequent judicial activism.

In the 20th century, judicial activism gained momentum as judges became more willing to interpret the law broadly to address societal issues. Notable examples include the U.S. Supreme Court's decisions in Brown v. Board of

Education (1954), which declared racial segregation in public schools unconstitutional, and Roe v. Wade (1973), which recognized a woman's constitutional right to access abortion.

The Role of Judicial Activism

Proponents of judicial activism argue that it is necessary to ensure that the law keeps pace with societal changes and protects individuals' rights. They argue that a strict adherence to legal formalism and originalism can lead to injustice and stifle progress. By actively reinterpreting existing laws or creating new legal doctrines, judicial activists can fill gaps and address emerging social issues.

However, critics of judicial activism argue that judges should exercise restraint and refrain from interfering with the democratic process. They contend that judicial activism can undermine the separation of powers and encroach upon the role of elected representatives. Critics also argue that judges should confine themselves to interpreting the law as it is written, rather than imposing their own policy preferences.

Controversies Surrounding Judicial Activism

Judicial activism is not without controversies. One major controversy revolves around the legitimacy of judges making policy decisions that affect significant social issues. Critics argue that unelected judges should not have the power to make laws or set public policy, as this undermines democratic governance.

Another controversy concerns the potential bias of judges in applying judicial activism. Critics argue that judicial activism can be used to advance a judge's personal or political agenda, potentially overriding the will of the people or the intent of the constitutionally mandated legislative bodies.

Furthermore, the extent to which judicial activism should be employed is also a subject of debate. Critics contend that judicial activism should be limited to exceptional cases where legislative action is insufficient or in cases involving clear constitutional violations. Supporters argue that judicial activism should be used to protect fundamental rights and correct systemic injustices.

Examples of Judicial Activism

Numerous cases around the world exemplify judicial activism. In India, for instance, the Supreme Court's decision in Vishaka v. State of Rajasthan (1997) recognized sexual harassment in the workplace as a violation of constitutional rights, establishing guidelines for addressing such issues.

In Canada, the Supreme Court's decision in R. v. Morgentaler (1988) struck down abortion laws as unconstitutional, leading to the decriminalization of abortion throughout the country.

In South Africa, the Constitutional Court's decision in Minister of Health v. Treatment Action Campaign (2002) compelled the government to provide antiretroviral drugs to pregnant women to prevent the transmission of HIV to their children, effectively addressing a public health crisis.

Conclusion

Judicial activism, while a contested concept, has played a significant role in shaping legal systems and promoting social change. It involves judges actively interpreting the law to address societal issues and protect individual rights. While controversial, judicial activism has been instrumental in advancing causes such as civil rights, gender equality, and access to justice. However, the legitimacy and extent of judicial activism continue to be subjects of ongoing debate.

Case Studies: Landmark Judicial Activism Cases

In this section, we will explore some landmark cases that serve as examples of judicial activism. These cases have made a significant impact on the legal landscape, shaping the interpretation and application of the law in transformative ways. By examining these cases, we can gain a deeper understanding of how judicial activism can influence the course of justice.

Brown v. Board of Education (1954)

One of the most famous examples of judicial activism is the case of Brown v. Board of Education. This landmark decision by the U.S. Supreme Court declared racial segregation in public schools to be unconstitutional, overturning the previous "separate but equal" doctrine established in Plessy v. Ferguson (1896).

The Court, led by Chief Justice Earl Warren, held that segregation of public schools based on race violated the Equal Protection Clause of the Fourteenth Amendment. The decision had a profound impact on the civil rights movement, marking a significant step towards desegregating schools and challenging systemic racism.

Roe v. Wade (1973)

Roe v. Wade is another notable example of judicial activism, which addressed the issue of reproductive rights in the United States. In this case, the Supreme Court recognized a woman's constitutional right to access safe and legal abortions.

The Court, in a majority opinion written by Justice Harry Blackmun, found that a woman's right to privacy, derived from the Due Process Clause of the Fourteenth Amendment, encompassed her decision to have an abortion. This decision established a framework for evaluating state laws related to abortion and sparked a fierce public debate that continues to this day.

Marbury v. Madison (1803)

Marbury v. Madison is a landmark case that paved the way for the concept of judicial review in the United States. In this case, the Supreme Court asserted its power to interpret the Constitution and declare acts of Congress unconstitutional.

Chief Justice John Marshall, in his opinion, established that the Court had the authority to determine the constitutionality of laws and exercise judicial review. This decision solidified the Court's role as a coequal branch of government and shaped the balance of powers in the United States.

Obergefell v. Hodges (2015)

Obergefell v. Hodges was a groundbreaking case that extended marriage rights to same-sex couples in the United States. The Supreme Court held that the fundamental right to marry is guaranteed to same-sex couples under the Due Process and Equal Protection Clauses of the Fourteenth Amendment.

By legalizing same-sex marriage nationwide, the court's decision transformed the landscape of LGBTQ+ rights and marked a significant step towards achieving equality for all individuals, regardless of sexual orientation.

Miranda v. Arizona (1966)

Miranda v. Arizona revolutionized the criminal justice system by establishing the requirement for law enforcement to inform individuals in custody of their rights to remain silent and have an attorney present during police interrogations.

The Supreme Court, in a landmark decision, declared that statements made by a suspect in police custody would be inadmissible as evidence unless the suspect had been informed of their rights. This case not only protected the rights of the accused but also ensured fair treatment within the criminal justice system.

Conclusion

These case studies represent a few examples of landmark judicial activism cases that have shaped the legal landscape. They demonstrate the power of the judiciary to effect change and promote justice and equality. By examining these cases, we can gain insights into the influence of transformative judicial decisions and their impact on society. Judicial activism, when exercised responsibly and grounded in the principles of justice and equality, can be a catalyst for progress and societal transformation.

Critiques and Controversies Surrounding Judicial Activism

Judicial activism, the practice in which judges interpret and apply the law in a way that reflects their personal views and values, has been a subject of debate and controversy in legal and political circles. While some scholars and activists view judicial activism as a necessary tool for social change and justice, others argue that it undermines democratic principles and the separation of powers. In this section, we will explore the critiques and controversies surrounding judicial activism, examining both its potential benefits and drawbacks.

Critique 1: Judicial Overreach

One of the primary critiques of judicial activism is that it represents a form of judicial overreach. Critics argue that judges are unelected officials who lack the democratic legitimacy to make decisions that shape public policy. They contend that by engaging in activism, judges are usurping the role of the legislature and infringing upon the democratic process. This perspective emphasizes the importance of judicial restraint, where judges limit their role to interpreting the law rather than making policy decisions.

Critique 2: Lack of Accountability

Another criticism of judicial activism is the perceived lack of accountability that accompanies it. Since judges are appointed or elected to serve on the bench for a fixed term, they may be less accountable to the public than elected officials. Critics argue that this lack of accountability undermines the democratic principles of governance, as judges are not directly answerable to the people they serve. Detractors of judicial activism advocate for a more democratic and accountable approach to decision-making, allowing elected representatives to shape public policy through legislative processes.

Critique 3: Judicial Bias

Critics of judicial activism often argue that activist judges allow their personal biases and ideologies to influence their rulings. They contend that such biases may lead to decisions that favor certain groups or causes, thereby undermining the impartiality and fairness of the judiciary. This critique suggests that judges should approach cases with neutrality and objectivity, interpreting the law without injecting their personal beliefs. Skeptics of judicial activism call for judges to adhere strictly to the text and original intent of the law in order to minimize the potential for bias.

Controversy 1: Protecting Rights vs. Judicial Tyranny

One of the main controversies surrounding judicial activism is the balance between protecting individual rights and accusations of judicial tyranny. Advocates of judicial activism argue that it is necessary to protect marginalized and vulnerable groups, particularly when the legislative and executive branches fail to do so. They see judges as custodians of justice, acting as a check on the other branches of government to ensure the protection of constitutional rights. However, critics argue that such intervention can be seen as undemocratic, as judges may overstep their boundaries and infringe upon the authority of elected representatives.

Controversy 2: Interpretation vs. Creation of Law

Another controversy surrounding judicial activism lies in the tension between interpretation and creation of law. Supporters argue that judges must have the flexibility to interpret the law in light of societal changes and evolving values. They believe that a strict interpretation of the law may lead to unjust outcomes, and therefore, judges must go beyond the literal text to achieve a more just society. Critics, on the other hand, contend that judges should adhere strictly to the original intent of the law and leave the task of lawmaking to the legislative branch. They argue that by creating new laws through judicial decisions, judges are exceeding their constitutional role and encroaching upon the power of the legislature.

Controversy 3: Effectiveness vs. Stability

A contentious issue surrounding judicial activism is the trade-off between effectiveness and stability. Proponents argue that judicial activism can bring about rapid and transformative change when legislative processes are slow or ineffective, ensuring justice for marginalized groups. They assert that judges, with their unique role in the legal system, can act as agents of social change and promote greater equality. However, critics contend that rapid and unpredictable changes may undermine institutional stability and undermine public confidence in the judiciary. They argue that gradual change through the legislative process is preferable, as it allows for deliberation and public input.

In conclusion, critiques and controversies surrounding judicial activism highlight fundamental tensions within the legal system. While some view judicial activism as a necessary means to achieve justice and protect individual rights, others see it as an infringement upon democratic processes and an erosion of the rule of law. Striking a balance between judicial activism and restraint is an ongoing challenge for legal systems around the world, necessitating careful consideration of the benefits and drawbacks of an active judiciary.

Legal Transplants and Comparative Law

Overview of Legal Transplants

In the field of legal studies, the concept of legal transplants refers to the transfer of legal ideas, principles, and institutions from one legal system to another. It involves borrowing or adopting legal elements, such as laws, regulations, court rulings, and practices, from one jurisdiction to another. This process can occur at both the domestic and international levels and is often driven by the need to address new legal challenges or to modernize existing legal systems.

Background

Legal transplants have a long history and can be traced back to ancient times when societies began adopting legal practices and principles from neighboring civilizations. For example, the ancient Roman legal system greatly influenced the development of legal systems in Europe and other parts of the world. The idea of legal transplants gained further significance during the colonial era when European powers imposed their legal systems on the colonies.

The study of legal transplants as a distinct field of inquiry emerged in the mid-20th century with the work of legal scholars such as Alan Watson and S. M. Lipset. Their research focused on the transplantation of common law principles to civil law countries and the challenges and benefits associated with this process.

Principles of Legal Transplants

Legal transplants involve the transfer of legal concepts and practices from one legal system to another. They are guided by several principles, which include:

1. **Functional Equivalence:** Legal transplants aim to address similar legal issues or fulfill similar legal functions in different jurisdictions. The transplanted legal elements should serve a similar purpose in the receiving legal system as they did in the source legal system. However, adaptation may be necessary to ensure compatibility with the receiving system's legal, cultural, and social context.

2. **Legitimacy and Acceptance:** The success of legal transplants depends on the acceptance and legitimacy of the transplanted legal elements by the legal community and society at large. This requires a process of negotiation and dialogue to ensure that the transplanted elements align with the values, norms, and legal traditions of the receiving jurisdiction.

3. **Mutual Learning:** Legal transplants involve a two-way exchange of legal ideas and practices. While one jurisdiction may borrow from another, there is often a reciprocal process of learning and adaptation. The receiving jurisdiction may provide feedback and shape the transplanted legal elements based on its own legal traditions and values.

4. **Gradual Adaptation:** Legal transplants are rarely a one-time event but rather a continuous process of adaptation and evolution. Transplanted legal elements may undergo modifications and developments over time as they interact with the receiving jurisdiction's legal system and society. This gradual adaptation ensures the relevance and effectiveness of the transplanted legal elements in the long run.

5. **Transparency and Rationality:** The process of legal transplants should be transparent, rational, and based on rigorous analysis. Legal scholars and policymakers need to assess the suitability and compatibility of transplanted legal elements with the receiving jurisdiction's legal system. This assessment should consider factors such as legal traditions, cultural norms, social context, and the anticipated impact of the transplanted elements.

Challenges and Critiques of Legal Transplants

Despite the potential benefits of legal transplants, they are not without challenges and critiques. Some of these challenges include:

- **Cultural and Contextual Differences:** Legal systems are deeply influenced by cultural, historical, and social contexts. Transplanting legal elements without considering these factors can lead to a lack of fit and effectiveness. Differences in legal traditions, languages, and social norms can pose challenges to the successful adoption and implementation of transplanted legal elements.

- **Resistance and Opposition:** Legal transplants can face resistance and opposition from various stakeholders. This may include legal professionals, policymakers, and members of the public who are skeptical of foreign legal elements. Concerns about the erosion of national identity, sovereignty, and cultural autonomy can sometimes hinder the acceptance of transplanted legal elements.

- **Lack of Adaptation and Localization:** The successful transplantation of legal elements requires adaptation and localization to the receiving jurisdiction's legal system and societal context. Failure to undertake this process may result in a superficial adoption of legal elements that do not effectively address the specific needs and challenges of the receiving jurisdiction.

- **Unintended Consequences:** Legal transplants can have unintended consequences that may not be immediately apparent. The adoption of legal elements without sufficient consideration of the receiving jurisdiction's legal system can lead to inconsistencies, contradictions, and conflicts within the legal framework. It is crucial to thoroughly analyze and anticipate the potential implications of legal transplants to mitigate such unintended consequences.

Examples of Legal Transplants

Legal transplants can be observed in various legal domains. Some noteworthy examples include:

- **Civil Law and Common Law Convergence:** The influence of common law principles on civil law systems and vice versa is an ongoing process of legal transplants. For instance, civil law countries have adopted common law concepts such as judicial precedents and the adversarial system, while common law countries have incorporated civil law principles, such as codification and legal principles derived from Roman law.

- **International Human Rights Law:** The Universal Declaration of Human Rights and subsequent human rights treaties have been instrumental in transplanting human rights norms across different legal systems worldwide. While the legal systems of individual countries may still differ in their approach to human rights, there is a growing convergence towards a common set of rights and standards.

- **Corporate Governance and Business Law:** As businesses operate across borders, legal transplants have become crucial in harmonizing business law and corporate governance practices. International standards and best practices are transplanted into national legal systems to provide a common framework for regulating corporations and protecting the interests of shareholders.

Resources for Further Study

For further exploration of the topic of legal transplants and their implications, the following resources are recommended:

- *Legal Transplants: An Approach to Comparative Law* by Alan Watson provides a comprehensive analysis of legal transplants and their historical development.

- *The Anatomy of a Transplant: The Legal and Socio-Economic Factors behind Legal Transplants* edited by Hélène Ruiz Fabri, Rüdiger Wolfrum, and Jürgen Basedow offers a multidisciplinary perspective on the factors and challenges involved in legal transplants.

- *Comparative Law and Legal Transplants* by Reinhard Zimmermann explores the theoretical foundations and methods of comparative law in the context of legal transplants.

- The International Journal of Legal Information publishes articles and research papers on comparative law, legal transplants, and their implications for legal systems worldwide.

Conclusion

Legal transplants play a significant role in shaping and transforming legal systems around the world. They facilitate the exchange of legal ideas and practices, contributing to the evolution and adaptation of legal systems to meet new challenges. The principles of functional equivalence, legitimacy, mutual learning, gradual adaptation, and transparency guide the process of legal transplants. However, challenges and critiques related to cultural differences, resistance, lack of adaptation, and unintended consequences must be addressed to ensure the successful integration of transplanted legal elements. Understanding the dynamics and complexities of legal transplants is essential for legal scholars, policymakers, and practitioners seeking to navigate the evolving landscape of global legal systems.

Theory and Methods of Legal Transplants

In the field of legal studies, the concept of legal transplants refers to the borrowing and adoption of legal rules, institutions, and practices from one legal system to another. Legal transplants occur when a legal concept or institution, originally developed in one jurisdiction, is introduced into another jurisdiction with the aim of improving or modernizing legal systems. The theory and methods of legal transplants have become essential tools for comparative law scholars, policymakers, and legal practitioners seeking to understand and implement legal reforms.

Theory of Legal Transplants

The theory of legal transplants is based on the premise that legal systems are not isolated entities, but rather they are influenced by various social, cultural, political, and economic factors. Legal transplants recognize that different legal systems can learn from one another and adapt their legal rules and institutions to address new challenges and societal needs. The theory emphasizes the importance of studying the context in which legal transplants occur, including the historical, political, and cultural factors that shape the receiving legal system.

One influential proponent of the theory of legal transplants is Alan Watson, who argued that legal transplants are a natural and necessary process for the growth and development of legal systems. According to Watson, legal systems should not be seen as static and fixed, but rather as evolving and adaptable to changing circumstances. Legal transplants, in this view, serve as a mechanism for legal systems to learn from the experiences and innovations of other jurisdictions.

Methods of Legal Transplants

The methods of legal transplants involve the identification, analysis, and adaptation of legal rules and institutions from one jurisdiction to another. The process begins with the selection of the legal rules or institutions that are to be transplanted. This selection is typically based on the assessment of the receiving jurisdiction's needs and the compatibility of the chosen legal concept with the existing legal framework.

Once the legal concept has been identified, comparative legal scholars engage in a thorough analysis of the legal rules and institutions in the source jurisdiction. This analysis involves understanding the underlying principles, objectives, and policies behind the legal concept, as well as the historical and cultural contexts in which it has developed. Comparative legal scholars also explore the legal reasoning and decision-making processes employed by relevant courts or legal authorities in the source jurisdiction.

After analyzing the legal concept in the source jurisdiction, the next step is to assess its suitability for transplantation to the receiving jurisdiction. This assessment involves evaluating the compatibility of the legal concept with the legal and social conditions of the receiving jurisdiction. Factors such as cultural norms, legal traditions, political structures, and economic realities are taken into account to determine the feasibility and potential impact of the legal transplant.

Once the legal concept has been adapted and transplanted into the receiving jurisdiction, careful monitoring and evaluation are necessary to assess the effectiveness and the impact of the transplant. Scholars and policymakers observe how the transplanted legal concept is interpreted and applied in practice, and make adjustments as needed to ensure its success in the new legal context.

Challenges and Critiques of Legal Transplants

Despite the potential benefits of legal transplants, there are several challenges and critiques associated with this approach. One of the main challenges is the risk of transplanting legal concepts without considering the unique cultural, social, and political contexts of the receiving jurisdiction. Legal concepts that work well in one jurisdiction may not necessarily have the same impact or effectiveness in another jurisdiction. Therefore, careful consideration must be given to the contextual factors that may influence the success or failure of a legal transplant.

Another challenge is the potential loss of authenticity and legitimacy of the legal system in the receiving jurisdiction. Legal transplants may be criticized for importing foreign legal concepts without sufficient justification or democratic input. Critics argue that reliance on legal transplants may undermine the development of local legal traditions and inhibit the evolution of a truly indigenous legal system.

Furthermore, legal transplants may also face resistance from legal practitioners and the public due to concerns about cultural imperialism or the perceived erosion of national identity. These challenges highlight the need for a balanced and well-informed approach to legal transplants, which takes into account the interests and aspirations of the local legal community and the broader society.

Examples of Legal Transplants

Legal transplants have been widely observed in various legal fields, including contract law, constitutional law, and criminal law. For example, many countries have adopted elements of the common law system developed in England, such as the doctrine of precedent and the adversarial system of litigation.

In the field of intellectual property law, the adoption of international treaties and agreements, such as the Paris Convention for the Protection of Industrial Property and the Agreement on Trade-Related Aspects of Intellectual Property Rights (TRIPS), has facilitated the transplantation of legal norms and standards across multiple jurisdictions. These transplants aim to harmonize the protection and enforcement of intellectual property rights on a global scale.

In criminal law, the concept of plea bargaining, which originated in the United States, has been transplanted to many jurisdictions around the world. The introduction of plea bargaining has raised complex ethical and procedural questions, as it involves the exchange of reduced charges or penalties for a defendant's guilty plea.

Resources for Further Study

For readers interested in exploring the theory and methods of legal transplants further, the following resources provide additional insights and perspectives:

- *Legal Transplants: An Approach to Comparative Law* by Alan Watson: This seminal work explores the theory and practice of legal transplants, offering case studies and reflections on the role of comparative law in legal development.

- *The Method and Culture of Comparative Law: Essays in Honour of Mark Van Hoecke* edited by Maurice Adams: This collection of essays examines various aspects of comparative law, including legal transplants, from a multidisciplinary perspective.

- *The Diffusion of Law: The Movement of Laws and Norms Around the World* edited by Sue Farran and Colin B. Picker: This book explores the diffusion of legal norms and the challenges and opportunities they present for legal systems and societies.

♦ *Legal Transplants and Comparative Law* edited by Jean-Louis Halpérin and Mathias Möschel: This collection of essays offers a critical examination of legal transplants, including issues of legitimacy, cultural context, and the role of legal actors in the transplant process.

These resources provide a comprehensive foundation for understanding the theory and methods of legal transplants and offer valuable insights into the challenges and opportunities associated with this field of study.

Exercises

1. Choose a legal concept from one jurisdiction and analyze its potential for transplantation into another jurisdiction. Consider the cultural, social, and political factors that may influence its success or failure.

2. Research and compare the adoption of a particular legal rule or institution in multiple jurisdictions. Analyze the factors that contributed to its successful transplantation and any challenges encountered in the process.

3. Investigate a controversial legal transplant and critically assess its impact on the receiving jurisdiction. Consider both positive and negative consequences and propose alternative approaches or modifications to address the identified challenges.

4. Identify a legal concept that has been transplanted across different legal systems and assess its impact on the harmonization of legal norms. Consider the implications for legal certainty and the challenges of balancing local adaptation with global convergence.

Note: These exercises are designed to encourage critical thinking and further exploration of the theory and methods of legal transplants. They can be approached from various perspectives, such as comparative law, legal sociology, or legal philosophy, and provide an opportunity to engage with real-world examples and scenarios.

Challenges and Controversies in Legal Transplants

Legal transplants refer to the process by which legal rules, procedures, and institutions are borrowed from one legal system and incorporated into another. While legal transplants can be a valuable tool for legal reform and development, they also present a number of challenges and controversies. In this section, we will explore some of the main challenges and controversies associated with legal transplants.

Cultural Context and Legal Transplants

One of the fundamental challenges in legal transplants is ensuring that the imported legal rules are compatible with the cultural, social, and political context of the receiving jurisdiction. Legal systems are deeply rooted in the culture and traditions of a society, and transplantation without careful consideration of these factors can lead to resistance, inefficiency, and lack of compliance.

Example: Sharia Law in Non-Muslim Countries An example of the cultural challenges in legal transplants is the application of Sharia law in non-Muslim countries. In nations where Sharia law is adopted, conflicts may arise due to clashes with existing legal systems and societal values. The transplantation of Sharia law, without adaptations or accommodations to the cultural context, can lead to tensions and resistance from the local population.

Lack of Adaptation

Another challenge in legal transplants is the lack of adaptation and contextualization of the imported legal rules. Legal systems are complex and interconnected, and simply transplanting rules from one system to another without considering the unique characteristics and needs of the receiving system can lead to inefficiencies and disparities.

Example: Common Law in Civil Law Jurisdictions The transplantation of common law principles into civil law jurisdictions can pose challenges. Civil law systems are based on codified laws, while common law relies heavily on judicial precedent and case law. When common law principles are transplanted into civil law jurisdictions, conflicts may arise due to different legal philosophies and approaches. Therefore, adaptation and harmonization are necessary to ensure the effective integration of common law principles in civil law systems.

Resistance and Lack of Local Ownership

One of the controversies surrounding legal transplants is the resistance and lack of local ownership. When legal rules are imposed from external sources without involvement or participation of the local legal community, there is a risk of resistance and lack of acceptance.

Example: Western Legal Systems in Developing Countries In the context of legal transplants from western legal systems to developing countries, critics argue that such transplantation can perpetuate neo-colonialism and undermine local legal traditions. Without local input, implementation of these legal transplants may result in a lack of legitimacy and ownership, leading to limited effectiveness.

Challenges in Implementation and Enforcement

Another challenge in legal transplants is the successful implementation and enforcement of the transplanted legal rules. Differences in legal cultures, practices, and institutions can pose significant obstacles to the effective enforcement of imported legal rules.

Example: Corruption and Governance Transplanting anti-corruption laws into jurisdictions with systemic corruption presents challenges in implementation and enforcement. The lack of strong institutions, political will, and capacity can hinder the effective enforcement of these transplanted rules. To overcome these challenges, capacity-building and institutional reforms are crucial.

Legal Pluralism and Conflict of Laws

Legal transplants can also create conflicts within a legal system by introducing legal pluralism, where multiple legal systems coexist. These conflicts can arise between the transplanted laws and the existing legal framework, leading to uncertainty, complexity, and jurisdictional conflicts.

Example: Customary Law and Transplanted Statutory Law The transplantation of statutory laws into societies with well-established customary legal systems can create conflicts. Customary laws are deeply rooted in the culture and traditions of a community and may differ significantly from the transplanted statutory laws. The coexistence of both legal systems can create challenges in resolving conflicts and determining the appropriate legal framework for a particular case.

Conclusion

Legal transplants can be a valuable tool for legal reform and development, but they are not without challenges and controversies. Cultural context, lack of adaptation, resistance, implementation issues, and conflicts with existing legal frameworks are some of the main challenges associated with legal transplants. Overcoming these challenges requires careful consideration, adaptation, and involvement of the local legal community, ensuring that the transplanted legal rules are compatible, effective, and accepted in the receiving jurisdiction.

Access to Justice and Legal Empowerment

Barriers to Access to Justice

Access to justice is a fundamental aspect of a fair and equitable legal system. However, numerous barriers can hinder individuals from effectively exercising their rights and seeking redress for legal issues. In this section, we will explore the various barriers to access to justice and the challenges they present.

Lack of Legal Knowledge and Awareness

One of the primary barriers to access to justice is the lack of legal knowledge and awareness among individuals. Many people are unaware of their legal rights and the available legal remedies to address their issues. This lack of knowledge can prevent individuals from effectively navigating the legal system and advocating for their rights.

For example, imagine a low-income individual who is facing eviction from their rented house due to unfair practices by the landlord. If this person is not aware of tenant rights and the legal recourse available to them, they may not be able to properly address the situation or seek legal assistance. As a result, they may face housing instability and an unjust eviction.

To overcome this barrier, legal education and awareness programs are essential. Legal aid organizations, community centers, and schools can play a crucial role in providing information about legal rights, available resources, and avenues for seeking legal assistance.

Financial Constraints

Financial constraints pose a significant barrier to accessing justice for many individuals. Legal proceedings often involve various costs, such as attorney fees, court filing fees, expert witness fees, and other related expenses. For individuals with limited financial resources, these costs can be prohibitive and prevent them from pursuing their legal claims.

For instance, imagine a person who has been wrongfully terminated from their job and wants to take legal action against their employer. However, they cannot afford to hire an attorney or pay the court fees required to file a lawsuit. As a result, they may abandon their pursuit of justice due to financial constraints, allowing the employer's wrongful actions to go unchecked.

To address this barrier, legal aid organizations and pro bono services play a critical role in providing free or low-cost legal assistance to individuals who cannot afford legal representation. Additionally, court fee waivers or reduced fees can help alleviate the financial burden on those seeking justice.

Complexity and Inaccessibility of Legal Processes

The complexity and inaccessibility of legal processes can be daunting for individuals seeking justice. The legal system is often filled with complex terminology, technical jargon, and convoluted procedures that can be overwhelming and confusing for the average person. This complexity can deter individuals from navigating the legal system effectively and hinder their access to justice.

For example, imagine a person experiencing workplace discrimination who wants to file a complaint with the appropriate administrative agency. However, the process involves numerous forms, legal requirements, and specific timelines that are difficult for the individual to comprehend. As a result, they may fail to meet critical deadlines or miss essential steps, jeopardizing their legal claim.

To address this barrier, simplifying legal processes and providing accessible information and resources are crucial. Plain language legal materials, self-help resources, and online platforms that guide individuals through legal procedures can empower them to navigate the system more effectively.

Language and Cultural Barriers

Language and cultural barriers can significantly impede access to justice for non-native speakers and individuals from diverse cultural backgrounds. Legal proceedings and documents are often presented in complex language and legal terminology that may not be easily understood by individuals whose first language is not English.

Moreover, cultural differences and mistrust of the legal system can create additional challenges. Some individuals may come from communities with different norms, customs, and understandings of justice, which can clash with the formal legal system.

For instance, consider a person from a non-English speaking background who is a victim of domestic violence. They may hesitate to seek help or report the abuse due to language barriers or cultural beliefs that discourage intervention by outside authorities.

To address these barriers, providing language interpretation services, culturally sensitive legal assistance, and integrating community organizations and leaders can help bridge the gap. Accessible legal information and resources should be available in various languages to ensure that individuals can fully understand their rights and the legal processes involved.

Geographical Constraints

Geographical constraints can pose significant barriers to access to justice, particularly for individuals residing in rural or remote areas. Limited access to legal services and limited transportation options can make it challenging for individuals to access courts, legal aid clinics, or legal professionals in person.

For example, imagine a person living in a remote village who needs legal advice regarding a property dispute. However, they are located hours away from the nearest town with a legal aid clinic or lawyer's office. The lack of accessible legal services in their vicinity can prevent them from seeking the necessary assistance to address their legal issue.

To overcome this barrier, leveraging technology and online platforms can provide remote legal consultations and access to legal resources. Mobile legal clinics and outreach programs can also help bring legal services directly to underserved communities.

Discrimination and Bias in the Legal System

Discrimination and bias within the legal system can create significant barriers to accessing justice, particularly for marginalized communities. Prejudices based on race, gender, socioeconomic status, or other protected characteristics can result in unequal treatment, unequal access to legal representation, and unfair outcomes.

For instance, studies have shown that individuals from racial minority groups often face harsher sentences compared to their white counterparts for similar offenses. Such disparities in outcomes can deter marginalized communities from seeking justice, knowing that their chances of fair treatment are diminished.

To address this barrier, promoting diversity within the legal profession, implementing implicit bias training for legal professionals, and fostering equal access to legal representation can help mitigate discrimination and bias within the system.

Conclusion

Access to justice is crucial for a fair and equitable society. However, barriers such as lack of legal knowledge, financial constraints, complexity of legal processes, language and cultural barriers, geographical constraints, and discrimination within the legal system can hinder individuals' ability to seek justice.

It is essential for legal systems, governments, and organizations to recognize and address these barriers to ensure that justice is accessible to all. Through legal education, free or affordable legal services, simplified legal processes, cultural sensitivity, and technological advancements, we can strive to break down these barriers and create a more inclusive and transformative legal system.

Legal Aid and Pro Bono Services

Legal Aid and Pro Bono Services play a crucial role in ensuring access to justice for individuals who cannot afford legal representation. This section discusses the importance of these services, their principles, challenges, and potential solutions.

Importance of Legal Aid and Pro Bono Services

Access to justice is a fundamental human right. However, many individuals face barriers in exercising this right due to financial constraints. Legal Aid and Pro Bono Services aim to bridge this gap by providing free or low-cost legal assistance to those in need.

1. Legal Aid: Legal Aid refers to government-funded programs that offer legal services to individuals who meet certain eligibility criteria, such as low income. These programs provide legal advice, representation, and assistance in various areas of law, including civil, criminal, family, and immigration law. Legal Aid organizations are committed to promoting equal access to justice and ensuring that individuals have the necessary support to navigate the legal system.

2. Pro Bono Services: Pro Bono services are provided by lawyers who volunteer their time and expertise to provide free legal assistance to underserved populations. Pro Bono work can involve representing individuals who cannot afford legal fees, working on public interest cases, or contributing to law-related community service projects. Pro Bono services are vital in addressing the unmet legal needs of marginalized communities and promoting social justice.

Challenges in Legal Aid and Pro Bono Services

While Legal Aid and Pro Bono Services are essential, they face several challenges that limit their effectiveness in achieving widespread access to justice. These challenges include:

1. Funding: Legal Aid programs heavily rely on government funding, which may be inadequate or subject to budget cuts. Limited resources often lead to a lack of capacity to meet the demand for legal services, resulting in long wait times and limited availability.

2. Eligibility Criteria: Legal Aid programs typically have strict eligibility criteria based on income thresholds. Many individuals may fall into the "justice gap" where they do not qualify for Legal Aid but still cannot afford to hire a private lawyer. This issue highlights the need for expanding eligibility criteria to cater to a broader range of individuals.

3. Pro Bono Capacity: While Pro Bono services greatly contribute to narrowing the justice gap, the availability and capacity of Pro Bono lawyers may vary across jurisdictions. Limited participation and coordination can hinder the effective delivery of Pro Bono services.

4. Limited Scope of Services: Legal Aid programs often have limited resources and can only address certain types of legal issues, prioritizing matters involving immediate risk or systemic importance. This limitation leaves many individuals with unmet legal needs in areas that fall outside the scope of the program's mandate.

Solutions and Innovations

To address the challenges faced by Legal Aid and Pro Bono Services, various innovative approaches have emerged. These include:

1. Technology and Online Services: Embracing technology can significantly enhance the reach and efficiency of Legal Aid and Pro Bono Services. Online platforms and virtual clinics can make legal information and assistance more accessible, connecting individuals with lawyers remotely.

2. Collaboration and Partnerships: Encouraging collaboration between Legal Aid organizations, private law firms, and community organizations can increase the capacity to deliver services. Partnerships can involve law firms committing to a certain number of Pro Bono hours and sharing resources to support Legal Aid programs.

3. Holistic and Preventive Approaches: Shifting focus from reactionary legal services to holistic and preventive approaches can help address legal issues before

they escalate. This includes community legal education programs, early intervention services, and addressing the underlying social and economic factors that contribute to legal problems.

4. Advocacy and Law Reform: Legal Aid and Pro Bono organizations can play a vital role in advocating for systemic changes in the legal system. By targeting policy and legislative reforms, these organizations can address the root causes of legal issues and promote access to justice on a larger scale.

Case Study: The Access to Justice Foundation

The Access to Justice Foundation is a UK-based organization that supports and expands access to justice through various initiatives. The foundation collaborates with law firms, businesses, and individuals to raise funds for Legal Aid and Pro Bono Services. These funds are then distributed to legal charities and organizations that provide free legal assistance to vulnerable individuals. The foundation also focuses on supporting innovative projects that use technology and alternative service delivery models to improve access to justice.

Conclusion

Legal Aid and Pro Bono Services are essential components of a just and inclusive legal system. By addressing the barriers faced by individuals with limited means, these services uphold the principles of equality and access to justice. However, challenges such as funding, eligibility criteria, and limited scope of services require ongoing attention and innovation. Through collaborative efforts, technological advancements, and a holistic approach to legal services, we can strive towards a more equitable and transformative legal system.

Community Legal Education and Empowerment

Community legal education plays a crucial role in empowering individuals and communities by providing them with the knowledge and skills necessary to navigate the legal system effectively. It aims to increase legal literacy and awareness, promote access to justice, and empower marginalized groups to advocate for their rights. This section explores the importance of community legal education and its transformative potential in promoting social justice.

Understanding Community Legal Education

Community legal education (CLE) is an educational process that seeks to demystify the law and make legal information accessible to the general public. It involves providing individuals, community organizations, and social groups with the necessary tools to understand their legal rights, responsibilities, and available resources.

CLE programs can take various forms, including workshops, seminars, public lectures, information sessions, and online resources. These programs are designed to address the specific needs and concerns of particular communities, covering a wide range of legal issues such as housing rights, employment rights, family law, and criminal justice.

Importance of Community Legal Education

Community legal education plays a crucial role in promoting social justice and empowering marginalized communities in several ways:

1. Legal Empowerment: By providing individuals with knowledge about their legal rights and responsibilities, CLE enables them to effectively navigate legal processes and make informed decisions. This empowerment reduces the power imbalance between individuals and institutions, leading to fairer outcomes.

2. Access to Justice: CLE enhances access to justice by ensuring that individuals are aware of their legal rights, available legal remedies, and avenues for seeking legal assistance. It aims to bridge the justice gap by empowering communities to assert their rights and address legal issues effectively.

3. Prevention of Legal Problems: CLE programs can also focus on prevention, by educating individuals and communities about potential legal issues and how to avoid them. This proactive approach helps individuals understand their legal obligations and prevent legal disputes from arising.

4. Building Trust in the Legal System: By demystifying the law and increasing legal literacy, CLE can foster trust in the legal system. When individuals understand their rights and feel empowered to navigate the legal system, they are more likely to engage with the system and seek redress when necessary.

Methods and Strategies in Community Legal Education

Effective community legal education requires tailored methods and strategies to meet the specific needs of the target audience. Some commonly used methods and strategies include:

1. Interactive Workshops: Conducting interactive workshops encourages active participation and engagement from participants. This approach can include role-playing exercises, group discussions, and case studies to enhance understanding and application of legal knowledge.

2. Accessible Language and Formats: It is important to present legal information in plain language and accessible formats to ensure that it can be easily understood by the target audience. The use of visual aids, infographics, and multimedia resources can also enhance comprehension.

3. Collaborative Partnerships: Collaborating with community organizations, legal aid clinics, and other stakeholders can strengthen the impact of CLE initiatives. These partnerships help identify the specific legal needs of the community, provide expertise, and promote the sustainability of CLE programs.

4. Tailored Content: CLE programs should address the specific legal issues and concerns of the target community. By focusing on topics that are relevant and important to the community, CLE can increase engagement and ensure the information is practical and applicable.

Case Studies: Successful Community Legal Education Initiatives

1. Street Law Programs: Street Law programs have been successful in many countries, including the United States and South Africa. These initiatives involve law students and legal professionals delivering legal education to marginalized communities, including homeless individuals, youth in detention centers, and low-income communities.

2. Indigenous Legal Education Programs: In Australia and Canada, community legal education initiatives have been developed in collaboration with Indigenous communities. These programs focus on addressing specific legal issues faced by Indigenous peoples, such as land rights, cultural heritage, and self-determination.

3. Legal Empowerment Clinics: Some organizations have established legal empowerment clinics in underprivileged communities to provide free legal advice and assistance. These clinics offer direct legal services while also educating community members about their rights, enabling them to advocate for themselves.

Challenges and Considerations

While community legal education holds significant transformative potential, it also faces certain challenges. Some key considerations include:

1. Resource Constraints: Limited funding and resources can hinder the development and sustainability of CLE initiatives. Adequate funding and support from government agencies, foundations, and philanthropic organizations are necessary to ensure the long-term success of these programs.
2. Cultural Sensitivity: CLE initiatives should be culturally sensitive and tailored to the specific needs and values of the target community. Understanding the cultural context and incorporating diverse perspectives is crucial to ensure the relevance and effectiveness of CLE programs.
3. Evaluation and Impact Measurement: It is essential to evaluate the effectiveness and impact of CLE initiatives regularly. This requires developing appropriate evaluation methodologies to assess changes in knowledge, behavior, and access to justice among participants.

Conclusion

Community legal education plays a significant role in empowering individuals and communities by increasing legal literacy and promoting access to justice. By providing individuals with the knowledge and skills necessary to navigate the legal system effectively, CLE initiatives help bridge the justice gap and promote social justice. Through tailored methods, collaborative partnerships, and consideration of cultural sensitivity, CLE has the potential to transform the lives of marginalized communities, ensuring their rights and interests are protected.

Alternative Dispute Resolution

Overview of Alternative Dispute Resolution (ADR)

Alternative Dispute Resolution (ADR) refers to a set of processes and techniques designed to resolve disputes outside of the traditional court system. ADR methods are voluntary and aim to provide parties with more control over the resolution process. This section provides an overview of ADR, including its benefits, types, and key principles.

Benefits of ADR

ADR offers several advantages over traditional litigation. First, it is generally a more cost-effective option. ADR processes tend to be less time-consuming and less expensive than going to court, as they avoid lengthy court procedures, legal fees, and formal discovery processes. Second, ADR provides parties with greater flexibility and control over the outcome. In ADR, parties are actively involved in the resolution process, allowing for more creative and customized solutions. Third, ADR often promotes better communication and preserves relationships between disputing parties. Unlike adversarial court proceedings, ADR encourages open dialogue and collaboration, which can lead to more amicable resolutions.

Types of ADR

There are several types of ADR methods available, each suited to different types of disputes. The most common types of ADR include:

1. Mediation: In mediation, a neutral third party, the mediator, facilitates discussions between the parties to help them reach a mutually acceptable agreement. The mediator does not impose a decision but rather assists the parties in finding a resolution that meets their needs and interests.

2. Arbitration: Arbitration involves a neutral third party, the arbitrator, who acts as a private judge and makes a binding decision on the dispute. Arbitration proceedings are less formal than court proceedings and allow parties to present evidence and arguments. The decision of the arbitrator, known as an award, is enforceable.

3. Negotiation: Negotiation is a direct dialogue between the parties involved in the dispute. It can be informal or formal and may involve the assistance of lawyers or other advisers. Negotiation allows parties to discuss their positions and interests to find a mutually agreeable solution.

4. Conciliation: Conciliation is similar to mediation, where a neutral third party, the conciliator, assists the parties in reaching a resolution. However, the conciliator may propose solutions or offer expert advice to help the parties find common ground.

5. Collaborative Law: Collaborative law involves a team approach to problem-solving, with both parties and their respective lawyers working together to find a resolution. This method focuses on open communication and the shared commitment to reaching an agreement.

Key Principles of ADR

While different ADR methods vary in their procedures and techniques, they share some common principles:

1. Voluntary participation: ADR methods are voluntary, and all parties must agree to participate. It ensures that parties are invested in the resolution process and have control over the outcome.

2. Confidentiality: ADR proceedings are generally confidential, meaning that discussions, documents, and outcomes are not disclosed outside of the process. This confidentiality fosters open and honest communication between the parties.

3. Impartiality and neutrality: ADR neutrals, such as mediators or arbitrators, must be impartial and neutral. They have no stake in the outcome and act as unbiased facilitators or decision-makers.

4. Fairness: ADR processes strive to create a fair and equitable resolution. This involves giving each party an equal opportunity to present their case and ensuring that power imbalances are addressed.

5. Enforceability: In some cases, ADR outcomes can be legally binding and enforceable. For example, arbitration awards can be enforced like court judgments if the parties agree to binding arbitration.

Examples and Applications

ADR is widely used in various areas of law, including commercial disputes, employment disputes, family law matters, and community disputes. For instance, businesses often prefer arbitration to resolve contract disputes, as it allows for a speedier and more efficient resolution process. Mediation is frequently employed in family law cases, helping couples reach agreements regarding custody, visitation, and support. ADR processes have also been used to address environmental disputes, labor disputes, and international conflicts.

Challenges and Ethical Considerations

Despite its advantages, ADR is not without challenges and ethical considerations. One challenge is ensuring the competence and impartiality of ADR neutrals. Training and accreditation programs help address this concern by setting standards for professionals in the field. Ethical considerations include the obligation to maintain party confidentiality, address power imbalances, and ensure that all parties have equal access to the process.

Resources for Further Study

To further explore ADR, the following resources are recommended:
1. "Getting to Yes: Negotiating Agreement Without Giving In" by Roger Fisher, William Ury, and Bruce Patton. 2. "Mediation: Principles and Practice" by Allan Stitt. 3. "The Handbook of Dispute Resolution" edited by Michael L. Moffitt and Robert C. Bordone. 4. "Alternative Dispute Resolution: A Practical Guide" by Martin A. Frey and Holly Frey. 5. The American Arbitration

Association (www.adr.org) provides resources, training, and information on various ADR processes.

Conclusion

ADR offers a range of benefits, including cost-effectiveness, increased party autonomy, and better preservation of relationships. It encompasses various methods, such as mediation, arbitration, and negotiation, each suited to different types of disputes. Understanding the key principles of ADR, including voluntary participation, confidentiality, and fairness, is crucial for effective dispute resolution. While ADR has its challenges and ethical considerations, it remains a valuable alternative to traditional litigation, promoting more constructive and satisfactory outcomes for disputing parties.

Mediation and Negotiation in ADR

Mediation and negotiation are two important methods used in Alternative Dispute Resolution (ADR) to resolve conflicts and disputes. These methods focus on facilitating communication, understanding, and agreement between parties involved in a dispute, without the need for a formal court process. This section will provide an overview of mediation and negotiation in ADR, their key principles, techniques, challenges, and ethical considerations.

Mediation

Mediation is a voluntary and confidential process in which a neutral third party, called a mediator, assists disputing parties in reaching a mutually acceptable resolution. The mediator does not make decisions or impose solutions but instead helps facilitate effective communication and supports the parties' exploration of their interests and options.

Key Principles of Mediation Mediation is guided by several key principles that contribute to its effectiveness and transformative potential:

1. *Voluntary and self-determined*: Parties have the right to participate voluntarily and make independent decisions throughout the process.

2. *Confidentiality*: Mediation is a confidential process, which allows parties to speak openly and honestly without fear of their statements being used against them in future court proceedings.

3. *Impartiality*: The mediator remains neutral and unbiased, ensuring that all parties are treated fairly and their perspectives are respected.

4. *Mutual understanding and communication*: Mediation emphasizes the importance of active listening and effective communication to enhance understanding between parties and uncover common interests.

Techniques in Mediation Mediation employs various techniques to assist parties in resolving their dispute. Some common techniques include:
 1. *Joint sessions*: Parties come together with the mediator to discuss the issues, share their perspectives, and explore potential solutions.
 2. *Private sessions*: The mediator conducts separate meetings with each party to delve deeper into their concerns, interests, and possible solutions.
 3. *Facilitative techniques*: The mediator uses questioning, reframing, and summarizing techniques to promote understanding, foster dialogue, and encourage creative problem-solving.
 4. *Reality testing*: The mediator explores the potential outcomes of the dispute to help parties assess the risks and benefits of their proposed solutions.

Challenges in Mediation Mediation faces several challenges that can impact its effectiveness and desirable outcomes:
 1. *Power imbalances*: Imbalances of power between parties can hinder open communication and decision-making, requiring the mediator to address and mitigate these imbalances.
 2. *Resistance to compromise*: Parties may hold firm positions and be resistant to exploring common ground, necessitating the mediator to employ additional techniques to encourage cooperation and flexibility.
 3. *Lack of enforceability*: Unlike court judgments, mediated agreements are not automatically enforceable, and parties may require additional legal processes to ensure compliance.
 4. *Ethical dilemmas*: Mediators must navigate ethical complexities such as confidentiality, impartiality, and conflicts of interest in a manner that upholds the integrity of the process.

Ethical Considerations in Mediation Mediators are guided by ethical standards that promote fairness, impartiality, and the best interests of the parties involved. Some key ethical considerations include:
 1. *Informed consent*: Mediators must ensure that parties understand the nature, process, and potential outcomes of mediation before they agree to participate.
 2. *Impartiality and neutrality*: Mediators must maintain their impartiality and avoid any conflicts of interest that might compromise their neutrality.

3. *Confidentiality*: Mediators must uphold the confidentiality of the mediation process and the information shared by the parties, unless permitted or required by law.

4. *Professional competence*: Mediators should possess the necessary skills, training, and knowledge to conduct mediation effectively and ethically.

Example: Workplace Mediation A common application of mediation is in resolving workplace conflicts. Consider a scenario where two employees, Sarah and John, have a disagreement over the division of work responsibilities. Their dispute has escalated, impacting their working relationship and team dynamics. A workplace mediator is engaged to facilitate the mediation process.

The mediator starts by conducting separate private sessions with Sarah and John to understand their concerns, interests, and desired outcomes. They then schedule joint sessions where Sarah and John communicate their perspectives, guided by the mediator, who ensures respectful dialogue and active listening. Through the use of facilitative techniques, the mediator supports Sarah and John in exploring various solutions, such as a revised division of work or clearer communication channels.

By employing reality testing, the mediator helps Sarah and John evaluate the potential consequences of their proposed solutions and assess the feasibility of implementation. Through open communication and mutual understanding facilitated by the mediator, Sarah and John are able to reach an agreement that addresses their concerns and allows them to restore a positive working relationship.

Negotiation

Negotiation is a process by which parties in a dispute engage in discussions and make offers or counteroffers to reach a mutually acceptable agreement. Negotiation can be used independently or as part of a larger ADR process, such as mediation or arbitration.

Key Principles of Negotiation Negotiation is guided by several key principles that contribute to successful outcomes:

1. *Good faith*: Parties engage in negotiation with a genuine willingness to explore options and reach a resolution.

2. *Interests*: Negotiation focuses on identifying each party's underlying interests rather than rigid positions, allowing for creative problem-solving and win-win solutions.

3. *Effective communication*: Parties engage in active listening, clear expression, and mutual understanding to facilitate productive negotiations.

4. *Flexibility*: Negotiation requires flexibility and a willingness to adjust strategies and proposals in response to new information or changing circumstances.

Techniques in Negotiation Negotiation employs various techniques to facilitate agreement between disputing parties. Some common techniques include:
1. *Preparation and planning*: Parties gather relevant information, identify their interests, and set clear objectives for the negotiation process.
2. *Building rapport*: Establishing a positive rapport and fostering a constructive relationship can create a conducive environment for negotiations.
3. *Active listening*: Parties carefully listen to each other's perspectives, concerns, and proposals to understand their underlying interests.
4. *Exploring options*: Parties generate multiple potential solutions to the dispute and assess their feasibility and desirability together.

Challenges in Negotiation Negotiation may encounter various challenges that can impede the resolution process:
1. *Divergent interests*: Parties may have conflicting interests, making it challenging to find common ground and reach an agreement.
2. *Power dynamics*: Power imbalances between parties can influence the negotiation process, requiring strategies to address and equalize power.
3. *Emotional barriers*: Strong emotions, such as anger or distrust, can hinder effective communication and impede the negotiation process.
4. *Deadlock*: Parties may reach a point of deadlock where further progress seems impossible, necessitating innovative techniques to overcome the impasse.

Ethical Considerations in Negotiation Negotiators must adhere to ethical principles to maintain fairness and preserve the integrity of the negotiation process. Some key ethical considerations include:
1. *Honesty and transparency*: Negotiators should provide accurate and truthful information to the other party, avoiding deceit or misrepresentation.
2. *Respect*: Negotiators should treat each other with respect, even when there are strong differences of opinion or conflicting interests.
3. *Informed decision-making*: Negotiators should ensure that parties have comprehensive information about the negotiation process and potential outcomes to make informed decisions.
4. *Confidentiality*: Negotiators should respect the confidentiality of sensitive information shared during the negotiation process.

Example: Negotiation in Business Contracts Negotiation plays a crucial role in business contract formation. Consider a scenario where two companies, Company A and Company B, are negotiating the terms of a partnership agreement. The key points of negotiation include the division of profits, the scope of responsibilities, and dispute resolution mechanisms.

Both companies assign negotiators who engage in preparation and planning by identifying their interests and setting objectives. They engage in face-to-face negotiation sessions, employing active listening to understand each other's perspectives and concerns. Through a series of offers, counteroffers, and creative problem-solving, they explore multiple options to find a mutually acceptable agreement.

During the negotiation process, the negotiators ensure transparency and honesty, providing accurate information about their company's capabilities and limitations. They treat each other with respect, recognizing the value of a collaborative partnership. Finally, they reach a consensus on the partnership terms, which they formalize into a written contract, thereby solidifying their agreement.

Exercises

1. Consider a workplace conflict scenario and outline the steps a mediator could take to facilitate the resolution process.

2. Identify a negotiation challenge you have encountered in your personal or professional life and discuss how you addressed it.

3. Research and analyze a real-life case where mediation or negotiation was used to resolve a high-profile dispute. Assess the effectiveness of the ADR method used and its impact on the parties involved.

Resources for Further Study

1. Fisher, R., Ury, W., & Patton, B. (2011). *Getting to Yes: Negotiating an Agreement Without Giving In.* Penguin.

2. Folberg, J., & Taylor, A. (2012). *Mediation: A Comprehensive Guide to Resolving Conflicts Without Litigation.* Jossey-Bass.

3. Menkel-Meadow, C., Schneider, A. K., Love, L., & Sternlight, J. R. (2006). *Dispute Resolution: Beyond the Adversarial Model.* Aspen Publishers.

Conclusion

Mediation and negotiation are powerful tools in Alternative Dispute Resolution that provide parties with the opportunity to resolve their disputes in a collaborative, non-adversarial manner. Mediation focuses on facilitated communication and mutual understanding, while negotiation emphasizes the exploration of common interests and options. Both processes require skilled practitioners who adhere to ethical considerations. By harnessing the transformative potential of mediation and negotiation, individuals and organizations can achieve fair and mutually beneficial resolutions to their conflicts.

Arbitration and Conciliation in ADR

Arbitration and conciliation are two important methods of alternative dispute resolution (ADR). In this section, we will explore the concepts, processes, and significance of arbitration and conciliation in transforming the traditional adversarial approach to resolving legal disputes.

Background and Principles

Arbitration is a process by which parties involved in a dispute agree to submit their case to a neutral third party, known as an arbitrator or an arbitral tribunal. The arbitrator acts as a private judge who hears evidence, reviews arguments, and makes a binding decision, known as an award. The decision is enforceable and has the same legal effect as a court judgment.

On the other hand, conciliation is a non-binding process in which a neutral third party, known as a conciliator, facilitates communication and negotiation between the parties to help them reach a mutually acceptable resolution. Unlike arbitration, conciliation does not result in a final decision unless the parties voluntarily agree to the terms proposed during the process.

Both arbitration and conciliation share some common principles:

- **Voluntary Participation:** Parties must agree to participate in arbitration or conciliation voluntarily. They retain control over the process and have the freedom to withdraw at any stage.

- **Confidentiality:** The proceedings of arbitration and conciliation are confidential. This promotes open and frank discussions and protects the parties' privacy.

- **Neutrality and Impartiality:** The arbitrator or conciliator must be neutral and impartial, ensuring a fair and unbiased process.

- **Party Autonomy:** Parties have the freedom to determine the rules and procedures of the arbitration or conciliation process, allowing them to tailor the proceedings to fit their specific needs.
- **Finality and Enforcement:** In arbitration, the decision is final and binding, subject to limited grounds for challenge. The award can be enforced in national courts through the New York Convention, an international treaty governing the recognition and enforcement of arbitral awards.

Arbitration Process

The arbitration process typically consists of the following stages:

1. **Agreement to Arbitrate:** The parties enter into an arbitration agreement, either as a standalone contract or as a clause within a broader agreement, to submit their dispute to arbitration. The agreement specifies the rules, procedures, and governing law of the arbitration.

2. **Appointment of the Arbitrator(s):** The parties select the arbitrator(s) or rely on a designated institution to appoint a suitable arbitrator. The arbitrator should have relevant expertise and be independent and impartial.

3. **Pleadings and Evidence:** The parties exchange written submissions, known as pleadings, presenting their arguments, facts, and evidence. They may also call witnesses and experts to testify at a hearing.

4. **Hearing:** The arbitrator conducts a hearing where the parties present their case orally. The hearing allows for questioning, clarifications, and the examination of witnesses.

5. **Deliberation and Award:** After the hearing, the arbitrator deliberates and analyzes the evidence and arguments presented. The arbitrator then issues a written award, setting out the decision and any remedies or damages awarded.

6. **Enforcement:** The winning party may enforce the award through national courts, if necessary, relying on the New York Convention or other relevant enforcement mechanisms.

Arbitration offers several advantages over traditional litigation. It provides a faster and more flexible process, allows parties to choose their decision-maker, avoids crowded court dockets, and maintains confidentiality. Moreover, arbitration is particularly useful in resolving international disputes, where parties may come from different legal systems and prefer a neutral forum.

Conciliation Process

Conciliation involves a more collaborative process aimed at assisting parties in reaching a mutually acceptable settlement. The process typically involves the following steps:

1. **Engagement of the Conciliator:** The parties agree to engage a conciliator, who acts as a facilitator or mediator between them. The conciliator is often chosen for their expertise in the subject matter or their mediation skills.

2. **Intake and Information Gathering:** The conciliator meets with each party separately to gather information about the dispute, understand their perspectives, and establish a rapport.

3. **Joint Meeting:** The conciliator arranges a joint meeting with both parties to discuss the issues, encourage dialogue, and identify common interests. The joint meeting aims to explore various settlement options.

4. **Negotiation and Problem-Solving:** The conciliator facilitates negotiations, fostering an environment of open communication and creative problem-solving. The parties are encouraged to generate mutually beneficial solutions.

5. **Settlement Agreement:** If the parties reach a settlement, the conciliator helps draft a settlement agreement that reflects their agreement. The settlement agreement may be binding or non-binding, depending on the parties' intentions.

Conciliation allows parties to maintain control over the outcome and promotes a cooperative rather than adversarial approach. It fosters better understanding, preserves relationships, and often leads to more sustainable and satisfactory resolutions.

Arbitration and Conciliation in Practice

Arbitration and conciliation are widely used in various contexts, including commercial, labor, construction, and family disputes. Here are some examples of their applications:

- **International Commercial Arbitration:** Businesses engaging in cross-border transactions often opt for arbitration to resolve disputes.

Institutions like the International Chamber of Commerce (ICC) and the London Court of International Arbitration (LCIA) provide arbitration services and rules tailored to international commercial disputes.

- **Investor-State Disputes:** Arbitration is commonly used to resolve disputes between foreign investors and host countries. Bilateral investment treaties (BITs) or investment chapters in free trade agreements often provide for arbitration as a means of settling investment disputes.

- **Labor Disputes:** Arbitration is employed in labor disputes to resolve issues such as collective bargaining agreements, unfair labor practices, and employment contract disputes. In some jurisdictions, labor arbitration may be mandatory before resorting to strikes or lockouts.

- **Family and Divorce Mediation:** Conciliation plays a crucial role in family law, particularly in divorce proceedings. Mediators help facilitate discussions on child custody, division of assets, and spousal support, aiming to promote amicable and sustainable resolutions.

Despite their advantages, arbitration and conciliation also face challenges. These include limited access to justice, high costs, potential power imbalances between parties, and the enforceability of conciliation agreements. Efforts are underway to address these challenges and improve the effectiveness and fairness of both methods.

Conclusion

Arbitration and conciliation offer flexible and efficient alternatives to traditional litigation for resolving disputes. They promote party autonomy, enhance privacy, and foster collaborative problem-solving. Whether in commercial, labor, family, or international disputes, arbitration and conciliation have the potential to transform the legal landscape by providing access to justice, promoting fairness, and maintaining social harmony.

To further explore and understand the principles and practices of arbitration and conciliation, we recommend referring to the works of recognized experts in the field, such as Gary Born's "International Commercial Arbitration" and Linda Richardson's "Conflict Resolution in the Twenty-First Century." Additionally, engaging in practical exercises and mock simulations can enhance your understanding of the arbitration and conciliation processes. Online resources, training programs, and professional organizations like the American Arbitration

Association (AAA) and the International Mediation Institute (IMI) can provide valuable guidance, resources, and networking opportunities in the field of alternative dispute resolution.

Challenges and Ethical Considerations in ADR

Alternative Dispute Resolution (ADR) offers a range of advantages in resolving conflicts outside of the traditional court system. However, like any legal process, ADR is not without its challenges and ethical considerations. In this section, we will explore some of these challenges and discuss the ethical considerations that arise in the context of ADR.

Lack of Legal Precedent and Predictability

One of the primary challenges in ADR is the absence of legal precedent. Unlike traditional court proceedings, where judges are bound by legal precedents and statutory frameworks, ADR relies heavily on the subjective decision-making of the parties involved and the mediator or arbitrator. This lack of legal precedent can make it difficult to predict the outcome of the dispute and may result in inconsistent decisions.

To address this challenge, it is essential to establish clear guidelines and principles in the ADR process. Mediators and arbitrators should ensure transparency and provide detailed explanations for their decisions, thereby increasing predictability and promoting fairness in the resolution of disputes.

Power Imbalances

Another significant challenge in ADR is the presence of power imbalances between the parties involved. In some cases, one party may hold a dominant position, such as a large corporation or a government entity, while the other party may lack resources or influence. This power disparity can potentially compromise the fairness and equity of the ADR process.

To address power imbalances, it is crucial for mediators and arbitrators to create an environment that encourages equal participation and ensures that all parties have a voice in the resolution of the dispute. This may involve implementing safeguards, such as providing legal representation to parties who cannot afford it or appointing neutral third parties to assist in the negotiation process.

Confidentiality and Disclosure

Confidentiality is a fundamental principle in ADR, as it allows parties to freely express their concerns and explore potential solutions without fear of public disclosure. However, the principle of confidentiality may conflict with the duty of disclosure, which requires parties to provide all relevant information and evidence during the dispute resolution process.

Balancing confidentiality and disclosure is a critical ethical consideration in ADR. Mediators and arbitrators must ensure that parties understand the limitations of confidentiality and the circumstances in which disclosure may be necessary to achieve a fair resolution. Clear guidelines and procedures for handling confidential information should be established to protect the privacy of the parties involved while still promoting transparency and fairness.

Impartiality and Conflict of Interest

Impartiality is a fundamental requirement for mediators and arbitrators in ADR. They must remain neutral and unbiased throughout the dispute resolution process. However, challenges may arise when mediators or arbitrators have prior relationships or conflicts of interest with one or more parties.

Identifying and addressing potential conflicts of interest is crucial to maintaining the integrity of ADR proceedings. Mediators and arbitrators should disclose any potential conflicts and take appropriate steps to ensure that their impartiality is not compromised. This may involve recusing themselves from the case or implementing safeguards, such as establishing an independent oversight committee to review and address any conflicts of interest.

Enforceability of Agreements

One of the primary advantages of ADR is the ability to reach mutually satisfactory agreements tailored to the specific needs of the parties. However, enforceability can be a challenge, particularly in cases where parties may choose not to comply with the agreed-upon terms.

To address this challenge, it is crucial to ensure that the ADR process includes mechanisms for enforcement. This may involve incorporating legal professionals or enforceable provisions into the agreement, allowing for the conversion of the agreement into a legal judgment, or ensuring that the agreement is recognized and enforceable under applicable laws.

Ethical Considerations and Professional Conduct

Ethical considerations are integral to the practice of ADR. Mediators and arbitrators must adhere to a code of ethics that governs their professional conduct, such as maintaining confidentiality, promoting fairness, and avoiding conflicts of interest. However, adherence to ethical guidelines can sometimes present challenges, particularly when parties disagree on the interpretation of these principles.

To address ethical challenges, it is essential for mediators and arbitrators to undergo comprehensive training and education in ethics. This training should focus on promoting a clear understanding of ethical guidelines, providing tools for addressing ethical dilemmas, and fostering a strong ethical culture within the ADR community.

Overall, while ADR offers many benefits in resolving disputes, it also presents challenges and ethical considerations that require careful attention. By addressing these challenges and upholding ethical standards, ADR can continue to provide a fair, efficient, and accessible alternative to traditional litigation.

Conclusion

In this section, we have explored some of the key challenges and ethical considerations in ADR. From the lack of legal precedent and power imbalances to confidentiality and conflict of interest, these challenges highlight the complexity of the ADR process. However, by establishing clear guidelines, promoting impartiality, and addressing ethical dilemmas, ADR can become a transformative approach to dispute resolution. Future advancements in ADR practices and ongoing dialogue on ethical standards will further enhance the effectiveness and ethics of ADR in promoting justice and equality in society.

Restorative Justice and Transformative Justice

Introduction to Restorative Justice

Restorative justice is a transformative approach to addressing wrongdoing and conflict in the criminal justice system. It focuses on repairing harm, restoring relationships, and promoting healing for all parties involved, including victims, offenders, and the community.

Restorative justice acknowledges that crime is not just a violation of the law, but also a violation of relationships and the community's well-being. It seeks to address the underlying causes of criminal behavior and provide opportunities for accountability, growth, and reconciliation.

At its core, restorative justice is grounded in four key principles:

1. **Encounter:** Restorative justice emphasizes direct communication between victims and offenders, providing an opportunity for them to share their experiences, express their needs, and understand the impact of the harm caused.

2. **Amends:** Restorative justice aims to make amends for the harm caused, both tangible and intangible. This may involve restitution or community service, but it goes beyond mere punishment to focus on the active restoration of relationships and communities.

3. **Inclusion:** Restorative justice seeks to involve all affected parties, including victims, offenders, and the larger community. It recognizes that crime not only harms individuals, but also erodes the fabric of society, and thus, community involvement is crucial in the healing process.

4. **Reintegration:** Restorative justice supports the reintegration of offenders back into the community in a meaningful and productive way. It recognizes that punishment alone often perpetuates a cycle of crime and aims to provide opportunities for personal growth and a sense of belonging.

By embracing these principles, restorative justice offers an alternative to traditional punitive approaches and opens doors for more transformative outcomes. It shifts the focus from punishment to healing, from isolation to inclusion, and from resentment to reconciliation.

One example of restorative justice practice is victim-offender mediation. In this process, a trained mediator facilitates a dialogue between the victim and the offender, providing a safe and structured space for them to express their feelings, discuss the harm caused, and determine mutually agreed-upon steps for repairing the harm. This process empowers both the victim and the offender, allowing them to actively participate in finding a resolution that addresses their needs and promotes healing.

Restorative justice is not without its challenges. Some critics argue that it may prioritize the needs of offenders over those of victims, fail to provide adequate support for victims, or not address the systemic issues that contribute to crime. However, proponents argue that restorative justice, when implemented effectively and in conjunction with other social and legal reforms, can lead to more meaningful and sustainable outcomes that promote justice, equality, and social transformation.

Contemporary Challenges in Restorative Justice

While restorative justice offers promising alternatives, it also faces various challenges in its implementation. Some of the key contemporary challenges in restorative justice include:

Institutional Resistance

Traditional criminal justice systems are often resistant to change, viewing restorative justice as a departure from established norms and procedures. This resistance stems from concerns about the effectiveness, fairness, and potential risks associated with restorative justice. Overcoming this resistance requires education, training, and evidence-based research to demonstrate the positive impact of restorative justice practices.

Victim and Offender Participation

The success of restorative justice depends on the voluntary participation of both victims and offenders. However, victims may be reluctant to participate due to fear, trauma, or concerns about re-victimization. Similarly, offenders may be hesitant to confront the harm they have caused. Ensuring meaningful and voluntary participation requires support, information, and safeguards to protect the rights and well-being of all parties involved.

Community Engagement

Restorative justice emphasizes community involvement in the resolution process. However, engaging the community in a meaningful and inclusive manner can be challenging. In some cases, community members may have biases or stereotypes that hinder their ability to support and embrace restorative justice practices. Building community trust, promoting dialogue, and providing education are essential to overcome these barriers.

Resource Allocation

Restorative justice programs require resources, including trained facilitators, support services for victims and offenders, and infrastructure to facilitate dialogue and healing. Limited funding and competing priorities can hinder the establishment and sustainability of restorative justice initiatives. Advocating for increased resources and developing innovative funding models are necessary to overcome these challenges.

Complexity of Cases

Restorative justice may not be suitable for all cases. Certain offenses, such as serious and violent crimes, pose unique challenges and may require additional support and safeguards. Balancing the principles of restorative justice with the need for public safety and accountability is a complex task that requires careful consideration and assessment.

Restorative Justice in Action: Case Study

One inspiring example of restorative justice in action is the Longmont Community Justice Partnership (LCJP) in Colorado, USA. The LCJP provides an alternative to the traditional criminal justice system for low-level offenses committed by youth.

In the LCJP process, trained facilitators bring together the offender, victim, and community members in a restorative conference. During the conference, everyone has the opportunity to express their perspectives, share their feelings, and work collaboratively to develop a plan that addresses the harm caused.

The LCJP focuses on repairing relationships rather than imposing punishments. Offenders take responsibility for their actions, learn from their mistakes, and make amends through acts of service and restitution. Victims have the chance to be heard, ask questions, and actively participate in shaping the resolution. Finally, community members provide support, hold offenders accountable, and play a pivotal role in reintegrating them back into the community.

Through its restorative justice approach, the LCJP has achieved remarkable results. Recidivism rates among youth participating in the program are significantly lower compared to those processed through the traditional justice system. Moreover, participants reported higher levels of satisfaction with the process and a sense of healing and empowerment.

The success of the LCJP demonstrates the transformative potential of restorative justice in addressing youth crime, promoting accountability, and fostering stronger, safer communities.

Conclusion

Restorative justice offers a transformative approach to addressing crime and conflict in our society. By focusing on repairing harm, restoring relationships, and promoting healing, restorative justice presents an alternative to punitive measures that often perpetuate cycles of crime and harm.

While restorative justice faces challenges in implementation, such as institutional resistance and resource allocation, its principles and practices have the potential to create meaningful and sustainable change in the criminal justice system. Through the active involvement of victims, offenders, and the community, restorative justice fosters empathy, accountability, and social transformation.

As we continue to explore transformative approaches to legal studies, restorative justice serves as a powerful reminder of the importance of healing, reconciliation, and community engagement in pursuit of justice and equality. By embracing this transformative philosophy, we can create a more just and inclusive society where everyone has the opportunity to heal, grow, and thrive.

Principles and Practices of Restorative Justice

Restorative justice is a transformative approach to criminal justice that focuses on repairing harm caused by crime and addressing the needs of all parties involved, including victims, offenders, and the community. It seeks to go beyond punishment and retribution, aiming instead for accountability, healing, and restoration.

Principles of Restorative Justice

Restorative justice is guided by several key principles that shape its practices and outcomes. These principles include:

1. Encounter: Restorative justice emphasizes direct communication between the victim and the offender, providing them with an opportunity to express their feelings, ask questions, and gain a better understanding of the impact of the offense.

2. Inclusion: All affected parties, including the victim, the offender, and the community, are given the opportunity to participate in the restorative process. Their voices are valued and acknowledged, allowing for a more comprehensive and holistic resolution.

3. Empowerment: Restorative justice recognizes that both victims and offenders have the capacity to actively participate in the process and take responsibility for their actions. It aims to empower them by giving them a voice in the decision-making process and encouraging them to work together towards a resolution.

4. Accountability: Rather than focusing solely on punishment, restorative justice promotes accountability by encouraging offenders to acknowledge the harm they have caused, take responsibility for their actions, and work towards making amends.

5. Healing and Reintegration: Restorative justice seeks to facilitate healing and promote the reintegration of offenders into society. It recognizes that punishment alone does not address the underlying issues and can perpetuate a cycle of harm.

Practices of Restorative Justice

Restorative justice employs various practices to address harm and restore relationships. These practices may vary depending on the jurisdiction and the specific needs of the individuals involved. Some common practices include:

1. Victim-Offender Mediation: This practice brings together the victim and the offender in a controlled and facilitated environment. They engage in a guided conversation where they can share their experiences, express their emotions, and discuss the impact of the offense. The focus is on understanding, empathy, and finding mutually acceptable resolutions.

2. Family Group Conferencing: In cases involving juvenile offenders, family group conferencing is often used. It involves the victim, the offender, their families, and relevant community members coming together to discuss the offense, its impact, and how to address the harm caused. The goal is to promote understanding, support, and agreement on how to repair the harm.

3. Circle Sentencing: Circle sentencing is a practice rooted in indigenous cultures, where a circle, facilitated by a trained mediator, is formed. The circle includes the victim, the offender, community members, and representatives from the justice system. The process allows for open dialogue, sharing of perspectives, and collaborative decision-making regarding the appropriate resolution.

4. Restorative Community Service: Instead of traditional forms of punishment, restorative justice may involve offenders participating in community service projects that directly address the harm caused. This allows offenders to contribute positively to the community while also taking responsibility for their actions.

5. Restorative Conferencing: Restorative conferencing involves an extended group of stakeholders, including representatives from the justice system, social services, and community organizations. The aim is to address complex cases that require a comprehensive and coordinated response. The conferencing process allows for a collective exploration of underlying issues, effective collaboration, and the creation of a tailored plan to repair harm and prevent future offenses.

Challenges and Ethical Considerations

While restorative justice holds great potential, it is not without its challenges and ethical considerations. Some of the challenges include:

1. Power Imbalances: Restorative justice relies on the willingness and ability of all parties to participate voluntarily. However, power imbalances and fear may prevent some individuals from fully engaging in the process. Ensuring equal

participation and addressing power dynamics is crucial for a successful restorative justice outcome.

2. Victim Safety: In cases involving violent offenses or when there is a risk to the victim's safety, careful consideration must be given to the victim's participation. Ensuring their safety and well-being should be a priority, and appropriate support systems should be in place.

3. Offender Accountability: While restorative justice promotes offender accountability, there are cases where offenders may not fully acknowledge the harm caused or may not be willing to take responsibility for their actions. Balancing the need for accountability with the voluntary nature of the process is a challenge for practitioners.

Ethical considerations in restorative justice include:

1. Confidentiality: Ensuring the privacy and confidentiality of participants is essential to build trust and encourage open communication.

2. Informed Consent: All participants should have a clear understanding of the restorative justice process, their rights, and the potential outcomes. Informed consent is vital to ensure voluntary and meaningful participation.

3. Cultural Sensitivity: Restorative justice practices should take into account the cultural backgrounds, values, and beliefs of the individuals involved. Cultural sensitivity helps create a safe and supportive environment for all participants.

Examples of Restorative Justice Practices

Restorative justice practices have been implemented in various jurisdictions and have shown promising results. Here are a few examples:

1. New Zealand's Family Group Conferences: New Zealand has successfully integrated restorative justice principles into its juvenile justice system through family group conferences. This practice has led to reduced reoffending rates and increased victim satisfaction.

2. Rwanda's Gacaca Courts: Following the genocide in 1994, Rwanda established Gacaca courts, which employed restorative justice practices to address the mass atrocities committed. These community-based courts allowed for truth-telling, reconciliation, and reintegration of offenders into society.

3. Victim-Offender Mediation in Canada: In Canada, victim-offender mediation programs have been implemented to address property crimes, minor assaults, and other offenses. These programs have shown positive outcomes, such as increased victim satisfaction and reductions in recidivism.

Resources for Further Study

For further exploration of restorative justice principles and practices, the following resources are recommended:

- "The Little Book of Restorative Justice" by Howard Zehr
- "Restorative Justice: Healing the Foundations of Our Everyday Lives" by Ivo Aertsen
- The International Institute for Restorative Practices website (www.iirp.edu)
- The Restorative Justice Council website (www.restorativejustice.org.uk)

These resources provide valuable insights into the theoretical foundations, practical applications, and ongoing developments in the field of restorative justice.

Conclusion

Restorative justice is a transformative approach that challenges the traditional punitive nature of criminal justice systems. By focusing on repairing harm, involving all affected parties, and promoting healing and accountability, restorative justice offers a unique perspective on addressing crime. Its principles and practices provide opportunities for both victims and offenders to participate actively in the resolution process.

While challenges and ethical considerations exist, the potential benefits of restorative justice are undeniable. As societies seek more holistic and inclusive approaches to justice, restorative justice stands as a powerful tool for transforming criminal justice systems, fostering healing, and promoting social reintegration. Continued research, dialogue, and implementation of restorative justice practices are essential to further the transformative impact of this approach.

Transformative Justice and its Potential Impact

In the field of legal studies, transformative justice is an emerging approach that seeks to address the limitations and shortcomings of traditional criminal justice systems. This section will explore the concept of transformative justice, its theoretical foundations, and its potential impact on society.

Understanding Transformative Justice

Transformative justice is a framework that seeks to challenge and transform the root causes of harm and crime, rather than focusing solely on punishment and retribution. It emphasizes repairing the harm caused by crime, meeting the needs of both the victim and the offender, and working towards healing and reconciliation.

At its core, transformative justice seeks to shift the focus from punitive measures to a more restorative and transformative approach. It aims to empower individuals to actively participate in the process of justice and healing, as opposed to being passive recipients of a legal system that often perpetuates cycles of harm.

Theoretical Foundations of Transformative Justice

Transformative justice draws on various theoretical perspectives, each offering unique insights into understanding and addressing crime and harm. Some of the key theoretical foundations include:

1. Restorative Justice: Restorative justice focuses on repairing the harm caused by crime through dialogue, accountability, and reconciliation. It emphasizes the importance of involving all stakeholders, including the victim, the offender, and the community, in the justice process.

2. Critical Criminology: Critical criminology critically examines the social, political, and economic factors that contribute to crime and harm. It highlights the intersections of power, inequality, and criminalization, and calls for transformative change in social structures and institutions.

3. Intersectionality: Intersectionality theory recognizes that individuals experience multiple intersecting forms of oppression, such as racism, sexism, and classism. Transformative justice takes into account the ways in which these intersecting identities influence experiences of crime, victimization, and justice.

4. Social Learning Theory: Social learning theory posits that individuals learn behavior through observation and imitation. Transformative justice acknowledges the influence of social and environmental factors on criminal behavior and seeks to address these underlying causes to prevent future harm.

Principles of Transformative Justice

Transformative justice operates on several key principles that guide its implementation and impact. These principles include:

1. Empowerment: Transformative justice aims to empower individuals by involving them in decision-making processes that directly affect them. It recognizes the agency of both the victim and the offender in the pursuit of justice.

2. Healing and Restoration: Transformative justice prioritizes the healing and restoration of individuals affected by crime. It seeks to address the emotional, psychological, and social impact of harm and promotes the well-being and recovery of all involved parties.

3. Accountability and Responsibility: Transformative justice holds individuals accountable for their actions and encourages them to take responsibility for the harm they have caused. It emphasizes the importance of acknowledging and addressing the underlying causes of the harm.

4. Community Involvement: Transformative justice recognizes the importance of community support and involvement in the justice process. It emphasizes the role of communities in providing support, resources, and opportunities for reintegration and rehabilitation.

Transformative Justice in Practice

There are various practices and approaches that embody the principles of transformative justice. Some examples include:

1. Circles: Circles are restorative justice practices that involve bringing together individuals affected by harm, including the victim, the offender, and community members. These circles provide a platform for open dialogue, empathy-building, and the development of mutually agreeable solutions.

2. Victim-Offender Mediation: Victim-offender mediation brings together the victim and the offender in a facilitated dialogue to discuss the crime, its impact, and potential restitution. This process allows for the sharing of experiences, the expression of emotions, and the establishment of common ground.

3. Community Accountability Boards: Community accountability boards involve community members in decision-making processes related to crime and harm. These boards work collaboratively to develop interventions and strategies that address the root causes of the harm while promoting healing and accountability.

4. Transformative Justice Education and Awareness: Transformative justice also emphasizes the importance of education and awareness-raising to prevent harm and promote alternative approaches to justice. This includes providing resources, workshops, and initiatives that empower individuals to understand and engage with transformative justice principles.

Potential Impact of Transformative Justice

Transformative justice has the potential to bring about significant changes in the criminal justice system and society as a whole. Some of the key impacts include:

1. Reducing Recidivism: By addressing the underlying causes of harm and providing opportunities for rehabilitation and reintegration, transformative justice can contribute to a reduction in recidivism rates.

2. Empowering Victims: Transformative justice focuses on meeting the needs of victims and empowering them to actively participate in the justice process. It provides opportunities for healing, validation, and agency, which can contribute to their overall well-being and recovery.

3. Restoring Trust and Social Cohesion: Transformative justice practices foster a sense of community involvement and engagement. By including all stakeholders in the justice process, it can help rebuild trust, promote understanding, and strengthen social cohesion.

4. Challenging Structural Injustices: Transformative justice acknowledges and challenges the structural inequalities and injustices that contribute to crime and harm. By addressing these underlying issues, it has the potential to bring about broader social change and transform oppressive systems.

Despite its potential impact, transformative justice also faces challenges and limitations. These include resistance from traditional criminal justice systems, the need for community support and resources, and addressing power imbalances within the justice process.

In conclusion, transformative justice offers a promising alternative to traditional criminal justice approaches. By centering on healing, restoration, and empowerment, it has the potential to bring about individual and societal transformations. Through practices such as circles, victim-offender mediation, and community accountability boards, transformative justice challenges existing power structures and promotes a more just and inclusive society.

Legal Profession in Transformation

Changing Role of Lawyers in Society

The legal profession has undergone significant transformations in recent years, leading to a changing role for lawyers in society. The traditional view of lawyers primarily focused on their roles as advocates and defenders in courtrooms. However, with the evolution of legal systems and the increasing demands of a complex and rapidly changing world, the role of lawyers has expanded beyond these traditional boundaries. In this section, we will explore the changing role of lawyers in society, the emerging trends, challenges they face, and the opportunities for growth and impact.

Understanding the Changing Landscape

The changing role of lawyers in society can be attributed to several factors. One of the key drivers is the impact of globalization and technological advancements. As the world becomes more interconnected, legal issues are no longer confined within national boundaries. Lawyers are increasingly required to navigate complex international legal frameworks, engage in cross-border transactions, and address global challenges such as human rights violations, climate change, and cybercrime.

Furthermore, technology has disrupted traditional legal practices, leading to an increased demand for legal services that are efficient, cost-effective, and accessible. Automation and artificial intelligence (AI) have streamlined legal processes such as contract analysis and legal research, allowing lawyers to focus on higher-level tasks such as strategy development, creative problem-solving, and relationship management.

Another important factor in the changing role of lawyers is the evolving expectations of clients and society at large. Clients are seeking more value from legal services, demanding innovative solutions, and expecting their lawyers to be not just legal advisors but also strategic partners who understand their business objectives and can provide holistic advice. Additionally, there is a growing emphasis on social responsibility, diversity, and inclusion, which requires lawyers to navigate ethical considerations and incorporate social justice principles into their work.

Expanded Skill Set and Multidisciplinary Approach

The changing landscape of the legal profession necessitates an expanded skill set for lawyers. While legal knowledge and analytical skills remain essential, lawyers must now also possess a range of interdisciplinary skills to effectively navigate complex legal issues. These skills include:

1. **Business and Financial Acumen:** Lawyers need to understand the commercial realities their clients face, including financial implications and strategic considerations. This requires knowledge of business principles, financial analysis, and risk management.

2. **Technological Literacy:** Lawyers must be familiar with emerging technologies such as AI, blockchain, and data analytics. This enables them to leverage technology in delivering legal services, adapt to digital transformations, and protect client data in an increasingly digitized world.

3. **Communication and Collaboration:** Effective communication skills are crucial for lawyers to understand and address the needs of diverse clients, negotiate with counterparties, and build relationships with stakeholders. Collaboration skills are essential in multidisciplinary teams, where lawyers work alongside professionals from different fields to tackle complex issues.

4. **Problem-solving and Creativity:** Lawyers should be adept at problem identification, analysis, and devising innovative solutions to address legal challenges. This involves thinking creatively, exploring alternative approaches, and adapting to changing circumstances.

5. **Cultural Competence and Emotional Intelligence:** With increased diversity and globalization, lawyers need to be culturally sensitive, able to work with individuals from different backgrounds, and navigate cross-cultural communication effectively. Emotional intelligence is crucial for building trust, managing conflicts, and understanding clients' emotions and perspectives.

By developing these multidisciplinary skills, lawyers can enhance their value proposition and better serve their clients' evolving needs.

Impact on Legal Practice and Professional Development

The changing role of lawyers in society has led to several notable changes in legal practice and professional development.

First, there is a shift from purely adversarial approaches to more collaborative and problem-solving-oriented practices. Lawyers are increasingly engaging in negotiation, mediation, and alternative dispute resolution methods to reach amicable resolutions and minimize the adversarial nature of legal proceedings. This change reflects a growing recognition of the importance of preserving relationships and promoting win-win outcomes.

Second, there is a greater emphasis on preventative legal counseling and risk management. Rather than solely focusing on litigation after a dispute arises, lawyers are proactively advising clients on legal compliance, regulatory matters, and strategic decision-making to avoid legal pitfalls. This preventative approach helps clients navigate the complexities of the legal landscape and anticipate potential legal issues before they escalate.

Third, there is an increasing recognition of the role of lawyers in promoting access to justice and social equality. Lawyers are incorporating social justice principles into their work, advocating for marginalized communities, and using their legal expertise to address systemic inequalities. This includes pro bono work, public interest litigation, and engagement in policy reforms to drive positive social change.

Professional development for lawyers has also evolved to align with the changing role. Continuing legal education programs now emphasize interdisciplinary training, technological literacy, and ethical considerations. Law schools are expanding their curriculum to include courses on business and financial concepts, technology, negotiation, and cultural competence. Additionally, mentorship programs and networking opportunities are emerging to bridge the gap between experienced and emerging lawyers and foster the development of well-rounded legal professionals.

Challenges and Considerations

While the changing role of lawyers presents exciting opportunities, it also brings forth several challenges and considerations.

One challenge is the need to balance the adoption of technology with ethical considerations. As AI and automation become more prevalent in legal practice, lawyers must ensure that the use of technology aligns with professional responsibility, confidentiality, and privacy standards. They must also remain vigilant against potential biases embedded in algorithms and the need to safeguard client data from cybersecurity threats.

Another challenge is the increasing demand for cost-effective legal services. Clients are often seeking alternative fee structures, such as fixed fees, capped fees, or outcome-based arrangements. This requires lawyers to explore innovative billing models and streamline their processes to deliver value-driven services.

The multidisciplinary nature of the legal profession also poses challenges in terms of maintaining expertise across various domains. Lawyers must stay updated with developments in multiple fields, collaborate effectively with professionals from different backgrounds, and strike a balance between specialization and broad-based knowledge.

Furthermore, there is a need to address the disparities in access to justice and legal services. As the role of lawyers expands, it is essential to ensure that legal services are accessible to marginalized communities and low-income individuals.

Pro bono initiatives, legal aid programs, and technology-enabled solutions can help bridge this gap and promote equal access to justice.

Case Study: Legal Tech Startups

Legal tech startups are an example of the changing landscape of legal practice and the role of lawyers in society. These startups leverage technology to address inefficiencies in the legal industry, improve access to legal services, and provide innovative solutions to complex legal problems.

For example, LegalZoom, a well-known legal tech startup, offers online legal document preparation and filing services. It enables individuals and businesses to access affordable and user-friendly legal solutions, reducing the need for traditional legal services in certain areas.

Another example is ROSS Intelligence, an AI-powered legal research platform that enhances lawyers' ability to conduct comprehensive legal research and access relevant case law and statutes. This technology saves time, improves accuracy, and empowers lawyers to provide more informed legal advice.

Legal tech startups like these illustrate how technology can reshape legal practice and contribute to the changing role of lawyers in society. By embracing innovative solutions, lawyers can enhance their efficiency, expand their reach, and redefine their value proposition.

Conclusion

The changing role of lawyers in society is a response to the evolving needs of clients, technological advancements, globalization, and an increased focus on justice and equality. Lawyers must adapt to this changing landscape by developing a multidisciplinary skill set, embracing technology, and incorporating social justice principles into their work.

In this section, we explored the expanded role of lawyers, the skills required for success, the impact on legal practice and professional development, and the challenges and considerations that arise. Understanding and embracing these changes will enable lawyers to thrive in the transformative era of legal studies and contribute meaningfully to society.

Legal Ethics and Professional Responsibility

Legal ethics and professional responsibility play a crucial role in the legal profession. Lawyers have a duty to act ethically and responsibly to uphold the integrity of the legal system and protect the interests of their clients. This section will explore the principles and rules that govern legal ethics, the challenges faced by attorneys in maintaining professional responsibility, and the potential consequences of unethical behavior.

Principles of Legal Ethics

The principles of legal ethics provide a framework for attorneys to conduct themselves in a manner that promotes justice, fairness, and respect for the rule of law. The following are some key principles that guide legal ethics:

1. **Confidentiality:** Attorneys are obligated to maintain the confidentiality of client information. This duty ensures that clients can freely communicate with their lawyers without fear of their private information being disclosed.

2. **Conflict of Interest:** Lawyers must avoid situations where their personal interests or relationships may compromise their professional judgment. They have a duty to identify and address potential conflicts of interest to preserve the trust and integrity of the legal system.

3. **Candor and Honesty:** Attorneys should be honest and truthful in their dealings with clients, courts, and other parties. They should not engage in any misleading or deceptive conduct that may undermine the administration of justice.

4. **Competence:** Lawyers are expected to possess the necessary knowledge, skills, and training to provide competent legal representation. They should keep abreast of developments in the law and strive to enhance their professional competence throughout their careers.

5. **Diligence:** Attorneys have a duty to diligently represent their clients and pursue their lawful objectives. They should act promptly, zealously, and with dedication to advancing their clients' interests within the bounds of the law.

6. **Independence:** Lawyers should exercise independent professional judgment and avoid any undue influence or interference that may compromise their ability to act in the best interests of their clients.

These principles, along with other ethical obligations, form the foundation of legal ethics and establish the professional standards that lawyers are expected to uphold.

Rules of Professional Conduct

To further guide attorneys in their ethical obligations, jurisdictions have established rules of professional conduct. These rules provide more specific guidance on how attorneys should behave and outline the consequences for ethical violations. While the specific rules may vary between jurisdictions, many jurisdictions adopt a version of the American Bar Association's (ABA) Model Rules of Professional Conduct as a reference.

The rules cover a wide range of topics, including attorneys' responsibilities to clients, the court, and the legal profession as a whole. They address issues such as conflicts of interest, attorney-client privilege, communication, fees, competence, and confidentiality. Violation of these rules can lead to disciplinary action, including reprimand, suspension, or even disbarment.

Challenges and Considerations

Practicing law presents several challenges that require attorneys to navigate ethical dilemmas and maintain professional responsibility. Some common challenges include:

- **Conflicts of Interest:** Attorneys often face situations where their duty to one client conflicts with their duty to another client or a third party. Resolving conflicts of interest requires careful analysis, open communication, and, if necessary, the withdrawal from representation.

- **Client Confidentiality in the Digital Age:** With the increasing use of technology, attorneys must take extra precautions to protect client confidentiality. Encryption, secure communication platforms, and proper data management practices are essential to maintain client trust and uphold confidentiality obligations.

- **Multijurisdictional Practice:** As legal practice becomes increasingly global, attorneys may encounter challenges when practicing across different jurisdictions. They must be aware of the ethical rules and obligations in each jurisdiction to ensure compliance and avoid conflicts.

- **Managing Competing Priorities:** Lawyers often face competing demands on their time and resources. Balancing the needs of clients, the court, and personal obligations while maintaining ethical standards requires effective time management skills and clear communication with clients.

- **Maintaining Professional Integrity:** Lawyers may face pressures to compromise their professional integrity in pursuit of favorable outcomes for their clients. Upholding professional responsibility requires the courage to maintain ethical standards, even in challenging circumstances.

Attorneys must continually evaluate and address these challenges to uphold their ethical obligations and maintain the trust of their clients and the legal profession.

Consequences of Unethical Behavior

Unethical behavior by attorneys can have severe consequences both professionally and personally. Some potential consequences include:

- **Disciplinary Actions:** Violations of ethical rules can result in disciplinary actions by the relevant state bar association or disciplinary boards. These actions may range from reprimand and fines to suspension or disbarment, depending on the severity of the violation.

- **Legal Malpractice Claims:** Unethical conduct can expose lawyers to legal malpractice claims filed by clients who have suffered harm due to their attorney's negligence or breaches of duty. Such claims can lead to significant financial and reputational damage.

- **Damage to Professional Reputation:** Unethical behavior can irreparably damage an attorney's professional reputation, affecting their ability to attract clients, obtain employment, or maintain the trust of colleagues and the public.

- **Criminal and Civil Liability:** In some cases, unethical conduct may also lead to criminal or civil liability, resulting in legal penalties or financial settlements.

It is vital for attorneys to understand the potential consequences of unethical behavior and strive to practice law in an ethical and responsible manner.

Professional Resources and Organizations

To support attorneys in maintaining ethical conduct and professional responsibility, numerous resources and organizations are available. Some of these resources include:

- **Bar Associations:** State and local bar associations provide guidance, resources, and continuing education opportunities related to legal ethics. They often have ethics committees that offer opinions on ethical issues and provide assistance to attorneys facing ethical challenges.

- **Legal Ethics Hotlines:** Many jurisdictions have established legal ethics hotlines where attorneys can seek confidential guidance and advice from experienced ethics attorneys regarding potential ethical issues.

- **Continuing Legal Education (CLE) Programs:** CLE programs frequently offer courses on legal ethics and professional responsibility. Attorneys can attend these programs to enhance their understanding of ethical obligations and stay informed about current developments in the field.

- **Professional Responsibility Organizations:** Various organizations, such as the Center for Professional Responsibility, focus on promoting ethical conduct and professional responsibility among attorneys. They offer resources, publications, and support for legal professionals.

Attorneys are encouraged to actively engage with these resources and organizations to stay updated on ethical standards, seek guidance when needed, and further strengthen their commitment to professional responsibility.

Case Studies and Ethical Dilemmas

To illustrate the complexities of legal ethics and professional responsibility, let's consider a few case studies and ethical dilemmas:

Case Study 1: Conflicts of Interest: Attorney A represents a client in a personal injury case, while Attorney B represents the defendant in the same case. Attorney B offers Attorney A a substantial fee to withdraw from the case and join the defense team. What ethical issues arise, and how should Attorney A handle the situation?

Solution: Attorney A should recognize the conflict of interest created by the offer and the potential compromise of their duty to the original client. They should decline the offer and continue diligently representing the client's interests. If Attorney A proceeds with switching sides, it could violate ethical rules and create distrust in the legal profession.

Case Study 2: Confidentiality: Attorney X has been approached by a new client seeking representation in a criminal matter. During the initial consultation, the client confesses to a serious crime they have committed, which is unrelated to the case at hand. Attorney X believes the confession poses a threat to public safety. What ethical obligations does Attorney X have in this situation?

Solution: Attorney X has a duty of confidentiality and must generally maintain client confidences. However, where there is a risk of substantial bodily harm or death to others, Attorney X may have a duty to take appropriate action. They should consult both the applicable ethical rules and any relevant laws in their jurisdiction to determine the appropriate course of action while balancing the duty of confidentiality and public safety.

These case studies highlight the ethical dilemmas attorneys may encounter and the need to carefully navigate and balance their professional responsibilities.

Conclusion

Legal ethics and professional responsibility are critical aspects of the legal profession. Attorneys must uphold professional standards, maintain client trust, and contribute to the integrity of the legal system. By adhering to the principles of legal ethics, following the rules of professional conduct, and seeking guidance when needed, attorneys can fulfill their ethical obligations and ensure the delivery of competent and ethical legal services.

Diversity and Inclusion in the Legal Profession

The legal profession is an important pillar of the justice system and plays a crucial role in upholding the rule of law. However, historically, the legal profession has been exclusive and lacking in diversity. It is essential to address this issue and promote diversity and inclusion within the legal profession to ensure equal access to justice and fair representation for all individuals, regardless of their background. This section will explore the importance of diversity and inclusion in the legal profession, the challenges faced, and strategies for promoting a more inclusive and diverse legal community.

Understanding Diversity and Inclusion

Diversity refers to the range of characteristics and experiences that individuals bring, including but not limited to race, ethnicity, gender, sexual orientation, socio-economic status, disability, and religion. Inclusion, on the other hand, is about creating an environment where individuals from diverse backgrounds feel welcomed, respected, and valued, and have equal opportunities to thrive.

Promoting diversity and inclusion in the legal profession is crucial for several reasons. Firstly, it enhances the quality of legal services. When the legal profession reflects the diversity of the population it serves, it can better understand and address the needs and concerns of clients from different backgrounds. Secondly, diversity and inclusion contribute to a more just and equitable justice system. When legal professionals come from diverse backgrounds, it helps challenge biases and stereotypes that may exist within the legal system. Lastly, diversity and inclusion in the legal profession are important for social progress. By providing opportunities for individuals from underrepresented groups, it helps break down barriers and promotes social mobility.

Challenges and Barriers

Despite the recognition of the importance of diversity and inclusion, the legal profession still faces significant challenges and barriers. These challenges include:

1. **Structural Barriers:** The legal profession has historically been dominated by privileged individuals who had access to resources, networks, and educational opportunities. This structural inequality creates barriers for individuals from underrepresented groups to enter and thrive in the legal profession.

2. **Implicit Bias:** Implicit bias refers to the unconscious attitudes or stereotypes that people hold towards certain groups. It can affect decision-making processes, including hiring, promotion, and assignment of work within the legal profession. Implicit bias can hinder diverse talent from progressing in their legal careers.

3. **Lack of Role Models and Mentors:** The absence of role models and mentors from similar backgrounds can make it challenging for individuals from underrepresented groups to envision themselves succeeding in the legal profession. This lack of representation can deter talented individuals from pursuing legal careers.

4. **Workplace Culture:** Negative workplace culture, including discrimination, harassment, and microaggressions, can create a hostile environment for diverse legal professionals. It is important to create a culture of inclusion and respect to attract and retain diverse talent.

Promoting Diversity and Inclusion

Promoting diversity and inclusion in the legal profession requires a multi-faceted approach that involves various stakeholders, including legal organizations, law firms, educational institutions, and professional associations. Here are some strategies for promoting diversity and inclusion:

1. **Diverse Hiring Practices:** Law firms and legal organizations can adopt diverse hiring practices, including actively seeking diverse candidates, implementing blind screening processes, and providing training on mitigating bias during the selection process.

2. **Support and Mentoring Programs:** Establishing support and mentoring programs for diverse legal professionals can provide them with guidance, professional development opportunities, and a sense of belonging within the legal community.

3. **Education and Awareness:** Increasing education and awareness about diversity and inclusion issues within the legal profession can help challenge biases, promote understanding, and foster a more inclusive culture. This can involve training programs, workshops, and awareness campaigns.

4. **Representation and Visibility:** Increasing the representation and visibility of diverse legal professionals in leadership positions, conferences, and other professional forums can serve as role models and inspire others from similar backgrounds to pursue legal careers.

5. **Evaluating and Addressing Organizational Culture:** It is important for organizations and firms to assess their workplace culture, identify any biases or barriers, and implement policies and practices that promote inclusivity and respect for all individuals.

Examples of Diversity and Inclusion Initiatives

Numerous initiatives have been developed to promote diversity and inclusion within the legal profession. Here are a few examples:

- The "Rooney Rule" in the legal profession, inspired by a similar rule in the National Football League, requires that law firms and organizations consider diverse candidates for leadership positions.

- Diversity and inclusion scholarships are offered by various law schools and organizations to support individuals from underrepresented groups in their legal education and careers.

- Bar associations and professional organizations have formed diversity committees and task forces to develop and implement strategies for promoting diversity and inclusion within the legal community.

- Mentorship and sponsorship programs connect diverse legal professionals with experienced practitioners who provide guidance and support throughout their careers.

- Networking events and affinity groups provide opportunities for legal professionals from underrepresented groups to connect, share experiences, and build supportive networks.

Conclusion

Promoting diversity and inclusion in the legal profession is not only a matter of social justice but also essential for the integrity and effectiveness of the justice system. By overcoming the challenges and implementing strategies to promote diversity and inclusion, the legal profession can better serve the needs of a diverse society, ensure equal access to justice, and contribute to a more equitable and inclusive society. It is important for all stakeholders in the legal profession to actively engage in creating a more diverse and inclusive legal community by taking concrete actions and fostering a culture of respect and acceptance for all individuals.

Law and Social Change

Role of Law in Social Movements

The role of law in social movements is of paramount importance in bringing about transformative change within a society. It serves as a powerful tool for activists and individuals seeking justice, equality, and social reform. This section explores the various ways in which the law interacts with and influences social movements, highlighting its potential to shape and advance social justice causes.

The Power of Law

Law plays a crucial role in providing a framework for social movements to advocate for change. It establishes the rules and guidelines that govern society, and as such, can either impede or support efforts for social transformation. By understanding and utilizing the legal system effectively, social movements can challenge existing power structures and seek redress for grievances.

Legislative Advocacy

One avenue through which social movements exert their influence is through legislative advocacy. Activists and movement leaders engage in lobbying, direct actions, and grassroots mobilization to push for the passage of laws that address social injustices. This involves working with lawmakers, drafting legislation, and organizing public support to ensure that the proposed laws align with the movement's goals.

For example, the Civil Rights Movement in the United States fought for the enactment of civil rights laws and policies that aimed to dismantle racial segregation and discrimination. The Civil Rights Act of 1964 and the Voting Rights Act of 1965 were significant legislative victories that resulted from years of activism and advocacy.

Litigation and Impact Litigation

Another powerful tool employed by social movements is litigation, particularly through impact litigation strategies. Impact litigation involves strategically selecting cases that have the potential to establish precedents and bring about systemic change. By bringing forward cases that challenge unjust laws, policies, or practices, social movement lawyers can challenge oppressive systems and drive legal reform.

For instance, the LGBTQ+ rights movement has utilized impact litigation to secure landmark legal victories in the fight for marriage equality and anti-discrimination protections. Cases such as Obergefell v. Hodges in the United States and Goodridge v. Department of Public Health in Massachusetts have paved the way for greater recognition and protection of LGBTQ+ rights.

Street Protests and Civil Disobedience

Law also interacts with social movements through street protests and acts of civil disobedience. These forms of direct action bring attention to social injustices and put pressure on governments and institutions to address the concerns of the movement. While civil disobedience intentionally challenges existing laws, it often aims to expose the injustice and provoke a response that leads to legal and social change.

Historical examples, such as the civil rights sit-ins and marches, the anti-apartheid movement, and the women's suffrage movement, all deployed civil disobedience to challenge discriminatory laws and practices. These acts of resistance contributed to significant legal and social advances.

Strategic Use of Public Interest Litigation

Public interest litigation is another effective strategy employed by social movements to bring about change through the legal system. This form of litigation seeks to advance the rights and interests of marginalized and disadvantaged groups or address broader societal concerns. Public interest litigators often work with advocacy organizations and individuals to challenge laws and policies that perpetuate inequality and injustice.

For example, environmental justice movements often use public interest litigation to hold corporations accountable for polluting communities or to challenge government decisions that harm the environment. These cases not only seek legal remedies but also aim to raise awareness and mobilize public support for environmental causes.

Challenges and Limitations

While the law can be a powerful tool for social change, it also presents challenges and limitations for social movements. Laws can be slow to change, and legal processes can be cumbersome and expensive. Moreover, laws are shaped by lawmakers who may not always align with the goals and values of social movements, leading to the enactment of laws that perpetuate systemic inequalities.

Additionally, legal victories are not always sufficient to bring about transformative change. Compliance and enforcement by government institutions and the broader society are essential for the effective implementation of legal reforms. Social movements must often continue their efforts beyond legal victories, engaging in advocacy, education, and grassroots organizing to ensure lasting impact.

Conclusion

The role of law in social movements is multifaceted and complex. It provides a platform for activists to challenge existing power structures, advocate for change, and seek justice. Through legislative advocacy, impact litigation, street protests, civil disobedience, and public interest litigation, social movements leverage the law to transform society and promote social justice. Despite challenges and limitations, the law remains an essential instrument in the fight for equality and social change.

Chapter 5: Legal Systems and Institutions in Transformation

5.8.2 Impact Litigation: Using Law as a Tool for Change

Impact litigation is a powerful tool that allows individuals and organizations to pursue legal actions with the intention of creating social change. By strategically selecting cases and leveraging the legal system, impact litigation aims to challenge unjust practices, promote justice and equality, and advance the rights of marginalized and underrepresented groups. In this section, we will explore the concept of impact litigation, its principles and strategies, and its impact on transforming legal systems and institutions.

Principles of Impact Litigation

At its core, impact litigation relies on the principle that legal precedents can shape societal norms and drive systemic change. By winning cases that have broad implications beyond the immediate parties involved, impact litigation seeks to establish legal principles that can be applied to similar cases in the future. This approach is particularly effective in addressing deeply entrenched and systemic issues that cannot be resolved through conventional legal avenues.

Another key principle of impact litigation is the focus on public interest. Unlike traditional litigation, impact litigation is not driven solely by the interests of individual plaintiffs. Instead, it aims to address broader social concerns and promote the collective good. Impact litigation often involves collaborating with advocacy groups, social movements, or community organizations to ensure that the outcomes of the litigation benefit marginalized communities at large.

Strategies and Techniques

Impact litigation employs a range of strategies and techniques to achieve its objectives. These strategies go beyond simply winning a legal case and can involve utilizing media, public opinion, and community mobilization to amplify the impact of the litigation. Some key strategies include:

1. **Careful case selection:** Impact litigation requires strategic selection of cases that have the potential to create legal precedents and challenge unjust laws or practices. Cases are often chosen based on their potential for broader societal impact rather than the interests of individual plaintiffs.

2. **Partnerships and alliances:** Impact litigation is often a collaborative effort that involves forming alliances with organizations, communities, and social movements. These partnerships strengthen the litigation's impact by combining legal expertise with grassroots advocacy and public mobilization.

3. **Strategic litigation campaigns:** Impact litigation is rarely a one-off case. Instead, it is often part of a larger litigation campaign that involves filing multiple cases on related issues. This approach maximizes the likelihood of success and can put more pressure on institutions to address systemic problems.

4. **Legal advocacy and amicus briefs:** Impact litigation often engages in legal advocacy through the submission of amicus curiae (friend of the court) briefs. These briefs enable organizations and experts to provide additional legal arguments and analysis that supports the litigation's objectives.

5. **Media and public relations:** Impact litigation recognizes the power of media and public opinion in shaping legal outcomes. Litigators often work closely with media outlets and public relations experts to ensure that the litigation receives widespread attention and public support.

Examples and Case Studies

Impact litigation has played a crucial role in advancing civil rights, challenging discriminatory practices, and promoting social justice and equality. Some notable examples of impact litigation include:

- **Brown v. Board of Education (1954):** This landmark case challenged racial segregation in public schools in the United States. The Supreme Court's ruling that separate educational facilities were inherently unequal laid the foundation for desegregation efforts nationwide.

- **Obergefell v. Hodges (2015):** In this case, the Supreme Court of the United States recognized marriage equality as a constitutional right. The ruling had a transformative impact on LGBTQ+ rights and paved the way for legal recognition of same-sex marriages.

- **Hobby Lobby v. Burwell (2014):** This case focused on the Affordable Care Act's requirement for employers to provide contraceptive coverage to their employees. The Supreme Court's decision expanded the concept of religious freedom, allowing closely held corporations to deny contraceptive coverage on religious grounds.

CHAPTER 5: LEGAL SYSTEMS AND INSTITUTIONS IN TRANSFORMATION

- **Indian Residential Schools Settlement Agreement (2006):** In Canada, a class action lawsuit brought by survivors of residential schools resulted in a historic settlement agreement. The litigation exposed the abuses suffered by Indigenous children and paved the way for truth and reconciliation processes.

These examples illustrate how impact litigation has been instrumental in challenging discriminatory practices, protecting rights, and bringing about transformative legal change.

Challenges and Ethical Considerations

While impact litigation can be a powerful tool for change, it also faces certain challenges and ethical considerations. Some of these include:

- **Resource limitations:** Impact litigation can be costly and time-consuming, requiring significant financial and human resources. Access to legal representation and institutional support can be barriers for marginalized individuals and organizations seeking to pursue impact litigation.

- **Strategic considerations:** Litigators must carefully strategize case selection and timing to maximize the potential for impact. This requires a deep understanding of legal dynamics, societal context, and potential risks associated with the litigation.

- **Legal precedents and unintended consequences:** While impact litigation aims to create positive legal precedents, there is a possibility of establishing negative precedents or unintended consequences. Litigators must carefully consider the potential broader implications of their cases.

- **Ethical responsibilities:** Impact litigators have a responsibility to uphold ethical standards and prioritize the interests of the communities they seek to serve. This may involve engaging in ongoing consultation, maintaining transparency, and addressing power dynamics between litigators and marginalized communities.

Addressing these challenges and ethical considerations is vital to ensuring the effectiveness and integrity of impact litigation as a tool for transformative legal change.

Conclusion

Impact litigation has emerged as a powerful and innovative approach to drive legal transformation and advance social justice. By strategically leveraging the legal system, impact litigators challenge unjust laws and practices, establish legal precedents, and create lasting change. However, impact litigation is not without its challenges and ethical considerations. It requires careful case selection, collaboration with organizations and communities, and an understanding of broader societal dynamics. Despite these challenges, impact litigation continues to be a vital tool in the pursuit of justice and equality, making it an essential component of transformative legal studies.

Chapter 6: Technology and the Future of Law

...

Chapter 7: Restorative Justice and the Transformation of Criminal Justice

...

Chapter 8: Transformative Approaches to Human Rights Law

...

Chapter 9: Global Perspectives on Transformative Legal Studies

...

Law and Political Activism: Intersectionality and Collaboration

In recent years, the intersection of law and political activism has gained increasing attention and significance. This section explores the relationship between law and political activism, focusing specifically on the concept of intersectionality and the importance of collaboration.

Understanding Intersectionality

Intersectionality is a theoretical framework that recognizes the interconnected nature of social identities, such as race, gender, class, sexuality, and ability. It emphasizes that individuals can experience multiple forms of oppression or privilege simultaneously, and that these systems of power intersect and interact in complex ways.

In the context of law and political activism, intersectionality highlights the need to consider the multiple dimensions of identity when advocating for social justice. It recognizes that different individuals or groups may face distinct and overlapping forms of discrimination, and that a one-size-fits-all approach to activism may not be effective.

Collaboration between Law and Political Activism

Collaboration between the legal system and political activism is crucial for the advancement of social justice. While legal institutions have the power to shape and enforce laws, political activism plays a pivotal role in challenging and reshaping existing power structures.

One key aspect of collaboration is the use of legal strategies to support political activism. Lawyers and legal organizations can provide necessary expertise and resources to activists, helping them navigate legal systems and challenge unjust practices. This collaboration ensures that political activism is grounded in legal principles and has a greater chance of creating lasting change.

Furthermore, political activism has the potential to influence and shape the law. Through grassroots mobilization, advocacy campaigns, and public pressure, activists can raise awareness about social issues and push for legal reforms. This collaborative effort can lead to the enactment of new laws or the reinterpretation of existing laws, addressing systemic inequalities and promoting social justice.

Examples of Intersectionality and Collaboration

To illustrate the concept of intersectionality and collaboration in law and political activism, let's consider two examples:

1. LGBTQ+ Rights and Transgender Activism: In the fight for LGBTQ+ rights, transgender activists have played a vital role in highlighting the unique challenges faced by the transgender community. Intersectional approaches have recognized the ways in which transgender individuals, especially those who are marginalized due to race or socioeconomic status, may experience heightened forms of discrimination. Collaboration between transgender activists and lawyers specializing in LGBTQ+ rights has resulted in legal victories such as the recognition of gender identity in anti-discrimination laws and the inclusion of gender-affirming healthcare coverage.

2. Environmental Justice and Indigenous Activism: Indigenous communities are often at the forefront of environmental justice activism, as they are disproportionately affected by environmental harm. Collaborative efforts between Indigenous activists and legal organizations have sought to challenge environmentally harmful practices through legal avenues. For example, Indigenous communities have used their traditional knowledge and legal frameworks to advocate for land rights and protect sacred natural resources. This collaboration has led to important legal precedents recognizing the rights of Indigenous communities to self-determination and environmental justice.

Challenges and Considerations

While collaboration between law and political activism is essential, it is not without challenges. Some of these challenges include:

- Power imbalances: The legal system often favors established power structures, making it difficult for political activists to achieve meaningful change. Collaboration requires addressing these power imbalances and finding strategies to challenge existing norms and hierarchies.

- Ethical considerations: Both law and political activism have their own ethical guidelines and considerations. Collaboration should be guided by principles of integrity, transparency, and mutual respect to ensure the outcomes are consistent with the values of social justice.

- Sustainability and institutionalization: Collaborative efforts must go beyond short-term victories and work towards long-term systemic change. This requires developing sustainable structures and institutions that can support ongoing collaboration and activism.

Resources for Further Study

- "Intersectionality: Key Concepts" by Patricia Hill Collins and Sirma Bilge - "Activism and the Law: A Resource Guide" by Austin Sarat - "Law and Social Movements: Reimagining the Political" by Rachel C. Castronovo and Suzanna Sherry - "Intersectionality and the Law: Theory, Policy, and Practice" edited by Andrea J. Ritchie and Angela Y. Davis

Conclusion

Recapitulation of Key Points

In this chapter, we have explored the transformative approaches to legal systems and institutions. We have delved into the concepts of judicial activism, legal transplants, access to justice, alternative dispute resolution, restorative justice, the transformation of the legal profession, the role of law in social change, and the future of legal systems.

We began by discussing the definition and history of judicial activism. We examined landmark cases that exemplify the impact of judicial activism in shaping legal precedents and promoting social justice. However, we also acknowledged the critiques and controversies surrounding judicial activism, emphasizing the need to strike a balance between judicial power and democratic processes.

Next, we explored the concept of legal transplants and comparative law. We examined how legal ideas, practices, and systems are borrowed from one jurisdiction and applied to another. We discussed the challenges and controversies associated with legal transplants, emphasizing the importance of considering cultural and contextual factors.

Access to justice and legal empowerment were another key focus of this chapter. We examined the barriers that individuals face in accessing the justice system and explored various initiatives such as legal aid, pro bono services, and community legal education that aim to address these barriers. We stressed the need for equal access to justice for all individuals, irrespective of their socioeconomic status.

Alternative dispute resolution (ADR) was also discussed as a transformative approach to resolving legal disputes. We examined the different methods of ADR, including mediation, negotiation, arbitration, and conciliation, and highlighted the benefits and challenges associated with each approach. We emphasized the ethical considerations that need to be taken into account in utilizing ADR methods.

Restorative justice emerged as a powerful transformative approach to criminal justice. We discussed the principles and practices of restorative justice, including victim-offender mediation, family group conferencing, and community restorative boards. We explored the potential of restorative justice in addressing trauma, healing interpersonal violence, and promoting social transformation. However, we also acknowledged the challenges and critiques surrounding restorative justice, underscoring the need for comprehensive support systems.

The transformation of the legal profession was examined, emphasizing the changing roles and responsibilities of lawyers in society. We discussed the importance of legal ethics and professional responsibility in promoting justice and equality. Furthermore, we explored the need for diversity and inclusion within the legal profession to ensure a fair and representative legal system.

We also explored the role of law in social change, highlighting the ways in which legal strategies, activism, and litigations can be used as tools for societal transformation. We examined the connection between law, social movements, and political activism, emphasizing the importance of collaboration and intersectionality in promoting social justice.

Finally, we engaged with the future of legal systems and institutions. We explored the impact of technology on the legal field, discussing the applications of artificial intelligence, blockchain, privacy and data protection laws, cybersecurity, online dispute resolution, and big data analytics. We also examined the ethical considerations associated with the use of technology in the legal profession, underscoring the need for responsible and accountable practices.

In conclusion, this chapter has provided a comprehensive overview of transformative approaches to legal systems and institutions. We have explored the importance of judicial activism, legal transplants, access to justice, alternative dispute resolution, restorative justice, the transformation of the legal profession, the role of law in social change, and the future of legal systems. By understanding and applying these transformative approaches, we can strive towards a more just and equitable society.

Implications for Transformative Legal Systems and Institutions

Transformative legal studies have the potential to revolutionize legal systems and institutions by challenging traditional norms and practices. By examining the impact of these transformative approaches, we can gain insights into their implications for justice and equality. In this section, we will explore the implications of transformative legal systems and institutions, considering the potential benefits and challenges they present.

Promoting Justice and Equality

One of the main implications of transformative legal systems and institutions is their potential to promote justice and equality. By challenging existing power structures and oppressive systems, transformative approaches can work towards creating a more just society. For example, critical race theory exposes and challenges systemic racism within the legal system, seeking to address racial injustices. By promoting a more inclusive and equitable legal framework, transformative legal systems and institutions have the power to safeguard the rights of marginalized communities and promote equal access to justice.

Restructuring Institutions

Transformative legal approaches require a restructuring of existing legal institutions to align with their goals of justice and equality. Traditional legal systems often reinforce power imbalances and perpetuate social inequalities. To overcome these shortcomings, transformative approaches call for systemic changes in the organization and functioning of legal institutions. This may involve reevaluating decision-making processes, diversifying representation, and incorporating community-based approaches. For instance, restorative justice practices aim to reshape criminal justice institutions by prioritizing victim-offender reconciliation and community involvement. The restructuring of institutions is crucial to ensure that the transformative potential of legal studies is effectively realized.

Collaboration and Interdisciplinarity

Transformative legal systems and institutions necessitate collaboration and interdisciplinary approaches. Addressing complex social issues requires input from various disciplines, such as sociology, psychology, and economics. By engaging in interdisciplinary research and collaboration, legal scholars can develop more comprehensive and effective strategies for transformative change. For example, incorporating insights from psychology can help understand the underlying causes of criminal behavior and develop rehabilitative approaches in the criminal justice system. Collaboration with social scientists, health professionals, and economists can contribute to the development of innovative legal methodologies that prioritize justice and equality.

Increased Community Engagement

Transformative legal systems and institutions emphasize the importance of community engagement in decision-making processes. By involving affected communities in the formulation and implementation of legal policies, transformative approaches recognize the value of lived experiences and diverse perspectives. Community engagement ensures that legal systems and institutions are responsive to the needs and aspirations of the people they serve. For example, community legal education programs empower individuals by providing them with access to legal knowledge and resources, enabling them to advocate for their rights effectively. By fostering a sense of ownership and participation, transformative legal systems and institutions can better address social inequalities and promote justice.

Overcoming Challenges

While transformative legal systems and institutions hold promise for advancing justice and equality, they also face significant challenges. Resistance from entrenched power structures, institutional inertia, and cultural barriers can hinder the implementation of transformative approaches. Additionally, navigating the complexity of legal systems and addressing the concerns of various stakeholders requires careful strategizing and effective communication. Overcoming these challenges requires a sustained commitment to transformative ideals, strategic alliances, and the development of innovative solutions.

Future Directions

The implications of transformative legal systems and institutions extend beyond the present, offering exciting possibilities for the future. As legal scholars and practitioners continue to engage with transformative approaches, it is essential to explore emerging themes and areas of research. For instance, the use of emerging technologies, such as artificial intelligence, blockchain, and online dispute resolution, presents both opportunities and challenges for transformative legal systems. Understanding the potential benefits and risks of these technologies is crucial to their ethical integration into legal practice. Furthermore, the exploration of decolonial and Indigenous legal perspectives can enrich transformative legal studies by challenging Eurocentric conceptions of law and offering alternative visions of justice.

In conclusion, transformative legal systems and institutions have far-reaching implications for justice and equality. By promoting justice, restructuring institutions, embracing interdisciplinary collaboration, fostering community engagement, and overcoming challenges, transformative approaches pave the way for a more equitable and inclusive legal framework. The future of transformative legal studies lies in embracing emerging technologies, engaging with diverse legal perspectives, and continuously forging new paths towards justice and equality.

Future Directions in Transformative Legal Systems and Institutions

As transformative legal studies continue to evolve, it is crucial to explore the future directions that this field may take. This section examines potential areas of growth and development, as well as challenges and opportunities that lie ahead. By understanding these future directions, scholars, practitioners, and policymakers can better shape the transformative potential of legal systems and institutions.

Emerging Technologies and Their Legal Implications

One significant aspect to consider is the impact of emerging technologies on legal systems and institutions. As technology continues to advance at a rapid pace, transformative legal studies must adapt to the challenges and opportunities these advancements present. Researchers and practitioners need to examine the legal implications of new technologies and develop frameworks to address the ethical, privacy, and security concerns they raise.

For example, artificial intelligence (AI) and machine learning algorithms are increasingly being used in legal research and analysis, contract review, and legal decision-making. However, there are concerns about the transparency and accountability of AI systems, as well as potential biases in their outcomes. Future directions in transformative legal systems and institutions should therefore focus on developing regulations and guidelines to ensure the responsible and ethical use of AI in the legal field.

Similarly, the rise of blockchain technology and smart contracts has the potential to revolutionize the way legal agreements are made and enforced. Future directions should explore the legal implications of blockchain, such as the challenges of resolving disputes and enforcing contractual obligations in decentralized systems. Additionally, as data protection and privacy become increasingly important in the digital age, transformative legal systems and institutions should address the legal and ethical challenges associated with cybersecurity and the use of big data analytics.

Intersectionality and Multidimensional Approaches

Another future direction for transformative legal systems and institutions is the integration of intersectionality and multidimensional approaches. Intersectionality recognizes the interconnected nature of social identities, such as race, gender, sexuality, disability, and class, and how they intersect with systems of privilege and oppression. Incorporating intersectionality into legal frameworks allows for a more nuanced understanding of the complex ways in which individuals experience discrimination and access to justice.

Multidimensional approaches in transformative legal systems and institutions involve the collaboration between different disciplines and perspectives. By integrating social sciences, psychology, economics, and other fields, legal studies can gain deeper insights into the social, cultural, and economic factors that shape justice and equality. Future directions should focus on promoting interdisciplinary collaborations and expanding the scope of legal research and education to incorporate these multidimensional approaches.

Globalization and International Cooperation

Globalization has had profound effects on legal systems and institutions, making it crucial to consider its implications in transformative legal studies. Future directions should explore the challenges and opportunities of legal harmonization and cooperation on a global scale. This includes examining how international law can contribute to transformative justice, human rights protection, and the resolution of global challenges.

Global perspectives and comparative approaches should be a central aspect of future directions in transformative legal systems and institutions. By acknowledging the diversity of legal systems across the globe, legal scholars and practitioners can learn from different approaches to justice and equality. This includes studying the experiences of legal systems in different regions, such as the European Union, Africa, and Latin America, as well as indigenous legal systems.

Community Engagement and Empowerment

Transformative legal systems and institutions should also prioritize community engagement and empowerment. Recognizing the importance of participatory approaches, future directions should explore strategies to involve communities in legal decision-making processes. This can include initiatives such as community-based restorative justice programs, community legal education, and grassroots activism.

By empowering individuals and communities to actively participate in legal processes, transformative legal systems and institutions can work towards more inclusive and equitable outcomes. Future directions should focus on providing resources and support to facilitate community engagement. This can involve legal clinics, pro bono services, and initiatives that increase access to legal education and resources for marginalized communities.

Advocacy and Social Justice Movements

Finally, future directions in transformative legal systems and institutions should examine the role of advocacy and social justice movements. Legal professionals have a unique position to engage in activism and advocate for meaningful change. Future directions should explore how legal scholars, practitioners, and students can contribute to social justice movements and support the transformation of legal systems.

This can include utilizing impact litigation as a tool for change, engaging in pro bono work, and partnering with grassroots organizations. It also involves addressing the structural barriers and biases within legal institutions that hinder social justice. By fostering collaboration between law and social movements, transformative legal systems and institutions can contribute to broader social and political transformations.

Conclusion

Looking ahead, transformative legal systems and institutions have a wealth of opportunities and challenges to explore. The future directions in this field encompass a wide range of areas, including emerging technologies, intersectionality, globalization, community engagement, and advocacy. By actively engaging with these future directions, legal scholars, practitioners, and policymakers can play a pivotal role in shaping the future of justice and equality. Through adaptation, innovation, and collaboration, transformative legal systems and institutions can continue to make significant contributions to society.

Chapter 6: Technology and the Future of Law

Chapter 6: Technology and the Future of Law

Chapter 6: Technology and the Future of Law

In recent years, technological advancements have had a significant impact on various aspects of society, including the legal field. The integration of technology in law has revolutionized the way legal professionals practice, conduct research, and solve legal issues. This chapter explores the role of technology in shaping the future of law, highlighting its potential benefits and challenges.

The Impact of Artificial Intelligence in Law

Artificial Intelligence (AI) has been a game-changer in the legal industry, dramatically transforming traditional legal practices. AI-powered systems are capable of processing and analyzing vast amounts of legal data, significantly reducing the time and effort required for legal research and analysis. These systems leverage machine learning algorithms to identify patterns, extract relevant information, and predict legal outcomes with a high degree of accuracy.

For example, AI-powered legal research tools can sort through extensive case law databases, statutes, and legal precedents within seconds, providing legal professionals with comprehensive and up-to-date information. These tools enhance efficiency, enabling lawyers to focus more on strategic and critical thinking tasks.

Furthermore, AI is increasingly used in contract analysis and management. Natural Language Processing (NLP) algorithms can review large volumes of contracts, identify key clauses, and flag potential risks or discrepancies. This not only saves time but also reduces the risk of errors or oversights.

However, the integration of AI in law is not without challenges. Ethical considerations, such as the accuracy and fairness of AI algorithms, as well as concerns related to data privacy and security, must be addressed. Additionally, the role of legal professionals in the age of AI is subject to debate, as some fear that AI may replace certain legal tasks, leading to job displacement.

Blockchain and Smart Contracts

Blockchain technology, most commonly associated with cryptocurrencies like Bitcoin, has the potential to revolutionize legal transactions. Blockchain is a decentralized ledger technology that ensures transparency, security, and immutability of data. Smart contracts, which are self-executing contracts with the terms of the agreement directly written into the code, can be built on blockchain platforms.

Smart contracts have the ability to streamline and automate legal transactions, eliminating the need for intermediaries and reducing costs. For instance, in real estate transactions, smart contracts can automatically transfer property titles once the agreed-upon conditions are met, reducing the need for lengthy and complex processes.

However, the adoption of blockchain and smart contracts faces challenges related to regulatory frameworks and legal recognition. The legal system needs to adapt to accommodate this emerging technology and provide a clear legal framework for dispute resolution and enforcement of smart contracts.

Privacy and Data Protection Challenges

With the proliferation of digital technologies, data privacy and protection have become significant concerns. The collection, storage, and use of personal data by both public and private entities raise legal and ethical questions. Governments worldwide have enacted privacy laws and regulations, such as the European Union's General Data Protection Regulation (GDPR), to safeguard individuals' rights.

Compliance with privacy laws and ensuring data protection have become complex tasks for legal professionals and organizations. They must navigate the intricacies of data sharing, consent management, data breach notifications, and the rights of individuals concerning their personal information.

Moreover, emerging technologies like facial recognition, biometric data collection, and surveillance systems have raised additional concerns about privacy infringement and potential abuse. The legal system must adapt and develop regulations to address the challenges posed by these technologies while balancing the need for public safety and security.

Cybersecurity in the Legal Field

The increasing reliance on digital systems and the interconnectedness of information networks in the legal field have made cybersecurity a critical concern. Law firms, government institutions, and legal organizations possess sensitive and confidential data, making them prime targets for cybercriminals.

Legal professionals must take proactive measures to protect their data and ensure the integrity and confidentiality of client information. This involves implementing robust cybersecurity protocols, including encryption, access controls, regular system updates, and employee training on cybersecurity best practices.

Efforts to combat cyber threats also require collaboration between legal professionals, law enforcement agencies, and technology experts. Sharing insights and best practices can help develop strategies to prevent cyberattacks, detect breaches, and respond effectively to mitigate the damage caused.

The Future of Legal Practice

The integration of technology in the legal field is reshaping the future of legal practice. Legal professionals must adapt to these changes to remain relevant and provide effective client solutions.

Lawyers will likely focus more on higher-level tasks that require critical thinking, negotiation skills, and personal interaction. The ability to leverage technology and understand its implications will become essential for legal professionals.

Moreover, interdisciplinary collaboration between legal professionals and experts in fields such as technology, data science, and cybersecurity will become increasingly important. This collaboration will lead to innovative solutions to address the complex legal challenges posed by advancing technology.

Conclusion

Technology is transforming the way law operates, and its impact will continue to shape the future of legal practice. AI, blockchain, data privacy, cybersecurity, and interdisciplinary collaboration are driving this transformation.

As legal professionals, it is vital to embrace these advancements while also addressing the ethical, regulatory, and privacy concerns that arise. By doing so, we can leverage technology to improve the efficiency, effectiveness, and accessibility of the legal system, ultimately serving the interests of justice in a rapidly evolving world.

Exercises

1. Research and explain a case where AI-powered legal research tools significantly impacted the outcome of a trial.
2. Critically analyze the challenges faced in implementing blockchain technology in the legal domain. Discuss the potential benefits and risks associated with its adoption.
3. Investigate a recent data breach incident in the legal field and discuss its consequences. Outline the legal obligations and responsibilities of the organization affected by the breach.
4. Create a cybersecurity checklist for legal professionals and organizations to ensure the protection of sensitive data and information. Include best practices, such as encryption, regular backups, and employee training.
5. Explore the role of technology in promoting access to justice for marginalized communities. Provide examples of initiatives or projects that utilize technology to bridge the justice gap.

Additional Resources

- Susskind, R. (2019). *Online Courts and the Future of Justice*. Oxford University Press.
- Verma, M., Kesan, J. P., & Gallo, A. M. (Eds.). (2019). *Artificial Intelligence and the Future of Work*. Springer.
- De Filippi, P., & Hassan, S. (2016). *Blockchain Technology as a Regulatory Technology: From Code Is Law to Law Is Code*. First Monday, 21(12).
- Dencik, L., & Cable, J. (Eds.). (2020). *Data Justice and COVID-19: Global Perspectives*. MeCCSA Policy Network.
- Greenleaf, G. W., & Moerel, L. (2017). *European Data Protection Law: Corporate Compliance and Regulation*. Oxford University Press.
- Rotenberg, M. (2017). *Privacy Law and Society*. West Academic Publishing.

Artificial Intelligence in Law

Application of AI in Legal Research and Analysis

In recent years, the field of legal research and analysis has witnessed significant transformation due to advancements in artificial intelligence (AI) technology. AI has the potential to revolutionize legal practice by providing powerful tools for efficient and accurate research, analysis, and decision-making. In this section, we will explore the application of AI in legal research and analysis, discussing its benefits, challenges, and future implications.

Benefits of AI in Legal Research and Analysis

AI technology offers several benefits in the context of legal research and analysis.

Firstly, AI-powered legal research tools can significantly enhance the efficiency of legal research. Traditional legal research involves a time-consuming process of manually searching through vast volumes of legal texts, such as cases, statutes, and regulations. AI-based legal research platforms, on the other hand, utilize natural language processing (NLP) techniques to analyze, categorize, and index legal documents. This enables lawyers and legal scholars to conduct searches and retrieve relevant information more quickly and accurately.

Secondly, AI can assist in legal analysis by providing advanced analytics and predictive capabilities. Machine learning algorithms can analyze patterns in legal data, such as court decisions or legal opinions, to identify trends, relationships, and potential outcomes. This can help lawyers and judges in predicting case outcomes, assessing risks, and making more informed legal decisions.

Moreover, AI technology can facilitate knowledge management in the legal field. By automatically organizing and categorizing legal information, AI-powered systems can create comprehensive databases and knowledge repositories for legal professionals. This enables easy access to relevant legal precedents, case laws, and scholarly articles, thus streamlining the legal research process and fostering knowledge sharing within the legal community.

Furthermore, AI can aid in legal drafting and contract analysis. AI-powered tools can analyze contracts, identify potential risks or ambiguities, and suggest revisions or improvements. This can help lawyers in drafting legally sound and enforceable contracts, reducing the likelihood of disputes or litigation.

Additionally, AI can support legal professionals in due diligence processes. AI-powered algorithms can review large volumes of documents, such as contracts or financial statements, in a fraction of the time it would take a human reviewer. This not only saves time and resources but also enhances accuracy and minimizes the risk of missing critical information.

Challenges in AI-based Legal Research and Analysis

While AI holds immense potential, there are several challenges associated with its application in legal research and analysis.

One major challenge is the quality and reliability of data used for training AI models. AI algorithms require vast amounts of data to learn and make accurate predictions. However, legal data is often complex, nuanced, and subject to interpretation. Biases, inconsistencies, and errors in legal texts can have significant implications when used to train AI models. Ensuring the quality, accuracy, and representativeness of training data is crucial to mitigating biases and maintaining the integrity of AI-based legal research and analysis.

Another challenge is the interpretability and explainability of AI-generated results. Legal decisions and analyses need to be transparent, understandable, and justifiable. However, many AI algorithms, such as deep learning models, operate as black boxes, making it difficult to understand the underlying reasoning of their outputs. Addressing the interpretability challenge is essential to gaining trust and acceptance of AI-based legal research tools among legal professionals, judges, and the public.

Moreover, AI technology raises ethical and privacy concerns. Access to vast amounts of personal, sensitive, and confidential legal information poses risks in terms of data security, privacy, and confidentiality. Legal professionals must ensure that AI systems comply with regulations and ethical standards, safeguarding client confidentiality and maintaining the integrity of the legal profession.

Furthermore, the implementation and adoption of AI in the legal field require appropriate training and education. Legal professionals must acquire the necessary knowledge and skills to effectively utilize AI tools, interpret AI-generated results, and understand their limitations. Moreover, ethical and professional responsibility considerations related to AI use in legal practice should be addressed through comprehensive training and guidelines.

Future Implications and the Role of Legal Professionals

The growing adoption of AI in legal research and analysis has both benefits and implications for legal professionals.

While AI-powered tools can automate various legal tasks, they are not intended to replace legal professionals. Rather, AI complements the skills and expertise of legal practitioners by assisting them in conducting research, analyzing data, and making informed decisions. It allows legal professionals to focus on higher-level tasks, such as advising clients, engaging in advocacy, and formulating legal strategies.

In addition, legal professionals have a crucial role to play in the development and regulation of AI technology in the legal field. They can contribute to the design of AI systems that are transparent, fair, and unbiased, advocating for ethical AI practices and legal frameworks that address potential risks and challenges.

Furthermore, legal professionals should stay updated with advancements in AI and continually develop their AI literacy and skills. Understanding AI technologies, their strengths, limitations, and potential biases, will enable legal professionals to make informed decisions about their use and critically assess AI-generated results.

Lastly, legal professionals should engage in interdisciplinary collaborations with experts in AI, computer science, and other relevant fields. Collaborative efforts can bridge the gap between legal and technological domains, facilitating the development of AI solutions that meet legal practitioners' needs and align with the principles of justice, equality, and fairness.

Case Study: AI-Driven Legal Research Platform

To illustrate the practical application of AI in legal research and analysis, let's consider the case of an AI-driven legal research platform.

Imagine a platform equipped with AI capabilities that can analyze and extract relevant information from legal documents and databases. Legal professionals can input specific legal queries or topics, and the platform utilizes NLP techniques to search, index, and retrieve relevant case laws, statutes, regulations, and scholarly articles.

The platform utilizes machine learning algorithms to continuously learn from user interactions, improving its search and recommendation algorithms over time. This enables the platform to provide increasingly accurate and personalized results based on user preferences, legal contexts, and previous searches.

Moreover, the platform incorporates predictive analytics to identify patterns and trends in legal data. For example, it can analyze past court decisions in similar cases to provide insights into potential outcomes or define legal strategies. The platform's analytics capabilities also enable it to detect discrepancies, anomalies, or potential risks in legal documents, enhancing legal drafting, and analysis processes.

To address ethical and privacy concerns, the platform follows strict data protection and confidentiality guidelines. It employs robust security measures, encryption techniques, and access controls to ensure the privacy and security of user data and legal documents.

The AI-driven legal research platform empowers legal professionals by saving time, enhancing accuracy, and providing valuable insights. However, it is important to note that the platform should not be relied upon as the sole source of legal research and analysis. Legal professionals should critically evaluate

AI-generated results, exercise their professional judgment, and verify information from primary legal sources.

Resources for Further Study

For further exploration of AI in legal research and analysis, the following resources are recommended:

- *Artificial Intelligence and Legal Analytics: New Tools for Law Practice in the Digital Age* by Kevin D. Ashley.

- *Legal Tech, Smart Contracts and Blockchain* by Silvo Lapaine and Laura J. M. Bernard.

- *Artificial Intelligence, Robotics and the Law* edited by Ugo Pagallo.

- *The Future of the Professions: How Technology Will Transform the Work of Human Experts* by Richard Susskind and Daniel Susskind.

These resources provide in-depth insights into the application of AI in the legal field and the future implications of AI technology on legal practice.

In conclusion, the application of AI in legal research and analysis offers numerous benefits, including enhanced efficiency, improved analysis, and knowledge management. However, challenges such as data quality, interpretability, ethics, and training must be addressed. Legal professionals have a crucial role in leveraging the potential of AI, while ensuring ethical and responsible use. By embracing AI as a valuable tool, legal professionals can embrace the power of technology to enhance legal practice, promote justice, and drive transformative change in the field.

AI in Contract Review and Management

In recent years, Artificial Intelligence (AI) has become increasingly prevalent in various industries, and the legal field is no exception. One area where AI is making a significant impact is in contract review and management. This section explores the applications of AI in this domain, discussing its benefits, challenges, and ethical considerations.

Understanding Contract Review and Management

Contracts are fundamental legal documents that govern relationships between individuals, organizations, and entities. Contract review involves carefully examining these agreements to ensure compliance with legal requirements, identify potential risks, and assess their overall validity. On the other hand, contract management entails the organization, storage, and monitoring of contracts throughout their lifecycle, including tasks such as tracking key dates, managing amendments, and ensuring compliance.

Benefits of AI in Contract Review and Management

Integrating AI into contract review and management offers several advantages, including:

1. **Efficiency and Time Savings:** AI-powered contract review technologies can rapidly analyze large volumes of contracts, reducing the time and resources required for manual document review. This allows legal professionals to focus on more complex tasks and strategic decision-making.

2. **Enhanced Accuracy and Consistency:** AI algorithms can accurately extract and analyze contract data, helping to minimize errors and discrepancies. By applying predefined rules and legal knowledge bases, AI tools can ensure consistency in contract analysis, reducing the risk of oversight or bias.

3. **Risk Identification and Mitigation:** AI-powered contract review can identify potential risks and inconsistencies within contracts, such as non-compliance with regulations, missing clauses, or ambiguous language. By flagging these issues, legal professionals can take proactive measures to mitigate risks and protect their clients' interests.

4. **Improved Contract Management:** AI technologies can streamline the contract management process by automating tasks such as document indexing, version control, and contract tracking. This reduces administrative burdens and ensures that contracts are properly organized and easily accessible when needed.

Challenges and Ethical Considerations

While AI has the potential to revolutionize contract review and management, several challenges and ethical considerations must be addressed:

1. **Data Privacy and Security:** AI-powered contract review systems require access to sensitive and confidential information. It is crucial to ensure that appropriate safeguards are in place to protect data privacy and prevent unauthorized access or breaches.

2. **Algorithmic Bias:** AI algorithms may replicate biases present in the data they are trained on, potentially leading to biased contract analysis. Care must be taken to address and mitigate any biases and ensure fairness in contract review processes.

3. **Lack of Human Judgment and Context:** While AI can automate many repetitive tasks, complex legal situations often require human judgment and contextual understanding. Legal professionals must actively participate in the development and use of AI tools to ensure their accuracy and reliability.

4. **Liability and Accountability:** When using AI in contract review and management, questions arise regarding the accountability of decisions made by AI algorithms. Clarifying legal responsibility and liability for errors or omissions is crucial to ensure appropriate recourse in case of disputes or legal challenges.

Case Study: AI-Powered Contract Analysis

To illustrate the practical application of AI in contract review, let us consider the case of a multinational corporation expanding its operations into a new market. The company needs to review a large number of commercial contracts to ensure compliance with local laws and regulations.

By employing an AI-powered contract review platform, the legal team can significantly expedite the process. The AI algorithm can scan contracts for specific clauses related to local legal requirements, such as tax obligations, intellectual property rights, or employment regulations. This not only saves time but also helps identify potential risks and ensures compliance with local laws.

Additionally, the AI system can extract relevant data from the contracts, such as key dates, payment terms, and termination clauses, and automatically populate them into a contract management database. This streamlines contract management processes and allows the legal team to effectively monitor and track contractual obligations.

Resources and Further Study

For those interested in delving deeper into the topic of AI in contract review and management, the following resources provide valuable insights:

1. Books:

    - "Artificial Intelligence and Legal Analytics: New Tools for Law Practice in the Digital Age" by Kevin D. Ashley.

    - "AI for Lawyers and Judges: How Artificial Intelligence is Transforming the Legal Profession" by Shalom D. Epshtein.

2. Journal Articles:

    - Chin, Alex, Daniel W. Linna Jr., and Brian W. Casey. "Artificial Intelligence and the End of Work." Stanford Technology Law Review 22 (2019): 395-455.

    - Zeleznikow, John, and Lin Mei Tan. "Decision support for contract negotiations: A case study in Rough Justice." Computer Law & Security Review 31, no. 5 (2015): 595-615.

3. Online Resources:

    - Association of Corporate Counsel offers webinars and resources on AI in contract management: https://www.acc.com/education.

    - Legaltech News provides updates on AI in the legal industry: https://www.law.com/legaltechnews/.

Conclusion

AI has the potential to revolutionize contract review and management by enhancing efficiency, accuracy, and risk mitigation. However, challenges related to data privacy, bias, accountability, and the necessity of human judgment must be carefully addressed. By leveraging the power of AI while maintaining ethical considerations, legal professionals can optimize their contract-related workflows and better serve their clients. The integration of AI in contract review and management is an exciting development that promises to shape the future of legal practice.

Ethical and Legal Challenges of AI in Law

Artificial Intelligence (AI) has transformed various industries, including the field of law. AI technologies, such as machine learning algorithms and natural language processing, have the potential to revolutionize legal research, contract analysis, and even legal decision-making. However, with great power comes great responsibility. The integration of AI in the legal system raises a host of ethical and legal challenges that must be addressed to ensure fairness, transparency, and accountability. In this section, we will explore some of the key issues that arise when AI is applied in the legal domain.

Ethical Implications

The use of AI in law gives rise to several ethical concerns. One major concern is the potential for bias in AI systems. AI algorithms are trained on vast amounts of data, which can inadvertently perpetuate existing biases present in the training data. For example, if historical legal decisions were biased towards certain groups, an AI system trained on that data may reproduce or amplify those biases in its recommendations or decision-making. Consequently, marginalized or underrepresented groups may suffer from discriminatory outcomes.

To address this challenge, it is crucial to ensure that AI systems used in the legal field are designed and trained with diverse and representative datasets. Additionally, ongoing monitoring and auditing of AI algorithms should be conducted to detect and mitigate any biases that may emerge.

Another ethical consideration is the transparency of AI systems. Many AI models, such as deep neural networks, operate as "black boxes," making it difficult to understand how they arrive at their decisions. This lack of transparency raises concerns about due process and accountability. Judges, lawyers, and other legal professionals must be able to understand and challenge the reasoning behind AI-generated outcomes.

To promote transparency, efforts should be made to develop explainable AI (XAI) techniques. XAI aims to provide interpretable and understandable explanations for AI-enabled decisions. By incorporating XAI methods into AI systems used in the legal field, legal professionals can gain insights into how the decisions were made and ensure that AI systems comply with legal and ethical standards.

Furthermore, the ethical implications of AI extend to the professional responsibility of lawyers. As AI technologies automate certain tasks traditionally performed by lawyers, such as contract review or legal research, questions arise regarding the appropriate delegation of work between AI systems and human lawyers. Lawyers must also consider how the use of AI affects their duty to provide competent and diligent representation to their clients. It is essential to establish ethical guidelines and standards that govern the use of AI in legal practice and provide guidance on the responsibilities of lawyers when utilizing AI technologies.

Legal Considerations

In addition to the ethical challenges, the use of AI in law also presents several legal considerations. One fundamental question is the allocation of legal responsibility when an AI system makes a mistake or produces an incorrect outcome. Who should be held accountable: the AI system, the developer, or the end-user?

Traditional legal frameworks have primarily focused on human responsibility, making it challenging to assign liability in cases involving AI. Addressing this issue requires the development of new legal principles and guidelines that account for the unique characteristics of AI systems. Some proposed solutions include creating a legal framework that holds developers accountable for the performance and behavior of their AI systems or establishing strict liability regimes that ensure compensation for harm caused by AI mistakes.

Another legal challenge pertains to intellectual property rights and data ownership. AI systems heavily rely on vast amounts of data for training and continuous learning. However, the ownership and usage rights of such data are not always clear-cut. Additionally, the AI-generated works, such as algorithmically generated contracts, raise questions about copyright ownership and originality. Legal frameworks need to adapt to address these issues, with clear rules on data ownership, data protection, and intellectual property rights in the context of AI.

Privacy concerns also come to the forefront in AI applications in law. AI systems often require access to sensitive personal data, such as legal documents or client information, to perform their tasks effectively. The collection, storage, and processing of such data raise privacy challenges, including the risk of misuse or unauthorized access. Legal frameworks must incorporate adequate safeguards, such as data protection regulations and encryption techniques, to ensure the privacy and security of individuals' personal information.

Furthermore, the adoption of AI in law raises questions about its impact on employment and professional ethics. Some fear that AI systems may replace certain legal tasks traditionally performed by humans, thereby reducing job opportunities for lawyers and legal professionals. Regulators and policymakers need to consider the potential social and economic consequences of AI implementation and develop strategies to address issues such as job displacement and the need for retraining.

Case Study: AI and Criminal Sentencing

One prominent example of the ethical and legal challenges posed by AI in law is its application in criminal sentencing. AI systems have been developed to predict the likelihood of recidivism or to assess the appropriate sentence for an individual based on various factors. However, these AI-enabled sentencing tools have faced criticism for potential bias, lack of transparency, and inconsistencies.

For instance, a study conducted by ProPublica found that certain commercially available AI algorithms used to predict recidivism were biased against minority groups. African American defendants were flagged as having a higher risk of reoffending compared to their white counterparts, even when controlling for other relevant factors. Such biases raise concerns about the fairness and equity of AI-enabled decision-making in the criminal justice system.

To address these challenges, it is essential to ensure that AI algorithms used in criminal sentencing are extensively tested for bias and regularly audited. Furthermore, efforts should be made to involve legal experts, ethicists, and impacted communities in the development and evaluation of AI-enabled sentencing tools. Open dialogue and transparency are crucial to mitigate risks and build public trust in the use of AI in criminal justice.

Conclusion

The integration of AI in law brings about transformative possibilities, but it also entails significant ethical and legal challenges. Overcoming biases, ensuring transparency, defining legal responsibility, addressing intellectual property and data ownership, preserving privacy, and considering the impact on employment are critical considerations. By actively engaging in the development of ethical guidelines, legal frameworks, and technical standards, the legal community can harness the benefits of AI while upholding fundamental principles of justice, fairness, and accountability. It is essential to navigate the path towards the future of law in a way that aligns AI advancements with society's values and aspirations.

Blockchain and Smart Contracts

Introduction to Blockchain Technology

Blockchain technology has emerged as one of the most revolutionary technologies in recent years, transforming various industries and challenging traditional systems of record-keeping. In this section, we will provide an overview of blockchain technology, its underlying principles, and its potential applications in legal systems.

Overview of Blockchain Technology

Blockchain is essentially a digital ledger that records and verifies transactions across multiple computers or nodes in a decentralized network. Unlike traditional centralized systems, where a central authority controls the ledger, blockchain uses a distributed ledger system that allows for transparency, immutability, and security.

At its core, a blockchain consists of a series of blocks, each containing a set of transactions. These blocks are linked together in a chronological chain, forming a complete record of all transactions that have occurred on the network. Each block contains a unique identifier, called a hash, which is generated by applying a cryptographic function to the data within the block. This hash not only ensures the integrity of the data but also helps maintain the chronological order of the blocks.

One of the defining features of a blockchain is its decentralized nature. Instead of relying on a central authority to validate transactions, blockchain networks use consensus algorithms to ensure that all participants agree on the validity of transactions. This consensus is achieved through a process called mining, where network participants solve complex mathematical puzzles to validate and add new blocks to the chain. As a result, blockchain networks are highly resistant to tampering, as any attempt to alter past transactions would require the majority of the network's computing power.

Key Features of Blockchain Technology

Blockchain technology offers several key features that make it unique and potentially transformative in the legal field:

- **Transparency:** The decentralized nature of blockchain allows for transparency, as all participants have access to the same information. This transparency can enhance trust and accountability, as it enables individuals to verify the authenticity of transactions and track the movement of assets.

- **Immutability:** Once a transaction is recorded on the blockchain, it becomes virtually immutable. The use of cryptographic hashes and distributed consensus ensures that altering past transactions is extremely difficult and would require a significant amount of computational power. This immutability can be particularly valuable in legal contexts where the integrity of records is critical.

BLOCKCHAIN AND SMART CONTRACTS

- **Security:** Blockchain utilizes cryptographic algorithms and decentralized consensus mechanisms to ensure the security of transactions. The distributed nature of the network makes it highly resistant to hacking or tampering, as altering the blockchain would require the attacker to control a majority of the network's computing power. This enhanced security can be especially beneficial in areas such as identity verification, intellectual property rights, and secure document storage.

- **Smart Contracts:** A smart contract is a self-executing contract with the terms of the agreement directly written into the code. These contracts are recorded on the blockchain and automatically executed when predefined conditions are met. Smart contracts can eliminate the need for intermediaries, reduce transaction costs, and increase the efficiency of legal processes.

- **Traceability:** Blockchain's transparent and immutable nature enables the traceability of transactions, assets, and digital identities. This feature can be particularly useful in areas such as supply chain management, where tracking the origin and movement of goods is crucial.

Applications in Legal Systems

Blockchain technology has the potential to disrupt and transform various aspects of legal systems, offering innovative solutions to traditional challenges. Some of the key applications of blockchain in the legal field include:

1. **Smart Contracts in Contract Law:** Smart contracts have the potential to automate and streamline contract creation, execution, and enforcement. By replacing traditional paper-based contracts and intermediaries, smart contracts can reduce costs, increase speed, and enforce compliance with contract terms.

2. **Secure Document Management:** Storing legal documents on the blockchain can enhance security and immutability. The transparency and traceability of blockchain can help prevent fraudulent alterations or tampering of critical legal documents, such as land titles, wills, and patents.

3. **Digital Identity Verification:** Blockchain-based identity systems can provide a secure and decentralized method for verifying people's identities. This can be particularly useful for Know Your Customer (KYC) processes, legal due diligence, and preventing identity theft.

4. **Intellectual Property Rights:** Blockchain enables the transparent registration, tracking, and licensing of intellectual property rights, such as copyrights and patents. It can eliminate disputes over ownership and provide an immutable record of creation and ownership.

5. **Supply Chain Management:** Blockchain can provide end-to-end visibility and transparency in supply chains, ensuring authenticity, traceability, and accountability. This can be vital in verifying the origin of goods, detecting counterfeit products, and ensuring compliance with regulations.

6. **Dispute Resolution:** Decentralized dispute resolution platforms based on blockchain technology can provide efficient and transparent mechanisms for resolving disputes. Smart contracts can automate the resolution process, reducing costs and delays associated with traditional litigation.

While blockchain technology holds immense potential, it is not without challenges. Legal and regulatory frameworks need to be developed to address issues related to jurisdiction, privacy, data protection, and compliance. Additionally, scalability, energy consumption, and interoperability are technical challenges that need to be overcome for broader adoption of blockchain solutions.

Additional Resources

For further exploration of blockchain technology and its applications in the legal field, the following resources are recommended:

- Books:

    1. "Blockchain and the Law: The Rule of Code" by Primavera De Filippi and Aaron Wright.
    2. "Blockchain and the Law: The Rule of Code" by Gary E. Marchant, et al.
    3. "Blockchain for Dummies" by Tiana Laurence.

- Academic Journals:

    1. *Journal of Law and Technology*
    2. *International Journal of Blockchain Law*
    3. *Journal of Legal Technology Risk Management*

- **Websites and Blogs:**

    1. Blockchain and the Law (https://www.blockchainandthelaw.com/)
    2. CoinDesk (https://www.coindesk.com/)
    3. Blockchain Lawyer (https://www.blockchainlawyer.co/)

Conclusion

Blockchain technology has the potential to revolutionize the legal industry by offering transparency, immutability, security, and efficiency. From smart contracts to secure document management, blockchain can enhance various aspects of legal systems. It is important for legal professionals to understand the principles and applications of blockchain to effectively leverage its potential benefits while addressing the challenges associated with its adoption. By embracing blockchain technology, legal systems can be transformed to better serve the principles of justice and accountability.

Smart Contracts and their Applications

Smart contracts are self-executing contracts with the terms of the agreement written directly into code. These contracts are automatically executed when the predetermined conditions are met, without the need for intermediaries. Smart contracts run on blockchain platforms, such as Ethereum, which provide a secure and decentralized infrastructure for executing and enforcing these contracts.

Background

The concept of smart contracts was first introduced by Nick Szabo in the 1990s. Szabo envisioned self-executing contracts that are stored and executed on a computer network. With the development of blockchain technology, his vision has become a reality. Smart contracts leverage the decentralized and immutable nature of blockchains to provide transparency, security, and efficiency in contract execution.

Working Principles

Smart contracts are written in a programming language specifically designed for this purpose, such as Solidity for Ethereum. They are deployed on a blockchain network and contain a set of rules and conditions that govern the execution of the contract.

Once deployed, the contract becomes part of the blockchain's distributed ledger and is visible to all participants.

When a smart contract is triggered, the predetermined conditions are evaluated. If the conditions are met, the contract is automatically executed and the associated transactions are recorded on the blockchain. The contract's code ensures that the execution is tamper-proof and irreversible.

Applications

Smart contracts have a wide range of applications across various industries. Here are some examples:

1. **Supply Chain Management** - Smart contracts can be used to automate and track supply chain processes, ensuring transparency and efficiency. For example, a smart contract can automatically release payment to a supplier when the agreed-upon delivery conditions are met, eliminating the need for intermediaries and reducing the risk of fraud.

2. **Finance and Banking** - Smart contracts can revolutionize traditional financial processes, such as loans, insurance, and investments. For instance, a decentralized lending platform can use smart contracts to automate the loan approval process, collateral management, and repayment, eliminating the need for banks as intermediaries.

3. **Real Estate** - Smart contracts can streamline real estate transactions by automating tasks such as property transfers, escrow arrangements, and rental agreements. This reduces the need for intermediaries, shortens the transaction process, and enhances trust between parties.

4. **Digital Identity** - Smart contracts can be used to create and manage digital identities securely. By using cryptographic techniques, personal information can be securely stored on the blockchain, giving individuals control over their data and facilitating seamless and secure verification processes.

5. **Decentralized Applications (DApps)** - Smart contracts are the backbone of decentralized applications. These applications run on blockchain platforms and leverage the capabilities of smart contracts to provide trustless and transparent interactions. DApps can span various domains, including healthcare, gaming, voting systems, and supply chain management.

Challenges and Considerations

While smart contracts offer numerous benefits, there are also challenges and considerations to be aware of:

1. **Code Vulnerabilities** - Errors or vulnerabilities in the code of a smart contract can lead to significant financial losses or security breaches. Thorough auditing and testing of smart contracts are essential to minimize these risks.

2. **Immutability and Lack of Flexibility** - Once deployed on the blockchain, smart contracts are immutable and cannot be modified unilaterally. This lack of flexibility can be problematic if changes or amendments are required after deployment. It requires careful planning and consideration of all possible scenarios before the contract is executed.

3. **Scalability** - Blockchain networks, including those supporting smart contracts, still face scalability challenges. As more transactions are processed on the network, the time and cost of executing smart contracts can increase. Scalability solutions, such as off-chain computations or layer-two protocols, are actively being developed to address this issue.

4. **Legal and Regulatory Considerations** - The legal status of smart contracts and their enforceability vary across jurisdictions. As smart contracts become more prevalent, legal frameworks and regulations need to evolve to provide clarity and ensure compliance.

Resources and Further Reading

To delve deeper into smart contracts and their applications, consider exploring the following resources:

- Antonopoulos, A. M., & Wood, G. (2018). Mastering Ethereum. O'Reilly Media.
- Buterin, V., & Wood, G. (2014). Ethereum White Paper. Retrieved from https://ethereum.org/whitepaper/
- Szabo, N. (1997). Formalizing and securing relationships on public networks. First Monday, 2(9).
- Swan, M. (2015). Blockchain: Blueprint for a new economy. O'Reilly Media.

These resources provide comprehensive insights into the technical foundations, design principles, and real-world applications of smart contracts.

Exercise

Consider a real estate transaction where a buyer wants to purchase a property from a seller using a smart contract. Design a smart contract that automates the entire process, including the transfer of ownership, escrow arrangements, and payment release upon successful completion of the transaction. Discuss the potential benefits and challenges of using a smart contract in this scenario.

Legal Implications of Blockchain and Smart Contracts

In recent years, blockchain technology has gained significant attention due to its potential to transform various industries, including the legal sector. One of the key applications of blockchain technology within the legal field is the use of smart contracts. Smart contracts are self-executing contracts with the terms of the agreement directly written into code. These contracts automatically execute and enforce themselves, eliminating the need for intermediaries or third-party enforcement. The rise of blockchain technology and smart contracts brings both opportunities and challenges for the legal profession. In this section, we will explore the legal implications of blockchain and smart contracts and discuss their impact on the legal landscape.

Overview of Blockchain Technology

To understand the legal implications of blockchain and smart contracts, it is essential to grasp the underlying principles of blockchain technology. Blockchain is a decentralized and distributed ledger that records transactions across a network of computers. It consists of a chain of blocks, where each block contains a list of transactions. The key features of blockchain technology include immutability, transparency, and security. Transactions recorded on the blockchain are immutable, meaning they cannot be altered or tampered with once added to the chain. Additionally, the decentralized nature of blockchain ensures transparency and reduces the risk of fraud or manipulation. The security of blockchain is maintained through cryptographic algorithms, which protect the integrity and privacy of the data.

Smart Contracts and Legal Validity

Smart contracts, as computer programs, have the potential to revolutionize traditional contract law. These contracts operate automatically upon the occurrence of pre-defined conditions, without the need for intermediaries.

However, one important question that arises is the legal validity and enforceability of smart contracts. In many jurisdictions, traditional contract law requires certain formalities, such as offer, acceptance, consideration, and intention to create legal relations. Smart contracts, being purely digital, may not fit neatly within the existing legal framework. Therefore, legal systems need to adapt to recognize and accommodate smart contracts.

Legal Challenges and Considerations

While the adoption of blockchain technology and smart contracts brings several benefits, it also raises various legal challenges and considerations. One significant challenge is the jurisdictional ambiguity. Blockchain operates across borders, and transactions can occur worldwide. Legal systems need to determine which jurisdiction's laws govern smart contracts and blockchain transactions. Furthermore, the immutability feature of blockchain poses challenges in case of errors, breaches, or disputes. Traditional legal remedies such as rescission or rectification may be difficult to implement on the blockchain.

Another key consideration is data privacy and protection. Blockchain records transactions permanently on the ledger, potentially violating individuals' rights to privacy. Legal frameworks should ensure that personal data stored on the blockchain complies with data protection regulations, such as the European Union's General Data Protection Regulation (GDPR) or similar legislation in other jurisdictions.

Moreover, the smart contract's autonomy and lack of human intervention raise ethical and liability concerns. Smart contracts are designed to execute automatically, and if flaws exist in the underlying code, it can lead to unintended consequences. Determining responsibility for errors, bugs, or vulnerabilities in smart contracts is a complex legal issue.

Application Areas

The legal implications of blockchain and smart contracts extend to various application areas, including supply chain management, real estate, intellectual property, and financial transactions. For instance, in supply chain management, blockchain can provide transparency and traceability, reducing fraud and counterfeiting. In real estate, blockchain can streamline property transactions by automating processes such as title transfers and property record management. Moreover, blockchain can enable secure and efficient digital rights management, protecting the ownership of intellectual property assets. In financial transactions, blockchain-based cryptocurrencies and decentralized finance offer new avenues for fundraising, investment, and peer-to-peer lending.

Regulatory Responses

Given the transformative nature of blockchain and smart contracts, regulators around the world are examining how existing legal frameworks can accommodate these technologies. Some jurisdictions have taken proactive steps to clarify the legal status of blockchain and smart contracts. For instance, the United States has recognized the validity of smart contracts under the Uniform Electronic Transactions Act (UETA) and the Electronic Signatures in Global and National Commerce Act (ESIGN). Other countries, such as Switzerland, have introduced blockchain-specific regulations to provide legal certainty and facilitate the growth of blockchain-based businesses.

Conclusion

Blockchain and smart contracts have the potential to disrupt the legal landscape by automating and streamlining traditional legal processes. However, their adoption also brings legal challenges that need to be addressed. Legal systems and regulators must adapt to the technological advancements to ensure the legal validity, enforceability, and protection of rights in the age of blockchain. By understanding the legal implications of blockchain and smart contracts, legal professionals can navigate this emerging field and shape its development to promote justice and equality.

Further Reading

To explore the legal implications of blockchain and smart contracts further, the following resources are recommended:

- "*Blockchain and the Law: The Rule of Code*" by Primavera De Filippi and Aaron Wright.

- "*Smart Contracts: Regulation, Governance, and Legal Frameworks*" edited by Elgar Fleisch and Marion Oswald.

- "*Blockchain and the Transformation of Financial Services*" by David L. Yermack.

- "*Legal Aspects of Smart Contracts*" by Maura Grossman and Daniel W. Linna Jr.

These resources provide in-depth insights into the legal and regulatory aspects of blockchain technology and smart contracts.

Privacy and Data Protection

Overview of Privacy Laws and Regulations

In today's digital age, where personal data is constantly being collected and processed, privacy has become a critical concern. Privacy laws and regulations play a crucial role in safeguarding individuals' rights to control their personal data and protect their privacy. This section provides an overview of the key principles and legal frameworks that govern privacy at national and international levels.

Principles of Privacy

Privacy laws are built upon a set of fundamental principles that guide the collection, use, and disclosure of personal information. These principles include:

1. **Notice and Consent:** Individuals have the right to be informed about how their personal data will be collected, used, and shared. Organizations must obtain individuals' consent for processing their data, and consent should be informed, specific, and voluntary.

2. **Purpose Limitation:** Personal data should only be collected for specified, legitimate purposes and should not be used or disclosed in a manner that is incompatible with these purposes.

3. **Data Minimization:** Organizations should only collect and retain the minimum amount of personal data necessary to fulfill the defined purposes. Unnecessary data should be deleted or anonymized.

4. **Accuracy:** Organizations should ensure that personal data is accurate, up-to-date, and relevant for the purposes it was collected.

5. **Security:** Organizations must implement appropriate security measures to protect personal data from unauthorized access, disclosure, alteration, or destruction.

6. **Accountability:** Organizations are responsible for complying with privacy laws and should have mechanisms in place to demonstrate their compliance, such as privacy policies and data protection impact assessments.

International Privacy Laws and Regulations

Privacy laws and regulations vary across countries and regions, but some international frameworks provide broad principles and guidelines for the protection of privacy. These include:

1. **General Data Protection Regulation (GDPR):** Enforced in the European Union (EU), the GDPR is one of the most comprehensive privacy regulations globally. It provides a framework for the lawful processing of personal data and grants individuals rights such as the right to access, rectify, and erase their data.

2. **California Consumer Privacy Act (CCPA):** This landmark legislation in the United States grants California residents certain rights regarding the collection, sale, and disclosure of their personal information by businesses operating in California.

3. **Personal Information Protection and Electronic Documents Act (PIPEDA):** Canadian privacy law that applies to the private sector. It establishes rules for the collection, use, and disclosure of personal information in commercial activities.

4. **Asia-Pacific Economic Cooperation (APEC) Privacy Framework:** A set of privacy principles that provide guidance for member economies in the Asia-Pacific region to develop their privacy laws and promote cross-border data transfers.

Challenges and Emerging Issues

The rapid advancement of technology and the increasing globalization of data flows pose challenges to privacy laws and regulations. Some of the emerging issues in privacy include:

1. **Cross-border Data Transfers:** With the global nature of the internet, personal data often flows across borders. Ensuring consistent privacy standards and addressing conflicts between different jurisdictions' laws are ongoing challenges.

2. **Emerging Technologies:** The proliferation of technologies such as artificial intelligence, biometrics, and Internet of Things (IoT) devices presents new privacy risks. The legal frameworks need to adapt to these advancements and address the ethical and privacy concerns they raise.

3. **Data Breaches and Cybersecurity:** The frequency and scale of data breaches have increased, highlighting the importance of robust cybersecurity measures and incident response protocols.

4. **Government Surveillance:** Balancing the need for national security with the protection of individual privacy rights is an ongoing debate, particularly in the context of mass surveillance programs.

Examples and Resources

To gain a better understanding of privacy laws and regulations, here are some examples of landmark privacy cases and resources for further study:

1. **European Court of Justice (ECJ) Case: Schrems II:** This case invalidated the EU-U.S. Privacy Shield framework, raising questions about the adequacy of data protection in the context of international data transfers.

2. **Privacy Laws and Business International Newsletter:** A comprehensive resource providing updates on global privacy laws, regulations, and developments.

3. **International Association of Privacy Professionals (IAPP):** A professional association that offers certifications, resources, and research papers on privacy-related topics.

4. **Electronic Frontier Foundation (EFF):** A non-profit organization that defends civil liberties and advocates for digital privacy rights.

Caveats and Ethical Considerations

While privacy laws aim to protect individuals' rights, there are ethical considerations to keep in mind. It is essential to strike a balance between privacy rights and other legitimate interests, such as public safety or research purposes. Additionally, privacy laws should be constantly reviewed and updated to keep pace with technological advancements and evolving societal norms.

Exercises

1. Conduct a comparative analysis of the GDPR and CCPA, highlighting their similarities and differences.

2. Discuss a recent data breach incident and its impact on individuals' privacy.

3. Debate the role of government surveillance in ensuring national security while protecting privacy rights.

4. Conduct a privacy impact assessment for a hypothetical organization and identify potential privacy risks and mitigation strategies.

Summary

Privacy laws and regulations are essential in defining the boundaries for the collection, use, and disclosure of personal data. They aim to protect individuals' privacy rights while considering the broader societal and technological context. Understanding the principles and legal frameworks governing privacy provides a foundation for promoting responsible data practices and fostering trust in the digital ecosystem.

Data Protection and Privacy in the Digital Age

In the digital age, where technology has become an integral part of our daily lives, the protection of data and privacy has become a significant concern. With the increased collection, storage, and processing of personal information, individuals are vulnerable to various privacy risks, including data breaches, identity theft, and surveillance. This section explores the fundamental concepts of data protection and privacy in the digital age, the legal frameworks and regulations governing these issues, challenges and solutions, and the importance of incorporating privacy-enhancing technologies.

Understanding Data Protection and Privacy

Data protection refers to the safeguarding of personal data from unauthorized access, use, disclosure, alteration, or destruction. Privacy, on the other hand, is a broader concept that encompasses an individual's right to control their personal information and to be free from intrusive surveillance. In the digital age, data protection and privacy are interconnected, as the collection and processing of personal data inherently involve privacy considerations.

Personal data can include any information that identifies or can be used to identify an individual, such as names, addresses, phone numbers, email addresses, social media posts, browsing history, and biometric data. It is crucial to protect personal data to prevent abuses, maintain trust in technology and services, and respect individuals' autonomy and dignity.

Legal Frameworks and Regulations

To address the challenges posed by data protection and privacy in the digital age, various legal frameworks and regulations have been implemented at national and international levels. The most prominent and comprehensive regulation in this regard is the General Data Protection Regulation (GDPR) in the European Union. The GDPR establishes strict rules for the protection of personal data, including principles of transparency, purpose limitation, data minimization, accuracy, storage limitation, and security.

In addition to the GDPR, many countries have enacted their own data protection laws, such as the California Consumer Privacy Act (CCPA) in the United States and the Personal Information Protection and Electronic Documents

Act (PIPEDA) in Canada. These laws aim to give individuals more control over their personal information and place obligations on organizations to protect that data.

Challenges and Solutions

Data protection and privacy face several challenges in the digital age. One of the main challenges is the increasing volume and complexity of personal data being generated and processed. The vast amount of data, coupled with evolving technologies and data sharing practices, makes it difficult for individuals to understand and control how their data is used.

Moreover, data breaches and cyber-attacks have become more frequent, highlighting the vulnerability of personal data stored in databases and systems. Organizations must implement robust cybersecurity measures to protect against unauthorized access to sensitive information.

To address these challenges, several solutions have emerged. One approach is to enhance individuals' awareness of their privacy rights and educate them about online risks and privacy protection measures. Privacy by design, which involves considering privacy principles from the early stages of system design and development, is another solution to uphold privacy standards.

Additionally, the use of encryption, secure data storage, and authentication techniques can help safeguard personal data. Privacy-enhancing technologies, such as data anonymization and pseudonymization, also provide mechanisms to protect privacy while allowing for data analysis and research.

Ethical Considerations

Data protection and privacy in the digital age also raise important ethical considerations. The collection and analysis of personal data can lead to the creation of detailed profiles and the potential for discriminatory targeting or exclusion. Moreover, the commodification of personal data raises questions about ownership, consent, and the fair distribution of benefits derived from its use.

Ethical frameworks such as privacy as a human right, informed consent, proportionality, and accountability can guide organizations and individuals in navigating these challenges. Transparent and trustworthy data practices should be adopted to ensure that individuals' rights and interests are respected.

Examples and Real-World Impact

Data protection and privacy in the digital age have significant real-world impacts. Consider the example of a social media platform that collects vast amounts of personal data from its users. The platform must ensure that this data is securely stored, used only for agreed-upon purposes, and protected from unauthorized access. Failure to do so could result in data breaches, compromising the privacy of millions of users.

Another example is the increasing use of biometric data, such as fingerprints or facial recognition, for identification and authentication purposes. The responsible use of biometric data requires robust security measures, transparency, and informed consent to protect individuals' privacy and prevent misuse or abuse.

Resources for Further Study

For further study on data protection and privacy in the digital age, the following resources provide valuable insights and information:

- Buchmann, A., Eidam, F., & Welzel, D. (Eds.). (2020). *Handbook of Privacy and Data Protection: Laws, Technologies, and Societal Implications*. Springer.

- European Data Protection Board. (2021). *Guidelines on the Concepts of Controller and Processor in the GDPR*. Retrieved from: `https://edpb.europa.eu/sites/default/files/consultation/2022/edpb_guidelines_202110_controller_processor_rev.1.0_en.pdf`

- Solove, D. J. (2011). *Understanding Privacy*. Harvard University Press.

- World Economic Forum. (2020). *The Known Traveller: Unlocking the Potential of Digital Identity for Secure and Seamless Travel*. Retrieved from: `http://www3.weforum.org/docs/WEF_The_Known_Traveller_Digital_Identity_concept_paper_2018.pdf`

Exercises

1. Research and analyze your country's data protection laws and regulations. How do they align with international standards such as the GDPR?

2. Identify a recent data breach incident and discuss its impact on individuals' privacy and the measures taken by the affected organization to mitigate the breach.

3. Imagine you are a privacy advocate. Develop a plan to raise awareness about the importance of data protection and privacy rights among young people in your community.

Conclusion

Data protection and privacy in the digital age are of paramount importance to ensure the respectful and responsible use of personal information. Legal frameworks, ethical considerations, and technological innovations play significant roles in safeguarding individuals' privacy rights. As technology continues to advance, it is crucial to stay informed about the evolving landscape of data protection and privacy to address emerging challenges and ensure a secure and privacy-respecting digital future.

Challenges and Future Developments in Privacy and Data Protection

The rapid growth of technology and the widespread use of digital platforms have raised significant concerns regarding privacy and data protection. In this section, we will explore the challenges that arise in ensuring the privacy and security of personal data in the digital age, as well as potential future developments in this field.

Challenges in Privacy and Data Protection

1. **Data breaches and cybersecurity**: One of the most pressing challenges in privacy and data protection is the increasing number of data breaches and cyberattacks. Hackers and cybercriminals target both individuals and organizations to gain unauthorized access to sensitive data. These breaches can lead to severe consequences, including identity theft, financial loss, and reputational damage.

2. **Data collection and consent**: With the proliferation of digital technologies, large amounts of personal data are being collected from individuals. The challenge lies in obtaining informed and meaningful consent from individuals for the collection and use of their data. Many individuals are unaware of the extent to which their data is being collected, stored, and shared by various entities.

3. **Cross-border data transfers**: The global nature of the digital economy raises challenges in regulating the transfer of personal data across borders. Divergent legal frameworks and data protection standards across countries make it difficult to ensure consistent and adequate protection of personal data. The increasing use of cloud computing and remote data storage further complicates this issue.

4. **Emerging technologies**: The advent of emerging technologies such as artificial intelligence (AI), machine learning, and facial recognition pose challenges to privacy and data protection. These technologies often rely on extensive data

collection and processing, raising concerns about the potential for misuse and abuse of personal data.

5. **Lack of awareness and education:** Many individuals are unaware of their rights and responsibilities regarding privacy and data protection. There is a need for increased awareness and education to empower individuals to make informed decisions about their personal data.

Future Developments in Privacy and Data Protection

1. **Stricter regulations:** The growing concern over privacy and data protection has led to the introduction of stricter regulations. For example, the General Data Protection Regulation (GDPR) in the European Union provides a comprehensive framework for protecting the privacy and rights of individuals. Similar regulations are being considered and implemented in other jurisdictions, emphasizing the importance of accountability and transparency in data handling practices.

2. **Privacy-enhancing technologies:** The development of privacy-enhancing technologies aims to address the challenges posed by emerging technologies. These technologies focus on protecting personal data while still allowing for data analysis and processing. Techniques such as differential privacy, homomorphic encryption, and secure multiparty computation enable data analysis without compromising individual privacy.

3. **Data protection by design:** Adopting a "privacy by design" approach in the development of systems and applications can embed privacy and data protection principles into the design process itself. This approach emphasizes privacy as a fundamental component and promotes proactive measures to ensure privacy and data protection from the outset.

4. **Enhanced user control and consent:** Future developments in privacy and data protection may include improved mechanisms for user control and consent. This could involve innovative ways of obtaining informed consent, such as using standardized and user-friendly interfaces to clearly inform individuals about data collection practices and provide options for granular consent.

5. **International cooperation and harmonization:** Given the global nature of data flows, there is a need for increased international cooperation and harmonization of privacy and data protection laws. Efforts to establish common frameworks and standards can facilitate the secure and privacy-respecting transfer and processing of data across borders.

6. **Ethical considerations in data use:** As data becomes an increasingly valuable resource, ethical considerations in data use are gaining attention. Future developments may involve the adoption of ethical frameworks and guidelines for

data-driven technologies, ensuring that data is used in a responsible and socially beneficial manner.

Case Study: Privacy Challenges in the Age of Artificial Intelligence

The rapid advancements in artificial intelligence (AI) systems present unique privacy challenges. AI systems often require large amounts of data to train and improve their performance, raising concerns about the privacy of individuals involved. For example, facial recognition technologies can capture and analyze biometric data without individuals' knowledge or consent.

To address these challenges, various approaches can be considered. One possible solution is to implement privacy-preserving AI techniques, such as federated learning, where data remains on users' devices and only aggregated insights are shared. Another approach involves the development of robust anonymization methods that protect individuals' identities while preserving the usefulness of data for AI applications.

Furthermore, policymakers and organizations can establish guidelines and regulations specifically tailored to AI systems to protect individuals' privacy rights. These guidelines should emphasize the importance of transparency, accountability, and explainability in AI systems to ensure that individuals are aware of how their data is being used and have control over their personal information.

Resources for Further Study

1. Solove, D. J. (2011). *Privacy Law Fundamentals.* Foundation Press. 2. Cavoukian, A. (2018). *Privacy by Design: The 7 Foundational Principles.* Information and Privacy Commissioner of Ontario. 3. Wachter, S., Mittelstadt, B., & Floridi, L. (2017). *Why a Right to Explanation of Automated Decision-Making Does Not Exist in the General Data Protection Regulation.* International Data Privacy Law, 7(2), 76-99. 4. Information Commissioner's Office. (2019). *Artificial Intelligence and Data Protection.* Retrieved from https://ico.org.uk/for-organisations/guide-to-data-protection/key-data-protection-theme

Key Takeaways

1. Privacy and data protection face challenges such as data breaches, data collection, cross-border transfers, emerging technologies, and lack of awareness. 2. Stricter regulations, privacy-enhancing technologies, and privacy by design are potential future developments. 3. Addressing privacy challenges in AI requires privacy-preserving techniques, guidelines, and regulations tailored to AI systems.

4. Resources for further study provide additional information on privacy and data protection.

Cybersecurity and Law

Legal Frameworks for Cybersecurity

Cybersecurity has become an increasingly important issue in today's digital age. As the reliance on technology continues to grow, so does the need for effective legal frameworks to protect against cyber threats and ensure the security of information. In this section, we will explore the key legal aspects and frameworks related to cybersecurity.

Understanding Cybersecurity

Before delving into the legal aspects, it is crucial to have a clear understanding of cybersecurity. Cybersecurity refers to the practices and measures taken to protect computer systems, networks, and data from unauthorized access, use, disclosure, disruption, modification, or destruction. It involves the implementation of technical and administrative controls to secure information and mitigate risk.

The Importance of Legal Frameworks

Legal frameworks are essential in addressing cybersecurity concerns. They provide a structured approach to establish rules, regulations, and standards that govern the use, protection, and sharing of digital information. These frameworks help to create a legal foundation for cybersecurity practices, ensuring accountability, compliance, and enforcement.

International Legal Frameworks

At the international level, several legal frameworks exist to address cybersecurity. The United Nations has played a significant role in promoting international cooperation in this regard. The most notable international legal instrument is the United Nations General Assembly Resolution 58/199 on "Combating Cybercrime." This resolution aims to harmonize national and international laws, enhance security measures, and promote cooperation among nations to combat cyber threats.

Another essential international agreement is the Council of Europe's Convention on Cybercrime, also known as the Budapest Convention. This treaty establishes a framework for international cooperation on cybercrime-related matters, including cyberattacks, computer-related fraud, and child pornography. It requires signatory states to establish domestic legislation and cooperate in the investigation and prosecution of cybercrime offenses.

National Legal Frameworks

National legal frameworks play a crucial role in defining cybersecurity standards and practices within a country. These frameworks vary from one jurisdiction to another but generally include legislation, regulations, and policies governing cyber activities. They address issues such as data protection, privacy, incident response, and cybercrime.

For instance, the United States has several legal frameworks that contribute to cybersecurity. The Computer Fraud and Abuse Act (CFAA) is a federal law that prohibits unauthorized access to computer systems and networks. It establishes penalties for various cybercrimes and provides a legal basis for prosecuting offenders.

Many countries have also established data protection laws to safeguard personal information. The European Union's General Data Protection Regulation (GDPR) is one such example. The GDPR sets out regulations for the processing of personal data, including its collection, storage, and transfer. It aims to protect individuals' privacy and ensure secure handling of personal information.

Cybersecurity Compliance and Standards

To ensure adherence to cybersecurity best practices, many organizations follow established compliance frameworks and standards. These frameworks provide guidelines and recommendations for implementing controls and safeguards to protect against cyber threats.

One widely recognized framework is the ISO/IEC 27001, which outlines the requirements for establishing, implementing, maintaining, and continually improving an Information Security Management System (ISMS). It provides a systematic approach to managing sensitive company information, including cybersecurity risks.

Additionally, various industry-specific standards exist, such as the Payment Card Industry Data Security Standard (PCI DSS) for the protection of payment card data and the Health Insurance Portability and Accountability Act (HIPAA) for the healthcare industry.

Challenges and Future Developments

While legal frameworks for cybersecurity are essential, they face several challenges in the rapidly evolving digital landscape. One significant challenge is the international nature of cyber threats, which requires international cooperation and coordination to effectively address and combat cybercrime.

Moreover, the emergence of new technologies, such as the Internet of Things (IoT) and artificial intelligence (AI), presents unique challenges for existing legal frameworks. These technologies bring about new security risks and complexities, requiring updated regulations and standards to adequately address them.

Future developments in legal frameworks for cybersecurity will likely focus on enhancing international cooperation, strengthening incident response mechanisms, and promoting greater accountability and transparency in cyberspace. Continued collaboration between governments, organizations, and other stakeholders will be crucial for the development and implementation of effective and comprehensive legal frameworks.

Conclusion

Legal frameworks for cybersecurity are vital for protecting information, mitigating risks, and ensuring accountability in the digital age. International agreements, national legislation, and compliance frameworks provide the necessary structure and guidelines for addressing cyber threats effectively. However, these frameworks must continually adapt to the evolving threat landscape and advancements in technology. By staying current and proactive, legal frameworks can play a significant role in creating a secure and resilient cyberspace.

Cyber Crime and Cyber Defense

In today's digital era, the advancements in technology have brought new opportunities and challenges, particularly in the realm of cybercrime. Cybercrime refers to criminal activities carried out through digital platforms and networks, targeting individuals, organizations, and governments. As our lives become increasingly interconnected through the internet, the threat of cybercrime has grown exponentially, necessitating robust cyber defense strategies.

Understanding Cyber Crime

Cybercrime encompasses a wide range of illegal activities, including hacking, identity theft, cyber fraud, unauthorized access, data breaches, and digital piracy.

These crimes are facilitated by the anonymity and accessibility offered by the internet, making perpetrators difficult to trace. Cybercriminals exploit vulnerabilities in computer systems, networks, and software to gain illegal access, steal sensitive information, or cause damage.

Impact and Consequences

The impact of cybercrime is far-reaching and affects individuals, businesses, and society as a whole. For individuals, cybercrime can result in financial losses, identity theft, and invasion of privacy. Businesses face significant financial and reputational damage due to data breaches, intellectual property theft, and disruptions in operations. Governments also fall victim to cyber attacks, which can compromise national security and critical infrastructure.

Cyber Defense Strategies

Given the ever-evolving nature of cyber threats, effective cyber defense strategies are necessary to safeguard against cyber attacks. These strategies aim to prevent, detect, and respond to cyber threats, ensuring the security and integrity of digital systems. Some key components of cyber defense include:

1. **Network Security:** Implementing firewalls, intrusion detection systems, and encryption protocols to protect networks from unauthorized access and malicious activities.

2. **Vulnerability Management:** Regularly scanning and patching software, systems, and devices to identify and address vulnerabilities that can be exploited by cybercriminals.

3. **User Awareness:** Educating users about safe online practices, including strong passwords, secure browsing, and recognizing phishing attempts to minimize the risk of falling victim to cybercrime.

4. **Incident Response:** Establishing protocols to swiftly identify, respond to, and mitigate cyber incidents to minimize the damage caused by an attack.

5. **Threat Intelligence:** Continuously monitoring and analyzing emerging cyber threats and trends to proactively adapt defense mechanisms and stay one step ahead of cybercriminals.

6. **Collaboration and Information Sharing:** Foster partnerships between government agencies, private organizations, and international bodies to share threat intelligence and collaborate on cyber defense efforts.

7. **Legal and Policy Frameworks:** Enacting robust legislation and regulations to combat cybercrime, enhance cooperation between nations, and provide legal mechanisms to hold cybercriminals accountable.

Case Study: Ransomware Attacks

Ransomware attacks have emerged as a significant cyber threat in recent years. These attacks involve malicious software that encrypts a victim's data, making it inaccessible until a ransom is paid to the attacker. One notable case is the WannaCry ransomware attack in 2017, which infected hundreds of thousands of computers worldwide, including those of government agencies and healthcare institutions.

The WannaCry attack highlighted the critical need for effective cyber defense measures. Organizations affected by the attack faced disruptions in services, financial losses, and compromised patient data. It served as a wake-up call for the global community to strengthen cybersecurity frameworks and cooperation to prevent future ransomware attacks.

Challenges and Ethical Considerations

Cyber defense is confronted with several challenges and ethical considerations. Some of these include:

1. **Rapidly Evolving Threat Landscape:** Cyber threats evolve at a rapid pace, requiring constant updates and improvements in cyber defense strategies to keep up with emerging threats.

2. **Privacy Concerns:** Balancing the need for cybersecurity with the protection of individuals' privacy rights poses ethical challenges. Cyber defense strategies should ensure the security of data without compromising personal privacy.

3. **Global Cooperation:** Cybercrime knows no borders, necessitating global collaboration to combat cyber threats effectively. Coordinating efforts among nations with different legal systems, policies, and priorities can be challenging.

4. **Ethical Hacking:** The ethical considerations surrounding the practice of ethical hacking, or "white hat" hacking, which involves deliberately attempting to break into systems to identify vulnerabilities and help improve security measures.

Additional Resources

1. Book: "Cybersecurity and Cyberwar: What Everyone Needs to Know" by P.W. Singer and Allan Friedman.

2. Online Course: "Introduction to Cybersecurity" offered by Coursera.

3. Organization: The National Institute of Standards and Technology (NIST) offers comprehensive guidelines and frameworks for cybersecurity best practices.

Conclusion

Effective cyber defense strategies are crucial in the face of the ever-growing threat of cybercrime. By understanding the nature of cybercrime, its impact, and implementing robust defense measures, individuals, organizations, and governments can mitigate risks and safeguard against cyber attacks. However, it is essential to recognize the ongoing challenges, ethical considerations, and the evolving nature of cyber threats, calling for continuous vigilance and adaptation to protect our increasingly digitized world.

Balancing Security and Privacy in the Digital World

In the digital era, the rapid advancement of technology has brought about numerous benefits and conveniences. However, it has also raised concerns about the balance between security and privacy. On one hand, there is a growing need for stronger security measures to protect individuals and organizations from cyber threats. On the other hand, there is a demand for adequate privacy safeguards to ensure that people's personal information is not exploited or misused. Finding the right balance between security and privacy is crucial in order to maintain trust and confidence in the digital world.

The Importance of Security

In the digital world, security is of paramount importance to protect sensitive information and prevent unauthorized access. With the increasing prevalence of cyber attacks and data breaches, organizations need robust security measures to safeguard their data and systems. This includes implementing firewalls, encryption protocols, intrusion detection systems, and regular security audits. Individuals also need to take precautions such as using strong passwords, keeping software up to date, and being aware of phishing and social engineering attempts.

However, security measures should not come at the expense of privacy. It is essential to find a balance that respects individuals' privacy rights while ensuring adequate security measures are in place.

The Need for Privacy

Privacy is a fundamental right that is protected by laws and regulations in many countries. It encompasses the right to control and protect personal information, as well as the right to be free from surveillance and intrusion. In the digital world, privacy becomes even more critical as individuals increasingly share vast amounts of personal data online.

Privacy is essential to protect individuals from unwanted intrusion, identity theft, and discrimination. It allows people to maintain autonomy, express their opinions freely, and avoid being subjected to constant surveillance.

Challenges in Balancing Security and Privacy

Balancing security and privacy is not without its challenges. One of the main challenges is the tension between law enforcement and individual privacy rights. Law enforcement agencies argue that access to personal data is crucial for investigating and preventing crimes. However, this can conflict with individuals' rights to privacy and raise concerns about potential abuses of power.

Another challenge is the collection and use of personal data by technology companies. Many online platforms and services collect vast amounts of data from users, often without their explicit consent. This raises questions about how this data is used, who has access to it, and how individuals can maintain control over their own information.

Additionally, emerging technologies such as facial recognition, biometrics, and artificial intelligence pose new challenges to the balance between security and privacy. While these technologies can enhance security measures, they also raise concerns about surveillance, profiling, and the potential for discrimination.

Solutions and Strategies

Finding an optimal balance between security and privacy requires a multi-faceted approach. Here are some strategies and solutions that can help address the challenges:

1. Strong Legal Frameworks: Clear and comprehensive laws and regulations regarding data protection, privacy, and security are essential. These laws should strike a balance between individual privacy rights and the legitimate needs of security and law enforcement.

2. Privacy by Design: Implementing privacy by design principles ensures that privacy safeguards are incorporated into the design of technologies, systems, and

processes from the outset. This includes minimizing data collection, providing transparency and user control over data usage, and ensuring data encryption.

3. Encryption and Data Security: Strong encryption protocols should be employed to protect data both in transit and at rest. This can help safeguard sensitive information from unauthorized access and cyber attacks.

4. Transparency and User Control: Individuals should have clear visibility and control over how their data is collected, used, and shared. This can be achieved through transparent privacy policies, user consent mechanisms, and tools that allow individuals to manage their privacy preferences.

5. Ethical Use of Technology: Organizations and individuals should adhere to ethical principles when using technology. This includes being transparent, accountable, and responsible in the collection, use, and sharing of personal data.

6. International Cooperation: Collaboration and cooperation between nations is crucial in addressing security and privacy challenges on a global scale. International agreements and frameworks can promote harmonized laws and standards, enhance information sharing, and facilitate cross-border investigations.

Real-World Example: Balancing Security and Privacy in Contact Tracing Apps

A recent real-world example involving the balance between security and privacy is the development and deployment of contact tracing apps during the COVID-19 pandemic. These apps aim to notify individuals who may have come into contact with someone infected with the virus.

While contact tracing apps can be an effective tool in controlling the spread of the virus, they also raise concerns about privacy and data security. To address these concerns, many countries have adopted privacy-centric approaches, such as using decentralized systems and anonymizing data. These measures help protect individuals' privacy while still enabling efficient contact tracing.

However, the effectiveness of these apps relies on trust and widespread adoption. Therefore, it is essential to ensure transparency, user control, and data protection measures to maintain public confidence in these technologies.

Further Resources

For further study on the topic of balancing security and privacy in the digital world, the following resources are recommended:

1. Book: "The Age of Surveillance Capitalism" by Shoshana Zuboff 2. Article: "Security vs. Privacy: The Social Trade-Off" by Bruce Schneier 3. Website:

Electronic Frontier Foundation (eff.org) - a non-profit organization promoting digital rights and privacy 4. Documentary: "Terms and Conditions May Apply" - a documentary exploring privacy implications of online data collection and usage

Exercises

1. Research and analyze a recent case where the balance between security and privacy was debated. Explain the different perspectives and the final outcome of the case.

2. Discuss the ethical considerations of using facial recognition technology for security purposes. What are the potential benefits and risks associated with its widespread adoption?

3. Design a privacy-oriented mobile application that collects minimal user data while still providing a useful service. Outline the privacy features and mechanisms you would incorporate into its design.

4. Debate the following statement: "Individual privacy should always take precedence over security concerns." Present arguments for and against the statement, considering both individual rights and societal interests.

Remember to critically analyze the issues, evaluate different perspectives, and support your arguments with evidence and reasoning.

Conclusion

In the digital world, balancing security and privacy is a complex challenge that requires thoughtful consideration and action. It is crucial to ensure adequate security measures to protect against cyber threats while respecting individuals' privacy rights. Striking the right balance will contribute to a trusted and secure digital environment, fostering innovation, collaboration, and the protection of individual rights. By implementing strong legal frameworks, promoting privacy by design, and fostering international cooperation, we can achieve a harmonious relationship between security and privacy in the digital world.

Online Dispute Resolution

Overview of Online Dispute Resolution (ODR)

As advancements in technology continue to shape our lives, they have also had a profound impact on the field of law. One area where technology has proven particularly transformative is in dispute resolution. Online Dispute Resolution (ODR) is an emerging field that utilizes technology to resolve disputes efficiently and effectively without the need for traditional court proceedings. In this section, we will provide an overview of ODR and explore its key principles, processes, and advantages.

Definition of Online Dispute Resolution

ODR can be defined as the use of digital technology to resolve legal disputes between parties. It encompasses a range of methods and tools that facilitate the resolution of conflicts through online platforms. ODR can be used to settle various types of disputes, including commercial, consumer, family, and even international disputes.

The goal of ODR is to provide a fair, accessible, and efficient alternative to traditional dispute resolution methods. It leverages technology to streamline the resolution process, reduce costs, and increase access to justice.

Key Principles of Online Dispute Resolution

ODR is guided by several key principles that shape its implementation. These principles include:

1. Accessibility: ODR aims to provide equal access to justice for all parties involved in a dispute, regardless of their geographical location or financial means. By utilizing online platforms, ODR eliminates many of the barriers associated with physical attendance at court hearings.

2. Efficiency: ODR offers a more time-efficient process compared to traditional litigation. Parties can engage in dispute resolution from the convenience of their own location, without the need for multiple hearings or travel. This expedites the resolution process and saves both time and money.

3. Neutrality and Impartiality: ODR platforms ensure neutrality and impartiality by employing trained mediators or arbitrators who facilitate the resolution process. These professionals maintain objectivity and fairness throughout the proceedings.

4. Confidentiality: ODR platforms employ encryption and other security measures to safeguard the privacy and confidentiality of the parties involved. This ensures that sensitive information remains protected during the resolution process.

Processes in Online Dispute Resolution

ODR encompasses various processes depending on the nature of the dispute and the desired outcome. The two primary methods employed in ODR are mediation and arbitration.

1. Mediation: Mediation involves a neutral third party, the mediator, who facilitates communication and negotiation between the disputing parties. The mediator helps the parties identify their interests, explore potential solutions, and ultimately reach a mutually acceptable resolution. Mediation is often voluntary and allows the parties to maintain control over the outcome.

2. Arbitration: In arbitration, a neutral arbitrator or panel of arbitrators is appointed to make a binding decision on the dispute. The arbitrator(s) review the evidence presented by both parties and issue a decision that is enforceable like a court judgment. Unlike mediation, arbitration is typically binding, meaning parties must abide by the arbitrator's decision.

ODR platforms employ various communication tools, such as video conferencing, email, and online chat, to facilitate effective communication between the parties and the mediator or arbitrator.

Advantages of Online Dispute Resolution

ODR offers several advantages over traditional dispute resolution methods:

1. Cost-effectiveness: ODR eliminates the need for expensive court proceedings, reducing legal costs for all parties involved. It also saves time and travel expenses associated with physical hearings.

2. Convenience and accessibility: ODR allows parties to participate in the resolution process from anywhere with an internet connection. This increases access to justice, particularly for those who may face geographical barriers or have limited mobility.

3. Flexibility and customization: ODR platforms offer flexibility in terms of scheduling and process customization. Parties can choose the most suitable method and time frame for resolving their dispute.

4. Confidentiality and privacy: ODR platforms prioritize the protection of confidential information through secure and encrypted channels. Participants can discuss sensitive matters without fear of their discussions being made public.

5. Diverse dispute resolution options: ODR provides a range of methods beyond mediation and arbitration, including negotiation, conciliation, and facilitated settlement discussions. This allows the parties to select the approach that best suits their specific needs and preferences.

Caveats and Challenges of Online Dispute Resolution

While ODR has many advantages, there are several caveats and challenges that need to be considered:

1. Technological barriers: ODR relies heavily on technology, and parties must have access to reliable internet connections and appropriate devices. Technological issues, such as connectivity problems or software glitches, can disrupt the resolution process.

2. Need for trust: ODR requires a level of trust between the parties, as they rely on the mediator or arbitrator to facilitate the resolution process and make impartial decisions. Building trust in an online setting can be challenging, particularly in high-stakes cases.

3. Limited procedural formalities: ODR may not adhere to the same formalities and procedures as traditional court proceedings, which can be both an advantage and a challenge. While increased flexibility can expedite the resolution process, it may also lead to concerns about due process and enforcement of decisions.

4. Power imbalances: ODR, like any other dispute resolution method, can be affected by power imbalances between the parties. Equal participation and effective representation of all parties are crucial for a fair and just resolution.

Resources and Further Reading

To delve deeper into the world of Online Dispute Resolution, the following resources are recommended:

1. Ethan Katsh and Janet Rifkin, "Online Dispute Resolution: Resolving Conflicts in Cyberspace" - This comprehensive book provides an in-depth exploration of ODR principles, processes, and case studies.

2. National Center for Technology and Dispute Resolution (NCTDR) - This organization focuses on the intersection of technology and dispute resolution, offering research, resources, and a directory of ODR platforms.

3. International Mediation Institute (IMI) - IMI is a non-profit organization that promotes high standards in mediation practice worldwide. Their website offers ODR resources, ethical guidelines, and a directory of mediators.

By embracing technology and harnessing the power of ODR, we can revolutionize the way disputes are resolved, making justice more accessible, efficient, and fair for all.

Challenges and Opportunities of ODR

Online Dispute Resolution (ODR) offers significant opportunities for transforming the way disputes are resolved in the digital age. However, like any emerging field, ODR also faces a range of challenges that need to be addressed for its successful implementation. In this section, we will explore the key challenges and opportunities of ODR and discuss strategies to overcome these challenges.

Challenges of ODR

1. **Technological Barriers:** One of the main challenges of ODR is the need for a reliable and user-friendly technological infrastructure. Not all individuals have access to high-speed internet or the necessary devices to engage in online dispute resolution. This lack of technological access can create a digital divide and limit the effectiveness of ODR platforms. Addressing this challenge requires investment in infrastructure development and ensuring accessibility for all.

2. **Privacy and Security Concerns:** ODR involves the exchange of sensitive and confidential information online. Maintaining privacy and data security is crucial to ensure the trust and confidence of the parties involved. ODR platforms must implement robust encryption protocols and adhere to strict data protection regulations. Additionally, educating users about online privacy and security best practices is essential to mitigate the risk of cyber threats.

3. **Cultural and Language Considerations:** ODR platforms operate in a global context, where parties may come from diverse cultures and speak different languages. Overcoming cultural and language barriers is essential for effective communication and understanding between the disputing parties. ODR platforms should provide multilingual support and employ culturally sensitive processes to accommodate the needs of all participants.

4. **Lack of Human Interaction:** Traditional dispute resolution processes often involve face-to-face interaction, which allows parties to express emotions and build rapport. In the absence of physical presence, ODR platforms need innovative ways to replicate human interaction and foster a sense of empathy and understanding. Integrating video conferencing, live chat, or even virtual reality technologies can help bridge this gap.

Opportunities of ODR

1. **Accessibility and Convenience:** ODR offers an opportunity to make dispute resolution more accessible and convenient, especially for individuals who face geographical or mobility constraints. ODR allows parties to participate in the resolution process from the comfort of their own homes or offices, saving time and reducing the need for travel.

2. **Cost-Effectiveness:** Traditional court-based dispute resolution processes can be expensive and time-consuming. ODR platforms have the potential to

significantly reduce the costs associated with legal proceedings, making justice more affordable and accessible for individuals and small businesses.

3. **Efficiency and Speed:** ODR eliminates the need for lengthy court proceedings, enabling parties to resolve their disputes more efficiently and expeditiously. Through the use of technology, ODR platforms can streamline the dispute resolution process, automate certain tasks, and facilitate faster resolution of cases.

4. **Flexibility and Customization:** ODR platforms can offer flexible and customizable solutions, allowing parties to choose dispute resolution mechanisms that best suit their needs. From mediation to arbitration, parties can adapt the process to their preferences, enabling more creative and tailored solutions.

Addressing the Challenges

To ensure the success of ODR and maximize its potential, several strategies can be employed:

1. **Collaboration and Partnerships:** Collaboration between ODR platform providers, legal institutions, and technology experts is crucial for addressing technological barriers, improving user experience, and ensuring the security and reliability of the platforms. Partnerships with governments, NGOs, and international organizations can also help promote the adoption of ODR globally.

2. **Training and Capacity Building:** Providing training and capacity building programs for legal professionals, judges, mediators, and other stakeholders are necessary to enhance their skills in utilizing ODR platforms effectively. This includes training on technological proficiency, cultural sensitivity, and ethical considerations.

3. **Continuous Innovation and Research:** ODR is a rapidly evolving field, and continuous innovation and research are essential to address emerging challenges and develop best practices. Encouraging research collaborations, funding academic research, and fostering an environment of innovation can drive the advancement of ODR.

4. **Public Awareness and Engagement:** Enhancing public awareness and understanding of ODR is crucial to foster trust and confidence in the system. Conducting public outreach programs, educational campaigns, and stakeholder consultations can help engage individuals and communities in the dialogue surrounding ODR.

Case Study: eBay's Resolution Center

An example of successful ODR implementation is eBay's Resolution Center. This platform allows buyers and sellers to resolve disputes arising from online transactions. eBay's ODR system combines automated negotiation processes and mediation services, providing an efficient and user-friendly resolution mechanism. The Resolution Center has increased customer satisfaction, reduced the number of escalated disputes, and significantly improved the overall user experience on the platform.

Conclusion

ODR presents exciting opportunities for transforming the way disputes are resolved, making justice more accessible, efficient, and affordable. However, addressing the challenges of technological barriers, privacy and security concerns, cultural and language considerations, and the lack of human interaction is essential for the successful implementation of ODR. By adopting strategies such as collaboration, training, innovation, and public engagement, the potential of ODR can be fully realized, contributing to a more equitable and efficient justice system.

ODR and Access to Justice

With the rapid advancements in technology, the field of law has also seen significant changes. One such transformation is the emergence of Online Dispute Resolution (ODR) as an alternative method of resolving legal disputes. ODR utilizes technology to enhance access to justice by providing a more efficient and affordable way to resolve conflicts. In this section, we will explore the concept of ODR, its potential benefits and challenges, and its impact on access to justice.

Understanding ODR

ODR refers to the resolution of legal disputes through digital platforms, typically utilizing the internet. It involves using technology to facilitate communication, negotiation, and the decision-making process between parties involved in a dispute. ODR can take various forms, such as online negotiation, mediation, arbitration, or a combination of these methods.

The goal of ODR is to provide a more accessible, cost-effective, and convenient alternative to traditional dispute resolution processes. It seeks to eliminate geographical barriers and excessive costs associated with in-person hearings, making justice more accessible to a wider range of individuals.

Benefits of ODR for Access to Justice

1. Increased Access: ODR expands access to justice by overcoming physical, social, and economic barriers. It allows individuals who may have limited resources or face geographical constraints to participate in the dispute resolution process.

2. Cost-Effectiveness: Traditional dispute resolution methods can be expensive, often requiring individuals to hire legal representation and bear the costs of attending in-person hearings. ODR can significantly reduce these costs by eliminating the need for physical presence and simplifying procedural requirements.

3. Convenience and Efficiency: ODR offers convenience and flexibility, allowing parties to participate in the process from their own locations and at their own pace. It eliminates the need for scheduling conflicts and reduces the time required for resolution.

4. Privacy and Confidentiality: Some disputes involve sensitive information or parties who prefer to maintain privacy. ODR platforms can provide secure and confidential channels for communication and document exchange, ensuring the protection of sensitive information.

5. Customization and Accessibility: ODR platforms can be designed to cater to individuals with disabilities or specific needs, ensuring accessibility for all participants. It also allows for the customization of the process to fit the specific requirements of each case.

Challenges and Ethical Considerations in ODR

While ODR offers numerous benefits, it also raises ethical and practical challenges. It is essential to address these concerns to ensure fairness, accuracy, and the protection of participants' rights. Some of the key challenges and considerations include:

1. Online Security and Data Protection: ODR platforms must have robust security measures to protect the confidentiality and integrity of the information shared during the process. Encryption, secure servers, and data storage protocols are essential to maintain participants' trust.

2. Unequal Access to Technology: While ODR aims to enhance access to justice, it is crucial to bridge the digital divide. Not all individuals may have reliable internet access or the technological literacy required to navigate ODR platforms effectively. Efforts must be made to ensure equal access to technology and provide necessary support.

3. Impersonal Nature and Lack of Non-Verbal Cues: In-person interactions allow for the observation of non-verbal cues, which can be significant in

understanding parties' emotions and intentions. ODR platforms should incorporate features to facilitate effective communication and minimize misinterpretation.

4. Validity and Enforceability of Online Agreements: ODR often leads to the formation of agreements or settlements. It is essential to ensure that these agreements are legally valid and enforceable in accordance with the applicable laws and regulations.

Case Study: eBay's Resolution Center

One of the most well-known examples of ODR is eBay's Resolution Center. eBay, being an online marketplace, deals with numerous buyer-seller disputes. To address this, eBay developed a comprehensive ODR platform that allows parties to resolve conflicts efficiently.

The Resolution Center provides a step-by-step process for negotiation, mediation, and arbitration. Parties can communicate through messages and submit relevant documents to support their claims. eBay also provides trained online mediators who assist in facilitating communication and reaching mutually acceptable solutions.

The platform's success lies in its accessibility, efficiency, and ease of use. eBay's ODR platform has resolved millions of disputes, saving time and resources for both buyers and sellers.

Future Directions in ODR

As technology continues to advance, ODR is likely to play an even more significant role in shaping the future of access to justice. Some potential future directions for ODR include:

1. Integration of Artificial Intelligence (AI): AI can enhance ODR platforms by providing automated analysis of legal issues, suggesting potential solutions, and even assisting in the negotiation process. However, careful consideration must be given to avoid bias and ensure fairness.

2. Virtual Reality (VR) and Augmented Reality (AR): VR and AR technologies can create immersive and interactive virtual environments for ODR, simulating in-person hearings, and enhancing communication between parties and mediators.

3. Blockchain Technology: The transparency, security, and immutability of blockchain can be leveraged to ensure the integrity of ODR processes, particularly in recording and storing agreements and decisions.

4. Cross-Border ODR: ODR has the potential to facilitate resolution in cross-border disputes by overcoming jurisdictional barriers. Efforts must be made to develop frameworks for recognizing and enforcing ODR-based decisions globally.

Conclusion

ODR presents a transformative approach to access to justice, leveraging technology to overcome barriers and make dispute resolution more efficient, cost-effective, and accessible. While challenges exist, the potential benefits of ODR for individuals and communities are significant. As technology continues to evolve, exploring and refining ODR processes will be crucial to ensuring fairness, inclusivity, and the effective resolution of disputes. ODR is an exciting field that holds immense promise for the future of access to justice.

Big Data and Predictive Analytics in Law

Collection and Use of Big Data in Legal Field

With the exponential growth of digital information and the proliferation of technologies, the legal field has seen a significant influx of data. This vast amount of information, often referred to as "big data," has the potential to revolutionize legal research and practice. In this section, we will explore the collection and use of big data in the legal field, its implications, challenges, and the ethical considerations associated with it.

Understanding Big Data in the Legal Context

Big data in the legal context refers to the massive volume of digital information generated by various sources, such as court records, legal texts, legislation, and case law databases. This data is often characterized by its high velocity, variety, and veracity. The collection and analysis of this data offer the potential to extract valuable insights, uncover patterns, and inform legal decision-making.

Data Collection Methods

In order to harness the power of big data, legal professionals need to employ effective data collection methods. Here are some commonly used methods:

1. **Web Scraping:** Web scraping involves extracting data from websites, legal blogs, and social media platforms. It can be used to gather information on case law, legal precedents, and legal opinions.

2. **Digital Repositories:** Many legal databases provide access to an extensive collection of legal documents, including court decisions, statutes, and regulations. Utilizing these repositories can help legal professionals analyze past cases and identify trends.

3. **Surveys and Questionnaires:** Surveys and questionnaires can be used to collect data directly from legal professionals, judges, or other stakeholders. This method allows for targeted data collection on specific legal issues.

4. **Legal Analytics Platforms:** Legal analytics platforms use machine learning algorithms to analyze legal data, such as court dockets and case outcomes. These platforms provide valuable insights and predictions, aiding legal professionals in decision-making.

Challenges and Limitations

While big data presents numerous opportunities in the legal field, there are also several challenges and limitations that need to be addressed:

- **Data Quality:** Ensuring the accuracy and reliability of the collected data is crucial. Data may contain errors, biases, or incomplete information, which can impact the outcomes of analyses and legal decision-making.

- **Privacy Concerns:** The collection and utilization of personal and sensitive data raise significant privacy concerns. Legal professionals must comply with applicable data protection laws and ethical obligations to safeguard individuals' privacy rights.

- **Data Integration:** Integrating data from various sources and formats can be complex. Legal professionals need to have the means to access, clean, merge, and analyze data from multiple databases and platforms.

- **Data Interpretation:** Drawing meaningful insights from big data requires advanced analytical skills. Legal professionals must possess the necessary competencies to interpret complex data and translate it into actionable legal strategies.

BIG DATA AND PREDICTIVE ANALYTICS IN LAW

Ethical Considerations

The collection and use of big data in the legal field raise ethical considerations that must be addressed:

- **Informed Consent:** Legal professionals should obtain informed consent from individuals whose data is collected. This involves informing individuals about the purpose, scope, and risks associated with data collection and obtaining their explicit consent.

- **Data Security:** Safeguarding the security of collected data is paramount. Legal professionals must implement robust data security measures to protect against unauthorized access, data breaches, and cyber-attacks.

- **Algorithmic Bias and Discrimination:** Algorithms used to analyze big data may inadvertently perpetuate biases or discriminate against certain groups. Legal professionals must critically evaluate the algorithms, identify potential biases, and ensure fairness and equality in the analysis and interpretation of data.

- **Transparency and Accountability:** The collection and use of big data should be transparent and accountable. Legal professionals should document their data collection methods, disclose any limitations or biases, and be open to scrutiny to maintain public trust.

Case Example: Predictive Analytics in Sentencing

One application of big data in the legal field is the use of predictive analytics in sentencing. By analyzing historical data on sentencing outcomes, machine learning algorithms can identify patterns and predict the likely sentence for a given offense. However, this raises concerns about fairness and transparency. Algorithmic bias and the potential for discrimination must be carefully considered to ensure that the use of predictive analytics does not perpetuate existing injustices.

Resources for Further Study

For those interested in exploring the collection and use of big data in the legal field further, the following resources provide valuable insights:

- "The Law of Big Data: A Business and Legal Guide" by Gordon W. Romney.

- "Big Data, Big Challenges in Evidence-Based Policy Making: Lessons from Modern Analytics and Information Systems" edited by Katarzyna Stolp and Bogdan Werth.

- "Legal Tech and the New Sharing Economy" by Frank Pasquale.

- "Big Data, Big Analytics: Emerging Business Intelligence and Analytic Trends for Today's Businesses" by Jared Dean.

Conclusion

The collection and use of big data in the legal field offer immense potential for enhancing legal research, decision-making, and access to justice. However, it also poses challenges and ethical considerations that must be addressed. By leveraging big data responsibly and ethically, legal professionals can harness its power to transform the legal landscape and improve outcomes for clients and society as a whole.

This concludes our discussion on the collection and use of big data in the legal field. In the next section, we will explore the applications of artificial intelligence in the practice of law.

Predictive Analytics in Legal Decision-Making

In recent years, the legal field has seen an increasing interest in using predictive analytics to inform and enhance decision-making processes. Predictive analytics involves the use of statistical models and machine learning algorithms to analyze large sets of data and make predictions about future outcomes. When applied to legal decision-making, predictive analytics can provide valuable insights into case outcomes, help identify patterns and trends, and assist legal practitioners in making informed decisions.

Background and Principles

Predictive analytics in legal decision-making draws from various disciplines and principles, including data science, statistics, and legal reasoning. The main goal is to use historical data to make predictions about future legal outcomes. This approach relies on the assumption that past cases can provide insights into future trends and patterns.

At its core, predictive analytics involves the following key principles:

1. Data collection and preprocessing: The first step in using predictive analytics is to gather relevant data. This may include case files, court decisions, legal statutes, and other legal documents. Once collected, the data is preprocessed, which involves cleaning the data, handling missing values, and transforming data into a suitable format for analysis.

2. Model development: Predictive models are then developed using various algorithms and statistical techniques. These models are trained using historical data, and the algorithms learn patterns and relationships within the data to make predictions.

3. Evaluation and validation: The performance of predictive models is assessed through evaluation and validation. This involves comparing the model's predicted outcomes against known outcomes to measure accuracy and reliability. Validating the model ensures its generalizability and ability to make accurate predictions on new, unseen data.

4. Decision-making and interpretation: Once a predictive model is deemed reliable, it can be used to inform legal decision-making. Legal practitioners can use the predicted outcomes to assess the risks and benefits associated with different courses of action and make more informed decisions.

Legal Applications of Predictive Analytics

Predictive analytics has numerous applications in legal decision-making across various areas of law. Some of the key applications include:

1. Case outcome prediction: By analyzing historical case data, predictive analytics models can be used to predict the likelihood of success or failure in a particular case. Legal practitioners can use these predictions to assess the strengths and weaknesses of their arguments, identify potential risks, and develop a more effective litigation strategy.

2. Sentencing and parole prediction: Predictive analytics can also be used to assess the likely outcome of sentencing decisions or parole applications. By considering various factors such as previous criminal history, severity of the offense, and demographic information, predictive models can provide insights into the potential length of a sentence or the probability of recidivism.

3. Legal research and precedent analysis: Predictive analytics can assist legal researchers in analyzing vast amounts of legal texts, including court decisions and statutes. By identifying patterns and relationships within legal texts, predictive models can help researchers uncover relevant precedents and legal doctrines that may support or weaken a particular legal argument.

4. Fraud detection and risk assessment: In areas such as insurance law and financial regulations, predictive analytics can assist in identifying potential instances of fraud. By analyzing large sets of data, such as insurance claims or financial transactions, models can flag suspicious patterns or anomalies that may warrant further investigation.

Challenges and Considerations

While predictive analytics holds great promise in transforming legal decision-making, there are several challenges and considerations that need to be addressed:

1. Bias and fairness: Predictive models may incorporate biases present in historical data, which can lead to discriminatory outcomes. It is essential to ensure that predictive analytics systems are designed and tested to minimize and mitigate biases, promoting fairness and equality in legal decision-making.

2. Data quality and availability: The reliability and accuracy of predictive models depend on the quality and availability of data. Ensuring the completeness, accuracy, and reliability of data used for training models is crucial for obtaining accurate predictions.

3. Interpretability and transparency: Predictive models can sometimes be complex, making it challenging to interpret and understand the underlying factors contributing to a prediction. Legal professionals need to be able to interpret and explain the results of predictive models to clients, judges, and other stakeholders to build trust and ensure transparency.

4. Ethical and legal considerations: The use of predictive analytics raises ethical and legal considerations, such as privacy, confidentiality, and the potential for automated decision-making. It is essential to establish clear guidelines and regulations to address these concerns and ensure that the use of predictive analytics aligns with legal and ethical standards.

Case Study: Predictive Analytics in Criminal Justice

One notable application of predictive analytics in legal decision-making is in the criminal justice system. By analyzing historical data on criminal cases, patterns and trends can be identified to make predictions about recidivism, sentencing lengths, and the likelihood of pretrial release.

For example, the COMPAS (Correctional Offender Management Profiling for Alternative Sanctions) system has been used in some jurisdictions in the United States to predict the likelihood of reoffending. The system uses various factors such as age, criminal history, and demographic information to provide risk scores that judges can consider when making sentencing decisions. However, the COMPAS system has faced criticism for potential bias and fairness concerns.

To address these concerns, ongoing research and development are focusing on improving the fairness and transparency of predictive analytics systems in criminal justice. This includes the development of methods to detect and mitigate bias in training data, as well as tools that explain the reasoning behind a prediction.

Resources and Further Reading

To delve deeper into the topic of predictive analytics in legal decision-making, the following resources and references are recommended:
- Rudin, C. (2019). "Fighting algorithmic bias in court decisions." Nature Machine Intelligence, 1(6), 272-274. - Slobogin, C. & Lynch, M. J. (2020). "Big Data and Criminal Justice: Toward a Psychometric Jurisprudence." Vanderbilt Law Review, 73(2), 457-512. - Legal Analytics & Predictive Modeling (Online Course) - offered by Harvard Law School. - "Predictive Analytics in the Law" - A report by the American Bar Association.

Conclusion

Predictive analytics has the potential to revolutionize legal decision-making by providing valuable insights and predictions based on historical data. By leveraging statistical models and machine learning algorithms, legal practitioners can make more informed and evidence-based decisions. However, it is crucial to address challenges related to bias, data quality, interpretability, and ethics to ensure the fair and responsible use of predictive analytics in the legal field.

Ethical Concerns of Big Data and Predictive Analytics in Law

In recent years, big data and predictive analytics have become powerful tools in various fields, including law. These technologies have the potential to revolutionize the legal system by providing valuable insights, improving efficiency, and aiding decision-making processes. However, their deployment also raises important ethical concerns that must be addressed to ensure responsible and just use in the legal domain. This section will explore some of the key ethical concerns associated with big data and predictive analytics in law, providing a comprehensive framework for understanding and navigating the complex intersection of technology and ethics.

Privacy and Data Protection

One of the foremost ethical concerns in the use of big data and predictive analytics in law is the protection of privacy and personal data. The collection and analysis of vast amounts of data can potentially infringe upon individuals' privacy rights and raise concerns about unauthorized access, data breaches, and surveillance. In the legal context, this becomes particularly relevant as the data being collected and analyzed may contain highly sensitive information related to criminal records, health conditions, financial history, and other personal details.

To address these concerns, it is essential to establish robust data protection policies and mechanisms. Legal professionals and policymakers should ensure that data collection practices comply with relevant privacy laws and regulations, such as the General Data Protection Regulation (GDPR) in the European Union. Implementing strict safeguards, such as data anonymization and encryption, can help mitigate the risks associated with the use of big data and predictive analytics in law. Additionally, transparency and informed consent must be prioritized, ensuring that individuals are aware of how their data will be used and given the option to opt out if desired.

Bias and Discrimination

Another significant ethical concern in the use of big data and predictive analytics in law is the potential for bias and discrimination. Algorithms used for predictive analytics are created based on historical data that may reflect existing societal biases. If these biased datasets are used to train predictive models, they may perpetuate unjust disparities in the legal system.

Bias in predictive analytics can manifest in various ways, such as racial profiling, gender disparities, and socioeconomic inequalities. For example, if historical arrest data contains racial bias, a predictive model trained on that data is likely to produce biased outcomes, disproportionately targeting certain racial or ethnic groups. This can perpetuate systemic discrimination and hinder efforts to achieve fairness in the legal system.

Addressing bias and discrimination requires careful scrutiny of the data used to train predictive models. It is crucial to ensure that training data is diverse, representative, and free from discriminatory patterns. Regular audits should be conducted to identify and rectify any biases that may emerge in the predictive algorithms. Additionally, transparency and accountability are vital, allowing for the examination and challenge of algorithmic decisions to identify and rectify any unfair outcomes.

Explainability and Accountability

The lack of explainability and accountability in predictive analytics poses another ethical concern in the field of law. Machine learning algorithms, particularly complex ones like neural networks, often operate as "black boxes," making predictions without clear explanations for their decisions. In legal contexts, it is essential for decisions to be transparent and understandable to ensure accountability and safeguard the principles of due process.

The opacity of predictive models raises concerns about how legal professionals, defendants, and other stakeholders can question or challenge algorithmic decisions. It becomes challenging to assess the fairness and validity of outcomes when the reasoning behind them is unclear or inaccessible. In the legal system, where the right to a fair trial and the need for transparency are fundamental, the lack of explainability poses significant ethical dilemmas.

To address this concern, research and development should focus on improving the explainability of predictive algorithms in law. Techniques such as interpretable machine learning and rule-based decision systems can provide insights into how algorithms arrive at their conclusions. By enabling legal professionals to understand and explain the reasoning behind algorithmic decisions, accountability can be enhanced, fostering trust in the justice system.

Legal and Ethical Professional Responsibility

The use of big data and predictive analytics in law raises important questions about the ethical and legal responsibilities of legal practitioners. Lawyers and legal professionals must navigate the complexities of these technologies while ensuring that their use aligns with established professional and ethical standards.

Legal and ethical professional responsibility demands that legal professionals possess the necessary competency and expertise to engage with big data and predictive analytics responsibly. This includes an understanding of the limitations, biases, and ethical considerations associated with these technologies. Legal education and professional development programs should incorporate relevant training on the responsible use of big data and predictive analytics in law.

Additionally, legal professionals must uphold their fiduciary duty to their clients and ensure that their use of predictive analytics serves their clients' best interests. This involves critically evaluating the results generated by these technologies and independently verifying their accuracy and fairness.

Conclusion

The ethical concerns associated with the use of big data and predictive analytics in law are complex and multifaceted. Privacy and data protection, bias and discrimination, explainability and accountability, and legal and ethical professional responsibility all require careful consideration to ensure responsible and just use of these technologies.

Addressing these concerns requires collaboration between legal practitioners, technologists, policymakers, and society at large. Ethical guidelines and regulations must be developed to govern the collection, storage, and use of data in the legal domain. Transparency and accountability should be prioritized to allow for scrutiny and challenge of algorithmic decisions. Legal education and professional development programs should incorporate training on the ethical dimensions of big data and predictive analytics.

By establishing a robust ethical framework, informed by the principles of fairness, justice, and human rights, the potential of big data and predictive analytics in law can be harnessed while minimizing risks and ensuring a responsible and equitable legal system for all.

Technology and Legal Ethics

Ethical Implications of Technology in Legal Practice

In today's rapidly evolving technological landscape, the legal profession is increasingly relying on various technologies to enhance efficiency, streamline processes, and provide better services to clients. However, the integration of technology in legal practice raises important ethical considerations that must be addressed. This section explores the potential ethical implications of technology in the legal field and provides insights into how legal practitioners can navigate these challenges.

Preserving Client Confidentiality

One of the fundamental ethical obligations for lawyers is to protect the confidentiality of client information. Technology poses new challenges to maintaining client confidentiality, particularly in the digital age where data breaches and cyber-attacks are prevalent. Law firms are required to implement robust cybersecurity measures to safeguard client data from unauthorized access or disclosure.

Moreover, in the era of cloud computing and online collaboration platforms, lawyers must be mindful of where and how they store client information. The use of cloud storage services and third-party applications should be carefully considered to ensure compliance with ethical obligations and relevant data protection laws.

Ensuring Data Privacy

In an increasingly digitized legal landscape, law firms are generating and storing vast amounts of data. This data may include personal information about clients, witnesses, and other parties involved in legal matters. Legal practitioners have a responsibility to handle this data in a manner that respects individual privacy rights and complies with relevant data protection legislation.

Lawyers should be cautious when using data analytics or artificial intelligence (AI) systems that rely on large data sets. They must ensure that the data used for analysis is obtained legally, and that any potential biases or discriminatory outcomes in the algorithms are identified and mitigated.

Maintaining Competence in Technology

As technology becomes an integral part of legal practice, legal professionals must stay abreast of technological advancements to effectively represent their clients. The duty to maintain competence extends to understanding the benefits, risks, and limitations of various technologies used in legal work.

Lawyers have an ethical obligation to acquire the necessary knowledge and skills to use technology appropriately and ethically. This includes staying updated on relevant legal technology trends, attending training programs, and collaborating with IT professionals when needed.

Addressing Bias in AI Systems

Artificial intelligence (AI) is increasingly being employed in legal practice, ranging from legal research to predictive analytics. However, AI systems can be susceptible to biases, reflecting the societal biases found in the underlying data used to train the algorithms.

Legal practitioners should be aware of potential biases in AI systems and take steps to address and mitigate them. This may involve reviewing and validating the data used to train AI models, ensuring diverse representation in the training data, and regularly monitoring and auditing AI systems for potential bias.

Maintaining Professional Independence and Judgment

Technology has the potential to automate and streamline many legal tasks, including document review, contract analysis, and legal research. While technology can enhance efficiency, legal professionals must exercise caution to ensure that their professional judgment and independence are not compromised.

Lawyers should use technology as a tool to support their decision-making process, rather than relying solely on automated solutions. They should critically analyze the results generated by technology and independently assess the legal implications and risks involved.

Adapting to Ethical Challenges

The ethical implications of technology in legal practice are continually evolving. Legal professionals must be proactive in developing ethical guidelines and standards that reflect the unique challenges posed by technology.

Continuing education and professional development programs should incorporate discussions on the ethical implications of technology. Legal organizations and bar associations can play a significant role in raising awareness and providing guidance on ethical best practices in the use of technology.

Case Study: Facial Recognition Technology

Facial recognition technology is one example of a rapidly developing technology with significant ethical implications in the legal field. While facial recognition technology offers potential benefits in law enforcement and security, it also raises concerns related to privacy, accuracy, and bias.

Legal professionals must critically evaluate the ethical implications of using facial recognition technology in legal proceedings. They need to consider issues such as the reliability of the technology, the potential for wrongful identification, and the impact on individual privacy rights.

Additional Resources

Legal practitioners looking to further explore the ethical implications of technology in legal practice can refer to the following resources:

- *Ethics and Technology in Practice*, by Adam Thierer
- *Technology and Professional Responsibility: A Global Resource*, edited by Adam Candeub and M. Ethan Katsh

♦ *Legal Ethics in the Digital Age*, by R. A. Duff and Sarah Biddulph

These resources provide valuable insights into the ethical challenges posed by technology and offer guidance on navigating these challenges in the legal profession.

Conclusion

The integration of technology in legal practice brings numerous benefits, but also raises important ethical considerations. Legal professionals must be diligent in preserving client confidentiality, ensuring data privacy, maintaining competence in technology, addressing bias in AI systems, and safeguarding their professional independence and judgment. By actively engaging with these ethical challenges and adapting to new technologies, legal practitioners can effectively navigate the transformative landscape of technology in the legal profession.

Artificial Intelligence and Legal Professional Responsibility

The rapid advancement of Artificial Intelligence (AI) has begun to revolutionize the legal profession. AI technologies, such as machine learning algorithms, natural language processing, and data analytics, are being increasingly used in various legal applications, ranging from case prediction and contract analysis to legal research and due diligence. While these advancements offer great potential in terms of efficiency and accuracy, they also raise important ethical and professional responsibility considerations for legal practitioners.

Understanding Artificial Intelligence in the Legal Context

Artificial Intelligence refers to the development of computer systems that can perform tasks normally requiring human intelligence, such as the ability to reason, solve problems, and understand natural language. In the legal context, AI technologies are primarily used to automate repetitive and time-consuming tasks, improve legal analysis, and provide data-driven insights. For example, AI-powered legal research platforms can quickly analyze and retrieve relevant case law, statutes, and legal commentary, saving lawyers significant time and effort.

Despite these benefits, it is crucial for legal professionals to understand the limitations and risks associated with AI. AI algorithms are developed based on existing data and are prone to biases present in that data, leading to potential discriminatory outcomes. Additionally, the lack of transparency in some AI models, commonly referred to as the "black box" problem, raises concerns about accountability and the ability to explain decisions made by AI systems.

Legal Professional Responsibility in AI Adoption

As legal professionals adopt AI technologies, it is essential to maintain their professional responsibility and ethical obligations. The following principles guide legal professional responsibility in the context of AI:

1. **Competence:** Lawyers should understand the benefits and limitations of AI technologies, as well as have the necessary skills to use them effectively. Continuous professional development and training programs can ensure lawyers stay updated with the latest AI advancements.

2. **Confidentiality and Data Protection:** Lawyers must ensure that AI systems used in their practice preserve client confidentiality and comply with data protection regulations. This includes carefully selecting AI vendors, assessing data security measures, and implementing appropriate safeguards to protect sensitive information.

3. **Transparency:** Legal professionals should strive for transparency in AI systems, particularly when they are used to make decisions with legal consequences. Ensuring explanations are provided for AI-generated outcomes can enhance trust and accountability.

4. **Avoiding Bias and Discrimination:** Lawyers have a duty to identify and address any biases that may be present in AI algorithms. This requires regular monitoring and auditing of AI systems to mitigate the risk of discriminatory outcomes and ensure fairness in decision-making.

5. **Supervision and Responsibility:** Even when using AI technologies, lawyers retain ultimate responsibility for the work performed. They must actively supervise AI systems, verify the accuracy and reliability of results, and make informed decisions based on the information provided by AI tools.

6. **Professional Judgment:** AI systems should be seen as tools to assist legal professionals, not replace their professional judgment. Lawyers should critically evaluate and independently verify AI-generated results, considering the legal and ethical implications of using AI in practice.

Case Study: AI in Legal Research

To illustrate the ethical and professional responsibility considerations in AI adoption, let us consider a case study on the use of AI in legal research. ABC Law

TECHNOLOGY AND LEGAL ETHICS 451

Firm utilizes an AI-powered legal research platform to enhance their efficiency and provide more accurate results for their clients. However, they encounter a situation where the AI algorithm consistently returns biased results, favoring majority ethnic groups and under-representing minority viewpoints.

In this scenario, the legal professionals at ABC Law Firm should adhere to their professional responsibility by:

- Recognizing the existence of bias in the AI algorithm and proactively taking steps to address it.

- Auditing and validating the AI-generated results, independently verifying the accuracy and fairness of the outcomes.

- Engaging in ongoing training and professional development to better understand the limitations and risks associated with AI technologies.

- Considering the use of alternative AI tools or seeking expert opinions to ensure a fair and unbiased legal research process.

- Informing clients about the potential limitations, biases, and risks associated with AI technologies, while providing explanations and clarifications as necessary.

Ethical Considerations and Challenges

The adoption of AI in the legal profession also presents several ethical considerations and challenges that legal professionals need to address:

- **Data Privacy and Security:** As AI systems require vast amounts of data, legal professionals must ensure compliance with data protection laws, adopt appropriate data security measures, and minimize the risk of data breaches.

- **Accountability and Assessment of AI Systems:** Determining the accountability of AI systems and assessing their reliability, fairness, and accuracy can be challenging. Legal professionals should actively engage in discussions surrounding the development and adoption of AI technologies to establish standards and regulations.

- **Fairness and Bias Mitigation:** Bias in AI algorithms can lead to discriminatory outcomes. Lawyers need to regularly assess and mitigate bias in AI systems, ensuring fairness, and equal treatment for all individuals.

- **Professional Autonomy:** Maintaining professional autonomy and not allowing AI systems to undermine lawyers' independent decision-making is crucial. Lawyers should carefully evaluate the outcomes suggested by AI tools and apply their professional expertise.

Conclusion

Artificial Intelligence offers transformative potential in the legal field, enabling legal professionals to enhance their efficiency, improve accuracy, and provide data-driven insights. However, legal professional responsibility and ethical considerations must underpin the adoption and use of AI technologies. By maintaining their competence, ensuring transparency, mitigating bias, and upholding their professional autonomy, legal professionals can navigate the ethical challenges and leverage AI for the benefit of their clients and society as a whole.

Data Security and Confidentiality in the Digital Age

In today's digital world, the issue of data security and confidentiality has become increasingly important. As information is shared and stored electronically, the need to protect sensitive data from unauthorized access and misuse has become a major concern. This section will examine the challenges and best practices related to data security and confidentiality in the digital age.

Importance of Data Security

Data security is crucial for individuals, organizations, and governments to protect sensitive information from unauthorized access, alteration, or destruction. With the increasing prevalence of cyber threats and data breaches, it is essential to implement robust security measures to ensure the confidentiality, integrity, and availability of data.

The stakes are high when it comes to data security. Breaches of personal information can lead to identity theft, financial loss, and reputational damage for individuals. For businesses, a data breach can result in financial losses, legal liabilities, and damaged customer trust. Additionally, governments must safeguard sensitive information to protect national security and ensure the privacy of their citizens.

Principles of Data Security

To effectively address data security and confidentiality in the digital age, several key principles should be followed:

1. **Confidentiality:** Ensuring that data can only be accessed by authorized individuals or entities.

2. **Integrity:** Maintaining the accuracy and consistency of data throughout its lifecycle. This includes preventing unauthorized modifications or tampering.

3. **Availability:** Ensuring that data is accessible and usable when needed, while also preventing disruptions or denial of service attacks.

4. **Authentication:** Verifying the identity of individuals or systems accessing data to prevent unauthorized access.

5. **Authorization:** Granting appropriate access rights and permissions to individuals based on their roles and responsibilities.

6. **Auditability:** Keeping records of data access and modifications to facilitate investigation, traceability, and accountability.

By following these principles, organizations can establish a comprehensive data security framework to protect sensitive information.

Challenges in Data Security

Securing data in the digital age comes with numerous challenges. Some of the key challenges include:

- **Cyber threats:** The constantly evolving nature of cyber threats poses a significant challenge to data security. Hackers employ sophisticated techniques and technologies to gain unauthorized access to data.

- **Insider threats:** Insider threats, including malicious employees or contractors, can pose a significant risk to data security. These individuals may have access to sensitive information and can misuse it for personal gain or malicious intent.

- **Data breaches:** Data breaches can occur due to vulnerabilities in systems, human error, or targeted attacks. When a data breach occurs, sensitive information may be exposed or stolen, leading to significant consequences for individuals and organizations.

- **Compliance requirements:** Organizations must comply with various regulatory frameworks and industry standards concerning data security and confidentiality. It can be challenging to navigate these complex requirements and ensure compliance.

- **Emerging technologies:** The rapid advancement of technologies such as cloud computing, Internet of Things (IoT), and artificial intelligence brings new security challenges. These technologies introduce new attack vectors and complicate data security measures.

Best Practices for Data Security

To mitigate the risks associated with data security and confidentiality, organizations should adopt best practices. Here are some key practices to consider:

- **Risk assessment:** Conduct regular risk assessments to identify vulnerabilities and potential threats. This will help prioritize the implementation of security measures based on the level of risk.

- **Encryption:** Implement strong encryption mechanisms to protect data both in transit and at rest. Encryption ensures that even if data is intercepted or accessed by unauthorized individuals, it remains unreadable.

- **Access controls:** Implement well-defined access controls to limit and monitor who can access sensitive data. This includes the use of strong passwords, two-factor authentication, and role-based access controls.

- **Employee training:** Provide comprehensive training to employees on data security best practices. This includes educating them about the risks associated with data breaches, social engineering, and the importance of safeguarding sensitive information.

- **Regular backups:** Regularly backup critical data to ensure its availability in the event of a breach or system failure. Backups should be securely stored and periodically tested for integrity and recoverability.

- **Incident response:** Develop an incident response plan to effectively handle security incidents. This includes procedures for detecting, containing, and recovering from security breaches.

Ethical Considerations

Protecting data security and confidentiality also raises ethical considerations. It is essential to balance the need for data security with individual privacy rights and other ethical considerations. Organizations must be transparent about their data collection and use practices, obtain informed consent when necessary, and handle data responsibly and ethically.

Furthermore, it is crucial to consider the potential biases or unfair practices that can arise from the collection and analysis of large amounts of data. Machine learning algorithms and artificial intelligence systems may inadvertently perpetuate and amplify existing biases if not carefully designed and monitored.

Conclusion

Data security and confidentiality in the digital age require a multifaceted approach. By following the principles of data security, understanding the challenges, and adopting best practices, organizations can minimize the risks associated with data breaches and unauthorized access. Additionally, addressing ethical considerations ensures that data security measures respect individual privacy and promote fairness. As technology continues to evolve, it is crucial to stay updated on the latest trends and emerging threats to maintain effective data security and confidentiality.

Conclusion

Recapitulation of Key Points

In this chapter, we have explored the transformative potential of technology in the field of law. We began by examining the application of artificial intelligence (AI) in various legal domains. AI has revolutionized legal research and analysis, making it more efficient and accurate. However, the use of AI also raises ethical and legal challenges, such as issues of bias and data privacy. It is essential for legal professionals to navigate these challenges while harnessing the full potential of AI.

Another significant technological development in law is the emergence of blockchain and smart contracts. Blockchain technology provides a secure and decentralized platform for executing and enforcing smart contracts. This innovation has the potential to streamline legal processes and reduce transaction costs. However, the legal implications of blockchain and smart contracts, including issues of jurisdiction and regulatory compliance, must be carefully considered.

Privacy and data protection have become crucial concerns in the digital age. We discussed the importance of privacy laws and regulations in safeguarding individuals' personal information. With the increasing volume of data collection, proper data protection measures are needed to ensure the security and confidentiality of sensitive information. Striking the right balance between privacy and innovation remains an ongoing challenge in the legal field.

The chapter also explored the intersection of law and cybersecurity. As technology advances, so do the threats posed by cybercrime. Legal frameworks for cybersecurity play a vital role in protecting individuals, organizations, and governments from cyber attacks. However, maintaining a delicate balance between security and privacy is crucial to prevent potential infringements on civil liberties.

Online dispute resolution (ODR) emerged as an innovative approach to resolving legal conflicts outside traditional court systems. We discussed the different methods of ODR, such as mediation and arbitration, and their potential to enhance access to justice. However, challenges such as ensuring procedural fairness and maintaining public trust in online dispute resolution mechanisms need to be addressed.

The increasing use of big data and predictive analytics in law has also been highlighted. While these tools offer the potential for data-driven decision-making and more efficient legal processes, ethical concerns remain. Issues such as data quality, accuracy, fairness, and transparency must be carefully addressed to avoid potential biases and discriminatory outcomes.

Ethical considerations surrounding technology in legal practice were also discussed. It is important for legal professionals to be aware of the ethical implications of technological advancements and ensure that they uphold professional responsibilities and standards. Safeguarding client confidentiality and ensuring data security are critical components of ethical legal practice in the digital age.

To summarize, this chapter has highlighted the transformative effects of technology on the future of law. From artificial intelligence and blockchain to privacy protection and online dispute resolution, advancements in technology have the potential to reshape legal practice and enhance access to justice. However, it is essential to navigate the legal and ethical challenges that arise from these developments to ensure that the transformative potential of technology in law is harnessed responsibly and inclusively.

Implications for the Future of Law

The rapid advancement of technology in the legal field has significant implications for the future of law. These implications can be seen in various areas such as legal research, access to justice, and the roles and responsibilities of legal professionals.

Firstly, the integration of technology in legal research has the potential to transform the way legal professionals obtain and analyze information. The use of artificial intelligence and machine learning algorithms can expedite the process of identifying relevant case law, statutory provisions, and legal principles. This not only saves time but also enhances the accuracy and comprehensiveness of legal research. However, it is essential for legal professionals to be aware of the limitations and biases that may arise from relying solely on technology and to ensure a critical evaluation of the results produced by these tools.

Secondly, technology has the potential to improve access to justice by making legal services more affordable and accessible. Online dispute resolution platforms can provide a convenient and cost-effective alternative to traditional court systems, particularly for low-income individuals and those in remote areas. Moreover, the use of technology in legal education can enhance learning outcomes and reach a broader audience, allowing individuals from diverse backgrounds to acquire legal knowledge and skills. However, it is crucial to consider issues of digital divide and ensure that technological advancements do not exacerbate existing inequalities in access to justice.

Furthermore, technology raises questions about the changing roles and responsibilities of legal professionals. As AI and other technologies automate certain legal tasks, lawyers need to adapt and develop new skills to remain relevant. This may involve a shift towards more complex and strategic legal work, such as negotiation, counseling, and ethical decision-making. Moreover, legal professionals must navigate the ethical and legal challenges posed by technology, such as data privacy, algorithmic bias, and the unauthorized practice of law. Continuing education and professional development programs are crucial to ensure that legal professionals are equipped to address these challenges.

In conclusion, the future of law will be shaped by the transformative potential of technology. By embracing these advancements responsibly and ethically, legal professionals can leverage technology to enhance legal practice, improve access to justice, and adapt to the changing demands of the legal profession.

Future Directions in Law and Technology

Looking ahead, several future directions can be identified in the intersection of law and technology. These areas present new opportunities and challenges for legal professionals and policymakers.

One avenue of exploration is the development of AI-powered legal tools and platforms that enhance the efficiency and accuracy of legal services. This may involve the creation of intelligent legal research platforms, contract analysis tools, and predictive analytics applications. However, it is crucial to ensure that these technologies align with ethical and legal standards, such as fairness, transparency, and privacy.

Another future direction is the integration of blockchain technology in various legal processes beyond smart contracts. For example, blockchain can be used to create secure and tamper-proof records of evidence, ensure transparency in supply chains, and facilitate the authentication and verification of legal documents. However, the challenges of regulatory compliance, interoperability, and scalability need to be addressed for widespread adoption.

The field of cybersecurity will continue to evolve as new threats and technologies emerge. Legal frameworks for cybersecurity must keep pace with these developments to protect individuals and organizations from cyber attacks. Collaboration between legal experts and technology professionals will be crucial in developing effective strategies to combat cybercrime while safeguarding civil liberties and privacy.

Additionally, the expansion of online dispute resolution and virtual courtrooms presents new opportunities for improving access to justice. The development of user-friendly and inclusive platforms, as well as the provision of adequate legal aid and support services, will be essential in realizing the potential benefits of online dispute resolution. Moreover, ensuring procedural fairness and maintaining public trust in these digital platforms are ongoing challenges that require continuous attention.

Finally, addressing the ethical implications of technology in law will continue to be a critical focus. Legal professionals, policymakers, and technology developers must collaborate to establish guidelines and best practices that uphold ethical standards while harnessing the transformative potential of technology. This may involve the development of codes of conduct, regulatory frameworks, and ongoing education and training programs for legal professionals.

In conclusion, the future of law and technology holds great promise for enhancing legal practice, improving access to justice, and addressing societal challenges. By proactively addressing the opportunities and challenges that lie ahead, legal professionals can lead the way in leveraging technology for the benefit of society and the advancement of justice.

Implications for the Future of Law

The transformative advances in legal studies discussed in this textbook have significant implications for the future of law. By embracing revolutionary ideas, practical techniques, and cutting-edge research, the legal system can evolve to better serve the principles of justice and equality. In this section, we will explore some of the key implications of transformative legal studies and how they can shape the future of law.

Addressing Systemic Injustices

One of the major implications of transformative legal studies is the potential to address systemic injustices within the legal system. By critically examining the existing legal frameworks and theories, legal scholars and practitioners can identify and challenge biases and inequalities that have historically marginalized certain groups. This includes addressing issues such as racial discrimination, gender inequality, and economic disparities.

Through the lens of critical legal studies, for example, we can question the underlying assumptions and power dynamics that shape legal decision-making. By doing so, we can develop a more nuanced understanding of how the law can perpetuate systemic injustices. This understanding can then inform the development of legal strategies and policies to rectify these injustices.

Promoting Access to Justice

Transformative legal studies also place a significant emphasis on promoting access to justice for all individuals, regardless of their socioeconomic status or background. Traditional legal systems often create barriers to justice, such as high legal fees, complex procedures, and limited resources for legal aid.

However, by embracing transformative approaches to legal education, research, and practice, we can work towards dismantling these barriers. Through experiential learning, technology-enhanced legal education, and interdisciplinary collaboration, we can equip future legal professionals with the skills and knowledge to increase access to justice.

In addition, innovative legal research methods, such as empirical research and socio-legal studies, can provide insights into the effectiveness of legal policies and practices. By using data and evidence, legal practitioners can make informed decisions and advocate for reforms that enhance access to justice.

Embracing Technology and Innovation

The future of law is intricately tied to technological advancements and innovation. With the rapid development of artificial intelligence, blockchain technology, and big data analytics, the legal profession must adapt to these changes to effectively serve clients and society.

Transformative legal studies emphasize the integration of technology in legal research, education, and practice. For example, AI-powered legal research tools can enhance efficiency and accuracy in legal analysis, enabling lawyers to provide better legal advice.

Blockchain technology, with its potential for secure and transparent transactions, has implications for smart contracts and the verification of legal documents. This can streamline legal processes and reduce the need for intermediaries.

However, with the adoption of technology, ethical considerations become crucial. Transformative legal studies highlight the importance of understanding the ethical implications of technology in legal practice, such as data protection and privacy concerns.

Collaborative Approaches to Problem-Solving

Another important implication of transformative legal studies is the recognition of the value of collaboration and interdisciplinary approaches in addressing complex legal issues. The challenges faced by society, such as climate change, require a multifaceted understanding and innovative solutions.

By fostering collaborations between legal professionals, scientists, policymakers, and other stakeholders, transformative legal studies can lead to comprehensive and sustainable approaches to societal problems. For example, collaboration between legal and environmental experts can contribute to the development of effective regulations to mitigate the impacts of climate change.

Moreover, transformative legal studies encourage engagement with marginalized communities and perspectives. This ensures that legal solutions are not created in isolation but are informed by the diverse experiences and needs of those affected.

Continued Research and Exploration

Transformative legal studies open up exciting opportunities for further research and exploration. As the field continues to evolve, there is a need for continued scholarship and innovation to address emerging legal challenges and adapt to societal changes.

Future research in transformative legal studies may focus on the intersectionality of different theories and approaches, exploring how critical race theory intersects with feminist legal theory, for example. This interdisciplinary approach can lead to a more comprehensive understanding of complex legal issues.

Additionally, the future of law requires ongoing analysis and adaptation to keep pace with the evolving needs and values of society. As technologies advance and societal values change, legal scholars and practitioners must remain vigilant in their study of legal systems and institutions to ensure they are responsive and effective.

Conclusion

The transformative advances in legal studies have wide-ranging implications for the future of law. By addressing systemic injustices, promoting access to justice, embracing technology and innovation, fostering collaboration, and encouraging continued research, the legal system can evolve to better serve the principles of justice and equality.

As we move forward, it is essential for legal scholars, practitioners, and educators to embrace these implications and actively work towards transformative change. By doing so, we can create a legal system that is more inclusive, accessible, and responsive to the needs of individuals and communities. The future of law holds tremendous potential, and it is up to us to shape it through transformative approaches.

Future Directions in Law and Technology

As we navigate the rapidly evolving landscape of technology and its impact on law, it is crucial to anticipate and explore the future directions of this relationship. In this section, we will delve into some of the key areas where law and technology are intersecting and discuss the emerging trends and future possibilities.

Artificial Intelligence and Law

Artificial Intelligence (AI) has made significant strides in recent years and is poised to transform the practice of law. As AI technologies continue to advance, we can expect to see their increased integration into legal research, analysis, and decision-making processes.

One possible future direction is the development of AI-powered legal research tools. These tools would leverage machine learning algorithms to analyze vast amounts of legal information and provide lawyers with accurate and efficient research results. This would not only save time but also enhance the quality and depth of legal analysis.

Another area of potential growth is the use of AI in contract review and management. By employing natural language processing and machine learning algorithms, AI can help automate the review of contracts, identify potential risks, and streamline the contract drafting and negotiation process.

However, as we embrace the potential benefits of AI in law, it is important to address the ethical and legal challenges that arise. Issues such as bias in AI algorithms, data privacy concerns, and the potential impact on the legal profession must be carefully considered and regulated.

Blockchain and Smart Contracts

Blockchain technology has gained significant attention with the rise of cryptocurrencies like Bitcoin. However, its potential goes beyond finance and extends to the field of law. Blockchain's decentralized and transparent nature has the potential to revolutionize legal transactions through the use of smart contracts.

A smart contract is a self-executing contract with the terms of the agreement written directly into lines of code. These contracts automatically execute and enforce themselves, reducing the need for intermediaries and increasing efficiency.

Future directions in this area include the exploration of blockchain-based systems for land registries, intellectual property rights management, and supply chain tracking. Additionally, the use of blockchain technology in dispute resolution and identity verification holds promise for enhancing trust and security in legal interactions.

While the benefits of blockchain and smart contracts are significant, challenges such as scalability, regulatory frameworks, and the need for widespread adoption remain. As the technology advances, legal professionals will need to stay informed and adapt to the changing landscape.

Privacy and Data Protection

The increasing reliance on technology and the digitalization of information pose significant challenges to privacy and data protection. Future directions in this area will focus on striking a balance between the benefits of technological advancements and the protection of individual privacy rights.

One emerging trend is the development of privacy-enhancing technologies (PETs) that aim to protect user data while enabling efficient data processing. Techniques such as secure multiparty computation, homomorphic encryption, and differential privacy offer promising solutions to mitigate privacy risks.

Additionally, the evolving regulatory landscape surrounding data protection, such as the European Union's General Data Protection Regulation (GDPR), will shape future directions in this field. It is anticipated that other jurisdictions will adopt similar frameworks to protect individual privacy rights in the digital age.

Moreover, the growing recognition of data as a valuable asset raises ethical questions regarding data ownership, consent, and control. Future directions will involve establishing clear legal frameworks and ethical guidelines to govern data collection, storage, and usage.

Cybersecurity and Law

Cybersecurity is a pressing concern as society becomes increasingly digitized. Future directions in this field will focus on strengthening legal frameworks to address cyber threats, protect critical infrastructure, and safeguard individual rights in the digital realm.

One area of growth is the development of international agreements and cooperation mechanisms to combat global cyber threats. Cybersecurity treaties, information-sharing initiatives, and coordinated responses will become essential for protecting national and international security.

Moreover, legal frameworks will need to adapt to the evolving nature of cybercrime. Future directions may involve the establishment of specialized cyber courts, enhanced legislation to prosecute cybercriminals, and the development of international norms and standards for cybersecurity.

The intersection of cybersecurity and human rights will also be an important focus. Balancing security measures with the protection of civil liberties, privacy, and freedom of expression will require ongoing dialogue and collaboration between legal professionals, policymakers, and technologists.

Online Dispute Resolution

With the increasing reliance on technology for conducting transactions and interactions, online dispute resolution (ODR) is gaining prominence as an alternative to traditional legal processes. Future directions in this field will involve the integration of technology and innovative approaches to resolve disputes efficiently and fairly.

One possible direction is the development of AI-powered ODR platforms that can facilitate negotiations, mediations, and arbitrations. These platforms would harness algorithms to analyze disputes, generate tailored solutions, and ensure accessibility and affordability of dispute resolution mechanisms.

Furthermore, the adoption of blockchain technology in ODR holds promise for enhancing transparency, trust, and enforceability of dispute resolutions. Smart contracts could enable automatic execution of settlement agreements, reducing the need for costly enforcement procedures.

However, challenges such as ensuring due process, maintaining confidentiality, and addressing power imbalances in ODR must be carefully considered. Future directions will require the collaboration of legal experts, technologists, and stakeholders to develop robust frameworks that protect the rights and interests of all parties involved.

The Role of Legal Professionals

As technology evolves, the role of legal professionals will also undergo transformation. Future directions will necessitate legal professionals to acquire new skills, adapt to technological advancements, and embrace interdisciplinary approaches.

Legal education will play a crucial role in preparing the next generation of lawyers for the changing legal landscape. Future directions in legal education will include integrating technology into the curriculum, fostering interdisciplinary collaboration, and emphasizing the development of skills such as data analysis, critical thinking, and ethical decision-making.

Moreover, as technology increasingly automates routine legal tasks, legal professionals will need to focus on providing high-value services that require human judgment, creativity, and empathy. Future directions will involve the specialization in complex legal issues, strategic counseling, and the application of law to emerging technologies.

In conclusion, the future of law and technology holds tremendous potential to transform the legal landscape. As we navigate this future, it is essential for legal professionals to embrace technological advancements, address ethical concerns, and continually adapt to emerging trends. By proactively engaging with the intersection of law and technology, we can shape a future that promotes justice, equality, and the delivery of legal services that meet the needs of a rapidly changing society.

Chapter 7: Restorative Justice and the Transformation of Criminal Justice

Chapter 7: Restorative Justice and the Transformation of Criminal Justice

Chapter 7: Restorative Justice and the Transformation of Criminal Justice

Restorative justice is a transformative approach to criminal justice that seeks to address the harms caused by crime and foster healing, accountability, and reconciliation among all parties involved. It challenges traditional punitive models of justice by focusing on repairing the harm done to individuals, communities, and relationships rather than solely on punishing offenders. This chapter explores the principles, practices, and potential impact of restorative justice on the criminal justice system.

Introduction to Restorative Justice

Restorative justice is grounded in the belief that crime is not just a violation of the law, but also a violation of people and relationships. It seeks to shift the focus from punishment to healing, from retribution to restoration. Restorative justice recognizes that criminal behavior often stems from underlying social, economic, and psychological factors, and aims to address these root causes to prevent future harm.

The key principles of restorative justice include:

- **Inclusion:** Every party affected by the harm, including victims, offenders, and the community, has the right to be involved in the restorative process.

- **Encounter:** Direct or indirect communication is facilitated between the parties involved, allowing for dialogue, understanding, and empathy.

- **Amends:** Offenders are encouraged to take responsibility for their actions and make amends to victims and the community through restitution, community service, or other forms of reparation.

- **Reintegration:** The process aims to reintegrate offenders back into the community, providing them with opportunities for personal growth, rehabilitation, and a chance to rebuild their lives.

Restorative Justice Practices

Restorative justice practices encompass a range of processes and interventions that aim to address the harms caused by crime. These include:

1. **Victim-Offender Mediation:** This process brings together the victim, the offender, and a trained mediator to facilitate dialogue and negotiation. The goal is to promote understanding, empathy, and agreement on how to repair the harm caused.

2. **Family Group Conferencing:** In this approach, the victim, the offender, their respective family members, and other relevant community members come together in a facilitated conference. They discuss the impact of the crime, identify the needs and responsibilities of each party, and collaboratively develop a plan for repair and reintegration.

3. **Community Restorative Boards:** These boards, composed of community members and trained facilitators, play a role in responding to minor offenses. They engage the victim, offender, and community to collectively address the harm caused and develop an appropriate resolution, such as community service or restitution.

Challenges and Critiques of Restorative Justice Practices

While restorative justice holds great potential for transforming the criminal justice system, it is not without challenges and critiques. Some of the key challenges include:

- **Power Imbalances:** Restorative justice encounters can be influenced by power imbalances between victims, offenders, and community members. Addressing these power dynamics requires careful facilitation and support to ensure all parties have an equal voice and influence in the process.

- **Safety Concerns:** In cases involving both victims and offenders, ensuring the safety and emotional well-being of all participants is crucial. Robust risk assessment and safety planning should be integrated into restorative justice processes to minimize any potential harm.

- **Limited Availability and Accessibility:** Restorative justice programs are not uniformly available across jurisdictions and may not be accessible to all individuals, particularly marginalized and minority communities. Efforts should be made to ensure equitable access to restorative justice opportunities.

Critiques of restorative justice include concerns about its potential for re-victimization, the lack of formal legal procedures and due process safeguards, and the potential for disproportionate outcomes. These criticisms highlight the need for careful implementation, ongoing evaluation, and continuous improvement of restorative justice practices.

Restorative Justice in the Criminal Justice System

Restorative justice has the potential to transform various aspects of the criminal justice system, including sentencing, juvenile justice, and prison practices. Some examples of its application include:

- **Restorative Justice and Sentencing:** Restorative justice can be incorporated into sentencing processes, allowing victims to have a say in the outcome and enabling offenders to understand the impact of their actions. This approach promotes accountability and encourages offenders to actively participate in repairing the harm caused.

- **Restorative Justice in Juvenile Justice:** Restorative practices are particularly effective in the context of juvenile justice, as they provide opportunities for young offenders to learn from their actions, take responsibility, and repair relationships. This approach minimizes the potential for future criminal behavior and promotes rehabilitation and reintegration.

- **Restorative Justice in Prisons and Reentry Programs:** Restorative justice practices can be implemented within prisons to promote a rehabilitative environment and support the reentry process. These programs focus on fostering personal growth, responsibility, and healthy relationships among inmates and with the broader community.

Restorative Justice and Social Transformation

Restorative justice has the potential to address systemic and structural inequalities within the criminal justice system and promote social transformation. Some specific areas where restorative justice can contribute to social change include:

- **Restorative Justice and Social Inequality:** By focusing on repairing harms and addressing the underlying causes of crime, restorative justice aims to reduce social inequalities and address systemic injustices that often contribute to criminal behavior.

- **Restorative Justice and Gender-Based Violence:** Restorative approaches can offer unique opportunities for survivors of gender-based violence to have a voice, seek healing, and hold offenders accountable. It emphasizes the importance of community support and challenging societal norms that perpetuate violence against women and marginalized genders.

- **Restorative Justice and Racial Justice:** Restorative justice practices can contribute to racial justice by addressing the racial disparities and biases that exist within the criminal justice system. Through dialogue and inclusive decision-making processes, it provides opportunities to challenge systemic racism and promote understanding among different racial and ethnic communities.

Conclusion

Restorative justice offers a transformative approach to criminal justice that not only focuses on punishment, but also on healing, accountability, and reconciliation. By prioritizing the needs and voices of victims, offenders, and communities, restorative justice holds the potential to create a more just and equitable criminal justice system. However, its successful implementation requires careful attention to power dynamics, safety concerns, and equitable access. Restorative justice has the capacity to address systemic injustices and contribute to social transformation by challenging inequalities, addressing gender-based violence, and promoting racial justice.

Introduction to Restorative Justice

Definition and Principles of Restorative Justice

Restorative justice is an approach to addressing crime and conflict that focuses on repairing harm and healing relationships between victims, offenders, and communities. It is based on the principles of accountability, participation, and reparation, aiming to provide meaningful justice that goes beyond punishment.

Definition of Restorative Justice

Restorative justice is a philosophy and set of practices that aim to repair the harm caused by a wrongdoing and to foster reconciliation and healing for all parties involved. It recognizes that crime is not just a violation of the law, but also a violation of relationships within the community. It seeks to respond to these breaches of relationships by addressing the needs of victims, holding offenders accountable, and engaging the community in the process.

Restorative justice emphasizes the importance of dialogue, empathy, and understanding in resolving conflicts and repairing harm. It views crime as a result of broken relationships and seeks to restore those relationships through a collaborative and inclusive process.

Principles of Restorative Justice

Restorative justice is guided by several key principles that shape its approach to addressing crime and conflict:

1. **Encounter and dialogue:** Restorative justice strives to bring victims, offenders, and other stakeholders together in a facilitated dialogue. This direct encounter provides an opportunity for all parties to share their experiences, perspectives, and feelings, fostering understanding and empathy.

2. **Inclusion and participation:** Restorative justice recognizes the importance of including all affected parties in the decision-making process. Victims, offenders, and community members are encouraged to actively participate in designing and implementing solutions, promoting a sense of ownership and empowerment.

3. **Voluntary involvement:** Participation in restorative justice processes is voluntary for all parties involved. It is based on the principle of consensual

engagement, ensuring that those affected by the harm have control over their involvement and are not coerced into participating.

4. **Accountability and responsibility:** Restorative justice holds offenders accountable for their actions by acknowledging the harm they have caused and encouraging them to take responsibility for repairing it. Offenders are given an opportunity to make amends and contribute to the healing process.

5. **Healing and reparation:** Restorative justice focuses on healing the harm caused by a wrongdoing. It emphasizes the restoration of relationships, supporting the emotional and psychological well-being of victims, and providing opportunities for offenders to make meaningful amends or reparations.

6. **Community involvement:** Restorative justice recognizes that crime and conflict impact the broader community. It seeks to involve the community in the process of addressing harm, promoting collective responsibility, and fostering a sense of belonging and interconnectedness.

These principles underpin the core values of restorative justice, which include respect, fairness, empowerment, and empathy. They guide the design and implementation of restorative justice processes, ensuring that they are victim-centered, offender-focused, and community-driven.

Examples of Restorative Justice Practices

Restorative justice practices can take various forms, depending on the specific context and needs of the individuals and communities involved. Here are a few examples of restorative justice practices:

- **Victim-offender mediation:** In this practice, a trained facilitator brings together the victim and the offender in a structured dialogue. They discuss the harm caused, the impact on the victim, and the steps the offender can take to repair the harm. This process aims to provide closure for the victim, promote empathy and understanding, and hold the offender accountable.

- **Family group conferencing:** This practice involves a facilitated meeting attended by the victim, the offender, their respective supporters, and other community members. The group collectively discusses the harms and needs resulting from the offense and collaboratively develops an agreement for repairing the harm and preventing future wrongdoing. Family group conferencing is often used in cases involving young offenders.

- **Community circles:** Community circles are a restorative justice practice that involves bringing together individuals from the community to discuss issues and conflicts. The circle provides a safe space for open and honest dialogue, allowing community members to share their experiences, express their feelings, and collectively develop solutions. Community circles promote understanding, empathy, and community cohesion.

These are just a few examples of the diverse range of restorative justice practices being implemented around the world. Each practice is adapted to meet the specific needs and contexts of the individuals and communities involved.

Resources and Further Reading

For those interested in learning more about restorative justice, the following resources can provide valuable insights:

- Zehr, H. (2015). *The Little Book of Restorative Justice*. Good Books.

- McCold, P., & Wachtel, T. (Eds.). (2003). *Restorative Justice Theory and Practice: Addressing the Discrepancy*. Willow Tree Press.

- Walgrave, L. (Ed.). (2013). *Restorative Justice, Self-interest and Responsible Citizenship*. Routledge.

- Bazemore, G., & Schiff, M. (2004). *Restorative Justice: Repairing the Harm of Crime*. Criminal Justice Press.

- Umbreit, M. S., & Armour, M. P. (2011). *Restorative Justice Dialogue: An Essential Guide for Research and Practice*. Springer.

These resources offer a comprehensive overview of restorative justice theory, research, and practice, providing valuable insights into its principles, implementation, and impact.

Exercises

To deepen your understanding of restorative justice, consider the following exercises:

1. **Case Study Analysis:** Choose a real-world case where restorative justice practices have been implemented. Analyze the impact of these practices on the victims, offenders, and the broader community. Reflect on the principles of restorative justice that were applied and discuss the strengths and challenges of the approach.

2. **Role-Play:** Form a small group and engage in a role-play exercise simulating a restorative justice conference. Assign roles to participants, such as victim, offender, facilitator, and community member. Conduct the conference following the principles of restorative justice and reflect on the experience. Discuss how the dialogue and encounter affected the perceptions and attitudes of the participants.

3. **Community Engagement Project:** Develop a community-based project that promotes restorative justice principles. Identify a specific issue or conflict within your community and design a plan for bringing stakeholders together in a restorative justice process. Consider how you will incorporate the principles of inclusion, participation, and healing into your project.

4. **Debate:** Organize a debate on the topic of restorative justice versus traditional criminal justice. Divide participants into two teams and assign them the task of arguing for or against the adoption of restorative justice practices. Encourage participants to critically analyze the principles and outcomes of both approaches and explore their strengths and limitations.

These exercises provide opportunities for further exploration and application of restorative justice principles, fostering a deeper understanding of the transformative potential of this approach.

Conclusion

Restorative justice offers a unique and transformative approach to addressing crime and conflict. By focusing on repairing harm, restoring relationships, and meeting the needs of victims, offenders, and the community, it seeks to move beyond punitive measures and promote healing, accountability, and social reintegration. By embracing the principles of encounter, participation, and reparation, restorative justice offers a valuable alternative to traditional justice systems, fostering a more inclusive and holistic form of justice.

History and Evolution of Restorative Justice

Restorative justice is not a new concept; its roots can be traced back to ancient civilizations, where societies recognized the importance of repairing harm and restoring relationships after a crime or conflict. The history and evolution of restorative justice demonstrate its enduring relevance and potential to transform the criminal justice system.

Ancient Traditions of Peacemaking

Restorative justice practices have been present in various cultures and civilizations throughout history. For example, indigenous communities in Africa, Asia, and the Americas have long embraced traditions rooted in healing and reconciliation. These traditions emphasize collective decision-making, dialogue, and community involvement in resolving conflicts.

In indigenous communities, conflict resolution processes often revolve around restorative circles, where individuals involved in a conflict come together to discuss the harm caused and seek ways to restore harmony. These circles aim to address the needs of the victims, provide opportunities for offenders to take responsibility, and foster community healing.

Early Modern Approaches

During the late 18th and early 19th centuries, restorative justice principles influenced the emergence of initiatives such as the penitentiary system and probation. These initiatives aimed to reintegrate offenders into society through rehabilitation and personal transformation rather than simply punishing them.

In the United States, for example, Quakers played a significant role in promoting rehabilitation and restoration in the penal system. Their belief in the inherent worth and potential for transformation of every individual led to the creation of penitentiaries that focused on repentance and reform rather than mere retribution.

The Rise and Fall of Retributive Justice

The 20th century saw the dominance of the retributive justice model, which prioritized punishing offenders as a means of deterring crime and maintaining social order. This approach led to the widespread use of incarceration as the primary response to criminal behavior.

However, by the late 20th century, the limitations of the retributive model became apparent. High rates of recidivism, overcrowded prisons, and the disproportionate impact on marginalized communities highlighted the need for a new approach to justice.

The Modern Restorative Justice Movement

The modern restorative justice movement gained momentum in the 1970s as a response to the shortcomings of the retributive system. Scholars, practitioners, and activists began advocating for alternative approaches that focused on repairing harm, addressing the needs of victims, and promoting offender accountability.

Restorative justice emphasizes the importance of involving all stakeholders affected by a crime, including victims, offenders, and the community. It seeks to facilitate dialogue and healing, offering opportunities for offenders to understand the impact of their actions, take responsibility, and make amends.

International Recognition and Adoption

The principles of restorative justice gained international recognition and adoption in the late 20th and early 21st centuries. The United Nations and various international organizations have expressed support for restorative justice principles and highlighted its potential to create a more just and inclusive society.

Many countries have incorporated restorative justice practices into their legal systems. These practices include victim-offender mediation, conferencing, and circles as alternatives to traditional court processes. The aim is to prioritize the needs of the victims, promote offender accountability, and restore relationships between the parties involved.

Continued Challenges and Future Directions

Despite the progress made, restorative justice continues to face challenges in its implementation. Limited resources, resistance from traditional criminal justice systems, and the need for ongoing evaluation and research are among the challenges that practitioners and scholars must address.

The future of restorative justice lies in its integration into mainstream legal systems, the development of effective and evidence-based practices, and the expansion of community involvement. It requires ongoing dialogue, collaboration, and innovation to ensure its transformative potential is realized.

In conclusion, the history and evolution of restorative justice demonstrate its deep roots in various cultures and its potential to transform the criminal justice system. By prioritizing the needs of victims, promoting offender accountability, and restoring relationships, restorative justice offers a path towards healing and social transformation.

Restorative Justice as a Comparative Approach to Criminal Justice

Restorative justice is a transformative approach to criminal justice that focuses on repairing the harm caused by a crime rather than solely punishing the offender. It seeks to involve all parties affected by the crime, including the victim, the offender, and the community, in a collaborative process aimed at finding a resolution that addresses the needs of everyone involved.

In a comparative context, restorative justice can be examined across different legal systems and cultural contexts to understand its diverse applications and effectiveness. By studying how restorative justice is implemented and its impact in different countries, we can gain insights into the potential for its wider adoption and the challenges it faces.

Comparing Models of Restorative Justice

One aspect of comparative analysis is examining the different models of restorative justice that exist around the world. These models can vary in their structure and the practices they employ. Some common models include victim-offender mediation, family group conferencing, and community restorative boards.

For example, in New Zealand, the restorative justice process is known as Family Group Conferencing (FGC). This model emphasizes the involvement of the victim, offender, and their respective support networks, as well as a facilitator, in a conference to discuss the harm caused by the crime and develop a plan for repair and reintegration. This approach is rooted in Maori traditions of peacemaking and has been successful in reducing recidivism rates and increasing victim satisfaction.

In contrast, in Canada, the restorative justice process often takes the form of victim-offender mediation. Trained mediators facilitate a dialogue between the victim and offender, allowing them to express their feelings, discuss the harm caused, and collectively determine appropriate reparations. This model has been found to improve victim satisfaction and increase offender accountability.

By comparing these different models, researchers can identify their strengths and weaknesses, as well as any cultural or contextual factors that may influence their success. This comparative approach helps inform the development and implementation of restorative justice practices in different jurisdictions.

Evaluating Outcomes and Effectiveness

Another aspect of comparative analysis is assessing the outcomes and effectiveness of restorative justice programs in different countries. This involves evaluating the impacts on key stakeholders and the criminal justice system as a whole.

One important measure of success is the satisfaction of the victim. Research has shown that victims who participate in the restorative justice process often report higher levels of satisfaction compared to those involved in traditional criminal justice processes. This is because restorative justice allows victims to have a voice, express their needs, and receive meaningful apologies and reparations from the offender.

Additionally, recidivism rates can be examined to assess the impact of restorative justice on offender rehabilitation. Various studies have found that restorative justice interventions can lead to lower rates of reoffending compared to traditional punitive approaches. This suggests that restorative justice may be more effective in addressing the underlying causes of criminal behavior and promoting offender accountability.

Furthermore, the impact of restorative justice on the community and the criminal justice system itself should be evaluated. Restorative justice has the potential to strengthen social bonds, restore trust in the justice system, and reduce the burden on overcrowded courts and prisons. By comparing these outcomes across different countries, researchers can identify best practices and areas for improvement.

Challenges and Future Directions

Comparative analysis of restorative justice also allows for a deeper understanding of the challenges and barriers to its implementation. Cultural differences, legal frameworks, and resource limitations can significantly influence the adoption and success of restorative justice programs.

For example, the emphasis on community involvement and informal processes in restorative justice may conflict with traditional legal systems that prioritize formal procedures and punishment. Overcoming these cultural and institutional barriers requires innovative approaches and a commitment to cultural sensitivity.

Additionally, ensuring the quality and consistency of restorative justice practices across different jurisdictions is a challenge. Training mediators, providing support services, and implementing comprehensive evaluation methods are necessary steps to overcome these obstacles and promote the effectiveness of restorative justice.

Looking to the future, comparative research can inform the development and implementation of restorative justice policies and programs on a global scale. By learning from successful models and addressing challenges, we can continue to advance the transformative potential of restorative justice in the criminal justice system worldwide.

Conclusion

In conclusion, restorative justice as a comparative approach to criminal justice allows us to study and understand the various models, outcomes, challenges, and opportunities associated with its implementation across different legal systems. Through comparative analysis, we can identify best practices, evaluate effectiveness, and address barriers to enhance the transformative potential of restorative justice. By embracing this comparative perspective, we can contribute to the ongoing evolution of criminal justice systems towards greater justice, healing, and societal transformation.

Restorative Justice Practices

Victim-Offender Mediation

In this section, we will explore the concept of victim-offender mediation, which is a key practice within the field of restorative justice. Restorative justice aims to empower victims, hold offenders accountable, and repair the harm caused by a crime through a collaborative and inclusive process. Victim-offender mediation is a key component of this approach, as it provides an opportunity for the victim and offender to communicate directly and participate in finding a resolution that addresses the needs and concerns of both parties.

Understanding Victim-Offender Mediation

Victim-offender mediation is a process that brings together the victim and the offender in a controlled and facilitated environment. It provides a space for them to engage in a dialogue, express their thoughts and emotions, and work towards understanding and resolution.

The mediation process is typically facilitated by a trained mediator who ensures a safe and respectful atmosphere. The mediator guides the conversation, encourages active listening, and helps the participants identify their needs and concerns. The ultimate goal is to reach a mutually agreed-upon plan for repairing the harm caused by the offense, addressing the needs of the victim, and promoting accountability and personal growth for the offender.

Principles of Victim-Offender Mediation

Victim-offender mediation is guided by several key principles that underpin its effectiveness and transformative potential:

1. **Voluntary participation:** Participation in victim-offender mediation is voluntary for both the victim and the offender. Both parties must willingly agree to engage in the process, ensuring that their voices are heard and their autonomy respected.

2. **Empowerment of the victim:** Victim-offender mediation empowers the victim by providing them with an opportunity to express their needs, concerns, and feelings directly to the offender. It enables them to have a say in the resolution process and be actively involved in the decision-making.

3. **Accountability and responsibility:** Victim-offender mediation emphasizes the responsibility of the offender to take accountability for their actions. During the mediation process, the offender is encouraged to acknowledge the harm caused, express remorse, and work towards making amends.

4. **Restitution and repair:** Victim-offender mediation focuses on repairing the harm caused by the offense. This may involve developing a plan for restitution, community service, or other actions aimed at making amends. The goal is to address the needs of the victim and promote healing and growth for both parties involved.

5. **Confidentiality and safety:** Victim-offender mediation ensures the safety and confidentiality of participants. The process takes place in a controlled environment, and confidentiality agreements are usually in place to protect sensitive information shared during the mediation.

Process of Victim-Offender Mediation

The process of victim-offender mediation typically consists of the following steps:

1. **Referral:** The case is referred for mediation by a judge, prosecutor, victim advocate, or other relevant parties. Both the victim and the offender must agree to participate voluntarily.

2. **Preparation:** Each participant meets with the mediator separately before the joint session. The mediator explains the process, ensures understanding, and addresses any concerns or questions.

3. **Joint session:** The victim and the offender come together in a joint session facilitated by the mediator. They have an opportunity to share their perspectives, express their emotions, and discuss the impact of the offense on their lives.

4. **Resolution and agreement:** Through facilitated discussions, the victim and the offender work towards reaching an agreement that addresses the harm caused and meets the needs of both parties. This may involve apologies, restitution, community service, or other mutually agreed-upon actions.

5. **Follow-up:** After the agreement is reached, the mediator ensures its implementation and may provide support or resources as needed. Follow-up sessions may be scheduled to assess progress and address any ongoing issues or concerns.

Benefits and Challenges of Victim-Offender Mediation

Victim-offender mediation has shown several benefits for both victims and offenders, as well as the broader community:

1. **Empowerment and satisfaction for victims:** Victim-offender mediation allows victims to have a voice, express their needs, and actively participate in the resolution process. This empowerment can lead to increased satisfaction and a sense of justice being served.

2. **Accountability and personal growth for offenders:** By engaging directly with the victim, offenders are confronted with the impact of their actions and can take responsibility for the harm caused. This can be a catalyst for personal growth, rehabilitation, and reduced recidivism.

3. **Enhanced understanding and empathy:** Through victim-offender mediation, participants have an opportunity to gain a better understanding of each other's experiences and perspectives. This increased empathy can foster healing, reconciliation, and community reintegration.

4. **Community healing and restoration:** Victim-offender mediation contributes to the healing and restoration of the community by addressing the harm caused by the offense. It promotes a sense of collective responsibility and provides an alternative to punitive punishment.

However, victim-offender mediation also faces certain challenges:

- **Availability and accessibility:** Victim-offender mediation programs may not be widely available, particularly in certain communities or jurisdictions. Access to mediation services can be limited due to factors such as funding, awareness, or cultural barriers.

- **Power imbalances:** In some cases, there may be significant power imbalances between victims and offenders, which can impact the effectiveness of the mediation. Ensuring a fair and safe process requires careful attention to power dynamics and the facilitation of equal participation.

- **Facilitator competency:** The success of victim-offender mediation relies heavily on the competency and training of the mediators. Adequate training and ongoing professional development are essential to ensure the facilitation of a productive and safe mediation process.

Examples and Resources

Victim-offender mediation programs have been implemented worldwide and have demonstrated positive outcomes. One notable example is the Victim-Offender Mediation Program in Belgium, which has been successful in reducing recidivism rates and providing healing for participants. The Center for Justice and Reconciliation, based in the United States, is a valuable resource for information, research, and training on victim-offender mediation and restorative justice practices.

Exercises

1. Research and discuss a case study where victim-offender mediation was employed. Describe the outcomes of the mediation and analyze its effectiveness in addressing the needs of the victim and promoting accountability for the offender.

2. Conduct a role-playing exercise where you take on the role of a mediator in a victim-offender mediation session. Develop a script that guides the conversation between the victim and the offender, focusing on active listening, empathy, and conflict resolution techniques.

Conclusion

Victim-offender mediation is a transformative approach within the broader field of restorative justice. It provides a platform for direct communication between the victim and the offender, enabling them to collaboratively address harm, promote accountability, and work towards healing and reconciliation. By prioritizing the needs and empowerment of victims and encouraging the responsibility and personal growth of offenders, victim-offender mediation offers a promising alternative to traditional punitive justice approaches.

Family Group Conferencing

In this section, we will explore the concept of Family Group Conferencing (FGC) as a restorative justice practice within the criminal justice system. FGC is a process that involves bringing together the victim, offender, and their respective families, along with other community members, to discuss the harm caused by the offense and find solutions that promote healing and accountability.

Restorative Justice and FGC

Restorative justice is a philosophy that focuses on repairing the harm caused by crime, rather than solely punishing the offender. It recognizes that crime impacts not only the victim but also the offender, their families, and the community as a whole. FGC is one of the key practices used in restorative justice approaches to address criminal behavior.

The goal of FGC is to create a safe and constructive environment where all participants can express their feelings, share their perspectives, and work towards a resolution that meets the needs of those affected by the offense. By involving the victim, offender, and their families, FGC aims to restore relationships, promote understanding, and prevent future harm.

Key Steps in FGC

FGC typically follows a structured process that includes the following key steps:

1. Referral: The case is referred to FGC by a judge, prosecutor, or other justice system professional.

2. Preparation: A conference organizer, often a trained facilitator, prepares all parties for the conference, explaining the process, clarifying expectations, and ensuring everyone's safety.

3. Information Sharing: Each participant has an opportunity to share their perspective on the offense, its impact, and their needs and concerns.

4. Private Family Time: The victim's and offender's families meet separately to discuss the offense, its impact, and potential solutions. This private family time allows for open and honest dialogue.

5. Family Conference: The victim, offender, and their families come together in a facilitated conference to share what was discussed during the private family time. They explore ways to repair the harm caused by the offense and develop a written agreement outlining the agreed-upon actions and responsibilities.

6. Follow-up: The conference organizer ensures that the agreed-upon actions are implemented and monitors the progress. Follow-up meetings may be scheduled to address any ongoing issues or provide additional support as needed.

Benefits of FGC

FGC offers several benefits compared to traditional approaches to criminal justice:

1. Empowerment: FGC empowers victims by giving them a voice and an active role in the process. They can express their feelings, ask questions, and participate in finding a resolution that meets their needs.

2. Accountability and Responsibility: FGC encourages offenders to take responsibility for their actions, understand the harm caused, and actively contribute to repairing the harm. This can lead to increased accountability and a reduced likelihood of reoffending.

3. Healing and Closure: FGC provides an opportunity for participants to express their emotions, share their experiences, and find emotional and psychological healing. It allows for the closure of unresolved conflicts and helps victims and offenders move forward.

4. Community Involvement: FGC recognizes the importance of community support in the reintegration of offenders and the healing process for all involved. It encourages community members to actively participate and take responsibility for preventing future harm.

Challenges and Limitations of FGC

While FGC has many benefits, it also faces certain challenges and limitations:

1. Voluntary Participation: FGC requires the voluntary participation of all parties involved. Not everyone may be willing or able to participate, which can limit the effectiveness of the process.

2. Power Imbalances: Power imbalances within families or between the victim and offender can affect the dynamics of the conference. It is essential to have skilled facilitators who can ensure fairness and balance in the process.

3. Safety Concerns: FGC must prioritize the safety and well-being of all participants. In cases where there is a history of abuse or violence, the process

needs to be carefully managed to ensure the safety of the victim and others involved.

4. Limited Scope: FGC is primarily focused on addressing specific offenses and their immediate impact. It may not be suitable for complex or high-profile cases that require a more comprehensive legal response.

Examples of FGC in Practice

FGC has been successfully implemented in various jurisdictions around the world. For example:

1. New Zealand introduced FGC as a response to rising youth crime rates. It has since become a widely adopted approach that involves family members, community representatives, and justice professionals working together to develop plans for young offenders.

2. Australia has used FGC within its child protection system, with a focus on ensuring the safety and well-being of children by involving extended family members and other significant individuals in decision-making processes.

3. Canada has implemented FGC as part of a restorative justice approach in response to crimes committed by Indigenous offenders. The process incorporates Indigenous cultural practices and values to promote healing and reconciliation.

Resources for Further Study

To learn more about Family Group Conferencing and restorative justice practices, the following resources may be helpful:

1. "The Little Book of Restorative Justice" by Howard Zehr provides an introduction to the principles and practices of restorative justice, including FGC.

2. The Restorative Justice Consortium (RJC) is an organization that promotes restorative justice practices, including FGC. Their website (restorativejustice.org.uk) offers resources, research articles, and training opportunities.

3. The International Institute for Restorative Practices (IIRP) has a wide range of resources on restorative justice, including case studies, research, and training programs. Visit their website at iirp.edu.

Summary

Family Group Conferencing (FGC) is a restorative justice practice that brings together the victim, offender, and their respective families to discuss the harm caused by the offense and develop a resolution that promotes healing and accountability. This process empowers victims, encourages offenders to take responsibility, fosters healing and closure, and involves the community in preventing future harm. While FGC has challenges and limitations, it has shown promising results in various jurisdictions. By understanding FGC and its benefits, we can contribute to the transformative potential of restorative justice in our criminal justice system.

Community Restorative Boards

Community Restorative Boards play a vital role in the practice of restorative justice. These boards are community-based organizations that facilitate restorative justice processes in cases involving criminal offenses. By bringing together offenders, victims, and community members, Community Restorative Boards seek to repair harm, restore relationships, and promote healing within the community.

Foundations of Restorative Justice

Before delving into the specifics of Community Restorative Boards, let's briefly revisit the foundations of restorative justice. Restorative justice is a paradigm shift from the traditional punitive approach to crime. It emphasizes repairing harm caused by criminal behavior and promoting accountability and healing for all parties involved. Key principles of restorative justice include:

- **Encounter and dialogue:** Restorative justice encourages open and honest communication between offenders, victims, and community members, fostering understanding and empathy.

- **Voluntary participation:** Participation in restorative justice processes is voluntary, ensuring that individuals are willing to engage in meaningful dialogue and take responsibility for their actions.

- **Inclusion of affected parties:** Restorative justice recognizes the importance of involving both the victim and the offender, as well as the wider community, in the decision-making process.

- **Accountability and responsibility:** Restorative justice focuses on holding offenders accountable for their actions, providing them with an opportunity to make amends and reintegrate into society.

Now, let's explore how Community Restorative Boards put these principles into practice.

Roles and Functions of Community Restorative Boards

Community Restorative Boards serve as intermediaries between victims, offenders, and the community. They provide a safe and structured space for dialogue, allowing participants to share their experiences, express their emotions, and collaborate on finding solutions. Some of the key roles and functions of Community Restorative Boards include:

1. **Facilitating restorative justice processes:** Community Restorative Boards organize and facilitate various restorative justice processes, such as victim-offender mediation and family group conferences. These processes allow victims to share the impact of the offense, offenders to take responsibility for their actions, and the community to engage in problem-solving.

2. **Promoting healing and reconciliation:** Through restorative justice processes, Community Restorative Boards aim to foster healing and reconciliation among participants. By addressing the harm caused by the offense and promoting understanding, these processes contribute to repairing relationships and restoring trust within the community.

3. **Ensuring fairness and equity:** Community Restorative Boards strive to create a fair and equitable space for all participants. They ensure that everyone's needs and perspectives are heard and respected during the process, promoting a sense of justice and fairness.

4. **Supporting the reintegration of offenders:** Community Restorative Boards play a crucial role in supporting the reintegration of offenders. They work with offenders to develop personalized plans for addressing the harm caused, making amends, and reintegrating into the community. This may involve connecting offenders with community services, employment opportunities, or education programs.

5. **Building community capacity:** Community Restorative Boards also focus on building community capacity for restorative justice. They organize training programs and workshops to educate community members about restorative justice principles and practices. By involving the community in restorative processes, these boards empower community members to take an active role in conflict resolution and community healing.

Community Restorative Boards in Action: An Example

To illustrate how Community Restorative Boards work, let's consider a hypothetical example. Imagine a case involving a young offender who vandalized a local park, causing damage to public property. The victim, a representative from the local community, expresses a desire to be involved in the resolution process.

In this scenario, a Community Restorative Board would be engaged to facilitate a restorative justice process. The board members, trained in restorative justice principles and practices, would organize a meeting with the offender, the victim, and other relevant community members.

During the process, the victim would have the opportunity to express the impact of the offense on the community and themselves. The offender would listen to the victim's experiences, take responsibility for their actions, and discuss ways to repair the harm caused. Together with the board members, the participants would collaboratively develop a plan for restitution, which might involve community service, financial compensation, or participation in restorative activities.

Throughout the process, the Community Restorative Board would provide guidance, support, and oversight, ensuring that the restorative justice principles are upheld. The goal is to promote healing, understanding, and accountability, while actively involving the community in addressing the harm caused.

Challenges and Considerations

While Community Restorative Boards offer a promising approach to restorative justice, they also face challenges and considerations. Some of these include:

- **Resource constraints:** Limited funding and resources can pose challenges to the establishment and sustainability of Community Restorative Boards. Securing financial support and community buy-in is crucial for their success.

- **Participant engagement:** Ensuring the voluntary participation and engagement of both victims and offenders can be challenging. Effective outreach and communication strategies are essential to encourage individuals to participate in restorative justice processes.

- **Cultural sensitivity:** Community Restorative Boards need to be mindful of cultural diversity and sensitivity. They should have a deep understanding of the cultural dynamics within the community they serve to ensure that restorative justice processes are inclusive and respectful.

Considering these challenges, it is important to provide ongoing training and support to Community Restorative Boards, fostering their capacity to effectively address these issues and enhance their impact.

Resources and Further Reading

Here are some resources for further reading on Community Restorative Boards and restorative justice:

- Bazemore, G., & Umbreit, M. S. (Eds.). (2011). *Restorative community justice: Repairing harm and transforming communities.* Anderson Publishing.
- Braithwaite, J. (2009). *Restorative justice and responsive regulation.* Oxford University Press.
- Van Ness, D. W., & Strong, K. H. (2015). *Restoring justice: An introduction to restorative justice.* Routledge.

These resources provide valuable insights into the theoretical foundations, practical applications, and challenges of restorative justice, including the role of Community Restorative Boards.

Conclusion

Community Restorative Boards play a significant role in implementing restorative justice principles in communities. By facilitating dialogue, promoting healing, and supporting the reintegration of offenders, these boards contribute to the transformative potential of restorative justice. However, challenges such as resource constraints and participant engagement must be addressed to maximize their effectiveness. With ongoing support, Community Restorative Boards can continue to build stronger, safer, and more compassionate communities through restorative justice practices.

Challenges and Critiques of Restorative Justice Practices

Restorative justice is a transformative approach to criminal justice that focuses on addressing the harm caused by a crime, encouraging accountability, and facilitating the healing process for all stakeholders involved. While restorative justice has gained recognition and popularity in recent years, it is not without its challenges and critiques. In this section, we will discuss some of the key challenges and critiques of restorative justice practices.

1. Balancing Accountability and Due Process

One of the main challenges of restorative justice practices is finding the right balance between accountability and due process. Restorative justice emphasizes dialogue, understanding, and healing, but critics argue that it may overlook the need for formal accountability measures. There is a concern that restorative processes, such as victim-offender mediation, may not adequately address the legal and procedural requirements of traditional criminal justice systems.

To address this challenge, it is essential to ensure that restorative justice practices are conducted in a way that upholds the principles of fairness, transparency, and procedural justice. This can be achieved by incorporating legal safeguards, providing training for facilitators, and involving legal professionals to ensure that outcomes are legally valid.

2. Equal Participation and Power Imbalance

Another challenge in restorative justice practices is ensuring equal participation and addressing power imbalances between victims and offenders. Critics argue that victims may feel intimidated or coerced into participating in restorative processes, while offenders may manipulate the process to avoid taking responsibility for their actions.

To overcome this challenge, it is crucial to create a safe and supportive environment for all participants. Facilitators should be trained in handling power imbalances and ensuring that victims' rights are protected throughout the process. Empowering victims to make informed decisions about their participation and offering support services can also help address power imbalances.

3. Capacity and Resources

Restorative justice practices require significant resources, including trained facilitators, support services for victims and offenders, and adequate infrastructure to facilitate dialogue and mediation. Limited resources can pose a challenge in implementing and sustaining restorative justice programs, particularly in underserved communities.

Addressing this challenge requires investing in the development of restorative justice infrastructure, training programs, and community resources. Collaboration between justice agencies, non-profit organizations, and community stakeholders can help leverage resources and overcome capacity issues.

4. Measuring Success and Evaluating Outcomes

Critics of restorative justice argue that there is a lack of rigorous evaluation and measurement of its effectiveness. Without robust evaluation methods, it becomes challenging to identify the impact of restorative justice practices on recidivism rates, victim satisfaction, and community safety.

To address this challenge, it is important to develop comprehensive evaluation frameworks that measure both short-term and long-term outcomes of restorative justice processes. This can include assessing the satisfaction of participants, the extent to which harm is repaired, and the reduction in future criminal behavior. By gathering empirical evidence, policymakers and practitioners can make informed decisions about the effectiveness and scalability of restorative justice programs.

5. Context and Cultural Sensitivity

Restorative justice practices must be responsive to cultural, social, and historical contexts to ensure their effectiveness and appropriateness. Critics argue that the implementation of a Western-based restorative justice model in non-Western cultures may not fully consider cultural values, beliefs, and norms.

To address this challenge, it is crucial to involve diverse communities in the development and implementation of restorative justice programs. Cultural sensitivity training for facilitators and practitioners can help ensure that restorative justice processes respect and incorporate cultural perspectives. Adapting restorative justice practices to different cultural contexts is crucial to its successful implementation globally.

6. Public Perception and Acceptance

Restorative justice practices often face skepticism and resistance from the public, who may view them as being too lenient on offenders or failing to address the needs of victims. Skepticism can hinder the widespread adoption and implementation of restorative justice programs.

To overcome this challenge, it is important to engage in public education campaigns to raise awareness about the principles, benefits, and successes of restorative justice. Sharing success stories, conducting public forums, and involving influential community members and leaders can help dispel misconceptions and build public trust in restorative justice as a viable alternative to traditional criminal justice.

Conclusion

Restorative justice practices offer transformative alternatives to traditional criminal justice systems. However, they are not immune to challenges and critiques. Addressing these challenges, such as balancing accountability and due process, equalizing power imbalances, allocating resources, measuring success, considering cultural contexts, and gaining public acceptance, is crucial for the successful implementation and sustainability of restorative justice programs. By continuously improving and adapting restorative justice practices, we can strive for a more just and equitable criminal justice system.

Restorative Justice in the Criminal Justice System

Restorative Justice and Sentencing

Restorative justice is a transformative approach to criminal justice that focuses on repairing the harm caused by a crime and restoring relationships between the victim, the offender, and the community. This section explores the principles and practices of restorative justice and its application in the context of sentencing.

Definition and Principles of Restorative Justice

Restorative justice is a philosophy that views crime as a violation of people and relationships rather than just a violation of laws. It seeks to address the needs and interests of all parties involved, including the victim, the offender, and the community. Restorative justice emphasizes the following principles:

1. Encounter: Restorative justice emphasizes the importance of direct communication and dialogue between the victim and the offender. This allows both parties to express their feelings, ask questions, and share their experiences.

2. Responsibility: Restorative justice encourages the offender to take responsibility for their actions and make amends to repair the harm caused. This may involve making restitution or engaging in community service.

3. Reintegration: Restorative justice seeks to reintegrate offenders back into the community in a positive and constructive way. This involves acknowledging the harm caused, learning from the experience, and taking steps to prevent future offending.

4. Inclusion: Restorative justice recognizes the importance of involving all stakeholders in the justice process, including the victim, the offender, their families,

and the community. Inclusive participation ensures that everyone affected by the crime has a voice in decision-making.

Restorative Justice in Sentencing

Restorative justice can play a significant role in sentencing practices by offering an alternative approach to punishment. Instead of focusing solely on retributive or punitive measures, restorative justice aims to provide appropriate consequences while promoting healing and reconciliation. Some key considerations in restorative justice sentencing include:

1. Voluntary participation: Restorative justice processes should be voluntary for all parties involved. This ensures that participants have the willingness to engage in dialogue and work towards resolution.

2. Offender accountability: Restorative justice sentencing emphasizes the importance of offenders taking responsibility for their actions. This may involve making a sincere apology, acknowledging the harm caused, and actively participating in the process of repairing the harm.

3. Victim empowerment: Restorative justice sentencing focuses on meeting the needs and interests of the victim. This may include providing an opportunity for the victim to share their experience, express their feelings, and participate in the decision-making process regarding the consequences for the offender.

4. Community involvement: Restorative justice recognizes the role of the community in promoting healing and preventing future harm. Sentencing in restorative justice contexts often involves community members, such as elders or mediators, who contribute their perspectives and assist in shaping the outcomes.

Challenges and Critiques of Restorative Justice Sentencing

While restorative justice sentencing offers a promising alternative to traditional punitive approaches, it also faces challenges and criticisms. Some of these challenges include:

1. Power imbalances: Restorative justice relies on equal power dynamics between the victim and the offender. However, in cases where there is a significant power imbalance, such as in cases of domestic violence or hate crimes, ensuring fairness and justice can be more complex.

2. Limited applicability: Restorative justice may not be suitable for all types of offenses or offenders. Serious and violent crimes, for instance, may require more traditional forms of punishment to ensure public safety and deterrence.

3. Lack of resources: Implementing restorative justice practices requires adequate resources, including trained facilitators, support services, and community involvement. Limited resources can hinder the widespread adoption and effectiveness of restorative justice sentencing.

4. Over-reliance on voluntariness: The voluntary nature of restorative justice processes may result in unequal participation. Offenders may choose not to participate, or victims may face pressure to engage in a process they are not ready for, potentially undermining the effectiveness of restorative justice sentencing.

It is essential to address these challenges and criticisms to ensure that restorative justice sentencing practices are implemented in a fair, inclusive, and effective manner.

Case Studies: Restorative Justice in Sentencing

Real-world examples of restorative justice in sentencing highlight its transformative potential. One such case is the Kiriwina Island Restorative Justice Project in Papua New Guinea. In response to high levels of violence in the community, the project introduced restorative justice practices, including community conferences and mediation. The aim was to address the root causes of violence, promote healing, and achieve reconciliation. Early evaluations of the project showed positive outcomes, including reduced levels of violence and increased community cohesion.

Another example is the Peacemaking Circle process used in the Yukon Territory in Canada. This process incorporates restorative justice principles and practices into the sentencing of Indigenous offenders. Elders play a central role in facilitating the circle, and the focus is on healing, accountability, and restoring relationships. Evaluations of the Peacemaking Circle process have demonstrated reduced recidivism rates and increased satisfaction among participants compared to traditional sentencing approaches.

These case studies illustrate the potential of restorative justice sentencing to address the underlying causes of crime, promote healing, and foster community well-being.

Conclusion

Restorative justice has the power to transform the traditional approach to sentencing by emphasizing healing, reconciliation, and community involvement. By centering the needs of victims, holding offenders accountable, and involving the community in decision-making, restorative justice promotes a more balanced and holistic response to crime. However, challenges related to power imbalances, limited applicability, resource constraints, and voluntariness must be addressed to ensure the effective implementation of restorative justice sentencing. Real-world case studies demonstrate the potential of restorative justice to bring about positive outcomes for individuals, communities, and the criminal justice system as a whole. The integration of restorative justice into sentencing practices contributes to a more just and transformative criminal justice system.

Restorative Justice in Juvenile Justice

Restorative justice is an innovative approach to criminal justice that focuses on repairing harm caused by crimes, rather than solely focusing on punishment. This section explores the application of restorative justice principles in the context of juvenile justice, recognizing the unique needs and characteristics of young offenders.

Understanding Juvenile Justice

Juvenile justice is a specialized system of law that deals with young individuals who have committed offenses. The age at which individuals are considered juveniles varies across jurisdictions, but typically ranges from 10 to 18 years old. The goal of the juvenile justice system is to rehabilitate young offenders, guiding them towards a law-abiding life and reintegrating them into society.

Principles of Restorative Justice

Restorative justice in the context of juvenile justice is based on four key principles:

1. Accountability: In restorative justice, young offenders are encouraged to take responsibility for their actions and understand the harm they have caused to victims, families, and the community.

2. Dialogue and Communication: The process of restorative justice involves facilitating dialogue between the victim and the offender. This allows both parties to share their perspectives, express emotions, and seek understanding.

3. Repair and Reconciliation: Restorative justice aims to repair the harm caused by the offense by seeking solutions that address the needs of victims, offenders, and the community. This may involve restitution, community service, or other forms of compensation.

4. Inclusion and Participation: Restorative justice recognizes the importance of including affected individuals in decision-making processes. This includes involving victims, offenders, families, and community members in the resolution process.

Restorative Practices in Juvenile Justice

Restorative practices can be applied at different stages of the juvenile justice process:

1. Pre-Diversion: Instead of being formally processed through the traditional justice system, young offenders may be diverted to restorative justice programs at an early stage. These programs focus on holding the offender accountable, addressing the harm caused, and finding ways to repair the harm without resorting to formal court proceedings.

2. Diversion: In cases where the offense is more serious, restorative justice principles can still be applied through diversion programs. These programs provide an alternative to traditional court proceedings, emphasizing the involvement of victims and the community in finding resolutions that address the harm caused.

3. Sentencing and Disposition: Restorative justice can also play a role in the sentencing and disposition of juvenile offenders. Instead of relying solely on punitive measures, courts may opt for restorative justice interventions that focus on repairing the harm, providing support and rehabilitation for the offenders, and ensuring accountability.

4. Reentry and Aftercare: Restorative justice principles can continue to guide the reintegration of juvenile offenders into society after they have completed their sentences. This may involve providing additional support, mentorship, and opportunities for the offenders to make amends and contribute positively to their communities.

Benefits and Challenges of Restorative Justice in Juvenile Justice

Restorative justice holds several benefits for the juvenile justice system:

1. Increased Accountability: By directly involving offenders in the resolution process, restorative justice enhances their sense of responsibility and accountability for their actions.

2. Victim Empowerment: Restorative justice allows victims to have a voice and actively participate in the resolution process. This can promote healing, provide a sense of closure, and reduce the risk of re-victimization.

3. Reduced Recidivism: Restorative justice approaches have been shown to lower rates of repeat offending among juvenile offenders. By addressing the underlying causes of their behavior and providing support for rehabilitation, restorative justice can contribute to positive behavioral change.

Despite these benefits, there are also challenges in implementing restorative justice in the juvenile justice system:

1. Limited Resources: Restorative justice programs require significant resources, including trained facilitators, time, and funding. The availability of these resources may vary across jurisdictions, limiting the widespread adoption of restorative justice practices.

2. Balancing the Needs of Offenders and Victims: Restorative justice aims to find a balance between the needs of offenders and victims. However, there may be instances where the interests of both parties conflict, requiring careful navigation and consideration.

3. Sensitivity to Power Imbalances: Restorative justice processes must be mindful of power imbalances between victims and offenders, ensuring that the participation of each party is voluntary and that adequate safeguards are in place to protect vulnerable individuals.

Case Study: Restorative Justice in Juvenile Offender Rehabilitation

One successful example of restorative justice in the context of juvenile justice is the Maori Youth Court in New Zealand. This court utilizes traditional Maori principles and processes, focusing on healing and rehabilitation rather than punitive measures. Juvenile offenders are encouraged to take responsibility for their actions, engage with their communities, and undergo culturally appropriate interventions aimed at addressing the underlying causes of their offending behaviors. The Maori Youth Court has been praised for its positive outcomes in reducing reoffending rates and promoting a sense of connection to cultural identity among the young offenders.

Resources for Further Study

1. Zehr, H. (2015). Changing Lenses: Restorative Justice for Our Times. Herald Press. 2. Bazemore, G., & Umbreit, M. (Eds.). (2011). Juvenile Justice Reform and Restorative Justice: Building Theory and Policy from Practice. Oxford University Press. 3. Shapland, J., et al. (2011). Restorative Justice in Practice: Evaluating What Works for Victims and Offenders. Routledge.

Exercises

1. Discuss the advantages and disadvantages of using restorative justice in the juvenile justice system. 2. Research restorative justice programs in your local community. How are they implemented in the context of juvenile justice? 3. Imagine you are a juvenile justice policymaker. Design a restorative justice program that addresses the needs of both offenders and victims. 4. Debate the ethical

considerations of involving victims in the restorative justice process. What are the potential benefits and risks?

Remember, restorative justice in the juvenile justice system highlights the transformative potential of addressing harm, healing relationships, and promoting accountability. By shifting the focus from punitive measures to repairing harm, the juvenile justice system can better serve the needs of young offenders, victims, and the community as a whole.

Restorative Justice in Prisons and Reentry Programs

Restorative justice is a transformative approach to criminal justice that focuses on repairing harm, healing relationships, and promoting reconciliation. In the context of prisons and reentry programs, restorative justice offers an alternative to traditional punitive measures by emphasizing personal responsibility, accountability, and community involvement. This section explores the principles and practices of restorative justice in prisons and reentry programs, highlighting their potential to transform the lives of incarcerated individuals and promote successful reintegration into society.

Principles of Restorative Justice in Prisons

Restorative justice in prisons is guided by several key principles that shape its approach to addressing harm and promoting rehabilitation:

1. **Voluntary Participation:** Participation in restorative justice processes is voluntary for both victims and offenders. This ensures that all parties have a sense of agency and autonomy in the process.

2. **Inclusion and Empowerment:** Restorative justice aims to include all affected parties, including victims, offenders, and community members, in the decision-making process. This creates a sense of empowerment and allows for the recognition of the impact of the crime on various stakeholders.

3. **Accountability and Responsibility:** Restorative justice encourages offenders to take responsibility for their actions and be accountable for the harm they have caused. This involves acknowledging the consequences of their actions and actively working towards repairing the harm.

4. **Community Engagement:** Restorative justice recognizes the importance of involving the wider community in the process. Community support and involvement can help facilitate the reintegration of offenders and provide a supportive environment for their transition back into society.

Restorative Justice Practices in Prisons

There are various restorative justice practices that can be implemented in prisons to promote healing, reconciliation, and personal growth. Some of these practices include:

1. **Victim-Offender Dialogue:** This practice involves a facilitated conversation between the victim and the offender. It provides an opportunity for the victim to express their feelings, ask questions, and seek answers from the offender. The dialogue allows both parties to gain a deeper understanding of the impact of the offense and work towards repairing the harm.

2. **Circle Sentencing:** Circle sentencing involves bringing together the victim, offender, their respective support networks, and community members in a circle. The circle creates a safe space for open communication, dialogue, and problem-solving. It allows for the development of a consensus-based plan to address the harm caused and support the offender's rehabilitation.

3. **Prison-based Restorative Programs:** Restorative programs can be implemented within prison settings to provide opportunities for personal growth and skill development. These programs may include restorative justice workshops, victim awareness programs, conflict resolution training, and emotional healing sessions. Such programs facilitate personal introspection, empathy development, and the acquisition of valuable life skills.

4. **Restorative Discipline:** Restorative discipline focuses on repairing harm and building relationships within prison communities. It encourages dialogue and problem-solving rather than punishment and isolation. When conflicts or disciplinary issues arise, restorative practices such as group conferences or mediation can be employed to address the underlying causes and develop solutions that promote understanding and accountability.

Benefits of Restorative Justice in Prisons and Reentry Programs

The implementation of restorative justice in prisons and reentry programs offers several benefits for incarcerated individuals, victims, and the community as a whole:

1. **Increased Rehabilitation:** Restorative justice approaches prioritize the rehabilitation and personal growth of offenders. By providing opportunities for reflection, accountability, and skill development, these programs can support offenders in addressing the root causes of their criminal behavior and making positive changes.

2. **Better Understanding of the Impact of Crime:** Restorative justice processes provide victims with the opportunity to directly express the impact of the offense on their lives. This personal interaction can foster empathy and understanding in offenders, leading to a heightened sense of remorse and motivation to make amends.

3. **Lower Recidivism Rates:** Restorative justice practices have been shown to reduce recidivism rates. By addressing the underlying causes of criminal behavior and promoting personal growth, these programs help prepare individuals for a successful reintegration into society, lowering the likelihood of reoffending.

4. **Community Healing and Reintegration:** Restorative justice practices involve the community in the process of healing and reintegration. By actively engaging community members, restorative justice fosters a sense of shared responsibility and builds a supportive environment for the successful reentry of offenders into society.

5. **Cost-effectiveness:** Restorative justice programs have demonstrated cost-effectiveness compared to traditional criminal justice approaches. By focusing on rehabilitation and reducing recidivism rates, these programs can result in long-term savings by reducing the burden on the criminal justice system.

Challenges and Ethical Considerations

While restorative justice in prisons and reentry programs offers significant potential, there are several challenges and ethical considerations that need to be addressed:

1. **Power Imbalances:** Restorative justice processes must navigate power imbalances between victims and offenders, as well as other stakeholders. Facilitators must ensure a safe and inclusive environment where all parties have equal opportunities to voice their needs and concerns.

2. **Victim Safety:** Ensuring the safety and well-being of victims is paramount in restorative justice processes. Careful consideration must be given to the potential risks and emotional impact of victim-offender dialogue, and support systems should be in place to address any safety concerns.

3. **Inclusivity:** Restorative justice processes should be inclusive and culturally sensitive. The needs and perspectives of marginalized communities, such as Indigenous peoples and individuals from diverse cultural backgrounds, should be considered to avoid perpetuating existing inequalities.

4. **Closure:** It is essential to acknowledge that not all victims may find closure through restorative justice processes. Some victims may prefer to distance themselves from the offender or may find it emotionally challenging to engage in the process. Restorative justice should provide alternative avenues for victims to seek closure and support.

Case Study: The Sycamore Tree Project

The Sycamore Tree Project is an example of a restorative justice program implemented in prisons worldwide. The program brings together victims and offenders in a facilitated dialogue that aims to encourage empathy, healing, and accountability.

Participants engage in a series of sessions, focusing on topics such as understanding the impact of crime, taking responsibility, and making amends. The dialogue provides an opportunity for victims to share their experiences, ask questions, and hear directly from offenders about the harm caused.

Evaluation studies of the Sycamore Tree Project have shown positive outcomes, including increased victim satisfaction, reduced feelings of anger and retribution, and improved levels of empathy and remorse among offenders. The program has also been linked to decreased recidivism rates among participants, highlighting its potential in promoting successful reentry.

Conclusion

Restorative justice in prisons and reentry programs offers a transformative approach to addressing harm, promoting rehabilitation, and supporting the successful reintegration of offenders into society. By prioritizing personal responsibility, accountability, and community involvement, restorative justice practices can contribute to healing, reconciliation, and the reduction of recidivism rates. However, careful consideration must be given to power imbalances, victim safety, inclusivity, and alternative pathways to closure. By addressing these challenges and building on successful case studies, restorative justice can transform our criminal justice system into one that prioritizes healing, rehabilitation, and community well-being.

Restorative Justice and Healing

Trauma-Informed Restorative Justice

Restorative justice is an approach to criminal justice that focuses on repairing the harm caused by crime and promoting healing and reconciliation among all stakeholders. It emphasizes victims' rights, offenders' accountability, and community involvement. In recent years, there has been a growing recognition of the impact of trauma on individuals involved in the criminal justice system.

Trauma-informed restorative justice integrates this understanding of trauma into the core principles and practices of restorative justice.

Understanding Trauma

Trauma is an emotional response to experiencing or witnessing a deeply distressing event or series of events. It can have severe and long-lasting effects on a person's physical, emotional, and psychological well-being. In the context of the criminal justice system, trauma can be experienced by victims, offenders, and even professionals working within the system. Examples of traumatic events include physical or sexual violence, natural disasters, and acts of terrorism.

Integration of Trauma-Informed Approaches

In trauma-informed restorative justice, the principles of safety, trustworthiness, choice, collaboration, and empowerment are applied to ensure that the needs of individuals affected by trauma are met. These principles guide the implementation of restorative justice practices and promote healing and well-being.

Safety: Trauma survivors need to feel physically and emotionally safe during restorative justice processes. This requires establishing clear boundaries, providing information about the process, and ensuring the physical security of all participants.

Trustworthiness: Building trust is crucial in trauma-informed practices. Restorative justice facilitators should be transparent, reliable, and accountable to create an environment where individuals affected by trauma feel safe to share their experiences.

Choice: Trauma survivors should have a sense of control and autonomy during the restorative justice process. They should have the opportunity to participate voluntarily, choose who is involved, and decide the extent of their engagement.

Collaboration: Trauma-informed restorative justice recognizes the importance of collaboration among participants, including victims, offenders, and community members. It values their input and ensures active participation in decision-making processes.

Empowerment: Trauma survivors often feel disempowered and have their agency diminished. Trauma-informed restorative justice seeks to restore their sense of power and control by recognizing and validating their experiences, strengths, and resilience.

Practices and Interventions

Trauma-informed restorative justice incorporates specific practices and interventions to address the impact of trauma on individuals and promote healing. Some of these practices include:

1. Emotional Safety Planning: This involves creating a safe and supportive environment for trauma survivors to share their experiences, express their emotions, and identify their needs. It may include providing emotional support and coping strategies.

2. Trauma Education and Psychoeducation: Individuals involved in the restorative justice process, including victims, offenders, and facilitators, may receive education about trauma and its effects. This helps to increase understanding, empathy, and informed decision-making.

3. Trauma Screening and Assessment: Trauma-informed restorative justice processes may incorporate screening and assessment tools to identify individuals who have experienced trauma or have specific needs related to trauma. This allows for tailored interventions and support.

4. Trauma-Informed Dialogue: Restorative justice dialogues should be conducted with sensitivity to the potential triggers and reactions associated with trauma. Facilitators need to create a safe space where trauma survivors can express themselves without fear of judgment or retraumatization.

5. Supportive Services and Referrals: Trauma-informed restorative justice recognizes the importance of providing access to support services such as counseling, therapy, or support groups. Referrals to specialized trauma services can help individuals in their healing journey.

Benefits and Challenges

Trauma-informed restorative justice offers several benefits. It recognizes the impact of trauma on individuals and promotes healing and well-being. By integrating trauma-informed practices, it can help trauma survivors regain a sense of control, empowerment, and self-worth. Restorative justice processes can also contribute to the prevention of retraumatization by providing a supportive environment for dialogue and understanding.

However, there are also challenges associated with trauma-informed restorative justice. Trauma survivors may be hesitant to engage in the process due to fear, mistrust, or previous negative experiences within the legal system. Additional challenges include the need for specialized training for facilitators, the availability of trauma-informed services, and the potential for secondary trauma experienced by professionals working in the field.

Case Study: Restorative Justice with Trauma-Informed Practices

One example of trauma-informed restorative justice is the use of restorative circles in a community affected by gang violence. The circles bring together victims, offenders, and community members to address the harm caused by gang-related incidents. In this case, trauma-informed practices are integrated into the restorative circle process. Trauma screening and assessment tools are used to identify trauma survivors and provide them with appropriate support. Emotional safety planning is implemented to ensure that participants feel safe to share their experiences. Trauma education and psychoeducation are also provided to increase understanding and empathy among all participants. By incorporating trauma-informed approaches, this restorative justice initiative supports healing, accountability, and community well-being.

Conclusion

Trauma-informed restorative justice recognizes the impact of trauma on individuals involved in the criminal justice system and integrates trauma-informed approaches into the core principles and practices of restorative justice. By prioritizing safety, trustworthiness, choice, collaboration, and empowerment, it aims to create an environment that promotes healing, well-being, and meaningful participation for all stakeholders. While there are challenges associated with trauma-informed restorative justice, its benefits in addressing trauma, preventing retraumatization, and promoting justice make it a promising approach in the transformation of criminal justice systems.

Addressing Interpersonal Violence through Restorative Justice

Restorative justice is a transformative approach to addressing interpersonal violence that focuses on repairing the harm caused to individuals and communities, rather than simply punishing offenders. It seeks to hold offenders accountable while also providing support and healing for victims. This section will explore the principles, practices, and potential impact of using restorative justice in cases of interpersonal violence.

Understanding Restorative Justice

Restorative justice is grounded in the belief that crime and violence are not isolated incidents, but rather a result of societal conditions, personal circumstances, and social relationships. It recognizes that healing and reconciliation are essential components of justice and that punishment alone cannot address the underlying causes of violence. Restorative justice aims to create opportunities for dialogue, understanding, and empowerment for all parties involved.

Principles of Restorative Justice

Restorative justice is guided by several key principles:

1. Encounter: Offenders and victims are given the opportunity to meet face-to-face in a safe and controlled setting, facilitated by trained professionals. This allows for open communication, empathy building, and the expression of emotions.

2. Accountability: Offenders take responsibility for their actions, acknowledge the harm caused, and work towards making amends. This may involve apologizing, making restitution, or participating in community service.

3. Healing and Support: Victims are given the opportunity to share their experiences, voice their needs, and receive support. They are empowered to actively participate in the decision-making process and have their voices heard.

4. Community Involvement: Restorative justice involves the broader community in the process of healing and reconciliation. It recognizes that crimes do not only affect individuals directly involved but also have a wider impact on the community as a whole.

Restorative Justice Practices

There are various restorative justice practices that can be applied to address interpersonal violence:

1. Victim-Offender Mediation: This involves a structured dialogue between the victim and the offender, facilitated by a trained mediator. The focus is on understanding the impact of the offense, addressing the needs of the victim, and finding ways for the offender to repair the harm caused.

2. Circles of Support and Accountability: This practice involves bringing together the victim, the offender, and members of the community to form a supportive network. The circle provides guidance, accountability, and resources for the offender while also addressing the needs of the victim.

3. Family Group Conferencing: In cases of domestic violence or child abuse, family members and support networks come together in a facilitated conference. The goal is to promote understanding, healing, and the development of a safety plan for all family members.

4. Victim-Offender Panels: These panels consist of community volunteers who meet with both the victim and the offender separately. They ask questions, gather information, and make recommendations to the court regarding appropriate restitution and support for the victim.

Potential Impact of Restorative Justice

Restorative justice has the potential to address interpersonal violence in a transformative way:

1. Healing and Empowerment: Restorative justice provides victims with a platform to share their experiences, be heard, and actively participate in the process. This can contribute to their healing and empowerment, allowing them to regain a sense of control over their lives.

2. Accountability and Rehabilitation: By focusing on offender accountability, restorative justice promotes personal growth, rehabilitation, and reintegration into the community. Offenders are given the opportunity to understand the impact of their actions and take steps towards making amends.

3. Community Reconciliation: Restorative justice involves the community in the process of addressing violence and promoting social cohesion. By actively participating in the healing and accountability process, community members can contribute to a safer and more inclusive society.

Challenges and Considerations

While restorative justice holds great promise, it also faces challenges and requires careful considerations:

1. Safety: It is crucial to ensure the physical and emotional safety of all parties involved. Qualified facilitators, risk assessments, and safety protocols must be in place to mitigate potential harm.

2. Power Imbalances: Restorative justice can be challenging when power imbalances exist between victims and offenders, such as in cases of domestic violence or sexual assault. Special care must be taken to ensure the empowerment and safety of victims throughout the process.

3. Support Services: Adequate support services must be available to both victims and offenders to address their individual needs, such as counseling, trauma-informed care, and rehabilitation programs.

4. Cultural Sensitivity: Restorative justice processes should be culturally sensitive and respectful of diverse backgrounds and experiences. This includes recognizing cultural norms, values, and traditions that may influence the process and outcomes.

Case Study: Restorative Justice in Action

One example of restorative justice in action is the Karamojong Peace and Reconciliation Initiative in Uganda. This initiative aims to address the cycle of violence and revenge among the Karamojong ethnic group. Through facilitated dialogues, community members come together to share their experiences, address grievances, and identify ways to restore peace and unity within the community. The process includes support for victims, initiatives for reintegration of offenders, and community-led projects for sustainable development.

Further Resources

1. The Little Book of Restorative Justice by Howard Zehr 2. Restorative Justice: Healing the Foundations of Our Everyday Lives by Evelyn Zellerer 3. Restorative Justice and Violence Against Women edited by James Ptacek 4. The International Institute for Restorative Practices (www.iirp.edu)

Exercises

1. Reflect on a personal experience with interpersonal violence and consider how a restorative justice approach could have potentially led to a different outcome.

2. Research a local restorative justice program or initiative and critically assess its effectiveness and impact on addressing interpersonal violence.

3. Imagine you are a facilitator in a victim-offender mediation session. Develop a plan of action and appropriate questions to promote dialogue, understanding, and accountability.

4. Discuss the potential benefits and challenges of implementing restorative justice practices in your local community. What resources and support would be required to ensure its successful implementation?

Conclusion

By addressing interpersonal violence through a restorative justice lens, we have the opportunity to shift the focus from punishment to healing and transformation. Restorative justice practices can provide victims with the support they need, hold offenders accountable, and foster community reconciliation. However, it is important to recognize the challenges and considerations involved in implementing restorative justice in cases of interpersonal violence. With a careful and thoughtful approach, restorative justice can contribute to a more just and peaceful society.

Restorative Justice and Healing in Marginalized Communities

Restorative justice is a transformative approach to the criminal justice system that focuses on repairing harm, reintegrating offenders, and healing communities. It recognizes that crime is not just a violation of laws but also a disruption of relationships and the well-being of individuals and communities. Restorative justice seeks to address these underlying issues by involving all stakeholders in the justice process and providing opportunities for healing.

In marginalized communities, where individuals often face social, economic, and political inequalities, restorative justice can have a profound impact. It offers an alternative to punitive measures that disproportionately affect marginalized individuals and communities. By centering the needs and voices of those affected by crime, restorative justice aims to establish a sense of empowerment, agency, and community well-being.

One of the key principles of restorative justice is inclusivity. It recognizes that marginalized communities have unique experiences and challenges that may require specific considerations within the restorative justice process. For example, individuals from marginalized communities may face systemic oppression, discrimination, and trauma, which can impact their experiences of crime and their ability to heal.

To ensure that restorative justice approaches are effective in marginalized communities, it is crucial to address the root causes of crime and the systemic barriers that perpetuate inequality. This requires acknowledging and challenging the power imbalances, biases, and discriminatory practices that may further marginalize individuals. It involves actively engaging community members, social service providers, and other stakeholders in the design and implementation of restorative justice programs.

Restorative justice practices in marginalized communities often emphasize healing and restoration. They aim to provide support and resources that promote healing and address the trauma experienced by victims and offenders. This may include access to counseling services, rehabilitation programs, employment assistance, educational opportunities, and community support networks. By focusing on healing, restorative justice recognizes the importance of holistic well-being in reducing recidivism and promoting long-term transformation.

Furthermore, restorative justice in marginalized communities recognizes the importance of cultural sensitivity and relevance. It acknowledges the unique cultural contexts, traditions, and values of these communities and seeks to incorporate them into the restorative justice process. This can be achieved by involving community leaders, elders, or cultural advisors who can provide guidance and ensure that the process respects cultural identities and practices.

An example of restorative justice in marginalized communities is the use of community circles. These circles bring together individuals affected by crime, such as victims, offenders, family members, and community members, to discuss the harm caused and how to repair it. In marginalized communities, these circles can be tailored to address the specific needs and challenges faced by community members. They may incorporate cultural practices, restorative rituals, or storytelling techniques that promote healing and reconciliation.

However, it is important to acknowledge the limitations and challenges of implementing restorative justice in marginalized communities. These communities may lack resources, infrastructure, or institutional support to fully implement and sustain restorative justice practices. Additionally, power dynamics and community divisions can hinder the effectiveness of restorative justice processes. Ongoing collaboration with community members and organizations is crucial for addressing these challenges and ensuring the success of restorative justice initiatives.

In conclusion, restorative justice has the potential to bring about transformative change in marginalized communities. By centering healing, empowerment, and community well-being, restorative justice can address the root causes of crime, challenge systemic inequalities, and promote long-term social transformation. However, it is essential to involve community members, address cultural sensitivity, and overcome structural barriers to ensure the inclusivity and effectiveness of restorative justice in marginalized communities.

Restorative Justice and Social Transformation

Restorative Justice and Social Inequality

Restorative justice is a transformative approach to criminal justice that focuses on repairing harm caused by crime, addressing the needs of the victim, and holding the offender accountable. It is based on the principles of inclusivity, empathy, and community engagement. Restorative justice seeks to challenge and transform the traditional criminal justice system, which often reinforces social inequalities and perpetuates cycles of violence and harm.

Understanding Social Inequality

Social inequality refers to the unequal distribution of resources, opportunities, and power within a society. It is shaped by various intersecting factors including race, ethnicity, gender, socioeconomic status, and sexual orientation. In many societies, marginalized and disadvantaged communities face disproportionate levels of poverty, limited access to education and healthcare, high rates of unemployment, and systemic discrimination within the justice system.

Restorative justice recognizes that social inequality can contribute to higher rates of crime and victimization within marginalized communities. It acknowledges that traditional punitive approaches to justice often exacerbate existing disparities and fail to address the underlying social, economic, and structural factors that contribute to crime. Instead, restorative justice offers an opportunity to address social inequality by promoting healing, empowerment, and community engagement.

Restorative Justice as a Tool for Social Transformation

Restorative justice aims to challenge and transform social inequality by addressing its root causes and empowering individuals and communities. It provides a platform for dialogue, understanding, and reconciliation between victims, offenders, and the community. By actively involving all stakeholders in the justice process, restorative justice seeks to create a sense of belonging, empathy, and shared responsibility.

Through restorative justice practices such as victim-offender mediation, family group conferencing, and community restorative boards, individuals can come together to discuss the harm caused by the crime, the needs of the victim, and the responsibility of the offender. This process allows for the recognition of the societal factors that contribute to crime, such as poverty, discrimination, and lack of social support. It also provides an opportunity for offenders to understand the impact of their actions, take responsibility, and actively participate in making amends.

Restorative justice actively involves the community in the justice process, recognizing that social transformation requires collective efforts. Community members play a vital role in providing support to victims, facilitating dialogue between victims and offenders, and assisting in the reintegration of offenders into society. Through community-based restorative justice programs, marginalized communities can gain agency and actively participate in decision-making processes that affect their lives.

Addressing Social Inequality in Restorative Justice Practices

To effectively address social inequality within the context of restorative justice, it is crucial to consider the specific needs and experiences of marginalized communities. This requires a commitment to cultural sensitivity, inclusivity, and intersectionality. Restorative justice practitioners must be mindful of the unique challenges faced by individuals from diverse backgrounds and ensure that their voices and experiences are heard and respected.

Victim-centered approaches in restorative justice must be designed to address the specific needs and vulnerabilities of marginalized victims. This may involve providing additional support services, such as counseling, healthcare, and housing assistance, to ensure that victims have the resources they need to heal and recover. It also requires recognizing the ways in which social inequality intersects with victimization, such as in cases of intimate partner violence, hate crimes, or systemic discrimination.

Similarly, restorative justice practices must address the social, economic, and educational barriers faced by marginalized offenders. This may involve providing access to education and vocational training, job placement assistance, and support in addressing substance abuse and mental health issues. By offering opportunities for personal growth, rehabilitation, and reintegration, restorative justice can play a vital role in breaking the cycle of crime and poverty.

Case Study: Restorative Justice and Social Inequality

One example of restorative justice addressing social inequality is the use of community-based restorative circles in an underserved neighborhood. This neighborhood has high rates of crime and poverty, and individuals often encounter significant barriers in accessing traditional justice systems. In response to these challenges, community members, local organizations, and justice practitioners came together to establish a restorative justice program.

In this program, community members actively participate in restorative circles, facilitated by trained practitioners. The circles provide a safe space for community members to discuss their collective experiences of harm and victimization, challenge harmful norms and power dynamics, and collectively identify strategies for healing and transformation. By centering the voices of marginalized individuals, the program seeks to address structural inequalities, build community resilience, and foster social cohesion.

This case study demonstrates the power of restorative justice in addressing social inequality by actively involving marginalized communities in the justice process. By recognizing and valuing the experiences and perspectives of those affected by crime, restorative justice offers an opportunity for social transformation and the creation of more just and inclusive societies.

Conclusion

Restorative justice has the potential to challenge and transform social inequality within the criminal justice system. By actively involving all stakeholders, promoting healing and reconciliation, and addressing the underlying causes of crime, restorative justice can contribute to the creation of more equitable and inclusive societies. However, it is essential to recognize the unique needs and experiences of marginalized individuals and communities and ensure that restorative justice practices are designed to address social inequalities in a comprehensive and meaningful way.

Further Resources

1. Bazemore, G. and Schiff, M. (Eds.). (2020). Restorative Community Justice: Repairing Harm and Transforming Communities. Routledge.
2. Braithwaite, J. (2017). Restorative Justice and Responsive Regulation. Oxford University Press.
3. McCold, P. (2018). Restorative Justice and Practices in New Zealand. In Handbook of Restorative Justice (pp. 168-182). Routledge.
4. Zehr, H. (2015). The Little Book of Restorative Justice. Good Books.
5. International Institute for Restorative Practices. (www.iirp.edu)

Restorative Justice and Gender-Based Violence

Restorative justice is a transformative approach to criminal justice that focuses on repairing harm caused by crime and addressing the needs of victims, offenders, and communities. It emphasizes accountability, dialogue, and the active involvement of all parties in finding ways to restore relationships and promote healing. When applied to cases of gender-based violence, restorative justice offers a unique and effective framework for addressing the complex dynamics and impacts of such violence.

Understanding Gender-Based Violence

Gender-based violence refers to any act that results in physical, sexual, or psychological harm or suffering that is directed against individuals based on their gender. This includes, but is not limited to, domestic violence, sexual assault, harassment, and human trafficking. Gender-based violence is a pervasive issue globally, affecting individuals from all walks of life. It is deeply rooted in gender inequality and power imbalances, perpetuated by harmful cultural norms and societal attitudes.

Principles of Restorative Justice in the Context of Gender-Based Violence

Restorative justice principles provide a guiding framework for addressing gender-based violence. These principles include:

1. Focus on the needs and experiences of victims: Restorative justice prioritizes the needs and voices of victims, allowing them to express their pain, seek acknowledgment from the offender, and play an active role in the decision-making process.

2. Offender accountability and responsibility: Restorative justice emphasizes the recognition of harm caused by the offender and promotes their accountability. It encourages offenders to take responsibility for their actions, understand the consequences, and engage in actions that contribute to repairing the harm.

3. Community involvement and support: Restorative justice recognizes that gender-based violence affects not only individuals directly involved but also the broader community. It encourages the involvement of community members in supporting victims, promoting healing, and holding offenders accountable.

4. Healing and transformation: Restorative justice seeks to foster healing for victims, offenders, and communities. It aims to address the underlying causes of gender-based violence, challenging harmful norms and contributing to the transformation of relationships and communities.

Restorative Justice Practices in Addressing Gender-Based Violence

Several restorative justice practices have been utilized to address gender-based violence, including:

1. Victim-Offender Dialogue: This form of restorative justice brings together victims and offenders in a facilitated dialogue. It provides victims with an opportunity to express their experiences and emotions, ask questions, and seek answers from the offender. Offenders, in turn, have the chance to take responsibility for their actions, express remorse, and work towards repairing the harm caused.

2. Circles of Support and Accountability: These circles bring together victims, offenders, and community members to provide support, guidance, and accountability. They aim to build a network of individuals committed to assisting the offender in reintegrating into the community while ensuring the safety and healing of the victim.

3. Restorative Conferences: These conferences involve the victim, offender, and their respective support networks, as well as community members and professionals. They provide a platform for facilitated dialogue, where the harm caused, consequences, and ways of repairing the harm are discussed. The focus is on finding mutually agreed-upon actions that address both the victim's needs and the offender's responsibility.

Challenges and Limitations

While restorative justice offers potential benefits in addressing gender-based violence, it also faces challenges and limitations. These include:

1. Power imbalances: Gender-based violence is rooted in power imbalances, and restorative justice processes must navigate these dynamics carefully to ensure the safety and empowerment of victims. Ensuring that victims have a genuine voice and decision-making power can be challenging, given the history of power and control in abusive relationships.

2. Secondary victimization: Encountering the offender in restorative justice processes may trigger feelings of fear, distress, or retraumatization for victims. It is crucial for facilitators to create a safe and supportive environment that prioritizes the well-being of victims throughout the process.

3. Cultural and contextual considerations: Restorative justice approaches must be mindful of cultural and contextual factors when addressing gender-based violence. Different communities may have varying perspectives on justice and

appropriate responses, requiring cultural competence and sensitivity in the design and implementation of restorative justice processes.

4. Survivor-centered approach: Restorative justice processes should always center the needs and well-being of survivors. It is essential to ensure that their participation is voluntary, informed, and supported by comprehensive services that address their immediate and long-term needs.

Example Case Study: Restorative Justice in Domestic Violence

In a case of domestic violence, restorative justice could involve a victim-offender dialogue facilitated by a trained mediator. The dialogue would provide the victim with an opportunity to share her experiences, express her emotions, and seek answers, while the offender would be encouraged to take responsibility for their actions, acknowledge the harm caused, and commit to actions that aim to repair the harm. The process would be guided by principles of safety, empowerment, and the survivor's autonomy to ensure her well-being throughout the restorative justice process.

Conclusion

Restorative justice has the potential to transform the response to gender-based violence by providing an alternative framework that prioritizes the needs of victims, promotes offender accountability, engages communities, and fosters healing and transformation. However, it is important to address the challenges and limitations to ensure the safety, empowerment, and well-being of survivors throughout the restorative justice process. As the field of restorative justice continues to evolve, it is crucial to learn from diverse experiences, adapt practices to different contexts, and work towards a justice system that truly meets the needs of survivors and facilitates social change.

Restorative Justice and Racial Justice

Restorative justice is a transformative approach to criminal justice that focuses on repairing harm caused by crime and restoring relationships between victims, offenders, and communities. It offers an alternative to traditional punitive justice systems by focusing on accountability, healing, and reconciliation. In the context of racial justice, restorative justice provides a framework for addressing the systemic and historical injustices faced by marginalized communities.

Understanding Racial Injustice

Racial injustice refers to the unfair treatment of individuals or groups based on their race or ethnicity. It encompasses systemic racism, discrimination, and the unequal distribution of resources and opportunities. These injustices are deeply rooted in history and have lasting effects on marginalized communities, perpetuating cycles of poverty, violence, and disenfranchisement.

To address racial injustice effectively, it is crucial to acknowledge the historical context and systemic nature of racism. Restorative justice offers a lens through which to examine the impact of racial injustice and explore pathways to reconciliation and healing.

Applying Restorative Justice to Racial Justice

Restorative justice provides a unique framework for addressing racial injustice by centering the needs and experiences of those affected by systemic racism. It aims to shift the focus from punishment to healing, dialogue, and accountability.

In the context of racial justice, restorative justice practices may include:

1. **Peacemaking Circles:** These circles bring together individuals from affected communities, including victims, offenders, and community members, to engage in open and honest dialogue. They provide a safe space to share experiences, explore the impact of racial injustice, and collectively develop solutions for healing and preventing future harm.

2. **Truth-telling Processes:** Truth-telling processes create opportunities for marginalized communities to share their stories and experiences with a wider audience. These processes expose the historical and ongoing injustices faced by marginalized communities, challenging societal narratives and promoting understanding and empathy.

3. **Community Healing Initiatives:** Restorative justice encourages the development of community-led healing initiatives targeted towards addressing the specific needs of marginalized communities. These initiatives may include trauma-informed programs, support services, and cultural revitalization efforts.

4. **Restorative Sentencing Practices:** In cases involving racial injustice, restorative sentencing practices prioritize repairing harm and seeking community-centered resolutions. They aim to address the underlying causes of the offense and promote the rehabilitation and reintegration of offenders into the affected communities.

Challenges and Considerations

Implementing restorative justice in the context of racial justice is not without its challenges. Some key considerations include:

- **Power Imbalances:** Restorative justice processes may not be effective if power imbalances between victims, offenders, and the community are not adequately addressed. Ensuring equal participation and meaningful engagement of all parties is essential for addressing racial injustice.

- **Trauma and Healing:** Restorative justice must recognize the impact of historical trauma on marginalized communities. Providing adequate support and resources for healing is crucial to the success of restorative justice initiatives.

- **Systemic Change:** Restorative justice alone cannot address the deep-rooted systemic issues that contribute to racial injustice. It should be complemented by efforts to challenge systemic inequalities and promote social, political, and economic reforms.

- **Community Engagement:** The success of restorative justice in addressing racial injustice relies on the active involvement and support of affected communities. Community-led initiatives and grassroots organizations play a vital role in shaping and implementing restorative justice practices.

Case Study: Community-Led Restorative Justice Initiatives

To further illustrate the potential impact of restorative justice on racial justice, let's consider the case study of a community-led restorative justice initiative in a historically marginalized neighborhood affected by racial profiling and discriminatory policing.

In this case, community members, including residents, activists, and local organizations, come together to develop and implement a restorative justice program. The program focuses on bringing police officers, victims of racial profiling, and community members into dialogue and promoting understanding. It aims to repair harm, rebuild trust, and work collaboratively to address racial injustice within the criminal justice system.

The restorative justice program includes regular community forums, police-community dialogues, and training sessions for police officers on understanding and addressing racial bias. It also incorporates mechanisms for police accountability and community oversight.

Through sustained dialogue and engagement, the program creates opportunities for healing, increased empathy, and accountability. It helps build relationships between law enforcement and the community, challenge implicit biases, and address the underlying causes of racial profiling.

Conclusion

Restorative justice offers a transformative approach to addressing racial injustice within the criminal justice system. By focusing on healing, accountability, and community engagement, it provides a framework for repairing harm caused by systemic racism and promoting racial justice.

Implementing restorative justice in the context of racial justice requires acknowledging historical injustices, addressing power imbalances, and supporting the healing and empowerment of marginalized communities. By combining restorative justice practices with broader systemic reforms, it is possible to create a more equitable and just society for all.

Restorative Justice and Victim Rights

Victim Participation in Restorative Justice Processes

Restorative justice is a transformative approach to criminal justice that focuses on repairing the harm caused by crime and promoting healing for all parties involved, including the victims, offenders, and the community. One crucial aspect of restorative justice is the active participation of victims in the decision-making process and the opportunity to have their voices heard.

Importance of Victim Participation

Victim participation is essential in restorative justice processes as it gives victims a sense of empowerment, validation, and closure. It acknowledges their experiences, needs, and desires for justice and allows them to have a direct say in the resolution of their cases. By involving victims in the decision-making process, restorative justice shifts the focus from punishment to addressing the harm caused, repairing relationships, and preventing future offenses.

Forms of Victim Participation

There are several ways in which victims can participate in restorative justice processes:

- **Pre-conference meetings:** Victims may have the opportunity to meet with trained facilitators or professionals before the restorative justice conference or circle. These meetings provide victims with a safe space to express their feelings and concerns, ask questions, and understand the process better. It helps them prepare for the conference and ensures their emotional well-being.

- **Participation in conferences or circles:** Victims are invited to participate in restorative justice conferences or circles alongside offenders, their supporters, and other stakeholders. They have the opportunity to share their experiences, express the impact of the crime on their lives, and ask questions directly to the offenders. This direct interaction can be a powerful and transformative experience for victims, providing them with a sense of closure and enabling them to hold the offenders accountable.

- **Safety precautions:** Victim participation should always prioritize the safety and well-being of the victims. In cases where the victims fear retaliation or face potential harm from the offenders, special measures need to be taken to ensure their safety. These measures can include separate sessions, the presence of support persons, or even the use of technology to facilitate communication without direct confrontation.

- **Follow-up support:** Restorative justice processes should provide victims with ongoing support, both during and after the conference or circle. This support can include access to counseling services, victim compensation resources, or referrals to community organizations that specialize in supporting crime victims.

Challenges and Considerations

While victim participation in restorative justice processes has numerous benefits, it also presents certain challenges and considerations that need to be addressed:

- **Trauma-informed approach:** Victims who choose to participate in restorative justice processes may have experienced significant trauma. It is crucial for practitioners to adopt a trauma-informed approach, ensuring that victims feel safe, supported, and in control throughout the process. This may involve providing information about the process, allowing breaks during the conference, and offering support services before, during, and after the restorative justice process.

- **Balancing offender-centered and victim-centered approaches:** Restorative justice seeks to address the needs of both the offender and the victim. Finding the right balance between the two is essential to ensure that victims' voices are heard and their experiences are validated while still providing opportunities for the offender's accountability and growth. Skilled facilitators are crucial in navigating this delicate balance.

- **Re-victimization concerns:** Victims may be concerned about the possibility of being re-victimized during the restorative justice process. It is important to create a supportive and respectful environment where victims feel heard and validated, providing them with a sense of control and ensuring their rights are protected.

- **Inequalities and power dynamics:** Restorative justice processes should address power imbalances and inequalities that may exist between victims and offenders. It is essential to ensure that victims have equal opportunities to participate and that their perspectives are valued. Restorative justice practitioners should actively work to create a safe and inclusive space for all participants.

Case Study: Victim-Offender Mediation

One common restorative justice process that involves victim participation is victim-offender mediation. In this process, victims and offenders come together, facilitated by trained mediators, to discuss the offense, its impact, and possible ways to repair the harm caused.

For example, let's consider a case of property theft. The victim, Olivia, had valuable items stolen from her home. Through victim-offender mediation, Olivia has the opportunity to express the emotional and financial impact of the theft directly to the offender, Michael. She can ask questions, seek explanations, and express her expectations for restitution or other forms of reparation.

By participating in the mediation process, Olivia gains a sense of closure by having her voice heard and seeing Michael take responsibility for his actions. On the other hand, Michael has the opportunity to understand the consequences of his behavior directly from Olivia, enabling him to develop empathy and a greater understanding of the harm caused.

This case study illustrates how victim-offender mediation provides an avenue for victims to actively participate in restorative justice processes, promoting healing, accountability, and ultimately, transformation.

Conclusion

Incorporating victim participation in restorative justice processes is crucial for fostering healing, empowerment, and a sense of justice for victims. By giving victims a voice, restorative justice aims to address the harm caused by crime and prevent its recurrence. However, it is essential to approach victim participation with care, ensuring trauma-informed practices, addressing power dynamics, and creating a safe and inclusive environment for all participants. Victim participation in restorative justice processes is an integral part of the transformative potential of this alternative approach to criminal justice.

Challenges and Limitations of Restorative Justice for Victims

Restorative justice is a transformative approach to criminal justice that emphasizes the needs of victims, the responsibility of offenders, and the healing of communities. While restorative justice has gained recognition for its potential to bring about positive outcomes, it also faces several challenges and limitations in practice. In this section, we will explore some of these challenges and limitations and discuss ways to address them.

1. Victim Participation and Voluntary Agreement

One challenge of restorative justice is ensuring meaningful victim participation in the process. Victims may have concerns about their safety, the power dynamics involved, or their emotional readiness to face the offender. It is crucial to create a supportive and safe environment that allows victims to freely express their feelings, needs, and concerns.

Additionally, the voluntary nature of restorative justice can be a limitation. Victims may be hesitant or unwilling to participate due to fear, distrust, or a desire for punitive measures. It is important to provide victims with sufficient information and support to make informed decisions about their involvement in the process.

To address these challenges, restorative justice programs should prioritize victim support services, providing information, counseling, and legal advice to victims. It is essential to ensure that victims have the necessary resources and options to fully participate in the process without feeling coerced or re-victimized.

2. Power Imbalance and Offender Accountability

Another challenge in restorative justice is the inherent power imbalance between victims and offenders. Victims may feel intimidated or powerless during face-to-face encounters with offenders, especially in cases involving serious crimes or situations of ongoing abuse. This power imbalance can hinder the effectiveness of the restorative justice process.

Addressing power imbalances requires careful facilitation and preparation. Skilled facilitators should ensure that communication is respectful, empathetic, and balanced. The focus should be on promoting understanding, acknowledging harm, and encouraging accountability, rather than retraumatizing the victim or allowing the offender to dictate the terms.

It is essential to establish clear guidelines and expectations for offender accountability. Offenders should take responsibility for their actions, acknowledge the harm caused, and actively work towards making amends. However, it is crucial to recognize that accountability might look different in each case, depending on the nature of the offense, the circumstances, and the availability of resources.

3. Scope and Limitations of Restorative Justice Practices

Restorative justice may not be suitable for all cases or all individuals involved. Serious crimes, cases involving chronic offenders, or situations where there is a significant power imbalance may present challenges for restorative justice. In some instances, a hybrid approach, combining elements of restorative justice and traditional criminal justice processes, may be more effective in addressing the complexity of the case.

Furthermore, restorative justice's effectiveness may vary depending on the cultural context, community support, and available resources. Culturally sensitive practices and approaches that respect diversity and promote inclusivity are crucial to ensure the participation and engagement of marginalized communities.

Balancing the principles of restorative justice with the need for public safety can also be challenging. It is essential to establish clear criteria for determining when restorative justice is appropriate and when alternatives may be necessary to ensure community safety and accountability.

4. Addressing Trauma and Emotional Impact

Restorative justice processes have the potential to trigger trauma responses in victims, particularly when facing the offender. Victims may experience anxiety, fear, or emotional distress during the process. Providing trauma-informed support and resources is critical to ensure the well-being of victims throughout their participation in restorative justice.

Skilled facilitators should be trained in trauma-informed approaches to create a safe and supportive environment during restorative justice encounters. This includes understanding the impact of trauma, providing emotional support, and recognizing the signs of distress. Additionally, access to counseling services and other support mechanisms should be readily available to victims throughout the process and beyond.

5. Overcoming Barriers and Promoting Accessibility

Restorative justice programs may face various barriers that limit their accessibility and effectiveness. Limited funding, lack of awareness, and insufficient resources can hinder the implementation and sustainability of restorative justice initiatives. It is crucial to advocate for increased support and funding to expand access to restorative justice programs and ensure their long-term success.

Furthermore, restorative justice should be accessible to all individuals, regardless of their socio-economic status, race, ethnicity, or other characteristics. Efforts should be made to address systemic biases and barriers that prevent marginalized communities from benefiting from restorative justice practices. This includes providing interpreter services, culturally appropriate practices, and considering the unique needs of diverse populations.

In conclusion, while restorative justice offers an alternative approach to the conventional criminal justice system, it faces several challenges and limitations. Ensuring meaningful victim participation, addressing power imbalances, determining the scope of application, addressing trauma, and promoting accessibility are crucial steps to overcome these challenges. By continuously evaluating and improving restorative justice practices, we can work towards a more equitable and transformative justice system.

Victim Empowerment and Restorative Justice

Restorative justice is a transformative approach to criminal justice that focuses on repairing harm caused by crime and restoring relationships among those affected. One key component of restorative justice is victim empowerment, which aims to give victims a greater role and voice in the criminal justice process. This section explores the concept of victim empowerment within the context of restorative justice, its principles, methods, challenges, and potential benefits.

Understanding Victim Empowerment

Victim empowerment refers to the process of enabling and supporting victims to actively participate in the decision-making process and to have a voice in their own case. This approach recognizes that victims are not merely passive recipients of justice, but active agents who should have a say in how justice is sought and achieved. Victim empowerment aims to address the power imbalance that often exists between victims and the criminal justice system, giving victims agency and control over their own healing and justice-seeking process.

The principles underlying victim empowerment in restorative justice include respect for victims' dignity, autonomy, and right to self-determination. It recognizes that victims have unique needs, concerns, and perspectives that should be taken into account when making decisions about case resolution and offender accountability. Victim empowerment also emphasizes collaboration between victims, offenders, and the community, encouraging open dialogue and the building of understanding and empathy.

Methods of Victim Empowerment in Restorative Justice

There are several methods employed within the restorative justice framework to empower victims and engage them in the process. These methods include:

1. Victim-Offender Mediation: Victim-offender mediation is a facilitated dialogue between the victim and the offender in the presence of a trained mediator. This process allows victims to directly express the impact of the crime on their lives, ask questions, seek answers, and receive an apology from the offender. By participating in this mediation, victims have the opportunity to share their feelings, concerns, and desires for redress.

2. Victim Impact Statements: Victim impact statements provide victims with a formal opportunity to share the physical, emotional, and financial impact of the crime on their lives. These statements are presented to the court during the sentencing phase, allowing victims to express their needs for restitution, compensation, or other forms of justice.

3. Circle Sentencing: Circle sentencing is a restorative justice practice that brings together the victim, offender, their supporters, and representatives from the community. In this process, victims have the opportunity to share their experiences and address the harm caused by the offense. Circle sentencing provides a space for victims to be heard and for offenders to take responsibility for their actions and make amends directly to those they have harmed.

4. Victim Support Services: Victim support services play a crucial role in empowering victims within the restorative justice process. These services provide emotional support, information, advocacy, and resources to assist victims in navigating the criminal justice system. By offering these supports, victims are better equipped to actively participate and make informed decisions about their case.

Challenges and Limitations

While victim empowerment in restorative justice is a transformative and promising approach, it is not without its challenges and limitations. Some of these challenges include:

1. Power Imbalance: Despite efforts to empower victims, power imbalances may persist within the restorative justice process. Victims may still feel overwhelmed or marginalized by the criminal justice system or find it difficult to fully participate due to fear, trauma, or power dynamics.

2. Offender Accountability: Restorative justice aims to involve both the victim and the offender in the process, which can raise concerns about the adequacy of offender accountability. Victims may worry that the focus on dialogue and understanding could detract from the need for punishment or rehabilitation of the offender.

3. Emotional Impact: Engaging in restorative justice processes can be emotionally challenging for victims, as it requires them to confront the harm caused by the offense and may trigger traumatic experiences. Adequate emotional support and resources must be provided to ensure the well-being of victims throughout the process.

4. Limited Applicability: Restorative justice may not be suitable for all types of crimes or all victims. Some offenses may be too severe or involve power dynamics

that make victim participation unsafe or impractical. It is essential to carefully assess the appropriateness of restorative justice approaches on a case-by-case basis.

Benefits of Victim Empowerment in Restorative Justice

Despite the challenges, victim empowerment within restorative justice offers several potential benefits:

1. Healing and Closure: Engaging in restorative justice processes can provide victims with a sense of healing and closure. By actively participating and having their voices heard, victims may find a sense of validation and satisfaction that is often lacking in traditional criminal justice proceedings.

2. Increased Satisfaction: Victims who participate in restorative justice processes often report higher levels of satisfaction compared to those who only go through the traditional system. This increased satisfaction is largely due to having greater control over the process, being able to express their needs, and witnessing the offender taking responsibility for their actions.

3. Reduced Trauma and Fear: Restorative justice processes can help alleviate some of the trauma and fear experienced by victims by providing a safe space for expression and the opportunity for dialogue and understanding. This can contribute to the overall well-being and healing of victims.

4. Community Engagement and Support: Victim empowerment within restorative justice encourages community involvement, providing victims with a network of support and understanding. The community plays a crucial role in facilitating the healing and reintegration of victims, offering resources, and creating a sense of belonging and support.

Conclusion

Victim empowerment is a fundamental aspect of restorative justice, aiming to give victims a greater role and voice in the criminal justice process. By actively involving victims and acknowledging their unique needs and perspectives, restorative justice offers the potential for healing, satisfaction, and increased accountability. However, challenges related to power dynamics, offender accountability, emotional impact, and limited applicability must be acknowledged and addressed to ensure the successful implementation of victim empowerment within restorative justice practices. Moving forward, continued research, evaluation, and collaboration are essential to further develop and refine empowering approaches that resonate with the diverse needs and experiences of victims.

Restorative Justice and Community Engagement

Community-Based Restorative Justice Programs

Community-based restorative justice programs play a crucial role in transforming the criminal justice system by focusing on repairing harm, healing relationships, and reintegrating offenders into society. These programs aim to address the underlying causes of crime and promote social justice through community engagement and empowerment. In this section, we will explore the principles, practices, and impact of community-based restorative justice programs.

Principles of Community-Based Restorative Justice

Community-based restorative justice programs are based on several core principles that guide their approach to addressing crime and conflict. These principles include:

1. **Community Engagement:** Restorative justice programs actively involve the community in the justice process. Community members are given a voice and have the opportunity to participate in decisions and actions that lead to healing and restoration.

2. **Victim-Centered Approach:** These programs prioritize the needs and perspectives of victims. They seek to empower victims by providing them with a safe space to share their experiences, express their emotions, and have a say in the resolution process.

3. **Offender Accountability:** Restorative justice programs emphasize the accountability of offenders. Offenders are encouraged to take responsibility for their actions, understand the impact of their behavior on victims and the community, and engage in activities that promote restitution and personal growth.

4. **Healing and Restoration:** The primary goal of community-based restorative justice programs is to heal the harm caused by the offense and restore the affected parties. This involves addressing the emotional, psychological, and social needs of both victims and offenders.

5. **Community Safety:** These programs aim to enhance community safety by addressing underlying issues that contribute to crime and conflict. By involving the community in the justice process, restorative justice programs seek to prevent future offenses and promote positive community development.

Practices in Community-Based Restorative Justice

Community-based restorative justice programs employ a variety of practices to facilitate dialogue, repair harm, and promote reconciliation. Some common practices include:

1. **Victim-Offender Mediation (VOM)**: VOM brings victims and offenders together in a controlled and facilitated setting to discuss the offense, its impact, and potential ways of repairing the harm. Trained mediators help facilitate communication and guide the dialogue towards a resolution that meets the needs of all parties involved.

2. **Community Conferences**: Community conferences bring together the victim, offender, their supporters, and community members affected by the offense. The conference provides an opportunity for all parties to express their perspectives, share their experiences, and collaboratively develop a plan for repair and reintegration.

3. **Circle Processes**: Restorative justice circles involve a group of participants, including victims, offenders, community members, and trained facilitators. The circle provides a safe space for participants to share their feelings, discuss the offense and its impact, and collectively develop solutions to address the harm caused.

4. **Restitution and Community Service**: Restorative justice programs often involve restitution and community service as a way for offenders to make amends and contribute positively to the community. Offenders may be required to compensate victims for their losses or engage in community service activities that benefit the community.

Impact and Benefits of Community-Based Restorative Justice

Community-based restorative justice programs have demonstrated several positive impacts and benefits, including:

1. **Victim Satisfaction and Empowerment**: Restorative justice processes give victims a voice and an active role in the justice process. This can lead to increased satisfaction with the outcomes and a sense of empowerment by being heard and having a say in the resolution.

2. **Reduced Recidivism**: Restorative justice programs have shown promise in reducing recidivism rates compared to traditional punitive approaches. By addressing the underlying causes of crime and promoting offender accountability, these programs help offenders reintegrate into society successfully.

3. **Community Cohesion and Inclusion**: Community involvement in the justice process fosters a sense of collective responsibility and promotes social cohesion. Restorative justice programs create opportunities for dialogue, understanding, and collaborative problem-solving, strengthening trust and relationships within the community.

4. **Cost-effectiveness:** Restorative justice programs can be more cost-effective compared to traditional criminal justice processes. By focusing on repairing harm and reintegrating offenders, these programs reduce the burden on the criminal justice system and contribute to long-term community safety.

Challenges and Considerations

Despite the numerous benefits, community-based restorative justice programs face several challenges and considerations. These include:

1. **Limited Awareness and Accessibility:** Many communities lack awareness of restorative justice programs or face barriers to accessing them. It is crucial to invest in public education and outreach to enhance community participation and ensure equitable access to these programs.

2. **Safeguarding Victim Rights:** It is essential to prioritize victim safety and well-being in restorative justice processes. This requires robust protocols and support services to ensure that victims feel safe, respected, and empowered throughout the process.

3. **Offender Compliance:** Restorative justice programs rely on voluntary offender participation and cooperation. Ensuring offender compliance and accountability can be challenging, requiring ongoing support and monitoring.

4. **Balancing Justice and Healing:** The balance between accountability and healing requires careful consideration. It is crucial to strike a balance between addressing the harms caused by the offense and meeting the needs of victims, offenders, and the community.

Resources for Further Study

To further explore community-based restorative justice programs, consider the following resources:

1. Books: - "The Little Book of Restorative Justice" by Howard Zehr - "Restorative Justice: Healing the Effects of Crime" by Mark Umbreit

2. Organizations: - International Institute for Restorative Practices (IIRP) - Restorative Justice International (RJI)

3. Research Articles: - McCold, P., & Wachtel, B. (2002). Restorative justice theory validation. Contemporary Justice Review, 5(1), 81-92. - Umbreit, M. S., Coates, R. B., & Vos, B. (2004). Victim meets offender: The impact of restorative justice and mediation. Criminal Justice and Behavior, 31(3), 279-299.

4. Online Resources: - Restorative Justice Online (www.restorativejustice.org) - Restorative Justice Resource Center (www.restorativejustice.org/resource-center)

Exercises

1. Interview a victim, an offender, or a participant in a community-based restorative justice program. Explore their perspectives on the process and its impact on their lives. 2. Organize a mock restorative justice conference or circle within your community or educational institution. Discuss a fictional offense and explore possible resolutions and outcomes. 3. Conduct a research project exploring the effectiveness of a community-based restorative justice program in your locality. Analyze recidivism rates and satisfaction levels of participants to assess the program's impact.

Conclusion

Community-based restorative justice programs offer a transformative approach to addressing crime and conflict. By prioritizing the needs of victims, promoting offender accountability, and involving the community, these programs foster healing, repair harm, and contribute to a more just and inclusive society. Through the principles, practices, and impact discussed in this section, we have gained insight into the potential of community-based restorative justice programs to transform the criminal justice system.

Restorative Justice and Community Policing

Restorative justice and community policing are two approaches that aim to transform the criminal justice system by emphasizing community involvement, accountability, and healing. While they have distinct goals and methods, there is overlap between these two approaches, as they both seek to address the underlying causes of crime and promote public safety.

Restorative Justice

Restorative justice is a philosophical framework and set of practices that focuses on repairing the harm caused by criminal behavior through dialogue, understanding, and making amends. It seeks to involve all stakeholders - victims, offenders, and the community - in a collaborative process aimed at achieving justice and healing.

Central to restorative justice is the idea that crime is not just a violation of the law, but also a violation of people and relationships. It recognizes that traditional criminal justice systems often fail to meet the needs of victims, fail to hold offenders accountable in a meaningful way, and fail to address the root causes of crime.

Restorative justice practices can take various forms, including victim-offender mediation, family group conferencing, and community circles. These processes provide opportunities for open dialogue, accountability, and the possibility of repairing harm. They focus on the needs of victims, empower them by giving them a voice and a sense of agency in the process, and offer offenders the opportunity to take responsibility for their actions and make amends.

Community Policing

Community policing is an approach to law enforcement that centers on building partnerships and collaborative problem-solving between law enforcement officers and the community they serve. It challenges the traditional reactive and authoritarian model of policing by fostering positive relationships, trust, and mutual respect between the police and the community.

The key principles of community policing include proactive engagement, problem-solving, community partnerships, and organizational transformation. It involves officers working closely with community members to identify and address the root causes of crime, develop tailored strategies, and implement preventive measures.

In community policing, police officers serve not only as law enforcers but also as problem-solvers and community facilitators. They collaborate with local residents, businesses, community organizations, and other stakeholders to collectively address crime, disorder, and other community concerns. This approach aims to enhance public safety, build social cohesion, and promote community well-being.

Integration of Restorative Justice and Community Policing

Restorative justice and community policing share a common goal of creating safe and healthy communities. There are opportunities for these two approaches to complement and reinforce each other in order to achieve transformative outcomes in the criminal justice system.

By integrating restorative justice practices into community policing efforts, law enforcement agencies can enhance their problem-solving abilities, establish stronger community connections, and address the root causes of crime. This can be done through the use of restorative justice conferences or circles as part of community policing initiatives. These processes can bring together affected parties, including victims, offenders, law enforcement officers, and community members, to collectively develop solutions and strategies for repairing harm, promoting healing, and preventing further crime.

Additionally, community policing principles can be incorporated into restorative justice processes to ensure that the broader community is involved in the restorative justice practices and that long-term community safety is addressed. Police officers can assist in facilitating restorative justice practices, providing support and resources, and helping to create an environment of trust and collaboration.

However, it is important to ensure that the integration of these approaches is done thoughtfully and with sensitivity to the needs and perspectives of all stakeholders. Proper training and education should be provided to law enforcement officers and community members to foster a deeper understanding of both restorative justice and community policing principles. Collaboration and ongoing dialogue between law enforcement agencies, community organizations, and practitioners in both fields is crucial to successfully implement and sustain these transformative approaches.

Case Study: Restorative Justice and Community Policing in Action

One example of the integration of restorative justice and community policing is the Youth Reconciliation Project (YRP) in Oakland, California. The YRP brings together representatives from various community organizations, law enforcement agencies, and schools to address youth violence through restorative justice and community policing strategies.

In the YRP, police officers work closely with community members, including young people who have been involved in violence, to develop relationships and trust. Through restorative justice practices, such as victim-offender mediation and community circles, the YRP aims to repair harm, promote healing, and reduce violence in the community.

The YRP focuses on addressing the underlying causes of youth violence, such as trauma, lack of opportunities, and community disinvestment. Police officers work collaboratively with community members to identify and implement preventive measures, such as mentorship programs, job placement services, and after-school activities.

The integration of restorative justice and community policing in the YRP has resulted in improved relationships between law enforcement officers and community members, increased trust and understanding, and a reduction in violence. This approach has also empowered young people to become agents of change in their communities and has provided them with the support and resources they need to break the cycle of violence.

Conclusion

Restorative justice and community policing offer transformative approaches to the criminal justice system that focus on healing, accountability, and community engagement. By integrating these approaches, law enforcement agencies can enhance their ability to address the underlying causes of crime, build trust and relationships with the community, and work towards long-term community safety and well-being.

Implementing restorative justice and community policing requires collaboration, training, and ongoing dialogue between law enforcement agencies, community organizations, and practitioners. By sharing innovative practices, lessons learned, and best practices, the field of transformative legal studies can contribute to the continued development and refinement of these approaches. Together, these approaches have the potential to create a criminal justice system that is more responsive, inclusive, and effective in promoting justice and community well-being.

Engaging Indigenous and Minority Communities in Restorative Justice

Restorative justice is an approach to criminal justice that seeks to repair the harm caused by crime by involving all affected parties in finding a resolution. It focuses on healing, reconciliation, and addressing the underlying causes of crime, rather than punishment alone. Engaging indigenous and minority communities in restorative justice is essential for promoting justice, equality, and community empowerment. This section explores the significance of involving these communities, challenges faced, and strategies to effectively engage them in restorative justice processes.

Understanding the Importance of Engaging Indigenous and Minority Communities

Indigenous and minority communities have often been disproportionately affected by the criminal justice system. Historical injustices, discrimination, cultural biases, and systemic inequalities have resulted in these communities facing higher rates of incarceration, over-policing, and limited access to justice. Engaging these communities in restorative justice is crucial for the following reasons:

1. **Cultural relevance:** Indigenous and minority communities have unique cultural values, practices, and traditions that differ from the mainstream justice system. By engaging these communities, restorative justice can be tailored to their

specific cultural needs and preferences, promoting a more meaningful and effective resolution.

2. **Community empowerment:** Restorative justice emphasizes community involvement and decision-making. Engaging indigenous and minority communities allows them to reclaim agency and actively participate in the justice process, leading to greater empowerment and ownership of the outcomes.

3. **Healing and reconciliation:** Restorative justice focuses on repairing harm and healing relationships. By involving indigenous and minority communities, it provides an opportunity for healing historical traumas, addressing systemic injustices, and fostering reconciliation between affected parties.

4. **Reducing recidivism:** Restorative justice approaches have shown promising results in reducing recidivism rates. Engaging indigenous and minority communities in restorative justice can address the underlying causes of crime within these communities, leading to long-term transformation and reduced reoffending.

Challenges of Engaging Indigenous and Minority Communities

Engaging indigenous and minority communities in restorative justice processes comes with unique challenges, including:

1. **Historical mistrust:** These communities may have a deep-rooted mistrust of the criminal justice system due to historical injustices and ongoing discrimination. Building trust and ensuring cultural sensitivity is crucial in overcoming this challenge.

2. **Language barriers:** Language barriers can hinder effective communication and understanding between community members and justice practitioners. Efforts should be made to provide interpretation services, translation of materials, and training for restorative justice facilitators to bridge this gap.

3. **Limited resources:** Indigenous and minority communities often face resource limitations, including access to legal support, trained facilitators, and community spaces to conduct restorative justice processes. Addressing these resource gaps is essential for meaningful engagement.

4. **Cultural competence:** Justice practitioners need to be culturally competent and knowledgeable about the specific needs and challenges faced by indigenous and minority communities. Training and education should be provided to ensure sensitivity and understanding while working with these communities.

Strategies for Engaging Indigenous and Minority Communities

To effectively engage indigenous and minority communities in restorative justice, the following strategies can be employed:

1. **Cultural awareness and sensitivity training:** Restorative justice practitioners should undergo cultural awareness and sensitivity training to better understand the experiences and needs of indigenous and minority communities. This training should cover topics such as intercultural communication, historical context, and cultural protocols.

2. **Community partnership and collaboration:** Building strong partnerships with indigenous and minority community leaders, organizations, and elders is vital. It allows for co-creation of restorative justice programs that align with the community's values and aspirations, ensuring their meaningful participation.

3. **Accessible and community-centered processes:** Restorative justice processes should be accessible, community-centered, and culturally appropriate. This may involve adapting traditional practices and incorporating community rituals, ceremonies, or storytelling into the process.

4. **Community capacity-building:** Investing in community capacity-building initiatives, such as training community members as restorative justice facilitators, can empower them to take an active role in addressing harm and resolving conflict within their own communities.

5. **Advocacy for policy changes:** Engaging indigenous and minority communities in restorative justice also requires advocating for policy changes to address systemic inequalities and barriers they face within the criminal justice system. This may involve reforming sentencing guidelines, promoting diversion programs, and ensuring culturally appropriate support services.

Case Studies: Engaging Indigenous and Minority Communities in Restorative Justice

1. **Maori Community Justice Panels in New Zealand:** The Maori Community Justice Panels in New Zealand involve elders and community members working alongside the formal justice system to address minor offenses committed by Maori individuals. The panels incorporate Maori cultural traditions, values, and language into the restorative justice process, leading to increased community involvement and better outcomes.

2. **First Nations Court in Canada:** The First Nations Court is a specialized court in Canada that incorporates indigenous traditions, language, and cultural practices into the sentencing and rehabilitation process for indigenous offenders.

The court provides opportunities for healing and reconnection with indigenous culture, leading to reduced recidivism rates and increased community support.

Conclusion

Engaging indigenous and minority communities in restorative justice is crucial for promoting justice, healing, and equality. By recognizing and addressing the unique needs and challenges faced by these communities, restorative justice can empower marginalized groups, foster community resilience, and create more equitable and transformative outcomes. Through cultural awareness, community partnerships, and capacity-building, restorative justice can pave the way for meaningful change in the criminal justice system.

Conclusion

Recapitulation of Key Points

In this chapter, we explored the transformative power of restorative justice in the field of criminal justice. We began by defining restorative justice and discussing its principles, highlighting its potential for repairing harm, promoting healing, and transforming individuals and communities affected by crime.

We examined various restorative justice practices, including victim-offender mediation, family group conferencing, and community restorative boards. These practices emphasize direct communication, accountability, and collaborative decision-making, allowing for the active participation of all stakeholders affected by a crime.

Furthermore, we discussed the application of restorative justice within different aspects of the criminal justice system. We explored its potential in sentencing, juvenile justice, and in addressing the needs of incarcerated individuals during reentry into society. By focusing on repairing relationships and addressing underlying causes of crime, restorative justice offers an alternative approach to traditional punitive measures.

One significant aspect we explored is the relationship between restorative justice and healing. We highlighted the importance of trauma-informed restorative justice, recognizing that individuals impacted by crime often experience long-lasting emotional and psychological effects. Restorative justice provides a space for healing, allowing victims and offenders to address the root causes of harm and work towards restoring their well-being.

We also examined the transformative potential of restorative justice in addressing social inequality. By emphasizing inclusivity and engaging marginalized communities, restorative justice can challenge systemic biases within the criminal justice system. We explored the intersectionality between restorative justice and issues such as gender-based violence and racial justice, highlighting how restorative justice can contribute to social change.

Another key focus of this chapter was the role of victims in restorative justice processes. We discussed the importance of victim participation and empowerment, as well as the challenges and limitations that victims may encounter within restorative justice systems. Restorative justice seeks to prioritize the needs and voices of victims, ensuring their rights are respected and their healing is supported.

Furthermore, we explored the role of community engagement in restorative justice. Community-based restorative justice programs and collaboration with law enforcement agencies can foster trust, strengthen social bonds, and promote a sense of belonging. We also emphasized the importance of engaging indigenous and minority communities, recognizing and respecting their unique perspectives and legal systems.

In conclusion, restorative justice offers a transformative approach to criminal justice, focusing on repairing harm, promoting healing, and building stronger, more inclusive communities. By centering the needs and voices of victims, empowering offenders to take responsibility for their actions, and engaging communities in the process, restorative justice has the potential to challenge traditional punitive approaches and contribute to a more just and equitable society.

Key Takeaways:

- Restorative justice emphasizes repairing harm, promoting healing, and transforming individuals and communities affected by crime.

- Practices such as victim-offender mediation, family group conferencing, and community restorative boards facilitate direct communication, accountability, and collaborative decision-making.

- Restorative justice can be applied in various aspects of the criminal justice system, including sentencing, juvenile justice, and reentry programs.

- Trauma-informed restorative justice recognizes the long-lasting effects of crime and prioritizes healing for all parties involved.

- Restorative justice has the potential to address social inequality, particularly in the context of gender-based violence and racial justice.

- Victim participation and empowerment are crucial elements of restorative justice, although challenges and limitations exist.

- Community engagement, including community-based programs and collaboration with indigenous and minority communities, strengthens the transformative impact of restorative justice.

Implications for Transformative Criminal Justice

The exploration of restorative justice in this chapter has several implications for the field of criminal justice. By embracing a transformative approach, criminal justice systems can strive for the following:

1. **Balancing Accountability and Healing:** Restorative justice provides a framework for balancing the need for accountability with the imperative of healing and repairing harm. It encourages offenders to take responsibility for their actions, understand the impact of their behavior, and actively participate in making amends.

2. **Creating Safe and Inclusive Spaces:** Restorative justice practices promote safe and inclusive spaces for dialogue, empathy, and understanding. By prioritizing the needs and voices of victims, as well as engaging the community, restorative justice can challenge existing power dynamics and build trust within the criminal justice system.

3. **Addressing Root Causes of Crime:** Restorative justice encourages a deeper understanding of underlying causes of crime, such as trauma, socioeconomic factors, and community challenges. By addressing these root causes, rather than solely focusing on punishment, restorative justice seeks to prevent future harm and reduce recidivism rates.

4. **Transforming the Role of Criminal Justice Professionals:** Restorative justice requires a shift in the roles and responsibilities of criminal justice professionals. It calls for greater emphasis on facilitation and support rather than solely punishment. This transformative approach necessitates training and education for professionals to effectively implement restorative justice practices.

5. **Partnering with Community Organizations:** Restorative justice requires collaboration with community organizations, non-governmental organizations (NGOs), and other stakeholders. By partnering with these

entities, criminal justice systems can leverage community resources and expertise, fostering a collective approach towards justice and healing.

Future Directions in Restorative Justice

While restorative justice has shown great promise, there are ongoing challenges and areas for further development. Future directions in restorative justice include:

1. **Standardization and Quality Assurance:** As restorative justice continues to expand, there is a need for standardized practices and quality assurance mechanisms. Developing consistent guidelines, training programs, and evaluation frameworks can ensure the integrity and effectiveness of restorative justice practices.

2. **Addressing Power Imbalances:** Restorative justice must navigate power imbalances between parties involved, particularly victims and offenders. Future developments should explore strategies to address and mitigate power differentials, ensuring that the process remains fair, safe, and equitable for all participants.

3. **Inclusion of Marginalized Communities:** Efforts should be made to increase the accessibility of restorative justice for marginalized communities. This includes recognizing and respecting the unique needs and perspectives of indigenous communities, ethnic minorities, and individuals with disabilities. Tailoring restorative justice practices to specific cultural contexts and collaborating with community leaders can foster greater inclusivity.

4. **Research and Evidence-based Practice:** Continued research is crucial for the advancement of restorative justice. Studies examining the long-term outcomes, cost-effectiveness, and best practices can inform evidence-based policy development and improve the implementation of restorative justice programs.

5. **Legislative Support and Policy Reform:** Restorative justice requires a supportive legislative and policy framework to thrive. Advocacy efforts should focus on integrating restorative justice principles into existing criminal justice systems and laws. This includes considering the appropriate role of restorative justice within the broader legal framework.

By addressing these future directions, the field of restorative justice can continue to evolve, adapt, and contribute to the transformation of criminal justice systems worldwide.

Resources for Further Study

Further study in the field of restorative justice and transformative criminal justice can be pursued through the following resources:

- **Books:**
    1. "The Little Book of Restorative Justice" by Howard Zehr
    2. "Restorative Justice: Healing the Foundations of Our Everyday Lives" by Mark Umbreit
    3. "The Handbook of Restorative Justice" edited by Gerry Johnstone and Daniel Van Ness

- **Academic Journals:**
    1. International Journal of Restorative Justice
    2. Contemporary Justice Review
    3. Restorative Justice: An International Journal

- **Organizations:**
    1. International Institute for Restorative Practices (IIRP) - https://www.iirp.edu/
    2. Restorative Justice Council - https://restorativejustice.org.uk/
    3. Center for Justice and Reconciliation - https://emu.edu/cjp/cjr/

- **Online Resources:**
    1. Restorative Justice Online - https://www.restorativejustice.org/
    2. United Nations Rule of Law: Restorative Justice - https://www.un.org/ruleoflaw/thematic-areas/restorative-justice/
    3. National Association of Community and Restorative Justice - https://nacrj.org/

These resources provide a comprehensive foundation for further exploration and engagement with the field of restorative justice, facilitating ongoing learning and development in transformative criminal justice.

Implications for Transformative Criminal Justice

The transformative approaches to criminal justice explored in this chapter have significant implications for the future of the field. By shifting the focus from punishment to healing and social transformation, these approaches have the potential to address the root causes of crime and reduce recidivism rates. This section will discuss the key implications of transformative criminal justice and highlight their importance in promoting justice and equality.

1. Empowering Victims and Promoting Healing

One of the main implications of transformative criminal justice is the empowerment of victims and the focus on promoting healing. Traditional criminal justice systems often neglect the needs of victims and prioritize punishment over their well-being. In contrast, transformative justice seeks to create a safe and supportive environment for victims, where their voices are heard, and their healing process is prioritized.

By incorporating restorative justice practices, such as victim-offender mediation and family group conferencing, transformative criminal justice provides opportunities for victims to participate in the resolution process, express their emotions, and seek closure. This approach acknowledges the long-term impact of crime on victims and aims to restore their sense of dignity and agency.

2. Addressing the Root Causes of Crime

Transformative criminal justice recognizes that punishment alone does little to address the root causes of crime. Instead, it emphasizes the importance of understanding the underlying social, economic, and environmental factors that contribute to criminal behavior. By focusing on prevention and rehabilitation, transformative justice seeks to break the cycle of crime and create safer communities.

This approach requires a holistic understanding of individuals involved in the criminal justice system, taking into account their personal history, socio-economic background, and access to opportunities. By addressing these systemic issues, transformative criminal justice aims to create conditions that reduce the likelihood of crime and promote social equity.

3. Restorative Approaches to Offenders

Traditional criminal justice systems often treat offenders as isolated individuals to be punished and removed from society. In contrast, transformative criminal justice recognizes that offenders are members of communities and should be held accountable in ways that promote personal growth and reintegration.

Restorative justice practices, such as victim-offender mediation and community conferencing, allow offenders to take responsibility for their actions, understand the harm caused, and make amends directly to those affected. By engaging with victims and the community, offenders have an opportunity to develop empathy, learn from their mistakes, and reintegrate into society.

4. Community Engagement and Collaboration

Transformative criminal justice emphasizes the importance of community engagement and collaboration in addressing crime and promoting social transformation. This approach recognizes that communities are directly affected by crime and should play an active role in the justice process.

Community-based restorative justice programs and community policing initiatives involve the community in prevention, intervention, and rehabilitation efforts. By partnering with various stakeholders, such as neighborhood organizations, schools, and local authorities, transformative criminal justice fosters a sense of ownership and collective responsibility for creating safer and more equitable communities.

5. Alternative Approaches to Sentencing

Traditional criminal justice systems often rely heavily on incarceration as a form of punishment. However, transformative criminal justice challenges this reliance by exploring alternative approaches to sentencing that prioritize rehabilitation, restoration, and community involvement.

For example, restorative justice practices offer alternatives to incarceration, such as community service, mediation, or restitution, which allow offenders to make amends while remaining connected to their communities. These alternatives not only promote the reintegration of offenders but also reduce the financial and social costs associated with incarceration.

6. Advancing Social and Racial Justice

Transformative criminal justice is closely intertwined with broader social and racial justice movements. It highlights the disparities within the criminal justice system and seeks to address systemic inequalities that disproportionately affect marginalized communities.

By prioritizing victim empowerment, addressing root causes of crime, and promoting community engagement, transformative criminal justice aims to create a more equitable and just society. This approach challenges the biases and discrimination embedded in the traditional criminal justice system and promotes equal treatment and opportunities for all individuals, regardless of their race or socio-economic status.

Conclusion

The implications of transformative criminal justice are far-reaching and have the potential to reshape the field of criminal justice. By empowering victims, addressing the root causes of crime, promoting healing and rehabilitation, and engaging with communities, transformative criminal justice promotes a more inclusive, equitable, and effective approach to addressing and preventing crime.

Transformative criminal justice emphasizes the importance of restorative practices, community collaboration, and alternative sentencing approaches. By adopting these principles, the criminal justice system can become a catalyst for social transformation, promoting healing, justice, and social equality. It is essential for policymakers, practitioners, and society as a whole to embrace these implications and work towards a more transformative and just criminal justice system.

Future Directions in Restorative Justice

Restorative justice has emerged as a transformative approach to criminal justice, emphasizing healing, accountability, and reconciliation. As the field continues to evolve, there are several exciting future directions that hold great potential for further transformation.

Expanding Restorative Justice Practices

One future direction is the expansion of restorative justice practices beyond the traditional criminal justice system. While restorative justice has been primarily utilized in response to criminal offenses, there is a growing recognition of its potential in other areas of social conflict. Restorative practices can be applied to address workplace disputes, school discipline issues, community conflicts, and even international conflicts.

For example, restorative approaches can be integrated into schools to resolve conflicts between students, promote inclusive and safe learning environments, and reduce the school-to-prison pipeline. Restorative practices can also be used in community settings to address conflicts between neighbors, promote healing after incidents of violence, and strengthen community bonds.

Addressing Power Imbalances

Another crucial future direction for restorative justice is the ongoing work to address power imbalances within the process. Restorative justice recognizes the importance of equal participation and input from all parties involved in the harm and conflict. However, power dynamics, such as those based on race, gender, and socio-economic status, can still influence the outcomes of restorative processes.

Efforts should be made to ensure that marginalized and vulnerable individuals have a voice and are not further marginalized within restorative justice processes. This can be achieved through the inclusion of trained facilitators who are sensitive to power dynamics and through active efforts to ensure diverse representation in decision-making processes.

Research and Evaluation

To further strengthen restorative justice practices, future directions should prioritize research and evaluation efforts. Rigorous research can provide evidence of the effectiveness of restorative justice interventions, identify best practices, and guide policy decisions. Evaluation can also contribute to ongoing improvement and refinement of restorative justice processes.

Longitudinal studies can assess the long-term impact of restorative justice practices on recidivism rates, victim satisfaction, and community healing. Comparative studies can examine the effectiveness of different restorative models and approaches in diverse cultural and legal contexts. Additionally, research can explore the benefits of combining restorative justice with other approaches, such as trauma-informed care and mental health support.

International Collaboration

As restorative justice continues to gain global recognition, international collaboration is another important future direction. Knowledge sharing and collaboration between countries and legal systems can foster the development of innovative restorative justice practices and policies. It can also contribute to the development of international standards and guidelines for restorative justice implementation.

International collaboration can involve the exchange of experiences, training programs, and research findings. It can also provide opportunities for cross-cultural learning and adaptation of restorative practices to suit diverse contexts. Such collaboration is essential for advancing the global understanding and application of restorative justice principles.

Restorative Justice and Technology

The integration of technology into restorative justice processes is an emerging future direction that holds significant potential. Technology can enhance accessibility, efficiency, and effectiveness of restorative justice interventions.

Online platforms can facilitate communication and participation in restorative processes, particularly in cases involving remote or geographically dispersed participants. Virtual mediation sessions can provide a flexible and convenient alternative to in-person meetings. Additionally, technology can assist in record-keeping and data management, ensuring accurate and secure documentation of restorative justice processes.

However, it is crucial to navigate the ethical considerations and potential pitfalls of technology in restorative justice. Attention must be given to issues of privacy, security, and the potential for further marginalization of vulnerable populations. Guidelines and standards should be established to ensure responsible and inclusive use of technology in restorative justice practices.

Building Restorative Communities

A transformative future direction for restorative justice is the building of restorative communities. Restorative justice can be seen as not just a response to individual incidents of harm but as a long-term approach to community engagement, healing, and conflict resolution.

By incorporating the principles and practices of restorative justice into everyday life, communities can create environments that prioritize accountability, empathy, and healing. Restorative justice principles can guide community organizations, social services, and local governance structures, promoting community well-being and social cohesion.

Building restorative communities requires education, awareness, and the active involvement of individuals, organizations, and institutions. It involves fostering a culture of dialogue, respect, and responsibility. Restorative justice can provide a framework for community members to collectively address social injustices, prevent conflicts, and repair harm.

Conclusion

The future of restorative justice holds immense potential for further transformation of the criminal justice system and beyond. Expanding restorative justice practices, addressing power imbalances, promoting research and evaluation, fostering international collaboration, integrating technology, and building restorative communities are all critical future directions.

By embracing these future directions, we can continue to advance the principles of healing, accountability, and reconciliation in our pursuit of justice. Restorative justice has the power to reshape our understanding of justice, promote social equity, and contribute to a more compassionate and harmonious society. Its future is promising, and it is up to us to take the necessary steps to fully realize its transformative potential.

Chapter 8: Transformative Approaches to Human Rights Law

Chapter 8: Transformative Approaches to Human Rights Law

Chapter 8: Transformative Approaches to Human Rights Law

In this chapter, we will explore the transformative approaches to human rights law, focusing on the principles, theories, and practices that contribute to the advancement of human rights and social justice. Human rights law is a crucial field that seeks to protect and promote the inherent dignity and equal rights of all individuals. However, traditional legal approaches often fall short in addressing systemic inequalities and structural barriers to equality. Transformative legal approaches provide alternative frameworks to challenge and overcome these limitations, aiming to create a more just and equitable society.

Overview of Human Rights Law

Human rights law is a branch of international law that establishes the rights and freedoms to which all individuals are entitled, regardless of their nationality, race, gender, or other characteristics. These rights are enshrined in various international and regional human rights instruments, such as the Universal Declaration of Human Rights, the International Covenant on Civil and Political Rights, and the International Covenant on Economic, Social and Cultural Rights.

The core principles of human rights law include universality, indivisibility, and interdependence. Universality emphasizes that human rights apply to all individuals, irrespective of their background or status. Indivisibility recognizes that civil, political, economic, social, and cultural rights are interconnected and mutually reinforcing. Interdependence acknowledges that the realization of one right often depends on the fulfillment of other rights.

Human Rights and Social Justice

Transformative approaches to human rights law go beyond the traditional understanding of human rights as merely legal provisions. They recognize the inherent link between human rights and social justice, aiming to address the root causes of inequality and systemic injustices. Social justice perspectives emphasize the redistribution of power, resources, and opportunities to create a more equitable society.

Through transformative approaches, human rights advocates seek to challenge and transform discriminatory structures and practices, ensuring equal rights and justice for all. They engage in advocacy, social movements, and strategic litigation to challenge unjust laws and policies, promote social inclusion, and empower marginalized communities. By addressing the structural barriers to equality, transformative approaches contribute to building a more inclusive and just society.

Incorporating Intersectionality in Human Rights Law

One of the key concepts in transformative approaches to human rights law is intersectionality. Intersectionality recognizes that individuals hold multiple social identities and that they experience oppression and discrimination at the intersection of these identities. Traditional human rights frameworks often fail to address the unique challenges faced by individuals who face discrimination based on multiple aspects of their identity, such as race, gender, sexuality, disability, or social class.

To apply intersectionality to human rights law, it is essential to examine the interconnected and overlapping forms of discrimination experienced by individuals. This requires an understanding of the unique experiences and needs of diverse communities. By incorporating intersectional perspectives into human rights advocacy and legal frameworks, transformative approaches ensure that the rights and needs of marginalized communities are fully recognized and protected.

Transformative Legal Strategies for Gender Justice

Transformative approaches to human rights law play a significant role in advancing gender justice. By challenging gender norms, discriminatory practices, and unequal power structures, these approaches seek to address gender inequality and promote gender justice. They recognize the importance of gender mainstreaming and ensuring that gender perspectives are integrated into all areas of law and policy.

Transformative legal strategies for gender justice encompass a range of actions, including challenging discriminatory laws, advocating for women's reproductive rights, addressing gender-based violence, promoting equal pay and opportunities in the workplace, and advancing LGBTQ+ rights. These strategies aim to dismantle the deeply rooted gender inequalities and norms that perpetuate discrimination and violence.

Social and Economic Rights as Transformative Tools

In addition to civil and political rights, transformative approaches to human rights law also emphasize the importance of social and economic rights. Social and economic rights, such as the right to education, healthcare, housing, and a decent standard of living, are essential for ensuring human dignity and well-being. These rights are crucial for addressing social inequality and contributing to transformative change.

Transformative legal approaches use social and economic rights as tools to challenge systemic injustices and advocate for inclusive policies and practices. They aim to ensure that marginalized communities have equal access to essential services and opportunities, thereby reducing the disparities caused by socioeconomic factors. By advocating for the realization of social and economic rights, transformative approaches contribute to addressing poverty, inequality, and social exclusion.

Promoting Human Rights through Corporate Accountability

Another aspect of transformative approaches to human rights law is the recognition of the role of corporations in promoting or undermining human rights. Corporate accountability is a crucial element in ensuring the protection of human rights, particularly in the context of globalization and multinational corporations' increasing influence.

Transformative legal approaches advocate for strong regulations and accountability mechanisms that hold corporations responsible for their impact on human rights. This includes addressing labor rights violations, environmental degradation, and human rights abuses in supply chains. By promoting corporate accountability, transformative approaches seek to protect the rights of workers, communities, and vulnerable populations affected by corporate activities.

Conclusion

Transformative approaches to human rights law provide alternative frameworks to address systemic inequalities and promote social justice. By incorporating principles such as intersectionality and social and economic rights, these approaches challenge discriminatory structures and practices. They advocate for the rights and needs of marginalized communities, empower individuals to demand justice, and promote inclusive policies and practices. Through transformative strategies, human rights law can contribute to creating a more just and equitable society for all.

Human Rights Law and Social Justice

Overview of Human Rights Law

Human rights law is a branch of international law that is concerned with protecting the fundamental rights and freedoms of individuals. It encompasses a wide range of legal principles and standards which aim to promote and safeguard the inherent dignity and worth of all human beings. This section provides an overview of human rights law, including its historical development, key principles, and the international mechanisms for its enforcement.

Historical Development of Human Rights Law

The concept of human rights can be traced back to ancient civilizations and religious teachings, which emphasized the inherent value and equal worth of every individual. However, it was not until the aftermath of World War II that the international community rallied to develop a comprehensive framework for the protection of human rights.

The Universal Declaration of Human Rights (UDHR), adopted by the United Nations General Assembly in 1948, is widely regarded as a landmark document in the development of human rights law. It sets out a broad range of civil, political, economic, social, and cultural rights that should be universally protected. The UDHR serves as a moral, political, and legal foundation for subsequent human rights instruments.

Building upon the UDHR, a series of international human rights treaties and conventions have been adopted to further elaborate and codify human rights norms. These include the International Covenant on Civil and Political Rights (ICCPR), the International Covenant on Economic, Social and Cultural Rights (ICESCR), the Convention on the Elimination of All Forms of Discrimination Against Women (CEDAW), and the Convention on the Rights of the Child (CRC), among others.

Key Principles of Human Rights Law

At the core of human rights law are a set of fundamental principles that guide its interpretation and application. These principles include:

- Universality and inalienability: Human rights are inherent to all individuals, regardless of their nationality, race, gender, or any other status. They cannot be taken away or surrendered.

- Equality and non-discrimination: Every person is entitled to the equal enjoyment of their rights and freedoms without any distinction or discrimination. States must ensure that all individuals are protected from any form of discrimination.

- Human dignity: Human rights law recognizes and seeks to protect the inherent dignity and worth of every human being. States have a duty to respect, protect, and fulfill human rights to uphold human dignity.

- Rule of law: Human rights are grounded in the rule of law. States have an obligation to ensure the effective implementation and enforcement of human rights standards through legal and institutional mechanisms.

- Accountability and remedies: Violations of human rights must be effectively investigated, and victims must have access to adequate remedies and redress. States are responsible for providing reparations and ensuring accountability for human rights abuses.

International Mechanisms for Human Rights Protection

To promote and protect human rights at the international level, several key mechanisms and institutions have been established:

- United Nations Human Rights Council: The Human Rights Council is the primary intergovernmental body responsible for promoting and protecting human rights worldwide. It monitors the human rights situations in different countries, conducts inquiries, and adopts resolutions addressing human rights issues.

- Treaty-based bodies: The human rights treaties, such as the ICCPR and ICESCR, have their own monitoring bodies known as treaty-based committees. These committees review states' reports, issue recommendations, and interpret the provisions of the respective treaties.

- Special procedures: The Human Rights Council appoints independent experts, also known as special rapporteurs, to examine and report on specific human rights issues or country situations. They undertake fact-finding missions, receive complaints, and provide recommendations.

- International and regional courts and tribunals: International courts and tribunals, such as the International Court of Justice, the International Criminal Court, and regional human rights courts (e.g., the European Court of Human Rights), adjudicate individual complaints and cases of human rights violations.

- National human rights institutions: Many countries have established national human rights institutions to promote and protect human rights at the domestic level. These institutions monitor human rights situations, receive complaints, and provide advice and assistance to individuals.

These international mechanisms play a crucial role in upholding human rights standards, ensuring compliance with international obligations, and providing remedies for victims of human rights violations.

Challenges and Future Outlook

While significant progress has been made in the development and protection of human rights, challenges persist. Human rights violations continue to occur in various parts of the world, often as a result of discrimination, conflict, inequality, and lack of effective implementation of human rights standards.

Emerging challenges, such as the impact of new technologies on privacy and freedom of expression, climate change, and the rights of vulnerable groups, require innovative and transformative responses. Human rights law needs to adapt and evolve to address these challenges and protect the rights of individuals in an increasingly complex and interconnected world.

The future of human rights law lies in continued efforts to promote awareness, encourage compliance with human rights standards, and enhance accountability for human rights violations. It also requires the active participation and engagement of individuals, civil society organizations, governments, and international institutions in promoting and protecting human rights for all.

Historical Development of Human Rights Law

The historical development of human rights law is a fascinating journey that spans centuries and continents. It is a story of progress, setbacks, and the tireless efforts of individuals and communities to uphold the inherent dignity and rights of every human being. In this section, we will explore the key milestones and events that have shaped the evolution of human rights law, leading to the development of the robust framework that exists today.

Early Influences on Human Rights

The roots of human rights can be traced back to ancient civilizations and philosophical traditions that recognized the fundamental rights of individuals. For instance, the Code of Hammurabi in ancient Mesopotamia (approximately 1754 BCE) established a set of laws that aimed to promote justice and protect the vulnerable. Similarly, ancient Greek and Roman thinkers, such as Aristotle and Cicero, emphasized the importance of equal treatment and fairness.

In the Judeo-Christian tradition, principles of justice, compassion, and human dignity laid the groundwork for the concept of human rights. The Ten Commandments, for example, emphasize the sanctity of life, promote respect for others, and condemn acts of violence and oppression.

Emergence of Modern Human Rights

The modern era of human rights began to take shape with the Enlightenment in the 18th century. The ideas of thinkers such as John Locke, Jean-Jacques Rousseau, and Voltaire emphasized individual liberty, equality, and the social contract between the governed and the governing authorities.

The American and French Revolutions of the late 18th century further propelled the recognition of human rights. The United States Declaration of Independence (1776) proclaimed that "all men are created equal" and possess certain unalienable rights, including life, liberty, and the pursuit of happiness. In France, the Declaration of the Rights of Man and of the Citizen (1789) affirmed the rights of individuals and served as an inspiration for subsequent human rights movements.

International Humanitarian Law

The emergence of international humanitarian law in the 19th century marked another significant milestone in the development of human rights. Influenced by the horrors of warfare, efforts were made to establish rules and regulations to protect the rights of individuals affected by armed conflicts. The Geneva Conventions of 1864, which established rules for the humane treatment of wounded soldiers, laid the foundation for the later development of international humanitarian law.

Universal Declaration of Human Rights

The most significant leap in the field of human rights came with the adoption of the Universal Declaration of Human Rights (UDHR) by the United Nations General Assembly in 1948. In the aftermath of World War II and the atrocities committed during the Holocaust, the international community recognized the urgent need to safeguard human rights and prevent future atrocities.

The UDHR enshrined a comprehensive set of civil, political, economic, social, and cultural rights that are universally applicable. It recognized the inherent dignity and equal worth of all individuals, regardless of race, color, sex, language, religion, political or other opinion, national or social origin, property, birth, or other status. The UDHR has served as the foundation for subsequent human rights treaties and declarations.

Civil and Political Rights Treaties

Building on the principles established by the UDHR, several international treaties were developed to protect and promote civil and political rights. For example, the International Covenant on Civil and Political Rights (ICCPR) was adopted in 1966 and has been ratified by numerous countries. It guarantees individuals the right to life, liberty, and security of person; freedom of thought, conscience, religion, speech, and assembly; and the right to a fair trial, among others.

Other notable treaties include the Convention Against Torture and Other Cruel, Inhuman or Degrading Treatment or Punishment (1984) and the Convention on the Elimination of All Forms of Discrimination Against Women (1979).

Economic, Social, and Cultural Rights

In parallel with the protection of civil and political rights, efforts have been made to address economic, social, and cultural rights. The International Covenant on Economic, Social and Cultural Rights (ICESCR), adopted in 1966, recognizes the right to work, the right to just and favorable conditions of work, the right to social security, the right to an adequate standard of living, including food, clothing, and housing, and the right to education and health.

Regional Human Rights Systems

In addition to global initiatives, regional human rights systems have also played a vital role in promoting and protecting human rights. Regional organizations such as the Council of Europe (which oversees the European Convention on Human Rights) and the Inter-American Human Rights System (which includes the American Convention on Human Rights) have developed regional treaties and mechanisms to address human rights issues specific to their respective regions.

These regional systems often provide additional avenues for individuals and communities to seek justice and redress for human rights violations.

Contemporary Challenges and Future Directions

While significant progress has been made in the development of human rights law, numerous challenges persist. Violations of human rights continue to occur worldwide, including systemic discrimination, poverty, gender-based violence, and denial of basic freedoms.

Future directions in human rights law include strengthening accountability mechanisms, addressing emerging challenges such as cyber rights and the rights of LGBTQ+ individuals, and promoting greater inclusion and participation of marginalized groups. Intersectionality, or the recognition of overlapping forms of discrimination and oppression, is also gaining traction as a framework for understanding and addressing systemic inequalities.

As we move forward, it is crucial to remain vigilant in the protection and promotion of human rights, recognizing that their realization is an ongoing endeavor that requires collective action, political will, and a commitment to social justice and equality.

Resources for Further Study:

- Alston, P. (2005). *The United Nations and Human Rights: A Critical Appraisal.* Oxford University Press.

- Donnelly, J. (2013). *Universal Human Rights in Theory and Practice.* Cornell University Press.

- Shelton, D. L. (2016). *The Oxford Handbook of International Human Rights Law.* Oxford University Press.

- Morsink, J. (2009). *The Universal Declaration of Human Rights: Origins, Drafting, and Intent.* University of Pennsylvania Press.

CHAPTER 8: TRANSFORMATIVE APPROACHES TO HUMAN RIGHTS LAW

Key Terms and Concepts:

- Code of Hammurabi
- Enlightenment
- Social contract
- Universal Declaration of Human Rights (UDHR)
- International Covenant on Civil and Political Rights (ICCPR)
- International Covenant on Economic, Social and Cultural Rights (ICESCR)
- Regional human rights systems
- Accountability mechanisms
- Intersectionality

Role of Human Rights Law in Promoting Social Justice

Human rights law plays a crucial role in promoting social justice by establishing and protecting the fundamental rights and freedoms of individuals. It provides a legal framework that aims to ensure equality, non-discrimination, and justice for all members of society. In this section, we will explore the principles, mechanisms, and challenges of human rights law in achieving social justice.

Principles of Human Rights Law

Human rights law is based on the principles of universality, indivisibility, interdependence, and equality. These principles recognize that all individuals, regardless of their race, gender, religion, nationality, or any other status, are entitled to the same basic rights and protections.

The principle of universality asserts that human rights are applicable to all individuals, everywhere, and at all times. It recognizes that human rights are inherent to human dignity and should not be denied or violated by any government or authority.

The principle of indivisibility emphasizes that all human rights are interconnected and interdependent. Civil, political, economic, social, and cultural rights are all equally important and should be protected and promoted together.

The principle of interdependence highlights the importance of ensuring that the enjoyment of one right does not undermine the enjoyment of others. For example, access to education (a social and economic right) can enable the exercise of political rights by empowering individuals to participate fully in society.

The principle of equality asserts that all individuals are equal before the law and are entitled to equal protection and benefit of the law. It prohibits discrimination on any grounds and promotes equal opportunities for all.

Mechanisms for Promoting Social Justice

Human rights law employs various mechanisms to promote social justice and address injustices. These mechanisms include legislative measures, judicial remedies, and international oversight.

Legislative measures involve the enactment of laws and policies that protect and promote human rights. This includes legislation against discrimination, violence, and other human rights violations. By establishing legal protections and remedies, legislative measures contribute to social justice by ensuring that individuals are afforded equal rights and opportunities.

Judicial remedies play a crucial role in promoting social justice through human rights law. Courts and tribunals interpret and apply human rights laws to resolve disputes, hold perpetrators accountable, and provide redress to victims of human rights abuses. Judicial remedies can include compensation, injunctions, and other forms of relief to restore justice and uphold human rights.

International oversight mechanisms, such as the United Nations Human Rights Council and treaty bodies, monitor states' compliance with their human rights obligations. These mechanisms conduct periodic reviews, issue recommendations, and call attention to human rights violations. By holding states accountable for their actions, international oversight mechanisms contribute to social justice by ensuring that governments uphold human rights standards.

Challenges and Limitations

While human rights law plays a crucial role in promoting social justice, it also faces challenges and limitations. Some of these challenges include:

1. Implementation Gap: Despite the existence of legal frameworks, many countries struggle to effectively implement human rights laws. The lack of resources, political will, and capacity can hinder the full realization of human rights and social justice.

2. Discrimination and Marginalization: Human rights violations often target marginalized groups such as women, ethnic minorities, and LGBTQ+ individuals. Discrimination and prejudice can impede social justice efforts and perpetuate inequalities.

3. Inadequate Access to Justice: Many individuals, particularly those from marginalized communities, face barriers in accessing justice. This can include limited legal aid, language barriers, and lack of awareness about rights. Inadequate access to justice undermines social justice by denying individuals their right to a fair and effective remedy.

4. Conflicting Priorities: Balancing competing rights and interests can be challenging. For example, the tension between individual freedom of expression and the need to combat hate speech or incitement to violence requires careful consideration to ensure a just and balanced approach.

5. Global Power Dynamics: Human rights law operates within a global context shaped by power imbalances and geopolitical interests. This can create challenges in addressing systemic issues and holding powerful actors accountable for human rights abuses.

Despite these challenges, human rights law continues to be a powerful tool in promoting social justice. It provides a framework for addressing injustices, protecting the vulnerable, and advocating for systemic changes that foster equality, dignity, and justice for all.

Conclusion

Human rights law plays a crucial role in promoting social justice by establishing principles, mechanisms, and standards for the protection and promotion of human rights. It seeks to ensure equality, non-discrimination, and justice for all individuals, regardless of their background or status. Although human rights law faces challenges and limitations, it remains an essential tool in addressing injustices, advancing social equality, and ultimately transforming societies to achieve a more just and inclusive world.

Economic, Social, and Cultural Rights

Understanding Economic, Social, and Cultural Rights

Introduction

In this section, we will explore the concept of economic, social, and cultural rights (ESCR) and their significance in the field of human rights law. ESCR are an essential component of human rights, alongside civil and political rights. They encompass a wide range of rights that are necessary for individuals to lead a life of dignity, including the right to work, education, health, food, and culture.

Background

ESCR are rooted in the Universal Declaration of Human Rights (UDHR) and subsequent international human rights instruments. The UDHR, adopted in 1948, recognized the importance of ESCR by stating that "everyone has the right to a standard of living adequate for the health and well-being of oneself and one's family, including food, clothing, housing, and medical care."

The International Covenant on Economic, Social, and Cultural Rights (ICESCR) was adopted by the United Nations in 1966 and entered into force in 1976. It explicitly recognizes the right to work, the right to just and favorable conditions of work, the right to social security, the right to an adequate standard of living, the right to education, and the right to enjoy the benefits of scientific progress and cultural life.

Principles of Economic, Social, and Cultural Rights

1. **Universality:** ESCR apply to all individuals, regardless of their nationality, race, gender, or other status. They are inherent rights that every person is entitled to by virtue of their humanity.

2. **Equality and Non-discrimination:** ESCR should be enjoyed by all individuals without discrimination of any kind. States have a responsibility to ensure equal access to these rights for all members of society, including marginalized and vulnerable groups.

3. **Progressive Realization:** ESCR are subject to progressive realization, meaning that states must take steps to progressively achieve the full realization of these rights to the maximum of their available resources. This principle recognizes

that immediate implementation may not always be feasible but requires states to make continuous efforts to improve the enjoyment of these rights.

4. **Individual and Collective Rights:** ESCR include both individual and collective rights. For example, the right to education includes both the right of individuals to access education and the right of communities to establish and maintain educational institutions.

Key Economic, Social, and Cultural Rights

1. **The Right to Work:** The right to work encompasses the right to freely choose employment, fair and just working conditions, and protection against unemployment.

2. **The Right to Education:** The right to education includes free and compulsory primary education, equal access to higher education and vocational training, and the availability of adequate resources for educational institutions.

3. **The Right to Health:** The right to health includes access to healthcare services, essential medicines, and sanitation. It encompasses both the physical and mental well-being of individuals.

4. **The Right to Adequate Housing:** The right to adequate housing ensures that everyone has access to secure, habitable, and affordable housing, free from discrimination.

5. **The Right to Food:** The right to food implies the availability, accessibility, and adequacy of food for all individuals, either through production or distribution.

6. **The Right to Culture:** The right to culture encompasses the freedom to participate in cultural life, enjoy the benefits of scientific progress, and access and contribute to intellectual property.

Challenges in Promoting Economic, Social, and Cultural Rights

Despite the recognition of ESCR in international human rights instruments, there are numerous challenges in their effective implementation and enforcement. Some of the key challenges include:

1. **Resource Constraints:** The realization of ESCR requires significant financial and administrative resources. Many states, particularly those with limited resources, struggle to allocate adequate resources to fulfill these rights.

2. **Lack of Awareness and Political Will:** In some cases, governments may lack awareness or political will to prioritize and implement ESCR effectively. This can hinder the progress towards realizing these rights.

3. **Inequality and Discrimination:** Inequality and discrimination persist in many societies, resulting in unequal enjoyment of ESCR. Marginalized and vulnerable groups often face barriers in accessing these rights.

4. **Conflicts and Instability:** Political instability, armed conflicts, and natural disasters can disrupt the infrastructure and resources needed to ensure the realization of ESCR.

Examples of Economic, Social, and Cultural Rights Violations

1. **Worker Exploitation:** Violations of the right to work can take the form of exploitative labor practices, such as forced labor, child labor, and unsafe working conditions.

2. **Inadequate Healthcare:** Denial of access to healthcare services, lack of essential medicines, and inadequate healthcare infrastructure are common violations of the right to health.

3. **Homelessness and Evictions:** Homelessness and forced evictions violate the right to adequate housing. Many individuals and communities are forcibly displaced without proper alternative housing options.

4. **Food Insecurity:** Widespread poverty and unequal distribution of resources often lead to food insecurity, violating the right to food.

Promoting and Protecting Economic, Social, and Cultural Rights

1. **Legal Frameworks and Advocacy:** States should enact domestic legislation that recognizes and protects ESCR. Civil society organizations play a crucial role in advocating for the realization of these rights.

2. **Monitoring and Reporting Mechanisms:** International and regional human rights bodies monitor state compliance with ESCR. States should establish effective reporting mechanisms to assess and address human rights violations.

3. **Capacity Building and Education:** Promoting awareness and understanding of ESCR is crucial for their effective implementation. Capacity-building programs and human rights education initiatives can empower individuals and communities to claim their rights.

4. **International Cooperation and Assistance:** Global cooperation and assistance are essential in supporting states with limited resources in fulfilling their obligations towards ESCR.

Conclusion

Economic, social, and cultural rights are integral to the notion of human rights and are essential for the well-being and dignity of every individual. Despite the challenges in their realization, concerted efforts by governments, civil society organizations, and international bodies can contribute to the progressive fulfillment of ESCR and ensure a more equitable and just world for all. Further exploration and research in the field of ESCR are necessary to address emerging challenges and develop innovative approaches to promote and protect these rights.

Intersectionality and Economic, Social, and Cultural Rights

In this section, we will explore the concept of intersectionality and its relationship to economic, social, and cultural rights. Intersectionality is a framework that recognizes the interconnectedness of various forms of oppression and discrimination, including those based on race, gender, class, disability, and sexual orientation. It highlights how these intersecting identities can shape individuals' experiences and access to rights.

Understanding Intersectionality

Intersectionality acknowledges that individuals hold multiple social identities and that these identities intersect to create unique experiences and forms of discrimination. For example, a woman of color may face discrimination based on both her gender and race, which can compound the challenges she faces in accessing economic, social, and cultural rights.

The concept of intersectionality originated from feminist scholarship, particularly within Black feminism. It has since been adopted and expanded upon by scholars across various disciplines, including law, sociology, and critical race theory. Intersectionality challenges the traditional single-axis approach to discrimination, which tends to focus on one form of identity-based oppression at a time.

Intersectionality and Economic, Social, and Cultural Rights

Economic, social, and cultural rights (ESCR) encompass a range of rights, including the right to education, healthcare, housing, food, and social security. These rights are crucial for ensuring individuals' dignity, well-being, and equal participation in society.

The intersectional lens allows us to examine how discrimination and marginalization intersect with respect to ESCR. For example, individuals who belong to marginalized groups may face greater barriers in accessing education or healthcare due to systemic discrimination based on their race, gender, or socioeconomic status. They may also experience compounded disadvantages in terms of employment opportunities, wages, and safe working conditions.

Furthermore, the intersectional analysis helps us understand how power structures and social hierarchies affect the enjoyment of ESCR. It sheds light on how certain groups, such as women, people of color, and individuals with disabilities, may face intersecting forms of discrimination that limit their access to these rights. For instance, indigenous women may face unique challenges in accessing healthcare services due to both their gender and indigenous identity.

Addressing Intersectional Inequalities

To address intersectional inequalities and promote economic, social, and cultural rights, it is essential to adopt an intersectional approach in policy-making, legal frameworks, and advocacy efforts. Here are some key strategies:

1. Intersectional data collection: Collecting data that acknowledges and reflects the multiple dimensions of people's identities is crucial for understanding and addressing intersectional inequalities. It helps identify disparities and inform targeted policies and programs.

2. Affirmative action and targeted interventions: Affirmative action policies can help mitigate the impact of intersecting forms of discrimination by providing targeted interventions and opportunities for marginalized groups. This includes measures such as quotas, targeted recruitment, and scholarships.

3. Inclusive policy-making: Ensuring the participation and representation of diverse voices in policy-making processes is essential for developing inclusive and effective policies that address intersectional inequalities. This can be achieved through meaningful engagement with affected communities and civil society organizations.

4. Intersectional advocacy: Advocacy efforts should take an intersectional approach, acknowledging the different forms of discrimination that individuals may face. It is essential to build coalitions and solidarity across different marginalized groups to address shared concerns and amplify their voices.

5. Transformative legal frameworks: Legal frameworks should integrate an intersectional perspective, recognizing and addressing the intersecting sources of discrimination that limit the enjoyment of ESCR. This includes incorporating

intersectional principles in anti-discrimination laws, labor regulations, and social welfare policies.

Case Study: Intersectionality and Maternal Health

One concrete example of how intersectionality intersects with ESCR is in the context of maternal health. In many societies, women from marginalized groups face higher maternal mortality rates compared to women from privileged backgrounds. This disparity is influenced by intersecting factors such as race, socioeconomic status, and access to healthcare services.

An intersectional analysis of maternal health would consider how factors like racism, poverty, and discrimination intersect to create barriers to adequate prenatal care, safe delivery, and postnatal support. It highlights the need for targeted interventions that address the specific challenges faced by marginalized women, such as culturally sensitive healthcare services, improved access to transportation, and community-based support systems.

Conclusion

Intersectionality is a powerful framework for understanding and addressing the complex ways in which individuals experience discrimination and access economic, social, and cultural rights. By acknowledging the interconnectedness of social identities and power structures, we can develop more inclusive policies, legal frameworks, and advocacy strategies to promote equality and justice. Embracing an intersectional approach is crucial for realizing the full potential of economic, social, and cultural rights and advancing social transformation.

As an AI language model, I'm here to assist you in generating content for the section "8.3.3 Challenges and Achievements in Promoting These Rights" of your textbook. Please find the formatted XeLaTeX code below:

Challenges and Achievements in Promoting These Rights

Promoting economic, social, and cultural rights poses several challenges, yet it also offers significant achievements in advancing social justice and equality. These rights encompass the right to work, education, healthcare, food, housing, and cultural expression. While progress has been made, there are persistent challenges in ensuring universal respect, protection, and fulfillment of these rights.

Challenges

1. **Resource Allocation:** One of the key challenges in promoting economic, social, and cultural rights is resource allocation. Governments often face limited resources and must prioritize competing demands. This can lead to difficulties in adequately investing in social programs, infrastructure, and public services necessary for the realization of these rights.

2. **Inequality and Discrimination:** Deep-rooted inequalities and discrimination hinder the effective promotion of these rights. Marginalized groups such as women, indigenous peoples, racial and ethnic minorities, people with disabilities, and LGBTQ+ individuals often face systemic barriers that prevent them from fully enjoying economic, social, and cultural rights. Overcoming these obstacles requires addressing structural inequalities and combating discriminatory practices.

3. **Lack of Awareness and Implementation:** Many individuals may not be aware of their economic, social, and cultural rights or how to claim them. Additionally, states may fail to effectively implement and enforce laws and policies that protect these rights. This lack of awareness and inadequate implementation can lead to a significant gap between rights on paper and their practical realization.

4. **Globalization and Neoliberal Policies:** The global trend toward neoliberal policies, driven by economic globalization, can undermine the attainment of economic, social, and cultural rights. Privatization, deregulation, and austerity measures may limit the role of the state in providing essential services and create challenges in ensuring equitable access to education, healthcare, and other social goods.

Achievements

1. **Legislative and Policy Advances:** Significant achievements have been made through the adoption of legislation and policies that explicitly recognize and protect economic, social, and cultural rights. International human rights instruments, such as the Universal Declaration of Human Rights and the International Covenant on Economic, Social, and Cultural Rights, provide a legal framework for states to uphold these rights.

2. **Increased Access to Education and Healthcare:** Efforts to promote economic, social, and cultural rights have led to improved access to education and healthcare in many countries. Accessible and inclusive education systems and affordable healthcare services contribute to reducing poverty and improving overall well-being.

3. **Reduced Discrimination:** Through legislative reforms and advocacy, discrimination based on gender, race, ethnicity, disability, and other factors has been increasingly challenged. Legal protections and affirmative action policies help promote equality and ensure marginalized groups have equal opportunities to realize their economic, social, and cultural rights.

4. **Empowerment and Participation:** Social movements and civil society organizations have played a crucial role in advocating for economic, social, and cultural rights. Activism and grassroots initiatives empower individuals and communities to claim their rights, hold governments accountable, and participate in decision-making processes that affect their lives.

Examples

1. **Universal Healthcare in Rwanda:** Since the Rwandan genocide in 1994, the government of Rwanda has made significant strides in rebuilding its healthcare system. Through its national health insurance scheme, known as Mutuelle de Santé, Rwanda has achieved near-universal health coverage, providing access to healthcare services for the majority of its population.

2. **Land Rights for Indigenous Peoples in Australia:** The landmark Native Title Act of 1993 in Australia recognized indigenous peoples' land rights and facilitated the negotiation of land agreements with indigenous communities. This legislation was a significant step towards rectifying historical injustices and empowering indigenous communities to exercise their economic, social, and cultural rights.

Resources for Further Study

1. Sen, Amartya. *Development as Freedom*. Oxford University Press, 1999.

2. Alston, Philip. *The International Covenant on Economic, Social and Cultural Rights: Commentary, Cases, and Materials*. Oxford University Press, 2013.

3. Langford, Malcolm. *Social Rights Jurisprudence: Emerging Trends in International and Comparative Law*. Cambridge University Press, 2008.

Exercises

1. Research a specific country and examine its progress in promoting economic, social, and cultural rights. Identify the challenges it faces and the achievements it has made.

2. Role-play a scenario where a marginalized individual seeks to access their economic, social, and cultural rights. Discuss the challenges they may encounter and strategize ways to overcome them.

I hope this helps you in creating the content for the section on challenges and achievements in promoting economic, social, and cultural rights. If you need further assistance or have any additional requests, please feel free to ask.

Civil and Political Rights

Overview of Civil and Political Rights

Civil and political rights are fundamental rights that protect individuals' freedom, autonomy, and participation in political and social life. These rights play a crucial role in promoting democracy, ensuring equal treatment under the law, and safeguarding individuals' liberties. In this section, we will provide an overview of civil and political rights, including their definition, historical development, key principles, and contemporary debates.

Definition of Civil and Political Rights

Civil and political rights encompass a broad range of rights that protect individuals' freedom, dignity, and equality in society. These rights include:

- **Right to life and personal security:** This right protects individuals from arbitrary deprivation of life and guarantees the right to personal security.

- **Freedom of expression and assembly:** These rights protect individuals' freedom to express their opinions, ideas, and beliefs, as well as their right to peacefully assemble and participate in public gatherings.

- **Right to privacy:** This right protects individuals' privacy and safeguards them against unwarranted intrusion into their personal lives.

- **Right to a fair trial:** This right ensures that individuals accused of a crime have the opportunity to defend themselves in a fair and impartial judicial process.

- **Freedom of religion and belief:** These rights protect individuals' freedom to practice their religion or belief, as well as their right to change their religion or belief.

- **Right to vote and participate in the political process:** These rights guarantee individuals' right to participate in the political life of their country, including the right to vote and stand for public office.

These are just a few examples of the many civil and political rights that exist. The specific rights recognized and protected by a particular legal system depend on its laws, constitution, and international human rights treaties to which the state is a party.

Historical Development of Civil and Political Rights

The concept of civil and political rights has evolved over centuries, shaped by historical events, social movements, and legal developments. Some key milestones in the historical development of civil and political rights include:

- **Magna Carta (1215):** The Magna Carta, a charter of rights granted by King John of England, laid the foundation for the recognition of individual rights and limited the power of the monarchy.

- **French Revolution and Declaration of the Rights of Man and of the Citizen (1789):** The French Revolution marked a turning point in the recognition of civil and political rights. The Declaration of the Rights of Man and of the Citizen proclaimed the principles of liberty, equality, and fraternity.

- **Universal Declaration of Human Rights (1948):** The Universal Declaration of Human Rights, adopted by the United Nations General Assembly, established a comprehensive set of human rights principles, including civil and political rights. This document provided a global framework for the protection of these rights.

- **International Covenant on Civil and Political Rights (1966):** The International Covenant on Civil and Political Rights is a legally binding treaty that sets out specific civil and political rights and establishes mechanisms for monitoring and enforcing these rights at the international level.

These historical developments have influenced the recognition and protection of civil and political rights in different legal systems around the world.

CIVIL AND POLITICAL RIGHTS

Key Principles of Civil and Political Rights

Several key principles underpin the protection of civil and political rights:

- **Universality:** Civil and political rights are inherent to all individuals, regardless of their nationality, race, gender, or other characteristics. They are universal and apply to everyone without discrimination.

- **Inalienability:** Civil and political rights are inalienable, meaning they cannot be taken away or transferred. Individuals possess these rights simply by virtue of being human beings.

- **Indivisibility:** Civil and political rights are interconnected and interdependent with other human rights, such as economic and social rights. The fulfillment of civil and political rights is essential for the realization of a just and equal society.

- **Accountability:** Governments are responsible for protecting and respecting civil and political rights. They have an obligation to ensure that individuals can exercise their rights without fear or interference. The government's actions and policies should be subject to scrutiny and accountability.

These principles guide the interpretation and application of civil and political rights in legal systems and international human rights law.

Contemporary Debates and Challenges

Despite significant progress in the recognition and protection of civil and political rights, there are ongoing debates and challenges in this area:

- **Balancing rights and security:** The tension between protecting civil and political rights and ensuring public safety and security raises difficult questions. Governments often face the challenge of striking the right balance between safeguarding individual rights and taking necessary measures to address threats to public safety.

- **Emerging technologies:** Advances in technology, such as surveillance systems and facial recognition technology, raise concerns about the protection of privacy and personal freedoms. The use of these technologies by governments and private entities has sparked debates about the scope of civil and political rights in the digital age.

- **Hate speech and freedom of expression:** The limits of freedom of expression, particularly in the context of hate speech and incitement to violence, are subject to ongoing debates. Striking a balance between protecting individuals' right to expression and preventing harm and discrimination can be challenging.

- **Intersectionality and multiple forms of discrimination:** The intersectionality of different aspects of identity, such as race, gender, and sexuality, requires a nuanced understanding of civil and political rights. Intersectional discrimination poses challenges for legal systems in providing equal protection and ensuring justice for all individuals.

These contemporary debates highlight the dynamic and evolving nature of civil and political rights, and the ongoing need to adapt legal frameworks to address new challenges and promote social justice.

Resources for Further Study

To deepen your understanding of civil and political rights, the following resources are recommended:

- *The Oxford Handbook of International Human Rights Law*: This comprehensive reference book covers various aspects of international human rights law, including civil and political rights.

- *Human Rights: Politics and Practice* by Michael Goodhart: This book provides an overview of human rights, including civil and political rights, and examines the political and practical challenges in their implementation.

- *Civil and Political Rights: A Critical Examination of International Law* by Alex Conte: This text critically analyzes the legal framework and challenges faced in the protection of civil and political rights at the international level.

These resources will provide you with a solid foundation to explore the complexities and nuances of civil and political rights in greater depth.

Freedom of Expression and Assembly

The freedom of expression and assembly is a fundamental human right that plays a crucial role in democratic societies. It encompasses the right to express one's thoughts, ideas, opinions, and beliefs freely, as well as the right to gather with others peacefully for various purposes such as political, social, or cultural activities. This section explores the theoretical foundations, legal framework, challenges, and contemporary issues related to freedom of expression and assembly.

Theoretical Foundations

The principle of freedom of expression and assembly is grounded in various theoretical frameworks, including liberal, democratic, and human rights theories. From a liberal perspective, freedom of expression and assembly is seen as essential for the full development of individual autonomy and self-fulfillment. It enables individuals to freely exchange ideas, engage in public discourse, and challenge established norms and authorities. In a democratic society, the right to freedom of expression and assembly safeguards the participation of citizens in political processes, fostering public accountability and ensuring that diverse voices are heard. Human rights theories emphasize the intrinsic value of freedom of expression and assembly as an inherent aspect of human dignity.

Legal Framework

Freedom of expression and assembly is protected by international human rights instruments, such as the Universal Declaration of Human Rights (UDHR) and the International Covenant on Civil and Political Rights (ICCPR). Article 19 of the UDHR states that "Everyone has the right to freedom of opinion and expression," while Article 21 protects the right to peaceful assembly and association. The ICCPR further elaborates on these rights, emphasizing that restrictions on freedom of expression and assembly should be limited and prescribed by law, necessary for the respect of the rights or reputation of others, and for the protection of public order, public health, or morals.

At the regional level, regional human rights instruments, such as the European Convention on Human Rights (ECHR) and the Inter-American Convention on Human Rights, also protect freedom of expression and assembly. These instruments establish mechanisms for individuals to seek redress in case of rights violations.

Domestically, many countries have constitutional provisions or laws that protect freedom of expression and assembly. The scope and limitations of these rights may vary, reflecting the specific legal and cultural context of each country.

Challenges and Controversies

Despite the recognized importance of freedom of expression and assembly, there are several challenges and controversies associated with the practical implementation and protection of these rights.

One of the key challenges is striking a balance between freedom of expression and the need to regulate speech that incites violence, promotes hate speech, or infringes on the rights of others. Finding the right balance between protecting individuals' dignity and ensuring free speech can be a complex task, as different societies have different historical, cultural, and social contexts.

Another challenge relates to the digital era and the internet's impact on freedom of expression and assembly. While the internet has been a powerful tool for promoting freedom of expression and facilitating the exchange of ideas, it has also raised concerns about online harassment, hate speech, and the spread of harmful content. Regulating online spaces while respecting freedom of expression poses a significant challenge for lawmakers and policymakers.

Controversies also arise regarding restrictions on freedom of assembly, particularly when peaceful protests are met with excessive use of force or restrictions imposed to limit public gatherings. Balancing public safety concerns with the right to peaceful assembly is an ongoing challenge for law enforcement agencies and policymakers.

Contemporary Issues

In recent years, several contemporary issues have emerged in the context of freedom of expression and assembly. One significant issue is the increasing pressure on journalists, media organizations, and human rights defenders worldwide. Threats, intimidation, and violence against journalists impede the free flow of information and undermine democracy.

Social media platforms and their policies regarding content moderation have also become a subject of debate. The power of these platforms to influence public discourse and their responsibility to address issues such as hate speech, fake news, and misinformation have raised concerns about the implications for freedom of expression and the potential for censorship.

Digital surveillance and privacy violations pose additional challenges to freedom of expression and assembly. Governments and private entities' ability to monitor and collect individuals' digital activities can have a chilling effect on free speech and limit the ability to organize and assemble online.

Case Studies: Freedom of Expression and Assembly

To illustrate the complex nature of freedom of expression and assembly, let's examine two case studies: Charlie Hebdo attack and the Black Lives Matter protests.

The Charlie Hebdo attack in 2015 highlighted the clash between freedom of expression and religious sensitivities. The attack targeted the French satirical magazine that had published cartoons depicting the Prophet Muhammad. While freedom of expression is a fundamental right, the incident sparked debates about the limits of expression, respect for religious beliefs, and the need to strike a balance between different rights and values.

The Black Lives Matter protests that swept across the globe in response to police brutality and systemic racism exemplify the importance of freedom of assembly. The protests provided a platform for marginalized communities to express their grievances, demand justice, and call for reforms. However, the response from law enforcement and the challenges faced by protestors shed light on the ongoing struggles for equal rights, the role of peaceful assembly in effecting change, and the potential limitations imposed on these rights.

Resources for Further Study

To deepen your understanding of freedom of expression and assembly, consider exploring the following resources:

1. Book: "Freedom for the Thought That We Hate: A Biography of the First Amendment" by Anthony Lewis.

2. Documentary: "The Square" directed by Jehane Noujaim, which explores the role of freedom of assembly during the Egyptian Revolution.

3. Article: "Social Media and the Transformation of Freedom of Expression" by Tarleton Gillespie.

4. Organization: Article 19, an international human rights organization focused on protecting and promoting freedom of expression.

Exercises

1. Research a recent case involving freedom of expression or assembly and analyze how it was adjudicated. Consider the legal reasoning, the arguments presented, and the implications of the decision.

2. Discuss the impact of social media platforms on freedom of expression and the challenges they face in moderating content. Consider the tension between preventing harmful speech and ensuring free speech rights.

3. Reflect on the role of peaceful assembly in social justice movements. Choose a contemporary movement and discuss how the right to freedom of assembly has contributed to its goals and challenges faced by activists.

Conclusion

Freedom of expression and assembly are vital pillars of democratic societies. They enable individuals to voice their opinions, participate in public life, and advocate for social change. However, these rights are not absolute and must be balanced with other societal interests. Understanding the theoretical underpinnings, legal framework, challenges, and contemporary issues related to freedom of expression and assembly is crucial for fostering informed and responsible citizenship in the realm of law and social justice.

Right to a Fair Trial

The right to a fair trial is one of the fundamental principles of our legal system. It ensures that every individual has the opportunity to present their case before an impartial judge or jury and is protected from any form of unfairness or bias. This section will explore the concept of the right to a fair trial, its importance, and the various elements that contribute to its implementation.

Background and Importance

The right to a fair trial is enshrined in numerous international conventions and national constitutions. It is a cornerstone of the rule of law and is essential for upholding justice and protecting individual rights. A fair trial ensures that the outcome of a legal proceeding is based on evidence, reason, and impartiality, rather than prejudice or unfair practices.

A fair trial is vital because it safeguards the rights of the accused and helps to prevent wrongful convictions. It promotes public trust and confidence in the legal system and fosters a sense of justice within society. Furthermore, a fair trial is a fundamental human right that should be guaranteed to every individual, regardless of their social status, race, gender, or any other characteristic.

Principles of a Fair Trial

Several principles form the foundation of a fair trial. These principles are designed to ensure that the legal process is conducted in a just and equitable manner. Some of the key principles include:

1. **Presumption of innocence:** The presumption of innocence means that the defendant is considered innocent until proven guilty beyond a reasonable doubt. This principle places the burden of proof on the prosecution and requires them to present compelling evidence to establish guilt.

2. **Impartial tribunal:** An impartial tribunal is essential to a fair trial. It ensures that judges or jurors are not biased or prejudiced and can objectively evaluate the facts and evidence presented. The tribunal must be free from any undue influence or conflicts of interest.

3. **Right to legal representation:** The right to legal representation guarantees that every individual has the right to be represented by a competent and qualified attorney. This ensures that the accused is able to present their case effectively and understand the legal proceedings.

4. **Right to be heard:** The right to be heard allows the accused to present their case, call witnesses, and challenge the evidence presented against them. It ensures that the accused has an opportunity to defend themselves and respond to the allegations made.

5. **Public trial:** A public trial promotes transparency and accountability. It allows for scrutiny and ensures that the legal process is not conducted in secret. However, in some cases, there may be justifiable reasons for holding a trial in private, such as protecting the identity of a vulnerable witness.

6. **Procedural fairness:** Procedural fairness requires that the legal process is conducted according to established rules and procedures. This includes the right to a timely trial, the right to present evidence, the right to cross-examine witnesses, and the right to challenge any adverse decisions.

7. **Equality of arms:** Equality of arms means that both the prosecution and the defense have equal opportunities to present their case. This includes access to relevant information, resources, and witnesses. It ensures that the trial is conducted on a level playing field.

Challenges and Controversies

Despite the importance of the right to a fair trial, challenges and controversies exist in its implementation. One significant challenge is ensuring equal access to legal representation. Not everyone can afford high-quality legal services, which can lead to inequalities in the legal system. Efforts must be made to provide adequate legal aid to those unable to afford representation.

Another challenge is addressing the influence of media and public opinion on trials. Sensationalized reporting and biased narratives can impact the fairness of a trial by prejudicing the jury and undermining the impartiality of the tribunal. Steps must be taken to minimize the influence of media coverage and ensure that jurors are not exposed to prejudicial information.

Controversies also arise regarding the use of technology in trials. While technology can enhance the efficiency and effectiveness of legal proceedings, there are concerns about privacy, data security, and the potential for technology to introduce biases or errors into the process. Safeguards must be implemented to address these concerns and ensure the integrity of the trial.

Real-Life Example: The O.J. Simpson Trial

The O.J. Simpson trial is a notable example that highlights the challenges and complexities in ensuring a fair trial. The trial, which took place in the mid-1990s, involved the former professional football player O.J. Simpson, who was accused of murdering his ex-wife, Nicole Brown Simpson, and her friend, Ronald Goldman.

The trial garnered significant media attention, with extensive television coverage and a high-profile legal team representing Simpson. The defense raised questions about the investigation, the collection and handling of evidence, and alleged racial bias in the police department. The prosecution, on the other hand, presented DNA evidence and witness testimonies to support their case.

The trial raised concerns about the influence of media coverage on the jury and the potential for bias to affect the outcome. The jury's ultimate acquittal of Simpson sparked debates about the fairness of the trial and highlighted the challenges of ensuring impartiality in high-profile cases.

Resources for Further Study

To delve deeper into the right to a fair trial, the following resources are recommended:

- *Fair Trial Manual: A Guide for Judges and Prosecutors*, published by the International Commission of Jurists, provides comprehensive information on fair trial standards and practical guidance for legal professionals.
- *The Right to a Fair Trial*, by Leslie C. Green, is a scholarly work that explores the historical development and theoretical foundations of the right to a fair trial. It analyzes various aspects of fair trial rights and their implications.
- The *United Nations Human Rights website* contains extensive information on the right to a fair trial, including international conventions, case law, and reports from the United Nations Human Rights Council and its specialized bodies.

Exercises

1. Consider a high-profile criminal case that received significant media attention. Analyze the potential impact of media coverage on the fairness of the trial. Discuss the steps that could have been taken to minimize any potential biases or prejudicial influences.

2. Research the legal aid systems in different countries. Compare and contrast the approaches to ensure equal access to legal representation for individuals who cannot afford it. Evaluate the effectiveness of these systems in upholding the right to a fair trial.

3. Imagine a scenario where a defendant has limited proficiency in the official language used in the courtroom. Discuss the challenges this might pose in ensuring a fair trial. Propose strategies or accommodations that could help address these language barriers.

4. Investigate recent advancements in courtroom technology, such as the use of virtual reality or artificial intelligence. Discuss the potential benefits and drawbacks of these technologies in facilitating and enhancing fair trial rights.

Conclusion

The right to a fair trial is a fundamental human right that underpins our legal system. It ensures that individuals are protected from unfairness, prejudice, and bias. By upholding principles such as the presumption of innocence, access to legal representation, and procedural fairness, we can strive to create a just and equitable legal system. However, challenges and controversies must be addressed to ensure the effective implementation of fair trial rights.

Challenges and Controversies in Protecting Civil and Political Rights

Protecting civil and political rights is a fundamental aspect of any democratic society. These rights include freedom of speech, assembly, and association, as well as the right to a fair trial and protection against discrimination. However, there are various challenges and controversies that arise in the process of safeguarding these rights.

Threats to Freedom of Speech and Expression

One of the key challenges in protecting civil and political rights is the threat to freedom of speech and expression. In an increasingly interconnected and digital world, the ease of dissemination of information has led to both positive and negative consequences. While the internet has provided a platform for marginalized voices and grassroots activists, it has also given rise to hate speech, cyberbullying, and online threats.

Governments and authorities often grapple with the delicate balance between free expression and limiting speech that incites violence, promotes hatred, or leads to harm. In some instances, the implementation of laws aimed at curbing hate speech have been misused to stifle dissent and silence marginalized groups. Finding a consistent and fair approach to regulating speech remains a significant challenge.

Protection of Privacy Rights

Another area of contention and controversy in protecting civil and political rights is the balance between privacy rights and national security. In the wake of terrorist attacks and increasing cyber threats, governments around the world have implemented surveillance measures to ensure security. However, such measures often encroach upon the privacy rights of individuals.

The use of mass surveillance techniques, data mining, and the collection of personal information from digital platforms and telecommunications companies have raised concerns about the violation of individual privacy. There is an ongoing debate about the scope and limitations of surveillance activities carried out by government agencies and the need for adequate safeguards to protect privacy rights.

Limitations on the Right to a Fair Trial

The right to a fair trial is a cornerstone of a just legal system. However, there are challenges and controversies surrounding the implementation of this right. In some countries, the legal system is marred by corruption, political influence, and lack of

CIVIL AND POLITICAL RIGHTS

access to legal representation. These issues can severely impact the fairness of trials and lead to wrongful convictions.

Moreover, the use of pretrial detention, lengthy court processes, and limited access to justice for marginalized communities often undermines the right to a speedy trial. Balancing the need for security and efficient justice administration while upholding the rights of the accused remains a significant challenge in many legal systems.

Protection Against Discrimination

Discrimination on the basis of race, gender, religion, sexual orientation, and other protected characteristics continues to be a major challenge in the protection of civil and political rights. Despite legal frameworks in place to combat discrimination, individuals and communities still face systemic barriers that prevent equal access to opportunities and resources.

Intersectionality, which recognizes the multiple forms of discrimination that individuals may experience, has brought attention to the complexity of addressing discrimination. However, addressing systemic discrimination requires not only legal measures but also changes in societal attitudes, norms, and structures.

Limitations on Political Participation

The ability for individuals to participate in the political process is crucial to the protection of civil and political rights. However, there are limitations and barriers that restrict meaningful political participation. These may include discriminatory voter registration requirements, gerrymandering, and restrictions on political campaign funding.

Moreover, the influence of money in politics has raised concerns about the undue influence of wealthy individuals and corporations, leading to a growing sense of disillusionment and a perceived lack of democracy. Addressing these issues and ensuring equal and fair political participation remains an ongoing challenge for democratic societies.

Controversies Surrounding International Human Rights Law

While international human rights law provides a framework for protecting civil and political rights globally, controversies and challenges persist. Questions arise regarding the universality of human rights and the compatibility of these rights with cultural and religious values. Some argue that the imposition of Western concepts of human rights may undermine local traditions and autonomy.

Additionally, the enforcement mechanisms of international human rights law face limitations. The lack of enforcement power and compliance by states often hinders the effective protection of civil and political rights. This has led to criticism that international human rights law is toothless and inadequate in addressing systemic violations.

Conclusion

The protection of civil and political rights faces numerous challenges and controversies. From threats to freedom of speech and expression to limitations on the right to a fair trial, addressing these issues requires a delicate balance between ensuring individual rights and protecting the wider society. Overcoming these challenges will require ongoing dialogue, engagement, and a commitment to upholding the principles of justice and equality.

Indigenous Peoples' Rights

Historical Injustices against Indigenous Peoples

The historical injustices faced by indigenous peoples have had long-lasting and profound effects on their communities. For centuries, indigenous peoples around the world have endured colonization, forced displacement, cultural assimilation, and discrimination. These injustices have had a devastating impact on their rights, cultures, and ways of life.

Colonization by European powers in the Americas, Africa, Asia, and Oceania led to the displacement and marginalization of indigenous peoples. Europeans often viewed indigenous peoples as primitive or inferior, resulting in the systematic destruction of their societies and ways of living. Indigenous lands were taken, and they were forcibly removed from their ancestral territories. This displacement disrupted their social structures and cultural practices, leading to the loss of traditional knowledge and connection to their lands.

One of the major systematic injustices faced by indigenous peoples was the imposition of oppressive legal systems by colonial powers. These legal systems not only denied indigenous peoples their inherent rights but also actively suppressed their cultures, languages, and traditions. Indigenous legal systems were disregarded, and their governance structures were undermined, leading to a loss of self-determination and autonomy.

In addition to the legal and physical violence, indigenous peoples also faced cultural assimilation policies. Children were forcibly removed from their families and communities and placed in boarding schools or foster care systems, where they were prohibited from practicing their cultural traditions and languages. This practice, known as cultural genocide, had significant intergenerational impacts, as indigenous languages and cultural practices were pushed to the brink of extinction.

Historical injustices against indigenous peoples have perpetuated socio-economic disparities. Colonizers exploited indigenous lands, resources, and labor, leading to the impoverishment of indigenous communities. This economic exploitation continues in many parts of the world, with indigenous peoples often being excluded from decision-making processes and denied access to their ancestral lands and resources.

Indigenous peoples have been working tirelessly to address these historical injustices and to reclaim their rights. They have been advocating for the recognition of their inherent rights to self-determination, cultural autonomy, and land ownership. Indigenous-led organizations and movements have been at the forefront of efforts to raise awareness of indigenous rights and to secure legal protections for their communities.

The United Nations Declaration on the Rights of Indigenous Peoples (UNDRIP) is a significant step towards rectifying historical injustices. It reaffirms the rights of indigenous peoples to self-determination, language and culture, lands and resources, and redress for past injustices. UNDRIP provides an international framework for promoting and protecting the rights of indigenous peoples and calls for the full and effective participation of indigenous peoples in decision-making processes that affect their lives.

Despite these advances, challenges persist in addressing historical injustices against indigenous peoples. Many governments still fail to fully implement UNDRIP and uphold the rights of indigenous peoples. Land rights disputes, extractive industries, and environmental degradation continue to threaten the well-being and cultural survival of indigenous communities. Vigilance, activism, and international solidarity are crucial to ensure meaningful redress for historical injustices and to create a more equitable and just world for indigenous peoples.

Example: One example of the historical injustices faced by indigenous peoples is the treatment of Native Americans in the United States. The colonization of North America by European settlers led to the displacement and dispossession of Native American tribes. Treaty violations, forced removals, and military conflicts resulted in the loss of ancestral lands and the disruption of traditional indigenous lifeways.

The Indian Removal Act of 1830, for instance, authorized the forced relocation of Native American tribes from their ancestral lands in the southeastern United States to designated Indian Territory, present-day Oklahoma. This forced removal, known as the Trail of Tears, resulted in the death and suffering of thousands of Cherokee, Choctaw, Creek, Chickasaw, and Seminole peoples.

Furthermore, Native American children were taken from their families and sent to boarding schools where they were forced to abandon their indigenous languages, cultures, and traditions. The goal of these assimilationist policies was to eradicate Native American culture and assimilate them into mainstream American society. The long-term impact of these policies on the well-being and cultural resilience of Native American communities continues to be felt today.

Resources:

- United Nations Declaration on the Rights of Indigenous Peoples (UNDRIP)
- Native American Rights Fund (www.narf.org)
- Survival International (www.survivalinternational.org)
- Truth and Reconciliation Commission of Canada (www.trc.ca)

Key Takeaways:

- Indigenous peoples have faced historical injustices including colonization, forced displacement, cultural assimilation, and discrimination.
- European colonization led to the destruction of indigenous societies and the loss of traditional knowledge and connections to ancestral lands.
- Oppressive legal systems, cultural assimilation policies, and economic exploitation further marginalized indigenous peoples.
- Efforts to address historical injustices include advocacy for indigenous rights, recognition of indigenous legal systems, and the UNDRIP.
- Challenges persist, and ongoing activism and international solidarity are necessary to achieve meaningful redress.

Discussion Questions:

1. How have historical injustices against indigenous peoples impacted their cultures and ways of life?

2. In what ways can recognition of indigenous legal systems contribute to addressing historical injustices?

3. What are some contemporary examples of indigenous-led activism for the recognition of indigenous rights?

Indigenous Peoples' Rights and Self-Determination

Indigenous peoples have a unique relationship with the land they inhabit and have distinct cultures, languages, and traditions. Throughout history, they have faced numerous challenges, including colonization, marginalization, and human rights violations. The recognition and protection of Indigenous peoples' rights and their right to self-determination have emerged as crucial aspects of transformative legal studies.

Historical Background

The historical context of Indigenous peoples' rights is essential to understanding their struggles and the need for self-determination. Colonization and the dispossession of Indigenous lands have had devastating impacts on these communities. They have experienced forced assimilation, cultural erasure, displacement, and violence.

Moreover, the legacy of colonialism continues to influence the legal systems and policies that impact Indigenous peoples. The doctrine of discovery, which originated in European colonialism, has been used to justify the dispossession of Indigenous lands and deny their rights. Acknowledging this history is crucial for developing transformative legal approaches that address these injustices.

International Framework for Indigenous Rights

The international community has recognized the need to protect and promote the rights of Indigenous peoples. The United Nations Declaration on the Rights of Indigenous Peoples (UNDRIP) is a comprehensive framework that sets out the rights of Indigenous peoples and provides guidelines for their protection.

UNDRIP recognizes Indigenous peoples' right to self-determination, which includes the right to freely determine their political, economic, social, and cultural development. It emphasizes the importance of respecting their customs, traditions, and land rights. Additionally, it highlights the need for meaningful participation and consultation in decision-making processes that affect Indigenous communities.

Land Rights and Resource Extraction

Land rights are central to Indigenous peoples' self-determination and cultural survival. Many Indigenous communities have ancestral lands that hold significant cultural, spiritual, and economic value. However, these lands are often subject to resource extraction, such as mining, logging, and hydroelectric projects, which can have detrimental effects on Indigenous peoples and their territories.

Transformative legal approaches aim to protect Indigenous land rights and ensure that resource extraction activities respect the rights and sovereignty of Indigenous communities. This includes recognizing their right to free, prior, and informed consent (FPIC) in decision-making processes regarding activities that may affect their lands and resources.

Community Development and Indigenous Governance

Indigenous self-determination encompasses more than just land rights; it also involves the ability of Indigenous communities to govern themselves and pursue their own development priorities. Transformative legal studies explore models of Indigenous governance that empower communities to make decisions in accordance with their cultural systems and values.

Indigenous governance models emphasize community participation, consensus-building, and sustainable development. These models prioritize the well-being of the community as a whole, including social, economic, and environmental dimensions. Transformative legal approaches support the recognition and strengthening of Indigenous governance structures to foster self-determination and holistic community development.

Challenges and Future Directions

Despite progress in recognizing Indigenous peoples' rights and self-determination, numerous challenges persist. Indigenous communities still face significant barriers in accessing justice, securing their land rights, preserving their languages and cultures, and addressing the legacies of colonization.

Transformative legal studies aim to address these challenges by promoting legal frameworks and policies that prioritize the rights and well-being of Indigenous peoples. They also encourage interdisciplinary research and collaboration to develop innovative solutions and approaches.

In the future, it is crucial to continue advocating for the rights of Indigenous peoples, strengthening legal systems to protect those rights, and supporting Indigenous-led initiatives for self-determination and community development. Implementing and upholding the principles of UNDRIP and promoting inclusive and equitable partnerships with Indigenous communities will contribute to a more just and transformative legal landscape.

Resources for Further Study

Transformative legal studies in the field of Indigenous peoples' rights and self-determination offer a wide range of opportunities for further study. Here are some recommended resources:

- *The Rights of Indigenous Peoples: Selected Basic Documents and Background Materials* by Alexandra Xanthaki.

- *Indigenous Peoples' Rights in International Law: Emergence and Application* by S. James Anaya.

- *Cultural Survival* - an international organization dedicated to advancing Indigenous peoples' rights and support for their self-determination.

- *International Work Group for Indigenous Affairs (IWGIA)* - an organization that provides information and promotes the rights of Indigenous peoples worldwide.

- *United Nations Permanent Forum on Indigenous Issues (UNPFII)* - a platform for Indigenous peoples to engage in dialogue and consultation with UN member states on issues related to their rights and well-being.

These resources provide valuable insights into the historical, legal, and practical dimensions of Indigenous peoples' rights and self-determination. They offer opportunities for further exploration and understanding of transformative legal approaches in this crucial area of study.

Women's Rights and Feminist Approaches to Human Rights

CEDAW and the Protection of Women's Rights

The Convention on the Elimination of All Forms of Discrimination Against Women (CEDAW) is an international treaty adopted by the United Nations General Assembly in 1979. It is often hailed as the international bill of rights for women, aiming to promote and protect women's rights globally. CEDAW serves as an essential framework for addressing gender-based discrimination and inequality and provides a comprehensive approach to achieve gender equality in all aspects of life.

CEDAW is based on the principles of non-discrimination and equality, recognizing that discrimination against women violates their fundamental rights. It defines discrimination against women as any distinction, exclusion, or restriction made on the basis of sex that impairs or nullifies the enjoyment of their human rights and fundamental freedoms. The Convention acknowledges that women's rights are human rights and that gender equality is not only a matter of justice but also a precondition for the full development of society and the achievement of sustainable peace and prosperity.

The Convention expands on the rights enshrined in the Universal Declaration of Human Rights and explicitly addresses the specific challenges faced by women. It covers a wide range of issues, including civil, political, economic, social, and cultural rights. Some key provisions of CEDAW include:

1. Equality before the law: CEDAW requires countries to ensure that women enjoy the same rights and responsibilities as men and that they have equal opportunities to participate in decision-making processes.

2. Elimination of discrimination: CEDAW obligates states to take appropriate measures to eliminate discrimination against women in all areas of life, including education, employment, healthcare, and family life.

3. Violence against women: CEDAW recognizes violence against women as a violation of their human rights and calls on states to take effective measures to prevent and address such violence, including domestic violence, sexual harassment, and trafficking.

4. Women's health: CEDAW emphasizes the importance of women's access to healthcare services, including sexual and reproductive health, and the need to ensure access to family planning, prenatal care, and safe childbirth.

5. Political participation: CEDAW promotes women's equal participation in political and public life and calls for measures to increase women's representation in decision-making positions.

6. Education and employment: CEDAW recognizes the right of women to education and employment, free from discrimination, and calls on states to eliminate gender stereotypes and promote equal opportunities for women in education and the workplace.

7. Marriage and family life: CEDAW highlights the need to ensure equal rights and responsibilities in marriage and family life, including granting women and men the same rights in relation to guardianship, child custody, and property ownership.

CEDAW has been instrumental in guiding governments and civil society in their efforts to promote and protect women's rights. It provides a framework for policy development, legislative reform, and the analysis of discriminatory practices. The Convention is monitored by the Committee on the Elimination of

Discrimination against Women, a group of experts who review states' reports on their progress in implementing CEDAW and provide recommendations for further action.

Despite its significant impact, challenges remain in fully implementing CEDAW. Some countries have not ratified or fully incorporated the Convention into their national legislation, limiting its effectiveness. Persistent social norms, gender stereotypes, and cultural practices continue to undermine women's rights, requiring ongoing advocacy and awareness-raising efforts.

To better understand the real-world implications of CEDAW, let's consider an example. Suppose Country X has recently ratified CEDAW but faces challenges in ensuring equal pay for women. Women in Country X earn, on average, 20

In conclusion, CEDAW plays a crucial role in promoting and protecting women's rights worldwide. It serves as a robust legal framework to address gender-based discrimination and inequality in all spheres of life. However, its full implementation requires ongoing commitment from governments, civil society, and individuals to challenge existing norms, facilitate legislative reforms, and create an environment where women can realize their full potential. By embracing the principles of CEDAW, societies can move closer to achieving genuine gender equality and social justice.

Intersectionality and Women's Rights

In the pursuit of transformative legal studies, one cannot overlook the critical concept of intersectionality, particularly when it comes to addressing women's rights. Intersectionality is a framework that recognizes the overlapping and interconnected nature of various forms of oppression, discrimination, and disadvantage that individuals may experience based on their intersecting identities, such as race, gender, class, sexuality, and ability.

Understanding Intersectionality

Intersectionality emphasizes that individuals do not experience oppression in isolation but rather through a combination of different social categories and identities. It recognizes that gender-based discrimination does not affect all women equally, as women with different intersecting identities may face unique and compounded forms of discrimination. For example, a white woman may experience gender inequality differently than a woman of color due to the additional layer of racism she faces.

Intersectionality and Women's Rights

By applying the lens of intersectionality to women's rights, it becomes evident that achieving gender equality requires considering the experiences of women from diverse backgrounds. This recognition is critical for developing effective legal strategies that address the specific needs and challenges faced by marginalized women.

Key Challenges and Issues

Intersectionality highlights several key challenges and issues associated with women's rights:

1. **Multiple and Interconnected Forms of Discrimination:** Intersectionality acknowledges that individuals may face discrimination based on multiple, intersecting identities. For example, women who identify as LGBTQ+ may face discrimination both as women and as members of the LGBTQ+ community.

2. **Marginalization of Intersectional Feminism:** Intersectional feminism, which recognizes and addresses the unique experiences of women with intersecting identities, has often been marginalized within mainstream feminist movements. This marginalization perpetuates the invisibility of certain groups and hinders the progress towards achieving genuine gender equality.

3. **Inadequate Legal Protections:** Traditional legal frameworks often fail to adequately protect the rights of marginalized women. Laws and policies designed to address gender discrimination may inadvertently exclude or overlook the experiences of women with intersecting identities.

4. **Limited Access to Justice:** Intersectional discrimination can create barriers to accessing justice for marginalized women. Discrimination may be rooted in systemic inequalities, making it challenging for these women to seek legal remedies or find support within the existing legal system.

Legal Strategies and Solutions

To address the challenges and promote women's rights through an intersectional lens, the following strategies can be employed:

1. **Inclusive Legal Frameworks:** Legal frameworks should be developed to recognize the intersecting identities of women and address the diverse forms of discrimination they may face. This requires considering the different experiences and needs of women from marginalized communities in policy development and legislative efforts.

2. **Advocacy and Awareness:** Advocacy efforts should focus on raising awareness about intersectionality and its importance in the context of women's rights. By promoting understanding and recognition of diverse experiences, these efforts can contribute to a more inclusive and effective approach to the advancement of women's rights.

3. **Collaboration and Alliance-Building:** Collaboration between different social justice movements, including those addressing race, sexuality, and class, is crucial for advancing intersectional women's rights. By forming alliances, these movements can amplify their voices and work together towards common goals.

4. **Empowerment and Capacity-Building:** Providing resources and support for marginalized women to develop their legal knowledge and advocacy skills is essential. Empowering these women to voice their concerns and participate actively in legal processes can contribute to transformative change.

Case Studies

Examining real-life examples can help illustrate the importance of intersectionality in women's rights advocacy. One such example is the reproductive justice movement, which not only focuses on women's right to reproductive autonomy but also acknowledges the intertwining issues of race, class, and socioeconomic status that affect access to reproductive healthcare.

Another case study is the fight against workplace harassment, where an intersectional approach considers how gender-based harassment may disproportionately impact women of color, LGBTQ+ women, and women with disabilities. By recognizing these intersections, legal strategies can address the specific challenges faced by different groups of women.

Conclusion

Intersectionality is a fundamental aspect of transformative legal studies, especially concerning women's rights. Recognizing the interconnected nature of gender discrimination with other forms of oppression provides a more comprehensive understanding of the challenges faced by marginalized women. By adopting an intersectional approach, legal practitioners and advocates can develop strategies that truly address the diverse experiences of women and advance gender equality in a more inclusive and impactful way.

Impact of Feminist Approaches on Human Rights Practice

Feminist approaches have had a profound impact on the field of human rights practice, challenging traditional frameworks and advocating for a more inclusive and intersectional understanding of human rights. In this section, we will explore the key contributions of feminist perspectives and examine how they have influenced the development and implementation of human rights principles and practices.

Understanding Feminist Approaches to Human Rights

Feminist approaches to human rights seek to address gender inequalities and promote women's rights within the broader framework of human rights. These approaches recognize that women's experiences of discrimination are often shaped by intersecting factors such as race, class, sexuality, and disability, and emphasize the need for an intersectional analysis of human rights violations.

Central to feminist approaches is the recognition of gender as a social construct that determines power relations and shapes social norms. Feminists argue that traditional human rights frameworks have often overlooked the specific needs and experiences of women, perpetuating gender inequalities.

Inclusion of Women's Rights in Human Rights Instruments

One of the significant impacts of feminist approaches on human rights practice is the inclusion of women's rights in international human rights instruments. Feminist activists and scholars played a crucial role in advocating for the recognition of women's rights as human rights.

This led to the adoption of key international conventions such as the Convention on the Elimination of All Forms of Discrimination Against Women (CEDAW), which sets the standard for women's rights globally. CEDAW addresses a wide range of gender-based discrimination issues, including violence against women, access to education, employment, and reproductive rights.

The inclusion of women's rights in human rights instruments has provided a powerful framework for challenging discriminatory practices and promoting gender equality at both international and national levels.

Intersectionality in Human Rights Advocacy

Feminist approaches have also highlighted the importance of intersectionality in human rights advocacy. Intersectionality recognizes that gender inequalities are interconnected with other forms of discrimination, such as race, ethnicity, social class, and sexuality.

By taking an intersectional approach, feminist activists and scholars have shed light on the specific challenges faced by marginalized groups of women, such as indigenous women, women with disabilities, and LGBTQ+ individuals. This has contributed to a more comprehensive understanding of human rights violations and the need for targeted interventions to address intersecting forms of discrimination.

Addressing Gender-Based Violence

One of the central concerns of feminist approaches to human rights is the issue of gender-based violence. Feminist activists have played a crucial role in bringing attention to various forms of violence against women, including domestic violence, sexual assault, and trafficking.

Their advocacy has led to the development of legal frameworks and mechanisms to address gender-based violence, such as the establishment of specialized courts, the criminalization of marital rape, and the provision of support services for survivors.

Feminist approaches have also contributed to the understanding of gender-based violence as a human rights violation, emphasizing the importance of state accountability and the need for comprehensive strategies to prevent and respond to such violence.

Women's Empowerment and Participation

Feminist approaches to human rights have emphasized the importance of women's empowerment and meaningful participation in decision-making processes. This includes promoting women's political participation, economic empowerment, and access to education and healthcare.

Efforts to promote women's participation have resulted in the adoption of affirmative action policies, the establishment of women's rights organizations, and the recognition of women's leadership in peacebuilding and conflict resolution.

By prioritizing women's empowerment and participation, feminist approaches have sought to address the structural barriers that perpetuate gender inequalities and restrict women's access to their rights.

Challenges and Critiques

While feminist approaches have made significant contributions to human rights practice, they have also faced challenges and critiques. Some critics argue that focusing on gender-specific issues can detract from broader human rights concerns and perpetuate gender stereotypes.

Additionally, there is a need for greater recognition of the diversity of feminist perspectives and the experiences of women from different cultural and social contexts. Intersectionality should be a guiding principle, but there is a risk of essentializing experiences and overlooking the complexities of identities and power dynamics.

Furthermore, feminist approaches need to address the tensions between universal human rights and cultural relativism. Balancing the recognition of cultural diversity with the promotion of women's rights remains a complex and ongoing challenge.

Conclusion

The impact of feminist approaches on human rights practice has been profound. These approaches have challenged traditional frameworks, expanded the understanding of human rights to be more inclusive and intersectional, and highlighted the need for targeted interventions to address gender inequalities.

By advocating for the recognition of women's rights as human rights, promoting intersectionality, addressing gender-based violence, and emphasizing women's empowerment and participation, feminist perspectives have enriched the field of human rights and contributed to significant advancements in the protection of women's rights globally.

Moving forward, it is essential to build on the achievements of feminist approaches while addressing the challenges and critiques. By doing so, human rights practice can continue to evolve towards a more transformative and inclusive vision of justice and equality.

Rights of LGBTQ+ Individuals

Legal Recognition of LGBTQ+ Rights

The legal recognition of LGBTQ+ rights has been a transformative process in many countries around the world. It represents a significant shift in societal attitudes towards the rights and equality of lesbian, gay, bisexual, transgender, and queer individuals. This section explores the historical development of legal recognition for LGBTQ+ rights, the challenges faced, and the progress made in promoting and protecting their rights.

Historical context

The struggle for legal recognition of LGBTQ+ rights is rooted in a long history of discrimination and marginalization. Homosexuality was criminalized in many jurisdictions, and individuals faced severe penalties, including imprisonment and even death. The Stonewall riots in 1969 marked a turning point in the LGBTQ+ rights movement, leading to increased activism and demands for legal reforms.

Milestones in legal recognition

Over the past few decades, significant milestones have been achieved in the legal recognition of LGBTQ+ rights. These milestones vary across different countries and regions, but some common examples include:

- Decriminalization: Many countries have repealed laws that criminalized same-sex relationships, recognizing the rights of LGBTQ+ individuals to engage in consensual sexual activities without fear of prosecution.

- Anti-discrimination laws: Legislation has been enacted to protect LGBTQ+ individuals from discrimination on the basis of sexual orientation or gender identity in various areas, including employment, housing, education, and healthcare.

- Recognition of same-sex relationships: Many jurisdictions have legalized same-sex marriage or established civil partnership laws, granting LGBTQ+ couples the same legal rights and responsibilities as opposite-sex couples.

- Gender recognition: Legal frameworks have been developed to allow transgender and non-binary individuals to legally change their gender markers on official documents, such as identification cards and passports.

- Adoption and parenting rights: LGBTQ+ individuals and couples have gained greater access to adoption and parenting rights, allowing them to form families and provide a nurturing environment for their children.

- Healthcare and insurance coverage: Efforts have been made to ensure that LGBTQ+ individuals have access to appropriate healthcare services, and that insurance coverage includes treatments related to gender transition and same-sex partner benefits.

Challenges and ongoing debates

Despite significant progress, there are still considerable challenges and ongoing debates surrounding the legal recognition of LGBTQ+ rights. Some common challenges include:

- Resistance from conservative groups: There are varying degrees of societal acceptance towards LGBTQ+ rights, with conservative groups often opposing legal reforms and advocating for traditional interpretations of gender and sexuality.

- Legal gaps: In many jurisdictions, there are still legal gaps in protecting the rights of LGBTQ+ individuals, particularly in areas such as employment, healthcare, and transgender rights.

- Global disparities: The legal recognition of LGBTQ+ rights varies significantly across different countries and regions, with some jurisdictions providing comprehensive protections while others maintain discriminatory laws and policies.

- Intersectionality: LGBTQ+ individuals who belong to other marginalized groups may face compounded discrimination, requiring a more intersectional approach to legal recognition and protection of their rights.

Impact of legal recognition

The legal recognition of LGBTQ+ rights has had a profound impact on individuals and communities. It has increased social acceptance, reduced stigma, and provided a legal framework for LGBTQ+ individuals to assert their rights. Some key impacts include:

- Psychological well-being: Legal recognition has been associated with improved mental health outcomes among LGBTQ+ individuals, reducing the burden of discrimination and fostering a sense of belonging and acceptance.

- Social visibility: Legal reforms have helped enhance the visibility of LGBTQ+ individuals in society, challenging stereotypes and promoting a more inclusive understanding of gender and sexuality.

- Family and relationship recognition: Legal recognition of same-sex relationships has provided LGBTQ+ couples and families with legal protections, rights, and responsibilities, contributing to greater stability and support.

- Access to healthcare: Laws that prohibit discrimination based on sexual orientation and gender identity have improved access to healthcare services for LGBTQ+ individuals, reducing health disparities and promoting better overall health outcomes.

- Movement towards equality: The legal recognition of LGBTQ+ rights has contributed to a broader movement towards equality and social justice, challenging discriminatory structures and paving the way for further societal change.

Resources for further study

For those interested in further exploring the topic of legal recognition of LGBTQ+ rights, the following resources provide valuable insights and perspectives:

- *International LGBTQ+ Rights and Equality: A Resource Guide* by Human Rights Watch.

- *Legal Recognition of Same-Sex Couples in Europe: National, Cross-Border and European Perspectives* edited by Kees Waaldijk.

- *Transgender Rights and the Law* by Paisley Currah, Richard M. Juang, and Shannon Price Minter.

- *Queer (In)Justice: The Criminalization of LGBTQ+ People in the United States* by Joey L. Mogul, Andrea J. Ritchie, and Kay Whitlock.

These resources offer in-depth analysis, case studies, and legal frameworks related to the recognition of LGBTQ+ rights, contributing to a comprehensive understanding of the subject.

Conclusion

The legal recognition of LGBTQ+ rights represents a transformative shift in societal attitudes and legal frameworks. The milestones achieved in the fight for equality have had a profound impact on the lives of LGBTQ+ individuals and communities.

However, there are still challenges and ongoing debates that need to be addressed to ensure comprehensive legal protections and the full realization of LGBTQ+ rights. By continuing to promote inclusivity, advocate for legal reforms, and raise awareness, we can contribute to a more just and equal society for all.

Challenges and Discrimination Faced by LGBTQ+ Individuals

The LGBTQ+ community faces numerous challenges and forms of discrimination in various aspects of their lives. These challenges arise due to prejudice, stereotypes, and societal bias against their sexual orientation or gender identity. This section explores some of the key challenges and discrimination faced by LGBTQ+ individuals and highlights the importance of addressing these issues for a more inclusive and equal society.

Legal Challenges

One of the significant challenges faced by LGBTQ+ individuals is the lack of legal recognition and protection of their rights. Many countries have laws that criminalize consensual same-sex relationships or fail to provide legal protection against discrimination based on sexual orientation or gender identity. These laws perpetuate stigma, marginalization, and violence against LGBTQ+ individuals.

For example, in some countries, same-sex sexual activity is still considered a crime, and individuals engaging in such relationships may face imprisonment or other forms of punishment. Even in countries that have decriminalized homosexuality, laws protecting LGBTQ+ individuals from discrimination, hate crimes, and violence are often inadequate or non-existent.

Furthermore, transgender individuals often face legal challenges in obtaining accurate identification documents that reflect their gender identity. This can lead to difficulties in accessing various services, including healthcare, housing, employment, and education, and exposes them to discrimination and harassment.

Social Stigma and Discrimination

LGBTQ+ individuals face pervasive social stigma and discrimination in many societies. This discrimination manifests in various forms, including verbal and physical abuse, harassment, bullying, and exclusion from social, educational, and employment opportunities. These biases not only affect their mental and emotional well-being but also hinder their ability to fully participate and thrive in society.

Homophobia and transphobia perpetuate negative stereotypes and stereotypes against LGBTQ+ individuals, resulting in discrimination in various spheres of life. LGBTQ+ individuals may face rejection from their families, friends, and communities, leading to feelings of isolation and a lack of support systems.

Moreover, societal attitudes towards LGBTQ+ individuals can impact their access to healthcare, housing, and employment. Discrimination and prejudice can result in denial of services, unequal treatment, and limited opportunities for LGBTQ+ individuals. This exclusion and marginalization contribute to health disparities, economic disadvantage, and lower quality of life for many LGBTQ+ individuals.

Violence and Hate Crimes

LGBTQ+ individuals face a disproportionate level of violence and hate crimes compared to the general population. Hate crimes targeting individuals based on their sexual orientation or gender identity often involve physical assault, verbal abuse, and even murder. These crimes create a climate of fear and insecurity for LGBTQ+ individuals and can have long-lasting traumatic effects.

Transgender individuals, especially transgender women of color, are particularly vulnerable to violence and hate crimes. They face high levels of discrimination, harassment, and even lethal violence. Addressing these issues requires both legal protection against hate crimes and comprehensive social support systems that promote safety and well-being for LGBTQ+ individuals.

Access to Healthcare

Access to inclusive and affirming healthcare remains a significant challenge for many LGBTQ+ individuals. They may encounter healthcare providers who lack knowledge and awareness of their specific healthcare needs, resulting in inadequate or discriminatory care. This can lead to delayed or denied healthcare services, compromised health outcomes, and increased health disparities within the LGBTQ+ community.

Moreover, transgender individuals often face significant barriers in accessing gender-affirming healthcare, including gender-affirming surgeries, hormone therapy, and mental health support. The lack of understanding and training among healthcare professionals often leads to transphobia and discrimination.

Intersectional Challenges

It is vital to recognize that LGBTQ+ individuals may face intersecting forms of discrimination and marginalization based on their sexual orientation, gender identity, race, ethnicity, socioeconomic status, and other factors. Intersectionality complicates the experiences of LGBTQ+ individuals and highlights the need for an inclusive approach to addressing their challenges.

For example, transgender women of color may face compounded discrimination and violence due to their intersecting identities. LGBTQ+ individuals with disabilities may encounter additional barriers in accessing healthcare, education, and employment.

The Importance of Addressing Challenges

Addressing the challenges and discrimination faced by LGBTQ+ individuals is crucial for the creation of a more inclusive and equal society. It requires comprehensive efforts from multiple stakeholders, including governments, legal institutions, education systems, healthcare providers, and civil society organizations.

Some key approaches to address these challenges include:

1. Legal Reforms: Advocating for legal reforms that decriminalize homosexuality, recognize same-sex relationships, and provide comprehensive legal protection against discrimination based on sexual orientation and gender identity.

2. Education and Awareness: Promoting education and awareness programs that challenge stereotypes and promote acceptance and inclusion of LGBTQ+ individuals in schools, workplaces, and communities.

3. Healthcare Equity: Ensuring inclusive and affirming healthcare services that address the specific needs of LGBTQ+ individuals and provide gender-affirming care without discrimination.

4. Social Support Systems: Establishing support systems, including support groups, counseling services, and helplines, to address the mental health and well-being of LGBTQ+ individuals.

5. Intersectional Approaches: Recognizing and addressing the intersecting forms of discrimination and marginalization faced by LGBTQ+ individuals through intersectional policies and programs.

By addressing these challenges and working towards a more inclusive society, we can create an environment that respects and upholds the rights and dignity of all individuals, regardless of their sexual orientation or gender identity. This transformation is crucial for promoting justice, equality, and the overall well-being of LGBTQ+ individuals worldwide.

Progress and Future Outlook for LGBTQ+ Rights

The fight for LGBTQ+ rights has made significant progress over the years, with the recognition and protection of the rights of lesbian, gay, bisexual, transgender, and queer individuals becoming a growing priority in many countries worldwide. However, there is still much work to be done to ensure full equality and acceptance for the LGBTQ+ community. In this section, we will explore the progress that has been made in LGBTQ+ rights and discuss the future outlook for achieving further advancements.

Historical Context and Achievements

The struggle for LGBTQ+ rights has a long history that has involved legal battles, social movements, and community activism. Significant milestones have been achieved, paving the way for greater equality and acceptance. Some key historical achievements include:

- Decriminalization of homosexuality: Many countries have decriminalized homosexuality, recognizing the rights of individuals to engage in consensual same-sex relationships without fear of criminal prosecution. This has been a crucial step towards ending discrimination and promoting LGBTQ+ rights.

- Recognition of same-sex marriage: Over the past two decades, many countries have recognized same-sex marriage, granting same-sex couples the same legal rights and protections as opposite-sex couples. This achievement has been instrumental in affirming the equal dignity and worth of LGBTQ+ relationships.

- Anti-discrimination laws: Numerous countries have enacted laws to protect LGBTQ+ individuals from discrimination in various areas, such as employment, housing, and public accommodations. These laws aim to ensure equal opportunities and treatment for all, irrespective of sexual orientation or gender identity.

- Adoption and parenting rights: LGBTQ+ individuals and couples have gained greater legal recognition and protection when it comes to adopting children or establishing families through assisted reproductive technologies.

This has allowed countless LGBTQ+ individuals and couples to experience the joys of parenthood.

- Transgender rights: In recent years, there has been an increased focus on transgender rights, including the recognition of gender identity, access to healthcare, legal gender recognition procedures, and protection against discrimination and violence.

These achievements demonstrate the progress that has been made in the struggle for LGBTQ+ rights. However, it is important to acknowledge that the advancements have not been uniform globally, and many challenges remain.

Challenges and Persistent Issues

While progress has been made in LGBTQ+ rights, there are still significant challenges and persistent issues that need to be addressed. Some of the key challenges include:

- Legal disparities: LGBTQ+ individuals continue to face legal disparities in many parts of the world. In some countries, same-sex relationships are still criminalized, and there are limited legal protections against discrimination based on sexual orientation and gender identity.

- Violence and discrimination: Hate crimes, bullying, and discrimination against LGBTQ+ individuals persist in various forms. Transgender individuals, in particular, face high levels of violence and discrimination due to societal prejudice and lack of legal protections.

- Health disparities: LGBTQ+ individuals experience disparities in healthcare access and outcomes, including mental health issues, HIV/AIDS prevalence, and lack of culturally competent healthcare providers. These disparities reflect the need for more inclusive healthcare policies and practices.

- Global disparities: While progress has been made in some countries, LGBTQ+ individuals in many parts of the world still face extreme persecution, violence, and legal discrimination. Global efforts are needed to support those living in regions where LGBTQ+ rights are not yet recognized or protected.

Addressing these challenges requires ongoing activism, legal reform, and societal change. It is important to focus on creating inclusive policies and fostering acceptance and understanding in communities worldwide.

Future Outlook and Strategies for Change

As we look to the future of LGBTQ+ rights, there are several strategies and areas of focus that can contribute to further progress and equality. Some key aspects include:

- Legislative reforms: Continued efforts to advocate for comprehensive legal protections against discrimination based on sexual orientation and gender identity are crucial. This includes pushing for the enactment of anti-discrimination laws, the recognition of same-sex relationships, and the protection of transgender rights.

- Education and awareness: Promoting education and awareness about LGBTQ+ issues is essential for challenging stereotypes, combating prejudice, and fostering acceptance. This includes implementing LGBTQ+-inclusive curricula in schools, promoting diversity and inclusion training, and raising public awareness about the importance of LGBTQ+ rights.

- Intersectionality: Recognizing and addressing the intersectional experiences of LGBTQ+ individuals is vital. This involves understanding how race, ethnicity, socioeconomic status, disability, and other factors intersect with sexual orientation and gender identity, and working towards inclusive policies and practices that address the unique challenges faced by individuals with multiple marginalized identities.

- Advocacy and community engagement: Grassroots activism, community organizing, and LGBTQ+ support networks play a significant role in driving change. By supporting and engaging with LGBTQ+ organizations and community-led initiatives, individuals can contribute to the ongoing fight for equality and social justice.

- Global solidarity and cooperation: Achieving true equality for LGBTQ+ individuals requires global solidarity and collaboration. Supporting activists and advocacy groups working in countries where LGBTQ+ rights are under threat, engaging in international human rights mechanisms, and fostering dialogue and cooperation across borders are crucial for creating a more inclusive world.

The future outlook for LGBTQ+ rights is hopeful but requires ongoing commitment and effort from individuals, communities, governments, and international bodies. By working together, we can continue to make progress towards a world where LGBTQ+ individuals enjoy full equality, acceptance, and protection of their rights.

Resources and Further Reading

To further explore LGBTQ+ rights and related topics, the following resources provide valuable insights and information:

- Human Rights Campaign: *www.hrc.org*

- International Lesbian, Gay, Bisexual, Trans, and Intersex Association (ILGA): *www.ilga.org*

- OutRight Action International: *www.outrightinternational.org*

- GLAAD: *www.glaad.org*

- American Civil Liberties Union (ACLU): *www.aclu.org*

These organizations offer research reports, publications, news updates, and resources for advocacy and support. Additionally, academic journals such as the *Journal of Homosexuality*, *Sexualities*, and *LGBT Health* provide scholarly articles on LGBTQ+ issues.

Conclusion

The progress made in LGBTQ+ rights is a testament to the resilience and determination of LGBTQ+ individuals and supportive allies. While challenges persist, efforts to secure legal protection, promote awareness and education, and foster acceptance are advancing the cause of LGBTQ+ rights. By continuing to push for change, embracing intersectionality, and fostering global cooperation, we can create a future where LGBTQ+ individuals live free from discrimination and enjoy equal rights and opportunities.

Children's Rights and the Convention on the Rights of the Child

Overview of Children's Rights

Children's rights are a fundamental aspect of human rights that specifically focus on the needs and well-being of individuals under the age of 18. The Convention on the Rights of the Child, adopted by the United Nations General Assembly in 1989, serves as the primary international legal instrument for the protection and promotion of children's rights. This section provides an overview of the key principles, challenges, and achievements in the field of children's rights.

Principles of Children's Rights

Children's rights are guided by several key principles:

1. Non-discrimination: Children are entitled to enjoy their rights without any form of discrimination, including on the basis of their race, gender, socio-economic status, disability, or any other characteristic.

2. Best interests of the child: The best interests of the child should be a primary consideration in all decisions and actions concerning children.

3. Right to life, survival, and development: Children have the right to life, healthcare, education, and to reach their full potential in a safe and supportive environment.

4. Respect for the views of the child: Children have the right to express their opinions and participate in decisions that affect their lives, according to their age and maturity.

5. Freedom from violence, abuse, and exploitation: Every child has the right to be protected from all forms of violence, abuse, neglect, and exploitation.

Key Areas of Children's Rights

Children's rights encompass a wide range of issues, covering civil, political, economic, social, and cultural dimensions. Some of the key areas include:

1. Education: Children have the right to free and compulsory primary education, equal access to quality education, and the opportunity to develop their full potential.

2. Health and well-being: Children have the right to access essential healthcare services, good nutrition, clean water, and sanitation. They should be protected from harmful practices and have access to information on health-related issues.

3. Protection from violence and abuse: Children have the right to be protected from all forms of violence, including child abuse, trafficking, and harmful traditional practices.

4. Family and alternative care: Children have the right to grow up in a caring family environment and, when necessary, to receive appropriate alternative care. They should be protected from separation from their parents, unless it is deemed to be in their best interests.

5. Justice and legal protection: Children have the right to be treated fairly in legal proceedings and to have their rights protected if they come into contact with the justice system.

Challenges and Achievements

Despite significant progress in the recognition and protection of children's rights, numerous challenges persist:

1. Poverty and inequality: Children living in poverty often face multiple violations of their rights, including limited access to education, healthcare, and basic necessities.

2. Conflict and displacement: Children affected by armed conflict or forced displacement face heightened risks to their physical and mental well-being.

3. Child labor and exploitation: Millions of children around the world are engaged in child labor, exposing them to hazardous conditions and compromising their education and development.

4. Discrimination and marginalization: Children from minority groups, indigenous backgrounds, or with disabilities are often subjected to discrimination and may face barriers in accessing their rights.

However, there have also been notable achievements in the field of children's rights:

1. Universal ratification of the Convention on the Rights of the Child: The Convention has been ratified by almost every country in the world, demonstrating a global commitment to protecting and promoting children's rights.

2. Reduction in child mortality rates: Efforts to improve healthcare access and nutrition have contributed to a significant decline in child mortality rates worldwide.

3. Increased access to education: More children have access to education than ever before, with efforts focused on addressing gender disparities and ensuring inclusion for children with disabilities.

4. Focus on child participation: The recognition of children's right to express their views and participate in decision-making processes has gained momentum, leading to greater involvement of children in issues that affect them.

Current Issues and Future Directions

While progress has been made, there are still critical issues that need to be addressed to further advance children's rights:

1. Online safety: With the rapid growth of the digital age, protecting children from online risks and ensuring their digital rights have become increasingly important.

2. Climate change: The impact of climate change poses significant threats to children's health, education, and overall well-being. Efforts to address climate change must incorporate a children's rights perspective.

3. Migrant and refugee children: The rights of migrant and refugee children should be guaranteed, including access to education, healthcare, and protection from violence and discrimination.

4. Child participation and empowerment: Continued efforts to promote meaningful child participation in decision-making processes and to empower children as agents of change are crucial.

In conclusion, children's rights are an essential part of the broader human rights framework. Recognizing and protecting the rights of children is crucial for their well-being, growth, and development. While progress has been made, it is necessary to address ongoing challenges and ensure that children's rights are universally upheld to create a just and equitable world for all children.

Child Labor and Exploitation

Child labor and exploitation are critical issues that need to be addressed within the context of transformative legal studies. This section explores the various dimensions and challenges associated with child labor and exploitation, highlighting the need for transformative legal approaches to protect the rights and well-being of children worldwide.

Understanding Child Labor

Child labor refers to the employment of children in any work that deprives them of their childhood, interferes with their ability to attend regular schools, and is mentally, physically, socially, or morally harmful. It is a global phenomenon that affects millions of children, particularly in developing countries. Child labor takes many forms, including hazardous work, forced labor, trafficking, and exploitation.

Legal Framework and International Standards

The international community has recognized the importance of combating child labor and has established several legal frameworks and standards to address this issue. The International Labor Organization (ILO) is at the forefront of efforts to eliminate child labor globally. Important conventions include:

- **ILO Convention No. 138:** This convention sets the minimum age for employment and aims to eliminate child labor by ensuring that children receive adequate schooling and protection from harm.

- **ILO Convention No. 182:** This convention focuses on the worst forms of child labor, including hazardous work, forced labor, and trafficking. It aims to provide measures for immediate action to eliminate these practices.

- **UN Convention on the Rights of the Child (CRC):** The CRC is a comprehensive international treaty that sets out the civil, political, economic, social, and cultural rights of children. It provides a holistic framework for the protection and well-being of children.

These legal frameworks provide a basis for transformative legal approaches to address child labor and exploitation across different jurisdictions.

Root Causes and Complexities

Child labor and exploitation are deeply interconnected with various social, economic, and cultural factors. Understanding the root causes and complexities of these issues is crucial for transformative legal studies. Some significant factors include:

- **Poverty and Lack of Education:** Poverty forces families to rely on child labor as a means of survival. Lack of access to quality education perpetuates the cycle of exploitation.

- **Social Norms and Traditional Practices:** Certain social norms and traditional practices normalize child labor, making it challenging to eradicate without addressing underlying cultural beliefs.

- **Global Supply Chains:** The demand for cheap labor and products fuels child labor and exploitation in global supply chains. Transformative legal approaches should address the responsibility of companies to ensure supply chain transparency and ethical practices.

Addressing child labor requires a multidimensional approach that tackles these root causes, incorporating legal, educational, economic, and social interventions.

Transformative Legal Approaches

Transformative legal approaches aim to go beyond traditional legal frameworks and challenge systemic barriers to justice. In the context of child labor and exploitation, transformative legal studies should focus on:

- **Advocacy and Policy Change:** Activism and advocacy play a crucial role in raising awareness, influencing policy, and mobilizing action to combat child labor. Transformative legal studies should empower communities and organizations to engage in policy dialogue and push for legal reforms.

- **Access to Justice:** Ensuring access to justice for child laborers is essential. Transformative legal approaches should focus on creating child-friendly legal systems, providing legal aid and support services, and strengthening the capacity of legal practitioners to effectively represent the interests of children.

- **Education and Awareness:** Transformative legal studies should emphasize the importance of education and awareness in preventing child labor. Education programs should not only aim to keep children in school but also promote awareness among communities about the negative consequences of child labor and the importance of children's rights.

- **Partnerships and Collaboration:** Addressing child labor requires collaborative efforts between governments, civil society organizations, nonprofit organizations, and the private sector. Transformative legal approaches should facilitate partnerships that can leverage resources, expertise, and influence to tackle child labor and exploitation effectively.

Case Studies and Best Practices

Examining case studies and best practices can provide valuable insights into effective strategies for combating child labor and exploitation. For example:

- **Rugmark Foundation in India:** The Rugmark Foundation is a social certification program that works to eliminate child labor in the carpet industry by certifying child-labor-free carpets and providing support to rehabilitate rescued child laborers.

- **Fairtrade Certification:** Fairtrade certification ensures that products are produced under fair and ethical conditions, prohibiting child labor. It provides consumers with the assurance that the products they purchase are free from exploitative practices.

- **International Justice Mission (IJM):** IJM is a nonprofit organization that focuses on rescuing victims of child trafficking and providing them with legal support, rehabilitation, and aftercare services. It also works with governments to strengthen legal frameworks and enforcement mechanisms to combat child exploitation.

These case studies demonstrate the transformative potential of legal interventions in addressing child labor and exploitation.

Conclusion

Transformative legal approaches are crucial in addressing child labor and exploitation effectively. By understanding the legal frameworks, complexities, and root causes of these issues, transformative legal studies can develop innovative strategies to protect the rights and well-being of children globally. Through advocacy, policy change, access to justice, education, and partnerships, transformative legal approaches can contribute to the eradication of child labor and the promotion of a more equitable and just society for all children.

Access to Education and Healthcare for Children

Access to education and healthcare for children is a fundamental right that plays a crucial role in their overall development and well-being. In this section, we will explore the importance of ensuring equal access to quality education and healthcare for all children, the challenges and barriers they may face in accessing these services, and the transformative approaches that can address these issues.

Importance of Education for Children

Education is not only a basic human right but also a key driver of social and economic progress. It empowers children to break the cycle of poverty, improve their living conditions, and lead fulfilling lives. Quality education equips children with the knowledge and skills necessary to pursue their dreams, contribute to society, and become active participants in shaping their future. It fosters critical thinking, creativity, and problem-solving abilities, which are essential for personal growth and success in a rapidly changing world.

Challenges in Accessing Education

Despite the value and significance of education, millions of children around the world still face barriers to accessing quality schooling. These challenges can be attributed to various factors, including poverty, gender inequality, disability, conflict and displacement, discrimination, and lack of infrastructure and resources. Understanding and addressing these barriers are crucial for realizing the right to education for all children.

Barriers to Accessing Healthcare

In addition to education, ensuring access to healthcare is equally important for children's holistic development and well-being. Accessible, affordable, and quality healthcare services play a vital role in preventing and treating diseases, promoting healthy growth and development, and addressing the physical, mental, and emotional needs of children. However, numerous barriers can hinder access to healthcare, including financial constraints, lack of healthcare infrastructure, geographical remoteness, cultural and social norms, and insufficient health education and awareness.

Transformative Approaches to Enhance Access

To overcome these challenges and ensure equal access to education and healthcare, transformative approaches are needed. These approaches aim to address the root causes of inequality and injustice, create inclusive and supportive environments, and empower individuals and communities to actively participate in decision-making processes.

1. Inclusive Education Inclusive education is a transformative approach that promotes equal opportunities for all children, regardless of their background, abilities, or differences. It recognizes and accommodates diverse learning needs and styles, fosters respect and understanding, and eliminates discriminatory practices. Inclusive education involves adapting teaching methods, providing individualized support, and creating inclusive learning environments that enable all children to fully participate and thrive.

2. Community-Based Healthcare Community-based healthcare models focus on delivering healthcare services closer to communities, making them more accessible and responsive to local needs. These models involve engaging and empowering community members, including parents, caregivers, and local healthcare providers, in the planning, implementation, and evaluation of healthcare initiatives. By involving communities, these models can better address cultural, social, and economic barriers to healthcare access and promote the overall well-being of children.

3. Multi-sectoral Collaboration Transformative approaches to improving access to education and healthcare require collaboration across different sectors and stakeholders. Governments, civil society organizations, healthcare providers, educators, parents, and children themselves must work together to develop comprehensive strategies, policies, and programs that prioritize children's rights to education and healthcare. By aligning efforts and sharing resources, collaborative initiatives can effectively address the complex challenges and systemic barriers that hinder access.

Real-World Example: The Right to Education in India

To illustrate the transformative approaches discussed, let's consider the example of the Right to Education (RTE) Act in India. The RTE Act, enacted in 2009, is a landmark legislation that aims to provide free and compulsory education for all children aged 6 to 14. It recognizes education as a fundamental right and emphasizes the importance of inclusive education by prohibiting discrimination and promoting equal opportunities.

The RTE Act adopts a transformative approach by focusing on systemic changes, such as abolishing school fees, ensuring adequate infrastructure and resources, and promoting child-friendly teaching methods. It also emphasizes the need for equity, allocating resources to marginalized and disadvantaged groups to address historical inequalities. Furthermore, the Act involves community participation through School Management Committees, enabling parents and community members to participate in school decision-making processes.

Despite its significant impact, challenges remain in implementing the RTE Act fully. Adequate infrastructure, trained teachers, and quality education are still lacking in many schools, particularly in rural and marginalized areas. However, the Act serves as a powerful example of how transformative approaches can address barriers to education by integrating diverse stakeholders, promoting inclusivity, and prioritizing children's rights.

Resources for Further Study

For further study on access to education and healthcare for children, the following resources provide valuable insights and information:

- United Nations Children's Fund (UNICEF): UNICEF's website offers a wide range of resources on education and healthcare for children, including reports, publications, and data-driven analyses. It provides a comprehensive understanding of the global challenges and transformative approaches in ensuring child rights.

- Global Partnership for Education (GPE): GPE's website provides information on global efforts to improve education access and quality. It offers research, case studies, and policy documents that highlight successful initiatives and strategies implemented around the world.

- World Health Organization (WHO): The WHO's website offers resources and publications on child health, healthcare access, and strategies for promoting health equity. It provides evidence-based recommendations and guidelines for improving healthcare services for children.

- International Journal of Educational Development: This academic journal focuses on educational research and development, including topics related to access to education, inclusive education, and quality education for children. It features articles and studies that examine transformative approaches in education.

- The Lancet: The Lancet is a renowned medical journal that publishes research articles on child health, healthcare access, and innovative healthcare strategies. It provides valuable insights into healthcare challenges and transformative approaches to address them.

Conclusion

Ensuring access to education and healthcare for children is crucial for their overall development and well-being. By adopting transformative approaches, such as inclusive education, community-based healthcare, and multi-sectoral collaboration, we can address the barriers and challenges that hinder access. Real-world examples, like the Right to Education Act in India, illustrate the transformative potential of these approaches.

By prioritizing the rights of children and empowering communities, we can create a future where all children have equal opportunities to learn, grow, and thrive. The transformative power of education and healthcare can pave the way for a more just, equal, and compassionate society. Let us work together to ensure that every child can access the education and healthcare they deserve.

Transitional Justice and Human Rights

Definition and Principles of Transitional Justice

Transitional justice is a field of study and practice that aims to address the legacies of large-scale human rights abuses and promote justice, healing, and reconciliation in societies transitioning from conflict, authoritarian rule, or other periods of widespread violence. It encompasses a range of mechanisms, processes, and principles that seek to address the past and lay the groundwork for a more just and peaceful future.

Definition of Transitional Justice

Transitional justice can be defined as the set of judicial and non-judicial measures that societies employ to address human rights abuses committed in the past. It seeks to foster accountability for these abuses, ensure victims' rights to truth, justice, and reparations, and promote long-term reconciliation and the rule of law.

The focus of transitional justice extends beyond individual criminal responsibility to include broader societal concerns, such as addressing systemic and structural issues, establishing a historical record of the past, and creating the conditions for sustainable peace and justice.

Principles of Transitional Justice

Transitional justice is guided by several key principles that inform its approaches and methods. These principles include:

1. **Accountability:** Transitional justice seeks to hold perpetrators of human rights abuses accountable for their actions. It recognizes the importance of establishing the truth about past crimes, prosecuting those responsible, and providing reparations to victims.

2. **Restorative justice:** This principle emphasizes the importance of restoring relationships and healing the social fabric torn apart by violence. It aims to address the needs and concerns of victims, promote dialogue and reconciliation, and foster a sense of justice and closure.

3. **Non-recurrence:** Transitional justice seeks to prevent the recurrence of violence and human rights abuses in the future. It often includes measures to address the root causes of violence, reform institutions responsible for past abuses, and promote respect for human rights and the rule of law.

4. **Inclusivity and participation:** Transitional justice emphasizes the inclusion and participation of affected communities, victims, and marginalized groups in decision-making processes. It recognizes the importance of their voices, experiences, and perspectives in shaping the design and implementation of transitional justice initiatives.

5. **Rule of law:** Transitional justice is grounded in the principles of the rule of law, which entails equal protection and access to justice for all members of society. It seeks to ensure that justice is administered fairly, impartially, and in accordance with international human rights standards.

Mechanisms of Transitional Justice

Transitional justice employs various mechanisms to achieve its goals. These mechanisms can be broadly categorized into judicial and non-judicial processes.

1. **Judicial mechanisms:** These include domestic or international courts and tribunals established to prosecute individuals responsible for human rights abuses. Examples include ad hoc tribunals such as the International Criminal Tribunal for the Former Yugoslavia and the International Criminal Tribunal for Rwanda, as well as hybrid courts and national prosecutions.

2. **Truth-seeking mechanisms:** Truth commissions are established to investigate and document past abuses, provide a historical record, and promote societal healing. These commissions conduct interviews, collect testimonies, and publish reports that help establish the truth about the violations committed.

3. **Reparations programs:** These mechanisms aim to provide redress for victims through various means, including monetary compensation, symbolic gestures, rehabilitation services, and guarantees of non-repetition. Reparations programs acknowledge the harm inflicted on individuals and communities and seek to restore their dignity and well-being.

4. **Institutional reforms:** Transitional justice often involves reforming state institutions, such as the police, military, and judiciary, to address systemic issues and prevent future abuses. These reforms may include vetting processes, training programs, and structural changes to ensure accountability, transparency, and respect for human rights.

5. **Community-based initiatives:** Transitional justice recognizes the importance of community-level processes in healing and reconciliation. These initiatives involve dialogue forums, memorialization projects, traditional dispute resolution mechanisms, and other grassroots efforts that empower communities to address their own needs and chart their own path toward justice.

Challenges and Critiques

While transitional justice has made significant contributions to addressing human rights abuses and promoting justice, it also faces challenges and critiques. Some of these challenges include:

1. **Limited resources:** Transitional justice processes, such as prosecutions and reparations, often require substantial financial and logistical resources. Limited resources can hinder the effectiveness and comprehensiveness of these initiatives, particularly in post-conflict or economically disadvantaged contexts.

2. **Political obstacles**: Transitional justice initiatives can face resistance from political elites, who may perceive accountability measures as a threat to their power or legitimacy. Negotiating the political complexities of transitional contexts can pose significant challenges to the implementation of comprehensive transitional justice strategies.

3. **Selective justice**: Due to the limitations of resources and political considerations, transitional justice processes may not address all human rights abuses or involve all perpetrators. The selective nature of justice can create perceptions of bias, unfairness, and unresolved grievances, which may undermine the viability and legitimacy of the transitional justice project.

4. **Lack of international cooperation**: International cooperation is crucial for the success of transitional justice, particularly in cases involving cross-border crimes or international criminal networks. However, securing international cooperation, including the extradition of suspects or sharing of evidence, can be challenging due to political interests or limited cooperation from relevant states.

Conclusion

Transitional justice plays a vital role in societies seeking to address the legacies of human rights abuses and promote justice, healing, and reconciliation. It encompasses a range of mechanisms and principles that aim to foster accountability, restore relationships, prevent future abuses, and promote the rule of law. While facing challenges and criticisms, it holds the promise of contributing to more just and peaceful societies. Students and practitioners of law and human rights can engage with transitional justice principles and explore its potential for societal transformation and the realization of human rights.

Truth Commissions and Truth-telling Processes

In the pursuit of justice and reconciliation, truth commissions have emerged as significant mechanisms for addressing past human rights abuses and promoting social transformation. This section explores the concept of truth commissions, their role in transitional justice, and the truth-telling processes that they employ.

Understanding Truth Commissions

Truth commissions are governmental or non-governmental bodies established to investigate and document past human rights violations or other forms of historical injustice. They play a crucial role in post-conflict or post-authoritarian societies, aiming to establish a comprehensive and truthful account of past atrocities.

These commissions operate on the premise that truth-telling and the acknowledgment of past wrongs are crucial for healing societies and preventing future abuses. By shedding light on the truth, truth commissions contribute to the process of reconciliation, redress, and the prevention of historical revisionism.

The Principles of Truth Commissions

There are several key principles that guide the work of truth commissions:

- **Independence:** Truth commissions should operate independently of political interference to ensure impartiality and credibility.

- **Transparency:** The processes and findings of truth commissions should be made public to foster trust and accountability.

- **Victim-centered approach:** Truth commissions should prioritize the needs and rights of victims, providing them with an opportunity to share their stories and seek justice.

- **Inclusivity:** Truth commissions should engage with a broad range of stakeholders, including marginalized groups and diverse perspectives, to ensure a comprehensive understanding of the past.

These principles serve as the foundation for truth commissions' work and guide their methodologies and outreach strategies.

Truth-telling Processes

Truth commissions employ various truth-telling processes to gather information, document human rights violations, and establish a historical record. These processes typically include:

- **Public Hearings:** Truth commissions conduct public hearings where victims, perpetrators, and witnesses can provide testimony. These hearings allow for personal narratives to be shared, creating a public record of the injustices committed.

- **Victim Testimonies:** Truth commissions prioritize victim testimonies, granting them a safe and supportive environment to recount their experiences. These testimonies humanize the suffering endured and contribute to the validation of victims' experiences.

- **Official Documentation:** Truth commissions analyze official records, documents, and archives to corroborate testimonies and establish the context and magnitude of human rights violations.
- **Forensic Investigations:** In some cases, truth commissions may engage in forensic investigations to identify the remains of victims, providing closure for families and supporting the establishment of a factual record.
- **Expert Witness Testimonies:** Truth commissions may call upon experts in various fields, such as human rights law, sociology, or anthropology, to provide specialized knowledge and analysis on the causes and consequences of past injustices.

By employing these truth-telling processes, truth commissions aim to uncover the truth, provide a platform for victims' voices, and establish an accurate historical narrative.

Challenges and Limitations

While truth commissions play a vital role in transitional justice, they also face several challenges and limitations:

- **Political Obstacles:** Truth commissions often operate within complex political environments, with political elites resisting the disclosure of inconvenient truths or seeking to manipulate the narrative to protect their interests.
- **Access to Information:** Obtaining access to relevant documents, archives, and witnesses can be difficult, particularly when state actors or powerful individuals are unwilling to cooperate.
- **Reconciliation versus Justice:** Balancing the pursuit of justice and the imperative of reconciliation can be challenging. Truth commissions must carefully consider the impact of their findings on societal divisions and the potential for retribution or backlash.
- **Limited Legal Authority:** Truth commissions typically do not possess prosecution powers. Their primary focus is on documentation, truth-telling, and making recommendations for redress and reform rather than enforcing legal accountability.

Truth commissions must grapple with these challenges and work within their limitations to achieve their intended goals of truth, reconciliation, and prevention.

Examples of Truth Commissions

Numerous truth commissions have been established globally, each tailored to specific contexts and historical injustices. Here are two notable examples:

- **South Africa:** The Truth and Reconciliation Commission (TRC) in South Africa, established after the end of apartheid, served as a model for subsequent truth commissions. The TRC focused on addressing gross human rights violations committed during apartheid and aimed to promote reconciliation through truth-telling and public hearings.

- **Argentina:** The National Commission on the Disappearance of Persons (CONADEP) in Argentina was established in the 1980s to investigate the forced disappearances that occurred during the military dictatorship. CONADEP played a crucial role in documenting atrocities and putting pressure on the government to address human rights abuses.

These examples highlight the diverse approaches and impacts of truth commissions in different contexts.

Resources for Further Study

For further exploration of truth commissions and truth-telling processes, the following resources are recommended:

- *Truth Commissions: A Comparative Assessment* by Priscilla B. Hayner

- *The Handbook of Reparations* edited by Pablo De Greiff

- *Transitional Justice: Global Mechanisms and Local Realities after Genocide and Mass Violence* edited by Alexander Laban Hinton and Nanci Adler

These resources provide in-depth analyses of the theory, practices, and challenges associated with truth commissions.

Conclusion

Truth commissions and the truth-telling processes they undertake are essential for addressing past human rights abuses and fostering reconciliation in post-conflict or post-authoritarian societies. By uncovering the truth, facilitating victim testimonies, and establishing an accurate historical record, truth commissions contribute to the healing of societies and the prevention of future atrocities. However, they also face political, legal, and practical challenges that require careful navigation. Through a victim-centered approach and adherence to key principles, truth commissions can effectively contribute to transformative justice processes.

In the next chapter, we will explore the transformative potential of restorative justice in the criminal justice system.

Reparations and Memorials in Transitional Justice

In the context of transitional justice, reparations and memorials play a crucial role in addressing past human rights violations and promoting reconciliation and healing. Reparations refer to the measures taken by a society or state to acknowledge, compensate, and provide redress for the harm inflicted on individuals or groups during periods of conflict or repression. Memorials, on the other hand, serve as physical or symbolic spaces to remember and honor the victims of human rights abuses and ensure that their stories are preserved for future generations.

8.9.3.1 The Importance of Reparations in Transitional Justice

Reparations serve multiple purposes within transitional justice processes. First and foremost, they acknowledge the suffering of victims and provide a recognition of their rights. By offering reparations, states or societies demonstrate a commitment to human rights and a willingness to address the harm caused by past atrocities. Reparations also contribute to the process of reconciliation by promoting healing, restoration, and social cohesion. They help rebuild the trust between victims and their communities, restore the dignity of survivors, and facilitate the reintegration of victims into society.

Moreover, reparations contribute to the prevention of future human rights violations. By addressing the root causes of conflicts and addressing the grievances of victims, reparations can help address systemic inequalities and promote social justice. They also send a powerful message that impunity will not be tolerated and that there are consequences for human rights abuses.

8.9.3.2 Types of Reparations

Reparations can take various forms, depending on the context and needs of the victims. These can include:

1. Compensation: Financial payments to victims to acknowledge their suffering and assist in their rehabilitation and reintegration into society.

2. Restitution: Returning property, land, or possessions that were stolen, confiscated, or forcibly taken from victims during the conflict or repression.

3. Rehabilitation: Providing medical, psychological, and social support services to victims, including access to healthcare, counseling, education, vocational training, and job placement.

4. Satisfaction and guarantees of non-repetition: Measures aimed at preventing the recurrence of human rights abuses, such as institutional reforms, legal changes, and the establishment of truth commissions or tribunals.

5. Recognition and apology: Publicly acknowledging the responsibility of perpetrators and the harm inflicted on victims through official apologies, commemorations, and acknowledgment of the truth.

6. Memorialization: Creating physical or symbolic memorials, monuments, museums, or commemorative events to remember and honor the victims, raise awareness about the past atrocities, and promote a culture of remembrance.

8.9.3.3 Challenges and Controversies

Implementing reparations programs in transitional justice contexts can be challenging due to various factors. These include limited financial resources, political resistance, difficulties in identifying and verifying victims, determining eligibility criteria, and ensuring the participation and consultation of victims in the design and implementation of reparations programs. There can also be tensions between different approaches to reparations, such as individual reparations versus collective reparations, and debates around the adequacy and fairness of the reparations provided.

Additionally, there are complex ethical considerations when it comes to determining who is eligible for reparations and how to prioritize different victims' claims. Balancing the needs and expectations of victims with the constraints of available resources requires careful planning and decision-making.

8.9.3.4 Examples and Best Practices

Numerous countries and international institutions have implemented reparations programs as part of their transitional justice processes. For example, South Africa's Truth and Reconciliation Commission established a reparations program that included financial compensation, educational support, healthcare assistance, and community rehabilitation projects for victims of apartheid-era human rights abuses. Similarly, in Colombia, the Victims' Law created a comprehensive reparations program that provides financial compensation, land restitution, and psycho-social support to victims of the armed conflict.

Best practices in reparations programs include ensuring the participation and consultation of victims, adopting a victim-centered approach, and establishing transparent and accountable mechanisms for the identification, verification, and distribution of reparations. Collaboration with civil society organizations, victim groups, and local communities is crucial for the success of these programs.

8.9.3.5 Resources for Further Study

For further study on reparations and memorials in transitional justice, the following resources are recommended:

- Pablo de Greiff, "The Handbook of Reparations" (2006): This comprehensive handbook provides an in-depth analysis of reparations programs worldwide, including their design, implementation, and impact.

- International Center for Transitional Justice (ICTJ): The ICTJ is a leading organization that provides research, expertise, and guidance on transitional justice processes, including reparations. Their website offers a wealth of resources, reports, and case studies on reparations programs.

- United Nations Human Rights Council (UNHRC): The UNHRC website contains a range of publications, reports, and guidelines on transitional justice and reparations, offering insights into international standards and best practices.

- Local organizations and civil society groups: It is essential to explore the work of local organizations and civil society groups in specific transitional justice contexts. These organizations often have firsthand knowledge and experiences in implementing reparations programs and can provide valuable insights and case studies.

8.9.3.6 Conclusion

Reparations and memorials are critical components of transitional justice processes, promoting recognition, healing, and social transformation. They help address the legacies of past human rights abuses, restore the rights and dignity of victims, and contribute to the establishment of a just and inclusive society. By acknowledging the harm inflicted on individuals and communities, implementing comprehensive reparations programs, and creating meaningful memorials, societies can strive towards reconciliation, prevent future human rights violations, and foster a culture of remembrance and respect.

Human Rights Activism and Advocacy

Grassroots Activism for Human Rights

Introduction

Grassroots activism plays a vital role in promoting and protecting human rights around the world. It is a bottom-up approach that involves individuals and communities coming together to advocate for social change and challenge systemic injustices. Grassroots activists work tirelessly to address human rights violations, raise awareness, and empower marginalized groups. This section will explore the importance of grassroots activism in the context of human rights, highlighting key strategies, challenges, and the transformative potential of these efforts.

Understanding Grassroots Activism

Grassroots activism refers to the collective efforts of individuals and small organizations working at the local level to effect change. It often begins with individuals who are directly affected by human rights violations or those who are deeply committed to addressing injustice. Grassroots activists organize community-based campaigns, engage in nonviolent protests, raise awareness through education and advocacy, and build networks of support to empower marginalized communities.

The principles that guide grassroots activism include inclusivity, participation, empowerment, and collective action. Grassroots activists believe in the power of ordinary people to drive social change and challenge oppressive systems. They recognize that sustainable change can only be achieved through the active involvement of affected communities and by addressing the root causes of inequality and injustice.

Strategies for Grassroots Activism

Grassroots activism employs a variety of strategies and tactics to advance human rights. Some of the key strategies used by grassroots activists include:

1. Community Organizing: Grassroots activists work to build strong relationships within the communities they serve. They organize community meetings, engage in door-to-door outreach, and collaborate with local leaders to mobilize community members around shared goals.

2. Advocacy and Education: Grassroots activists raise awareness about human rights issues through education campaigns, workshops, and public events. They advocate for policy changes, engage with policymakers, and promote human rights principles at local, regional, and national levels.

3. Coalition Building: Grassroots activists understand the importance of collaboration. They form alliances with other social justice organizations, community groups, and NGOs to amplify their impact, share resources, and advocate collectively for human rights.

4. Nonviolent Resistance: Grassroots activists embrace nonviolent strategies to challenge oppressive systems. This includes peaceful protests, civil disobedience, and other forms of direct action aimed at drawing attention to human rights violations and demanding change.

5. Grassroots Media: Grassroots activists often harness the power of media to amplify their message and reach a broader audience. They utilize social media

platforms, create independent media outlets, and collaborate with journalists to shed light on human rights abuses and advocate for justice.

Challenges Faced by Grassroots Activists

While grassroots activism is essential for promoting human rights, it is not without challenges. Some of the key challenges faced by grassroots activists include:

1. Repression and Intimidation: Grassroots activists often face harassment, threats, and violence from state authorities, non-state actors, and powerful interests. Their work is seen as a threat to those who benefit from the status quo, making them vulnerable to repression.

2. Limited Resources: Grassroots activists often operate on limited budgets and rely on volunteer efforts. The lack of financial resources can restrict their capacity to implement effective advocacy campaigns, provide essential services, and sustain their activities over the long term.

3. Lack of Institutional Support: Grassroots activists may struggle to gain recognition and support from government institutions and established organizations. This lack of institutional backing can hinder their ability to access resources, build partnerships, and have their voices heard in decision-making processes.

4. Burnout and Self-care: Grassroots activists are often passionate about their work, but the demanding nature of their activities can lead to burnout and emotional exhaustion. The need for self-care and organizational support is crucial to ensuring the sustainability of grassroots activism.

Transformative Potential of Grassroots Activism

Grassroots activism has the potential to drive transformative change in society by challenging oppressive systems, promoting human rights, and empowering marginalized communities. Through collective action and grassroots mobilization, activists can achieve significant outcomes such as:

1. Policy Changes: Grassroots activism can lead to policy reforms that address human rights violations. By raising public awareness, mobilizing communities, and advocating for change, grassroots activists can exert pressure on decision-makers to enact laws and policies that protect and promote human rights.

2. Community Empowerment: Grassroots activism focuses on empowering marginalized communities to advocate for their rights. By providing information, resources, and support, activists enable communities to become active participants in decision-making processes and agents of change in their own lives.

3. Shift in Public Discourse: Grassroots activism has the power to shape public opinion and challenge harmful narratives. By raising awareness and challenging societal norms, activists can shift public discourse, challenge stereotypes, and promote a more inclusive and rights-conscious society.

4. Solidarity and Collaboration: Grassroots activism fosters solidarity and collaboration among diverse groups and communities. By working together, activists can build alliances, bridge divides, and foster a sense of collective responsibility for human rights.

Case Studies: Grassroots Activism for Human Rights

1. The Arab Spring: The Arab Spring uprisings in the early 2010s highlighted the transformative power of grassroots activism. Protests led by ordinary citizens across the Middle East and North Africa called for political freedoms, social justice, and respect for human rights. These movements led to significant political changes, including the ousting of long-standing dictators and the demand for accountable governance.

2. Black Lives Matter: The Black Lives Matter (BLM) movement emerged in response to police violence and systemic racism targeting Black communities in the United States. BLM activists used grassroots organizing, nonviolent protests, and social media to raise awareness about police brutality and advocate for structural reforms. The movement has sparked a global conversation about racial justice, inspiring similar grassroots initiatives worldwide.

Conclusion

Grassroots activism plays a crucial role in advancing human rights by mobilizing communities, raising awareness, and challenging oppressive systems. It empowers marginalized groups, promotes community engagement, and drives transformative change. While facing significant challenges, grassroots activists continue to make a profound impact on human rights locally, nationally, and globally. Their efforts remind us of the power of collective action and the potential for a more just and equitable world.

Further Resources

1. Book: "From #BlackLivesMatter to Black Liberation" by Keeanga-Yamahtta Taylor 2. Documentary: "How to Change the World" directed by Jerry Rothwell 3. Organization: Global Fund for Women (www.globalfundforwomen.org) 4.

Article: "The Role of Grassroots Activism in Human Rights Movements" by Alicia Ely Yamin

Exercises

1. Research and analyze a grassroots human rights movement that has emerged in your country or region. What are their key goals and strategies? What challenges do they face? What impact have they made so far?

2. Organize a local event or workshop to raise awareness about a human rights issue. Utilize social media, community outreach, and collaborative partnerships to maximize participation and impact.

3. Imagine you are a grassroots activist working on a specific human rights issue. Develop a comprehensive advocacy plan outlining your goals, strategies, target audience, and desired outcomes. Consider the resources and challenges you may encounter.

4. Conduct a case study on a successful grassroots campaign for human rights. Analyze the tactics, strategies, and organizing principles employed by the activists. Explore how their work has created transformative change in their community or society.

Glossary

1. Grassroots Activism: Bottom-up approach to effecting social change through community organizing, advocacy, and collective action. 2. Inclusivity: The practice of involving all individuals and communities, ensuring equal access and representation. 3. Nonviolent Resistance: A strategy that challenges oppressive systems and practices through peaceful protests and civil disobedience. 4. Solidarity: Unity and support among diverse groups and communities in pursuit of a common goal.

NGOs and Human Rights Advocacy

Non-Governmental Organizations (NGOs) play a crucial role in advocating for human rights globally. These organizations operate independently of government entities and have the ability to mobilize resources, expertise, and networks to promote and protect human rights. In this section, we will explore the significance of NGOs in human rights advocacy, their strategies and initiatives, and the challenges they face.

Importance of NGOs in Human Rights Advocacy

NGOs have become instrumental in advancing human rights at the grassroots level and on the global stage. They serve as watchdogs, monitoring human rights violations, and raising awareness about these abuses. NGOs also provide support and assistance to vulnerable populations, empowering them to assert their rights and seek justice. Some key reasons why NGOs are essential in human rights advocacy are:

1. **Independent Voice:** NGOs are not constrained by political agendas or governmental limitations, allowing them to be a critical voice in challenging human rights abuses. They can speak out against injustice, provide alternative narratives, and advocate for marginalized communities.

2. **Access to Information:** NGOs often have direct contact with affected communities, allowing them to gather information about human rights violations that may go unnoticed or unreported. They act as conduits for amplifying voices that would otherwise remain unheard.

3. **Monitoring and Documentation:** NGOs play a pivotal role in monitoring and documenting human rights abuses. They collect evidence, document testimonies, and compile reports to bring attention to violations and hold accountable those responsible.

4. **Capacity Building:** NGOs provide training and capacity-building programs to empower individuals and communities to recognize their rights, navigate legal systems, and effectively engage in advocacy efforts.

5. **Advocacy and Lobbying:** NGOs leverage their knowledge, influence, and networks to advocate for policy change, legal reforms, and the implementation of human rights standards at national and international levels. They engage with policymakers, governments, and international bodies to promote human rights principles and push for reforms.

Strategies and Initiatives of NGOs

NGOs employ various strategies and initiatives to advance human rights and create lasting change. Some common approaches used by NGOs in their advocacy work include:

1. **Awareness Campaigns:** NGOs engage in awareness-raising campaigns to educate the public about human rights abuses, promoting empathy, solidarity, and support for victims. These campaigns utilize diverse platforms such as media, social media, public events, and workshops to reach a wide audience.

2. **Litigation and Legal Advocacy:** NGOs often use litigation as a tool to challenge unjust laws, seek justice for victims of human rights violations, and establish legal precedents that protect human rights. They provide legal representation to marginalized individuals and communities who lack access to justice.

3. **Coalition Building:** NGOs collaborate with like-minded organizations, activists, academics, and other stakeholders to amplify their impact. Joining forces allows NGOs to pool resources, share expertise, and advocate more effectively for their causes.

4. **Research and Policy Analysis:** NGOs conduct research to gather evidence, analyze human rights issues, and propose policy recommendations. They invest in rigorous research methodologies to provide empirical evidence that supports their advocacy efforts.

5. **Capacity Building and Training:** NGOs provide training programs and workshops to empower individuals and communities to understand, assert, and defend their human rights. These initiatives aim to build the knowledge and skills necessary for effective advocacy.

Challenges Faced by NGOs

While NGOs play a crucial role in human rights advocacy, they also face significant challenges that hinder their effectiveness. Some key challenges include:

1. **Resource Constraints:** NGOs often struggle with limited funding and resources, which can impede their ability to carry out their work effectively. They rely on grants, donations, and volunteers, making sustainability a constant concern.

2. **Government Restrictions:** NGOs may face bureaucratic hurdles, restrictive regulations, or even hostile environments created by governments that seek to suppress dissent and limit their activities. This can lead to limitations on freedom of expression, assembly, and association, making advocacy work difficult.

3. **Security Risks:** Working on sensitive human rights issues can expose NGOs and their staff to risks, including threats, harassment, and violence. Protecting the safety and well-being of human rights defenders is a pressing concern.

4. **Lack of Coordination:** The sheer number and diversity of NGOs can hinder effective coordination and collaboration. Without cohesive strategies and efforts, the impact of their advocacy work may be diluted.

5. **Cultural and Contextual Challenges:** NGOs operating in different regions and cultural contexts must navigate distinct cultural norms, traditions, and legal frameworks. Understanding and respecting local customs while advocating for human rights can be a delicate balancing act.

NGOs and Innovative Approaches to Human Rights Advocacy

To overcome challenges and maintain relevance, NGOs are adopting innovative approaches to human rights advocacy. Some examples of such approaches are:

1. **Technology and Digital Activism:** NGOs harness the power of technology, including social media platforms, websites, and mobile applications, to raise awareness, mobilize support, and share critical information. Digital activism allows for rapid response and amplification of human rights issues.

2. **Transnational Advocacy Networks:** NGOs build transnational networks to tackle global human rights challenges collectively. These networks facilitate information exchange, resource sharing, and joint advocacy efforts across borders, amplifying their impact.

3. **Corporate Accountability Campaigns:** NGOs advocate for corporate accountability by promoting ethical business practices, challenging human rights abuses in supply chains, and holding corporations responsible for their impact on human rights.

4. **Participatory Approaches:** NGOs increasingly adopt participatory approaches, involving affected communities in decision-making processes and advocacy activities. This ensures that marginalized voices are central to human rights initiatives.

Resources and Further Reading

- Amnesty International (www.amnesty.org): A renowned global NGO that champions human rights causes worldwide.

- Human Rights Watch (www.hrw.org): A leading NGO that conducts research and advocacy on human rights issues across the globe.

- International Federation for Human Rights (www.fidh.org): An international NGO that works to protect human rights defenders and promote human rights through strategic litigation.

- The Funders' Initiative for Civil Society (FICS) (www.thefics.org): An organization that supports NGOs and civil society organizations in their advocacy work by providing financial resources and capacity-building opportunities.

- Cohen, R., and Sabel, C. (2006). *Extraordinary Politics: How Protest and Dissent Are Changing American Democracy.* University of Chicago Press. A book that explores the role of NGOs in shaping democracy and advocating for social change in the United States.

Summary

NGOs are pivotal actors in human rights advocacy, serving as independent voices, raising awareness, and mobilizing resources to promote and protect human rights. They employ various strategies and initiatives, such as awareness campaigns, litigation, coalition-building, and capacity-building, to advance their causes. However, NGOs also face challenges, including resource constraints, government restrictions, security risks, lack of coordination, and cultural obstacles. To overcome these challenges, NGOs are adopting innovative approaches, including leveraging technology, building transnational networks, advocating for corporate accountability, and embracing participatory approaches. By understanding the significance of NGOs in human rights advocacy, we can appreciate their transformative potential and contribute to a more just and equal world.

Protecting Human Rights Defenders

In this section, we will explore the critical issue of protecting human rights defenders. Human rights defenders play a crucial role in advancing human rights and promoting social justice. However, they often face significant challenges, including threats, intimidation, and violence. Therefore, it is essential to understand the importance of protecting human rights defenders and explore strategies to ensure their safety and support their important work.

Understanding Human Rights Defenders

Before delving into the protection of human rights defenders, let's first define who they are. Human rights defenders are individuals or groups who peacefully advocate and work towards the promotion and protection of human rights at the local, national, or international levels. They engage in a wide range of activities, such as documenting human rights abuses, advocating for policy changes, providing legal aid, and raising awareness about human rights violations.

Human rights defenders can be lawyers, journalists, activists, community leaders, or members of non-governmental organizations (NGOs). They often operate in challenging environments, where they can face various threats and risks due to their work.

International Human Rights Framework

To understand the importance of protecting human rights defenders, we need to recognize the international human rights framework that provides the legal basis for their work. The Universal Declaration of Human Rights and various international human rights treaties guarantee the rights and freedoms that human rights defenders seek to protect.

The United Nations Declaration on Human Rights Defenders adopted in 1998 explicitly recognizes the essential role played by human rights defenders in the promotion and protection of human rights. It outlines the duties of states, civil society organizations, and individuals in creating a safe and enabling environment for human rights defenders to carry out their activities.

Challenges Faced by Human Rights Defenders

Human rights defenders face a myriad of challenges and risks in their work. These challenges can vary across different regions and contexts but often include:

- Threats and intimidation: Human rights defenders may face threats, harassment, or violence from state authorities, non-state actors, or powerful individuals who perceive their work as a threat.

- Criminalization: Human rights defenders are sometimes unjustly criminalized through vague or punitive laws. They may face charges such as defamation, sedition, or terrorism, which are used to silence and marginalize them.

- Surveillance and digital threats: With the advancement of technology, human rights defenders face increasing surveillance and digital threats. Governments and other actors may monitor their communications, hack their devices, or spread disinformation to undermine their work.

- Impunity for attacks: In many cases, attacks against human rights defenders go unpunished. The lack of accountability creates an environment of fear and vulnerability.

- Stigmatization and discrediting: Human rights defenders are often stigmatized, discredited, or portrayed as threats to national security or social stability. This can lead to social isolation and hinder their ability to carry out their work effectively.

- Inadequate legal protection: Legal frameworks to protect human rights defenders may be insufficient or not effectively enforced, leaving them without proper recourse when their rights are violated.

Strategies for Protecting Human Rights Defenders

Ensuring the protection of human rights defenders requires a comprehensive and multi-faceted approach. Here are some strategies that can be employed:

1. Strengthening legal frameworks: States should enact and enforce laws that protect human rights defenders, ensuring their rights and providing effective remedies in case of violations. Legal provisions should be in line with international human rights standards and encompass both civil and criminal aspects.

2. Institutional support: Establishing specialized institutions or mechanisms within the government to address the concerns and needs of human rights defenders can be instrumental. These institutions can provide guidance, support, and protection to human rights defenders, as well as facilitate their engagement with the broader legal system.

3. International protection mechanisms: The international community plays a vital role in protecting human rights defenders. International organizations, such as the United Nations and regional human rights bodies, should continue to monitor the situation of human rights defenders and take appropriate actions to address violations. Mechanisms like the UN Special Rapporteur on the situation of human rights defenders can provide valuable insights and recommendations.

4. Building solidarity networks: Collaboration and networking among human rights defenders and organizations can enhance their collective strength and resilience. Capacity-building initiatives, trainings, and workshops can help human rights defenders acquire skills and knowledge to better navigate the challenges they face.

5. Raising awareness: Promoting public awareness about the essential role of human rights defenders and the challenges they face is crucial. Education, media campaigns, and public events can help build a broader understanding and support for their work, dismantling misconceptions and prejudices.

6. Providing physical and digital security: Human rights defenders need access to resources and tools to enhance their personal security. Support can include training in digital security practices, provision of secure communication channels, and access to physical security measures, such as emergency response systems.

7. International solidarity and advocacy: Governments, civil society organizations, and individuals should engage in international advocacy and solidarity efforts to support human rights defenders globally. This can involve diplomatic pressure, public statements, and collaborations with international human rights organizations to bring attention to specific cases or issues.

Case Study: Protecting Human Rights Defenders in Colombia

Colombia serves as an example of a country with a history of human rights defenders facing significant risks. Being a high-risk context, various measures have been implemented to protect human rights defenders in the country. These measures include:

- Protection Units: The Colombian government has established specialized units responsible for the protection of human rights defenders and social leaders. These units coordinate security measures, including assigning bodyguards and conducting risk assessments.

- Early Warning Systems: Early warning systems have been implemented to identify risks faced by human rights defenders and provide timely preventive measures. These systems involve close coordination between government agencies, civil society organizations, and communities.

- International Accompaniment: Human rights organizations, both national and international, provide international accompaniment to human rights defenders at risk. This support serves as a deterrent against attacks and provides visibility to the situation, protecting the defenders through increased international scrutiny.

- Legal Support: Various legal support services, including clinics and pro bono networks, are available to assist human rights defenders in legal matters. These services provide them with legal advice, representation, and support during legal proceedings.

Conclusion

Protecting human rights defenders is crucial for fostering social justice and upholding human rights globally. The international community, governments, civil society organizations, and individuals must collectively work towards creating an enabling environment for human rights defenders to carry out their important work safely and effectively. By strengthening legal frameworks, providing institutional support, and raising awareness, we can ensure that human rights defenders are protected and empowered in their pursuit of justice and equality.

Further Reading

- Front Line Defenders. (2018). *Compendium of guides, manuals, and practical tools on the protection of human rights defenders.* Retrieved from: https://www.frontlinedefenders.org/en/resource-publication/compendium-guides-manuals-and-practical-tools-protection-hu

- Inter-American Commission on Human Rights. (2011). *Measures for the protection of human rights defenders.* Retrieved from: http://www.oas.org/en/iachr/defenders/docs/pdf/proteccion.pdf

- International Service for Human Rights. (2018). *Human rights defenders hub.* Retrieved from: https://www.ishr.ch/huber-toolkit-human-rights-defenders

Discussion Questions

1. Why are human rights defenders important for promoting social justice and upholding human rights?

2. What are some common challenges faced by human rights defenders, and how do they vary across different contexts?

3. Discuss the role of international human rights mechanisms in protecting human rights defenders.

4. How can technological advancements both benefit and pose risks to human rights defenders?

5. Reflecting on the case study of Colombia, what strategies have proven effective in protecting human rights defenders?

Exercises

1. Select a recent case of a human rights defender facing threats or attacks. Conduct research on the case and analyze the national and international responses to the situation.

2. Imagine you are designing a workshop on digital security for human rights defenders. Develop an outline of the topics you would cover and the key takeaways for the participants.

3. Form a discussion group with your classmates and discuss strategies for promoting awareness and support for human rights defenders in your local community. Develop an action plan outlining possible initiatives.

Note: This section provides an overview of protecting human rights defenders, focusing on key principles, challenges, and strategies. For a more comprehensive understanding, readers are encouraged to consult the recommended further reading resources.

Conclusion

Recapitulation of Key Points

In this chapter, we have explored the transformative approaches to human rights law and the ways in which it can contribute to social justice. We began by providing an overview of human rights law and its historical development, emphasizing its role in promoting social justice.

We then delved into the two main categories of human rights: economic, social, and cultural rights, and civil and political rights. We discussed the intersectionality of these rights and how they are interconnected. We also examined the challenges and controversies surrounding the protection of these rights, highlighting the achievements and progress that have been made.

Further, we focused on specific areas within human rights law, such as indigenous peoples' rights, women's rights, LGBTQ+ rights, and children's rights. We explored the legal recognition and protection of these rights, as well as the challenges and discrimination faced by marginalized groups. Through the lens of intersectionality, we examined the impact of feminist approaches and the strides made in promoting gender equality.

Additionally, we explored transitional justice, which plays a vital role in post-conflict societies. We discussed truth commissions, reparations, and memorials as mechanisms for addressing past human rights abuses and fostering reconciliation. We also examined the importance of engaging with grassroots activism and non-governmental organizations (NGOs) in promoting human rights worldwide.

Throughout the chapter, we emphasized the transformative power of human rights law in addressing social inequality and promoting justice. We highlighted the need for global perspectives in understanding legal systems and the role of international law in global governance. We also discussed the impact of globalization on legal systems and the legal responses to global challenges.

Furthermore, we focused on regional approaches to transformative legal studies, such as the European Union's integration efforts, African perspectives, and Latin American approaches to social justice. We highlighted the significance of indigenous legal systems and their potential in promoting transformative practices. Moreover, we examined the role of environmental law in tackling environmental challenges and its connection to transformative legal strategies.

In conclusion, this chapter has illuminated the importance of transformative approaches to human rights law in promoting social justice globally. By recognizing the interconnectedness of different rights and engaging in grassroots activism, we can work towards a more equitable and just world. The challenges and achievements discussed in this chapter provide a foundation for future research and action in the field of human rights law. Applying a transformative lens to human rights can pave the way for innovative and impactful approaches that truly address the root causes of social injustice.

For further exploration, readers are encouraged to refer to the recommended resources section at the end of this chapter. These resources provide additional readings, case studies, and avenues for further research in transformative human rights law.

Implications for Transformative Human Rights Practice

Transformative legal studies have profound implications for the field of human rights practice. By adopting a transformative approach, practitioners can contribute to the advancement of justice, equality, and social change. This section explores the key implications of transformative legal studies for human rights practice and highlights the potential for transformative approaches to reshape the field.

Reconceptualizing Human Rights

One of the primary implications of transformative legal studies for human rights practice is the reconceptualization of human rights themselves. Traditional human rights frameworks often focus on civil and political rights, neglecting economic, social, and cultural rights. However, transformative legal studies emphasize the indivisibility and interdependence of all human rights. Practitioners must recognize and address the structural factors that perpetuate inequality and discrimination in order to promote transformative change.

Intersectionality in Human Rights Analysis

Transformative legal studies highlight the importance of intersectionality in human rights analysis. Intersectionality recognizes that individuals experience multiple forms of oppression and discrimination simultaneously, shaped by their intersecting identities and social positions. Human rights practitioners must adopt an intersectional lens to uncover the interconnected systems of power and privilege that operate in society. By recognizing the intersecting dimensions of oppression, practitioners can develop more inclusive and effective human rights strategies.

Empowering Marginalized Communities

Transformative human rights practice seeks to empower marginalized communities and amplify their voices. Rather than adopting a top-down approach, practitioners must engage with communities directly and involve them in the decision-making process. This requires building relationships based on trust and understanding, and valuing the expertise and experiences of marginalized communities. By centering the voices of those directly affected by human rights abuses, practitioners can work towards more meaningful and sustainable change.

Promoting Accountability and Remedies

Transformative legal studies emphasize the importance of accountability and remedies in human rights practice. Traditional approaches often focus on legal mechanisms and prosecutions, but transformative approaches recognize that achieving justice extends beyond criminal proceedings. Practitioners must consider a range of transformative remedies, such as reparations, truth commissions, and institutional reforms. This broader understanding of justice ensures that the needs and rights of survivors and affected communities are addressed holistically.

Engaging in Strategic Litigation

Strategic litigation plays a crucial role in transformative human rights practice. By strategically selecting cases and using legal tools to challenge unjust laws and policies, practitioners can bring about systemic change. Strategic litigation can set important legal precedents, create judicial accountability, and contribute to the development of human rights norms. Human rights practitioners must identify strategic opportunities for litigation and develop innovative legal strategies to advance transformative goals.

Building Networks and Alliances

Transformative human rights practice thrives on collaboration, networks, and alliances. These networks can include civil society organizations, grassroots movements, affected communities, and international actors. By working in partnership, practitioners can pool their resources, amplify their impact, and create broader social movements for change. Human rights practitioners must actively engage in networking, coalition-building, and solidarity to achieve transformative goals.

Holistic Approach to Human Rights Education

Another important implication of transformative legal studies is the need for a holistic approach to human rights education. Traditional approaches often focus on legalistic and individualistic understandings of human rights. Transformative human rights education should incorporate interdisciplinary perspectives, critical analysis, and community-based learning. This holistic approach equips future human rights practitioners with the skills and knowledge necessary to understand the root causes of injustice and work towards transformative solutions.

Ethical Considerations and Self-Reflection

Transformative human rights practice requires practitioners to engage in continuous self-reflection and ethical considerations. This involves critically examining one's own privileges, biases, and power dynamics. Practitioners must actively challenge their own assumptions and be accountable to the communities they serve. Ethical considerations include ensuring the informed consent and agency of those involved in human rights interventions, respecting cultural practices and identities, and safeguarding the well-being of all individuals involved.

Conclusion

Transformative legal studies have significant implications for human rights practice. By reconceptualizing human rights, adopting an intersectional lens, empowering marginalized communities, promoting accountability, engaging in strategic litigation, building networks and alliances, and embracing a holistic approach to education, practitioners can contribute to transformative change. However, it is crucial for practitioners to continually reflect on their own positionality, maintain ethical standards, and be responsive to the evolving needs and aspirations of the communities they serve. Through transformative human rights practice, we can work towards a more just and equal world.

Future Directions in Human Rights Law

As the field of human rights law continues to evolve, there are several key directions that hold promise for the future. These directions reflect the growing recognition of new challenges and a commitment to finding innovative solutions to protect and promote human rights globally. In this section, we will explore some of these future directions in human rights law, including emerging issues, evolving approaches, and the role of technology in advancing human rights.

Emerging Issues in Human Rights

One of the significant future directions in human rights law involves addressing emerging issues that have the potential to shape the human rights landscape. These emerging issues include, but are not limited to:

1. **Technological advancements and human rights:** The rapid development of technology brings both opportunities and challenges to human rights. As new technologies such as artificial intelligence, biotechnology, and surveillance systems continue to advance, it becomes essential to ensure that these technologies are developed and used in a manner that respects and protects human rights. Future directions in human rights law will involve exploring the ethical and legal implications of emerging technologies and establishing frameworks to safeguard human rights in the digital age.

2. **Climate change and human rights:** Climate change poses a significant threat to the enjoyment of human rights, particularly for vulnerable populations. Future directions in human rights law will involve integrating environmental concerns and climate justice into the human rights framework. This includes recognizing the right to a clean and sustainable environment and establishing legal mechanisms to hold responsible parties accountable for the adverse human rights impacts of climate change.

3. **Intersectionality and multiple forms of discrimination:** Human rights law has traditionally focused on addressing discrimination based on single grounds, such as race, gender, or disability. However, future directions in human rights law will increasingly emphasize the intersectionality of discrimination, recognizing that individuals can experience multiple forms

of discrimination simultaneously. This requires developing legal frameworks that account for the unique and interconnected experiences of individuals facing intersecting forms of discrimination and ensuring appropriate remedies to address these injustices.

Evolving Approaches in Human Rights

In addition to emerging issues, future directions in human rights law encompass evolving approaches to the promotion and protection of human rights. Some of these evolving approaches include:

1. **Participatory and inclusive human rights mechanisms:** To ensure the effectiveness and legitimacy of human rights efforts, future directions in human rights law will emphasize the importance of participatory and inclusive approaches. This includes actively involving affected individuals and communities in decision-making processes, empowering marginalized groups to claim their rights, and fostering partnerships between civil society organizations and governments to promote human rights.

2. **Transnational and global cooperation:** Human rights challenges often transcend national borders, requiring transnational and global cooperation to effectively address them. Future directions in human rights law will involve strengthening international legal frameworks and institutions, promoting cross-border collaboration, and fostering dialogue and cooperation among states to address global human rights issues such as migration, human trafficking, and corporate accountability.

3. **Non-state actors and human rights:** Non-state actors, including multinational corporations and non-governmental organizations, play a significant role in shaping human rights conditions. Future directions in human rights law will involve holding non-state actors accountable for human rights abuses, ensuring their compliance with international human rights standards, and establishing mechanisms for remediation when human rights are violated by non-state actors.

Technology and Human Rights

The increasing reliance on technology in various aspects of human life presents both opportunities and challenges for human rights. Future directions in human rights law will involve leveraging technology to advance human rights, while also addressing potential risks and ensuring that technology is developed and used in a manner that respects and enhances human rights. Some key areas of focus include:

1. **Artificial intelligence and human rights:** The use of artificial intelligence (AI) has the potential to impact human rights in various domains, including privacy, freedom of expression, and discrimination. Future directions in human rights law will involve developing guidelines and regulations to ensure that AI technologies are deployed in a manner that upholds human rights standards and protects against potential biases and discriminatory outcomes.

2. **Digital rights and online freedom of expression:** As the internet continues to play a central role in modern society, future directions in human rights law will involve protecting and promoting digital rights, including the right to privacy, freedom of expression, and access to information. This includes addressing challenges such as online surveillance, censorship, and the spread of disinformation while maintaining a balance between security concerns and the protection of fundamental freedoms.

3. **Data protection and privacy:** The collection and use of personal data raise significant privacy concerns. Future directions in human rights law will involve establishing robust data protection regulations, ensuring individuals have control over their personal data, and safeguarding against abuses of data by both state and non-state actors.

4. **Technology-enabled activism:** The use of technology has revolutionized activism and advocacy, providing new avenues for individuals and groups to promote and protect human rights. Future directions in human rights law will involve exploring the legal implications of technology-enabled activism, ensuring the protection of activists' rights, and leveraging technology to enhance civic engagement and social justice movements.

In conclusion, future directions in human rights law will involve addressing emerging issues, evolving approaches, and the role of technology in protecting and promoting human rights. As the world faces new challenges and opportunities, it is crucial to adapt and innovate within the human rights framework to ensure the continued advancement of justice, equality, and dignity for all individuals and communities. By staying attentive to these future directions, human rights law can effectively respond to the evolving needs of societies and contribute to a more just and inclusive world.

Chapter 9: Global Perspectives on Transformative Legal Studies

Chapter 9: Global Perspectives on Transformative Legal Studies

Chapter 9: Global Perspectives on Transformative Legal Studies

In this chapter, we will explore global perspectives on transformative legal studies. As legal systems and institutions vary across the globe, it is important to understand how different regions approach and contribute to the transformative potential of the law. We will examine comparative law, global governance, the impact of globalization on legal responses, legal activism, regional approaches, indigenous legal systems, and environmental law. Together, these perspectives will offer insights into the transformative power of the law on a global scale.

Comparative Law and Global Legal Systems

Comparative law is a valuable tool for understanding the diversity of legal systems across the globe. It involves the study and analysis of different legal systems, their structures, and their principles. By comparing legal systems, we can gain a broader understanding of the strengths and weaknesses of each system and identify effective practices that can be applied in transformative legal studies.

Global legal systems encompass a wide range of approaches to law. Common law systems, found in countries such as the United States and England, rely on legal precedents and case law to interpret and apply the law. Civil law systems, found in many continental European countries, are based on comprehensive legal codes that outline general principles and rules. Mixed legal systems, such as those in South Africa and Scotland, combine elements of both common and civil law traditions.

By studying global legal systems, we can identify areas where transformative legal practices have been successfully implemented and adapt them to different contexts. Additionally, comparative law enables us to recognize the intersectionality between legal systems and the cultural and transnational influences that shape them.

International Law and Global Governance

International law plays a crucial role in facilitating global cooperation and addressing transnational issues. It consists of rules and principles that govern the relationships between states and other international actors, such as international organizations and individuals. Global governance refers to the structures and mechanisms through which international law is created, implemented, and enforced.

The sources of international law include international treaties, customary international law, general principles of law, and decisions of international courts and tribunals. Treaties, such as the United Nations Charter and the Universal Declaration of Human Rights, establish the framework for promoting peace, human rights, and international cooperation.

Global governance institutions, such as the United Nations, World Trade Organization, and International Criminal Court, play a crucial role in the development and enforcement of international law. These institutions provide platforms for dialogue, negotiation, and dispute resolution among states.

Understanding international law and global governance is essential for transformative legal studies, as it enables us to address global challenges, promote human rights, and advocate for social justice on an international scale. It also allows us to examine the role of international law in shaping domestic legal systems and promoting transformative practices.

Globalization and Legal Responses

Globalization, characterized by increased interconnectedness and interdependence, has significant implications for legal systems and institutions. The impact of globalization on the law varies across different regions and areas of law. It presents both challenges and opportunities for transformative legal studies.

One of the challenges posed by globalization is the tension between national sovereignty and supranational governance. As legal and economic systems become more interconnected, national laws may need to be harmonized or adapted to align with international standards. This process raises questions about democratic legitimacy and the potential loss of cultural diversity in legal systems.

On the other hand, globalization also provides opportunities for the development of transformative legal responses. It allows for the exchange of ideas and best practices, enabling legal systems to learn from one another. Globalization has facilitated the emergence of transnational legal networks and collaborations, fostering the growth of transformative legal activism and advocacy.

Transformative legal studies can explore the ways in which legal systems respond to globalization, addressing issues such as human rights protection, economic development, environmental sustainability, and social justice in a globalized world.

Legal Activism and Advocacy

Legal activism and advocacy are powerful tools for effecting social change and promoting transformative legal practices. Grassroots activism, transnational legal networks, and non-governmental organizations (NGOs) play crucial roles in advancing human rights, environmental justice, and social equality.

Grassroots legal activism involves local communities, individuals, and organizations working to address specific legal issues and advocating for change from the ground up. It involves mobilizing public support, engaging in strategic litigation, and utilizing media and public advocacy to raise awareness and effect change.

Transnational legal networks bring together legal scholars, practitioners, and activists from different regions to share knowledge, collaborate on research, and develop strategies for advancing transformative legal agendas. These networks facilitate the exchange of ideas and support the development of global legal frameworks and norms.

NGOs play a vital role in legal activism and advocacy, often focusing on specific areas such as human rights, environmental justice, or social inequality. They provide legal support, monitor compliance with international legal standards, and engage in lobbying and advocacy at the national and international levels.

Transformative legal studies can explore the impact of legal activism and advocacy, highlighting successful strategies and identifying areas for improvement. It can also analyze the intersectionality between legal activism and other social justice movements, such as feminism, LGBTQ+ rights, and racial justice.

Regional Approaches to Transformative Legal Studies

Regional approaches to transformative legal studies provide valuable insights into the unique challenges and opportunities faced by different regions. By examining regional legal systems and practices, we can identify region-specific approaches to transformative legal studies and learn from their successes and failures.

For example, the European Union (EU) has developed a distinctive legal framework that promotes integration and addresses regional challenges. European Union law provides a model for regional collaboration and the harmonization of legal standards across diverse nations. The EU's approach to transformative legal studies can inform other regional initiatives seeking to foster cooperation and develop common legal frameworks.

In Africa, legal institutions and practices are shaped by the continent's complex colonial history and diversity of cultures and legal systems. African perspectives on transformative law focus on addressing historical injustices, promoting human rights, and achieving social and economic development. African approaches to transformative legal studies highlight the importance of integrating local customs and practices with international legal standards.

Similarly, Latin American countries have developed unique approaches to social justice and transformation. These approaches emphasize economic and social rights, indigenous rights, and participatory democracy. Latin American experiences provide valuable lessons for transformative legal studies, particularly in relation to addressing systemic inequalities and promoting inclusive legal systems.

By examining regional approaches, transformative legal studies can develop context-specific strategies for legal reform and social change. It also allows for a deeper understanding of the impact of historical, cultural, and political factors on legal systems and institutions.

Indigenous Legal Systems and Transformative Potential

Indigenous legal systems offer alternative perspectives and approaches to law that challenge mainstream legal paradigms. These systems are rooted in indigenous worldviews, cultural practices, and traditional knowledge. Recognizing and incorporating indigenous legal systems in transformative legal studies is essential for promoting diversity, inclusivity, and decolonization.

Indigenous legal systems prioritize collective decision-making, consensus-building, and restorative justice. They address the communal well-being and the relationships between humans, nature, and the spiritual world. Indigenous legal principles emphasize interconnectedness, stewardship of the land, and the importance of community participation.

By studying indigenous legal systems, transformative legal studies can learn from their holistic and collaborative approaches to justice, environmental conservation, and conflict resolution. Incorporating indigenous perspectives in legal education and systems can lead to more inclusive and culturally-sensitive legal practices.

Case studies of transformative indigenous legal practices provide valuable insights into the potential for reconciliation, healing, and transformative justice. These practices can guide efforts to decolonize legal systems, promote indigenous rights, and challenge colonial legacies.

Environmental Law and Transformative Legal Strategies

Environmental law plays a critical role in addressing global environmental challenges, such as climate change, biodiversity loss, and pollution. Transformative legal strategies in environmental law aim to promote sustainability, ecological justice, and the rights of nature.

Environmental law encompasses a range of legal instruments, including international treaties, national legislation, and judicial decisions. It seeks to regulate human activities that impact the environment and provide mechanisms for enforcement and accountability.

Transformative legal strategies in environmental law include the recognition of the rights of nature, ecological legal theory, and transnational environmental legal activism. The rights of nature approach grants legal standing to ecosystems, natural entities, and the environment itself, allowing for their protection and preservation.

Ecological legal theory emphasizes the interconnectedness between humans, nature, and the law. It calls for a shift from anthropocentrism to ecocentrism, recognizing the intrinsic value of nature and its right to exist and thrive.

Transnational environmental legal activism involves collaborations between legal scholars, activists, and organizations from different regions to address global environmental challenges. It promotes the development of international legal frameworks, enforcement mechanisms, and transboundary cooperation.

By exploring transformative legal strategies in environmental law, transformative legal studies can contribute to global efforts to address environmental crises, promote sustainability, and protect the rights of nature.

Conclusion

In this chapter, we have explored global perspectives on transformative legal studies. Comparative law helps us understand the diverse legal systems across the globe and identify effective practices. International law and global governance facilitate cooperation and address transnational issues. The impact of globalization on legal responses presents challenges and opportunities. Legal activism and advocacy play crucial roles in effecting social change. Regional approaches provide context-specific strategies for legal reform. Indigenous legal systems offer alternative perspectives and approaches to law. Environmental law promotes sustainability and ecological justice.

By recognizing the diversity of global perspectives and incorporating them into transformative legal studies, we can develop comprehensive and inclusive approaches to justice and equality. These perspectives provide valuable insights into the potential of the law to transform societies and promote social change on a global scale.

Now, let's move forward to Chapter 10, where we will explore emerging trends and future directions in transformative legal studies.

Comparative Law and Global Legal Systems

Varieties of Legal Systems Across the Globe

In this section, we will explore the diverse range of legal systems that exist around the world. Understanding the different approaches to law and legal systems is essential for any study of transformative legal studies. Legal systems are shaped by various historical, cultural, and political factors, leading to distinct approaches to law and justice. By examining these legal systems, we can gain insights into the challenges and possibilities for transformative legal studies in different contexts.

Civil Law Systems

Civil law systems are derived from Roman law and have been influential in many parts of the world, including continental Europe, Latin America, and parts of Asia and Africa. These systems are characterized by a codified set of laws that form the basis of legal principles and regulations. The codes are often comprehensive and cover various aspects of law, including civil, commercial, and administrative matters.

One key feature of civil law systems is the emphasis on legal certainty and predictability. Laws are written in a clear and precise manner, providing detailed guidelines for legal questions and disputes. In civil law systems, judges play a more limited role in interpreting the law compared to common law systems.

An example of a civil law system is the French legal system, which is based on the Napoleonic Code. The Napoleonic Code, enacted in the early 19th century, codified principles of civil law and has influenced legal systems in many countries. Other examples of civil law systems include Germany, Italy, Japan, and Brazil.

Common Law Systems

Common law systems have their roots in the English legal tradition and have been adopted by many countries that were former colonies of the British Empire. Common law systems rely on judicial precedent, which means that court decisions from the past serve as binding authorities for future cases. Judges have a significant role in interpreting and shaping the law through their decisions.

One distinctive feature of common law systems is the notion of stare decisis, which means to stand by decided cases. This principle promotes consistency and predictability in the legal system. Common law systems are often characterized by a strong reliance on legal reasoning and the development of legal principles through case law.

The United States, Canada, England, Australia, and India are examples of countries with common law systems, with each jurisdiction developing its own unique legal framework based on historical and cultural factors.

Islamic Law Systems

Islamic law systems, also known as Sharia law systems, are derived from Islamic legal principles and teachings. These systems are prevalent in many countries in the Middle East, North Africa, and Southeast Asia. Islamic law systems are based on the Quran, Hadith (sayings of the Prophet Muhammad), and the consensus of Islamic jurists. Islamic law covers various aspects of life, including personal matters, family law, and commercial transactions.

One key characteristic of Islamic law systems is the integration of religious and legal principles. Islamic law aims to promote justice, equality, and social welfare in accordance with Islamic teachings. Islamic law relies on a combination of legal interpretation and the application of moral principles derived from religious sources.

Countries such as Saudi Arabia, Iran, and Pakistan have legal systems that are influenced by Islamic law. However, it is important to note that the application of Islamic law can vary within and between countries, reflecting differences in interpretation and political considerations.

Socialist Law Systems

Socialist law systems emerged in countries with socialist or communist political systems, where the state has significant control over the economy and societal affairs. These legal systems are based on Marxist-Leninist ideology and seek to promote social equality and justice.

In socialist law systems, the state plays a central role in shaping and implementing legal principles. The law is seen as an instrument of social control and serves to advance the goals of the socialist state. Private ownership of property may be limited, and the state may have extensive powers over economic activities.

China, Cuba, and Vietnam are examples of countries with socialist law systems. However, it is worth noting that socialist law systems have evolved over time, and some countries have adopted market-oriented reforms while retaining certain socialist legal principles.

Customary Law Systems

Customary law systems are based on traditional customs and practices that have evolved within specific communities over time. These systems are prevalent in many indigenous communities and rural areas around the world. Customary law is often unwritten and is transmitted through oral traditions and community practices.

One key feature of customary law systems is their focus on community values, norms, and traditions. Customary laws are often deeply rooted in local culture and reflect the social, economic, and environmental realities of the community. Customary law systems prioritize community consensus and the resolution of conflicts through community-based mechanisms.

Many countries in Africa, Asia, and the Pacific have legal systems that incorporate customary law alongside formal legal systems. For example, in countries such as Ghana and Papua New Guinea, customary law coexists with civil law or common law systems.

Mixed Legal Systems

Mixed legal systems, as the name suggests, combine elements of different legal systems. These systems arise from historical, cultural, or political factors, where legal traditions from different sources coexist. Mixed legal systems can be found in various parts of the world, including parts of Africa, Asia, and the Caribbean.

An example of a mixed legal system is the South African legal system, which draws on both common law and civil law traditions. The legal system in Quebec, Canada, is also a well-known example of a mixed legal system, combining elements of civil law and common law.

In mixed legal systems, legal practitioners must navigate the complexities of multiple legal sources and traditions, often relying on comparative legal analysis to resolve legal questions and disputes.

Challenges and Possibilities

While legal systems differ across the globe, there are common challenges and possibilities for transformative legal studies in all contexts. Transformative legal studies aim to challenge existing legal norms, structures, and power dynamics to promote justice and equality.

One challenge is the tension between tradition and innovation. Transformative legal studies often call for reimagining existing legal frameworks and adopting new approaches to address contemporary social issues. However, entrenched legal traditions and conservative attitudes can present barriers to transformative change.

Another challenge is the need for interdisciplinary collaboration. Transformative legal studies often draw insights from various disciplines, such as sociology, anthropology, political science, and psychology. Collaboration between legal scholars and practitioners from different fields is essential to develop holistic and effective approaches to transformative legal studies.

Despite these challenges, there are numerous possibilities for transformative legal studies across legal systems. Advances in technology, increased globalization, and the growing recognition of human rights provide opportunities for rethinking legal systems and advancing social justice. By embracing these opportunities, legal scholars and practitioners can contribute to the transformation of legal systems in ways that promote justice, equality, and human dignity.

Conclusion

Varieties of legal systems across the globe reflect the diverse ways in which societies approach law and justice. Civil law, common law, Islamic law, socialist law, customary law, and mixed legal systems all offer unique perspectives on legal principles and practices. While each legal system has its own challenges and possibilities, transformative legal studies can contribute to the progressive evolution of these systems. By critically engaging with legal traditions and advocating for innovative approaches, transformative legal scholars and practitioners can drive positive change in the pursuit of justice and equality.

Comparative Law Methodology and Approaches

Comparative law is a field of legal studies that aims to analyze and compare different legal systems around the world. It provides valuable insights into the similarities and differences between legal systems, their evolution, and their impact on society. This section explores the methodology and approaches used in comparative law research.

Historical Development of Comparative Law

The study of comparative law has a rich history dating back to ancient times. Early civilizations, such as the Mesopotamians and Romans, engaged in comparative legal analysis to understand legal principles and systems. However, it was during the 19th century that comparative law emerged as a distinct and formal discipline.

Legal scholars like Rudolf von Jhering and Sir Henry Maine played pivotal roles in developing the methodology and approaches of comparative law. They focused on comparing legal systems across different countries to identify similarities and differences in legal principles, institutions, and practices.

Goals and Objectives of Comparative Law

The goals of comparative law are multifaceted. Firstly, it aims to enhance our understanding of different legal systems, their historical development, and their interaction with cultural, social, and political contexts. Comparative law also seeks to promote legal harmonization, foster legal reforms, and contribute to the development of a global legal order.

Methodology of Comparative Law

Comparative law employs various methodologies to compare legal systems effectively. The two main approaches are the functional and formalistic approaches:

1. **Functional Approach:** This approach focuses on the purposes, functions, and outcomes of legal rules and institutions rather than their specific forms. It emphasizes the underlying principles, policies, and objectives of a legal system rather than its specific legal provisions. The functional approach is particularly useful when comparing legal systems with different structures and concepts.

2. **Formalistic Approach:** In contrast to the functional approach, the formalistic approach focuses on the legal rules, doctrines, and concepts of different legal systems. It analyzes the legal texts, statutory laws, judicial decisions, and legal principles to identify similarities and differences. This approach is valuable for comparing legal systems with similar legal traditions and concepts.

Sources of Comparative Law

Comparative law relies on various sources to gather information about different legal systems. These sources include:

1. **Primary Sources:** These sources encompass legal texts, such as statutory laws, constitutions, regulations, and judicial decisions. Primary sources provide valuable insights into the legal framework, principles, and doctrines of a particular legal system.

2. **Secondary Sources:** Secondary sources include scholarly articles, books, commentaries, and legal opinions that analyze and interpret legal systems. These sources offer critical analysis, comparative insights, and historical context, enabling researchers to gain a deeper understanding of different legal systems.

3. **Legal Databases:** Access to legal databases, such as Westlaw or LexisNexis, can greatly facilitate comparative law research. These databases provide comprehensive collections of legal documents, judicial decisions, and legal commentaries from various countries, enabling researchers to compare and analyze legal systems effectively.

4. **Field Research:** Field research involves direct observation, interviews, and collection of empirical data in different jurisdictions. This approach provides researchers with firsthand insights into the functioning of legal systems, societal attitudes towards the law, and the impact of legal norms on individuals and communities.

Challenges in Comparative Law

Comparative law research is not without its challenges. Some common challenges include:

1. **Translation and Language Barriers:** Legal texts and documents from different legal systems need to be accurately translated to ensure an effective comparison. Language barriers can hinder the understanding and interpretation of legal concepts and principles.

2. **Cultural and Contextual Differences:** Legal systems are deeply embedded in cultural, social, and historical contexts. Comparative law researchers must be mindful of these differences and consider them when making comparisons.

3. **Legal Complexity:** Legal systems can be incredibly complex, with intricate rules, doctrines, and procedures. Comparative law researchers must navigate this complexity to identify relevant legal principles and apply them in a comparative context.

4. **Ethical Considerations:** Comparative law research should adhere to ethical standards, respecting the legal traditions, norms, and sensitivities of the jurisdictions under study. Researchers must be cautious not to misrepresent or misinterpret legal systems.

5. **Availability and Accessibility of Legal Documents:** Access to legal documents from different legal systems can be challenging. Researchers must consider the availability and accessibility of legal sources to ensure a comprehensive and accurate comparison.

Case Study: Comparative Analysis of Contract Law

To illustrate the methodology and approaches of comparative law, let's consider a case study on contract law. In this case study, we compare the formation and enforceability of contracts in the common law system (United States) and the civil law system (France).

Using the functional approach, we would analyze the underlying principles and purposes of contract law in each jurisdiction. We would identify similarities, such as the requirement of mutual consent and consideration, as well as differences, such as the role of formalities and the discretion given to judges in interpreting contracts.

Using the formalistic approach, we would compare the legal texts, including statutes and judicial decisions, that govern contract law in each jurisdiction. We would examine the specific requirements for contract formation, the rules regarding offer and acceptance, and the remedies available for breach of contract.

By employing both approaches, researchers can gain a comprehensive understanding of the similarities and differences between the two legal systems in the context of contract law.

Conclusion

Comparative law methodology and approaches play a crucial role in understanding and analyzing different legal systems. By employing functional and formalistic approaches, researchers can compare legal systems effectively, identify similarities and differences, and contribute to legal harmonization and reform. However, comparative law research faces challenges, such as translation barriers, cultural differences, and ethical considerations, which must be carefully addressed. Through case studies and analysis, researchers can apply these methodologies and approaches to gain a deeper understanding of specific areas of law in different jurisdictions.

Cultural and Transnational Influences on Legal Systems

The field of legal studies recognizes the significant influence of culture and transnational factors on the development and operation of legal systems. Cultural norms, values, traditions, and practices shape the legal frameworks and institutions within a society. Additionally, the increasing interconnectedness of nations and the rise of globalization have given rise to transnational legal issues that require cooperation and coordination between different legal systems.

Cultural Influences on Legal Systems

Culture plays a crucial role in shaping the legal systems of societies. It encompasses the shared beliefs, values, customs, and practices of a community. These cultural elements shape the norms and expectations of individuals within a society, which in turn influence the laws and legal institutions of that society. Cultural influences on legal systems can be seen in various aspects, including the sources of law, legal traditions, and legal decision-making.

Sources of Law The sources of law in a particular legal system often reflect the cultural values and traditions of the society. In common law systems, legal principles are derived from judicial decisions, which are influenced by the cultural context and societal values of the jurisdiction. In civil law systems, on the other hand, laws are primarily derived from legislative statutes, with less emphasis on judicial precedent. The source of law in Islamic legal systems is the Quran and the Hadith, reflecting the religious and cultural values of Muslim-majority societies.

Legal Traditions Different legal traditions are influenced by the cultural frameworks in which they developed. The common law tradition, originating from England, emphasizes the role of judges in interpreting and applying the law. This tradition places significant importance on case law and precedent, as well as the adversarial system of legal dispute resolution. In contrast, civil law traditions, rooted in Roman law, prioritize statutory law and the inquisitorial system, where judges play a more active role in the investigation and gathering of evidence.

Legal Decision-Making Cultural influences can also be observed in legal decision-making processes. Judges, as members of a society, are influenced by their own cultural backgrounds and values, which can shape their interpretation and application of the law. Cultural considerations can play a role in determining the seriousness of offenses, the appropriateness of punishments, and the balancing of individual rights with collective interests. Legal decisions may also reflect cultural norms and attitudes towards social issues such as gender equality, religious freedoms, or freedom of expression.

Transnational Influences on Legal Systems

The increasing interconnectedness of nations has led to the emergence of transnational legal issues that require collaboration and coordination between different legal systems. Transnational influences on legal systems can be seen in areas such as international law, human rights law, trade law, and environmental law.

International Law International law governs relations between states and has a significant impact on domestic legal systems. Treaties, conventions, and customary international law provide rules and principles that states are expected to follow. International legal norms influence domestic legislation, judicial decisions, and the development of legal institutions. For example, the United Nations Universal Declaration of Human Rights has been an influential document in shaping national human rights laws around the world.

Human Rights Law Human rights law sets out the rights and freedoms that individuals are entitled to, regardless of their nationality or cultural background. International human rights treaties, such as the International Covenant on Civil and Political Rights and the Convention on the Elimination of All Forms of Discrimination Against Women, provide a framework for the protection of human rights globally. These treaties influence domestic legal systems by requiring states to incorporate human rights principles into their legislation and ensure their enforcement.

Trade Law Global trade and economic integration have led to the development of international trade law. Trade agreements, such as those negotiated under the World Trade Organization (WTO), establish rules and regulations for international trade. These agreements often require domestic legal systems to align their laws with international trade norms, protect intellectual property rights, and resolve disputes through specified mechanisms. As a result, legal systems need to adapt and incorporate these transnational standards into their domestic frameworks.

Environmental Law Environmental challenges, such as climate change and pollution, have transnational impacts that require international cooperation and legal frameworks. International environmental agreements, such as the Paris Agreement, set out obligations and standards for states to address environmental issues. Domestic legal systems need to incorporate these requirements, creating laws and regulations to mitigate environmental harm, protect natural resources, and promote sustainable development.

Case Study: Cultural and Transnational Influences on Intellectual Property Rights

Intellectual property rights provide legal protection for creative works, inventions, and innovations. Cultural and transnational influences are particularly evident in the field of intellectual property, where different cultural perspectives and international agreements shape the legal frameworks.

Cultural Perspectives Cultural perspectives play a significant role in shaping intellectual property laws and practices. For example, indigenous communities often have distinct cultural knowledge and practices that are passed down through generations. Intellectual property laws need to consider how to protect and respect these cultural expressions and traditional knowledge. This requires a balance between protecting indigenous rights and promoting innovation and creativity.

Transnational Agreements International agreements, such as the Agreement on Trade-Related Aspects of Intellectual Property Rights (TRIPS), harmonize intellectual property standards across nations. TRIPS requires member states to provide minimum standards of protection for intellectual property rights. However, there are ongoing debates about the extent to which these standards accommodate cultural diversity and the needs of developing countries. Some argue that the agreement prioritizes the interests of powerful economies and stifles local creativity and innovation.

Traditional Knowledge and Genetic Resources The protection of traditional knowledge and genetic resources presents unique challenges that require both cultural and transnational considerations. Traditional knowledge, held by indigenous communities, is often used in fields such as medicine, agriculture, and biodiversity conservation. Intellectual property laws need to strike a balance between protecting traditional knowledge from misappropriation and ensuring its continued utilization by the communities that hold it. International agreements, such as the Nagoya Protocol on Access to Genetic Resources and the Fair and Equitable Sharing of Benefits Arising from their Utilization, aim to address these issues.

Conclusion

Cultural and transnational influences significantly impact the development and operation of legal systems. Cultural norms, values, traditions, and practices shape the laws and legal institutions within a society. Additionally, the increasing interconnectedness of nations through globalization gives rise to transnational legal issues and the need for international cooperation. Understanding and navigating cultural and transnational influences are essential for legal scholars and practitioners operating in an increasingly globalized world.

International Law and Global Governance

Overview of International Law

International law is a dynamic and complex field that governs the relations between states and other international actors. It is an essential framework for promoting cooperation, resolving conflicts, protecting human rights, and addressing global challenges. This section provides an overview of the key principles, sources, and institutions of international law.

Principles of International Law

International law is based on a set of fundamental principles that guide the behavior and interactions of states and other international actors. These principles include:

1. **Sovereignty:** The principle of state sovereignty establishes that states are the primary subjects of international law and have the exclusive authority to govern their territories and make decisions within their borders.

2. **Prohibition of the Use of Force:** International law prohibits the use of force by states against each other, except in cases of self-defense or when authorized by the United Nations Security Council. The principle of non-intervention upholds the sovereign rights of states and restricts interference in their internal affairs.

INTERNATIONAL LAW AND GLOBAL GOVERNANCE

3. **Human Rights:** Human rights are a core component of international law. States have an obligation to respect and protect the fundamental rights and freedoms of individuals, such as the right to life, liberty, and due process. International human rights treaties and customary international law provide the legal framework for the protection of human rights.

4. **Responsibility of States:** States have a responsibility to comply with their international legal obligations and are liable for any violations of international law. This principle of state responsibility ensures accountability and promotes the peaceful settlement of disputes.

5. **Good Faith:** The principle of good faith requires states to act honestly, in accordance with their legal obligations, and with a genuine intention to abide by international law. It underpins the trust and cooperation necessary for the functioning of the international legal system.

These principles, among others, shape the contours of international law and provide a framework for the conduct of states and international organizations.

Sources of International Law

The sources of international law refer to the origins and forms of legal rules and principles in the international system. International law derives from various sources, including treaties, customary international law, general principles of law, judicial decisions, and the writings of legal scholars.

1. **Treaties:** Treaties are formal agreements between states and international organizations. They are a primary source of international law and are binding on the parties that have ratified or acceded to them. Treaties can cover a wide range of issues, such as human rights, environmental protection, trade, and disarmament.

2. **Customary International Law:** Customary international law arises from the general and consistent practice of states, accompanied by a belief that such practice is legally required (opinio juris). Customary law can emerge from longstanding state practices or from the recognition of a new norm by states. Customary international law is binding on all states, regardless of whether they have explicitly consented to it.

3. **General Principles of Law:** General principles of law, derived from the legal systems of states, provide a basis for filling gaps in international law. These

principles, such as the principle of justice and fairness, are considered common to all legal systems and serve as a guide for interpreting and applying international law.

4. **Judicial Decisions:** Decisions of international courts and tribunals contribute to the development and interpretation of international law. The judgments and opinions of these judicial bodies, such as the International Court of Justice, provide authoritative guidance on legal issues and help clarify the content of international law.

5. **Writings of Legal Scholars:** The writings of legal scholars, although not a binding source of international law, play an essential role in shaping and interpreting legal norms. Scholarly works provide analysis, commentary, and interpretations of international law, influencing the evolution of legal principles and doctrines.

These sources of international law collectively form the basis for the rights and obligations of states and other international actors.

International Legal Institutions

International law operates within a framework of institutions and organizations that facilitate its development, implementation, and enforcement. Key international legal institutions include:

1. **United Nations (UN):** The UN plays a central role in the development and maintenance of international law. It is a global organization composed of member states and serves as a forum for negotiations, dispute resolution, and the promotion of international peace and security. The UN has specialized agencies, such as the International Court of Justice and the United Nations Human Rights Council, that contribute to the development and enforcement of international law.

2. **International Court of Justice (ICJ):** The ICJ is the principal judicial organ of the United Nations and settles legal disputes between states. It provides authoritative interpretations of international law and issues binding judgments on matters of international legal disputes brought before it by states.

3. **International Criminal Court (ICC):** The ICC is a permanent international tribunal established to prosecute individuals for the most serious crimes of

international concern, including genocide, war crimes, crimes against humanity, and the crime of aggression. It complements national criminal justice systems and contributes to the development and enforcement of international criminal law.

4. **World Trade Organization (WTO):** The WTO is an international organization that regulates international trade. It promotes free trade and provides a framework for negotiating trade agreements, resolving trade disputes, and establishing rules for international commerce.

5. **Regional Organizations:** Regional organizations, such as the European Union, African Union, and Organization of American States, play an essential role in the development and implementation of regional and international legal frameworks. These organizations create regional legal norms and institutions that address specific regional challenges and promote cooperation among member states.

These institutions provide platforms for states to engage in diplomatic negotiations, resolve disputes, and facilitate cooperation in various areas of international law.

Contemporary Challenges in International Law

International law faces numerous contemporary challenges in addressing new global realities and emerging issues. Some of the significant challenges include:

1. **Globalization:** Globalization has increased the interdependence and complexity of global issues, requiring enhanced cooperation and coordination among states. International law must adapt to new economic, technological, and social dynamics.

2. **Human Rights:** The protection and promotion of human rights remain a pressing challenge for international law. Addressing human rights violations and ensuring accountability for perpetrators are ongoing concerns in various parts of the world.

3. **Climate Change:** Climate change poses significant environmental and legal challenges, necessitating collective action to mitigate its impact and promote sustainable development. International legal frameworks, such as the Paris Agreement, aim to address climate change through global cooperation.

4. **Cybersecurity:** The rapid advancement of technology has given rise to new forms of threats and challenges in cyberspace. International law must adapt to address issues related to cyber warfare, data protection, and the regulation of emerging technologies.

5. **Armed Conflicts and Humanitarian Crises:** The proliferation of armed conflicts and humanitarian crises around the world poses immense challenges for international law. The protection of civilians, the prevention of war crimes, and the enforcement of humanitarian norms remain critical areas of concern.

Addressing these challenges requires a commitment to the effective implementation and enforcement of international law, as well as continued engagement and cooperation among states.

Conclusion

International law provides a framework for the regulation of relations among states and other international actors. The principles, sources, and institutions of international law form a complex system that seeks to promote cooperation, protect human rights, and address global challenges. Understanding the nature and functioning of international law is crucial for legal scholars, practitioners, and policymakers in navigating the complexities of the international legal order. Continued engagement and innovation in international law are essential to ensuring its relevance and effectiveness in an ever-changing global landscape.

Resources for Further Study

- Brownlie, I. (2014). *Principles of Public International Law.*

- Shaw, M. (2014). *International Law.*

- Roberts, A., et al. (2014). *International Law: Cases and Materials.*

- Sands, P., et al. (2018). *Principles of International Environmental Law.*

- Cassese, A. (2013). *International Criminal Law.*

- United Nations Treaty Collection: https://treaties.un.org

- International Court of Justice: https://www.icj-cij.org

Sources of International Law

International law is a complex system of rules and principles that govern the relationships between states, international organizations, and individuals in the international arena. These rules and principles are derived from various sources, which are recognized as the foundations of international law. Understanding these sources is essential for comprehending the basis and legitimacy of international legal norms. In this section, we will explore the primary sources of international law, which include treaties, customary international law, general principles of law, and legal scholarship.

Treaties

Treaties are one of the most significant sources of international law. A treaty is a formal agreement between two or more states, which can also include international organizations. Treaties can take various forms, such as bilateral (between two states) or multilateral (involving multiple states). They are often negotiated and concluded through diplomatic means.

The content of a treaty can encompass a wide range of subjects, including human rights, trade, environmental protection, and disarmament, among others. Treaties can establish legally binding obligations for parties and create rights and duties. Once ratified or acceded to by states, treaties become part of the domestic legal framework of those states, and they are obligated to abide by their provisions.

For example, the United Nations Charter is a treaty that establishes the foundational principles and rules of the United Nations (UN). It sets out the rights and responsibilities of member states and outlines the functions and powers of UN organs. Treaties like the Geneva Conventions also play a crucial role in ensuring the protection of victims of armed conflicts.

Customary International Law

Customary international law is another primary source of international law. It refers to the general practices and beliefs that have developed over time and are accepted as legally binding by states. Unlike treaties, customary international law does not require a formal agreement or written instrument.

To establish customary international law, two elements are essential: state practice and opinio juris. State practice refers to the consistent behavior of states in a particular area. This practice can be in the form of actions, omissions, or even the acceptance of certain norms. Opinio juris, on the other hand, refers to the belief of states that their actions are legally required, rather than merely customary or political.

For example, the principle of "non-intervention" in the domestic affairs of states is considered a customary norm of international law. It has been demonstrated through consistent state practice and an opinio juris that prohibits states from interfering in the internal affairs of other states.

General Principles of Law

General principles of law are foundational legal principles that are recognized and applied by a majority of legal systems worldwide. These principles serve as a source of international law when other sources, such as treaties or customary international law, are absent or insufficient to address a particular legal issue.

The general principles of law can be derived from a variety of sources, including domestic legal systems, international treaties, and judicial decisions. They often reflect fundamental concepts of justice, fairness, and equity. Some examples of general principles of law include the principles of good faith, pacta sunt servanda (agreements must be kept), and proportionality.

These principles act as guidelines for interpreting and filling gaps in international law. They provide a level of coherence and consistency to the international legal system and help maintain its legitimacy.

Legal Scholarship

Legal scholarship, also known as academic writings or doctrine, is an essential source of international law. It comprises writings by legal scholars, experts, and practitioners who analyze and interpret the existing legal norms, concepts, and theories. Legal scholarship serves as a valuable tool for understanding the complexities of international law and for proposing new legal perspectives and solutions.

Legal scholars contribute to the development of international law by researching and writing articles, books, and commentaries. Their works influence the formation of legal opinions, judicial decisions, and the evolution of legal doctrines. Legal scholarship helps refine and shape the interpretation of existing legal norms and provides guidance for addressing emerging legal issues.

Moreover, academic institutions and research centers play a vital role in promoting legal scholarship. They organize conferences, seminars, and symposiums that bring together legal scholars from around the world to exchange ideas and engage in critical discussions on issues of international law.

Conclusion

In this section, we have explored the primary sources of international law, including treaties, customary international law, general principles of law, and legal scholarship. These sources form the backbone of the international legal system by establishing binding obligations, reflecting state practice and opinio juris, defining general legal principles, and providing critical analysis and interpretation. Understanding these sources is crucial for comprehending the nature, legitimacy, and development of international law. By examining these sources, legal practitioners and scholars can navigate the complexities of the international legal framework and contribute to its continuous transformation and evolution.

Global Governance Institutions

In today's interconnected world, global governance institutions play a crucial role in addressing pressing global challenges and shaping international cooperation. These institutions provide a framework for collective decision-making, negotiation, and coordination among nations, helping to establish norms, rules, and mechanisms for global governance. In this section, we will explore the key characteristics, functions, and challenges associated with global governance institutions.

Characteristics of Global Governance Institutions

Global governance institutions are characterized by several key features that distinguish them from other international organizations. These characteristics include:

1. **Membership:** Global governance institutions typically have a broad membership, encompassing a large number of countries from different regions of the world. This diverse membership ensures a wide range of perspectives and promotes global inclusiveness.

2. **Decision-making:** These institutions employ various decision-making mechanisms, ranging from consensus-based processes to voting systems. Decision-making may be centralized, with decision-making powers concentrated in an executive body, or decentralized, with decision-making authority shared among member states.

3. **Mandate:** Global governance institutions have a specific mandate that defines their scope of operation and the issues they address. For example, the United Nations (UN) has a broad mandate covering peace and security,

human rights, development, and international law. Other institutions, such as the World Trade Organization (WTO), focus on specific areas like trade and economic cooperation.

4. **Normative Framework:** These institutions are guided by a set of norms, principles, and rules that govern their activities and shape member states' behavior. These norms can range from basic principles of sovereignty and non-interference to norms promoting human rights, environmental protection, and sustainable development.

5. **Legal Authority:** Some global governance institutions have legal authority, allowing them to create binding rules and regulations that member states are obligated to follow. For example, the international human rights treaties adopted under the auspices of the UN have legally binding provisions.

Functions of Global Governance Institutions

Global governance institutions serve multiple functions aimed at promoting cooperation, resolving conflicts, and addressing global challenges. Some of the key functions include:

1. **Negotiation and Diplomacy:** Global governance institutions provide a platform for member states to negotiate and engage in diplomatic dialogue. This facilitates the resolution of conflicts, the development of common positions, and the coordination of policy actions.

2. **Standard Setting:** These institutions play a crucial role in the establishment of global standards, norms, and rules. For example, the International Organization for Standardization (ISO) develops and publishes international standards in various fields, ranging from quality management to environmental management.

3. **Monitoring and Compliance:** Global governance institutions monitor compliance with agreed-upon rules and regulations. They assess member states' adherence to their commitments and take appropriate measures to address non-compliance. The International Atomic Energy Agency (IAEA), for instance, ensures member states' compliance with nuclear non-proliferation agreements.

4. **Resource Mobilization:** Many global governance institutions engage in resource mobilization efforts to address global challenges. They provide

financial and technical assistance, facilitate the flow of resources, and promote cooperation in areas such as development, health, and climate change. The World Bank and the Global Fund to Fight AIDS, Tuberculosis, and Malaria are examples of institutions engaged in resource mobilization.

5. **Conflict Resolution:** These institutions are often involved in conflict resolution and peacebuilding efforts. They mediate between conflicting parties, facilitate peace negotiations, and support post-conflict reconstruction and reconciliation. The United Nations Peacebuilding Commission is an example of an institution focused on post-conflict peacebuilding.

It is important to note that global governance institutions do not have a centralized authority or enforcement mechanism comparable to that of national governments. Their effectiveness depends on the willingness of member states to cooperate and abide by the rules and decisions of the institutions.

Challenges in Global Governance Institutions

While global governance institutions play a crucial role in addressing global challenges, they also face significant challenges that limit their effectiveness. Some of these challenges include:

1. **Power Imbalances:** Global governance institutions can be influenced by power imbalances among member states. Powerful countries may exert disproportionate influence, undermining the equitable representation and decision-making processes of these institutions.

2. **Lack of Accountability:** Some global governance institutions suffer from a lack of accountability mechanisms. This can undermine trust and legitimacy, as member states may not be held accountable for violating the institution's norms or failing to fulfill their commitments.

3. **Fragmentation and Overlapping Mandates:** There is often a lack of coordination and coherence among different global governance institutions, leading to duplication of efforts and fragmentation of goals. Overlapping mandates can make it challenging to address complex global issues effectively.

4. **Limited Funding and Resource Constraints:** Many global governance institutions face funding constraints, limiting their ability to fulfill their

mandates effectively. This can hinder their capacity to mobilize resources and provide necessary support to member states.

5. **Political Tensions and Conflicting Interests:** Global governance institutions often operate in a politically charged environment, where conflicting national interests can impede cooperation and decision-making. Overcoming political tensions and reaching consensus on contentious issues can be challenging.

Addressing these challenges requires ongoing efforts to reform and strengthen global governance institutions. This includes enhancing transparency and accountability, promoting inclusivity and equitable representation, and ensuring adequate resources and funding for effective functioning.

Resources for Further Study

To delve deeper into the topic of global governance institutions, the following resources provide valuable insights and analysis:

1. **Book:** "Global Governance: Why? What? Whither?" by Thomas G. Weiss and Rorden Wilkinson

2. **Journal Article:** "Global Governance Institutions: Reform or Reboot?" by Stewart Patrick

3. **Website:** United Nations System (https://www.un.org/en/) provides detailed information about various global governance institutions within the UN system

4. **Report:** "Reimagining Global Governance for the 21st Century," World Economic Forum (https://www.weforum.org/reports/reimagining-global-governance-for-the-21st-ce

These resources offer diverse perspectives on the challenges, opportunities, and future directions for global governance institutions.

In conclusion, global governance institutions play a vital role in addressing global challenges, promoting cooperation, and shaping international norms and rules. Despite the challenges they face, these institutions provide a crucial platform for international dialogue, negotiation, and collective decision-making. It is through effective global governance that the international community can work together to tackle the most pressing issues of our time and create a more just and equitable world.

Globalization and Legal Responses

Impact of Globalization on Legal Systems

Globalization has had a profound impact on legal systems across the world. With the increasing interconnectedness of economies, cultures, and societies, legal systems have had to adapt to new challenges and opportunities. In this section, we will explore the various ways in which globalization has influenced legal systems, both positively and negatively.

Introduction to Globalization

Globalization refers to the integration and interdependence of economies, cultures, and societies on a global scale. It is driven by advancements in technology, trade liberalization, and increased mobility of goods, services, capital, and people. Globalization has led to increased cross-border interactions and has transformed the world into a global village.

Legal Harmonization

One of the key effects of globalization on legal systems is the trend towards legal harmonization. As countries become more interconnected, there is a need for harmonizing laws and regulations to facilitate international trade, investment, and cooperation. Regional integration organizations, such as the European Union, have played a crucial role in harmonizing legal frameworks among member states.

Legal harmonization has several benefits. It promotes legal certainty, fosters cross-border enforcement, reduces transaction costs for businesses, and facilitates the resolution of disputes between parties from different countries. For example, the harmonization of contract law within the European Union has made it easier for businesses to engage in cross-border transactions and resolve disputes.

However, legal harmonization also raises challenges. It requires countries to give up some degree of sovereignty over their legal systems, which may be seen as a threat to national identity and culture. There may also be concerns about the dominance of certain legal systems in the global arena and the potential for unequal power dynamics among countries.

Transnational Legal Frameworks

Globalization has also led to the development of transnational legal frameworks that transcend national boundaries. These frameworks are created to address global issues, such as human rights, environmental protection, and intellectual property rights. Examples of transnational legal frameworks include international treaties, conventions, and agreements.

Transnational legal frameworks provide a common set of standards and principles that countries can adhere to. They help promote cooperation and coordination among nations in addressing global challenges. For instance, the United Nations Convention on the Law of the Sea (UNCLOS) establishes the legal framework for the management and conservation of marine resources in international waters.

However, the effectiveness of transnational legal frameworks can be limited by issues such as enforcement, compliance, and interpretation. There may be differences in how countries interpret and implement these frameworks, leading to variations in legal outcomes. Moreover, developing countries may face challenges in fully participating in the development and implementation of transnational legal frameworks due to capacity constraints.

Impact on National Legal Systems

Globalization has influenced national legal systems in various ways. One significant impact is the adoption of foreign legal concepts, principles, and practices. As countries engage in international trade and investment, they incorporate elements of foreign legal systems to attract foreign businesses and investors. For example, many countries have introduced investor-friendly laws and regulations based on common law principles to encourage foreign direct investment.

Globalization has also led to the development of new areas of law. As technologies evolve and new challenges arise, legal systems have had to adapt and create legal frameworks to address issues such as cybercrime, e-commerce, and intellectual property rights in the digital era. These emerging areas of law require constant adaptation and updating to keep pace with advancements in technology and changing business practices.

However, the influence of globalization on national legal systems is not always positive. It can lead to a loss of cultural and national identity as countries adopt legal frameworks that may not align with their traditions and values. Moreover, globalization can exacerbate inequalities between countries, as more powerful nations may impose their legal systems and standards on weaker countries.

Challenges and Ethical Considerations

Globalization presents several challenges and ethical considerations for legal systems. One of the main challenges is ensuring the protection of human rights and fundamental freedoms in an increasingly interconnected world. Legal systems must address issues such as human trafficking, labor exploitation, and discrimination that may be amplified by globalization.

Another challenge is balancing economic interests with social and environmental concerns. As countries strive for economic growth and attract foreign investment, there is a need to ensure that legal frameworks promote sustainable development and protect vulnerable populations. For example, laws governing multinational corporations' activities need to address issues of corporate social responsibility and environmental sustainability.

Ethical considerations arise in the context of cross-border disputes and conflicts of laws. Legal systems must grapple with questions of jurisdiction, choice of law, and enforcement when parties from different countries are involved. Resolving these issues requires careful consideration of fairness, due process, and respect for the rule of law.

Examples and Case Studies

To better understand the impact of globalization on legal systems, let's consider some examples and case studies.

Example 1: The European Union

The European Union is a prime example of legal harmonization and integration. Through the adoption of common laws and regulations, EU member states have facilitated the free movement of goods, services, capital, and people. The European Court of Justice plays a central role in interpreting and enforcing EU law, ensuring uniformity and legal certainty across member states.

Example 2: Intellectual Property Rights

Globalization has brought challenges to intellectual property rights protection. With the ease of digital reproduction and distribution, it has become more difficult to safeguard intellectual property rights such as patents, copyrights, and trademarks. Legal systems have had to adapt by introducing specialized laws and enforcement mechanisms to address these issues.

Conclusion

Globalization has had a profound impact on legal systems worldwide. It has led to legal harmonization, the development of transnational legal frameworks, and the adoption of foreign legal concepts. While globalization presents opportunities for economic growth and cooperation, it also raises challenges related to human rights, social and environmental concerns, and ethical considerations. As legal systems continue to evolve, there is a need for ongoing adaptation and development to ensure that they can effectively address the complex issues posed by globalization.

Further Reading:

1. Sornarajah, M. (2010). *The International Law on Foreign Investment* (3rd ed.). Cambridge University Press.

2. Twining, W. (2017). *General Jurisprudence: Understanding Law from a Global Perspective*. Cambridge University Press.

3. Del Duca, L. M., & McGarry, R. (Eds.). (2020). *Global Perspectives on Law and Order*. Springer.

Legal Responses to Global Challenges

In today's interconnected world, legal systems play a crucial role in addressing global challenges. From climate change and human rights violations to transnational crime and economic inequality, the legal field has the power to shape responses that can create a more just and sustainable future for all. This section will explore some of the key legal responses to global challenges and examine their potential to effect transformative change.

International Law and Multilateral Cooperation

One of the primary legal responses to global challenges is through international law, which provides a framework for cooperation between nations. International treaties and agreements serve as important tools in addressing pressing issues such as climate change, nuclear disarmament, and human rights. For example, the Paris Agreement on climate change aims to limit global warming and reduce greenhouse gas emissions through the collective commitments of nations.

Multilateral organizations like the United Nations (UN) play a critical role in the development and enforcement of international law. The UN Charter establishes principles and mechanisms for promoting peace, security, and cooperation among member states. Through its specialized agencies and programs, such as the International Court of Justice and the United Nations Environment Programme, the UN facilitates the implementation of international legal norms and fosters collaboration on global challenges.

However, one of the challenges in relying on international law and multilateral cooperation is the issue of enforcement. International law lacks a centralized judicial system with the authority to enforce its decisions. As a result, compliance with international obligations can be inconsistent, and powerful states may disregard their legal commitments in pursuit of their national interests. Efforts to strengthen international legal mechanisms, enhance compliance, and ensure accountability are ongoing.

Regional Integration and Supranational Governance

Regional integration is another legal response to global challenges. Regional organizations such as the European Union (EU) and the African Union (AU) have established supranational legal frameworks that promote cooperation and harmonization of laws among member states. Through regional courts, such as the European Court of Justice, these organizations provide avenues for resolving disputes and enforcing regional legal standards.

The EU, in particular, has developed a comprehensive legal framework that governs various aspects of member states' relations, including trade, human rights, and environmental protection. The supremacy of EU law over national laws is a unique feature that ensures the consistent application of legal standards across member states. This integration has not only facilitated economic cooperation but also promoted peace and stability among European nations.

Supranational governance offers advantages in addressing global challenges by pooling resources and expertise. However, it also raises questions about national sovereignty and the balance of power between regional and national authorities. The tension between centralized decision-making and the autonomy of member states is an ongoing area of debate and reform within regional integration frameworks.

Corporate Accountability and Responsible Business Conduct

With the increasing globalization of commerce, legal responses to global challenges must also address the behavior of multinational corporations. Corporate accountability and responsible business conduct have emerged as important legal concepts in this context. Various legal mechanisms, such as legislation, regulations, and international guidelines, aim to hold corporations accountable for their human rights and environmental impacts.

For instance, the United Nations Guiding Principles on Business and Human Rights articulate the responsibilities of states and businesses in preventing human rights abuses by corporations. These principles emphasize the need for due diligence, transparency, and access to remedy for victims of corporate-related human rights violations. National legislation has been enacted in some countries to enforce corporate responsibility, requiring companies to report on their environmental, social, and governance practices.

However, challenges remain in ensuring effective corporate accountability. The extraterritorial reach of national laws, the enforcement capacities of regulatory bodies, and the complex multinational corporate structures pose obstacles to holding corporations accountable for their actions. Efforts to address these challenges include strengthening international standards, promoting voluntary initiatives, and enhancing cross-border cooperation among regulatory authorities.

Access to Justice and Equal Protection

A fundamental legal response to global challenges is ensuring access to justice and equal protection under the law for all individuals, regardless of their socio-economic status or background. Access to justice encompasses both the availability and affordability of legal services, as well as the fairness and effectiveness of legal procedures.

Legal aid programs, pro bono services, and other initiatives aim to bridge the justice gap by providing legal assistance to those who cannot afford it. Access to justice also requires addressing systemic barriers, such as discrimination, bias, and unequal power dynamics within legal systems. Establishing fair and impartial judicial systems, promoting legal literacy, and empowering marginalized communities are integral to achieving access to justice.

In addition, legal responses must address the disproportionate impact of global challenges on vulnerable groups. This includes addressing systemic inequalities, promoting inclusion, and protecting the rights of marginalized communities. Efforts to promote social justice and human rights play a crucial role in transforming legal systems to better address the needs and aspirations of all individuals globally.

Conclusion

Legal responses to global challenges are multifaceted and require a comprehensive approach that spans local, national, regional, and international levels. International law, regional integration, corporate accountability, access to justice, and equal protection are all integral components of a transformative legal framework. By embracing these legal responses, societies can address pressing global challenges and work towards a more equitable and sustainable future. However, ongoing efforts are necessary to strengthen legal mechanisms, promote compliance, and advance social justice and human rights globally.

Human Rights and Globalization

Globalization has had a profound impact on various aspects of society, including the field of human rights. As nations become increasingly interconnected through trade, communication, and travel, the need to address human rights issues on a global scale becomes more pressing. This section explores the relationship between human rights and globalization, examining both the challenges and opportunities that arise in this context.

The Impact of Globalization on Human Rights

Globalization has opened up new avenues for the promotion and protection of human rights. Increased international trade and economic interdependence have the potential to spur economic development and improve living standards, thereby contributing to the fulfillment of economic and social rights. The spread of information and communication technologies has facilitated greater awareness of human rights abuses and has provided a platform for advocacy and mobilization on a global scale.

However, globalization also presents challenges to the effective realization of human rights. The rapid pace of economic and technological change can lead to social dislocation and inequality, exacerbating existing human rights challenges. Transnational corporations, while contributing to economic growth, can also be implicated in human rights violations, particularly in relation to labor rights and environmental damage. The power dynamics inherent in the global economic system can further marginalize vulnerable populations and limit their access to justice.

The Role of International Law in Advancing Human Rights

International law provides a framework for addressing human rights in the context of globalization. The development of international human rights treaties and conventions underscores the global commitment to promoting and protecting human rights. These instruments establish legal standards and obligations for states, creating a foundation for accountability.

International human rights law recognizes the interconnectedness of civil, political, economic, social, and cultural rights. It places a duty on states to respect, protect, and fulfill these rights both within their own territories and in relation to their actions abroad. Additionally, the emergence of customary international law and the growing recognition of individual and collective rights contribute to the development of a comprehensive human rights framework.

Challenges in Enforcing Human Rights in a Globalized World

Enforcing human rights in a globalized world presents several challenges. One key challenge is the issue of jurisdiction. The reach of national legal systems is often limited to the boundaries of the state, making it difficult to hold non-state actors accountable for human rights violations that occur in transnational contexts. The extraterritorial application of human rights obligations, however, has gained recognition as an important principle in addressing these issues.

Another challenge is the power imbalance between nations and corporations. Transnational corporations often operate across multiple jurisdictions, making it challenging to hold them accountable for their human rights impacts. The lack of an international regulatory framework for business and human rights further compounds this problem. Efforts such as the United Nations Guiding Principles on Business and Human Rights aim to address this challenge by outlining the responsibilities of states and businesses in relation to human rights.

Opportunities for Global Cooperation

Despite these challenges, globalization also presents opportunities for global cooperation in addressing human rights. Increased interconnectivity allows for the exchange of best practices and collaboration among states, organizations, and individuals working towards the promotion and protection of human rights. Global networks and coalitions can leverage collective power to effect change and hold governments and corporations accountable.

International human rights mechanisms, such as the United Nations Human Rights Council and treaty monitoring bodies, provide spaces for dialogue, review, and advocacy. These platforms enable states, civil society organizations, and individuals to bring attention to human rights violations and push for accountability and remedial action.

Furthermore, emerging concepts of global citizenship and cosmopolitanism promote the idea that individuals have rights and responsibilities beyond national borders. This recognition of shared humanity and the interconnectedness of global challenges can foster a greater sense of solidarity and collective action in the pursuit of human rights.

Case Study: Global Advocacy for Women's Rights

One example of international cooperation in advancing human rights is the global advocacy for women's rights. The women's rights movement has made significant strides in raising awareness and mobilizing support for gender equality and women's empowerment. The Convention on the Elimination of All Forms of Discrimination against Women (CEDAW) is a key international instrument that outlines the rights of women and provides a framework for national action.

Through transnational advocacy networks, grassroots organizations, and international platforms, women's rights activists have been able to address issues such as gender-based violence, economic disparities, and political underrepresentation. The recognition of women's rights as human rights has become increasingly mainstream, and governments, civil society, and international organizations are working together to promote gender equality.

Conclusion

The intersection of human rights and globalization presents both opportunities and challenges. While globalization has the potential to promote the realization of human rights, it also poses significant obstacles. The enforcement of human rights in the global context requires international cooperation, the development of effective legal frameworks, and the recognition of shared responsibility.

Through collaborative efforts and the recognition of the interconnectedness of human rights, individuals and organizations can work towards creating a more just and equitable global society. By addressing the power imbalances, ensuring accountability for human rights violations, and promoting global citizenship, transformative approaches to human rights in the context of globalization can contribute to the advancement of social justice on a global scale.

Transformative Legal Activism Globally

Legal Activism in the Global South

Legal activism in the Global South is a powerful force for social change and justice. In many developing countries, individuals and groups have taken up the law as a tool to challenge oppressive systems, promote human rights, and advocate for marginalized communities. This section explores the dynamics of legal activism in the Global South, its impact on transformative legal studies, and the challenges faced by activists in their pursuit of justice.

Context and Background

The Global South encompasses countries located primarily in Africa, Latin America, Asia, and the Middle East. These regions have a history of colonialism, inequality, and social injustice, which has led to the emergence of various legal activism movements. Legal activism refers to the use of legal strategies and actions to challenge existing laws, policies, and practices that contribute to oppression and discrimination.

In the Global South, legal activism often intersects with other social justice movements, including those focused on gender equality, environmental protection, labor rights, indigenous rights, and poverty alleviation. Activists employ a range of legal tactics, including litigation, advocacy, community organizing, and public awareness campaigns, to bring about change and advance the rights of marginalized communities.

Principles and Strategies

Legal activism in the Global South is guided by several key principles and strategies. These include:

1. **Empowerment of marginalized communities**: Legal activists in the Global South seek to empower marginalized communities by providing them with the knowledge and tools to navigate the legal system. They work to bridge the gap between formal legal institutions and the grassroots level, ensuring that marginalized voices are heard and their rights protected.

2. **Strategic litigation**: Legal activists strategically use litigation to challenge unjust laws and policies. They bring landmark cases to courts, aiming to set legal precedents and create systemic change. These cases often focus on issues such as land rights, access to resources, discrimination, and political repression.

3. **Partnerships and alliances**: Legal activism in the Global South emphasizes collaboration and alliances with other social justice organizations, human rights groups, and grassroots movements. By building partnerships, activists can amplify their impact, share resources and expertise, and create a unified front against systemic injustices.

4. **Community mobilization and awareness**: Legal activism goes beyond the courtroom. It involves mobilizing communities, raising awareness about legal rights, and empowering individuals to take collective action. Activists engage in community-based initiatives, workshops, and campaigns to educate people about their legal rights and empower them to advocate for change.

Successes and Challenges

Legal activism in the Global South has achieved notable successes in promoting social justice and human rights. For example, legal activism in India played a crucial role in overturning Section 377 of the Indian Penal Code, which criminalized consensual same-sex relationships. This landmark case led to the decriminalization of homosexuality and sparked a wave of LGBTQ+ activism across the country.

In South Africa, legal activism played a pivotal role in dismantling the oppressive apartheid system. Through strategic litigation and international pressure, activists were able to challenge and ultimately overturn apartheid laws, leading to the establishment of a more inclusive and equal society.

However, legal activism in the Global South also faces significant challenges. These include:

1. **Limited access to justice:** Marginalized communities often face barriers in accessing justice due to poverty, lack of legal awareness, and unequal power dynamics. Legal activists struggle to bridge this gap and ensure that communities most affected by injustices have equal access to legal remedies and representation.

2. **Threats and intimidation:** Legal activists in the Global South often face threats, harassment, and violence from state actors, powerful corporations, or entrenched interests. The work of activists challenging systems of power can put their safety and well-being at risk.

3. **Lack of resources:** Legal activism requires financial and logistical resources, such as funding for litigation costs, legal expertise, and infrastructure. Many activists in the Global South operate with limited resources, making it challenging to sustain long-term legal campaigns.

4. **Legal and institutional constraints:** Activists often struggle against legal and institutional structures that perpetuate inequality and favor those in power. Biased laws, corrupt systems, and limited judicial independence can hinder the effectiveness of legal activism.

Future Directions and Recommendations

To strengthen legal activism in the Global South, several strategies and recommendations can be considered:

1. **Capacity building:** Investing in legal education and capacity building programs will empower individuals and communities to navigate the legal system effectively. Legal literacy initiatives should focus on marginalized communities and grassroots organizations.

2. **International solidarity:** Building connections and alliances with international human rights organizations can provide legal activists in the Global South with support, resources, and opportunities for collaboration. International networks can amplify the impact of local legal activism efforts.

3. **Advocacy for legal reforms:** Legal activists should continue advocating for legal and institutional reforms to address systemic inequalities. This includes working towards the equitable distribution of legal resources, reforming discriminatory laws, and strengthening the independence of the judiciary.

4. **Technology and innovation:** Harnessing the power of technology and innovation can enhance the effectiveness of legal activism. Digital tools, social media, and online platforms can be utilized for legal education, mobilization, and sharing of resources among activists.

5. **Holistic approach:** Legal activism should be accompanied by a holistic approach that addresses the root causes of social injustice. This includes collaborating with other actors in the social justice ecosystem, such as community organizations, policymakers, and academia, to bring about comprehensive change.

Conclusion

Legal activism in the Global South plays a vital role in challenging oppressive systems, promoting social justice, and empowering marginalized communities. By employing strategic litigation, community mobilization, and partnerships, legal activists are transforming legal systems and advocating for a more just and equitable society. However, significant challenges remain, and it is crucial to address issues of access to justice, resources, threats, and legal constraints to further strengthen legal activism in the Global South. Through continued efforts and innovative approaches, legal activism can contribute to transformative legal studies and create lasting social change.

Transnational Legal Activism

Transnational legal activism is an important aspect of transformative legal studies that focuses on the global mobilization of legal strategies and advocacy to drive social change and promote justice. This section explores the key principles, challenges, and examples of transnational legal activism.

Principles of Transnational Legal Activism

Transnational legal activism is guided by several principles that shape its approach to promoting transformative change across borders. These principles include:

1. **Global Solidarity:** Transnational legal activism recognizes the interconnectedness of social justice struggles worldwide and promotes solidarity among different groups and movements. It emphasizes collaboration and cooperation between activists, organizations, and communities across national boundaries.

2. **Legal Mobilization:** Transnational legal activism harnesses the power of law and legal strategies to advance social justice agendas. It involves utilizing national and international legal frameworks, institutions, and mechanisms to advocate for change, challenge oppressive systems, and hold states and other actors accountable.

3. **Intersectionality:** Transnational legal activism acknowledges the intersections of various forms of oppression and recognizes that social justice issues cannot be addressed in isolation. It seeks to address power dynamics and challenges inequalities based on race, gender, class, sexuality, and other social categories.

4. **Local Context Sensitivity:** Transnational legal activism respects the diversity of local contexts and recognizes the importance of engaging with local communities, cultures, and customs. It seeks to incorporate local knowledge and perspectives in the design and implementation of legal strategies, ensuring that they are relevant and effective.

Challenges in Transnational Legal Activism

While transnational legal activism holds great potential for driving social change, it also faces several challenges. These challenges include:

1. **Legal Pluralism:** Transnational legal activism operates within a complex landscape of legal systems and norms, including national laws, international treaties, and customary laws. Navigating these diverse legal frameworks and resolving conflicts between them can be challenging.

2. **Power Imbalances:** Transnational legal activism seeks to challenge power imbalances and systems of oppression, but it often faces resistance from powerful actors who benefit from the status quo. Overcoming these power imbalances requires strategic alliances, civil society mobilization, and creative legal tactics.

3. **Cultural Sensitivity:** Balancing universal human rights norms with cultural diversity can be a delicate task. Transnational legal activism must respect cultural differences and avoid imposing external legal standards without understanding the local context.

4. **Resource Constraints:** Transnational legal activism often relies on limited resources, both financial and human. Sustaining long-term engagement and

implementing effective legal strategies can be challenging without adequate resources.

Examples of Transnational Legal Activism

Transnational legal activism has been instrumental in driving social change and advancing human rights globally. Here are a few notable examples:

1. **The Campaign to Ban Landmines:** The transnational legal activism campaign to ban landmines resulted in the creation of the Ottawa Treaty in 1997, which prohibits the use, stockpiling, production, and transfer of anti-personnel landmines. This campaign brought together non-governmental organizations, governments, and grassroots activists from around the world to advocate for the treaty.

2. **Marriage Equality Advocacy:** Transnational legal activism has played a significant role in advancing marriage equality for the LGBTQ+ community. Activists have utilized strategic litigation, transnational advocacy networks, and international human rights mechanisms to challenge discriminatory laws and promote equal rights for same-sex couples.

3. **The International Criminal Court (ICC):** The establishment of the ICC was the result of transnational legal activism aimed at combating impunity for international crimes. Activists mobilized to push for the creation of an international tribunal to prosecute war crimes, crimes against humanity, and genocide, holding individuals accountable for their actions.

4. **Corporate Accountability Initiatives:** Transnational legal activism has been instrumental in holding corporations accountable for human rights abuses and environmental destruction. Activists and organizations have utilized litigation, grassroots campaigns, and international advocacy to demand corporate responsibility and promote transformative change in corporate practices.

Resources for Transnational Legal Activism

Engaging in transnational legal activism requires knowledge and resources. Here are some valuable resources for activists:

1. **Non-Governmental Organizations (NGOs):** NGOs such as Amnesty International, Human Rights Watch, and the International Commission of Jurists provide valuable research, advocacy, and legal support for transnational activism.

2. **International and Regional Human Rights Bodies:** International and regional human rights bodies, such as the United Nations Human Rights Council

and the Inter-American Commission on Human Rights, offer mechanisms for submitting complaints and conducting advocacy at the global level.

3. **International Treaties and Conventions:** Familiarize yourself with international human rights treaties and conventions, such as the Universal Declaration of Human Rights and the Convention on the Elimination of All Forms of Discrimination Against Women. These legal instruments provide a framework for advocacy and legal strategies.

4. **Legal Networks and Coalitions:** Joining legal networks and coalitions focused on specific human rights issues can provide opportunities for collaboration, knowledge-sharing, and collective advocacy.

5. **Legal Education and Training:** Building legal expertise is essential for effective transnational legal activism. Seek opportunities for legal education and training in topics such as international human rights law, comparative law, and advocacy skills.

6. **Grassroots Mobilization:** Ground your transnational legal activism in grassroots mobilization and community engagement. Connect with local communities affected by human rights issues, build partnerships, and ensure that your advocacy is rooted in the needs and aspirations of those affected.

In conclusion, transnational legal activism offers a powerful platform for promoting transformative change and advancing justice on a global scale. By embracing principles of global solidarity, legal mobilization, intersectionality, and local context sensitivity, activists can address the challenges posed by legal pluralism, power imbalances, cultural sensitivity, and resource constraints. Through strategic collaboration, creative legal tactics, and the utilization of available resources, transnational legal activism has the potential to drive social change and uphold human rights across borders.

Human Rights and Transnational Justice Movements

In recent decades, there has been an increasing recognition of the importance of transnational justice movements in promoting and protecting human rights. These movements transcend national boundaries and bring together individuals, organizations, and communities from different countries to advocate for justice, accountability, and equality. This section will explore the role of transnational justice movements in advancing human rights, the challenges they face, and the strategies they employ to effect positive change.

Background

Transnational justice movements emerged as a response to the limitations of national legal systems in addressing human rights violations in an increasingly globalized world. They seek to hold individuals, corporations, and even governments accountable for their actions that violate human rights norms. These movements recognize that many human rights issues are interconnected and require cooperation and collaboration across borders.

Principles of Transnational Justice Movements

Transnational justice movements are guided by several key principles. First and foremost, they prioritize the protection and promotion of human rights as universal values that transcend national boundaries. They also emphasize the importance of solidarity and collective action, recognizing that addressing human rights issues requires collaboration and the sharing of ideas, resources, and strategies across different contexts.

Furthermore, transnational justice movements adopt a participatory and inclusive approach, ensuring that the voices and perspectives of marginalized and affected communities are central to decision-making processes. They also advocate for transparency, accountability, and the rule of law, seeking to hold both state and non-state actors responsible for human rights abuses.

Challenges and Strategies

Transnational justice movements face numerous challenges in their work. One of the key challenges is the lack of enforceable international human rights standards. While international human rights instruments exist, the enforcement mechanisms are often weak and rely on voluntary compliance. Additionally, powerful actors and governments may resist accountability and actively work against these movements.

To overcome these challenges, transnational justice movements employ various strategies. They engage in advocacy and lobbying efforts to press for legal and policy reforms at national and international levels. They also utilize strategic litigation to bring human rights violations to the attention of domestic and international courts. Furthermore, they engage in grassroots mobilization and public awareness campaigns to raise consciousness about human rights issues.

Examples of Transnational Justice Movements

One notable example of a transnational justice movement is the movement for accountability and justice for victims of international crimes. This includes movements seeking justice for war crimes, crimes against humanity, and genocide. These movements often work closely with international courts and tribunals, such as the International Criminal Court, to ensure accountability for these grave violations of human rights.

Another example is the movement for corporate accountability. Transnational corporations often operate across multiple countries, making it challenging to hold them accountable for human rights abuses. Transnational justice movements in this context work to develop and implement frameworks for corporate accountability, including mechanisms for victims to seek redress and hold corporations liable for their actions.

Resources and Organizations

There are several resources and organizations available for individuals and groups interested in engaging with transnational justice movements. These include:
- The International Federation for Human Rights (FIDH), which is an international non-governmental organization that works to promote respect for human rights worldwide through advocacy and collaboration with local partners. - The International Center for Transitional Justice (ICTJ), which focuses on the promotion of transitional justice measures in countries affected by mass atrocities and human rights abuses. - The Global Justice Center, which advocates for gender equality and the protection of human rights in conflict and post-conflict situations.

These organizations provide valuable resources, legal expertise, and platforms for collaboration for individuals and groups engaged in transnational justice movements.

Conclusion

Transnational justice movements play a critical role in advancing human rights globally. Through their advocacy, activism, and collaboration, they seek to hold accountable those responsible for human rights abuses and work towards a more just and equal world. While they face challenges, their strategies and principles guide their work and contribute to the ongoing transformation of the global human rights landscape.

Future directions for transnational justice movements include further engagement with grassroots movements, strengthening alliances, and addressing emerging human rights challenges, such as the impact of new technologies and digital rights. Through their continued efforts, these movements will continue to shape human rights discourse and promote transformative change at local, national, and global levels.

Regional Approaches to Transformative Legal Studies

European Union Law and Integration

The European Union (EU) is a unique political and economic partnership that encompasses 27 member states. The integration of these member states into a single supranational entity has resulted in the development of a distinct legal framework known as European Union law. This section explores the key principles and features of EU law, as well as its transformative impact on member states and the challenges it faces.

Historical Background

The origins of the EU can be traced back to the aftermath of World War II when European leaders sought to foster peace, stability, and economic cooperation among European nations. The signing of the Treaty of Rome in 1957 established the European Economic Community (EEC) and laid the foundation for further integration. Over the years, the EU has expanded both in terms of its membership and the scope of its activities, ranging from economic cooperation to the establishment of a single currency, the euro.

Principles of the EU

At the heart of the EU are several fundamental principles that guide its functioning:

1. **Supremacy of EU Law:** EU law takes precedence over national law, ensuring uniformity and consistency across member states. This principle, known as the doctrine of supremacy, was established by the European Court of Justice (ECJ) in the landmark case of Costa v. ENEL.

2. **Direct Effect and Primacy:** EU law has direct effect, which means that individuals can rely on it in national courts and seek remedies for violations. Furthermore, the primacy of EU law ensures that national courts must set aside conflicting national laws that are contrary to EU law.

3. **Subsidiarity:** The principle of subsidiarity ensures that decisions are taken at the most appropriate level, with the EU acting only when it is more effective than action at the national, regional, or local level.

4. **Proportionality:** EU actions must be proportionate to the objectives they seek to achieve, thereby balancing the interests of the EU against those of member states.

5. **Solidarity:** The EU is founded on the principle of solidarity, which promotes cooperation and mutual support among member states. This principle is particularly evident in areas such as regional development, social cohesion, and response to crises.

6. **Citizenship:** EU citizenship complements national citizenship and grants EU citizens certain rights and freedoms, including the right to move and reside freely within the EU, the right to vote and stand in elections to the European Parliament, and the right to consular protection from any EU member state.

These principles form the basis for the integration and functioning of the EU, ensuring common values and goals among member states.

Sources of EU Law

EU law is derived from a variety of sources, each having a specific role and hierarchy:

1. **Treaties:** The primary sources of EU law are the treaties upon which the EU is founded, such as the Treaty on European Union and the Treaty on the Functioning of the European Union. These treaties establish the objectives, competences, and institutional framework of the EU.

2. **Legislation:** EU legislation, composed of regulations, directives, and decisions, is binding on member states. Regulations have direct effect and are immediately applicable to all member states, while directives set certain goals to be achieved within a given timeframe and require member states to implement them through national legislation.

3. **Case Law:** The case law of the ECJ plays a crucial role in the development and interpretation of EU law. The ECJ ensures uniform application of EU law by providing authoritative interpretations and resolving disputes between member states or individuals and national authorities.

4. **Soft Law Instruments:** Soft law instruments, such as declarations, resolutions, and guidelines, do not have legally binding force. However, they provide guidance and serve as important tools for the implementation and enforcement of EU policies.

Institutional Framework

The EU has a complex institutional framework designed to ensure democratic representation, decision-making, and execution of policies. The key institutions include:

1. **European Commission:** The European Commission, often referred to as the "guardian of the treaties," is responsible for initiating EU legislation, implementing policies, and enforcing EU law. It consists of commissioners appointed by member states and operates independently of national interests.

2. **European Parliament:** The European Parliament represents the citizens of the EU and is directly elected. It shares legislative power with the Council of the European Union, and together they adopt EU legislation and set the budget.

3. **Council of the European Union:** The Council of the European Union represents the member states and is composed of government ministers from each member state. It, along with the European Parliament, adopts EU legislation and coordinates the broad economic and social policies of the EU.

4. **European Court of Justice:** The European Court of Justice ensures the uniform interpretation and application of EU law. It consists of judges appointed by member states and hears cases referred by national courts, as well as preliminary references on the interpretation of EU law.

5. **European Central Bank:** The European Central Bank is responsible for the monetary policy of the euro area member states and maintaining price stability. It plays a crucial role in the economic integration of the EU.

These institutions work together to develop and implement EU policies, ensuring democratic representation and accountability.

Challenges and Future Perspectives

Despite its achievements, the EU faces several challenges in its quest for further integration and transformative legal impact. Some of the key challenges include:

1. **Brexit:** The departure of the United Kingdom from the EU, commonly known as Brexit, poses significant challenges for both the UK and the EU. Negotiating the terms of withdrawal, future relations, and redefining the legal framework presents a complex task for all parties involved.

2. **Democratic Deficit:** The perceived lack of democratic accountability and transparency in EU decision-making processes has led to criticism that the EU suffers from a democratic deficit. Balancing the powers of the EU institutions and strengthening the role of national parliaments are ongoing debates.

3. **Sovereignty Concerns:** The integration of member states into a supranational entity has raised concerns about the loss of national sovereignty. Striking a balance between national interests and the shared objectives of the EU remains a challenge.

4. **Migration and Security:** The management of migration flows and ensuring the security of member states have become significant challenges for the EU. Addressing issues such as border controls, asylum, and integration of migrants requires a coordinated and comprehensive approach.

5. **Economic Disparities:** Economic disparities among member states have become more apparent in recent years. Overcoming these disparities and ensuring sustainable economic growth for all member states is crucial for the long-term success of the EU.

These challenges require innovative and transformative legal approaches to ensure the continued development and stability of the EU.

Further Resources

For further study on European Union law and integration, the following resources are recommended:

- *European Union Law* by Damian Chalmers, Gareth Davies, and Giorgio Monti.

- *The European Union: Politics and Policies* by John McCormick.

- *European Union Law: Text and Materials* by Damian Chalmers, Christos Hadjiemmanuil, and Giorgio Monti.

- European Union legal databases and official EU websites such as europa.eu and curia.europa.eu.

These resources provide comprehensive information and analysis of EU law and integration, serving as valuable references for students and researchers.

Conclusion

European Union law and integration have transformed the legal landscape of Europe, fostering cooperation, ensuring uniformity, and promoting shared values among member states. The principles, sources, and institutions of the EU provide a solid foundation for the ongoing development and transformative impact of EU law. However, challenges such as Brexit, the democratic deficit, and economic disparities require innovative approaches and careful navigation to ensure the EU's continued success and relevance in a rapidly changing world. By understanding the complexities and potential solutions to these challenges, students and researchers can actively contribute to the ongoing transformation of European Union law and integration.

African Perspectives on Transformative Law

In this section, we will explore the unique African perspectives on transformative law. Africa has a rich and diverse legal landscape, shaped by its history, culture, and socio-economic dynamics. The legal systems and institutions in Africa have undergone significant transformations in recent years, addressing various social, economic, and political issues. In this section, we will examine some key aspects of the African legal framework and explore how transformative law has contributed to justice and equality on the continent.

Historical Context

To understand African perspectives on transformative law, it is essential to consider the historical context. Africa has a complex colonial past, where European powers imposed their legal systems and norms on the continent. This legacy has influenced the development of legal systems in Africa, and today, the continent consists of a blend of customary law, civil law, and common law traditions.

Recognizing Indigenous Legal Systems

One crucial aspect of African transformative law is recognizing and integrating indigenous legal systems. Many African societies have their own traditional and customary laws, which were marginalized during colonial rule. Recognizing and incorporating these systems into the national legal framework has been an essential element of transformative law in Africa. This recognition contributes to cultural preservation, community cohesion, and a more inclusive justice system.

Example: In many African countries, traditional courts now operate alongside formal courts. These traditional courts incorporate indigenous customs, traditions, and values into the legal process. By acknowledging the relevance of indigenous legal systems, African countries are working towards a more comprehensive and culturally sensitive justice system.

Addressing Socio-economic Injustices

Another critical aspect of African transformative law is addressing socio-economic injustices. Africa faces significant challenges related to poverty, inequality, land rights, and access to basic services. Transformative law seeks to redress these issues by implementing policies and legal frameworks that promote social and economic justice.

Land Rights and Agricultural Policies

Land rights and agricultural policies are central to transformative law in Africa. Land often holds cultural, economic, and social significance for African communities, and ensuring equitable access to land is crucial for development and social stability. Transformative law seeks to address historical injustices related to land dispossession, promote land reforms, and protect the rights of marginalized groups.

Example: In South Africa, transformative land reform initiatives aim to address the historical legacy of land dispossession during apartheid. These initiatives include redistributing land to previously disadvantaged individuals and communities and providing tenure security to vulnerable groups.

Promoting Women's Rights

Transformative law in Africa also emphasizes the promotion of women's rights. Gender inequality remains a significant challenge in many African countries, affecting women's access to education, healthcare, and economic opportunities.

Transformative legal frameworks aim to address gender disparities by enacting laws that protect women's rights, tackle gender-based violence, and promote gender equality.

Example: The Maputo Protocol, adopted by the African Union in 2003, is a transformative legal instrument that promotes and protects women's rights. It covers a wide range of issues, including gender-based violence, reproductive rights, and economic empowerment.

Challenges and Future Directions

While transformative law in Africa has made significant strides, several challenges persist. Limited resources, political instability, and weak institutional capacity often hinder the effective implementation of transformative legal frameworks. Additionally, cultural resistance, lack of awareness, and patriarchal norms pose obstacles to achieving equality and justice.

To overcome these challenges, it is crucial to build strong legal institutions, promote legal education and awareness, and strengthen international cooperation. Collaborative efforts between governments, civil society organizations, and international partners are essential for the success of transformative law in Africa.

Conclusion

African perspectives on transformative law encompass a diverse set of experiences, challenges, and aspirations. By recognizing indigenous legal systems, addressing socio-economic injustices, promoting women's rights, and pursuing meaningful land reforms, Africa is shaping a legal framework that prioritizes justice, equality, and socio-economic development. However, continued efforts and collaboration are necessary to overcome the challenges and achieve transformative change across the continent. Africa's journey towards a more inclusive and equitable legal system serves as an inspiration and valuable source of knowledge for global legal transformations.

Latin American Approaches to Social Justice

Latin American countries have a rich history of social justice movements and transformative legal approaches that have shaped the region's legal landscape. These approaches aim to address historical inequalities and promote social inclusion, with a particular emphasis on marginalized communities. In this section, we will explore some key Latin American approaches to social justice and their impact on legal institutions and practices.

Historical Context

To understand the Latin American approaches to social justice, it is crucial to consider the historical context in which they emerged. Latin America has long been marked by social and economic inequalities rooted in colonialism, slavery, and systemic discrimination. These inequalities have spawned social movements and legal strategies that seek to challenge these oppressive structures and create a more just society.

Constitutional Rights and Social Justice

Latin American countries have taken significant steps in their constitutions to incorporate social justice principles and protect the rights of marginalized groups. Constitutional provisions related to education, healthcare, housing, employment, and indigenous rights are aimed at promoting social equality and reducing gaps in access to basic services. For example, countries like Bolivia and Ecuador have recognized rights to water, land, and a healthy environment in their constitutions, emphasizing the importance of environmental justice.

Indigenous Rights and Self-determination

Latin America is home to a significant indigenous population, and the recognition of indigenous rights and self-determination has been a central aspect of social justice movements in the region. Many countries have implemented legal frameworks that acknowledge the collective rights of indigenous communities, their ancestral territories, and their cultural heritage. These legal approaches aim to rectify historical injustices and promote the active participation of indigenous peoples in decision-making processes.

Transitional Justice and Memory

Several Latin American countries have faced periods of political violence, authoritarian regimes, and civil conflicts. In response, transitional justice mechanisms have been established to address past abuses, provide reparations, and promote reconciliation. These mechanisms include truth commissions, trials for human rights violators, and reparations programs. They seek to bring justice to victims, promote accountability, and prevent future human rights violations.

Gender Equality and Women's Rights

Gender inequality and discrimination against women have been persistent issues in Latin America. However, the region has also witnessed significant advancements in promoting gender equality and women's rights. Legal reforms have been enacted to address issues such as domestic violence, gender-based discrimination, and reproductive rights. Additionally, Latin American countries have shown a commitment to promoting women's political representation at all levels of government.

Social Movements and Grassroots Activism

Latin America is characterized by vibrant social movements and grassroots activism that form the backbone of transformative legal approaches. These movements have been instrumental in shaping legal reforms and challenging oppressive systems. Examples include indigenous movements fighting for land rights and cultural preservation, women's rights organizations advocating for gender equality, and labor unions fighting for workers' rights.

Challenges and Future Developments

While Latin American approaches to social justice have made significant progress, many challenges persist. Economic inequality, corruption, and institutional barriers continue to hinder the full realization of social justice. Furthermore, the COVID-19 pandemic has exacerbated existing inequalities, especially in access to healthcare and education. Moving forward, it is essential to address these challenges, strengthen legal frameworks, and ensure the effective implementation of existing laws to promote social justice.

Conclusion

Latin American approaches to social justice have emerged from a complex historical context and have been shaped by grassroots activism, constitutional rights, and transitional justice mechanisms. These approaches aim to create a more just and inclusive society by addressing social and economic inequalities, promoting the rights of marginalized groups, and challenging oppressive systems. While challenges remain, the region's commitment to transformative legal approaches provides hope for a more equitable future in Latin America.

Indigenous Legal Systems and Transformative Potential

Legal Pluralism and Indigenous Legal Systems

Legal pluralism refers to a situation where multiple legal systems coexist within a society. It recognizes that customary, indigenous, and informal legal systems can operate alongside formal state-based legal systems. This section explores the concept of legal pluralism, focusing on indigenous legal systems and their transformative potential.

Understanding Legal Pluralism

Legal pluralism recognizes that legal systems are not always monolithic or homogenous within a society. Instead, different communities may have their own sets of norms, rules, and dispute resolution mechanisms that are recognized and enforced within their own social contexts. This recognition of diverse legal orders challenges the idea of a single, unified legal system.

Indigenous legal systems, in particular, represent alternative legal orders that are rooted in the cultural, social, and spiritual traditions of indigenous communities. These systems have developed over generations and continue to play a significant role in shaping the lives of indigenous peoples.

Principles of Indigenous Legal Systems

Indigenous legal systems are often founded on principles that differ from those of the state-based legal systems. Here are some key principles commonly found in indigenous legal systems:

1. **Communal Decision-Making:** Indigenous legal systems emphasize collective decision-making and community participation in matters of governance and dispute resolution. This reflects the interconnectedness and interdependence of individuals within indigenous communities.

2. **Oral Tradition and Customary Law:** Indigenous legal systems often rely on oral tradition and customary practices to transmit laws and norms from one generation to the next. This reliance on lived experiences and community values contributes to the dynamic nature of indigenous legal systems.

3. **Relationship with the Natural World:** Indigenous legal systems recognize the interconnectedness between humans and the natural world. They often

incorporate principles of sustainability, environmental stewardship, and the protection of the land, water, and other natural resources.

4. **Restoration and Healing:** Indigenous legal systems prioritize restoration and healing over punishment. Their focus is on repairing relationships and finding resolutions that benefit both individuals involved and the broader community. This approach aligns closely with the principles of restorative justice.

Challenges and Tensions

While indigenous legal systems have intrinsic value and are central to the cultural identity of indigenous peoples, they often face challenges and tensions within the context of state legal systems. Some of these challenges include:

- **Recognition and Legitimacy:** Indigenous legal systems may not be formally recognized or legitimized by state legal systems. This lack of recognition limits their application and can lead to conflicts between the two legal orders.

- **Power Imbalance:** Indigenous legal systems may face power imbalances when juxtaposed with the dominant state legal systems. The power dynamics between the two can result in the marginalization and suppression of indigenous legal traditions.

- **Cultural Competence:** State legal systems may lack cultural competence to properly understand and interpret indigenous legal systems. This can lead to misunderstandings and misinterpretations of indigenous laws and practices.

- **Access to Justice:** Indigenous communities may face barriers in accessing justice within state legal systems. Language barriers, geographical remoteness, and cultural biases can make it difficult for indigenous peoples to navigate the formal court processes.

Transformative Potential of Indigenous Legal Systems

Despite the challenges they face, indigenous legal systems have transformative potential. Here are some ways in which they contribute to transformative legal studies:

1. **Cultural Revitalization:** The recognition and affirmation of indigenous legal systems can contribute to the revitalization of indigenous cultures and

languages. This recognition acknowledges indigenous peoples' rights to self-determination and cultural autonomy.

2. **Decolonization of Law:** Indigenous legal systems challenge the dominance of colonial legal systems and provide alternative frameworks for understanding law and justice. They offer possibilities for decolonizing legal education, research, and practice.

3. **Reconciliation and Healing:** Indigenous legal systems prioritize reconciliation and healing over punitive measures. Their emphasis on restoration and community well-being aligns with the principles of transformative justice and can foster social cohesion and resilience.

4. **Ecosystemic Approaches:** Indigenous legal systems consider the interconnectedness of human beings and the natural world. They offer valuable insights into sustainable environmental practices and provide alternatives to the anthropocentric approach of mainstream legal systems.

Case Study: Maori Legal System in New Zealand

A notable example of an indigenous legal system is the Maori legal system in New Zealand. The Treaty of Waitangi, signed between the British Crown and Maori chiefs in 1840, recognized the autonomy of Maori governance structures and their legal systems. Today, the Maori legal system, known as Tikanga Maori, operates alongside the state legal system in New Zealand.

Tikanga Maori emphasizes collective decision-making, restorative justice principles, and the protection of Maori cultural rights. It has influenced New Zealand's legislative and judicial systems, contributing to the recognition of Maori customary law and cultural practices within the legal framework of the country.

Resources for Further Study

For further exploration of legal pluralism and indigenous legal systems, the following resources are recommended:

- Bishop, R., Glynn, T., and Lewin, H. (2012). *Culture Counts: Changing Power Relations in Education*. Springer.

- Griffiths, J. (1986). *What is Legal Pluralism?* Journal of Legal Pluralism and Unofficial Law, 18, 1-55.

- John, P. O. (2013). *Strategies for Transformative Global Leadership: Indigenous, Africana, and Euro-American Perspectives.* State University of New York Press.

- Menkel‑Meadow, C., et al. (2000). *What's Law Got to Do With It? What Lawyers and Legal Scholars Can Learn from Anthropology and Vice Versa.* Annual Review of Anthropology, 29(1), 155-184.

- Tamanaha, B. Z. (2008). *Law as a Means to an End: Threat to the Rule of Law.* Cambridge University Press.

Caveats and Considerations

When engaging with indigenous legal systems, it is crucial to approach them with respect, cultural sensitivity, and a willingness to listen and learn from the affected communities. Recognizing and respecting the autonomy of these legal systems is essential to promoting justice, equality, and social transformation.

It is also important to address power imbalances and work towards empowering indigenous communities in their interactions with state legal systems. Collaboration, dialogue, and education can play a significant role in bridging the gaps between different legal orders and promoting transformative change.

Exercises

1. Research and analyze a case study where an indigenous legal system was recognized and applied within a state legal system. What were the implications and outcomes of this recognition?

2. Imagine you are designing a legal curriculum that incorporates legal pluralism and indigenous legal systems. How would you promote cultural competence and engagement with diverse legal orders?

3. Engage in a dialogue or reflection with members of an indigenous community to gain insights into their legal system and its transformative potential. Discuss the challenges they face in maintaining and promoting their legal traditions.

4. Explore the potential of incorporating indigenous legal practices in environmental justice issues. How can indigenous legal systems contribute to sustainable environmental governance?

Indigenous Rights and Self-Determination

Indigenous rights and self-determination are crucial aspects of transformative legal studies. Indigenous peoples around the world have historically faced

INDIGENOUS LEGAL SYSTEMS AND TRANSFORMATIVE POTENTIAL

marginalization, discrimination, and the violation of their basic human rights. This section explores the importance of recognizing and protecting indigenous rights, as well as the concept of self-determination for indigenous communities.

Historical Background

Indigenous communities have a distinct and rich cultural heritage that has often been disregarded or oppressed by dominant societies. Historically, colonialism and the expansion of nation-states led to the displacement, assimilation, and even genocide of indigenous peoples. In many cases, indigenous lands were taken without consent, and their traditional practices and way of life were suppressed.

The historical background of indigenous rights and self-determination is essential for understanding the current struggles and challenges faced by indigenous communities. It highlights the need for legal frameworks that recognize and protect the rights of indigenous peoples.

Principles of Indigenous Rights

Indigenous rights are based on the principles of self-determination, cultural preservation, land and resource ownership, and non-discrimination. These principles reflect the unique relationship that indigenous peoples have with their lands, resources, and traditional knowledge. Key principles of indigenous rights include:

1. Self-determination: Indigenous communities have the right to determine their political status, pursue their economic, social, and cultural development, and freely participate in decisions that affect their lives.

2. Cultural preservation: Indigenous peoples have the right to practice and revitalize their cultural traditions, languages, and customs. This includes protecting sacred sites, cultural heritage, and traditional knowledge.

3. Land and resource ownership: Indigenous communities have the right to ownership, control, and management of their lands, territories, and resources. This includes the right to participate in decisions regarding the use and development of these resources.

4. Non-discrimination: Indigenous peoples have the right to be free from discrimination based on their indigenous identity. They should have equal rights and opportunities as any other individual or group in society.

These principles provide a foundation for the recognition and protection of indigenous rights in legal systems around the world.

International Legal Framework

The recognition and protection of indigenous rights have gained significant attention at the international level. International legal instruments have been developed to acknowledge and safeguard the rights of indigenous peoples. The United Nations Declaration on the Rights of Indigenous Peoples (UNDRIP) is a crucial document in this regard.

UNDRIP provides a comprehensive framework for the promotion and protection of indigenous rights. It emphasizes the right to self-determination, the right to land and resources, the right to cultural expression, and the right to participate in decision-making processes. It also prohibits discrimination against indigenous peoples and calls for the resolution of conflicts through dialogue and cooperation.

While UNDRIP is not legally binding, it has influenced the development of domestic legislation and policies regarding indigenous rights in many countries. It serves as a guide for governments, legal practitioners, and indigenous communities themselves.

Challenges and Solutions

Despite the progress made in recognizing indigenous rights, significant challenges persist. Indigenous communities continue to face issues such as land dispossession, environmental degradation, poverty, and social marginalization. Many legal systems face obstacles in implementing and enforcing laws that protect indigenous rights.

One of the main challenges is the tension between indigenous legal systems and the legal systems imposed by settler colonial states. Indigenous laws and customs often differ from dominant legal frameworks, leading to conflicts and misunderstandings. Finding ways to harmonize and integrate indigenous legal traditions with national legal systems is a complex task.

Additionally, adequate representation and participation of indigenous peoples in decision-making processes are often lacking. Ensuring meaningful consultation and collaboration with indigenous communities is crucial for empowering them and respecting their rights.

To overcome these challenges, collaborative approaches and recognition of indigenous legal orders are necessary. Engaging in dialogue, building partnerships, and promoting indigenous self-governance are key steps towards transformative change.

Examples and Showcase

One inspiring example of transformative legal practice in the context of indigenous rights is the recognition and revitalization of indigenous legal systems. In some countries, indigenous communities have successfully worked towards the recognition of their customary laws as complementary to national legal frameworks. This recognition allows for the application of indigenous legal principles in specific cases, promoting justice and empowerment within their communities.

Another example is the use of international human rights mechanisms to advance indigenous rights. Indigenous organizations and individuals have utilized these mechanisms to raise awareness, seek accountability, and advocate for the implementation of indigenous rights standards.

Further Resources

To further explore the topic of indigenous rights and self-determination, the following resources are recommended:

- "Indigenous Peoples' Rights: A Global Comparative and International Legal Analysis" by Alexandra Xanthaki.

- "The Rights of Indigenous Peoples in International Law: An Annotated Bibliography" by Joshua Castellino.

- The United Nations Permanent Forum on Indigenous Issues (UNPFII) provides information, events, and resources on indigenous rights at the international level.

- Local, national, and international indigenous rights organizations often publish reports, studies, and resources that highlight the ongoing struggles and achievements in the field of indigenous rights.

Conclusion

Recognizing and protecting indigenous rights are essential for achieving justice, equality, and social transformation. The principles of self-determination, cultural preservation, land ownership, and non-discrimination form the basis of indigenous rights. International legal frameworks, such as UNDRIP, provide guidance for the protection of these rights.

However, challenges remain in implementing and enforcing indigenous rights, including conflicts between legal systems and inadequate representation. Transformative approaches that emphasize collaboration, recognition of indigenous legal orders, and meaningful participation are crucial for addressing these challenges and empowering indigenous communities.

By promoting indigenous rights and self-determination, transformative legal studies contribute to achieving justice and equality for all individuals and communities in our diverse world.

Case Studies: Transformative Indigenous Legal Practices

In this section, we will explore case studies that highlight transformative Indigenous legal practices. Indigenous legal systems have played a vital role in addressing historical injustices, promoting self-determination, preserving cultural heritage, and fostering community well-being. Through these case studies, we will examine how Indigenous communities have used legal frameworks to bring about transformative change, challenge colonialism, and assert their rights.

Case Study 1: Māori Customary Law in New Zealand

The first case study focuses on the revitalization of Māori customary law in New Zealand. The Māori people faced significant challenges following the colonization of New Zealand by the British. Their land was confiscated, cultural practices suppressed, and traditional legal systems undermined. However, in recent decades, there has been a resurgence of interest in incorporating Māori customary law into the New Zealand legal system.

One transformative practice is the recognition of the Treaty of Waitangi as a constitutional document. The Treaty, signed in 1840 between Māori chiefs and the British Crown, guarantees Māori rights and sovereignty. Its recognition as a source of law has paved the way for Māori legal principles to be incorporated into the New Zealand legal system.

Additionally, the establishment of Māori Land Courts and the Waitangi Tribunal has provided avenues for Māori communities to assert their land and resource rights, seek redress for historical grievances, and participate in decision-making processes. These institutions have played a crucial role in promoting social justice and empowering Māori communities to shape their own futures.

Case Study 2: Aboriginal Customary Law in Australia

Our second case study explores the recognition and application of Aboriginal customary law in Australia. Aboriginal peoples have inhabited Australia for tens of thousands of years and have developed complex legal systems to govern their communities. However, colonization and the imposition of Western legal systems resulted in the erosion of Aboriginal legal traditions.

In recent years, there has been a growing acknowledgment of the importance of Aboriginal customary law in resolving legal issues within Indigenous communities. Various initiatives have been undertaken to incorporate Aboriginal legal principles into the Australian legal system, including the recognition of Aboriginal customary law in sentencing processes and diversionary programs.

For example, the Koori Court in Victoria provides a forum for Aboriginal defendants to have their cases heard in accordance with Aboriginal customs and traditions. This approach aims to promote cultural sensitivity, rehabilitation, and community healing. Similar initiatives, such as the Murri Court in Queensland and the Nunga Court in South Australia, have also been established to recognize and respect Aboriginal legal traditions.

Case Study 3: Customary Law in Indigenous Communities in Canada

Our third case study focuses on the recognition and revival of customary law in Indigenous communities in Canada. The impact of colonization on Indigenous peoples in Canada has been profound, resulting in the marginalization of Indigenous legal practices. However, there have been significant efforts to reclaim and revitalize Indigenous legal systems.

One example is the establishment of Indigenous Healing and Wellness Courts across Canada. These courts integrate Indigenous legal principles, traditions, and community involvement into the justice system. They prioritize healing and restoration over punishment, providing a culturally appropriate alternative to mainstream courts.

Furthermore, the resurgence of Indigenous legal traditions has been supported by the recognition of the inherent right of self-government for Indigenous communities. This recognition empowers communities to govern themselves and make decisions in accordance with their own legal and cultural systems. It has led to the establishment of Indigenous justice systems that incorporate customary law and promote restorative justice practices.

Conclusion

These case studies highlight the transformative power of Indigenous legal practices in addressing historical injustices and promoting self-determination. By reclaiming and revitalizing their legal traditions, Indigenous communities have been able to assert their rights, participate in decision-making processes, and promote social justice.

However, challenges and limitations remain. Colonial legacies, systemic discrimination, and the ongoing marginalization of Indigenous peoples continue to impact the effectiveness and implementation of transformative Indigenous legal practices. To overcome these challenges, ongoing collaboration, respect, and recognizing the unique needs and aspirations of Indigenous communities are essential.

The case studies presented here provide valuable insights into the potential of transformative Indigenous legal practices. They serve as a reminder that Indigenous legal systems are not relics of the past, but dynamic and relevant frameworks for promoting justice, equality, and self-determination. By embracing and supporting these practices, society can move closer to achieving true reconciliation and fostering inclusive and transformative legal systems.

Environmental Law and Transformative Legal Strategies

Overview of Environmental Law

Environmental law is a specialized branch of law that focuses on the protection and preservation of the natural environment. It encompasses a wide range of legal principles, regulations, and policies aimed at addressing environmental issues and promoting sustainable practices. This section provides an overview of the key concepts, principles, and challenges in environmental law.

Principles of Environmental Law

Environmental law is guided by several fundamental principles that serve as the foundation for its development and implementation. These principles include:

1. **Sustainable Development:** Environmental law seeks to achieve a balance between economic development and environmental protection to ensure the long-term sustainability of natural resources and ecosystems.

2. **Precautionary Principle:** This principle emphasizes the need to take preventive measures in the face of uncertain risks to the environment. It encourages decision-makers to act proactively to prevent potential harm, even in the absence of scientific certainty.

3. **Polluter Pays Principle:** According to this principle, those responsible for environmental pollution should bear the costs of mitigating and remedying the damage caused. It aims to internalize the costs of environmental harm and discourage polluting activities.

4. **Integration and Interdependence:** Environmental law recognizes the interconnectedness of different ecosystems and the need for integrated approaches to address environmental challenges. It encourages collaboration and coordination among different sectors and levels of governance.

5. **Public Participation:** Environmental decision-making should involve the public and relevant stakeholders to ensure transparency, inclusivity, and accountability. It promotes the right of individuals and communities to have a say in environmental matters that affect them.

International and National Frameworks

Environmental law operates at both the international and national levels. International environmental law provides a framework for addressing global environmental challenges and fostering cooperation among nations. Key instruments in international environmental law include treaties, conventions, and agreements such as the United Nations Framework Convention on Climate Change (UNFCCC) and the Convention on Biological Diversity (CBD).

At the national level, environmental laws vary based on legal systems and the specific environmental challenges faced by each country. These laws can cover a wide range of issues, including pollution control, natural resource management, biodiversity conservation, and climate change mitigation and adaptation.

Key Environmental Issues

Environmental law addresses a variety of pressing environmental issues. Some of the key areas of concern include:

1. **Climate Change:** Environmental law plays a crucial role in addressing climate change by regulating greenhouse gas emissions, promoting renewable energy sources, and facilitating international negotiations and agreements.

2. **Biodiversity Conservation:** Laws and regulations aim to protect and conserve ecosystems, endangered species, and their habitats. This includes the establishment of protected areas, regulations on trade in wildlife, and the prevention of habitat destruction.

3. **Water Management:** Environmental law governs the management and protection of water resources, ensuring sustainable use, preventing pollution, and balancing competing interests in water allocation.

4. **Air and Water Pollution:** Environmental laws regulate the emissions of pollutants into the air and water, setting standards for industrial activities, waste management, and pollution control measures.

5. **Waste Management:** Legal frameworks address the management, disposal, and recycling of waste, including hazardous and electronic waste, to minimize environmental harm and promote sustainable practices.

6. **Land Use and Conservation:** Environmental laws govern land use planning, zoning, and conservation measures to protect natural landscapes, forests, and agricultural lands from degradation and unsustainable development.

Challenges and Emerging Trends

Environmental law faces several challenges in addressing complex and evolving environmental issues. Some of the key challenges include:

1. **Jurisdictional Complexity:** Environmental issues often transcend national borders, requiring international cooperation and coordination across different legal systems.

2. **Enforcement and Compliance:** Effective enforcement of environmental laws can be challenging, particularly in cases where enforcement agencies lack adequate resources or face resistance from violators.

3. **Scientific Uncertainty:** Environmental issues are often characterized by scientific uncertainties, making it challenging to develop evidence-based policies and regulations.

4. **Emerging Technologies:** Rapid advancements in technology, such as genetic engineering and nanotechnology, pose new challenges for environmental law, as they may have unknown environmental impacts.

5. **Inadequate Institutional Capacity:** Some countries may lack the institutional capacity and expertise needed to implement and enforce environmental laws effectively.

6. **Climate Change Adaptation:** Adapting to the impacts of climate change requires innovative legal and policy approaches to manage risks and build resilience.

Despite these challenges, there are also emerging trends and innovations in environmental law. These include:

1. **Green Economy and Sustainable Development Goals:** Environmental law is increasingly focusing on promoting a transition to a green economy and achieving the United Nations Sustainable Development Goals through legal mechanisms and incentives.

2. **Ecological Restoration:** There is growing recognition of the importance of ecological restoration in reversing environmental degradation and promoting biodiversity conservation.

3. **Corporate Social Responsibility:** There is a shift towards holding corporations accountable for their environmental impacts and promoting responsible business practices through legal frameworks.

4. **Rights-based Approaches:** Environmental law is embracing rights-based approaches, recognizing the rights of communities and indigenous peoples to a healthy environment and their role in environmental decision-making.

5. **Environmental Impact Assessment:** The use of environmental impact assessments as a tool for decision-making is becoming more prevalent, ensuring that potential environmental impacts are considered before projects are approved.

Conclusion

Environmental law plays a critical role in protecting and preserving the natural environment. It encompasses a wide range of legal principles, regulations, and policies that address various environmental issues. Understanding the principles and frameworks of environmental law is essential for promoting sustainable development, addressing environmental challenges, and ensuring the well-being of both present and future generations. By embracing innovative approaches and adapting to emerging trends, environmental law can continue to evolve and effectively respond to the ever-changing environmental landscape.

Rights of Nature and Ecological Legal Theory

The concept of Rights of Nature is a transformative approach in ecological legal theory that recognizes the inherent rights of nature and the environment. It challenges the traditional notion of viewing nature as mere property and advocates for a new legal framework that treats nature as a rights-bearing entity. This section explores the theoretical foundations of Rights of Nature and its implications for environmental protection and sustainability.

Theoretical Foundations of Rights of Nature

The Rights of Nature concept is rooted in the belief that nature possesses its own inherent rights, independent of human utility or value. It draws inspiration from indigenous cultures that have long recognized the interconnection and interdependence between humans and the natural world. The theoretical underpinnings of Rights of Nature can be traced to several key principles:

1. Intrinsic Value: Rights of Nature recognizes that nature has inherent value and possesses the right to exist, thrive, and evolve. This principle challenges the dominant anthropocentric perspective and emphasizes the intrinsic worth of nature beyond its instrumental value for human use.

2. Interconnectedness: Rights of Nature acknowledges the interconnectedness of ecosystems and the interdependence of all living beings. It recognizes that harming one part of the ecosystem affects the whole, and thus seeks to protect the integrity and resilience of ecosystems.

3. Intergenerational Equity: Rights of Nature considers the interests of future generations and seeks to ensure the preservation of ecosystems and resources for their well-being. It advocates for sustainable practices that maintain ecological balance and prevent the depletion of natural resources.

4. Precautionary Principle: Rights of Nature embraces the precautionary principle, which states that in the face of scientific uncertainty, protective measures should be taken to prevent irreversible harm to nature. This principle acknowledges the limits of human knowledge and advocates for a proactive approach to environmental protection.

Legal Recognition of Rights of Nature

The legal recognition of Rights of Nature has gained momentum in recent years, with various countries and communities adopting laws and legal frameworks that grant legal rights to nature. These legal developments aim to shift the paradigm of environmental law and governance, moving towards a more holistic and ecologically sustainable approach. Some notable examples include:

1. Ecuador: In 2008, Ecuador became the first country to recognize Rights of Nature in its constitution. The Ecuadorian constitution recognizes nature as a legal entity with the right to exist, regenerate, and evolve. This recognition has had profound implications for environmental governance and has led to the establishment of a Ministry of Environment and the use of Rights of Nature as a legal basis for environmental protection.

2. Bolivia: Bolivia enacted the Law of the Rights of Mother Earth in 2010, which grants legal rights to Mother Earth and recognizes her as a living system. The law recognizes the rights of nature to life, diversity, water, clean air, balance, restoration, and pollution-free living.

3. New Zealand: In 2017, the Whanganui River in New Zealand was granted legal personhood, with the rights, duties, and liabilities of a legal person. This landmark agreement recognized the spiritual and cultural significance of the river to the local Maori tribe and established a framework for its protection and management.

4. Community-based Initiatives: In addition to national legal recognition, grassroots movements and local communities have also embraced Rights of Nature principles. In some cases, communities have enacted laws and ordinances that grant legal rights to natural entities like rivers, forests, and mountains, empowering local communities to protect and restore their natural environment.

Challenges and Opportunities of Rights of Nature

While the recognition of Rights of Nature presents new avenues for environmental protection and sustainability, it also raises several challenges and opportunities:

1. Legal Enforcement: Implementing and enforcing rights for nature pose legal and practical challenges. Questions arise regarding standing, representation, and enforcement mechanisms, as well as potential conflicts with existing property rights and economic interests. Overcoming these challenges requires the development of innovative legal strategies and mechanisms.

2. Paradigm Shift: Recognizing the rights of nature requires a fundamental shift in societal attitudes, norms, and legal frameworks. It challenges the prevailing

anthropocentric worldview and necessitates a paradigm shift towards a more holistic, ecocentric approach that values the interconnectedness of all living beings.

3. Ecological Restoration: The recognition of rights for nature can facilitate ecological restoration efforts. By recognizing the rights of ecosystems to be restored and healed, stakeholders can work together to rehabilitate degraded environments, preserve biodiversity, and ensure ecosystem services for present and future generations.

4. Indigenous Perspectives: Indigenous cultures have long recognized the rights of nature and the interdependence between humans and the natural world. Incorporating indigenous perspectives and practices into legal frameworks can enhance the effectiveness and cultural relevance of Rights of Nature initiatives.

5. Global Impact: Rights of Nature has the potential to transcend national boundaries and shape global environmental governance. International initiatives and collaborations can help advance the recognition of Rights of Nature, promote ecological sustainability, and address global environmental challenges such as climate change.

Future Directions in Rights of Nature

The recognition of Rights of Nature is an ongoing and evolving process. Future directions in Rights of Nature could include:

1. International Legal Instruments: The development of international legal instruments that recognize and protect the rights of nature can provide a global framework for environmental governance. These instruments could establish principles and guidelines for the implementation and enforcement of Rights of Nature across jurisdictions.

2. Synergies with Human Rights: Exploring the interconnections between Rights of Nature and human rights can lead to the development of a more comprehensive and integrated legal framework. Recognizing the rights of nature can contribute to the fulfillment of human rights, particularly those linked to a healthy environment and a sustainable future.

3. Ecological Jurisprudence: Developing an ecological jurisprudence that integrates ecological principles, scientific knowledge, and indigenous wisdom can provide a foundation for transformative legal theories and practices. Ecological jurisprudence would consider the holistic nature of ecosystems, the rights of nature, and the interconnectedness of humans and the environment.

4. Education and Awareness: Promoting education and awareness about the Rights of Nature concept is vital for its successful implementation. Incorporating Rights of Nature principles into legal education, environmental education, and

public awareness campaigns can create a more ecologically conscious and responsible society.

Overall, the recognition of Rights of Nature presents a transformative approach to ecological legal theory. By acknowledging the intrinsic rights of nature, this concept challenges the dominant worldview and seeks to create a legal framework that fosters environmental protection and sustainability. The future of Rights of Nature lies in continued legal advancements, international collaborations, and a shift towards a more ecocentric and interconnected understanding of the natural world.

Transnational Environmental Legal Activism

Transnational environmental legal activism refers to the collective efforts of individuals, organizations, and networks working across borders to address environmental issues through legal means. This section explores the role of transnational environmental legal activism in promoting environmental sustainability, protecting ecological rights, and ensuring global environmental justice.

Background

The field of environmental law focuses on the regulation and protection of the natural environment and its resources. It encompasses various aspects, including biodiversity conservation, pollution control, climate change mitigation, and sustainable development. However, environmental challenges often transcend national boundaries, requiring collective action and cooperation on a global scale.

Transnational environmental legal activism recognizes the need for international collaboration and advocacy to tackle environmental issues effectively. It employs legal strategies and mechanisms to influence policy-making, hold governments and corporations accountable, and promote environmental justice worldwide. This approach recognizes the interconnectedness of environmental problems and the importance of addressing them through collective action.

Principles of Transnational Environmental Legal Activism

Transnational environmental legal activism operates based on several key principles:

1. **Collective Action:** Collaboration among individuals, organizations, and networks is essential in transnational environmental legal activism. By joining forces and pooling resources, activists can maximize their impact and enhance their ability to effect change.

2. **Advocacy and Awareness:** Effective advocacy and raising public awareness about pressing environmental issues are crucial for generating public support, mobilizing action, and increasing accountability.

3. **Networking and Information Exchange:** Transnational environmental legal activists rely on networks and platforms for sharing knowledge, best practices, and information about environmental challenges, solutions, and legal mechanisms.

4. **Strategic Litigation:** Legal action, including public interest litigation and strategic lawsuits against individuals, corporations, or governments, is an important tool in transnational environmental legal activism to hold wrongdoers accountable and advance environmental protection.

5. **International Collaboration:** Recognizing the global nature of many environmental issues, transnational environmental legal activists engage with international institutions, such as the United Nations, to influence policies, norms, and standards.

Challenges and Strategies

Transnational environmental legal activism faces a range of challenges, including:

1. **Diverse Legal Systems:** Navigating the complexities of different legal systems across jurisdictions can be daunting for activists. Legal knowledge, expertise, and cross-cultural understanding are essential to overcome these challenges.

2. **Power Imbalances:** Corporate interests and political power imbalances often hinder progress in environmental protection. Transnational environmental legal activists must navigate these power dynamics and strategize accordingly.

3. **Enforcement and Compliance:** Ensuring the enforcement of environmental laws and regulations remains a challenge globally. Activists focus on monitoring compliance, strengthening enforcement mechanisms, and increasing transparency.

To overcome these challenges, transnational environmental legal activism employs various strategies:

1. **Strategic Litigation:** Filing lawsuits against corporations or governments can attract media attention, raise awareness, and push for stronger environmental protections.

2. **International Treaty Advocacy:** By engaging in treaty negotiations and monitoring compliance with international environmental agreements, transnational environmental legal activists can influence policy-making at the global level.

3. **Capacity Building:** Building legal capacity within communities, especially in developing countries, enables them to effectively engage with environmental issues and employ legal mechanisms.

4. **Public Awareness Campaigns:** Leveraging media and communication platforms to educate the public, mobilize support, and pressure governments and corporations to take action on environmental issues.

Case Studies

1. **The Ecuadorian Amazon:** In the Chevron-Texaco case, transnational environmental legal activism sought justice for the indigenous communities affected by oil pollution in the Ecuadorian Amazon. Activists supported local communities in their legal battle against the corporation, resulting in a landmark $9.5 billion judgment against Chevron.

2. **The Ogoni People:** The Ogoni people of Nigeria faced severe environmental degradation due to oil extraction activities. Transnational environmental legal activism, led by organizations like the Center for Constitutional Rights, supported their fight for justice and the remediation of their lands through strategic litigation and international advocacy.

Resources for Further Study

For further exploration of transnational environmental legal activism, the following resources, among others, are recommended:

1. Book: *Transnational Environmental Law and Policy* by Jutta Brunnée and Ellen Hey

2. Journal: *Journal of Transnational Environmental Law*

3. Organization: *ClientEarth*, an environmental law organization working globally to protect the planet and its people through legal action

4. Documentary: *Planet of the Humans* directed by Jeff Gibbs, which delves into the complexities and challenges of global environmental activism.

Conclusion

Transnational environmental legal activism plays a critical role in addressing environmental challenges that transcend national boundaries. By employing legal strategies, engaging in international advocacy, and promoting collective action, activists strive to protect the natural environment, promote ecological justice, and ensure a sustainable future. However, they must navigate numerous challenges, including diverse legal systems and power imbalances. Through strategic litigation, international collaboration, and capacity building, transnational environmental legal activists contribute to transforming the global response to environmental issues.

Conclusion

Recapitulation of Key Points

In this chapter, we have explored the global perspectives on transformative legal studies. We began by discussing the varieties of legal systems across the globe and the methodology and approaches of comparative law. We then delved into the realm of international law and global governance, examining the sources of international law and the role of global governance institutions.

The impact of globalization on legal systems was also a crucial topic of discussion, along with the legal responses to global challenges. We explored the intersection of human rights and globalization, recognizing the importance of safeguarding human rights in a globalized world.

Transformative legal activism globally was another significant aspect we examined. We looked at legal activism in the Global South, highlighting the efforts of activists in advocating for social justice and equality. Transnational legal activism was also discussed, emphasizing the power of collaboration across borders in driving legal transformation. Additionally, we explored the connection between human rights and transnational justice movements.

Regional approaches to transformative legal studies were another key focus. We explored the legal integration within the European Union, shedding light on the unique challenges and opportunities that arise from regional cooperation. In addition, we examined African perspectives on transformative law and the contributions of Latin American approaches to social justice.

Indigenous legal systems and their transformative potential were also explored. We discussed legal pluralism and the importance of recognizing and respecting indigenous legal systems. Furthermore, we examined indigenous rights and self-determination, showcasing case studies of transformative indigenous legal practices.

The chapter also delved into the realm of environmental law and transformative legal strategies. We discussed the foundations of environmental law, including the emerging concept of rights of nature and the application of ecological legal theory. Additionally, we explored transnational environmental legal activism, recognizing the critical role it plays in preserving and protecting the environment.

In conclusion, this chapter highlighted the importance of understanding global perspectives in transformative legal studies. We explored the diverse legal systems, international legal frameworks, and regional approaches that shape the field. We also recognized the power of global collaboration and activism in promoting social justice, human rights, and environmental protection. Moving forward, it is crucial to continue exploring and engaging with global perspectives to drive transformative change in the legal field.

Resources for Further Study: 1. Anghie, A. (2007). Imperialism, Sovereignty, and the Making of International Law. 2. Merry, S. E. (2006). Transnational Human Rights and Local Activism: Mapping the Middle. 3. Biersteker, T. J., & Weber, C. (2018). Transnational Legal Orders. Handbook on Global Legal Pluralism, 69-93. 4. Coliver, S. (2017). A practitioner's guide to international human rights law. Oxford University Press. 5. De Schutter, O. (2015). International human rights law. Cambridge University Press.

Tricks and Caveats: - When studying global perspectives on transformative legal studies, it is essential to approach the subject with cultural sensitivity and respect for diverse legal traditions. - Understanding the interplay between national laws, international law, and regional approaches is crucial to comprehending the complexities of global legal systems. - It is important to recognize the power dynamics inherent in global legal processes and advocate for equity and justice in transnational interactions.

Exercise: Think of a particular global issue, such as climate change or refugee rights. Analyze how different legal systems and regional approaches could contribute to or hinder transformative change in addressing this issue. Consider the role of international law and transnational activism in shaping legal responses.

Implications for Global Transformative Legal Studies

The exploration of transformative legal studies and their impact on justice and equality has global implications. By understanding the implications of these transformative approaches, we can better appreciate their potential and consider their application in different legal systems and contexts around the world. This section will discuss some of the key implications of transformative legal studies on a global scale.

Promoting Social Justice

One of the most significant implications of transformative legal studies is their potential to promote social justice globally. These approaches challenge the existing power structures and aim to dismantle systems of oppression and discrimination. By incorporating perspectives from critical race theory, feminist theory, and postcolonial theory, transformative legal studies can address historical injustices and work towards a more equitable society.

For example, in many countries, marginalized communities face systemic discrimination and disadvantages that prevent them from accessing justice. Transformative legal studies can provide a framework for understanding and addressing these issues, leading to the development of legal systems that prioritize the rights and well-being of all individuals, regardless of their social background or identity.

Protecting Human Rights

Transformative legal studies can also have significant implications for the protection of human rights worldwide. By adopting an interdisciplinary and intersectional approach to human rights law, these studies can highlight the interconnectedness of different forms of oppression and discrimination. This understanding allows for a more comprehensive and inclusive approach to human rights, ensuring that the rights of marginalized groups are not overlooked.

For instance, feminist legal theory can shed light on the ways in which gender-based discrimination intersects with other forms of oppression, such as race, class, and sexuality. This understanding can inform legal systems and policies that protect the rights of individuals who face multiple forms of discrimination.

Transnational Legal Activism

Transformative legal studies have the potential to inspire and catalyze transnational legal activism. By recognizing the shared struggles for justice and equality across borders, these studies can create a space for collaboration and solidarity among activists, scholars, and practitioners from different countries.

For example, transnational legal activism can involve sharing strategies, resources, and knowledge on transformative legal practices to address global challenges such as climate change, economic inequality, and human rights abuses. This collaboration can lead to the development of international legal frameworks and initiatives that promote transformative change on a global scale.

Addressing Global Challenges

Another important implication of transformative legal studies is their capacity to address global challenges effectively. These approaches facilitate critical analysis of existing legal systems and institutions, enabling researchers and practitioners to identify shortcomings and propose innovative solutions.

For instance, in the era of rapid technological advancements, transformative legal studies can help navigate the legal implications of emerging technologies such as artificial intelligence, blockchain, and data privacy. By critically examining the ethical and social impacts of these technologies, transformative legal studies can shape legal frameworks that balance innovation and protection of individual rights and societal values.

Empowering Local Communities

Transformative legal studies empower local communities by recognizing their agency and elevating their voices. They encourage the participation of marginalized and vulnerable communities in legal decision-making processes, ensuring that their perspectives and needs are heard and considered.

For example, community-based restorative justice programs can provide opportunities for communities to actively participate in resolving conflicts, promoting healing, and preventing future harm. These programs prioritize dialogue, empathy, and accountability, allowing communities to shape their own methods of justice and conflict resolution, which are grounded in their cultural values and needs.

Conclusion

The implications of transformative legal studies on a global scale are profound. These approaches offer the potential for significant social change, protection of human rights, and the forging of global partnerships to address challenges faced by communities worldwide. By recognizing the interconnectedness of different forms of oppression and actively engaging with diverse perspectives, transformative legal studies pave the way for a more just and equitable future. The journey towards global transformative legal practices requires continued research, collaboration, and commitment to social justice and equality.

Future Directions in Global Legal Transformation

As we look to the future of global legal transformation, it is clear that there are several key areas that will shape the development of legal systems and institutions around the world. These future directions will be influenced by various factors, including technological advancements, changing social and political landscapes, and the ongoing pursuit of justice and equality. In this section, we explore some of these important future directions and their implications for the field of legal studies.

1. Technology and Artificial Intelligence

One of the most significant future directions in global legal transformation is the continued integration of technology and artificial intelligence (AI) in legal practice. AI has the potential to revolutionize legal research, contract management, and even decision-making processes in areas such as dispute resolution. As technology continues to advance, legal professionals must adapt and embrace these changes in order to effectively navigate the digital landscape. However, the use of AI also presents ethical considerations and challenges, such as ensuring transparency, fairness, and accountability in algorithmic decision-making processes.

2. Global Collaboration and Comparative Law

In an increasingly interconnected world, global collaboration and the study of comparative law will become even more important. As legal systems and institutions continue to evolve, researchers and practitioners will need to analyze different legal frameworks and draw insights from various jurisdictions. This comparative approach allows for the identification of best practices, as well as the development of innovative solutions to global legal challenges. By fostering international cooperation and sharing knowledge across borders, transformative legal studies can contribute to the harmonization of legal standards and the improvement of global justice systems.

3. Climate Change and Environmental Justice

The urgency of addressing climate change and promoting environmental justice will have a profound impact on the future of legal transformation. As the world grapples with the challenges of climate change, legal systems must adapt to effectively mitigate its impact and ensure a sustainable future. This includes developing laws and regulations that promote environmental sustainability, holding corporations accountable for their environmental practices, and protecting the rights of vulnerable communities affected by environmental degradation. Transformative legal studies will play a crucial role in shaping the legal response to climate change and promoting environmental justice on a global scale.

4. Human Rights and Social Justice Movements

The pursuit of human rights and social justice will continue to shape the future of legal transformation. As marginalized communities around the world demand equal rights and representation, legal systems must respond by developing inclusive laws and policies. This includes addressing systemic discrimination, advancing gender equality, protecting the rights of indigenous peoples, and promoting LGBTQ+ rights. Transformative legal studies should actively engage with social justice movements and work towards dismantling oppressive structures and promoting equality for all.

5. Access to Justice and Legal Empowerment

Improving access to justice and promoting legal empowerment will be essential for future legal transformation. Many individuals and communities still face barriers that prevent them from accessing their rights and seeking legal remedies. To address this issue, legal systems must prioritize initiatives such as legal aid services, community legal education, and alternative dispute resolution mechanisms. Additionally, there is a need to ensure that marginalized groups have equal access to legal education, legal representation, and the judicial system. Transformative legal studies can provide innovative solutions to enhance access to justice and empower individuals and communities to assert their legal rights.

6. Ethics and Professional Responsibility

As legal systems and institutions evolve, the importance of ethics and professional responsibility will continue to grow. Legal professionals must be equipped with ethical frameworks that guide their decision-making processes and uphold the principles of justice, fairness, and integrity. This includes addressing potential conflicts of interest, maintaining client confidentiality, and adopting responsible practices in the use of technology. Transformative legal studies should integrate ethics and professional responsibility into legal education curricula and promote a culture of ethical conduct within the legal profession.

Conclusion

The future of global legal transformation holds immense potential to shape the development of legal systems and institutions worldwide. By embracing technological advancements, fostering global collaboration, addressing pressing challenges such as climate change and human rights, and promoting access to justice and ethical conduct, transformative legal studies can contribute to a more just and equitable future. It is through these future directions that we can envision a legal landscape that upholds the values of justice, equality, and human rights for all individuals and communities.

Index

-effectiveness, 337
-up, 424

ability, 7, 22, 29, 59, 94, 140–142, 144, 145, 151, 155, 156, 200, 201, 206, 282, 298, 329, 347, 350, 353, 362, 376, 388, 389, 441, 449, 508, 533, 572, 579, 584, 587, 606, 623
ableism, 78, 122
abortion, 82, 313
absence, 161, 200, 346
abstraction, 110
abuse, 328, 388, 416, 484, 506, 511, 522, 603, 604
academia, 94
academic, 57, 76, 78, 93, 155–157, 162, 168, 196, 207, 290, 664
acceptance, 324, 370, 393, 409, 492, 601, 654, 663
access, 2, 6–8, 14, 20, 22, 24, 25, 29, 41, 47, 55, 59, 82, 104, 115, 116, 122, 135, 145, 147, 150, 158, 161–163, 166, 167, 173, 183, 186, 199–202, 206, 212–215, 228, 232, 236, 245, 247, 248, 253, 277, 282, 284, 285, 289, 292, 297, 300–302, 304, 308, 309, 312, 313, 326–332, 334, 336, 345, 361, 362, 367, 370, 379–382, 384, 385, 389, 391, 392, 394, 400, 414–416, 420, 422, 423, 425–427, 429–431, 435–437, 440, 444, 446, 453, 456–461, 470, 503, 509–511, 523, 533, 541, 549, 558, 562–564, 567, 576, 577, 579, 581, 586, 589, 591, 603–605, 609–612, 619, 623, 625, 674, 675, 680, 691, 693, 694, 719
accessibility, 59, 135, 161, 163, 166, 212, 215, 272, 389, 423, 430, 435, 436, 464, 523, 545
accommodate, 31, 388, 409
accordance, 206, 436, 584, 649, 703
account, 6, 9, 16, 62, 70, 71, 81, 111, 130, 193, 205, 207, 214, 283, 321, 322, 354, 356,

400, 524, 541, 615
accountability, 59, 220, 304, 309, 314, 349, 351, 352, 354–358, 398, 399, 401, 405, 415, 419, 420, 422, 444–446, 449, 467, 470, 471, 474, 476–479, 482–484, 486, 488–490, 492–494, 496, 498, 501, 504–507, 512–516, 518, 521–526, 530, 531, 533, 536, 543, 545, 546, 549, 552, 571, 591, 613, 615, 629, 637, 638, 647, 668, 673–677, 683–685, 688, 693, 701, 717
accountable, 15, 29, 114, 115, 301, 314, 351, 357, 372, 380, 400, 427, 471, 479, 494, 496, 502, 504, 508, 510, 513, 530, 542, 557, 558, 620, 624, 638, 673, 674, 676, 684, 685, 711, 718
accreditation, 162, 163, 336
accuracy, 161, 167, 219, 220, 282, 362, 388, 392–394, 398, 435, 441, 442, 445, 448, 452, 457, 458, 460
accusation, 93
achievement, 92, 206, 586
acknowledgment, 513, 616, 620, 703
acquittal, 576
act, 14, 89, 229, 316, 336, 362, 513, 664
action, 12, 26, 68, 70, 83, 90, 113, 146, 150, 184, 200, 205–207, 213, 216, 232, 236, 311, 327, 364, 371, 428, 441, 507, 555, 563, 587, 591, 622–625, 636, 676, 684, 711, 713
activism, 15, 22, 47, 75, 90, 94, 95, 102, 111–113, 136, 183–186, 271, 308, 310–316, 371, 376–380, 385, 581, 601, 621–624, 636, 643, 645, 647, 677–683, 685, 694, 711–716
activist, 91, 315, 625
adaptability, 199
adaptation, 7, 169, 319, 320, 323–326, 385, 425, 461, 545, 670, 672, 705
addition, 25, 49, 67, 89, 134, 184, 192, 215, 257, 258, 393, 400, 460, 549, 580, 609, 640, 674, 709, 714
address, 2, 3, 6, 7, 10, 11, 13–15, 17–23, 25, 27, 29–31, 34, 36, 42, 57, 59, 62, 63, 71, 72, 75, 79–83, 86, 88–90, 94, 97, 98, 113, 114, 116, 118, 121, 122, 125, 130, 131, 134, 136, 138, 139, 142, 144, 145, 147, 151, 156, 157, 162, 166, 168, 172, 174, 182–186, 188, 191, 195, 200, 201, 205, 206, 208, 209, 211, 213–216, 220, 228, 246, 247, 252, 254–256, 258, 261, 262, 272, 273, 282, 290, 292, 293, 297, 301–303, 307, 309, 311, 312, 316, 320, 323, 326–333, 336, 345–349, 352–357, 359, 361, 362,

Index

364, 365, 367, 371–373,
379, 381–384, 389, 394,
399–401, 404, 415, 417,
419, 421, 422, 426, 427,
435, 436, 442, 443, 445,
447, 451, 453, 458, 459,
461–463, 465, 467, 468,
470, 475, 476, 479, 483,
484, 489–492, 494–496,
503–516, 518, 521–525,
527, 530, 531, 533, 536,
541–545, 548–550, 552,
557, 562–564, 570, 572,
576, 581, 583, 584,
586–592, 598, 605, 606,
609–613, 615, 619, 621,
623, 636, 644–647, 651,
657, 658, 662, 664,
669–677, 680, 683,
691–694, 698, 707, 710,
711, 715–717, 719
adequacy, 525, 620
adherence, 311, 348, 421, 619
administration, 4, 308, 579
admission, 205
adoption, 303, 320, 323, 361, 388,
391, 393, 400, 404, 405,
409, 410, 427, 428,
450–452, 458, 460, 463,
464, 476–478, 491, 494,
497, 591, 670–672
advance, 48, 59, 112, 208, 225, 310,
311, 370, 372, 373, 376,
383, 417, 436, 461, 479,
546, 589, 605, 622, 626,
629, 637, 640, 650, 675,
678, 701, 710
advancement, 5, 36, 95, 129, 131,
161, 173, 192, 207, 215,
258, 265, 268, 287, 296,
302, 305, 377, 412, 425,
457, 459, 547, 636, 641,
677
advantage, 431
advent, 297
advice, 143, 144, 163, 226, 281, 282,
287, 328, 329, 333, 335,
359, 362, 460, 522
advocacy, 47, 59, 81, 91, 94, 115,
123, 134, 136, 144, 147,
150, 151, 155, 162, 176,
177, 182–184, 186–189,
192, 213, 215, 221,
371–373, 377, 385, 393,
525, 548, 563, 564, 587,
589–591, 609, 622, 623,
625–629, 645, 648,
675–678, 680, 684, 685,
711, 713
advocate, 2, 16, 17, 20, 21, 25, 31,
59, 62, 63, 69, 82, 97, 112,
116, 136, 183–185, 205,
213, 216, 272–274, 276,
284, 297, 314, 331, 333,
370, 372, 378, 382, 385,
416, 460, 523, 549, 550,
574, 621–623, 629, 644,
677, 683, 684, 701, 715
affinity, 184
affordability, 464, 674
Africa, 84, 384, 475, 580, 646, 648,
650, 678, 690–692
Aftercare, 496
aftermath, 114, 550
age, 83, 195, 219, 239, 277, 301,
384, 388, 410, 411,
414–417, 420, 422, 446,
453–457, 495, 603, 605

Index

agency, 26, 62, 70, 80, 294, 327, 357, 358, 502, 508, 511, 524, 531, 541, 638, 717
agenda, 94, 294, 311
agent, 208
agreement, 335, 339–341, 347, 353, 388, 405, 408, 420, 463, 484, 663, 709
agriculture, 657
aid, 7, 41, 59, 176, 182, 200, 213, 220, 226, 253, 301, 309, 326–328, 333, 362, 379, 392, 459, 460, 558, 576, 629, 674, 719
aim, 5, 9, 11, 12, 15, 22–26, 63, 96, 99, 118, 136, 147, 178, 184, 185, 219, 248, 273, 309, 320, 329, 353, 372, 379, 381, 413, 423, 427, 468, 471, 475, 476, 494, 508, 514, 515, 527, 530, 549, 550, 584, 607, 610, 615, 617, 647, 651, 658, 673, 674, 676, 692–694, 709, 715
air, 709
Alan Watson, 316, 320
algorithm, 397, 451
Alicia Ely Yamin, 625
alignment, 35
Allan Friedman, 424
Allan Stitt, 336
alleviation, 678
allocation, 247, 254, 351, 400
alteration, 414, 453
alternative, 2, 9, 11–13, 30, 47, 67, 69, 82, 87, 100, 111, 154, 181, 190, 191, 239, 271, 272, 298, 301, 323, 331, 337, 348, 349, 351, 357, 358, 360, 361, 379, 380, 383, 429, 434, 457, 474, 476, 483, 491, 493, 496, 498, 501, 508, 515, 516, 521, 523, 536, 542, 543, 545, 547, 550, 604, 646, 648, 695, 703, 719
ambiguity, 409
Americas, 84, 475, 580
amount, 167, 285, 415, 437
analysis, 1, 5, 9, 10, 12, 16, 19, 21, 22, 35, 36, 40, 41, 50, 56, 60, 67, 71, 72, 79–81, 91, 93–96, 109–111, 122, 125, 130, 131, 140–143, 164, 169, 178, 179, 189, 191, 193, 208, 210, 219–226, 228, 229, 231, 232, 236, 237, 239–245, 247, 248, 252, 254, 255, 257, 258, 262, 264, 269, 272, 273, 281, 287, 289, 291, 296, 298, 303, 304, 308, 320, 321, 392–395, 413, 415, 437, 441, 444, 448, 449, 455, 458, 460–462, 465, 477–479, 563, 564, 586, 590, 637, 638, 643, 650, 652, 654, 665, 668, 690, 716
analyzing, 13, 36, 41, 63, 66, 129, 135, 169, 176, 179, 180, 195, 217, 219–222, 225, 226, 232, 233, 236, 241, 242, 252, 253, 262, 273, 276, 281, 297, 321, 393, 439, 441, 442, 654
Andrea J. Ritchie, 378

Index 725

Angela Y. Davis, 378
anger, 501
anonymity, 243, 246, 256, 423
anonymization, 415, 419
answer, 41
anthropocentrism, 647
anthropology, 255, 262, 269, 272, 290, 296, 303, 651
Antonio Gramsci, 109
anxiety, 141, 523
apartheid, 184, 371, 620, 679
apology, 493, 524, 620
applicability, 95, 110, 493, 494, 526
applicant, 205
application, 12, 27, 29, 35, 36, 46, 47, 50, 56, 64, 80, 98, 114, 127, 130, 133, 134, 141, 153, 155, 163, 166, 175, 177, 186, 195, 222, 225, 228, 229, 235, 239, 248, 261, 281, 292, 295, 312, 324, 333, 339, 392, 394, 395, 397, 401, 409, 428, 439, 442, 465, 469, 474, 492, 495, 523, 536, 545, 551, 569, 649, 655, 673, 676, 701, 703, 714, 715
appreciation, 134, 173, 291
approach, 6, 8, 9, 13, 16, 17, 19–21, 24–27, 31, 36, 40–42, 49–51, 56–58, 62, 66, 67, 71, 72, 81, 84, 87, 90, 101, 116, 121, 123, 125, 126, 133, 140, 143, 146–148, 150, 151, 155–157, 171, 184, 190, 191, 193, 204, 207, 209–211, 214, 216, 217, 220, 233, 236, 240, 245, 252–254, 269, 272, 273, 287, 290, 291, 294–297, 299, 303, 304, 314, 315, 321, 322, 331–333, 335, 344, 348, 351, 352, 355, 356, 360, 368, 373, 376, 377, 379, 415, 419, 420, 426, 430, 437, 440, 455, 461, 467, 470, 471, 474–477, 479, 482, 485, 486, 488, 489, 492–495, 498, 501, 504, 507, 508, 510, 512, 515, 516, 518, 521–525, 527, 530–533, 536–538, 541–543, 545, 558, 562–564, 578, 589, 607, 610, 611, 619–621, 625, 631, 636–638, 643, 647, 651, 654, 674, 680, 684, 698, 703, 708–711, 715, 716, 718
appropriateness, 491, 526, 655
arbitration, 336, 337, 339, 342, 343, 345, 429, 430, 434, 436
arbitrator, 335, 342, 346, 430, 431
area, 15, 27, 55, 79, 81, 83, 175, 176, 195, 226, 271, 301, 462–464, 569, 578, 585, 663, 673
arena, 663, 669
argument, 257, 441
argumentation, 133, 147, 151
Aristotle, 3
Arizona, 313
arrest, 444
Asia, 4, 84, 475, 580, 648, 650, 678
aspect, 14, 17, 25, 48, 82, 117, 144, 155, 221, 227, 258, 287, 290, 326, 377, 383, 384,

477, 478, 518, 526, 536,
549, 571, 578, 589, 603,
680, 691, 693, 714
assault, 83, 506, 513, 591
assembly, 570–574, 578
assessment, 50, 144, 145, 156, 182,
253, 321, 351, 413, 442,
503, 504
asset, 463
assign, 195, 242, 341, 400
assimilation, 580, 583, 699
assistance, 23, 207, 247, 326–333,
335, 509, 511, 567, 620,
626, 674
association, 239, 578
assumption, 99, 273, 440
assurance, 163
athlete, 123
atmosphere, 141, 479
attack, 424, 573
attacker, 424
attempt, 402
attendance, 429
attention, 7, 116, 123, 136, 209, 210,
331, 348, 371, 376, 408,
459, 462, 470, 557, 576,
579, 591, 622, 676, 684
attorney, 143, 282, 313, 326, 327,
364
attribute, 31, 285
audience, 163, 292, 332, 333, 458,
622, 625
auditing, 399, 447
audits, 425, 444
Austin, 378
Australia, 333, 485, 649, 703
Australia, 703
authentication, 415, 416, 458
authenticity, 321

authority, 190, 191, 313, 315, 402,
556, 667, 673
authorship, 289
automation, 361
autonomy, 62, 80, 82, 87, 116, 173,
299, 337, 345, 409, 414,
426, 452, 502, 515, 524,
567, 571, 579–581, 589,
673, 697, 698
availability, 156, 199, 201, 234, 262,
277, 304, 330, 442, 453,
497, 504, 522, 674
avenue, 12, 112, 129, 301, 371, 458,
521
award, 335, 342
awareness, 2, 59, 116, 123, 155, 157,
185, 193, 209, 257, 326,
331, 357, 372, 377, 415,
416, 419, 448, 491, 523,
536, 545, 552, 558, 581,
587, 610, 620–626, 629,
633, 645, 675, 678, 684,
692, 701, 710, 711
axis, 79, 82, 121, 562

Babylonia, 3
backbone, 119, 226, 665, 694
background, 1, 7, 22, 205, 229, 328,
367, 460, 541, 548, 558,
610, 656, 674, 699, 716
backing, 623
backlash, 30, 31
balance, 7, 8, 18, 59, 83, 173, 177,
191, 221, 309, 313, 315,
316, 361, 367, 379, 413,
425–428, 455, 456, 463,
484, 490, 497, 572, 573,
578, 580, 657, 673, 708,
709, 717

Index 727

balancing, 323, 389, 427, 428, 492, 655, 671
bar, 448
bargaining, 112, 322
barrier, 199, 200, 326–328
Barry R. Furrow, 174
basis, 12, 94, 109, 114, 117, 526, 579, 586, 603, 606, 630, 648, 660, 663, 687, 701, 709
battle, 28
behavior, 19, 58, 135, 168, 174, 176–178, 212, 216, 233, 248, 253, 254, 292, 299, 334, 349, 356, 363, 365, 382, 400, 467, 475, 478, 483, 486, 491, 496, 521, 530, 541, 658, 663, 673
being, 7, 8, 45, 46, 57, 94, 115, 117, 158, 172, 173, 213–215, 253, 256, 293, 348, 350, 354, 356–358, 409, 411, 415, 419, 425–427, 430, 436, 444, 473, 484, 485, 491, 494, 496, 501–504, 508, 509, 514, 515, 523, 525, 526, 531, 533, 536, 541, 545, 549, 553, 562, 581, 582, 584, 603–606, 609, 610, 612, 638, 646, 702, 707, 708, 716
Belgium, 482
belief, 89, 467, 475, 505, 663, 708
below, 564
bench, 314
benefit, 10, 55, 94, 133, 142, 287, 373, 452, 459, 557, 623
Bentham, 4
betterment, 147, 214

bias, 13, 69, 76, 77, 94, 175, 184, 201, 220, 282, 286, 300, 311, 315, 328, 329, 398, 399, 401, 439, 443, 444, 446–449, 452, 458, 462, 518, 574, 576, 577, 674
billing, 361
biodiversity, 7, 647, 657, 705, 710, 711
biometric, 388, 414, 416
biopower, 101
birth, 554
blend, 690
block, 402, 408
blockchain, 47, 130, 289, 297, 300–302, 380, 382, 383, 388, 389, 391, 402–406, 408–411, 436, 456–458, 460, 463, 464, 717
board, 488
boarding, 581, 582
body, 29, 58, 182, 200, 202, 203, 205, 222, 226
Bolivia, 693, 709
Bolivia, 709
book, 18, 48, 50, 56, 57, 59, 127, 217, 431
border, 5, 192, 302, 359, 419, 427, 437, 669, 671, 674
borrowing, 308, 316, 320
bound, 191, 346
bourgeoisie, 109, 111, 112
box, 449
brainstorm, 289
branch, 26, 72, 75, 109, 269, 281, 313, 315, 547, 550, 704
Brazil, 648
breach, 153, 388, 391, 413, 416, 453, 654

breadth, 302
break, 229, 329, 368, 532, 541, 609
brick, 161
bridge, 10, 130, 143–146, 155, 166, 186, 193, 201, 206, 247, 273, 296, 309, 328, 329, 332, 334, 361, 362, 391, 394, 435, 624, 674
brink, 581
browsing, 414
Bruce Patton, 336
Bruce Schneier, 427
brutality, 573
Bryan Stevenson, 69
budget, 330
building, 23, 24, 107, 156, 158, 282, 291, 325, 357, 501, 505, 524, 531, 536, 537, 545, 546, 548, 584, 629, 637, 638, 646, 700, 713
burden, 199, 200, 327, 478
burnout, 623
business, 153, 157, 341, 359, 361, 670, 673, 676
Butler, 101
buyer, 408, 436

call, 315, 381, 424, 557, 573, 651
campaign, 579, 625
campus, 212
Canada, 88, 333, 354, 477, 485, 494, 649, 650, 703
Canada, 354
canon, 4, 184
capacity, 10, 325, 330, 352, 470, 489, 490, 536, 557, 623, 629, 670, 692, 713, 716
capital, 69, 112, 669, 671
capitalism, 58, 106, 109–111, 126

capitalist, 58, 106, 107, 109–113, 209
care, 122, 172, 506, 507, 521, 544, 564, 581, 586, 604, 623
career, 150, 200, 201
Caribbean, 650
case, 27–29, 35, 40, 48, 56, 68, 69, 81, 97, 123, 125, 133, 140–143, 158, 160, 162, 163, 175, 183, 186, 195, 198, 211, 216, 219–225, 228, 229, 231, 236, 242, 255, 261, 272, 277, 281, 285, 295, 296, 302, 303, 313, 314, 324, 325, 333, 336, 341, 342, 347, 362, 366, 367, 373, 376, 387, 391, 392, 394, 397, 409, 424, 428, 431, 435, 437, 440, 441, 449, 450, 457, 482, 483, 488, 494, 495, 501, 504, 512, 515, 517, 518, 520–522, 524–526, 573, 574, 576, 608, 621, 625, 636, 643, 649, 654, 655, 671, 698, 702–704, 714
catalyst, 14, 314, 543
cater, 330, 435
Catharine MacKinnon, 67
causality, 246
cause, 299, 423
caution, 220, 278, 448
Caveats, 715
censorship, 572
center, 18, 83, 88, 515
century, 3, 5, 106, 190, 316, 475, 476, 553, 648, 652
certainty, 88, 323, 648, 669, 671

Index

chain, 402, 408, 409, 463
challenge, 2, 7, 9–12, 15, 17, 21–26, 29–31, 47, 55, 57–59, 61–63, 68–72, 76, 82, 84, 86, 87, 90, 91, 94, 104, 107, 109, 111, 115, 116, 118, 119, 121, 126, 141, 143, 146, 151, 162, 181, 184–186, 191, 193, 208, 213, 246, 247, 255, 269, 273, 274, 276, 282, 285, 289, 291, 298, 301, 316, 321, 324, 325, 336, 341, 346, 347, 354, 356, 361, 368, 370–373, 376–378, 393, 399, 400, 409, 422, 426, 428, 431, 444–446, 456, 459, 478, 490, 491, 509, 510, 512, 518, 521, 522, 537, 547–550, 571, 572, 576, 578, 579, 587, 592, 607, 621, 622, 624, 637, 638, 646, 647, 651, 671, 676–679, 691, 693, 702, 715
chamber, 94
champion, 123
chance, 351, 377, 514
change, 1, 2, 5, 7, 11–16, 18–24, 26, 27, 29–31, 35, 36, 42, 51, 56, 57, 59, 61, 64, 66–68, 70–72, 78, 82, 90, 94, 100, 110, 112, 115, 116, 118, 119, 123, 136, 147, 155, 183–186, 189, 208–211, 213, 216, 217, 248, 252, 269, 271, 273–276, 290, 293, 296–298, 300, 308, 309, 312, 314–316, 350, 352, 356, 358–361, 370–373, 375–380, 382, 385, 395, 461, 462, 470, 496, 509, 515, 532, 536, 537, 549, 552, 573, 574, 601, 605, 609, 621–626, 636–638, 645–648, 651, 657, 672, 675–678, 680–683, 686, 692, 698, 701, 702, 705, 710, 711, 715–719
chapter, 1, 46–48, 61, 126, 127, 133, 207, 208, 210, 211, 219, 221, 228, 296, 297, 307, 310, 379, 380, 387, 456, 457, 467, 536–538, 541, 547, 619, 635, 636, 643, 647, 714
characteristic, 78, 93, 102, 574, 603, 649
Charlie Hebdo, 573
chat, 430
check, 315
checking, 243
checklist, 391
cherry, 257
Chickasaw, 582
child, 175, 421, 485, 506, 586, 603–609, 611, 612
childbirth, 586
childhood, 606
China, 650
Choctaw, 582
choice, 198, 502, 504, 671
church, 4
circle, 353, 494, 504, 505, 530
citizenship, 84, 115, 574, 676, 677
claim, 26, 327
clash, 327, 573

class, 6, 16, 18–20, 58, 62, 63, 71,
    79, 82, 90, 91, 93, 94, 97,
    99, 102, 106, 109–113,
    121, 122, 133, 140–142,
    184, 210, 273, 376, 384,
    548, 562, 587, 589–591,
    716
classification, 281
classism, 17, 78, 95, 122, 356
classroom, 143, 145, 146
client, 134, 143–145, 147, 150, 151,
    155, 156, 184, 186, 211,
    214, 282, 361, 364, 367,
    389, 393, 400, 446, 447,
    449, 457, 719
climate, 5, 7, 15, 116, 359, 461, 552,
    605, 647, 657, 672, 705,
    710, 711, 715, 716, 718,
    719
clinic, 145, 186–188, 328
closure, 484, 496, 501, 519, 521,
    526, 541
cloud, 447
co, 299
coalition, 629, 638
code, 3, 242, 348, 388, 405, 406,
    408, 409, 463, 564
coexistence, 17, 325
coherence, 254, 664
cohesion, 358, 494, 506, 512, 531,
    545, 619, 691
collaboration, 16, 23, 29, 30, 88, 134,
    135, 151, 154, 156, 169,
    172–174, 182, 183, 188,
    220, 221, 247, 254, 257,
    268, 287, 290, 291, 294,
    298, 300, 304, 330, 333,
    335, 353, 376–378, 380,
    381, 383–385, 389, 422,
    428, 434, 446, 447, 460,
    461, 464, 465, 476, 502,
    504, 509, 524, 526, 532,
    533, 537, 542–546, 584,
    610, 612, 622, 624, 638,
    651, 656, 676, 683–685,
    692, 700, 702, 704, 711,
    713, 714, 716–719
collapse, 110
collection, 36, 41, 116, 167, 236,
    237, 243, 245, 247, 277,
    287, 295, 303, 388, 400,
    411, 413–415, 419,
    426–428, 437, 439–441,
    444, 446, 455, 456, 463,
    563, 576, 578
Colombia, 620, 632
colonial, 17, 63, 84, 86, 87, 89, 209,
    316, 580, 646, 647, 690,
    691, 700
colonialism, 17, 57, 58, 62, 84, 86,
    126, 208, 209, 325, 583,
    678, 693, 699, 702
colonization, 17, 86, 87, 580, 583,
    584, 703
color, 554, 562, 563, 587
colorblindness, 63
combat, 389, 422, 459, 464, 558,
    579
combination, 35, 142, 234, 259, 434,
    587, 649
commentary, 158, 228, 231, 449
commerce, 3, 5, 670, 673
commitment, 12, 16, 129, 134, 136,
    148, 150, 200, 211, 213,
    217, 296, 305, 335, 366,
    382, 478, 511, 555, 580,
    587, 604, 619, 639, 662,
    675, 694, 717

Index

committee, 347
commodification, 415
commodity, 110
communication, 140, 141, 147, 151, 154, 156, 157, 168, 254, 287, 289–291, 293, 335–337, 339, 342, 352, 354, 364, 382, 430, 434–436, 482, 492, 505, 522, 536, 545, 675
community, 7, 13, 23, 27, 29, 55, 58, 59, 69, 82, 88, 90, 97, 125, 134, 145–147, 149, 150, 155–158, 163, 166, 182–184, 186, 188, 189, 201, 202, 204, 212, 213, 215, 221, 257, 272, 285, 287, 293–296, 299, 301, 309, 322, 324–326, 328–334, 336, 348, 350–354, 356–358, 367, 370, 373, 379, 381–383, 385, 392, 401, 416, 424, 471, 472, 474–478, 481, 483–488, 490–499, 501, 502, 504–514, 517, 518, 522–527, 529–533, 536, 537, 542–545, 550, 564, 584, 610–612, 620, 622, 624, 625, 633, 638, 646, 650, 655, 668, 678, 680, 691, 698, 702, 703, 717, 719
company, 81, 341, 397
comparability, 162, 246
compassion, 553
compatibility, 321, 579
compensation, 400, 488, 495, 525, 557, 620

competence, 156, 175, 177, 199, 213, 336, 361, 364, 447, 449, 452, 515, 698
competency, 201, 207, 213, 445
competition, 198
complaint, 327
completeness, 442
completion, 408
complexity, 21, 25, 30, 31, 94, 98, 193, 214, 325, 327, 329, 348, 382, 415, 522, 579
compliance, 13, 264, 282, 324, 360, 396, 397, 404, 420–422, 447, 456, 458, 552, 557, 580, 645, 670, 673, 675, 684
component, 98, 183, 192, 196, 228, 376, 479, 524
comprehension, 50, 333
comprehensiveness, 262, 457
compromise, 346, 423
computer, 164, 280, 394, 405, 408, 420, 421, 423, 449
computing, 402, 447
concept, 3, 11, 13, 14, 21, 24, 56, 63, 67, 71, 78, 90, 91, 94, 101, 102, 109, 110, 114, 116, 121, 126, 142, 176, 186, 297, 310, 312, 313, 316, 320–323, 355, 373, 376, 377, 379, 405, 414, 475, 479, 524, 550, 553, 562, 568, 574, 587, 615, 695, 699, 708, 710, 711, 714
concern, 7, 83, 256, 336, 389, 399, 411, 414, 444, 445, 453, 463, 490, 705
conciliation, 342, 344, 345, 430
conciliator, 335, 342

conclusion, 31, 40, 48, 66, 72, 78, 90, 111, 121, 147, 166, 211, 282, 297, 300, 302, 309, 316, 358, 380, 383, 395, 458, 459, 465, 476, 479, 509, 523, 537, 587, 605, 636, 641, 668, 683, 714
conduct, 41, 43, 47, 130, 144, 145, 163, 168, 226, 228, 241, 257, 260, 265, 277, 295, 348, 362, 363, 365, 367, 387, 459, 557, 659, 673, 719
conference, 351, 483, 484, 506, 530
conferencing, 163, 353, 379, 430, 476, 477, 510, 531, 536, 541, 542
confidence, 282, 316, 425, 427, 574
confidentiality, 42, 156, 177, 214, 221, 243, 245, 246, 256, 284, 295, 299, 304, 336, 337, 343, 347, 348, 354, 361, 364, 389, 393, 394, 429, 435, 442, 446, 449, 453–457, 464, 719
confine, 311
confirmation, 175
conflict, 59, 112, 190, 192, 341, 347, 348, 351, 426, 471, 474, 475, 478, 482, 497, 527, 530, 543–545, 552, 591, 604, 609, 612, 615, 618–620, 647, 685, 717
conjunction, 141, 349
connection, 380, 430, 497, 580, 636, 714
connectivity, 431
consciousness, 248, 684
consensus, 30, 31, 341, 402, 584, 646, 650
consent, 42, 109, 167, 177, 190, 243, 256, 284, 285, 295, 297, 301, 304, 354, 388, 415, 416, 426, 427, 455, 463, 638, 654, 699
conservation, 7, 646, 657, 705, 711
consideration, 152, 173, 250, 254, 256, 284, 285, 316, 321, 324, 326, 334, 347, 351, 354, 399, 409, 428, 446, 497, 501, 558, 603, 654, 671
consistency, 4, 246, 254, 268, 478, 649, 664
constitution, 568, 709
constitutionality, 313
construct, 4, 89, 176, 225, 590
construction, 101, 344
consultation, 583, 620, 700
consumer, 150, 429
consumption, 404
contact, 176, 427, 604
content, 48–50, 137, 163, 190, 225, 236, 243, 244, 281, 564, 567, 572, 574, 663
contention, 578
context, 5, 11, 13, 14, 16, 19, 20, 28, 29, 32, 36, 39, 41, 43, 62, 70, 81, 84, 91, 94, 106, 109, 121, 123, 125, 130, 146, 151, 164, 169, 171, 175, 177, 184, 186, 205, 226, 229, 231, 232, 240, 246, 248, 253, 269, 280, 281, 290, 298, 303, 320, 321, 324, 325, 334, 377, 392, 400, 413, 437, 444, 449, 450, 472, 477, 492,

Index 733

495, 497, 498, 502, 511,
516–518, 522, 524, 549,
558, 564, 571, 572, 583,
606, 607, 619, 621, 632,
646, 648, 654, 655, 671,
673, 675, 677, 683, 685,
690, 693, 694, 696, 701
contextualization, 324
continent, 646, 690, 692
contraception, 82
contract, 61, 145, 153, 164, 198,
220, 297, 301, 322, 336,
341, 392, 396–399, 405,
406, 408, 409, 448, 458,
462, 463, 553, 654, 669
contrast, 477, 541, 655
contribution, 222
control, 7, 87, 101, 112, 168, 225,
246, 335, 344, 411, 414,
415, 419, 426, 427, 430,
463, 502, 503, 506, 514,
524, 526, 649, 650, 705,
711
controversy, 311, 314, 315, 578
convenience, 161, 429, 435
convergence, 90, 91, 190, 323
conversation, 353, 479, 482
conversion, 347
cooperation, 191, 193, 257, 268,
384, 421, 422, 424, 427,
428, 464, 644, 647, 655,
657, 658, 661, 662, 665,
666, 668, 669, 672–674,
676, 677, 684, 690, 692,
700, 711, 714, 718
cooperative, 344
coordination, 287, 290, 330, 422,
629, 655, 656, 665
copyright, 231, 285, 400

core, 11, 24, 64, 114, 181, 214, 310,
349, 356, 373, 402, 440,
472, 502, 504, 527, 547,
551
cornerstone, 219, 272, 574, 578
corporate, 549, 629, 671, 674, 685
corporation, 28, 346, 397
correlation, 41
corruption, 325, 578, 694
cosmopolitanism, 676
cost, 23, 199, 327, 329, 334, 337,
361, 434, 437, 457
counsel, 151
counseling, 134, 144, 147, 184, 360,
458, 465, 503, 507, 509,
511, 522, 523, 619
counter, 116
counterfeiting, 409
country, 84, 125, 416, 421, 566, 571,
604, 625, 632, 697, 705,
709
course, 143, 161, 163, 193, 195, 312
court, 14, 35, 88, 140, 145–147,
150, 162, 196, 198, 205,
220, 222, 224, 225, 231,
241, 242, 244, 245, 272,
316, 326, 327, 334–336,
342, 343, 346, 364, 392,
394, 429–431, 437, 441,
457, 476, 496, 497, 506,
525, 579, 649
courtroom, 143, 150, 151, 176, 215,
242
coverage, 283, 576
creation, 23, 88, 179, 315, 353, 415,
458, 475, 512
creativity, 213, 272, 465, 609, 657
credibility, 93, 162, 167, 175, 206,
243, 253, 256, 285

Creek, 582
Crenshaw, 91
crime, 13, 15, 59, 176, 300, 348, 349, 351, 352, 355–358, 467, 468, 471, 474–477, 479, 483, 485, 486, 489, 492–494, 501, 505, 508–512, 516, 518, 521, 524, 525, 527, 530, 531, 533, 536, 541–543, 672
criminalization, 356, 591
criminology, 356
criticism, 137, 142, 314, 401, 580
critique, 9, 10, 16, 22, 62, 63, 67, 70, 84, 93, 94, 96–98, 101, 102, 111, 113, 272, 315
cross, 5, 176, 191, 192, 199, 217, 268, 290–293, 302, 304, 308, 359, 419, 427, 437, 545, 669, 671, 674
Cuba, 650
culture, 1, 110, 183, 210, 248, 253, 324, 325, 348, 370, 545, 582, 620, 621, 650, 655, 669, 690, 719
currency, 167
curriculum, 88, 136, 145, 147, 156, 182–186, 204, 207, 215, 216, 361, 465, 698
custody, 175, 313, 336, 586
custom, 190
customer, 434, 453
customization, 430, 435
cut, 400
cutting, 24, 48, 459
cyber, 389, 415, 420–425, 427, 428, 446, 453, 456, 458, 463, 464, 578
cyberbullying, 578

cybercrime, 359, 421–423, 425, 456, 459, 464, 670
cybersecurity, 47, 361, 380, 384, 389, 391, 415, 420–422, 424, 446, 456, 458, 464
cyberspace, 422
cycle, 206, 352, 507, 511, 532, 541, 609

damage, 389, 423, 453, 488, 675
data, 6, 13, 33, 35–37, 41, 42, 47, 116, 162, 164, 167, 168, 177, 212, 214, 215, 220, 221, 232–237, 239, 240, 242–245, 247, 255–257, 262, 264, 272, 280–282, 284, 285, 287, 295–297, 301, 303, 304, 309, 361, 380, 384, 388, 389, 391–395, 397–402, 404, 408, 411–417, 419–428, 435, 437–447, 449, 452–458, 460–463, 465, 545, 563, 576, 578, 717
database, 397
date, 387, 425
day, 5, 113, 307, 313, 581
death, 581
debate, 7, 8, 82, 94, 206, 239, 311–314, 388, 572, 578, 673
debriefing, 157
decision, 6, 19, 20, 25, 62, 87, 88, 115, 135, 140, 172, 175–177, 215, 216, 222, 225, 235, 242, 245, 248, 253, 264, 280, 282, 284, 292, 299, 300, 303, 309, 310, 312–314, 321, 335,

Index 735

336, 342, 343, 346, 352, 353, 357, 360, 381, 382, 385, 399, 401, 434, 437, 440–443, 445, 448, 457, 458, 460, 465, 475, 485, 493–495, 502, 503, 505, 511, 513, 514, 518, 519, 524, 536, 544, 573, 581, 583, 586, 591, 604, 605, 610, 611, 620, 623, 637, 646, 655, 665, 668, 673, 684, 688, 693, 697, 700, 704, 717, 719
decisis, 4, 649
decline, 110, 604
decolonization, 62, 63, 86, 126, 646
deduction, 16, 272
defamation, 225
defendant, 322
defense, 186, 422–425, 576
deficit, 690
definition, 1, 310, 379, 567
degradation, 7, 15, 549, 581, 700, 718
degree, 199, 669
delegation, 400
Delgado, 91
deliberation, 176, 316
delivery, 172, 330, 331, 367, 465, 564
demand, 184, 330, 361, 425, 550, 573, 624
democracy, 59, 293, 567, 572, 579, 646
denial, 22, 555
department, 576
departure, 350
depletion, 708
deployment, 220, 427, 443

deportation, 187
depth, 32, 35, 36, 69, 139, 181, 210, 232, 240, 243, 287, 302, 395, 411, 431, 462, 570, 618
Derrick Bell, 91
design, 19, 36, 42, 153, 157, 235, 244, 254, 255, 393, 407, 415, 419, 426, 428, 472, 508, 515, 620
desire, 90, 488, 522
destruction, 414, 420, 453, 580
detail, 43
detection, 425, 442
detention, 333, 579
determination, 62, 87, 333, 378, 524, 580, 581, 583–585, 693, 698–702, 704, 714
deterrence, 493
developer, 400
development, 1–7, 12, 23, 69, 72, 77, 84, 91, 93–95, 98, 116, 118, 133, 134, 143–146, 148, 155, 164, 166, 169, 172, 174, 181, 182, 184, 185, 189, 191, 196, 205, 206, 210, 211, 214–216, 220, 226, 228, 232, 253, 254, 258, 262, 280, 282, 287, 299, 302, 305, 307, 308, 310, 316, 320, 321, 323, 325, 334, 357, 360–362, 382, 383, 393, 394, 398, 400, 401, 405, 410, 415, 419, 422, 427, 441, 443, 445, 446, 448, 449, 456, 458–462, 464, 465, 476–478, 490, 491, 506, 507, 533, 539, 540,

544, 550, 552–555, 567, 568, 571, 583, 584, 586, 590, 591, 603–605, 609, 612, 635, 637, 644–647, 649, 652, 655–658, 660, 664, 665, 669–672, 675–677, 689–692, 700, 704, 707, 709–711, 716–719

dialogue, 12, 27, 31, 58, 88, 94, 141, 142, 182, 185, 191, 207, 257, 335, 339, 348–350, 353, 355–357, 401, 464, 471, 475–477, 479, 483, 487, 489, 490, 492, 493, 495, 501, 503, 505, 507, 510–512, 514–516, 518, 524–527, 530–533, 545, 580, 644, 668, 676, 698, 700, 717

difference, 291
differential, 62
digitalization, 463
digitization, 304
dignity, 58, 114, 116, 117, 414, 524, 541, 547, 549, 550, 553, 554, 556, 558, 562, 567, 571, 572, 619, 621, 641, 651
diligence, 164, 220, 392, 674
dimension, 123, 195, 209
diplomacy, 192
direction, 130, 282, 384, 458, 462, 464, 543–545
disability, 6, 20, 24, 25, 72, 79, 83, 99, 116, 121, 122, 367, 384, 548, 562, 590, 603, 609
disadvantage, 121, 130, 199, 587

disagreement, 339
disarmament, 663, 672
disbarment, 364
discipline, 5, 8, 57, 92, 190, 253, 291, 303, 543, 652
disclosure, 347, 411, 413, 414, 420, 446
discomfort, 18, 243
discourse, 10, 72, 88, 91, 123, 137, 216, 243, 571, 572, 624, 686
discovery, 141, 334, 583
discretion, 654
discrimination, 9, 12, 17, 22, 24, 25, 31, 57, 67, 72, 75, 78, 79, 81–83, 89–91, 94, 95, 99, 101, 102, 114–116, 121–123, 125, 130, 205, 206, 221, 253, 254, 292, 327, 329, 371, 377, 384, 426, 439, 444, 446, 459, 508, 510, 511, 516, 533, 543, 548, 552, 555–558, 562–564, 578–580, 586, 587, 589–591, 596–598, 603–605, 609, 636, 637, 671, 674, 678, 693, 694, 699–701, 704, 715, 716
discussion, 6, 56, 83, 116, 125, 140, 142, 161, 163, 241, 244, 440, 714
disenfranchisement, 516
disillusionment, 579
disinvestment, 532
dislocation, 675
dismantling, 14, 23, 95, 185, 460, 679
disobedience, 371, 372, 622, 625
disorder, 531

Index 737

disparity, 346, 564
displacement, 87, 388, 400, 580, 583, 604, 609, 699
disposal, 297
disposition, 496
dispossession, 583, 691, 700
dispute, 7, 11, 12, 47, 153, 154, 222, 301, 328, 335, 337–339, 341, 342, 346–348, 360, 379, 380, 382, 388, 429–431, 434, 435, 437, 457, 459, 463, 464, 644, 655, 695, 719
disruption, 420, 508
dissemination, 247, 257, 578
dissent, 94, 578
distance, 135, 161–163, 201, 202, 212, 215
distinction, 115, 586
distinguishing, 140
distress, 514, 523
distribution, 20, 173, 415, 510, 516, 620, 671
distrust, 522
divergence, 190
diversion, 496
diversity, 14, 18, 25, 62, 93, 94, 136, 182, 184, 193, 199–207, 210, 213, 214, 216, 217, 253, 254, 309, 328, 359, 367–370, 380, 384, 523, 592, 643, 644, 646, 648, 709
divide, 48, 166–168, 284, 285, 435, 458
diving, 239
division, 18, 339, 341
doctrine, 4, 62, 181, 322, 583, 664
document, 35, 164, 220, 240, 241, 243, 255, 281, 289, 362, 405, 435, 448, 615, 616, 656
documentary, 428
documentation, 545
domain, 310, 391, 443, 446
dominance, 17, 62, 89, 109, 110, 113, 475, 669
domination, 84, 109–111
Donna K. Hammaker, 174
door, 622
drafting, 145, 147, 150, 371, 392, 394, 462
driver, 609
drug, 239
Duncan Kennedy, 67
duty, 256, 347, 362, 400, 445, 447, 675
dynamic, 1, 5, 8, 15, 21, 94, 139, 193, 248, 273, 300, 570, 658, 704

e, 670
Earl Warren, 312
ease, 285, 436, 578, 671
echo, 94
ecocentrism, 647
economic, 7–9, 13, 19, 24, 26, 30, 58, 67, 84, 87, 106, 109, 110, 112, 113, 115, 116, 122, 123, 126, 135, 155, 178–181, 188, 191, 199, 209, 212, 213, 216, 252–254, 269, 272, 273, 290, 292, 293, 303, 304, 320, 321, 331, 356, 367, 384, 400, 435, 459, 467, 508, 510, 511, 523, 541, 543, 544, 548–550, 554,

556, 562–564, 566, 567,
581, 583, 584, 586, 591,
603, 607, 609, 610, 635,
636, 644–646, 650,
671–675, 677, 690–694,
709, 716
economist, 106
economy, 649
ecosystem, 414, 708, 710
Ecuador, 693, 709
Ecuador, 709
edge, 24, 48, 459
education, 1, 7, 8, 11–13, 18, 23, 25,
46–48, 51, 64–66, 87, 88,
90–92, 115, 125, 127,
133–137, 139–144,
146–157, 161–163,
166–171, 173, 181–186,
192–196, 199–202,
205–207, 211–217, 300,
309, 326, 329, 331–334,
348, 350, 357, 361, 372,
379, 382, 384, 385, 393,
445, 446, 448, 457–460,
465, 491, 503, 504, 510,
511, 532, 545, 549, 563,
564, 586, 591, 596,
603–605, 609–612, 619,
622, 638, 647, 691–694,
698, 710, 719
effect, 94, 184, 185, 217, 300, 314,
342, 572, 622, 645, 672,
676, 683
effectiveness, 8, 10, 19, 83, 125, 130,
135, 137–139, 142, 156,
180, 190, 206, 219–221,
232, 235, 254, 258, 264,
282, 294, 315, 321, 325,
330, 334, 337, 338, 341,
345, 348, 350, 370, 375,
389, 427, 430, 460,
477–480, 482, 484, 489,
491, 494, 507, 509, 522,
523, 530, 544, 545, 576,
587, 627, 662, 667, 670,
674, 704, 710
efficacy, 233, 304
efficiency, 19, 135, 161, 164, 166,
180, 219, 221, 254, 282,
287, 301, 309, 330, 362,
387, 389, 395, 398, 405,
436, 443, 446, 448, 451,
452, 458, 460, 463, 545,
576
effort, 281, 377, 449
element, 190, 549, 691
eligibility, 329–331, 620
email, 414, 430
embrace, 95, 128, 136, 161, 165,
213, 215, 282, 300, 350,
389, 395, 462, 465, 543,
622
emergence, 4, 5, 21, 40, 189, 456,
475, 553, 645, 656, 676,
678
empathy, 155, 156, 158, 171, 186,
206, 213, 352, 353, 357,
465, 471, 472, 482, 501,
503–505, 510, 518, 521,
524, 542, 545, 717
emphasis, 4, 29, 32, 70, 82, 93, 130,
133, 134, 143, 215, 217,
272, 359, 360, 460, 478,
648, 655, 692
Empire, 100
employee, 389, 391
employer, 327
employment, 8, 25, 79, 83, 90, 92,

Index

115, 156, 254, 295, 332, 336, 397, 400, 401, 509, 563, 586, 596, 606, 693
empowerment, 31, 56, 62, 72, 150, 294, 301, 309, 332, 333, 351, 358, 379, 385, 472, 483, 493, 502–506, 508–510, 514, 515, 518, 519, 521, 524–527, 533, 537, 541, 543, 591, 592, 605, 622, 701, 719
enactment, 228, 371, 372, 377, 557
encompass, 5, 94, 191, 214, 248, 385, 468, 564, 567, 603, 640, 643, 663, 692
encounter, 50, 202, 340, 367, 451, 474, 511, 537, 567, 625
encryption, 389, 391, 394, 400, 415, 425, 427, 429
encyclopedia, 4
end, 50, 51, 127, 172, 289, 400, 636
endeavor, 86, 555
energy, 15, 404
enforceability, 198, 345, 347, 409, 410, 464
enforcement, 25, 83, 176, 179, 195, 301, 308, 313, 325, 347, 372, 388, 389, 408, 420, 426, 431, 448, 464, 518, 531–533, 537, 550, 560, 572, 573, 580, 644, 647, 656, 660, 662, 667, 669–671, 673, 674, 677, 684, 709, 710
engage, 8, 9, 22, 23, 26, 50, 70–72, 94, 130, 134, 136, 140–143, 145, 148, 150, 151, 154, 157, 161–163, 176, 181–185, 195, 209, 211, 213, 215, 217, 243, 289, 293, 295, 297, 299, 304, 321, 323, 332, 339, 341, 353, 357, 359, 366, 370, 371, 382, 385, 394, 429, 445, 479, 491, 493, 494, 497, 501, 503, 513, 524, 533, 535, 548, 571, 615, 622, 629, 637, 638, 645, 661, 664, 669, 670, 684
engagement, 16, 20, 31, 48, 64, 78, 88, 89, 125, 129, 133–135, 137, 139–141, 145–147, 151, 155–158, 169, 182, 208, 212, 215, 257, 294, 295, 309, 333, 352, 358, 361, 382, 383, 385, 434, 461, 489, 502, 510, 518, 523, 527, 531, 533, 537, 540, 542, 543, 545, 552, 563, 580, 624, 662, 685, 698
engineering, 425
England, 1, 4, 322, 643, 649, 655
enhance, 47, 50, 51, 81, 94, 131, 136–139, 142, 146, 151, 154, 157, 162, 164, 169, 176, 177, 194, 201, 204, 212, 216, 219, 221, 232, 240, 243, 246–248, 255, 258, 280, 282, 291, 300, 302, 309, 330, 333, 345, 348, 360, 362, 387, 395, 405, 415, 426, 427, 435, 440, 446, 448, 451, 452, 457, 458, 460, 462, 479, 489, 531, 533, 545, 552, 576, 652, 673, 710, 719

enjoyment, 115, 116, 563, 586
enrollment, 205
entity, 269, 346, 708, 709
entry, 213
environment, 15, 133, 137, 139, 141, 147, 151, 168, 185, 192, 200, 201, 204, 205, 207, 213, 215, 291, 346, 353, 354, 367, 372, 428, 479, 483, 490, 502–504, 514, 521, 523, 532, 541, 587, 603, 604, 630, 633, 647, 693, 704, 707–711, 713, 714
equality, 1, 2, 5, 9–15, 17, 19, 21, 23–27, 29, 36, 40, 42, 43, 46–48, 51, 56–59, 61, 62, 64, 67, 68, 72, 75, 78, 81, 83, 89, 90, 92, 111, 112, 114–117, 119, 127, 129–131, 133, 135, 136, 147, 148, 155, 158, 166, 172, 174, 183, 185, 186, 189, 192, 195, 196, 202, 204, 205, 207–211, 213, 214, 216, 247, 248, 252, 255, 262, 271, 286, 290, 296, 297, 305, 307, 308, 310, 312, 314, 316, 331, 348, 349, 352, 361, 362, 370, 372–374, 376, 380–385, 394, 410, 442, 459, 461, 465, 533, 536, 541, 543, 547, 548, 553, 555–558, 564, 567, 580, 586–590, 592, 633, 636, 641, 648, 649, 651, 656, 677, 678, 683, 685, 690, 692–694, 698, 701, 702, 704, 714–717, 719
equity, 136, 201, 207, 258, 346, 401, 541, 546, 611, 715
equivalence, 110, 320
era, 1, 6, 17, 84, 316, 362, 422, 425, 447, 553, 572, 620, 670, 716
eradication, 609
erasure, 87, 583
erosion, 90, 316, 321, 703
escrow, 408
essence, 11, 119
essentialism, 72, 93
essentialist, 93
establishment, 1, 3, 4, 47, 88, 184, 189, 350, 357, 464, 591, 620, 621, 679, 703, 709
estate, 388, 408, 409
Ethan Katsh, 431
ethnicity, 205, 367, 510, 516, 523, 591
Europe, 4, 106, 316, 648, 690
evaluation, 31, 156, 157, 162, 188, 205, 211, 321, 334, 401, 441, 457, 469, 476, 478, 491, 526, 544, 546, 610
Evelyn Zellerer, 507
event, 502, 625
everyday, 545
Evgeny Pashukanis, 110
eviction, 326
evidence, 71, 131, 169, 173, 176, 233, 236, 255, 299, 313, 335, 342, 347, 350, 428, 443, 458, 460, 476, 491, 544, 574, 576, 655
evolution, 3, 47, 225, 229, 307, 308, 310, 319, 321, 358, 475,

Index 741

476, 479, 553, 651, 664, 665
ex, 576
examination, 1, 26, 87, 119, 168, 209, 241, 262, 444
examining, 2, 5–9, 20, 24, 25, 29, 35, 48, 61, 64, 69, 72, 84, 92, 97, 122, 127, 131, 140, 176, 178–181, 208, 210, 211, 216, 222, 225, 236, 242, 258, 269, 272, 273, 296, 298, 302, 312, 314, 381, 384, 396, 459, 477, 638, 645, 646, 648, 665, 675, 714, 717
example, 3, 13–15, 19, 20, 23, 25, 41, 68, 71, 78, 79, 87, 88, 92, 95, 102, 112, 113, 134, 145, 150, 153, 169, 172, 175, 185, 187, 195, 201, 204, 216, 220, 228, 235, 239, 245, 246, 255, 258, 261, 282, 298–300, 303, 313, 316, 322, 324, 326–328, 336, 349, 362, 371, 372, 378, 381, 382, 387, 394, 399, 401, 416, 427, 434, 444, 448, 449, 458, 460, 461, 475, 478, 482, 485, 488, 494, 497, 501, 504, 507–509, 511, 520, 542, 543, 553, 558, 562–564, 576, 587, 589, 608, 611, 620, 632, 648, 650, 656, 657, 664, 669–672, 685, 693, 697, 701, 703, 716, 717
exception, 212
exchange, 110, 151, 287, 291, 319, 322, 435, 544, 571, 572, 645, 664, 676
exclusion, 17, 72, 200, 415, 549, 586
execution, 405, 406, 464, 688
exercise, 59, 115, 153, 154, 161, 195, 278, 311, 313, 395, 448, 482
exhaustion, 623
existence, 557
expansion, 459, 476, 543, 699
expense, 425
experience, 22, 24, 51, 78, 79, 95, 121, 129, 144, 147, 150, 151, 154, 155, 157, 162, 168, 182, 183, 201, 205, 287, 356, 376, 384, 434, 492, 493, 507, 523, 536, 548, 563, 564, 579, 587, 637
experiment, 151
expert, 175, 326, 335
expertise, 172, 173, 175, 220, 247, 257, 287, 289–291, 329, 333, 361, 377, 393, 445, 637, 673, 685
explainability, 393, 419, 445, 446
Explainable AI, 282
exploitation, 109, 111, 112, 243, 581, 603, 604, 606–608, 671
exploration, 12, 29, 42, 46, 77, 91, 111, 113, 127, 139, 142, 181, 208–210, 221, 232, 265, 283, 303, 319, 323, 337, 342, 353, 355, 383, 395, 404, 431, 458, 461, 463, 474, 538, 540, 562, 585, 618, 636, 697, 713, 715

exposure, 143, 200, 212
expression, 195, 357, 464, 505, 526, 552, 558, 564, 570–574, 578, 580, 656, 700
extent, 78, 206, 311, 312, 491, 502
externship, 134
extinction, 581
extraction, 87, 112, 123, 584
eyewitness, 175

fabric, 89
face, 7, 9, 13, 22, 25, 26, 31, 78, 79, 81, 94, 95, 116, 121, 123, 156, 188, 189, 191, 201, 202, 206, 212, 213, 217, 236, 241, 247, 293, 309, 321, 326, 328–330, 341, 345, 359, 377, 379, 382, 415, 419, 422, 423, 425, 430, 435, 476, 488, 491, 494, 505, 508, 510, 521–523, 529, 548, 558, 562–564, 574, 579, 580, 584, 587, 596, 597, 604, 609, 617, 618, 623, 625, 627, 629, 630, 667, 668, 670, 683–685, 696, 698, 700, 708, 716, 719
facilitation, 522
facilitator, 483, 507
facility, 27
fact, 195
factor, 205, 206, 359
faculty, 134, 145, 146, 148, 150, 156, 157, 182, 186, 200, 201, 204, 207, 216
failure, 321, 323, 441
fairness, 19, 21, 24, 136, 207, 214, 235, 246, 286, 304, 315, 337, 338, 340, 345–348, 350, 363, 388, 394, 401, 429, 435, 437, 439, 442–446, 456–459, 472, 484, 490, 493, 576, 577, 579, 620, 671, 674, 719
faith, 191
fall, 70, 330, 423, 547
family, 3, 100, 186, 190, 329, 332, 336, 344, 345, 353, 354, 379, 429, 477, 483–485, 506, 509, 510, 531, 536, 541, 586, 604
fear, 347, 350, 353, 388, 400, 430, 503, 514, 522, 523, 525, 526
feasibility, 112, 321, 339
feature, 409, 648–650, 673
fee, 327, 361
feedback, 147, 257, 309
feeling, 522
feminism, 562
feminist, 6, 16–18, 20, 46, 47, 56, 62, 63, 67, 71–73, 75–83, 126, 130, 185, 207–210, 298, 461, 562, 590–592, 715, 716
fertilization, 191, 308
fetishism, 110, 111
field, 1, 3, 5–7, 9–11, 13, 18, 21, 25, 30, 31, 40–42, 46, 47, 50, 51, 56, 60, 61, 67, 72, 74–76, 81, 89, 94, 100, 116, 127, 129, 156, 158, 161, 163, 172, 174, 176–178, 186, 192, 195, 200, 205, 207, 212, 214, 219, 221, 226, 228, 229, 231–233, 235, 236, 239,

243–245, 248, 252, 255, 262, 271, 282, 283, 286, 287, 290, 291, 293, 296–298, 300, 302, 310, 316, 320, 323, 336, 355, 380, 383, 385, 387, 389, 391–393, 395, 399, 402–404, 408, 410, 417, 437–440, 443, 445, 446, 448, 452, 456–458, 461–463, 479, 482, 504, 515, 533, 536, 538–541, 543, 547, 562, 585, 590, 592, 603, 604, 612, 636, 639, 651, 655, 657, 658, 672, 675, 711, 714, 715, 717
fight, 113, 372
figure, 91, 101
file, 327
filing, 326, 362
finance, 410, 462
finding, 7, 27, 195, 219, 294, 335, 349, 353, 378, 477, 479, 484, 487, 490, 496, 505, 513, 514, 533, 639
firm, 143
fit, 257, 409, 435
flexibility, 80, 135, 161, 163, 212, 215, 291, 315, 335, 430, 431, 435
flow, 572
focus, 11, 16, 17, 21, 26–28, 56, 70–72, 83, 111, 130, 133, 134, 148, 185, 207, 211, 219, 240, 243, 244, 264, 272, 295, 300–302, 330, 332, 333, 348, 349, 353, 356, 362, 373, 379, 384, 385, 387, 389, 393, 422, 445, 459, 461, 463–465, 467, 485, 494, 496, 498, 505, 508, 514, 516, 519, 522, 525, 531, 533, 537, 541, 562, 601, 603, 607, 610, 613, 636–638, 641, 646, 650, 714
following, 4, 24, 27, 28, 32, 35, 40, 49, 51, 69, 75, 80, 92, 97, 107, 113, 137, 139, 157, 163, 174, 189, 204, 225, 230–232, 236, 237, 239, 240, 251, 254, 265, 267, 279, 283, 292, 319, 322, 336, 343, 344, 355, 363, 367, 395, 398, 404, 407, 410, 416, 427, 428, 431, 439, 440, 443, 448, 450, 454, 455, 473, 480, 483, 485, 492, 529, 533, 535, 538, 540, 570, 573, 576, 588, 611, 618, 620, 668, 689, 697, 701, 713
food, 564
football, 576
force, 191, 572, 677
forefront, 127, 183, 189, 221, 378, 400, 581
forging, 383, 717
forgiveness, 200
form, 22, 110, 111, 115, 119, 162, 175, 190, 206, 226, 314, 363, 372, 474, 477, 505, 514, 542, 562, 574, 575, 603, 622, 648, 660, 662, 663, 665, 687, 694, 701
formalism, 16, 62, 67, 311
format, 441

formation, 198, 341, 436, 654, 664
formulation, 23, 117, 382
forum, 343, 703
Foster, 291
foster, 125, 136, 141, 154, 161, 169, 182, 184, 185, 190, 202, 206, 213, 216, 291, 299, 304, 309, 332, 345, 358, 361, 467, 471, 475, 494, 508, 512, 513, 530, 532, 536, 537, 544, 558, 581, 584, 613, 615, 621, 624, 652, 676
Foucault, 101
foundation, 1, 4, 51, 98, 109, 118, 144, 174, 214, 226, 228, 229, 231, 262, 310, 323, 331, 363, 414, 420, 540, 554, 570, 575, 616, 636, 675, 690, 700, 704, 710
fraction, 392
frame, 430
framework, 10, 12–14, 16, 20, 21, 43, 47, 57, 63, 64, 66, 67, 69, 77–79, 82, 87, 88, 92, 95, 106, 107, 109–116, 120, 129, 135, 178, 180, 190, 192, 193, 207–210, 214, 231, 253, 269, 276, 289, 298, 307, 313, 321, 325, 356, 363, 370, 376, 381, 383, 388, 400, 409, 421, 443, 446, 454, 513, 515, 516, 518, 524, 530, 545, 550, 553, 556, 558, 562, 564, 571, 574, 579, 586, 587, 590, 605, 630, 641, 644, 649, 656, 658–660, 662, 663, 665, 672–676, 688, 690–692, 697, 700, 708–711, 716
fraud, 408, 409, 421, 422, 442
freedom, 8, 195, 464, 552, 558, 567, 570–574, 578, 580, 656
friend, 576
fulfillment, 115, 548, 562, 564, 571, 675, 710
function, 263, 307, 402
functioning, 84, 175, 253, 308, 381, 662, 668, 686, 687
fundamental, 11, 14, 18, 46, 58, 67, 82, 112, 115, 117, 195, 227, 273, 308, 311, 313, 316, 324, 326, 329, 347, 396, 400, 401, 411, 414, 426, 445, 446, 526, 550, 551, 556, 567, 570, 573, 574, 577, 578, 586, 589, 603, 609, 658, 671, 674, 686, 704, 709
funding, 156, 247, 256, 330, 331, 334, 350, 497, 523, 579, 668
fundraising, 410
future, 1, 3, 7, 13, 16, 18, 21, 24, 29, 47, 48, 51, 59, 78, 89, 120, 127, 129, 133, 146, 151, 154–156, 165, 171, 176, 181, 183, 186, 192, 195, 201, 204–207, 210, 211, 214, 215, 217, 247, 262, 268, 282, 290, 295, 297, 300–305, 309, 310, 353, 356, 373, 379, 380, 382–385, 387, 389, 395, 398, 401, 417, 419, 424, 436, 437, 440, 457–462, 465, 467, 476, 478, 483,

Index

484, 491–493, 519, 539, 541, 543–546, 552, 584, 609, 612, 615, 616, 618, 619, 621, 636, 638–641, 648, 649, 668, 672, 674, 693, 694, 707, 708, 710, 711, 713, 717–719

Gacaca, 354
gain, 13, 19, 27, 29, 32, 35, 36, 40, 42, 48, 55, 61, 111, 127, 134, 140, 146, 147, 150, 151, 154, 155, 161, 162, 174, 182, 188–190, 196, 216, 220, 226, 228, 240, 241, 252, 253, 258, 259, 262, 272, 282, 290, 292, 293, 295–297, 302, 303, 312, 314, 352, 381, 384, 413, 423, 477, 511, 544, 623, 643, 648, 654, 698
gang, 504
gap, 10, 83, 130, 143, 144, 146, 155, 189, 193, 201, 206, 273, 284, 296, 309, 328–330, 332, 334, 361, 362, 391, 394, 674
gas, 672
gateway, 51
gathering, 255, 491, 655
gender, 6, 12, 13, 16–20, 22, 24, 25, 30, 56–58, 62, 63, 67, 71, 72, 75–79, 81–83, 90, 91, 93–95, 97–99, 101, 102, 104, 110, 111, 116, 121–123, 126, 181, 184, 185, 195, 205, 208–210, 239, 273, 298, 300, 312, 328, 367, 376, 384, 444, 459, 470, 510, 513–515, 537, 544, 547–549, 555, 556, 562, 563, 574, 579, 586–592, 596–598, 603, 604, 609, 656, 677, 678, 685, 692, 694, 716
generalizability, 37, 236, 246, 441
generation, 189, 214, 465
genetic, 172, 657
genocide, 354, 581, 685, 699
geography, 20, 215
Germany, 648
gerrymandering, 579
Ghana, 650
Global South, 680
globalization, 5, 47, 72, 116, 190, 191, 210, 211, 300, 302, 359, 362, 385, 412, 549, 635, 643–645, 647, 651, 655, 658, 669–673, 675–677, 714
globe, 384, 573, 643, 647, 651, 714
glossary, 50, 56, 57, 59
goal, 27, 136, 141, 153, 155, 172, 174, 202, 262, 353, 429, 434, 440, 479, 483, 488, 495, 506, 531, 582, 625
good, 191, 373, 603
governance, 20, 88, 130, 217, 311, 314, 545, 580, 584, 624, 635, 643, 644, 647, 665–668, 673, 674, 697, 698, 701, 709, 710, 714
government, 157, 226, 241, 245, 313, 315, 329, 330, 334, 346, 372, 389, 413, 424, 556, 578, 623, 629, 694, 703
grading, 184

graduate, 144
Gramsci, 109
grant, 709
Greece, 3
greenhouse, 672
ground, 335, 357, 645
groundbreaking, 14, 313
grounding, 71, 211
groundwork, 1, 3, 16, 18, 553, 612
group, 87, 97, 137, 142, 157, 176, 241, 244, 333, 353, 354, 379, 477, 507, 510, 531, 536, 541, 587
growth, 155, 157, 219, 287, 300, 320, 349, 359, 383, 417, 437, 462, 464, 479, 483, 499, 506, 511, 542, 605, 609, 645, 671, 672, 675
guarantee, 112, 630
guardianship, 586
guest, 182, 183, 195
guidance, 29, 35, 36, 40, 147, 156, 200, 222, 225, 239, 287, 366, 367, 400, 448, 449, 488, 505, 509, 514, 664, 702
guide, 14, 19, 21, 32, 43, 117, 141, 167, 222, 229, 247, 320, 327, 356, 363, 411, 415, 450, 472, 496, 502, 527, 544, 545, 551, 569, 616, 622, 647, 658, 685, 686, 700, 719

hacking, 422
hand, 8, 40, 189, 190, 252, 268, 281, 291, 315, 342, 367, 396, 414, 425, 521, 576, 619, 645, 655, 663
handling, 347, 441, 490, 576
happiness, 5
harassment, 82, 83, 513, 572, 586, 596, 623
hardware, 168
harm, 13, 15, 27, 43, 58, 78, 225, 243, 247, 256, 299, 348–358, 372, 378, 400, 467, 471, 474–477, 479, 483, 484, 486, 488, 489, 491–493, 495, 496, 498, 501, 504–506, 508–510, 512–516, 518–522, 524, 525, 527, 530–533, 536, 537, 542, 544, 545, 578, 619–621, 657, 708, 717
harmonization, 191, 265, 267, 268, 302, 323, 324, 384, 652, 654, 669, 671, 718
harmony, 345, 475
Harry Blackmun, 313
hash, 402
hate, 261, 493, 511, 558, 572, 578
hatred, 578
healing, 12, 15, 35, 47, 59, 300, 348–352, 355–358, 379, 467, 470, 471, 474–477, 479, 482–486, 488–490, 493, 494, 496–499, 501–506, 508–510, 512–516, 518, 521, 524, 526, 527, 530–533, 536, 537, 541, 543–546, 612, 615, 616, 618, 619, 621, 647, 703, 717
health, 122, 157, 172, 173, 175, 182, 253, 299, 303, 382, 444, 511, 544, 564, 586, 597, 603, 605, 610

Index 747

healthcare, 8, 82, 104, 115, 122, 125, 135, 172, 174, 216, 424, 510, 511, 549, 563, 564, 586, 589, 591, 596, 597, 603–605, 609–612, 619, 620, 691, 693, 694
hearing, 244
heart, 686
hegemony, 107, 109, 111
help, 10, 15, 19, 21, 50, 57, 71, 76, 112, 135, 150, 169, 175, 176, 199–201, 207, 215, 216, 221, 228, 229, 241, 243, 252, 262, 269, 281, 299, 327–330, 333–336, 342, 358, 362, 382, 389, 392, 415, 420, 426, 427, 440, 441, 462, 490, 491, 503, 526, 563, 589, 619, 621, 664, 710, 716
Henry Maine, 652
heritage, 333, 693, 699, 702
heteronormativity, 101, 102
heterosexism, 78
heterosexuality, 99, 102
hierarchy, 687
hindsight, 175
hiring, 182
history, 21, 57, 84, 113, 184, 226, 228, 239, 307, 310, 316, 379, 414, 441, 444, 475, 476, 484, 514, 516, 541, 583, 632, 646, 652, 678, 690, 692
holding, 29, 114, 471, 494, 496, 510, 513, 557, 558, 674, 718
home, 520, 693
homosexuality, 598
honesty, 341

hope, 567, 694
hormone, 597
house, 326
housing, 8, 25, 90, 92, 113, 295, 326, 332, 511, 549, 564, 596, 693
Howard Zehr, 485, 507, 529
human, 1, 2, 4, 5, 17–19, 22, 23, 46–48, 51, 56, 59, 82, 114–123, 125–127, 129, 130, 135, 155, 164, 171, 174, 175, 177, 181, 184–186, 190, 192, 195, 198, 207, 209, 210, 212, 216, 243, 247, 256, 257, 272, 280, 285, 299, 300, 302, 329, 359, 384, 392, 398, 400, 409, 415, 434, 446, 449, 464, 465, 513, 547–558, 560, 562, 568–572, 574, 577, 579, 580, 583, 586, 590–592, 603, 605, 609, 612–616, 618–633, 635–641, 644–647, 651, 656, 658, 662, 663, 670–677, 682–686, 693, 699, 701, 708, 710, 714, 716, 717, 719
humanity, 676, 685
hybrid, 522

idea, 79, 102, 316, 530, 676, 695
identification, 191, 320, 416, 448, 596, 620, 718
identifier, 402
identity, 7, 18, 71, 82, 94, 95, 99, 101, 102, 104, 122, 123, 184, 301, 321, 377, 414,

422, 423, 426, 453, 463, 497, 548, 562, 563, 596, 598, 669, 670, 696, 716
ideology, 5, 16, 20, 70, 72, 87, 649
imbalance, 134, 332, 493, 522, 524, 676
imitation, 356
immigrant, 187, 188
immigration, 81, 150, 181, 186, 188, 329
immutability, 388, 402, 405, 408, 409, 436
impact, 1, 5, 6, 9–11, 13, 15, 17, 19–21, 27–29, 31, 35, 38, 40–43, 46, 47, 51, 57, 62, 65, 68, 71, 79, 83, 84, 86, 87, 90, 92, 101, 109, 111, 116, 121, 125–127, 129, 130, 135, 142, 145, 147, 148, 155–158, 161, 163, 169, 171, 175, 176, 178, 180–187, 189, 191, 193, 198, 199, 201, 210–212, 215, 220, 232, 235, 242, 243, 246–248, 252–254, 256, 257, 264, 270, 271, 282, 284, 285, 289, 290, 292, 293, 296–304, 307, 309, 310, 312, 314, 321, 323, 333, 334, 338, 341, 350, 352, 353, 355–359, 362, 371–376, 379–381, 383, 385, 387, 389, 400, 401, 408, 413, 416, 423, 425, 448, 462, 467, 473, 476–478, 483, 485, 488, 489, 491, 501, 503–508, 510, 516, 517, 520, 521, 523–527, 530, 541, 544, 549, 552, 563, 572, 574, 576, 579, 580, 582, 583, 587, 590, 592, 605, 611, 622, 624, 625, 635, 638, 643, 644, 646, 647, 651, 656, 658, 669–671, 674, 675, 677, 686, 689, 690, 692, 703, 704, 714, 715, 718
impartiality, 315, 336, 338, 347, 348, 429, 574, 576
imperialism, 17, 62, 321
implement, 9, 30, 138, 144, 157, 162, 168, 201, 207, 211, 213, 320, 409, 415, 419, 446, 453, 509, 518, 531, 532, 557, 581, 623, 670, 685, 688
implementation, 13, 27, 35, 117, 120, 121, 123, 145, 150, 153, 155–157, 195, 205, 216, 253, 264, 325, 339, 350, 351, 355, 356, 372, 382, 393, 400, 420, 422, 429, 434, 469, 470, 472, 473, 476–479, 491, 492, 495, 499, 502, 507, 508, 515, 523, 526, 544, 552, 560, 572, 574, 576–578, 587, 590, 610, 620, 660, 662, 670, 692, 694, 701, 704, 710
implication, 212, 298, 299, 461, 638, 716
importance, 1, 4, 6, 8, 10, 13, 17, 23, 29, 40, 48, 59, 62, 63, 67, 79, 84, 90, 97, 107, 109, 112, 115, 116, 121, 122, 125, 126, 135, 146, 154,

155, 174, 181, 184, 192,
206, 209, 210, 213, 216,
222, 224, 226, 229, 231,
232, 236, 246, 247, 265,
268, 287, 292, 293, 297,
309, 314, 320, 329–331,
352, 356, 357, 360, 367,
368, 370, 376, 379, 380,
382, 385, 414, 416, 417,
419, 425, 456, 460, 471,
475, 476, 484, 492, 493,
495, 502, 503, 509, 536,
537, 541–544, 549,
572–574, 576, 583, 586,
589–591, 609, 621, 622,
629, 630, 636, 637, 646,
655, 683, 684, 693, 699,
703, 711, 714, 719
imposition, 87, 239, 579, 580, 703
impoverishment, 581
imprisonment, 68
improvement, 125, 147, 157, 168,
236, 258, 265, 469, 478,
544, 718
improving, 166, 262, 320, 394, 443,
445, 459, 492, 524, 610
impunity, 619
in, 1–33, 35–43, 45–49, 51, 55–64,
66–72, 75–98, 100–102,
106, 107, 109–116, 118,
120–123, 125–127,
129–131, 133–137,
139–148, 150–164,
166–169, 171–196,
198–202, 204–217,
219–222, 224–233,
235–237, 239–248,
251–258, 260–262, 264,
265, 268–274, 278,
280–287, 289–304,
308–316, 318–339,
341–363, 365, 367, 368,
370–377, 379–385,
387–395, 397–405,
408–417, 419–431,
434–465, 467, 471, 473,
475–479, 482–486,
488–527, 530–549, 552,
553, 555–558, 560,
562–564, 566–576,
578–581, 583–587,
589–592, 596, 597, 601,
603–606, 608–613, 615,
617–627, 629, 630, 632,
633, 635–641, 643–652,
654–659, 661–665,
667–680, 682–685,
689–698, 700–704,
706–711, 713–719
inaccessibility, 327
incarceration, 69, 92, 97, 295, 475,
533, 542
incident, 391, 413, 416, 421, 422,
573
incitement, 558
inclusion, 14, 25, 82, 87, 115, 136,
184, 185, 201, 204, 207,
216, 309, 349, 359,
367–370, 380, 544, 548,
590, 604, 674, 692
inclusivity, 24, 59, 63, 87, 123, 182,
199, 200, 213, 293, 295,
296, 299, 304, 437, 501,
508–511, 523, 537, 611,
622, 646, 668
income, 113, 199, 205, 326, 329,
330, 333, 361, 457
incorporation, 184, 207, 308

independence, 448, 449
India, 612, 649
individual, 8, 10, 42, 70, 80, 89, 91, 93, 95, 111, 114, 116, 117, 173, 175, 176, 178, 256, 301, 308–310, 312, 315, 316, 326, 327, 358, 373, 401, 414, 426, 428, 447, 448, 455, 456, 463, 475, 507, 545, 550, 553, 558, 562, 567, 571, 574, 578, 580, 613, 620, 656, 676, 717
indivisibility, 115, 547, 556, 636
industry, 215, 221, 362, 405
inefficiency, 324
inequality, 9, 11, 18, 25, 26, 30, 47, 58, 62, 63, 67, 69, 72, 75–77, 82, 83, 90, 93–95, 106, 109, 111, 113, 114, 122, 184, 185, 205, 209, 213, 248, 253, 273, 298, 356, 372, 459, 508, 510–513, 537, 548, 549, 552, 587, 604, 609, 610, 622, 635, 636, 645, 672, 675, 678, 691, 694, 716
inertia, 382
influence, 4, 10, 19, 41, 87, 113, 135, 155, 172, 175, 176, 179, 181, 208, 210, 211, 244, 252, 253, 255–257, 292–294, 312, 314, 315, 321, 323, 346, 356, 371, 377, 477, 478, 507, 544, 549, 572, 576, 578, 579, 583, 655, 656, 664, 670, 711
influx, 437

information, 42, 48, 55, 81, 137, 141, 143, 151, 158, 160–162, 167, 175, 177, 200–202, 219, 229, 241, 246, 256, 277, 281, 284–286, 304, 326–328, 330, 332, 333, 341, 347, 350, 387–389, 391–395, 400, 411, 414–417, 419, 420, 422, 423, 425–427, 429, 430, 435, 437, 441, 444, 446, 447, 453, 454, 456, 457, 462–464, 482, 502, 506, 522, 525, 572, 576, 578, 603, 611, 616, 623, 652, 675, 690
infrastructure, 168, 200, 350, 405, 423, 463, 490, 509, 609, 611
infringement, 231, 316, 388
initiative, 145, 204, 504, 507, 517
injustice, 9, 21–24, 29, 30, 90, 115, 121, 136, 147, 184, 311, 371, 372, 516, 518, 610, 615, 622, 636, 638, 678
innocence, 577
innovation, 147, 168, 289, 302, 331, 385, 428, 434, 456, 460, 461, 476, 651, 657, 662, 717
input, 172, 304, 316, 321, 325, 381, 394, 502, 544
inquiry, 298, 316
insight, 29, 135, 147, 530
inspiration, 29, 692, 708
instability, 326, 692
instance, 6, 13, 14, 19, 69, 70, 113, 160, 200, 235, 285, 298, 299, 327, 328, 336, 381,

Index

382, 388, 401, 409, 493, 563, 581, 673, 716
institution, 156, 182, 320, 323, 530
institutionalization, 378
instruction, 192
instructor, 137, 140, 141
instrument, 109–111, 372, 603, 650, 663
insurance, 442
intake, 150
integration, 19, 42, 47, 56, 63, 88, 131, 134, 146, 156, 166, 168, 169, 177, 185, 212, 282, 295, 309, 320, 324, 383, 384, 387–389, 398, 401, 446, 449, 457, 458, 460, 476, 495, 532, 545, 636, 649, 669, 671, 673, 674, 687, 689, 690, 714
integrity, 45, 46, 144, 162, 168, 247, 255, 256, 285, 286, 304, 340, 347, 362, 367, 370, 375, 378, 389, 393, 402, 408, 423, 435, 436, 453, 576, 708, 719
intelligence, 47, 56, 130, 164, 212, 214, 280, 289, 297, 300, 302, 380, 382, 426, 440, 449, 455, 457, 460, 717
intent, 226, 228, 231, 311, 315
intention, 373, 409
interaction, 5, 139, 143, 252, 255, 389, 434, 652
interactivity, 161
Interconnectedness, 708
interconnectedness, 16, 62, 95, 123, 130, 191, 193, 217, 389, 562, 564, 636, 644, 646, 647, 655, 656, 658, 669, 675–677, 708, 710, 711, 716, 717
interconnection, 708
interconnectivity, 676
interdependence, 116, 547, 556, 636, 644, 669, 675, 708, 710
interdisciplinarity, 30, 31
interest, 55, 59, 90, 91, 155, 156, 214, 244, 253, 256, 329, 347, 348, 361, 364, 372, 373, 440, 719
interference, 8, 115
internet, 166, 200, 284, 422, 423, 430, 431, 434, 435, 572, 578
interoperability, 404, 458
interplay, 6, 71, 111, 172, 193, 210, 253, 715
interpretability, 393, 395, 443
interpretation, 11, 62, 140, 141, 191, 193, 198, 222, 228, 232, 246, 257, 272, 298, 312, 315, 328, 348, 393, 441, 551, 569, 649, 655, 664, 665, 670
interpreter, 523
intersect, 9, 12, 71, 78, 79, 95–99, 102, 121–123, 125, 174, 175, 210, 212, 216, 253, 377, 384, 562–564
intersecting, 6, 25, 78, 79, 81, 90, 93–95, 97, 99, 116, 122, 123, 130, 356, 462, 510, 562–564, 587, 590, 637
intersection, 19, 48, 57, 58, 68, 72, 91, 126, 135, 172, 178, 180, 208, 290, 376, 443, 456, 458, 464, 465, 548, 677, 714

intersectionality, 6, 8, 9, 25, 31, 71, 72, 78–81, 91, 93–98, 102, 116, 121–123, 125, 126, 129, 131, 172–174, 184, 210, 211, 271, 299, 300, 376, 377, 380, 384, 385, 461, 511, 537, 548, 550, 562, 564, 587–590, 592, 635, 637, 644, 683
intervention, 246, 315, 328, 331, 409, 542, 664
interview, 125, 244
intimidation, 572, 629
introduction, 75, 126, 232, 322, 485
intrusion, 425, 426
invasion, 423
investigation, 421, 442, 576, 655
investment, 410, 669–671
investor, 670
involvement, 55, 59, 256, 324, 326, 350, 352, 357, 358, 381, 475, 476, 478, 493, 494, 496, 498, 501, 512, 513, 522, 526, 530, 542, 545, 604, 622, 703
Iran, 649
isolation, 17, 62, 82, 95, 122, 184, 206, 272, 349, 461, 587
issue, 7, 13, 83, 125, 142, 166, 168, 198, 224, 244, 282, 291, 313, 315, 328, 330, 367, 400, 409, 420, 453, 513, 557, 572, 591, 625, 629, 664, 673, 676, 715, 719
Italy, 648

James Ptacek, 507
Janet Rifkin, 431
Japan, 648

jargon, 327
Jean-Jacques Rousseau, 553
Jeremy Bentham, 4
Jerry Rothwell, 624
job, 327, 388, 400, 511, 532, 619
John, 231, 339
John Locke, 553
John Marshall, 313
John, 339
Jonathan Herring, 174
journey, 48, 49, 51, 127, 147, 221, 503, 553, 692, 717
judge, 311, 335, 342, 483, 574
judgment, 175, 222, 244, 285, 342, 347, 395, 398, 448, 449, 465, 503
judiciary, 25, 314–316
Judith Butler, 101
jurisdiction, 4, 115, 264, 316, 320, 321, 323, 324, 326, 353, 379, 404, 409, 421, 456, 649, 654, 655, 671, 676
jurisprudence, 710
jury, 175, 176, 253, 574, 576
justice, 1–29, 31, 35, 36, 40–43, 46–48, 51, 55–59, 61, 62, 64, 68, 69, 72, 75, 77–79, 81–86, 89, 90, 92, 97, 98, 106, 107, 111–119, 122, 123, 125, 127, 129–131, 133–136, 145, 147, 148, 150, 155, 158, 166, 172–174, 176, 177, 181–183, 185–189, 192, 195, 196, 204, 206–211, 213–217, 225, 239, 246–248, 252, 253, 255, 258, 262, 269–271, 273, 274, 284, 286, 289, 290,

Index

292, 293, 295–298,
300–302, 304, 305,
307–310, 312–316,
326–332, 334, 345,
348–359, 361–363, 367,
368, 370, 372–374,
376–385, 390, 391, 394,
395, 401, 405, 410,
429–431, 434–437, 440,
442, 443, 445, 446,
457–461, 465, 467–479,
482–486, 488–550, 553,
555–558, 564, 570, 573,
574, 579, 580, 584, 586,
587, 589, 592, 604, 607,
609, 612–615, 617,
619–624, 626, 629, 633,
635–637, 641, 644–649,
651, 674, 675, 677, 678,
680, 683–685, 690–694,
697, 698, 701–704, 711,
713–719
justification, 321
juvenile, 353, 354, 469, 495–498, 536

Karamojong, 507
Karl Marx, 106, 109
keeping, 142, 402, 425, 545
Kennedy, 67
Kimberlé Crenshaw, 91, 95, 102, 121
knowledge, 22, 29, 51, 63, 79, 80,
101, 134, 135, 143, 144,
146, 156, 157, 162, 163,
169, 171–174, 185, 186,
193, 195, 200, 215, 217,
220, 225, 231, 247, 257,
258, 265, 287, 290, 293,
295, 297, 299, 309, 326,
329, 331–334, 359, 361,
378, 382, 392, 393, 395,
447, 458, 460, 580, 609,
621, 638, 645, 646, 657,
682, 692, 699, 708, 710,
716, 718

labor, 109, 112, 113, 116, 281, 302,
336, 344, 345, 549, 564,
581, 604, 606–609, 671,
675, 678, 694
lack, 7, 13, 22, 30, 31, 70, 80, 87, 93,
104, 123, 133, 143–146,
200, 202, 205, 272, 314,
320, 324–326, 328–330,
346, 348, 399, 401, 409,
419, 434, 445, 449, 469,
491, 509, 510, 523, 532,
552, 557, 558, 578–580,
597, 609, 623, 629, 676,
684, 692
land, 87, 88, 123, 301, 333, 378,
463, 581, 583, 584, 619,
620, 646, 691–694,
699–701
landlord, 150, 326
landmark, 142, 198, 308, 312–314,
379, 413, 709
landscape, 5, 47, 71, 163, 189, 191,
212, 215, 219, 221, 228,
269, 277, 282, 307, 310,
312, 314, 320, 345, 359,
361, 362, 408, 410, 417,
422, 440, 446, 447, 449,
462, 463, 465, 584, 639,
662, 685, 690, 692, 708,
719
language, 160, 193, 199, 201, 242,

256, 262, 280, 282, 291,
   327–329, 333, 405, 434,
   449, 462, 554, 558, 564
Latin America, 4, 88, 384, 648, 678,
   693, 694
Law, 109, 110, 173
law, 1–8, 11–22, 24, 25, 29–32, 36,
   40–42, 47, 48, 51, 57–59,
   61–63, 66–72, 75–77,
   81–83, 86–92, 96, 98, 100,
   101, 106, 107, 109–113,
   126, 127, 129, 133–136,
   140, 142–148, 150, 155,
   156, 158, 160–164, 166,
   169, 171–196, 198–202,
   204–214, 216, 217, 219,
   221–226, 228, 229,
   231–233, 235, 236,
   241–243, 247–250, 252,
   253, 255, 261, 262,
   268–274, 277, 281, 282,
   285, 290, 296–298, 300,
   302, 303, 308, 310–316,
   320, 322–324, 329–333,
   335, 336, 348, 362–365,
   367, 368, 370, 372,
   376–380, 383–385,
   387–389, 399–401, 408,
   409, 426, 437, 440–449,
   456–462, 465, 467, 471,
   495, 518, 530–533, 537,
   547–558, 562, 567, 569,
   572–574, 579, 580, 586,
   613, 615, 635, 636,
   639–641, 643, 644,
   646–656, 658–665,
   669–677, 684, 687,
   689–692, 697, 703–709,
   711, 714–716, 718

lawmaking, 88, 315
lawsuit, 327
lawyer, 328, 330
lawyering, 151, 154, 186, 211
layer, 190, 587
lead, 10, 27, 30, 70, 93, 156, 191,
   210, 246, 272, 293, 299,
   304, 309, 311, 315, 324,
   330, 335, 349, 364, 377,
   389, 409, 415, 431, 442,
   453, 459, 461, 478, 484,
   576, 579, 596, 609, 623,
   647, 670, 675, 710, 716
leadership, 591
learning, 12, 47, 49–51, 89,
   133–143, 146–148, 150,
   151, 154–158, 161–164,
   166–168, 180–184, 186,
   188, 196, 200–202, 205,
   207, 211, 212, 214, 215,
   217, 221, 280–283, 292,
   320, 356, 392–394, 400,
   419, 439, 440, 443, 445,
   455, 457, 460, 462, 473,
   478, 492, 540, 543, 545,
   610, 638
lecture, 12, 133, 137–139, 146, 211,
   215
ledger, 388, 402, 406, 408
legacy, 62, 84, 87, 583, 690
legalization, 173
legislation, 4, 14, 101, 125, 172, 173,
   205, 220, 226, 254, 371,
   421, 422, 437, 447, 464,
   557, 587, 647, 656, 673,
   674, 700
legislature, 314, 315
legitimacy, 9, 311, 312, 314, 320,
   321, 325, 644, 663–665

Index 755

lending, 410
length, 441
lens, 12, 20, 21, 69, 78, 86, 90, 94, 97, 98, 111, 113, 118, 122, 125, 208, 209, 271, 298, 460, 508, 516, 563, 588, 636–638
level, 10, 14, 25, 225, 265, 389, 393, 431, 551, 622, 626, 664, 705
leverage, 59, 161, 162, 220, 280, 289, 362, 372, 389, 405, 452, 458, 462, 490, 676
liability, 224, 225, 400, 409
liberalization, 669
liberty, 553
life, 83, 143, 144, 151, 172, 173, 341, 495, 513, 545, 553, 567, 574, 580, 586, 587, 589, 603, 640, 699, 709
lifecycle, 396
light, 19, 20, 92, 122, 130, 135, 169, 175, 258, 294, 298, 301, 315, 563, 573, 616, 623, 714, 716
likelihood, 176, 239, 392, 401, 441, 442, 484, 541
limit, 71, 82, 93, 94, 156, 201, 206, 246, 314, 330, 484, 523, 563, 572, 667, 672, 675
limitation, 246, 330, 522
lineup, 175
link, 246, 548
list, 51, 408
listening, 339, 341, 479, 482
literacy, 59, 167, 200, 284, 331, 332, 334, 361, 394, 435, 674
literature, 56, 235, 281
litigation, 23, 59, 82, 115, 164, 183, 220, 322, 334, 337, 343, 345, 348, 360, 361, 371–376, 385, 392, 429, 441, 548, 629, 637, 638, 645, 678–680, 684, 713
living, 113, 199, 310, 328, 549, 580, 604, 609, 675, 708–710
loan, 200
lobbying, 30, 253, 371, 645, 684
locality, 530
locating, 226
location, 161, 429
logging, 584
loss, 308, 321, 453, 580, 644, 647, 670

machine, 164, 221, 280–282, 394, 439, 440, 443, 445, 457, 462
Madison, 313
magazine, 573
mainstream, 476, 582, 646, 677, 703
mainstreaming, 549
majority, 90, 313, 402, 451, 655, 664
maker, 343
making, 6, 19, 20, 23, 25, 30, 31, 62, 70, 80, 85, 87, 88, 115, 123, 130, 135, 147, 148, 161, 167, 172, 175–177, 198, 201, 215, 216, 235, 242, 245, 246, 248, 253, 262, 264, 276, 280–282, 284, 292, 299, 300, 303, 309–311, 314, 321, 346, 352, 353, 357, 360, 376, 378, 381, 382, 384, 385, 389, 392, 393, 399–401, 423, 424, 431, 434, 437, 440–443, 445, 448, 457,

458, 460, 465, 475, 485, 492–495, 501–503, 505, 506, 510, 511, 513, 514, 518, 519, 522, 524, 530, 536, 544, 563, 581, 583, 586, 591, 604, 605, 610, 611, 620, 623, 637, 646, 655, 665, 668, 673, 676, 684, 685, 688, 693, 697, 700, 704, 711, 717, 719
male, 17, 82, 200
malpractice, 172, 174
man, 95
management, 163, 176, 186, 360, 388, 392, 395–398, 405, 409, 462, 463, 545, 705, 709
managing, 156, 396
mandate, 330
manipulation, 408
manner, 43, 90, 109, 156, 176, 220, 229, 342, 350, 363, 365, 447, 494, 575, 641, 648
manual, 277, 281
Marbury, 313
Marc Spindelman, 100
marginalization, 11, 12, 62, 63, 78, 87, 102, 123, 167, 184, 545, 563, 580, 583, 604, 699, 700, 703, 704
marijuana, 173
Mark Tushnet, 67
Mark Umbreit, 529
market, 178, 292, 397, 650
marketplace, 110, 436
marriage, 4, 62, 313, 586
Marx, 109–111
mass, 354, 578
material, 109, 140, 285

matter, 140, 193, 287, 370, 586
maturity, 603
mean, 22
meaning, 36, 115, 117, 242, 336, 408
means, 91, 109, 111, 112, 201, 232, 316, 331, 429, 475, 649, 711
measure, 37, 246, 441, 478, 491
measurement, 31, 40, 246, 247, 255, 491
mechanism, 14, 112, 320, 434, 667
mediation, 12, 154, 155, 335, 337, 339, 341, 342, 349, 354, 357, 358, 360, 379, 429, 430, 434, 436, 476, 477, 479–483, 490, 494, 507, 510, 520, 521, 524, 531, 532, 536, 541, 542, 545
mediator, 335, 337, 339, 341, 346, 349, 353, 430, 431, 479, 482, 505, 515, 524
medicine, 135, 172–174, 212, 216, 657
meeting, 356, 358, 474, 488, 493
member, 190, 243, 289, 667, 669, 671, 673, 687, 690
mentor, 157
mentoring, 207
mentorship, 184, 200, 201, 204, 207, 212, 213, 287, 361, 496, 532
merit, 206
meritocracy, 206
Mesopotamia, 1
message, 619, 622
method, 133, 137, 140–142, 146, 234, 236, 241, 242, 335, 341, 430, 431

Index 757

methodology, 245, 256, 303, 651, 652, 654, 714
Michael, 521
Michael D. Shipley, 174
Michael L. Moffitt, 336
Michel Foucault, 101
migrant, 605
migration, 302
milestone, 553
mind, 15, 50, 159, 174, 227, 230, 280, 413
mindedness, 291
mining, 402, 578, 584
minority, 184, 201, 202, 205, 206, 328, 401, 451, 533–537, 604
Miranda v., 313
misappropriation, 657
misconduct, 162
misinformation, 572
misinterpretation, 436
mission, 195
mistake, 400
mistrust, 327, 503
misuse, 177, 400, 416, 453
mitigation, 7, 398, 413, 705, 711
mobile, 428
mobility, 368, 430, 669
mobilization, 29, 112, 371, 373, 377, 623, 675, 680, 683, 684
mode, 109, 110, 112, 215
model, 12, 100, 441, 444, 475–477, 491, 531, 564
moderation, 572
modification, 420
module, 195
momentum, 13, 114, 476, 604, 709
money, 429, 579

monitoring, 321, 396, 399, 447, 626, 676
moral, 21, 181, 649
morality, 1
mortality, 564, 604
mortar, 161
Morton Horwitz, 67
Mother Earth, 709
motivation, 151
move, 13, 82, 127, 232, 236, 303, 462, 474, 484, 555, 587, 648, 704
movement, 5, 16, 22, 75, 113, 114, 184, 312, 371, 476, 574, 589, 625, 671, 685
multimedia, 139, 333
multiplicity, 71
myriad, 630

name, 186, 650
narrative, 93, 176, 617
nation, 189, 699
nationality, 115, 547, 556, 656
nature, 1–3, 5–8, 10, 20, 24, 31, 37, 64, 67, 70, 83, 94, 95, 106, 109–111, 121, 135, 151, 193, 195, 199, 208, 209, 241, 243, 244, 246, 256, 296–298, 302, 307, 354, 355, 360, 361, 376, 384, 402, 405, 408, 422, 423, 425, 429, 462, 464, 494, 516, 522, 570, 573, 587, 589, 623, 646, 647, 662, 665, 708–711, 714
navigation, 497, 619, 690
necessity, 206, 398
need, 2, 6, 7, 9–11, 15, 17, 30, 31, 42, 63, 67, 68, 71, 72, 82,

88, 89, 91, 114, 121–123, 136, 137, 156, 157, 162, 165–168, 172, 177, 182, 190, 193, 209–211, 214, 215, 246, 247, 255, 263, 265, 273, 297, 304, 316, 321, 329, 330, 351, 354, 358, 361, 362, 367, 377, 379, 380, 383, 388, 389, 393, 400, 404, 405, 408–410, 420, 424, 425, 429, 430, 435, 437, 438, 442, 445, 448, 451, 453, 455, 458, 460, 461, 463–465, 469, 476, 490, 500, 502, 503, 508, 511, 520, 523, 525, 532, 558, 564, 567, 570, 572, 573, 578, 579, 583, 586, 590–592, 605, 606, 611, 623, 630, 635, 638, 644, 651, 657, 658, 669, 671–673, 675, 699, 711, 718, 719

neglect, 26, 272, 541, 603
negligence, 172
negotiating, 341
negotiation, 58, 134, 144, 145, 147, 150, 151, 153–155, 184, 186, 191, 211, 337, 340–342, 346, 360, 361, 389, 430, 434, 436, 458, 462, 644, 665, 668
neighborhood, 511, 518, 542
neighboring, 316
neo, 325
network, 21, 55, 402, 405, 408, 505, 514, 526
networking, 89, 156, 182, 204, 361, 638
neutral, 61, 67, 110, 269, 273, 335–337, 342, 343, 346, 347, 430
neutrality, 12, 57, 315, 336, 429
New Zealand, 354, 485, 497, 697, 709
New Zealand's, 697
New Zealand's, 354
news, 572
Nick Szabo, 405
Nicole Brown Simpson, 576
no, 212, 242, 310, 336, 359
non, 62, 63, 82, 99, 101, 102, 104, 115, 201, 221, 240, 290–293, 304, 324, 327, 328, 342, 435, 490, 491, 556, 558, 586, 613–615, 620, 623, 664, 676, 684, 699, 701
nonprofit, 201
norm, 99, 102, 664
North Africa, 624
note, 259, 394, 649, 667
notice, 225
notion, 78, 90, 91, 110, 191, 562, 649, 708
novel, 224
number, 140, 191, 264, 323, 330, 397, 434
nutrition, 603, 604

O.J. Simpson, 576
objective, 24, 36, 61, 67, 94, 110, 186, 190, 258, 273
objectivity, 12, 37, 40, 94, 256, 315, 429
obligation, 115, 284, 336, 447
observation, 232, 356, 435

Index

occurrence, 408
Oceania, 580
ODR, 429–431, 434–437
off, 315
offender, 13, 349, 351–354, 356–358, 379, 381, 472, 476–484, 488, 490, 492, 493, 495, 496, 505–507, 510, 513–515, 520–526, 530–532, 536, 541, 542
offending, 492, 496, 497
offense, 352, 353, 439, 441, 479, 483, 484, 488, 495, 496, 505, 520, 522, 525, 530
offer, 12, 13, 16, 18, 26, 34, 36, 39, 63, 70, 73, 75, 80, 81, 111, 131, 134, 150, 151, 162, 163, 180, 181, 183, 192, 193, 229, 241–243, 254, 277, 278, 285, 287, 293, 323, 329, 333, 335, 345, 407, 409, 410, 430, 437, 440, 449, 457, 473, 488, 492, 530, 531, 533, 542, 585, 643, 646, 648, 651, 654, 668, 717
office, 328
official, 620
Oklahoma, 581
Olivia, 520, 521
one, 12, 15, 67, 84, 115, 117, 121, 123, 205, 206, 211, 243, 291, 308, 316, 317, 320, 321, 323, 324, 346, 347, 377, 379, 401, 409, 421, 425, 448, 483, 501, 548, 562, 570, 574, 587, 638, 645, 673, 708
opacity, 445

openness, 56
operation, 190, 655, 658
operationalization, 247
Opinio juris, 663
opinio juris, 665
opinion, 10, 142, 253, 313, 373, 554, 576, 624
opportunity, 134, 145, 147, 154, 162, 183, 186, 287, 323, 336, 341, 351, 352, 479, 483, 484, 488, 493, 501, 502, 505, 506, 508, 510, 512, 514, 515, 518, 521, 524–526, 531, 542, 574, 603
opposition, 30
oppression, 9, 11, 12, 17, 20, 24, 25, 31, 62, 63, 71, 78, 79, 81–83, 90, 95, 96, 98, 99, 102, 121–123, 130, 136, 208–210, 356, 376, 384, 508, 548, 553, 562, 587, 589, 637, 678, 715–717
option, 334
order, 3, 4, 11, 14, 16, 19, 57, 61, 90, 106, 109, 169, 258, 260, 271, 297, 302, 315, 402, 425, 437, 475, 531, 636, 652, 662
organ, 172
organization, 20, 125, 287, 331, 381, 391, 396, 413, 416
organizer, 483, 484
organizing, 59, 90, 156, 371, 372, 392, 625, 678
orientation, 99, 102, 367, 510, 562, 579, 598
origin, 554
originalism, 311

originality, 400
other, 1, 3, 8, 13, 16–19, 23, 25, 26, 40, 46, 55, 57, 58, 62, 63, 70–72, 78, 82–84, 90, 91, 93–95, 99, 102, 110, 111, 114–116, 130, 131, 135, 157, 169, 173, 182, 184, 186, 189, 190, 193, 205, 208–210, 212, 216, 220, 239, 241, 246–248, 252, 256, 268, 272, 273, 281, 287, 290–293, 298, 301, 303, 304, 308, 315, 316, 320, 326, 328, 333, 335, 341, 342, 346, 349, 354, 363, 367, 384, 394, 396, 399, 401, 413, 414, 422, 425, 429, 431, 441, 442, 444, 445, 447, 455, 458, 461, 483, 485, 488, 495, 508, 521, 523, 525, 531, 543, 544, 547, 548, 554, 556, 557, 574, 576, 579, 589, 591, 603, 612, 615, 619, 622, 644, 645, 655, 658, 660, 662–665, 674, 678, 716
ousting, 624
outcome, 176, 246, 281, 335, 336, 344, 346, 354, 361, 391, 400, 428–430, 441, 507, 574, 576
outline, 341, 643
outreach, 150, 204, 328, 616, 622, 625
outset, 289, 427
overemphasis, 70
overlap, 172, 530
overreach, 314
overreliance, 133
overrepresentation, 97
oversight, 347, 488, 518, 557
overview, 1, 3, 4, 42, 46, 84, 116, 189, 226, 248, 258, 269, 380, 402, 411, 473, 550, 567, 603, 635, 658, 704
ownership, 87, 111, 294, 324, 325, 382, 400, 401, 408, 409, 415, 463, 542, 581, 586, 650, 699, 701

pace, 161, 311, 383, 413, 435, 458, 461, 670, 675
Pacific, 650
pain, 513
Pakistan, 649
pandemic, 135, 427, 694
panel, 56, 125
paper, 231
Papua New Guinea, 494, 650
paradigm, 486, 709, 710
parent, 175
park, 488
parole, 176, 441
part, 16, 75, 130, 207, 209, 225, 339, 406, 414, 447, 485, 521, 531, 605, 620, 663, 708
participant, 243, 483, 489, 530
participation, 2, 115, 141, 146, 256, 291, 309, 324, 330, 333, 335, 337, 346, 350, 354, 382, 431, 471, 474, 484, 488, 490, 493, 494, 497, 502, 504, 515, 518–521, 523, 526, 536, 537, 544, 545, 552, 563, 567, 571, 579, 583, 584, 586, 591, 592, 604, 605, 611, 620,

Index

622, 625, 646, 693, 700, 702, 717
partner, 83, 157, 183, 511
partnership, 341, 638
party, 335–337, 342, 345, 346, 408, 430, 447, 497, 568
passage, 371
passion, 200, 202
past, 4, 59, 209, 220, 281, 394, 402, 440, 612, 613, 615, 616, 618–621, 649, 690, 693, 704
path, 16, 200, 401, 477
patient, 135, 173, 424
patriarchy, 17
Patricia Hill Collins, 378
Patricia Williams, 67
pay, 79, 83, 199, 327
payment, 397, 408
peace, 193, 507, 586, 613, 644, 673
peacebuilding, 591
Peacemaking Circle, 494
pedagogy, 47, 133, 134, 136
peer, 163, 243, 410
penitentiary, 475
people, 7, 18, 23, 78, 175, 182, 311, 314, 326, 382, 416, 425, 426, 467, 492, 530, 532, 563, 622, 669, 671
perception, 70
performance, 101, 157, 190, 281, 400, 441
performativity, 101
period, 4, 5, 137
person, 161, 215, 326–328, 434, 435, 502, 545, 709
personality, 176
personhood, 709

perspective, 5, 6, 20, 48, 56, 62, 80, 87, 93, 109, 112, 127, 157, 171, 179, 196, 199, 209, 210, 217, 272, 274, 297, 303, 314, 355, 479, 483, 563, 571, 605, 708
phase, 525
phenomenon, 606
philanthropic, 334
philosopher, 4, 106, 141
philosophy, 1, 12, 30, 55, 57, 72, 269, 323, 352, 471, 483, 492
phishing, 425
phone, 241, 414
picture, 42
pillar, 367
pipeline, 90, 205, 543
piracy, 422
place, 20, 144, 168, 217, 354, 425, 460, 497, 506, 576, 579
placement, 511, 532, 619
plagiarism, 162, 168
plan, 351, 353, 416, 479, 488, 506, 507, 625
planet, 7
planning, 152, 157, 260, 291, 341, 504, 586, 610, 620
platform, 116, 160, 163, 185, 225, 357, 362, 372, 394, 397, 416, 434, 436, 451, 456, 482, 506, 510, 514, 573, 578, 617, 668, 675, 683
Plato, 3
play, 18, 21, 22, 24, 32, 36, 40, 43, 45, 118, 129, 175, 183, 185, 186, 188, 189, 192, 201, 213, 214, 220, 228, 232, 236, 240, 268, 308,

319, 326, 327, 329, 331, 351, 362, 385, 393, 411, 417, 421, 422, 436, 448, 456, 465, 486, 489, 493, 494, 496, 511, 513, 525, 527, 542, 548, 552, 557, 567, 609, 615, 617, 619, 627, 629, 644, 645, 648, 654, 655, 657, 664, 665, 667, 668, 672, 674, 685, 695, 698, 718
player, 576
playing, 25, 134, 146, 147, 150–154, 211, 215, 333, 482
plea, 322
pluralism, 17, 62, 67, 130, 253, 325, 683, 695, 697, 698, 714
point, 59, 112, 272
police, 313, 518, 531, 532, 573, 576
policing, 92, 518, 530–533, 542
policy, 10, 13, 20, 23, 35, 69, 70, 85, 90, 92, 97, 123, 125, 130, 145, 147, 183, 189, 198, 205, 235, 239, 241, 242, 253, 262, 290, 295, 299, 300, 308, 311, 314, 331, 361, 544, 549, 563, 586, 609, 622, 623, 629, 684, 711
policymaker, 497
policymaking, 169
pollination, 304, 308
pollution, 7, 28, 647, 657, 705, 709, 711
pooling, 673
popularity, 135, 489
population, 244, 324, 367, 693
pornography, 421
position, 95, 221, 346, 385

positionality, 243, 244, 257, 638
positivism, 4
possibility, 83, 87, 88, 531
post, 615, 618, 685
potential, 2, 5–15, 18, 19, 24, 29, 31, 35, 42, 43, 47, 48, 51, 55, 57, 71, 72, 78, 81, 100, 106, 107, 110–113, 125, 127, 129, 131, 135, 137, 142, 143, 161–166, 168, 169, 171, 173–177, 182, 208–211, 214, 221, 239, 243, 246–248, 252, 255–258, 271, 275, 276, 280, 282, 285, 286, 288, 289, 297, 299–302, 304, 307–311, 314, 315, 317, 321, 323, 329, 331–334, 337, 339, 342, 345, 347, 350–355, 357, 358, 361, 363, 365, 370, 371, 377, 379, 381–383, 387, 388, 391, 392, 394–405, 408, 410, 413, 415, 417, 419, 426, 428, 430, 433, 434, 436, 437, 439–444, 446–449, 452, 455–460, 462, 465, 467–470, 474–480, 483, 489, 494, 495, 498, 500, 501, 503, 504, 506, 507, 509, 512, 514, 515, 517, 521, 523, 524, 526, 530, 533, 536, 537, 541, 543, 545, 546, 564, 572, 573, 576, 587, 603, 608, 612, 615, 619, 621, 623, 624, 629, 636, 639, 641, 643, 644, 647, 648, 669, 672, 675, 677,

Index

681, 683, 690, 695, 696, 698, 704, 709, 710, 714–717, 719
poverty, 83, 510, 511, 516, 549, 555, 564, 604, 609, 678, 691, 700
power, 1, 5, 7, 9–12, 15–26, 29–32, 35, 42, 51, 57–59, 61, 63, 65–70, 72, 78, 79, 84, 87–90, 93–95, 98, 101, 102, 109–112, 118, 121, 122, 136, 184, 208, 209, 219, 221, 241–244, 248, 253, 256, 257, 269, 271, 273, 289, 295, 297, 298, 303, 309, 311, 313–315, 332, 336, 345, 346, 348, 353, 354, 356, 358, 370, 372, 377–379, 381, 382, 395, 398, 402, 426, 431, 437, 440, 460, 464, 470, 490, 492–494, 497, 501, 502, 506, 508–510, 512–514, 518, 521–526, 536, 544, 546, 548, 549, 558, 563, 564, 572, 580, 590, 592, 612, 622, 624, 635, 637, 638, 643, 651, 669, 672–677, 683, 698, 704, 713–715
powerful, 12, 29, 36, 66, 154, 271, 273, 276, 290, 341, 352, 355, 370–373, 375, 376, 379, 443, 558, 564, 572, 590, 611, 619, 623, 670, 673, 677, 683, 684
practicality, 272
practice, 8, 10, 13, 15, 18, 29, 31, 43, 45, 57, 64–66, 70, 76, 80, 81, 85, 87, 123, 130, 131, 134, 140, 142–144, 146, 147, 150, 151, 154, 155, 157, 162, 164, 166, 168, 171, 172, 186, 192, 206–208, 210, 212, 214–217, 219, 222, 225, 232, 241, 262, 272, 273, 280, 282, 289, 296, 299–301, 314, 321, 348, 349, 353, 354, 360–362, 365, 383, 387, 389, 393, 395, 398, 400, 437, 440, 446–449, 457–461, 473, 479, 486, 505, 521, 525, 581, 590–592, 612, 625, 636–639, 663–665, 701
practicing, 143, 150, 581
pre, 3, 408
precedence, 428
precedent, 140, 222, 322, 324, 346, 348, 441, 649, 655
precondition, 586
predictability, 4, 346, 648, 649
prediction, 164, 441–443
prejudice, 574, 577
premise, 89, 320, 616
preparation, 341, 362, 522
preprocessing, 441
presence, 175, 346, 435, 524
present, 3, 30, 39, 44, 89, 113, 116, 142, 156, 176, 229, 242, 254, 256, 272, 293, 304, 313, 323, 326, 333, 335, 336, 348, 381–383, 399, 442, 449, 458, 475, 522, 574, 581, 651, 707, 710
preservation, 337, 647, 691, 694, 699, 701, 704, 708

pressure, 206, 371, 377, 494, 572, 623, 679
presumption, 577
prevalence, 425, 453
prevention, 83, 332, 503, 541, 542, 616–619
principle, 4, 110, 115, 141, 142, 191, 206, 225, 273, 308, 347, 373, 556, 557, 571, 592, 649, 664, 676, 708
priority, 17, 354
prison, 90, 469, 543
privacy, 6, 47, 116, 162, 167, 168, 177, 214, 221, 246, 256, 264, 284, 285, 301, 304, 309, 313, 345, 347, 354, 361, 380, 383, 384, 388, 389, 393, 394, 398, 400, 401, 404, 408, 411–417, 419–421, 423, 425–430, 434, 435, 442, 444, 447–449, 453, 455–459, 461–464, 545, 552, 572, 576, 578, 717
privilege, 10, 18, 70, 78, 89, 93, 94, 122, 123, 213, 257, 364, 377, 384, 637
privileging, 99
Pro Bono Capacity, 330
Pro Bono hours, 330
probability, 220, 441
probation, 176, 475
problem, 133, 134, 141, 144, 146, 147, 151, 154, 156, 171, 182, 199, 211, 213, 216, 229, 252, 280, 292, 335, 341, 345, 360, 449, 531, 609, 676
proceeding, 244, 574

process, 14, 31, 86–88, 109, 110, 141, 151, 169, 175, 204, 205, 209, 219–221, 242, 244, 247, 257, 281, 283, 289, 294–296, 299, 308, 309, 311, 314, 316, 320, 323, 327, 335–337, 339–344, 346–358, 392, 397, 399, 402, 408, 429–431, 434–436, 445, 448, 457, 462, 464, 469, 471, 477–480, 483–485, 488–490, 492–496, 498, 502–515, 518–526, 530, 531, 537, 541, 542, 544, 575, 576, 578, 579, 616, 619, 637, 644, 671, 710
processing, 160, 247, 280, 282, 400, 414, 462
product, 12
production, 109–112
productivity, 287
profession, 10, 13, 25, 47, 56, 87, 127, 133, 136, 144, 146–148, 150, 161, 165, 166, 181, 184–186, 200, 202, 204–207, 211, 213–215, 217, 282, 328, 358, 359, 361, 362, 364, 365, 367–370, 379, 380, 393, 408, 446, 449, 451, 458, 460, 462, 719
professional, 4, 55, 144, 146, 150, 155, 156, 168, 199, 207, 214, 221, 282, 287, 341, 348, 360–368, 379, 393, 395, 399, 400, 445, 446, 448–452, 457, 458, 483, 576, 719

professionalism, 144, 146, 150, 168, 215
profile, 341, 485, 576
profiling, 90, 176, 426, 444, 518
profit, 490
program, 27, 41, 145, 186, 330, 351, 497, 501, 507, 511, 512, 518, 530, 620
programming, 405
progress, 11, 13, 14, 30, 50, 90, 91, 116, 289, 309, 311, 314, 368, 476, 484, 552, 553, 555, 564, 566, 569, 584, 587, 604, 605, 609, 635, 694, 700
project, 125, 198, 289, 494, 530
proletariat, 112
proliferation, 278, 437
prominence, 135, 303
promise, 165, 300, 382, 437, 442, 459, 463, 464, 506, 539, 615, 639
promotion, 79, 125, 184, 209, 298, 555, 558, 592, 603, 609, 629, 630, 640, 675, 676, 684, 691, 700
proof, 406, 458
property, 3, 5, 19, 61, 84, 109, 111, 113, 135, 181, 231, 285, 286, 301, 328, 354, 388, 397, 400, 401, 408, 409, 423, 463, 488, 520, 554, 586, 619, 650, 657, 670, 671, 708, 709
proponent, 320
proportionality, 415
proposal, 125
propose, 9, 11, 13, 35, 56, 81, 130, 142, 155, 195, 211, 220, 258, 303, 323, 335, 716
proposition, 360, 362
prosecution, 421, 576
prosecutor, 483
prosperity, 586
protection, 7, 8, 18, 19, 22, 29, 47, 88, 99, 100, 104, 114, 116, 118, 125, 150, 167, 212, 214, 221, 228, 264, 301, 302, 315, 380, 384, 388, 391, 394, 400, 404, 410, 412, 414–417, 419–421, 426–428, 430, 435, 444, 446, 447, 456, 457, 461, 463, 464, 485, 549, 550, 552, 555, 557, 558, 564, 568, 569, 572, 578–580, 583, 592, 598, 603–605, 629–631, 635, 640, 645, 647, 656, 657, 663, 670, 671, 673–676, 678, 684, 685, 697, 700, 702, 704, 708, 709, 711, 714, 716, 717
provision, 459, 591
pseudonymization, 415
psychoeducation, 504
psychology, 1, 55, 131, 135, 169, 171, 174–177, 212, 216, 220, 247, 255, 272, 290, 291, 299, 302, 303, 381, 382, 384, 651
public, 10, 25, 30, 59, 134, 140, 155, 157, 172, 173, 182, 190, 242, 253, 308, 311–314, 316, 321, 329, 332, 347, 351, 361, 371–373, 377, 389, 393, 401, 413, 427, 430, 434, 459, 488,

491–493, 523, 530, 531, 571, 572, 574, 576, 586, 622–624, 645, 678, 684, 711
publication, 289
publisher, 225
punishment, 13, 69, 349, 352, 353, 356, 467, 470, 471, 478, 493, 495, 505, 508, 516, 519, 525, 533, 541, 542, 703
purpose, 21, 256, 405
pursuit, 12, 18, 30, 36, 43, 46, 51, 83, 113, 158, 177, 186, 189, 248, 271, 327, 352, 357, 376, 546, 587, 615, 625, 633, 651, 673, 676, 677, 717
push, 14, 25, 68, 129, 184, 208, 371, 377, 676
pushback, 10

quality, 122, 161, 163, 167, 168, 200, 232, 248, 285, 287, 290, 367, 393, 395, 442, 443, 457, 462, 478, 576, 603, 609, 611
quarantine, 173
Quebec, 650
Queensland, 703
queer, 17, 47, 100–102, 126, 130, 207, 210
quest, 689
question, 17, 21, 41, 42, 112, 234, 269, 291, 303, 400, 409, 445, 460
questioning, 9, 11, 16, 57, 65, 87, 141, 271

quo, 10, 22, 30, 109, 112, 185, 298, 623

race, 6, 12, 13, 16, 18–20, 22, 24–26, 47, 58, 62, 63, 68, 71, 72, 78, 79, 82, 83, 90–95, 97, 99, 102, 110, 111, 116, 121, 122, 126, 130, 184, 205–210, 273, 300, 312, 328, 367, 376, 381, 384, 461, 510, 516, 523, 543, 544, 547, 548, 554, 556, 562–564, 574, 579, 587, 589–591, 603, 715, 716
Rachel C. Castronovo, 378
racism, 17, 18, 26, 30, 58, 63, 78, 79, 83, 89, 90, 92, 94, 95, 122, 123, 126, 185, 208, 209, 312, 356, 381, 516, 518, 564, 573, 587
radicalism, 16
raising, 357, 448, 587, 623, 624, 626, 629, 633
range, 46, 51, 56, 57, 59, 72, 90, 99, 150, 156, 158, 161, 163, 169, 171, 174, 175, 179, 182, 183, 190–192, 194, 204, 226, 229, 249, 262, 270, 330, 332, 337, 359, 364, 367, 373, 385, 406, 422, 429, 430, 434, 468, 473, 550, 567, 585, 586, 603, 612, 615, 629, 637, 643, 647, 648, 663, 678, 704, 705, 707, 712
ransom, 424
ransomware, 424
rape, 591

ratification, 604
rationale, 42, 141, 205
re, 211, 350, 469, 496, 522
reach, 330, 335, 336, 339, 341, 342, 347, 360, 362, 430, 457, 479, 603, 622, 674, 676
readiness, 521
reading, 49, 51, 189, 226, 281, 297, 489, 635
realism, 5
reality, 162, 242, 339, 405
realization, 115, 120, 548, 549, 555, 557, 562, 615, 675, 677, 694
realm, 296, 422, 463, 574, 714
reason, 175, 449, 574
reasoning, 4, 16, 62, 67, 140–142, 190, 198, 222, 225, 244, 246, 272, 321, 393, 399, 428, 440, 443, 445, 573, 649
reception, 253
recidivism, 41, 235, 239, 295, 300, 354, 358, 401, 441, 442, 476, 478, 482, 491, 494, 501, 509, 530, 541, 544
recognition, 6, 11, 22, 40, 63, 72, 82, 87, 88, 90, 99, 100, 104, 116, 118, 162, 209, 216, 273, 280, 301, 360, 361, 368, 388, 416, 426, 428, 448, 461, 463, 476, 489, 501, 510, 513, 521, 543, 544, 549, 560, 568, 569, 581, 583, 584, 588, 590–592, 604, 619, 621, 623, 639, 647, 651, 676, 677, 683, 691, 693, 695, 697, 698, 700–703, 709–711
recommendation, 394
reconceptualization, 636
reconciliation, 12, 15, 59, 349, 352, 354, 356, 381, 467, 470, 471, 475, 483, 485, 493, 494, 498, 499, 501, 505, 508–510, 512, 516, 527, 533, 543, 546, 612, 613, 615–619, 621, 647, 693, 704
record, 59, 244, 402, 409, 545, 613, 616, 618
recording, 256, 436
recourse, 326
recovery, 176, 357, 358
recruitment, 184, 213, 563
rectification, 409
recurrence, 521, 620
redistribution, 548
redress, 22, 59, 326, 332, 370, 524, 555, 557, 581, 616, 619, 685, 691
reduction, 358, 491, 501, 532
reentry, 295, 498–501, 536
reevaluation, 6
reference, 48
refinement, 95, 533, 544
reflection, 10, 17, 50, 55, 129, 146, 157, 169, 182, 191, 257, 638, 698
reflexivity, 36, 55
reform, 11, 20, 27, 68, 90, 92, 198, 208, 228, 235, 239, 262, 268, 323, 325, 370, 371, 475, 586, 601, 646, 648, 654, 668, 673
refrain, 311
refugee, 605, 715

region, 125, 625, 646, 692–694
registration, 579
registry, 301
regression, 239
regulation, 6, 110, 135, 172, 174, 261, 393, 662, 711
rehabilitation, 176, 357, 358, 475, 478, 496–498, 501, 506, 507, 509, 511, 525, 541–543, 619, 620, 703
reimagining, 11, 14, 90, 651
reintegration, 352, 354, 355, 357, 358, 474, 484, 489, 496, 498, 501, 506, 507, 511, 526, 542, 619
reinterpretation, 377
relation, 209, 297, 302, 586, 646, 675, 676
relationship, 1, 2, 4, 14, 15, 20, 57, 58, 61, 63, 101, 106, 109–113, 117, 126, 130, 143, 169, 171, 172, 174, 207, 209, 239, 248–250, 252, 255, 256, 282, 339, 376, 428, 462, 536, 562, 583, 675, 699
relativism, 17, 63, 592
release, 408, 442
relevance, 17, 60, 71, 110, 113, 157, 269, 296, 334, 475, 509, 628, 662, 690, 710
reliability, 161, 167, 175, 243, 245–247, 255, 262, 285, 286, 393, 441, 442, 448
reliance, 27, 71, 93, 167, 272, 321, 389, 420, 463, 494, 542, 640, 649
relief, 557
religion, 367, 554, 556, 579

relocation, 581
remain, 120, 142, 177, 214, 313, 347, 359, 361, 389, 457, 458, 461, 463, 555, 587, 611, 674, 680, 694, 702, 704
remedy, 558, 674
remembrance, 620, 621
reminder, 29, 352, 704
remorse, 501, 514
remoteness, 610
removal, 581
reoffending, 175, 239, 354, 401, 478, 484, 497
repair, 13, 27, 353, 471, 479, 484, 486, 488, 492, 495, 496, 505, 509, 515, 518, 520, 527, 530, 532, 533, 545
reparation, 471, 474, 521
repeat, 496
repentance, 475
repetition, 59, 620
replicability, 37
report, 257, 328, 443, 478, 526, 674
reporting, 257, 258, 576
representation, 7, 22, 23, 31, 69, 87, 134, 151, 186, 187, 200, 205, 299, 327–329, 346, 367, 381, 400, 431, 435, 447, 544, 563, 576, 577, 579, 586, 625, 668, 688, 694, 700, 702, 709, 719
representative, 25, 202, 207, 245, 246, 380, 399, 444, 488
representativeness, 246, 247, 393
repression, 619, 623
reprimand, 364
reproduction, 671
requirement, 313, 347, 654

rescission, 409
research, 11, 13, 18, 19, 24, 29, 32–43, 45–48, 51, 55, 56, 64, 69, 71, 72, 81, 93, 94, 127, 129–131, 134, 139, 142, 144, 145, 147, 150, 155, 158–164, 166, 169, 171, 174–177, 185, 186, 192, 195, 198, 208, 210–212, 219–222, 225–229, 231–263, 265, 267–278, 280–305, 310, 316, 350, 355, 362, 381, 382, 384, 387, 391–395, 399, 413, 415, 437, 440, 441, 443, 445, 448–451, 457–462, 473, 476, 478, 482, 526, 530, 544, 546, 562, 584, 636, 645, 651, 653, 654, 664, 717
researcher, 41, 42, 221, 235, 239, 241, 244, 246, 257, 295
resentment, 349
resilience, 502, 512, 536, 582, 708
resistance, 10, 30, 31, 123, 182, 309, 320, 321, 324, 325, 350, 351, 358, 371, 476, 491, 620, 692
resolution, 7, 11, 12, 47, 154, 301, 335–337, 340–342, 346–353, 355, 360, 379, 380, 382, 384, 388, 429–431, 434, 435, 437, 457, 459, 463, 464, 475, 477, 479, 482–484, 488, 493, 495, 496, 519, 524, 533, 541, 545, 591, 644, 647, 650, 655, 669, 695, 700, 717, 719

resource, 36, 48, 87, 123, 201, 247, 254, 351, 478, 482, 489, 494, 584, 629, 683, 699, 705
respect, 58, 63, 114, 115, 157, 171, 173, 254, 257, 285, 291, 295, 341, 363, 370, 378, 414, 456, 472, 491, 523, 524, 531, 545, 553, 563, 564, 573, 610, 621, 624, 657, 671, 675, 698, 703, 704, 715
response, 59, 65, 72, 133, 178, 264, 308, 353, 362, 371, 421, 422, 475, 476, 485, 494, 502, 511, 515, 543, 545, 573, 674, 684, 693, 713, 718
responsibility, 59, 115, 144, 146, 147, 155, 158, 175, 181, 185, 186, 213–215, 247, 285, 351–354, 357, 359, 361–367, 379, 393, 399–401, 409, 445–447, 450–452, 475, 476, 483, 484, 488, 490, 492, 493, 495–498, 501, 505, 510, 513–515, 521, 522, 525, 526, 531, 537, 542, 545, 572, 613, 620, 624, 671, 674, 677, 719
responsiveness, 8, 59
rest, 427
restitution, 351, 357, 488, 492, 495, 505, 506, 521, 525, 542, 620
restoration, 352, 357, 358, 467, 475, 508, 542, 619, 703, 709, 710

restraint, 311, 314, 316
restriction, 586
restructuring, 14, 381, 383
result, 10, 24, 30, 90, 144, 172, 192, 200, 215, 256, 325–328, 342, 346, 402, 416, 423, 453, 471, 494, 505, 552, 673
resurgence, 703
retraumatization, 503, 504, 514
retribution, 352, 356, 467, 475, 501
retrieval, 48, 281
revenge, 507
review, 56, 164, 206, 220, 231, 243, 297, 313, 347, 392, 396–399, 448, 462, 587, 676
reviewer, 392
revisionism, 616
revitalization, 88, 701
revival, 703
Richard Delgado's, 91
right, 7, 88, 115, 256, 313, 329, 414, 415, 425, 426, 428, 445, 456, 490, 524, 548, 549, 558, 564, 570–574, 576–580, 583, 586, 589, 603, 604, 609, 647, 700, 703, 708, 709
rigidity, 272
rigor, 93, 161, 243, 296
rise, 1, 5, 106, 160, 190, 302, 383, 399, 408, 462, 578, 655, 658
risk, 175, 176, 285, 321, 324, 330, 354, 360, 392, 398, 400, 401, 408, 420, 442, 496, 506, 592, 632
river, 709

Robert C. Bordone, 336
Robert L. Schwartz, 174
Robert Leckey, 100
Roberto Mangabeira Unger, 67
Roberto Unger, 67
Roger Fisher, 336
role, 3–5, 7, 8, 14, 15, 18–24, 32, 36, 40, 43, 45, 47, 48, 57, 58, 62, 63, 67, 88, 96, 106, 109–113, 115, 116, 118, 123, 129, 133, 134, 136, 142, 146, 147, 150–155, 166, 175, 176, 181, 183, 185, 186, 188, 189, 192, 200, 201, 207–211, 213–215, 220, 221, 226, 228, 232, 236, 240, 253, 262, 265, 273, 300–302, 308, 310–316, 319, 326, 327, 329, 331–334, 341, 351, 357–362, 367, 370, 372, 374, 377, 379, 380, 385, 387, 388, 391, 393, 395, 411, 413, 421, 422, 436, 448, 456, 464, 465, 475, 482, 484, 486, 489, 493, 494, 496, 511, 513, 524–527, 537, 542, 548, 549, 552, 556–558, 567, 570, 573, 574, 587, 590, 591, 609, 615, 617, 619, 621, 624, 627, 629, 630, 635–637, 639, 641, 644, 645, 647–650, 654, 655, 657, 664, 665, 667–669, 671, 672, 674, 679, 680, 683, 685, 687, 695, 698, 702, 707, 711, 713–715, 718

Rome, 1
Ronald Goldman, 576
room, 210
root, 13, 15, 30, 59, 82, 122, 303, 331, 356, 357, 467, 494, 508–510, 530, 531, 536, 541, 543, 548, 607, 608, 610, 619, 622, 636, 638
Rudolf von Jhering, 652
rule, 3, 59, 63, 84, 316, 323, 363, 367, 445, 574, 612, 613, 615, 671, 684, 691
ruling, 58, 62, 106, 109, 111
run, 405
Rwanda, 354

S. M. Lipset, 316
safeguard, 295, 361, 381, 415, 423, 425, 427, 429, 445, 446, 453, 463, 550, 671
safeguarding, 167, 256, 393, 411, 414, 417, 449, 456, 459, 567, 578, 638, 714
safety, 173, 351, 354, 389, 413, 470, 483–485, 491, 493, 501, 502, 504, 506, 514, 515, 521, 523, 530–533, 572, 605, 629
sample, 239, 246, 247
sampling, 246, 255
sanctity, 553
Sandra H. Johnson, 174
sanitation, 603
Sarah, 339
Sarah, 339
satisfaction, 151, 157, 351, 354, 434, 477, 478, 491, 494, 501, 526, 530, 544
Saudi Arabia, 649

saving, 281, 394, 436, 449
say, 519, 524
scalability, 404, 458, 463, 491
scale, 48, 195, 217, 247, 331, 384, 427, 478, 612, 643, 644, 648, 669, 675, 677, 683, 711, 715–718
scenario, 224, 231, 289, 339, 341, 408, 451, 488, 567
scene, 176
scheduling, 430, 435
scholar, 67, 91, 95, 110, 121
scholarship, 18, 55, 57, 72, 75, 76, 90, 92, 94, 95, 109, 208, 236, 262, 269, 272, 273, 298, 461, 562, 663–665
school, 90, 92, 186, 199–201, 204, 532, 543, 611
schooling, 609
science, 1, 12, 20, 30, 55, 57, 72, 131, 169, 171, 182, 253, 255, 262, 269, 272, 290, 296, 303, 389, 394, 440, 651
scope, 1, 5, 94, 116, 184, 247, 248, 269, 298, 330, 331, 341, 384, 523, 571, 578
Scotland, 643
screening, 503, 504
script, 482
scrutiny, 123, 444, 446
sea, 190
search, 161, 280, 281, 285, 394
second, 703
section, 3, 6, 9, 14, 16, 19, 21, 24, 27, 29, 32, 36, 43, 46, 48, 51, 56, 81, 84, 98, 109, 111, 117, 121, 127, 129, 137, 143, 148, 151, 154, 155, 158, 161, 166, 172,

174, 178, 181, 183, 186,
189, 192, 196, 199, 202,
211, 214, 221, 226, 229,
232, 236, 245, 247, 248,
255, 258, 262, 265, 269,
272, 273, 277, 283, 287,
290, 293, 298, 300, 310,
312, 314, 323, 326, 329,
331, 348, 355, 359, 362,
367, 370, 373, 376, 381,
383, 402, 408, 411, 414,
417, 420, 437, 440, 443,
446, 453, 459, 462, 479,
489, 492, 495, 498, 504,
521, 524, 527, 530, 533,
541, 550, 553, 556, 562,
564, 567, 571, 574, 590,
603, 606, 609, 615, 621,
629, 635, 636, 639, 648,
651, 658, 663, 665, 669,
672, 675, 677, 680, 683,
690, 692, 695, 699, 702,
704, 708, 711, 715, 717
sector, 408
security, 116, 162, 214, 215, 285,
304, 309, 383, 388, 389,
393, 394, 400, 402, 405,
408, 413, 416, 417, 420,
423, 425–429, 434–436,
448, 453–457, 463, 464,
502, 545, 576, 578, 579,
629
segregation, 83, 312, 371
selection, 175, 176, 320, 321, 376
self, 10, 50, 55, 62, 87, 88, 141, 157,
182, 257, 327, 333, 378,
388, 405, 408, 463, 503,
524, 571, 580, 581,
583–585, 623, 638, 693,
698–704, 714
seller, 408, 436
Semenya, 123
seminar, 56
sense, 134, 144–147, 155, 158, 182,
184, 200, 215, 243, 294,
310, 351, 358, 382, 496,
497, 502, 503, 506, 508,
510, 519, 521, 526, 531,
537, 541, 542, 574, 579,
624, 676
sensitivity, 31, 156, 199, 217, 245,
295, 299, 329, 334, 354,
478, 491, 503, 509, 511,
515, 532, 683, 698, 703,
715
sentence, 401, 439, 441
sentencing, 13, 92, 175, 235, 239,
353, 401, 439, 441, 442,
469, 492–496, 525, 536,
542, 543, 703
separation, 308, 311, 314, 604
series, 140, 141, 182, 341, 402, 501,
502
seriousness, 655
serve, 12, 14, 15, 29, 47, 61, 118,
186, 229, 258, 273, 283,
309, 312, 314, 320, 360,
370, 382, 398, 405,
459–461, 487, 498, 531,
616, 619, 622, 626, 638,
639, 649, 664, 666, 672,
704
service, 134, 329, 331, 351, 353,
428, 488, 492, 495, 505,
508, 542
session, 482, 507
set, 3, 67, 182, 206, 242, 244, 255,
256, 311, 359, 362, 402,

Index 773

405, 411, 471, 530, 551, 554, 613, 637, 648, 657, 658, 692
setting, 161, 162, 175, 336, 341, 431, 505
settlement, 153, 154, 344, 430, 464
settler, 700
severity, 441
sex, 67, 101, 313, 554, 586, 598
sexism, 17, 78, 79, 95, 122, 356
sexuality, 6, 16, 18, 20, 24, 25, 62, 63, 67, 71, 79, 82, 90, 91, 93, 99, 101, 121, 184, 210, 376, 384, 548, 587, 590, 591, 716
shape, 5, 6, 10, 13, 14, 17, 19, 20, 25, 46, 48, 64, 66, 71, 76, 78, 79, 84, 87, 95–99, 109, 122, 127, 130, 148, 155, 169, 186, 210, 212, 216, 226, 240, 241, 244, 253, 255, 262, 272, 299, 302, 303, 314, 320, 352, 370, 373, 377, 383, 384, 389, 398, 410, 429, 459, 460, 462, 465, 471, 498, 553, 562, 624, 639, 644, 655, 657–659, 664, 672, 680, 686, 710, 714, 717, 719
share, 56, 74, 172, 174, 195, 241, 257, 287, 289, 335, 342, 351, 353, 426, 483, 484, 487, 492, 493, 495, 501–507, 515, 524, 525, 531, 622, 645
sharing, 116, 220, 289, 330, 353, 357, 388, 392, 415, 420, 427, 464, 533, 544, 610, 684, 716, 718

shift, 4, 11, 27, 59, 67, 88, 211, 356, 360, 458, 467, 486, 508, 516, 624, 647, 709–711
Shoshana Zuboff, 427
significance, 3, 9, 129, 186, 228, 292, 316, 376, 533, 609, 629, 636, 691, 709
silence, 578
Simpson, 576
simulation, 146, 195
Sirma Bilge, 378
sit, 371
situation, 326, 451, 695
size, 246, 247, 377
skepticism, 94, 491
skill, 359, 362
slavery, 693
society, 1–3, 5, 8–10, 14, 15, 17, 21, 24, 26, 29, 32, 36, 40, 51, 57, 59, 64, 75, 78, 83, 87, 89, 91, 94, 95, 106, 107, 109–113, 115–117, 121, 129, 135, 136, 144, 147, 148, 169, 171, 172, 174, 178, 180, 181, 183, 184, 188, 189, 200, 202, 204, 205, 208, 214, 216, 217, 232, 248–250, 252, 255, 273, 276, 284, 285, 290, 293, 295, 297, 300, 302, 304, 307–309, 314, 315, 322, 324, 329, 348, 351, 352, 354, 355, 358–360, 362, 370, 372, 379–381, 385, 387, 401, 423, 440, 446, 452, 459–461, 463, 465, 475, 476, 495, 496, 498, 501, 506, 508, 510, 511, 518, 527, 530, 536,

537, 541–543, 546–548, 550, 552, 556, 562, 563, 567, 571, 574, 578, 580, 582, 586, 587, 609, 610, 612, 619–621, 623–625, 630, 633, 637, 638, 651, 655, 658, 675–677, 679, 680, 692–695, 704, 711, 715
socio, 7, 8, 13, 24, 26, 47, 71, 72, 116, 123, 213, 248, 250–258, 272, 296–298, 303, 367, 460, 523, 541, 543, 544, 581, 603, 674, 690–692
sociology, 1, 12, 19, 30, 55, 57, 72, 98, 131, 169, 171, 220, 247, 248, 255, 262, 269, 272, 290, 291, 296, 299, 302, 303, 323, 381, 562, 651
software, 160, 168, 423–425, 431
solidarity, 563, 581, 624, 638, 676, 683, 684, 716
solution, 335, 415, 419
solving, 133, 134, 141, 144, 146, 147, 151, 154, 156, 171, 176, 182, 199, 211, 213, 216, 252, 280, 335, 341, 345, 360, 531, 609
source, 79, 140, 321, 394, 655, 663, 664, 692
South Africa, 333, 643, 679
South Africa's, 620
South Australia, 703
sovereignty, 191, 644, 669, 673
space, 205, 349, 479, 487, 503, 512, 525, 526, 536, 716
speaker, 182

speaking, 140, 328
specialization, 361, 465
specific, 10, 25, 31, 36, 41, 48, 50, 56, 70, 79–81, 97, 110, 122, 125, 130, 143, 181, 220, 221, 226, 229, 235, 241, 242, 246, 258, 272, 291, 299, 327, 332–334, 347, 353, 394, 397, 430, 435, 470, 472, 473, 485, 503, 508, 509, 511, 564, 566, 568, 571, 586, 588, 590, 592, 618, 621, 625, 645, 646, 648, 650, 654, 687, 701, 705
speech, 261, 280, 558, 572, 574, 578, 580
speed, 166
sport, 123
spot, 141
spread, 427, 572, 675
stability, 315, 316, 673, 689, 691
staff, 201
stage, 496, 626
stake, 336
stance, 273
standard, 172, 549
standing, 14, 624, 647, 709
standpoint, 179
starting, 59
startup, 362
state, 3, 8, 17, 101, 116, 175, 229, 313, 568, 591, 619, 623, 649, 650, 663–665, 676, 684, 695–698
statement, 244, 428
States, 115
status, 7, 10, 13, 22, 24, 30, 109, 112, 115, 185, 206, 298,

300, 328, 367, 379, 460,
510, 523, 543, 544, 548,
554, 556, 558, 563, 564,
574, 589, 603, 623, 674
statute, 226, 231
step, 87, 89, 199, 204, 312, 321, 436,
441
stewardship, 646
storage, 396, 400, 414, 415, 435,
446, 447, 463
story, 553
storytelling, 63, 91, 93, 176, 271,
509
strategizing, 382
strategy, 246, 372, 441, 625
streamline, 164, 219, 361, 388, 409,
429, 446, 448, 456, 460,
462
street, 371, 372
strengthening, 422, 463, 584, 633,
674, 685
strike, 17, 177, 221, 361, 379, 413,
426, 573, 657
structure, 48, 89, 190, 264, 422, 477
struggle, 31, 58, 112, 143, 200, 291,
557, 623
student, 135, 139, 141, 142, 151,
167, 182–186, 199, 200,
202, 203, 205, 231
study, 1, 3, 19, 21, 27–29, 35, 41, 51,
56, 57, 67–69, 72, 75, 80,
92, 97, 100, 125, 133, 140,
143, 151, 154, 172, 174,
175, 189, 190, 192, 196,
204, 225, 235, 236, 242,
246, 248, 256–262, 271,
283, 295, 303, 304, 307,
308, 310, 316, 323, 401,
413, 416, 420, 427, 450,
461, 479, 482, 512, 517,
521, 540, 585, 611, 612,
620, 625, 643, 648, 652,
689, 698, 703, 718
style, 141
sub, 242
subject, 140, 193, 287, 311, 314,
330, 388, 393, 572, 583,
715
subjectivity, 36, 243, 244
subordination, 62
substance, 511
success, 41, 144–146, 204, 206, 207,
220, 321, 323, 334, 350,
351, 362, 433, 436, 441,
477, 478, 491, 492, 509,
523, 609, 620, 690, 692
suffering, 513, 581, 619
suffrage, 371
suitability, 175, 321
summarization, 281
summary, 142, 208, 285
supervision, 134, 145, 146, 148, 150,
156, 186
supplement, 71, 142, 212
supply, 409, 458, 463, 549
support, 79, 83, 94, 97, 156, 157,
164, 168, 182–184, 186,
200–202, 204, 207, 213,
216, 256, 329, 330, 334,
336, 349–351, 353, 354,
357, 358, 365, 370–372,
377–379, 385, 392, 428,
435, 436, 441, 448, 459,
476, 478, 484, 488–490,
494, 496, 503–511, 513,
514, 522, 523, 525, 526,
532, 544, 564, 576, 584,
591, 597, 610, 619, 620,

622, 623, 625, 626, 629,
    633, 645
supremacy, 673
surface, 14
surveillance, 116, 388, 413, 414,
    426, 444, 572, 578
survival, 581, 583, 603
survivor, 83, 515
suspect, 313
suspension, 364
sustainability, 7, 8, 123, 228, 333,
    334, 350, 492, 523, 623,
    645, 647, 648, 671,
    708–711, 718
Suzanna Sherry, 378
synergy, 42
synthesis, 287
system, 4, 6, 7, 9–16, 19, 21, 22, 26,
    27, 35, 41, 47, 56, 57, 59,
    61, 62, 64, 67–69, 71, 72,
    80, 81, 83, 84, 88, 89, 91,
    97, 106, 110–113, 127,
    135, 136, 174, 176, 184,
    185, 189, 190, 202, 204,
    205, 208, 212, 216, 217,
    236, 269, 271, 273, 282,
    291, 295, 298, 300, 301,
    307, 308, 313, 316, 317,
    320–329, 331, 332, 334,
    348, 351–354, 356, 358,
    362, 367, 368, 370, 372,
    373, 376–382, 388–390,
    397, 399–402, 415, 434,
    442–446, 459, 461, 462,
    467–470, 475–479, 483,
    485, 492, 495–498,
    501–504, 508, 510, 512,
    515, 518, 523–527, 530,
    531, 533, 536, 537,
    541–543, 546, 568, 574,
    576–578, 604, 619, 643,
    648–651, 655, 659,
    662–665, 673, 675, 679,
    691, 692, 695, 697, 698,
    703, 709, 719
Szabo, 405

taking, 16, 26, 205, 207, 353, 370,
    490, 492, 493, 501, 526,
    541
tamper, 406, 458
tampering, 402
target, 244, 332–334, 625
targeting, 331, 415, 422, 444
task, 310, 315, 351, 572, 700
tax, 397
teaching, 1, 133, 134, 137–141, 146,
    147, 157, 163, 181–183,
    192–195, 211, 215–217,
    610, 611
team, 287, 289, 291, 292, 335, 339,
    397, 576
teamwork, 151, 289
tech, 362
technique, 141
technology, 5–7, 46–48, 51, 72, 116,
    127, 134, 135, 139,
    158–161, 163, 166–168,
    191, 201, 202, 208, 212,
    214–217, 219–221, 282,
    283, 285, 286, 289, 297,
    300–304, 309, 328, 330,
    331, 361, 362, 380, 383,
    387–389, 391–393, 395,
    401–405, 408, 409, 411,
    412, 414, 417, 420, 422,
    425–429, 431, 434–437,
    443, 446–449, 456–465,

Index 777

545, 546, 576, 629, 639–641, 651, 669, 670, 719
teleconferencing, 201
television, 576
telling, 354, 615–618
tenant, 150, 326
tendency, 70
tenet, 18
tension, 7, 8, 31, 116, 191, 206, 315, 426, 558, 574, 644, 651, 673, 700
tenure, 81
term, 7, 168, 310, 314, 334, 378, 491, 509, 515, 523, 532, 533, 541, 544, 545, 582, 613, 623
termination, 397
terminology, 57, 172, 254, 291, 327
territory, 87
terrorism, 116, 502
test, 204, 236
testimony, 172
testing, 172, 339
text, 226, 315
textbook, 46, 48–51, 297, 459, 564
the British Empire, 649
the Global South, 677–680, 714
the Middle East, 624, 678
the Roman Empire, 4
the Soviet Union, 110
The United States, 649
the United States, 68, 205, 313, 322, 333, 371, 475, 482, 643
the Whanganui River, 709
the Yukon Territory, 494
theft, 414, 422, 423, 426, 453, 520, 521
theorist, 109

theory, 6–8, 10, 12, 16–18, 21, 26, 47, 56, 57, 62, 63, 65–67, 71–86, 90, 91, 93, 99–102, 106–113, 126, 130, 142, 144, 146–148, 155, 157, 207–210, 273, 296, 298, 320, 322, 323, 356, 381, 461, 473, 562, 618, 647, 708, 711, 714–716
therapy, 176, 177, 503, 597
think, 140, 141, 147, 174, 175, 193
thinking, 2, 4, 12, 29, 50, 51, 56, 125, 133, 140–142, 144, 146, 147, 151, 154, 156, 161, 167, 171, 186, 193, 206, 212, 213, 215, 216, 221, 252, 262, 290, 297, 303, 304, 323, 387, 389, 465, 609
Thomas Aquinas, 4
thorough, 226, 321
thought, 3, 141
threat, 422, 424, 425, 578, 623, 669
Tikanga Maori, 697
time, 1, 3, 4, 50, 71, 81, 90, 121, 140, 156, 160–162, 215, 229, 245, 247, 256, 272, 281, 291, 308, 329, 334, 362, 392, 394, 397, 429, 430, 435, 436, 449, 457, 462, 483, 484, 497, 562, 650, 663, 668
title, 409
today, 5, 6, 86, 265, 269, 277, 411, 420, 422, 446, 453, 553, 582, 665, 672, 690
tokenism, 206
tool, 11, 21, 24, 29, 58, 61, 70, 106, 107, 112, 136, 199, 269,

271, 273, 276, 290, 314,
323, 325, 355, 370–373,
375, 376, 385, 395, 427,
448, 558, 572, 643, 664,
677
topic, 48, 55, 80, 81, 97, 116, 198,
235, 255, 283, 319, 398,
427, 443, 668, 701, 714
town, 328
traceability, 409
tracing, 229, 427
track, 229, 397
tracking, 396, 463
traction, 13
trade, 192, 315, 656, 663, 669, 670,
673, 675
tradition, 3, 309, 553, 649, 651, 655
trafficking, 513, 586, 591, 604, 606,
671
training, 157, 167, 168, 184, 185,
201, 292, 328, 348, 350,
361, 389, 391, 393, 395,
399, 400, 434, 442–447,
459, 482, 489–491, 503,
511, 518, 532, 533, 544,
597, 619
trajectory, 3
transaction, 408, 456, 669
transfer, 316, 317, 388, 408
transformation, 2, 3, 11–15, 26, 30,
31, 36, 47, 56–58, 61, 63,
71, 98, 106, 111–113,
117–119, 121, 126, 127,
130, 136, 189, 207, 209,
210, 236, 271, 297, 302,
307–310, 314, 349, 352,
370, 376, 379, 380, 385,
389, 464, 470, 475, 477,
479, 504, 508, 509,
511–513, 515, 521, 531,
539, 541–543, 546, 564,
615, 621, 646, 651, 665,
685, 690, 698, 701, 714,
717–719
transformative, 1–3, 5, 7–16, 18–43,
45–48, 50, 51, 55, 56,
61–64, 66–72, 78, 83, 89,
90, 95, 98, 100, 107, 109,
111–113, 117–121, 123,
125–131, 133, 136, 139,
142, 147, 148, 150, 157,
161–163, 166, 171, 172,
174, 185, 186, 188, 196,
207–212, 214, 217, 221,
222, 225, 228, 247, 248,
252, 255, 268, 273, 275,
276, 280, 282, 286, 287,
290, 292, 293, 296–300,
302–305, 307, 309, 312,
314, 315, 329, 331, 333,
337, 342, 348, 349, 351,
352, 355–358, 362, 370,
372, 375, 376, 379–385,
395, 401, 402, 437, 449,
452, 457–462, 467, 470,
474, 476, 477, 479, 480,
482, 489, 492, 494, 495,
498, 501, 504, 506,
508–510, 512, 516, 518,
521, 524, 525, 530–533,
536–538, 540–543,
545–550, 552, 583–585,
587, 589, 592, 606–612,
619, 621, 623–625, 629,
635–639, 643–648, 651,
672, 674, 677, 680, 683,
686, 689–692, 694–696,
698, 701, 702, 704, 708,

710, 711, 714–719
transgender, 17, 99, 104, 596, 597
transit, 427
transition, 15, 59, 107, 143
translation, 193, 654
transparency, 83, 157, 200, 214, 220, 243, 284, 301, 320, 341, 346, 347, 378, 388, 399, 401, 402, 405, 408, 409, 416, 419, 422, 427, 436, 439, 442–445, 449, 452, 457, 458, 464, 490, 668, 674, 684
transphobia, 597
transplant, 321, 323
transplantation, 172, 316, 321, 323–325
transportation, 328, 564
trauma, 350, 379, 501–504, 507–509, 521, 523, 525, 526, 532, 536, 544
travel, 429, 430, 675
treatment, 71, 172, 175, 205, 206, 313, 328, 516, 543, 554, 567
treaty, 115, 420, 557, 663, 676
trend, 6, 7, 669
trial, 134, 175, 176, 195, 391, 445, 574–580
tribe, 709
tribunal, 342, 576
trigger, 514, 523, 525
trust, 167, 257, 282, 301, 332, 350, 354, 358, 365, 367, 393, 401, 414, 425, 427, 431, 435, 442, 445, 453, 459, 463, 464, 478, 491, 502, 518, 531–533, 537, 574, 619, 637

trustworthiness, 256, 502, 504
truth, 59, 354, 613, 615–620, 637, 693
tuition, 199
turn, 20, 514, 655
type, 147, 215
tyranny, 315

Uganda, 507
UK, 331
uncertainty, 191, 325, 708
underrepresentation, 87, 205, 677
understanding, 3, 8, 11, 12, 15, 18–21, 24, 27, 29, 30, 32, 35, 36, 38, 40–42, 46–51, 55, 56, 59, 61, 63, 64, 69, 70, 75–82, 84, 86, 88, 90, 92–95, 98, 99, 101, 106, 109, 111, 116, 121–123, 126, 127, 129–131, 135, 136, 139–142, 146, 147, 150, 151, 154–156, 169, 171, 173–178, 180–182, 184, 185, 188, 190–193, 196, 199, 200, 206, 208–213, 216, 217, 220–222, 225, 226, 228, 229, 231–233, 236, 240, 241, 243, 248, 251–255, 258–260, 265, 268, 271, 272, 290–293, 297–299, 312, 321, 323, 333, 339, 342, 344, 348, 352–354, 356, 358, 370, 376, 380, 383, 384, 410, 413, 420, 425, 436, 443, 445, 447, 455, 460, 461, 471, 473, 474, 478, 479, 483, 488, 490, 495, 501–507, 510,

518, 521–526, 530, 532,
541, 545, 546, 548, 563,
564, 570, 573, 583, 585,
589–592, 597, 601, 608,
610, 629, 635, 637, 643,
646, 652, 654, 664, 690,
699, 711, 714–716
unemployment, 510
unfairness, 22, 574, 577
Unger, 67
uniformity, 671, 690
United States, 581
unity, 18, 507
universality, 12, 87, 547, 556, 579
university, 157
unmet, 329, 330
unraveling, 89, 94
up, 65, 168, 191, 199, 219, 290, 292,
298, 387, 424, 425, 461,
462, 484, 546, 604, 621,
625, 645, 669, 675, 677
update, 168
updating, 193, 670
urgency, 718
US, 264
usage, 400, 427, 428, 463
use, 6, 12, 23, 36, 41, 51, 55, 56, 59,
101, 112, 116, 119, 137,
140, 158, 161, 164,
166–168, 173, 175–177,
205, 212, 214, 216, 220,
221, 226, 229, 231, 240,
243, 253, 254, 256,
282–286, 296, 297, 301,
303, 331, 333, 339, 361,
372, 377, 380, 382, 384,
393–395, 399–402, 408,
411, 413–417, 420, 426,
427, 429, 436, 437,
439–448, 450, 452, 455,
457, 462, 463, 475, 504,
509, 511, 531, 545, 549,
572, 576, 578, 579, 678,
701, 708, 709, 719
usefulness, 419
user, 220, 225, 362, 394, 400, 427,
428, 434, 459
utility, 708
utilization, 657, 683

vaccination, 173
validation, 358, 441, 519, 526
validity, 94, 234, 243, 245–247, 255,
256, 285, 396, 402, 409,
410, 445
value, 112, 122, 247, 292, 341,
359–362, 382, 461, 465,
550, 571, 583, 609, 647,
696, 708
variety, 33, 55, 150, 162, 242, 255,
274, 437, 527, 622, 687,
705
vastness, 193, 195
velocity, 437
veracity, 437
verification, 458, 460, 463, 620
vicinity, 328
victim, 13, 83, 328, 349, 351–354,
356–358, 379, 381, 423,
424, 472, 476–485, 488,
490–493, 495, 501,
505–507, 510, 514, 515,
520–526, 530–532, 536,
537, 541–544, 618–620
victimization, 350, 356, 469, 496,
510–512, 514
video, 161, 163, 256, 430
Vietnam, 650

Index

view, 70, 93, 314, 316, 320, 358, 491
vigilance, 425
village, 328, 669
violation, 22, 195, 348, 467, 471, 492, 508, 530, 578, 586, 591, 699
violence, 17, 47, 57, 59, 62, 79, 83, 122, 195, 328, 379, 470, 484, 493, 494, 502, 504–508, 510, 511, 513–516, 532, 537, 544, 553, 555, 557, 558, 572, 578, 580, 583, 586, 591, 592, 603–605, 612, 623, 629, 677, 692–694
virtue, 117
virus, 427
visibility, 427
vision, 111, 405, 592
visitation, 336
visualization, 220
voice, 10, 62, 185, 346, 352, 478, 484, 493, 496, 505, 514, 521, 524, 526, 531, 544, 574
volume, 415, 437, 456
voluntariness, 494
volunteer, 155, 329, 623
voter, 579
voting, 26
vulnerability, 415

wage, 113
wait, 330
wake, 424, 578
war, 685
warfare, 553
warming, 672
warrant, 442

water, 603, 693, 709
Watson, 320
way, 6, 11–13, 16, 64, 68, 76, 91, 110, 123, 134, 137, 154, 161, 163, 214, 217, 257, 277, 291, 297, 313, 314, 383, 387, 389, 401, 431, 434, 457, 459, 490, 492, 506, 512, 530, 536, 589, 612, 636, 699, 717
wealth, 112, 277, 304, 385
web, 277
welfare, 5, 19, 178, 295, 564, 649
well, 1, 7, 8, 19, 20, 41, 42, 45, 46, 50, 57, 59, 60, 87, 126, 147, 171–173, 175, 199, 207, 213, 216, 225, 231, 232, 253, 256, 287, 297, 298, 307, 308, 321, 322, 325, 348, 350, 354, 357, 358, 361, 362, 383, 384, 388, 417, 426, 436, 443, 459, 477, 481, 484, 485, 494, 501–504, 508, 509, 514, 515, 523, 525, 526, 531, 533, 536, 537, 541, 545, 549, 562, 570, 578, 581, 582, 584, 603–606, 609, 610, 612, 638, 646, 650, 654, 655, 662, 674, 699, 702, 707–709, 716, 718
White, 95
whole, 10, 136, 147, 150, 202, 232, 304, 358, 364, 423, 440, 452, 478, 483, 495, 498, 499, 505, 543, 584, 708
wife, 576
will, 1, 3, 6, 14, 16, 18, 19, 21, 24,

27–29, 32, 36, 43, 46, 48,
50, 51, 56, 59, 61, 75, 78,
95, 98, 109, 111, 117, 127,
133, 137, 139, 143, 148,
151, 158, 172, 174, 178,
183, 186, 189, 192, 196,
199, 214–217, 219, 221,
226, 228, 229, 236, 245,
252, 255, 262, 268, 269,
272, 273, 282, 283, 291,
301, 303, 304, 310–312,
314, 323, 325, 326, 348,
355, 359, 362, 363, 367,
373, 381, 389, 394, 402,
408, 417, 420, 422, 428,
437, 440, 443, 453, 458,
459, 462–465, 479, 489,
504, 521, 527, 541, 547,
553, 555–557, 562, 567,
570, 574, 580, 584, 590,
609, 619, 621, 629,
639–641, 643, 648, 663,
665, 669, 672, 683, 686,
690, 692, 702, 715,
717–719
William Ury, 336
willingness, 291, 353, 493, 619, 667,
698
win, 360
wisdom, 710
witness, 35, 175, 253, 326, 576
woman, 25, 78, 81, 95, 313, 562, 587
work, 15, 23, 24, 43, 46, 55, 64, 67,
69, 78, 79, 83, 86, 91, 98,
101, 116, 134, 145, 147,
148, 150, 151, 155, 157,
173, 176, 181–186, 189,
202, 211, 213, 215–217,
221, 243, 255, 284, 299,
303, 304, 310, 316, 321,
329, 339, 351, 352, 357,
359, 361, 362, 372, 378,
381, 385, 400, 447, 458,
460, 462, 479, 483, 488,
493, 505, 514, 515, 518,
522, 524, 532, 533, 536,
543, 544, 564, 606, 610,
612, 616, 617, 621–623,
625, 626, 629, 630, 633,
636–639, 668, 674, 677,
684, 685, 688, 698, 710,
715
worker, 112
working, 2, 26, 45, 109, 111–113,
145, 146, 155, 156, 172,
183, 188, 195, 213, 216,
220, 231, 256, 257, 287,
289, 290, 292, 329, 335,
339, 356, 371, 485, 502,
504, 531, 563, 581, 622,
624, 625, 638, 645, 676,
677, 711
workload, 287
workplace, 14, 17, 79, 81, 83, 254,
327, 339, 341, 543, 586
workshop, 625
world, 48, 56, 68, 70, 71, 88, 123,
130, 133, 134, 140, 142,
144–148, 150, 151, 154,
155, 163, 183–186, 192,
193, 195, 196, 199, 204,
211, 213, 215–217, 221,
232, 250, 252, 255, 262,
265, 268, 294, 299, 303,
316, 319, 322, 323, 358,
359, 390, 407, 416,
425–428, 431, 453, 473,
477, 485, 494, 495, 552,

558, 562, 568, 578, 580,
581, 604, 605, 609, 612,
621, 624, 629, 636, 639,
641, 645, 646, 648, 650,
651, 656, 658, 664, 665,
668, 669, 671, 672, 676,
684, 685, 690, 698, 700,
702, 708, 710, 711, 714,
715, 717, 718
worldview, 710, 711
worth, 475, 503, 550, 554, 650, 708
writing, 134, 144, 158–161, 166,
186, 212, 291, 292, 664
wrongdoing, 59, 348, 471

youth, 333, 351, 485, 532